MY LIFE

A Memoir of a pilot who was hijacked twice

by

Bennett Shelfer

Unabridged, Uncut, Uncensored, and Barely Edited

For the Kideroos

The tree of life has many branches

This is the story of

but one of those branches

From which you come

Author's note: This is a work of representative dialogue. The portrayed conversations actually happened, or are similar to what happened, or probably happened, based on the author's knowledge of characters and events.

Prologue

October 30, 1970

This was a trip I did not want to take. It was almost 11 o'clock on a Friday night when the big DC-8 airliner that was National Airlines Flight 43 taxied into takeoff position on runway nine left at Miami International Airport. Carl Greenwood, a veteran Captain, was in the left seat at the controls. I was the copilot in the right seat.

During the previous week I had tried desperately to avoid flying this four-day trip. Two days prior, my pregnant wife and I had moved into a new house in Pine Acres, a development in the West Kendall area of Southwest Miami. The house was newly constructed and, other than a bed, we had no furniture. We had taped newspapers to the windows for privacy, until we could purchase curtains. My presence was needed at our new house to make it a home.

There was another reason I didn't want to be on this trip. The Florida State University Seminoles were playing the Miami Hurricanes in the Orange bowl on the very Friday night the trip departed. My beloved Marching Chiefs were in town and I did not want to miss this rare opportunity to see them. Nonetheless, despite all my efforts, I was unable to swap or drop this trip.

"National 43, wind 070 at 10, cleared for takeoff runway nine left," the tower operator said over the radio.

"National 43 rolling, nine left," I answered.

"Takeoff power," Capt. Greenwood said. He pushed throttles forward and the four Pratt & Whitney turbojet engines roared to life.

Vance Stanley, the flight engineer, leaned forward from his seat behind me and trimmed the throttles to the takeoff setting.

"80 knots, airspeed checked," I called out. "V1, rotate, V2."

Capt. Greenwood pulled back on the controls and gently lifted the big jet into the air.

"Positive rate," I said, announcing that the aircraft was climbing.

"Gear up," Capt. Greenwood commanded.

I lifted the gear handle to the up position and the landing gear retracted. Up ahead, below me to the right, I could see the lights of the Orange Bowl. My thoughts immediately drifted to the game I was missing. I had checked the score in operations before boarding the airplane and was so happy that into the fourth quarter my Seminoles were trouncing the Hurricanes.

"National 43, Miami Departure 119.5," the tower operator transmitted.

"119.5, National 43. So long," I said.

When I switched the radio to departure control frequency, there was chatter on the air so I waited my turn to check in. We retracted the flaps from the takeoff position so the aircraft was in a clean configuration as we continued to climb past the Orange Bowl. Staring down, I could see the players on the field and was once again sorry I couldn't be there for this great victory.

The cockpit door opened, then closed, behind me. I didn't look around because I knew it was Terri Martindale, the good-looking blonde stewardess working First Class, coming in to make sure our coffee cups were full. She knew it was going to be a long night by the time we got to San Francisco.

"Captain...." Terri said in a meek voice. Carl was busy flying the airplane. We had now entered a cloud layer with a little bit of turbulence.

"Captain..." Terri said, again.

This time there was something different about her voice that made me turn around to look. The first thing I saw was the barrel of a gun aimed right between my eyes.

"Habana! Habana! No trouble!" the man screamed. His finger was on the trigger and the gun was shaking in his hand. He had a chokehold on Terri's neck with his left arm as he stood behind her, using her body as a shield. He was a slight built man with a dark complexion, wearing a narrow-brimmed Panama hat. He went on a tirade, waving the gun around and shouting commands in Spanish. Even in the dim light I could tell his face was flushed and his eyes showed a look of desperation and fear.

Carl connected the airplane to the autopilot and turned to face the hijacker, showing both his hands in a calming manner.

"Hey, hey… Calm down," Carl said. "It's okay. We'll take you to Havana. Just put the gun down."

The hijacker either didn't believe him or didn't understand him, and proceeded into another tirade of shouting and gun waving. The turbulence from flying in and out of the clouds continued. I was afraid he might even accidentally shoot someone. I knew if the gun fired, someone would have to go after hijacker, no matter what. Very quietly, I slid my right hand to my waist and disconnected my seatbelt and shoulder harness. If the gun went off, I would lunge for him. I knew Vance, the flight engineer, would help me, if he had not been shot.

"Let's go to Havana," Carl said to me.

"You want me to tell departure?" I asked.

"Yes, tell them."

I had no idea how the hijacker would react to me talking on the radio. Reluctantly, I picked up the mic, not knowing if I was about to speak my last words.

"Miami Departure, this is National 43, we have a man with a gun in the cockpit that wants to go to Havana, and were going to take him," I said.

"National 43… Say again. Confirm you have a hijacker on board," Departure said.

"That's affirmative, National 43."

"National 43, turn right heading 180, climb to one 17,000."

"Roger, 180, leaving 5000 for 17000," I said.

When I turned back around the hijacker once again had the gun inches from my face, pointed directly between my eyes. There was a look of contempt and hatred on his face. This time the gun wasn't shaking and his aim was steady. I could see his finger tightening on the trigger…

Chapter 1

October 16, 1940.

She heard the screen door slam closed from the front porch below. She heard the heavy footsteps of him lumbering up the steep stairs to their two-room apartment on the second floor. The door opened quickly and she saw him standing there with his usual two shots of Seagram-7 smirk on his face.

"Howard, where have you been," she asked? "I was beginning to worry. Your supper is cold. It's waiting for you on the stove."

He said nothing. He looked at her, across the room in the tiny kitchen. The smell of pork chops and turnip greens remained heavy in the room. He slowly made his way to the small table and sat opposite her. An old radio was playing softly between them.

"Are you okay," he asked?

"Am I okay? I'm nine months pregnant and you ask if I'm okay?"

"I was doing what I had to do."

"You didn't have to do it, Howard. You don't turn 26 until eight more days."

"Well, I done it, Dot. I registered for the draft. I done my duty."

"I guess hanging out with Joe B. and Herschel down at the bar on Main Street was something you had to do too?"

"We was just listening to the news. Has Roosevelt talked yet?"

"No. All they talk about is war, war, war! Hitler, Hitler, Hitler! I tell you, Howard, I'm worried. Hitler won't stop at nothing until he takes everything, including us." She leans forward and turns her head to the radio. "Wait! This might be it."

"Turn it up, Dot. Turn it up."

They both listened intently to the radio on the table between them.

"This is WJAX in Jacksonville, Florida. We switch you now to the White House in Washington DC. Ladies and gentlemen, the president of the United States:"

"On this day, October 16, 1940, more than sixteen million young Americans are reviving the three-hundred-year-old American custom of the muster. They are obeying that first duty of free citizenship by which, from the earliest colonial times, every able-bodied citizen was subject to the call for service in the national defense.

"It is a day of deep and purposeful meaning in the lives of all of us. For on this day we Americans proclaim the vitality of our history, the singleness of our will and the unity of our nation. We prepare to keep the peace in this New World which free men have built for free men to live in. The United States, a nation of one hundred and thirty million people, has today only about five hundred thousand-half a million-officers and men in Army and National Guard. Other nations, smaller in population, have four and five and six million trained men in their armies.

"Our present program will train eight hundred thousand additional men this coming year and somewhat less than one million men each year thereafter. It is a program obviously of defensive preparation and of defensive preparation only.

"Calmly, without fear and without hysteria, but with clear determination, we are building guns and planes and tanks and ships-and all the other tools which modern defense requires. We are mobilizing our citizenship, for we are calling on men and women and property and money to join in making our defense effective. Today's registration for training and service is the keystone in the arch of our national defense.

"In the days when our forefathers laid the foundation of our democracy, every American family had to have its gun and know how to use it. Today we live under threats, threats of aggression from abroad, which call again for the same readiness, the same vigilance. Ours must once again be the spirit of those who were prepared to defend as they built, to defend as they worked, to defend as they worshipped. The duty of this day has been imposed upon us from without. Those who have dared to threaten the whole world with war-those who have created the name and deed of total war-have imposed upon us and upon all free peoples the necessity of preparation for total defense. But this day not only imposes a duty; it provides also an opportunity for united action in the cause of liberty-an opportunity for the continuing creation on this continent of a country where the people alone shall be master, where the people shall be truly free.

"To the sixteen million young men who register today, I say that democracy is your cause-the cause of youth. Democracy is the one form of society which guarantees to every new generation of men the right to imagine and to attempt to bring to pass a better world. Under the despotisms the imagination of a better world and its achievement are alike forbidden. Your act today affirms not only your loyalty to your country, but your will to build your future for yourselves. We of today, with God's help, can bequeath to Americans of tomorrow a nation in which the ways of liberty and justice will survive and be secure. Such a nation must be devoted to the cause of peace. And it is for that cause that America arms itself. It is to that cause-the cause of peace-that we Americans today devote our national will and our national spirit and our national strength."

"Sounds like Delano is gettin' ready for fight," Dot said. The tone of her voice matched the expression on her face. Worry and concern.

"He ain't gonna start no fight, but I'll tell you one thing…" Howard stared straight ahead, contemplating.

"What's that, Howard?" Dot finally asked.

"If somebody else starts it, he'll sure as hell end it."

Dot placed her hand on the top of her huge tummy and felt two sharp kicks. She grimaced at the pain then giggled at the site of the little foot causing a bulge on the outside of her tummy.

"Hey, Howard! Feel this."

"No, that's okay. I don't want to," Howard said. He had a quiet shyness about him regarding members of the opposite sex, even with his young bride. And especially with matters of maternity.

"Oh! Come on Howard don't be a wuss." She grabbed his hand and pulled it to her tummy. He tolerated her antics, but he would not look at her. Right on cue, he felt a jolting kick, and smiled.

9

"He wants out of there," Howard said. He would never even consider that his first born might be a girl.

"I hope so. I'm ready to get this over with." She grimaced again from a different kind of pain that seemed to be getting worse and occurring more often. More worry and concern. "You need something solid in your stomach, Howard. Go eat your supper."

Later that evening, I, Bennett Howard Shelfer, Junior, was born in St. Luke's Hospital in Jacksonville, Florida. My mother, Dorothy Alberta VanMeter was born January 18, 1921, in Wilmington Delaware. My father, Bennett Howard Shelfer, was born October 24, 1914, in Sneads, Florida.

Chapter 2

"Beeeeneey!"

I brought my tricycle to a screeching halt and looked down the street at my Aunt Versie waving at me.

"Hey Benny! Time to come home." I could see she was waving at me holding something in her hand. "Hurry up! I got a "purty" for you."

I took another quick lap around the old oak tree in front of my friend's house, and stopped when I got to where she was sitting on tricycle.

"Bye, Mary Lou. I have to go now."

I thought Mary Lou was so cute. She had lots of freckles and reddish blond hair that was totally curly and fell all the way to her shoulders. She was my girlfriend. Well, actually, she was my only friend. But that was okay, because we liked to do all the same things…run, wrestle, and ride tricycles. And, we were about the same age, just a few months short of three years old.

"Bye," Mary Lou said. She sat there expressionless, but raised the palm of her hand and gave me a little four-fingered wave. So cute.

I raced nearly a block down the sidewalk on my tricycle to where Aunt Versie was sitting on a short stone wall in front of our apartment on 16th St. She was talking with my Aunt Sis, who had come to sit beside her.

"Look, Benny. I got you something from the PX," Aunt Versie said.

Even then I had already learned that the word "purty" referred to something pretty, which was how my family described a toy. And this "purty" Aunt Versie was holding in her hand was the prettiest toy I had ever seen. It was an airplane. Red and blue, and was no bigger than a deck of cards. She handed it to me and I smiled shyly and stared at it for the longest time.

"What do you say, Benny?" She asked.

"Thank you, Aunt Versie." I began walking up and down the sidewalk doing figure eights with my new airplane.

"He's such a good boy," Aunt Sis said.

"He's the sweetest thing I've ever seen," Aunt Versie said.

"Well, he is the Boy Champion of Jacksonville," Aunt Sis chuckled.

She was referring to a citywide baby contest of Jacksonville last year. My mother had dressed me in my best (and probably only) 18-month outfit and entered me in the contest. I made it to the finals, probably because I was smiling and everyone else was crying. So, there I was, going for the title, against a set of twins. I mean, really, was that fair? I guess not, because I won. I guess because one smile beats two cries every time. I was boy Champion of Jacksonville, 1942. I won a huge trophy and my picture was in the Florida Times Union.

"I'll tell you, Versie," Aunt Sis said, "I just can't figure this whole situation out. How could Dot not want to be with this precious little boy?"

I continued playing on the sidewalk getting the feel for my new airplane. Obviously, being precious.

"You tell me, Sis," Aunt Versie said. "You were closer to her than any of us."

"I know. I'm not afraid to say I liked Dot. We were kind of a kindred spirit."

"Yes, you do have a wild side, Sis."

"Adventuresome, Versie, adventuresome," Sis said. She had a bit of a twinkle in her eye. "Mama liked her too."

"Mama liked everybody."

"That's cause Mama could find the good in everybody. And Dot did have a good side. Yeah, she liked to go out drinking and smoking and dancing and playing cards just like Sing…"

"Yeah, but Sing's a guy."

"And Dot was one of the guys too. She could hold her own with any of them. Just like that last job she had, driving a big ole bus all over town. Not every man can do that."

I was having lots of fun running up and down the sidewalk flying my new airplane, which had a loud engine, "brrrrrroooooooom!" And guns! "Rat-a-tat-tat-tat!" I heard my Aunts talking about my daddy, Sing. That's what everybody called him. Except my mother…she called him by his middle name, Howard. He worked for the city of Jacksonville sewer department. But then, he had to go in the Army and left to fight the war. I miss my daddy.

"She might have a good side, but I can never forgive her for what she did," Versie said. "Benny was 11 months old and she just walked out and left him one morning in his bed all alone. She disappeared. I came home from working at the cigar factory that night and heard him screaming. He was wet and dirty and starving. I got him cleaned up and fed by the time Sing got home from work. He said he had no idea what happened to Dot. Finally, after most of a year had passed, Sing filed for divorce and got full custody of Benny."

"Then she came back."

"Yeah, she came back. That's another mystery. After nobody hears from her for more than a year, she shows up out of the blue just like nothing happened and is all lovey-dovey to Sing."

"And he marries her again," Aunt Sis said.

"I couldn't believe it. I thought Sing had lost his mind."

"He loved her, Versie. Maybe he thought it was worth a try, for Benny's sake if nothing else.

"There was no way it was going to work. They fought like cats and dogs, especially when they were drinking, which was most of the time."

I was getting really good at flying my new airplane. I would defend my territory against all intruders. I saw the postman riding his bicycle down the street returning to the post office after delivering the mail. I buzzed him, "brrrrrrooooooom! Rat-a-tat-tat-tat!" He smiled and waved at me.

"Stay away from the street, Benny," Aunt Versie said.

"I will," I said.

"Sing is not easy to live with," Aunt Sis said.

"I know he's no bargain, but Dot did not even try. After three months she is gone again and nobody's heard from her since. Good riddance, I say. Then Sing gets his second divorce from Dot, once again with full custody, and then is immediately drafted into the Army."

"And here we are…Dot's out of the picture, Sing's off to fight the Germans or the Japs or whoever, and God knows if he will ever come home. I'm just so worried about what might happen to Benny," Aunt Sis said. She watched me as I flew my airplane at full throttle and full volume up and down the sidewalk. "Just look at him, playing and having fun without a worry in the world."

"He doesn't have a worry in the world. I'm going to take care of him until Sing comes home. Or forever, if he doesn't make it back."

"Oh! Versie, how are you gonna do that? You and Larry just got married, and you didn't even have time for a honeymoon before he had to leave for basic training. We were all shocked at that, by the way. We never thought you would fall for a Marine."

"Just tell 'em it was the uniform, Sis. That tall, dark, and handsome football player that was really just a big old teddy bear didn't interest me at all." Versie beamed a slow, yearning smile at no one in particular.

"Yeah but where you gonna live, Versie? Y'all had to let the apartment go and you gotta be out in a few days."

"We're going home, Sis. Back to the farm. Day after tomorrow, Benny and I are getting on a Greyhound bus and going to Sneads. We're gonna live with mama and daddy 'til the war's over. Momma's gonna love Benny…she's only seen him a couple of times."

I was flying my airplane down the sidewalk towards Mary Lou's house when I noticed an intruder approaching my territory from the East. It was a huge dog, much taller than I, with brown coloring and a blackish face, pointed ears, and a long tail. He was trotting along at a deliberate pace, like he knew where he was going…and he was on my sidewalk. So, of course, I buzzed him. Brrrrrroooooom! Rat-a-tat-tat-tat!

He did not smile and wave at me like the mailman had done. He lunged at me snarling and growling and knocked me to the ground. He was on top of me, attacking me with all the fury of a vicious, killer dog. I felt the pain of his teeth sinking into my flesh.

Chapter 3

Amidst the mayhem of the snarling and growling and biting I heard a scream and a loud, resounding thud. In an instant, Aunt Versie had me in her arms, holding me tight, still screaming at the dog. She had kicked him in the gut and the attacker was now limping away down the street, yelping with every breath.

I was lying on a table in my underwear under a bright light in St. Luke's hospital. A lady wearing a white dress and a white cap was washing my arms and neck and face with soap and water. Everywhere she touched me would sting and hurt. I was whimpering but I tried my best not to cry.

"Nurse, what do we have here?" A tall man with a mustache wearing a white shirt and tie had walked into the room and was looking at me.

"Oh! Hi Doctor. We have a brave young man whose name is Benny that was attacked by a big old bad dog." She then turned to the doctor and whispered, "I've got him pretty much cleaned up. The worst seems to be the right arm but I believe I have the bleeding stopped." I heard everything she said.

"Let me take a look," the doctor said. And he did.

A lady wearing a blue dress and carrying a clipboard stuck her head in the door and said to my Aunt Versie, "ma'am, I need some information from you."

"Okay," Aunt Versie said. She walked over to where the lady was standing, but kept looking back at me being examined by the doctor.

"What's the boy's name?"

"Benny."

"What's his full name?"

"Bennett Howard Shelfer, Jr."

"Are you his mother?"

"No. I'm his aunt. My name is Versie Mae Shelfer Collins. I'm his legal guardian while his daddy is away with the Army."

The doctor finished checking me out then turned to my Aunt Versie who was now standing beside the bed. "Ma'am, the boys gonna be just fine. He has some abrasions from falling down, and a couple of scratches from the dog's paws on his neck. The only deep bite is in his right arm and that's going to need a few stitches. Where is the dog that attacked him?

"I don't know. He ran away."

"That's a problem. We've been having an outbreak of rabies, and if you can't find the dog and place him in quarantine, the boy is going to have to be inoculated for rabies."

"He has to take a shot? Aunt Versie asked.

"He has to take a series of shots, one a day for 12 days." The doctor could see that Aunt Versie was very concerned and perplexed. "Ma'am, this is not something you can play around with. If you can't find the dog, the boy must begin the shots no later than day after tomorrow. Otherwise, if the dog is rabid, the boy could die… We will notify the police and they will help you look for the dog."

Two days later, Aunt Versie and I were sitting in the Duval County health clinic awaiting my first rabies shot. The police were very helpful. They searched the neighborhood regularly for two days…all to no avail. I was resigned to my fate of taking the shots. Especially since aunt Versie had promised me an ice cream cone after every shot, if I would be brave and not cry.

"Bennett Shelfer?" A young lady wearing a gray dress with black shoes and white stockings with the seams running up the back of her legs called my name. She smiled at me as Aunt Versie and I walked into the room. "Good morning, Bennett! Aren't you a handsome young man? And you and I have a date here every morning for the next 12 days. What you think about that?"

"I wanted to talk to about that," Aunt Versie said. "We leave tomorrow morning for Sneads."

"Leaving? Sneads? Where is that? How long will you be gone?"

"Sneads, Florida. It's a small town in Jackson County about 50 miles west of Tallahassee. Benny and I are going to live out in the country there until the war is over."

"You can't wait for 12 days?"

"I wrote a letter to Mama. Pappa's going to drive into town tomorrow with the horse and buggy and pick us up at the bus stop."

"Let me look at something," the young lady said. She opened a big book on her desk. "Actually, there is a County clinic in Sneads. You can finish Bennett's shots there."

Aunt Versie smiled and nodded. "That's good," she said. "Thank you."

"But I'll get you started," the young lady said. She appeared to be looking forward to something that I was not. She laid me down upon her table and pulled up my shirt. After swabbing my bellybutton with alcohol, she pulled out the biggest needle I'd ever seen and stuck it in my stomach.

Chapter 4

There is something mysterious and magical about a bus station. At least I thought so standing there in wide-eyed awe holding my Aunt Versie's hand. Her other hand was clutching a large suitcase, which I'm sure contained all the clothes we owned. A booming singsong voice reverberated throughout the large waiting room.

"Now loading in zone two, passengers for Baldwin, Macclenny, Lake City, Live Oak, Madison, Greenville, Monticello, Tallahassee, Quincy, Chattahoochee, Sneads, Marianna, Chipley, DeFuniak Springs, Crestview, Pensacola, Mobile, New Orleans, and all points West. All aboard please."

"Let's go, Benny. We don't want to miss our bus," Aunt Versie said.

We walked outside and joined a short line of people boarding the biggest bus I'd ever seen. It had a picture of a blue dog on its side, which looked nothing like the picture of the mean dog that bit me a few days ago. Aunt Versie gave our tickets and our luggage to the driver who was standing at the door the bus.

"Welcome aboard, ma'am," the driver said. "Hello, young man." He reached down and patted me on the head and tousled my hair. He was a short, portly man. He was wearing a hat with a slick bill, a cane ventilated rim, and a silver Greyhound emblem on the front. In fact, everything he was wearing, except his dark blue pants, was emboldened with a Greyhound, even his white shirt and his tie. The driver punched our tickets and then returned the ticket puncher to its holster on his big black belt, which of course had a big silver buckle with a Greyhound on it. "Sneads, aay? Looks like y'all will be with us for a while. Sit anywhere you like."

There were several young soldiers in uniform waiting to get on the bus. They didn't carry suitcases but they all had large green canvas bags.

Two of them were the last ones to get on the bus because they kept hugging and kissing their girlfriends, who were sobbing.

Aunt Versie let me sit on the aisle in the first seat behind the driver. It was a long bus ride. I was fascinated watching the driver do his job, and watching all the oncoming traffic scarcely miss us on the narrow highway which was US 90. Soon my fascination turned to drowsiness and I was napping more than I was watching.

After six or seven hours and rest stops in Lake City and Tallahassee, I was happy to have Aunt Versie awakened me.

"Wake up, Benny," she said. "We're almost there. Look! There's the Chattahoochee River!"

The bus came down a steep hill and entered a long narrow bridge, crossing a wide muddy river. "Ladies and gentlemen, we are now entering the central time zone," the bus driver said in a loud voice. "Please set your watches back one hour."

"We are on slow time now," Aunt Versie said.

In a few minutes the bus began slowing down. There was a railroad track on the left and we were passing a red brick school on the right. We rounded a curve and the driver pulled over at a gas station. It had a large sign with a green dinosaur. Hanging below that was a smaller sign with a Greyhound on it. The Sinclair station was also the bus station.

"Sneads, Florida," the driver announced as he opened the door.

"Look! There's Papa with Nellie and the buggy!" Aunt Versie said. She was very excited, and I was suddenly a little bit shy.

"Thank you for the safe ride," Aunt Versie said to the driver, as he handed her our suitcase. He tipped his shiny-billed, cane ventilated hat to her, tousled my hair once again, and got back on the bus and roared away, leaving a trail of black exhaust behind.

I looked across the street and saw my granddaddy for the first time I could remember. He was a tall slender man with a sinewy build. He wore a buttery colored Sunday best straw hat, a white open collared shirt, and dark gray pants that mostly covered his black leather high-top shoes. He walked slowly across the road to meet us.

"Papa!" Aunt Versie yelled. She ran to meet Granddaddy and hugged him for the longest time. He had taken off his hat unleashing a full head of gray hair that was almost as tousled as mine.

"Papa, this is Benny," Aunt Versie said.

Granddaddy put his hat back on and looked down at me with a little half smile. I couldn't tell if he was happy to see me or thought I was up to something. Anyway, I was glad he didn't tousle my hair again.

"What happened to his arm?" Granddaddy asked. He was looking down at my arm which was still bandaged.

"He got dog bit, Papa," Aunt Versie said. "We have to get him some shots. Do you know if the health clinic is still open?"

"I think it's open all day. Why does he have to take shots? Was the dog mad?

Aunt Versie told the whole story of my dog bite to Granddaddy, and about how they never found the dog and therefore didn't know if he had rabies are not. So that meant that I had no choice but to take the shots.

"Y'all hop in the buggy and we'll run down to the community center and see if the clinic is open. I can tie Nellie up at the hitching post down there in the shade," Granddaddy said. In one swooping motion, he lifted me off the ground and stood me in the center of the buggy behind the buckboard, which I could barely see over. "Hold on, son. Nellie gets a little skittish now and then. She's scared of just about anything, especially the 4 o'clock train which should be here directly." He reached down and pulled up on a gold chain and lifted a shiny gold watch out of a small pocket just below his belt. He looked at the watch and I could see that it had a picture of a locomotive engine engraved on the back. "Yep. Just about time."

"Giddyup," Granddaddy said. He rustled the reins of the buggy and made a clucking noise with his mouth. I almost fell down as I began my first buggy ride, but I could feel Aunt Versie holding on to me from behind. Soon I could hear the sound of Nellie's hooves clopping along on US 90, the only paved road in Sneads. I peeked over the buckboard, but straight ahead all I could see was the East end of westbound Nellie. And her big long tail swishing around. On the left was McDaniel's grocery store. On the right, under a large oak tree, was the post office and then Lanier's grocery store. We took a sharp turn down the first road to the left and stopped in front of a large brown building which was completely built from logs.

"Looks like it's open, Versie," Granddaddy said. He quickly stepped out of the buggy and tied Nellie to the hitching post.

Aunt Versie and I were walking into the log building when I first heard it. Then I felt it in my feet because the ground was beginning to shake. The 4 o'clock train was right on time. I heard a commotion behind me and looked back to see Nellie trying to rear up, but was constrained by the buggy rig and the hitching post. She was wide-eyed and made a loud neighing sound that horses make.

I looked down the street and could see the train station which was called the depot. It also contained the telegraph office. Next to it was a small building made of concrete blocks with bars on the window. That was the jail, or the hoosecow, as everyone called it. The train roared to a stop in front of the depot with dense black smoke billowing from its smokestack and white steam spouting from below.

The inside of the log building, the community center, was one large open room with a few doors to smaller rooms at the back of the building. We walked towards the only door that was open when a lady wearing a flowered dress and white stockings and shoes came out of the room.

"May I help you?" The lady asked.

"We were looking for the clinic," Aunt Versie said.

"You found it. I'm Mrs. Carlisle, the county nurse here. What can I do for you?"

Aunt Versie took a piece of paper from her purse that she had brought from the Jacksonville clinic and handed it to the lady. Mrs. Carlisle looked at the paper and then looked at me. Then she did it again.

"Oh, my! We're going to have to take care of this young man. We can't be having any rabies around here." And she did.

Chapter 5

'... Didn't take long," Granddaddy said. He sounded like it was an afterthought that surprised him.

"I think Mrs. Carlisle was ready to go home, but she took good care of us," Aunt Versie said.

"Did he get his shot? I didn't hear any squalling in there."

"Oh, he won't cry. He's a big boy. So now he gets an ice cream cone." Aunt Versie looked down and saw the little grin on my face. "Does Lanier still sell ice cream cones?"

"I don't remember," Granddaddy said. "We do most of our trading at McDaniels."

And we began the process we repeated for the next 11 days. I got a shot in the stomach with a big needle, I didn't cry, and I had a big ice cream cone.

The buggy ride to my new home in the country was fun and exciting, as they always were when Nellie was hooked up to the rig. She spooked at just about anything unusual that happened and she liked to run. Especially when she realized she was headed back to the barn, where her tub of water and bale of hay was always waiting. Granddaddy was constantly battling to hold her to a slow trot with tight reins and an occasional "whoa Nelly."

"Gotta stop by the mill, Versie," Granddaddy said. "Need to pick up the meal."

"Okay, Papa. You think it's ready?"

"Ought to be... I dropped the corn off yesterday."

After we had gone about a quarter of a mile down the road, Granddaddy stopped the buggy in front of an old building that looked like a one-story barn. Almost immediately, the door opened and I saw a strange sight. A man walked out carrying a large white dusty cotton bag that appeared to be about half full. On the side of the bag written in crayon was the letter "M" and "SHELFER". But the strange thing was the man was totally covered in white powder; hat, hands, shoes and all, except for his eyeballs.

"Here you go, Mr. Shelfer." He lifted the heavy bag into the back of the buggy.

"Much obliged Joe." Granddaddy tipped his hat to the man covered in white, clucked to Nellie, and we were off again.

"You didn't pay him. Do you want me to pay him, Pappa?" Aunt Versie asked.

"We trade for halves. I bring him a sack of corn. He shells it, grinds it, and we split it. He sells his half, and mama makes the best cornbread in Jackson County with our half.

"Mr. Braswell looks like a big catfish ready for the skillet," Aunt Versie said.

Granddaddy said nothing but nodded at her with a tightlipped grin.

"Mama always like her cornmeal medium?"

"Joe can make it course, medium, or fine. Your mama likes to get it medium because she says it's best for both cornbread and fish."

"That talk's making me hungry, Pappa. I sure do miss Mama's cooking."

"None like it, nowhere," Granddaddy said.

I held on tight to the buckboard as Nellie spirited the three of us in the little buggy northward up River Road. Soon we were out in the country with acres and acres of peanut fields and cornfields everywhere you looked. There were only a few white puffy clouds in the sky and the scorching sun of the dog days of summer was having its way. Everything along the road was dusty because even our buggy kicked up a cloud of dust. We met a farm truck loaded with peanut hay on its way in the town and we were engulfed in the brown cloud of dust for several minutes afterwards.

Even though we were clopping along at a respectable clip, the horseflies were pestering Nellie continuously. I was quite amused by Nellie swishing her tail in a passive defense against the never-ending harassment. We passed Charlie Mitchell's house on the right, which was shaded with three enormous pecan trees. The road turned to red clay as we climbed a steep hill and eventually passed Tommy Lanier's place, a white ranch-style house set off in the distance amidst a dense stand of tall, longleaf yellow pines.

The road took a gentle turn to the left and went down another steep hill. More red clay, with deep ditches cut into high banks on either side of the road.

"Papa! Papa! Look at that snake!" Aunt Versie was almost coming out of her seat and pointing towards an enormous snake stretched out on the high bank on the right side of the road.

"He's dead, Versie," Granddaddy said. "He's a big 'un, ain't he? Over 6 feet long… biggest rattler I've seen in a while. Charlie Mitchell took care of him this morning…thinks it might have been the one that killed his best bird dog."

At the bottom of the hill, we crossed a small branch of trickling water, formed by a clear water spring bubbling from the ground called Cat Springs. As we started up the hill on the other side, we met a man that had a mule pulling a ground slide with a 55-gallon drum on it. Granddaddy tipped his hat to him.

"Ain't that Mr. Anderson?" Aunt Versie asked. "Where's he going?"

"Every day or so he goes down to Cat Springs and fills that drum up with fresh drinking water. Glad we don't have to do that. We get pure, good tasting water pumped up to us from an underwater stream below the flint rock 120 feet down from that well you had drilled for us. Were much obliged to you for that, Versie."

"You're welcome, Papa."

"Not everybody has electricity, and were still one of the few up this way who has indoor plumbing."

"I know, Papa…"

25

The road was headed due West as we passed Buford Sneads' house on the right and then Walter Sneads' house on the left. About 100 yards up ahead, the road took a 90° turn to the right. But, when we got there, we turned left. I was looking directly at a big white house with four brick and wood columns fronting a porch that was almost as wide as the house. On the porch in a wooden rocker sat a gray-haired, matronly lady, wearing a flowered dress and a white apron. It was my grandmother.

I was home.

Chapter 6

"Whoa, Nellie," Granddaddy said. He tightened the reins and brought the buggy to a stop at the wooden gate in front of the house.

Grandmother bounded down the steps like a teenager and hurried towards the buggy with outstretched arms. "Hey, Benny. It's good to see you. I'm so glad you're here." She swept me from the buckboard and swung me around holding me tight.

"Hey Mama," Aunt Versie said.

Grandmother put me down and the two of them hugged like there was no tomorrow. It looked like Aunt Versie was trying not to cry.

A light brown dog with white spots came running at me from around the house. He had a happy hassle and was wagging his tail, but I recoiled, covering the bandage on my right arm.

"That's Fido. He won't hurt you, Benny," Grandmother said.

Aunt Versie started towards me, but by then Fido had already nudged me and licked me and was on his way to doing the same to her.

"Nice doggie, Fido," Aunt Versie said, patting his head. "Benny might be a little skittish of dogs. He was just attacked a few days ago by a big old German police dog in Jacksonville. What kind of dog is Fido?"

"He's a Heinz 57, but we think he's mostly cocker spaniel. He took up with us a few months ago," Grandmother said.

I looked around at my new surroundings. To the left side of the house a dark green wisteria vine draped over a large arbor. The remnants of deep purple blossoms covered the ground below. Beyond that towards the back of the house was a huge woodpile with an ax sticking into a block of wood waiting to be chopped. There were already a few leaves beginning to fall from several tall oak trees in the yard around both sides of the house. To the right of the house the terrain sloped downward to the pumphouse. Beyond that was a pear tree covered with ripe green pears. Then there was a stable where Nellie stayed, adjacent to an old gray barn. To the right of that was a vegetable garden with tomatoes, okra, squash, cantaloupes, radishes, potatoes, peppers, corn, and even a few watermelons. Nearby was a chicken yard with dozens of hens scratching around. Most of them were red in color with a few white and a few gray speckled chickens mixed in. Standing tall above them all was a big red rooster, sporting long, sharp spurs.

We entered the front of the house through the screen door which was held closed by a strong spring. There was also a heavy wooden door, with most of the top half being a clear pane of thick glass. The door was seldom closed and never locked. In fact, it didn't even have a lock. Standing in the corner behind the door was a long barreled 12-gauge shotgun.

"Oh! Mama," Aunt Versie said. "I can't believe what Papa has done to this place." She looked up at the freshly painted high ceilings above the living room, the dining room, and then the kitchen on the left side of the house. On the left wall of the living room was the fireplace, adorned with a wooden mantle and a brick hearth. Grouped nearby was a large wooden rocker, a wicker settee, and a grand glider rocker covered with dark blue fabric with armrests accentuated by goosenecks carved from dark wood. At the foot of the rocker was a country ottoman, which was actually just a footstool made from gallon-sized tin cans tied together and covered with dark blue fabric. Asleep on the stool, totally indifferent to us, was a portly white cat. Colorful braided oval rugs were scattered about on the tongue-and-grooved hardwood floor.

"Harde done a good job, like he always does," Grandmother said. "But he had a lot of good help. Hardy did a lot of the cuttin' and totin' and nailin', and Bud came over from Jacksonville and wired it for us. He's quite a good 'lectrician, you know."

My Grandmother, and all their friends, called Granddaddy "Harde" (pronounced Hard). Hardy Anderson Shelfer married my grandmother, Laura Minerva Neel, in 1896. Within the next 28 years, they had 12 children, seven boys and five girls. There were all born at their home on the farm, without complications.

My Grandfather was a man of many talents. He was a master carpenter and generally considered the best in the county. He was the sole go-to dentist in the area, even though he specialized only in extractions. And he played a mean fiddle, providing music for many Saturday night hoedowns.

"Versie, you and Benny take the third bedroom. Verdayne's in the middle bedroom. No tellin' how long, though, 'cause he's threatening to go join the Army to help with the war. I tried to talk to him, but he won't listen to me. He's taken a likin' to one of those Dennis girls, Minnie Lee, who lives down near Shady Grove South of town. Maybe she can talk some sense into him."

We walked into the dining room where there was a long narrow serving table against the wall along with at least half a dozen chairs. In the center of the room was a heavy wooden table covered by a white tablecloth with crocheted corners. It was currently configured to seat six people, but it was expandable to accommodate at least 12 people by adding up to two additional leaves in the center. There were several dishes of food in the center of the table covered with cloths to keep them warm. I especially noticed a large platter of homemade biscuits that satiated the room with a tantalizing aroma. There were four places set at the table, accentuated by four large sweating glasses of sweet tea.

Through the next door was the kitchen, a room almost as large as the others, but the floor was completely covered with a brown colored linoleum. Along the left wall was the sink with a drain counter for dishes. Next to that, was a jet-black wood-burning stove with white porcelain handles to the firebox, the oven, and the warming pantry above. A black metal flu vented the smoke from the stove to a small chimney outside. On the right wall of the kitchen, emitting a low humming noise, was the new electric refrigerator, or icebox, as everyone called it.

"Versie, y'all washup. Supper's ready. We'll eat soon as Harde gets back from putting Nellie in the barn," Grandmother said.

Aunt Versie put her suitcase in the third bedroom and left her purse on the double bed. It was covered with a white chenille bedspread and had a black metal frame. White Priscilla curtains with ruffled valances billowed softly from the warm breeze of the two open West-facing windows. Looking down the hill beyond the pumphouse I could see Nellie drinking water from a wooden trough. Granddaddy gave her half of a bale of hay and closed the gate to the barn yard.

"Benny, come wash your hands." Aunt Versie was calling me from another room.

I turned to look for her to find Grandmother standing just outside the door smiling at me. I returned a sheepish smile and ran to find Aunt Versie in the bathroom, which was through one of two doors off the back of the kitchen.

"He's such a happy boy, Mama," Aunt Versie said. "He's smart, and he's a good boy, too. Ain't that right, Benny?"

"Yes, ma'am," I said. I was already learning that being good meant saying yes ma'am and no ma'am, yes sir and no sir, to speak when spoken to, and to be seen and not heard.

The bathroom was a narrow room off the back of the house that consisted of a small linen closet, a sink, which was called a washbasin, a white porcelain tub standing on little clawed feet, and a white toilet, called a commode.

I climbed up on another tin can footstool Grandmother had placed for me beside the washbasin so I could reach the faucets. I turned on the water but was surprised when I reached for the soap. It was a block about half the size of brick, with sharp corners like a piece of cheese that had been cut with a knife. It was a weird color, with marbling between caramel brown and deep purple. I glanced at Aunt Versie.

"Go ahead, Benny. It's alright. It's homemade lye soap that your grandmother made in that big black kettle in the backyard. On the farm, we have to make do."

I washed my hands, but the lye soap didn't lather up too well and it did not smell like flowers.

We walked through the screen door at the rear of the kitchen which led to the back porch. Fido was curled up beneath the Maytag washing machine, one of the latest models complete with a hand-cranked clothes wringer. A clothes wire was strung along one side of the porch, well beneath the overhang to provide for rainy day clothes drying. Hanging from nails on the wall were two number 2 wash tubs. Off the right side of the porch at the back of the house was a storage area, usually called the junk room for obvious reasons.

Six wide-plank steps led from the porch down to the backyard. A large hydrangea plant bloomed on either side of the steps. Also scattered along the side of the house were a few azalea plants. Dark green oleander bushes with pink blossoms dotted the side yard. The black iron kettle sat on spiked legs and red bricks in a makeshift fire pit in the back of the yard. On the East side of the house, where it could catch the morning sun, was a long clothes line strung taunt between two trees. The yard itself was mostly just plain old dirt. The large oak trees, which provided the much-needed shade for the house, would not allow grass to grow.

Grandmother walked to the edge of the porch and looked around the corner down towards the barn. Granddaddy was slowly making his way up the path towards the house. In the corner of the yard was a small weathered wood building with a shingled roof about half the size of a one car garage.

"Harde, step in the smokehouse and get us a side of meat," Grandmother said. "We'll need it for breakfast in the morning."

Granddaddy stooped to go through the small door and quickly emerged with a slab of meat the color of dark honey and about the size of first base on a baseball diamond. It had been hanging in the smokehouse by a loop inserted in the corner of the meat fashioned from a piece of bear grass. Granddaddy used his pocketknife to cut the bear grass and remove it from the meat.

Grandmother, Aunt Versie, and I walked back to the dining room and took our places at the dinner table waiting for Granddaddy to wash up.

"Versie, tell me about Sing," Grandmother said. She had a tone of concern in her voice.

"Well, after Sing and Dot got divorced again, and Dot went back up north again, Sing was drafted into the Army. When he got orders to report to Camp Blanding down south of Jacksonville for basic training, he was going crazy worrying about Benny. By then, I'd married Larry and he had enlisted in the Marines and had gone to Camp Lejeune in North Carolina for his training. So, I told Sing, don't worry about Benny, I'll take care of him 'til you come home. Just make sure you come home."

"That's what I'm worried about. I'm afraid we'll never see him again. Seems like every week or so around here somebody's getting' a telegram 'bout their boy being killed."

"Sing says he thinks he gets a few days leave after basic training, and if he does, he'll come see us."

"Oh, I hope he does…" Grandmother's voice trailed off as she watched Granddaddy walk around to take his seat at the head of the table. His hands and face were washed and his wiry, damp hair had been combed. Grandmother nodded to him.

31

"Smile on us, Heavenly Father, and make us be thankful for these and all our many blessings. Amen."

Amen, indeed.

Chapter 7

A couple of months had passed since I had my last rabies shot and therefore my last ice cream cone. Aunt Versie and I had made an easy adjustment to life on the farm. She was always helping grandmother with the cooking, cleaning, and sewing. The last few days, they had been busy "putting up vegetables," as Grandmother called it. Aunt Versie said they were "canning vegetables," even though no cans were involved. All I know is they would go down to the garden and pick something like tomatoes, okra, or butter beans, dump them in a large pot and cook them for a long time, filling the house with crazy smells. After they cooled, they were poured into dozens of brand-new Mason jars with shiny gold-colored lids to be stored on several shelves in the junk room for later use.

There were many chores to be done on the farm. Strangely enough, almost all of them involved food; doing something that would put food on the table. Food and water, the basic necessities that made everything else possible. It wasn't long before grandmother gave me my first chore.

"Benny, do you think you could be the one to fetch the eggs from the henhouse for us?" Grandmother asked.

"Yes ma'am, I said." I wasn't sure, but I was feeling a sense of pride that Grandmother would trust me to get the eggs.

"Good. What you do is, ever' day about dinner time, take this egg basket and bring in the eggs. Be careful not to leave the gate open and let the chickens out. And, watch out for that old red rooster...he thinks he owns that chicken yard. Oh! Don't go barefooted, you're bound to cut your foot."

Grandmother handed me the basket and I marched out the back door and down to the chicken yard on a mission with purpose and commitment. The large brood of hens was scattered about the yard, scratching and clucking. I noticed that the rooster was in the back of the yard beneath the shade of a nearby pear tree, so I darted through the front gate and into the henhouse in the middle of the yard.

It was a small house, not even as big as the smokehouse, and built with slatted sides so the air could pass through. There were several wall-to-wall poles at different heights for the chickens to roost above ground at night. Even though the house was ventilated, the smell was…different. Malodorous. The dirt floor of the house was covered with manure, so it was impossible to walk through here without cutting your foot, stepping in it.

There were several nests on the ground scattered around the walls of the house. I gathered a total of about a half a dozen eggs into my basket and went back through the door of the house, only to find myself nose to nose with the big red rooster. His head, with the yellow beak, piercing eyes, and blood flushed comb, was almost as tall as me. He billowed his crimson feathers as he stretched and strutted, accentuating the sharp three-inch spurs on his long yellow legs.

I wanted to run, but I was afraid I would drop the eggs and break them. After a few moments of a staring contest, which seemed like an eternity, I began walking slowly towards the gate. The rooster began angling around, trying to get behind me, looking for a chance to attack. As he did so, I kept turning to face him and ended up backing out through the gate. The big red rooster flapped his wings and crowed and strutted around amongst the hens, obviously proud of having vanquished the threat to his kingdom.

It was a proud moment when I placed the basket of uncracked eggs on the drain board for Grandmother to wash and put away. I heard someone talking on the front porch so I ran through the house to tell them of my accomplishment.

"Grandmother! Aunt Versie! I did it. I got the eggs," I said. I burst through the screen door to the front porch, then quickly turned around to catch it from slamming shut. Granddaddy, who was sitting in the big rocker in the middle of the porch, did not like to hear the front door slam.

"That's real good, Benny," Grandmother said. She and Aunt Versie were sitting in the rocking chairs towards the wisteria vine. And they both were looking at me with this cat-that-ate- the-canary smile, with occasional glances behind me.

"Benny, look who's here," Aunt Versie said. She nodded at someone behind me.

I turned to look at the man sitting and smiling at me in the front porch swing. He was tall and thin, with deeply tanned leathery skin and had black, wavy hair and a thin mustache. He was wearing an olive drab gabardine uniform with a shiny brass belt buckle and a black tie that was tucked into his shirt below the second button. Atop his head was a green folding overseas cap cocked with a certain flair off to one side.

"Daddy!" I ran to him at full speed. He swept me up and lifted me almost to the ceiling, swinging me around and around.

"Look how much you've grown," Daddy said. "You're gittin' to be such a big boy."

"I didn't know you were coming, Daddy."

"I didn't have time to write. I just jumped on the next bus to come see you when I finished my training and got my orders."

"If I'd known you was comin', I'd a hitched Nellie to the buggy and picked you up," Granddaddy said. He took another deep draw from his mahogany-colored half bent Dublin pipe and directed a puff of white smoke at some of the ever-present gnats.

"That's all right, Papa. It's not more than a mile. At Camp Blanding, we'd march five times that distance just to get to breakfast."

"Breakfast? Don't look like they fed you at all. Yor' skinny as a rail," Grandmother said. "We need to fatten you up."

"Either that or worm 'im," Granddaddy said. He had a twinkle in his eye and a hint of a grin as he dispatched some more gnats with another puff of smoke.

"Oh! They've already wormed me, Pappa. And gave me a shot for every disease in the world, 'cause I'm going overseas."

"You going after the Japs or the Krauts?" Granddaddy asked.

"The Japs, Pappa. My orders are to report to board a troop carrier in San Francisco at the end of next week. I have to catch the Gulf Wind for California on Saturday."

"God be with you, son. Go kill every one of them damn squinty-eyed bastards. Make 'em pay for Pearl Harbor." Granddaddy no longer had a hint of a grin, or a twinkle in his eye. Grandmother gave him that "look," obviously disapproving of his language.

"We'll git 'em, Pappa. Don't you worry 'bout that." Daddy sat back down in the swing, watching me intently as he tousled my hair and placed me beside him. And I couldn't take my eyes off of his new mustache.

"I hear you're being a good boy… and you're doing chores?" Daddy asked.

"Yes sir. I brought in the eggs, but that old rooster tried to git me."

"Just show him who's boss, son. If he tries to mess with you again, just give him a good kick."

"Yes, sir." I couldn't help but smile thinking about what Daddy had just said. And I kept staring at his mustache.

"Wake up, Benny! They're bitin' down at Rock Pond. Let's go fishin'," Daddy said.

I was sleeping so soundly that Daddy had to shake the bed twice to wake me. It was so nice to have Daddy home. I got to sleep with him in the middle bedroom, and we had talked and talked until it was, I'm sure, long past my bed time.

"Git your fishin' clothes on, washup, and hurry to the dining room. Breakfast is waitin'," Daddy said.

There was no harder working woman on earth than my grandmother. Between the animals, the garden, the housecleaning, the cooking, the dishwashing, the sewing, the clothes washing, and the ironing, she was busy doing something all day long. But she did have one passionate pastime…fishing. She loved it more than anything and cherished each moment she could get away to go fishing.

"Sing, soon as you and Benny finish your breakfast, go down by the barn and dig us some wigglers," Grandmother said. "Me and Versie will clean up the kitchen and meet you down there with the fishing poles."

"You might want to grunt some earthworms, too," Granddaddy said. He was sitting at his usual spot at the head of the table pouring his piping hot black coffee back and forth between his cup and his saucer to cool it.

Grandmother paused for a moment to give him what I again recognized as "the look." He returned her gaze with that twinkle in his sky-blue eyes, and he almost smiled. After 12 children and almost 50 years of marriage not many words were needed between these two.

"You comin' with us, Pappa?" Daddy asked.

"No y'all go ahead. My arthritis is actin' up, so I think I'll just hang around the house today."

Granddaddy seemed to be having trouble moving around, but he never complained. He just walked slower, but never with a cane.

The scrambled eggs, grits with red-eye gravy, and the fresh bacon from the smokehouse were very tasty. But nothing could compare to Grandmother's biscuits. She showed me how to poke my finger into the side of the biscuit, wiggle it around and pull it straight out, leaving a hole in the biscuit. I would then pour that hole full of fresh sugar cane syrup from the syrup pitcher that was always on the table. Yummy.

Daddy grabbed an empty gallon can from the back porch and a six-pronged tilling hoe from under the house and we went down by the barn to dig bait. There was a plot of soft dirt just outside of Nellie's stall. With one quick motion Daddy planted the hoe in the soft dirt and flipped over a big clump. A dozen worms longer than a dollar bill danced on the ground.

"Benny, grab those wigglers and put 'em in the can," Daddy said.

"Will they bite me? They look like baby snakes." The more I watched them the more I hesitated.

"No, they won't bite you," Daddy said. "Snakes will bite you, even baby snakes. But not worms. Worms are just fish bait." The tone of his voice and his gentle smile was reassuring. He reached down with one swoop of his big hand and threw several wigglers into the can. So, then I grabbed one of those slimy, squirmy, squishy things and put him in the can. Daddy gave me an approving smile and a nod, and I did it again. It didn't take me long to learn that you had to hold a worm just right; tight enough they don't get away, but not so tight you squish them into pieces.

"Y'all findin' any bait?" Grandmother asked. She and Aunt Versie had walked down from the house carrying several long cane polls. I noticed

Aunt Versie was carrying the short fishing pole that Daddy had rigged especially for me.

"I think we got plenty, Mama," Daddy said. "What do you think?" He showed her the can that was now almost half full of worms. "Y'all done good. Let's go fishing," Grandmother said.

We began walking single file past the corn crib beside Nellie's stall and entered a narrow trail into the woods. Daddy led the way with me right behind him, then Grandmother and Aunt Versie. Off to our left was a wire fence bordering a cornfield. Everywhere else there were lots of tall pine trees with thick underbrush, and knee-deep wire grass covering the ground.

After about 10 minutes, which seem like a long time to me, the woods thinned out a bit. There were fewer pine trees but more blackjack oaks and scrub oaks, as Daddy called them.

"Benny, look at this." Daddy had stopped and was pointing to something a few feet off the trail. "Do you know what that is?" He asked.

"It's a turtle," I said. I was looking at this creature with a big pewter colored shell that was covered with a pattern of ornate ridges.

"No, that's a gopher," Daddy said. "Turtles live in the water, and gophers live on the land."

"Actually, it's a land tortoise," Aunt Versie said. "But we always called them gophers. I love gophers. They carry their house with them everywhere they go." She walked right up to him and picked him up. The gopher had pulled his head and feet inside his shell.

"Will he bite you?" I asked.

"He won't bite you, but them snappin' turtles in the pond shore will," Grandmother said. "And he won't turn loose 'til it thunders."

"Now Mama, quit trying to scare 'im. After that big ole' dog bit 'im, he's just trying to figure out what'll bite and what won't," Aunt Versie said. She brought the gopher over to me and held him near me. "Here, you can touch 'im, Benny. It's okay"

And I did. With one finger. His shell was hard as a rock.

"Y'all quit messin' with gophers, and let's go fishin'," Grandmother said.

"Let's put 'im back near his home, Benny," Aunt Versie said. She took us few steps off the trail and gently placed the gopher down near a large hole in the ground. "See, that's where he lives. Bye-bye, sweet gopher," Aunt Versie said, as we walked away.

"There's more snakes in them holes than there are gophers. And all snakes will bite you," Grandmother said. "Right up the hill there was where the ground rattler bit Tots. We almost lost her. She was sick for two weeks." Grandmother had already passed us and was now leading the way on the trail down a steep hill.

As I followed along, I noticed many gopher holes on either side of the trail. I didn't see any snakes, but now I was looking for them. We reached a clearing at the bottom of the hill and all I could see was water in front of us. It was Rock Pond, our fishing hole.

Grandmother went straight to her favorite spot to fish. She unwound the line from her fishing pole, slid the cork up the line to the right depth, and baited her hook with one of the wigglers. With one sweeping familiar motion, she threw her line out into the pond and rested the pole on a tree branch to keep it out of the water. She reached into her apron pocket and retrieved a tin box about the size of a large lemon that she always carried. After opening the tin and tapping an ample dip of Railroad snuff into her lower lip, she sat down on the bank and relaxed, but never taking her eyes off her cork. The expression on her face was revealing. The world was at war, but for Grandmother, at this moment, all was well.

"Come here, Benny," Daddy said. "Here's a good fishing spot for you, close to Mama." He had already unwound the line from my little pole and was digging into the bait can for a wiggler. I had found some small rocks on the side of the hill and I threw one into the pond, just to see it splash.

"No, Benny. Don't throw rocks into the water. You have to be real quiet or you'll scare the fish." The tone of Daddy's voice was very kind, not admonishing at all. I gently placed the rocks on the ground, because I wanted to be a good boy. I had heard Aunt Versie and Grandmother talking and saying that I was a good boy, and I wanted to be perfect for them. And I wanted to be perfect for Daddy, too.

Daddy baited my hook, flipped my line out into the pond, and rested my pole on a nearby tree branch so it would not make ripples in the water.

"Sit right here," Daddy said. He patted the ground beside him. "Just keep an eye on your cork, and when it goes under, pull 'im."

"Look! Mama's gittin' a bite," Aunt Versie said. She was sitting up on the hill, just watching.

Grandmother's cork was bobbing up and down, and then it went under. She tightened the line with gusto and pulled a small fish, a very small fish, out of the pond.

"Nice going, Mama," Daddy said. "You caught the first fish."

"Throw that little thing back, Mama," Aunt Versie said.

"I'll do no such thing, Versie." Grandmother said it like she meant it.

"Awe, throw 'im back, Mama. Tell 'im to 'go grow'. He ain't no bigger than a soda cracker."

"You know it's bad luck not to keep the first fish you catch. I'm gonna fry 'im up for dinner, and I'll eat 'im on a soda cracker, if I have to," Grandmother said.

Aunt Versie, Daddy, and now even Grandmother were all laughing. And I was learning that all fishermen are superstitious, and fishing with family is great fun.

"Pull 'im, Benny! Pull 'im!" Grandmother shouted at me and pointed at my cork.

I looked, trying to see my cork, but there were only ripples where the cork had been. And the end of my little fishing pole was being dipped forcefully into the water.

"Pull 'im, Benny, before he drags your pole into the pond," Daddy said.

I grabbed the pole and lifted it with all my might, but the fish had other ideas. He was pulling hard, doing circles towards the deep water, and I could barely keep the end of my pole out of the pond.

"Hold 'im, Benny! That's a nice one," Aunt Versie said.

After a few of the most exciting moments of my life, the fish grew tired and I was so excited I jerked him out of the water up over my head on the bank behind me. This big beautiful fish of many colors, about the size of my daddy's hand, was flopping around on the hill behind me.

"Benny's caught his dinner," Grandmother said. "Nice red belly."

"Good job, Benny," Daddy said. "You had him hooked real good, right in the upper lip. We'll put 'im on the stringer with Mama's fish."

We had fished for a couple more hours when Grandmother glanced up at the midday sun and announced that we had a "mess" of fish and it was about time for us to go home and fry 'em up for dinner. I had caught a few more fish. Of course, Grandmother caught the most fish, followed by Daddy, and then me. Aunt Versie didn't fish at all. She kept the comments coming from her nearby perch up on the hill. Especially about Grandmother and the little fish she caught which was on the stringer next to my big fish. I had caught my first fish and I hooked him good. But he hooked me good also. I loved to fish.

"Mama, please pass the hushpuppies," Aunt Versie said.

We had all assumed our positions at the dinner table. There was a big plate of fish, fried to a golden brown in peanut oil and heavily coated with corn meal. The hushpuppies covered another platter. They were also fried to a golden brown; a concoction of corn meal and onions and were slightly larger than a golf ball. The usual fare of turnip greens, rutabagas, green beans, and okra were also on the table. I wasn't too sure about the hushpuppies, so I had my eye on the biscuits that were left over from breakfast.

"Here you go, Benny, here's your fish," Daddy said. "And here's a hushpuppy to go with it."

I looked at the hushpuppy. Still not sure.

"Go ahead, Benny," Aunt Versie said. "They're real good. Take a bite."

"Put one of them hushpuppies up on your head," Granddaddy said. He leaned forward a bit and almost smiled. "Your tongue'll slap your brains out trying to git to it."

Everyone laughed and laughed, like they had never heard that one before. I was still staring at the hushpuppy. Then I saw the pitcher of cane syrup that was always on the table along with the salt and pepper and the bottle of pepper sauce. Without thinking, I did my biscuit trick with the hushpuppy. I punched a hole in it with my finger and filled it with syrup. So good. I then knew it would be good even without the syrup, but I was taking no chances.

"That boy's got a sweet tooth," Grandmother said.

"Yes, he does," Aunt Versie said. "And he especially loves him some ice cream."

"Benny, you ain't never had no ice cream 'till you've had Mama's homemade peach ice cream," Daddy said.

"Sing, don't be teasing Benny about peach ice cream," Aunt Versie said. "The peaches are all gone this year."

"No, I put a few up back in July, and I think I have a few jars left," Grandmother said. "Now y'all quit talking 'bout sweets so Benny can eat his dinner."

"Here, Benny, let me show you how to eat a bream," Daddy said. He picked up the red belly I had caught and held it for me to see. "First, you can munch on the tail fin, which is always crunchy and good. Then you pull out this big fin in the back, the dorsal fin. Now you can just eat it like a ham sandwich." He held it up like he was going to take a big bite, and smiled. Instead, he handed it to me and I took a big bite. It tasted different, but not bad. So, I took another bite.

"Now, Benny, be careful not to get any bones," Aunt Versie said. "If you do, you have to spit them out, or they'll get caught in your throat."

Eating the fish did present a few problems, deciding what was meat and what was bones. So, I picked at it and scattered it around the plate and devoted most of my time to the hushpuppy.

"Papa, how long you had that hoss? What's her name, Nellie?" Daddy asked.

"Longer than I'm gonna have 'er, if she don't straighten up and fly right," Granddaddy said. "She's a little too much on the wild side for my likin'."

"Has she been broke?"

"They said she had, but she ain't."

"I'll break her for you, Pappa."

"No need, son. She'll either eventually come around, or she won't."

"She just needs somebody to ride her. Let me have a go at her. I'll meet you down at the barn soon as we're done with dinner."

"You're starting to sound as wild and stubborn as she is," Granddaddy said. "But I guess it wouldn't hurt to try."

Granddaddy already had the bridal reins on Nellie when daddy and I got down to the barn after dinner. She was hitched to the fencepost on the outside of the barn yard.

"I ain't got a saddle son, 'cause I ain't never gonna ride her," Granddaddy said.

"That's okay, Papa," Daddy said. "I'll just ride her bareback."

Daddy approached Nellie walking very slowly and talking to her in low, gentle tones. "Hello Nellie… nice horsey… pretty horsey… what a sweet girl…" He quietly untied the reins from the fencepost and lovingly petted her long face and rubbed her tiny little ears. Nellie neighed and whinnied and shook her head from side to side. It was difficult to tell whether she liked what Daddy was doing, or was just annoyed.

"Here, Pappa, hold the reins a minute. It might be easier for me to mount her if I climb up on the fence," Daddy said. He handed the reins to Granddaddy and walked through the barn yard gate, and carefully climbed up high on the fence. "Nice horsey…pretty horsey…what a sweet girl…" Daddy eased off the fence and delicately lowered himself onto Nellie's back. He leaned forward with his arms on either side of Nellie's neck and stroked her ever so gently. "Nice horsey…pretty horsey…what a sweet girl…"

Granddaddy handed Daddy the reins and slowly backed away. I was standing out of the way near the pump house, and I could see Grandmother and Aunt Versie watching intently from up the hill in the backyard. Daddy sat up straight on Nellie's back and tightened the reins against the bit in her teeth.

"Let's go, Nellie. Let's go for a little walk," Daddy said to her, almost in a whisper. He made a clucking sound to her and twitched the reins. Nellie remained still for a moment, then began walking slowly away from the fence; two steps, three steps, four steps, five…

Without warning, Nellie bucked her rear end high into the air and simultaneously kicked both hind legs straight at the clouds! Daddy sailed towering over her head, turned a complete flip in the air, and landed flat of his back on the hard dirt with a frightening thud.

"Daddy!" I yelled at the top of my lungs. Grandmother and Aunt Versie ran down the hill screaming. Granddaddy walked towards Daddy, looking stunned. Nellie took a victory gallop around the yard, then bucked and pranced into the barnyard. Daddy did not move.

Chapter 8

Daddy lay still in the bed. His eyes were closed like he was asleep, but I knew he wasn't. Well, maybe he was. I wasn't sleepy at all, even though everyone else had gone to bed and the house was dark and quiet. I had heard them talking about Daddy leaving tomorrow. I didn't know why he was going and I didn't want him to go. And I couldn't clear my head of the memory of Nellie bucking Daddy head-over-heels onto the hard ground. He had laid there for the longest time and I thought he was dead. Finally, after all of us had gathered around, he coughed a few times and opened his eyes. Granddaddy said he would be okay, that he just had the wind knocked out of him. He didn't look okay to me. After he sat up, I could see blood oozing from scrapes on both of his elbows and a large area on the backside of his left shoulder about the size of the red belly I caught. Grandmother had splashed the dirt off the wounds with a bucket of water she got from the pump house, and dried him off with the backside of her apron. Daddy winced from the burning pain when Aunt Versie doused his wounds with red merthiolate.

"Daddy… Daddy." I tapped Daddy on the shoulder, being careful not to touch his wounded shoulder. "Daddy, wake up."

"Huh…what is it, Benny?" Daddy opened his eyes and propped his head up higher on the pillow and looked at me. Now that I had him awake, I didn't know what to say.

"Daddy, are there any alligators in the ocean?" I blurted out. Daddy doubled the pillow and propped his head up a little higher and gave me the look. The look that simultaneously showed amusement, agitation, and amazement. The AAA look.

"No, Benny. There ain't no alligators in the ocean. The ocean is saltwater and gators like freshwater and warm weather," Daddy said. He relaxed a bit and closed his eyes again.

"Can fish fly?" I asked.

"No, fish don't fly… Except for in the ocean there is a fish that jumps out of the water and glides on real thin fins that act like wings. They call him a flying fish." My daddy was a patient man.

"Daddy, are you leaving tomorrow?"

"Yes… I'm leaving tomorrow." Daddy sat straight up in the bed like he realized that I was finally getting around to what was really bothering me.

"Why? Why do you want to leave me?" I couldn't look at Daddy. I just stared into the darkness. What I really wondered was why he wanted to leave me, too. My mother had left me twice, and now my daddy was leaving me too.

"I don't want to leave you, Benny. I don't ever want to leave you."

"Then why are you going?" I asked.

"Sometimes, you can't do what you want to do because you have to do what you have to do," he said. "Does that make sense, Benny? Do you understand?"

"Yes sir. I understand."

I laid my head on the pillow and I saw that Daddy did the same. Sleep came almost immediately.

Granddaddy had hitched Nellie to the buggy and pulled him around to the front of the house and hitched them to a post outside the front gate. I was already standing in the buggy holding on to the buckboard. Granddaddy and Aunt Versie were waiting on the seat behind me.

Daddy and Grandmother were talking quietly on the porch. They hugged each other, longer than normal, and exchanged kisses on the cheek. Daddy picked up his large green duffel bag and walk slowly down the front porch steps towards the buggy.

"Bye, Mama," he said. He looked back over his shoulder but Grandmother had already gone into the house. I guess she didn't want Daddy to see her crying. Or maybe she didn't want to watch us drive away because she thought she had said goodbye to her fifth son, her eighth child, for the last time.

Nellie turned to look at Daddy who was walking a little more gingerly than normal towards the buggy. She shook her head and swished her tail and after a little neigh and whinny looked away as if everything was normal. That was not exactly the way Daddy was looking at her.

"Pappa, can you trust this crazy horse with all of us in the buggy?" Daddy asked.

"She might be a little skittish but she won't buck when she's hitched to the buggy. She does, I'll snatch this bit clear up behind her ears," Granddaddy said. He said it like he meant it. I believed him, and I think Nellie did, too.

Daddy threw his duffel bag behind the buggy seat and continued to stare at Nellie.

"You need some help getting' in son?" Granddaddy asked. "You seem to be a little puny today." There it was again, that wry little smile and the twinkle in Granddaddy's eye.

"Thanks, Pappa, but I can make it just fine." Daddy smiled back at Granddaddy, acknowledging his good-natured concern. Daddy had insisted that he was none the worse off from yesterday's rodeo trick, yet his movements were very deliberate.

It was mostly a quiet ride into town. Daddy and Granddaddy made occasional small talk about the weather and how dry it was.

"Looks like Mr. Tommy's corn's goin' to the bad if we don't get some rain," Daddy said. "It's all twisted up and turning brown. You think it'll ever rain again?"

"I don't much care if it ever rains again, not for me," Granddaddy said. He lifted the straw hat from his head and wiped his glistening brow as he waited for effect. The hint of that little grin betrayed him again. "I've seen it rain," he continued, "but Benny here is almost four years old and he ain't never seen it rain."

Daddy and Aunt Versie laughed and laughed, like they had never heard that one before.

"Hardy came by the other day and said down at the Long Pond there were three-year-old catfish that ain't never learned how to swim." Granddaddy was on a roll and there was more laughter from Daddy and Aunt Versie.

Nellie clopped along at a spirited trot down the big clay hill and then past Charlie Mitchell's house on the left and then the Edwards' place on the right. I noticed that Daddy gave it a long look as we rode by. It was widely believed Hubert Edwards was the local go-to moonshiner. With Jackson County being a dry county, the long driveway through the sage field up to the Edwards house was a well-traveled road. Everyone knew that Edwards kept his pints and half-pints of white lightning buried in the sage field so that if the sheriff raided his house, he would find no illegal alcohol.

"I'll tell you what, Sing," Granddaddy said. He saw Daddy staring at the field. "As dry as it is, if that sagebrush ever catches on fire, it'll be like 4th of July."

"That would be a shame," Daddy said. Somehow, I knew he meant it.

Granddaddy tied Nellie and the buggy to the hitching rail at the post office so Nellie wouldn't be scared when the big iron horse came puffing into Sneads. The little town was buzzing with the usual flurry of activity that coincided with the daily arrival of the 4 o'clock westbound train. There were a few cars and trucks parked around, but just as many mules and wagons. We all walked slowly together the short block and a half down the hill to the depot. I would normally run ahead exploring all the sites, but today I held Daddy's hand. It just seemed the right thing to do. We crossed US 90 at GD Malloy's filling station and past Lanier's grocery store.

There was a young Pentecostal preacher standing on the corner with a tattered Bible in his hand shouting fire and brimstone like he was speaking to a thousand people, when actually there were only a handful gathered on the sidewalk. He was dripping with sweat, yet he refused to loosen his tie or shed the coat of his navy-blue wool suit. He delivered each line of his message with a singsong rhythm until he completely ran out of breath. Then he would verbally inhale in rhythm and do it all over again. I couldn't understand a word he was saying except for an occasional Jesus and hell which were always elongated and emphasized. Perhaps it was just as well.

As we ambled towards the depot we passed Carlisle's furniture store, Joe Cogburn's barbershop, and BL Watsons dry goods store. Across the street was Boy Glisson's café, Doc O'Hara's office, and Edgar Bailey Liddon's general merchandise store.

The train depot was an austere cream-colored building along the tracks on the west side of the street, with an attached loading platform for incoming and outgoing freight. Inside the building, sharing a room, was the telegraph office and the ticket office with a window to the waiting room. Granddaddy, Aunt Versie, and I sat in the wooden seats that were built all around the room. I could hear the click clack of the telegraph machine as Daddy handed a copy of his orders to the agent at the window. The man said something to Daddy, handed him a ticket, and pointed to the clock on the wall.

"He said it's right on time," Daddy said.

"Usually is," Granddaddy said. "What did it cost you, son?"

"Didn't cost me nothing, Pappa," Daddy said. "Soldiers traveling on orders get to ride free. Sometimes they even have special cars on the train for us."

In the distant I heard the unmistakable whistle of the steam locomotive engine.

"My advice is the same, son. Go kill every one of them damn squinty-eyed sumbitches over there that you can, so we don't have to kill 'em over here," Granddaddy said. They shared a long, firm handshake.

"I'll do my best, Papa."

"I know you will, son. I'm proud of you."

Now I could hear the roar of the train on the rails and the choo-chooing of the locomotive...getting louder. Daddy walked over and hugged Aunt Versie. They were talking in hushed tones and I couldn't hear what they were saying, but from their glances my way, I knew they were talking about me. Aunt Versie was fighting tears and didn't want to let him go.

The depot door was open, so I walked over and peeked outside down the tracks towards River Junction. There it was, the big iron horse, puffing dense black smoke from its smokestack and spewing steam from underneath, around its mammoth wheels. It was like an unstoppable agitated bull, pawing and prancing towards me. The menacing cowcatcher, an enormous iron grate that extended from the front of the engine inches above the tracks, cleared the way. I could now see the engineer in the engine cab. He was continuously ringing the bell and pulling down on the cord above his head for one more full blast of the whistle before the train crossed Main

Street. The deafening sound reverberated through the little town leaving no doubt that the 4 o'clock train had arrived.

For a few moments I was mesmerized by the scene around me…until I was grabbed from behind, spun around, and thrown high into the air. Daddy caught me, then playfully tossed me up again, just like he had always done when we were playing. I giggled and he laughed and smiled like we were the only ones around.

" All 'board…" The conductor had stepped off the train and was pointing to the boarding door.

Daddy hugged me tight and walked slowly down the tracks toward the boarding door. The door to the mail car slid open and a bag of mail was thrown out on the ramp. The depot agent countered by throwing a bag of outgoing mail onto the train. Daddy walked slower and squeezed me tighter.

"'board," the conductor shouted again, looking at Daddy holding me and shouldering his green duffle bag, knowing that he was the only passenger to board.

Daddy lifted me high into the air again, no longer smiling, but with moistening eyes. He stood me on the loading platform by the depot and just looked at me for a moment.

"You have to do what you have to do," he said. I said nothing, but he knew that I understood. He turned and in an instant was on the train, which had started moving away. I watched as he walked through the passenger car and jumped into a seat by the window. He waved. I responded with a timid little goodbye wave.

I stood on the platform alone and bewildered. My mother had left me and now my daddy was leaving me, on a disappearing train to who knows where.

Chapter 9

The days on the farm during the war years of the 1940s were pretty much all the same. There was immense uncertainty about the future, and it was all because the war. The dictators of Germany, Italy, and Japan, that is Hitler, Mussolini and Tojo, were determined to take over the entire world. And their armies were murdering millions of innocent people across Europe and Southeast Asia to prove their point. The people of the United States, a relatively young country born for freedom and liberty, basically wanted to just live and let live. They were reluctant to spend our nation's money and the blood of our young men to fight a battle on foreign soil, even to aid our friends and allies. That all changed on December 7, 1941. The Japanese launched a surprise attack on Pearl Harbor and Honolulu and it became very personal for us. President Roosevelt and the Congress immediately declared war on Japan. This was a fight for the survival of not only our lives, but our way of life. It was understood that this war would end with the total defeat and unconditional surrender of either them or us. So, everyone was totally committed to make sure it was them.

My dad and uncle were deployed on active duty in the military. But, for the four of us in a church-converted farm house in the country, the war effort was mostly a role of day-to-day existence on our own. Actually, there were five of us, but Verdayne wasn't around very much. There was very little money, so basically everything we ate came from the farm, and Grandmother and Aunt Versie made most of our clothes.

There was a place in town that collected all junk metal and rubber materials to be recycled into weapons for the war. We had very little to contribute along those lines except for an occasional farm tool like an old plow or an old saw.

Each and every day on the farm started the same way, and started early with the alarm sounding at daylight. The alarm was the big red rooster who had saved his voice all night so he could strut out of the chicken house at the crack of day to crow blaringly about the fact that he and his brood had survived another night. And they were hungry and thirsty.

Granddaddy would get out of bed and go straight to the kitchen and build a fire in the stove. He was moving slower as the days passed, but always got the job done. Grandmother and Aunt Versie followed shortly afterwards to cook breakfast. The menu was usually the same: coffee, fried eggs, grits with redeye gravy, bacon, ham, and of course there were always plenty of Grandmother's biscuits. I usually drank milk for breakfast. The milk, straight from the cow, was kept in a big glass pitcher in the icebox. They still called it an icebox, even though it was now an electric refrigerator. If I was hesitant about drinking the milk, Grandmother would mix it with a spoonful of Ovaltine to make chocolate milk. I fell for that every time.

After breakfast, I would follow Granddaddy as he would pick up the slop bucket from near the kitchen door and head down to the barn yard. He would dump the contents of the bucket, all the kitchen scraps from the previous day, into the feeding trough in the pigpen. If there weren't enough scraps, he would supplement that with hog shorts which came in a bag and had to be purchased from the store. Not an option Granddaddy liked to use. Then we went to the stable to give Nellie fresh water and a half a bale of peanut hay. The cows only needed fresh water because they were on their own to roam around in the pastures and woods and graze. The chickens got fresh water and scratch feed, which was kernels of corn that had been crushed. It was called scratch feed because we scattered it by hand throughout the chicken yard so they could scratch around in the dirt and find it. Every other week, we would scatter limestone that had been crushed into tiny bits and pieces about the yard for them. Grandmother said that would help them produce harder egg shells. I would gather the eggs from the nests in the chicken house and take them back to the house.

Grandmother and Aunt Versie did the never-ending inside chores: cooking breakfast, dinner and supper, then washing and drying the dishes by hand; washing the clothes, hanging them out to dry, then ironing them; cleaning, sweeping, mopping; sewing, making new clothes and repairing the old ones.

Granddaddy worked outside. He worked the garden, cut weeds and grass with a hand sling, raked leaves, and spent part of everyday on the wood pile chopping wood for the kitchen stove and for the fireplace in the wintertime. Grandmother and Aunt Versie seemed to be spending more time in the garden to help him. They said Granddaddy's rheumatism was acting up. He was, after all, in his mid-60s. Even though he and Grandmother were the same age, she seemed to be showing no sign of slowing down, as was he.

My main chores were feeding Fido and gathering eggs. In addition to that I was expected to 'help out.' That meant that if I saw someone doing something and there was a way for me to make it easier for them to do it, I should. If I saw something that needed to be done, I should do it without having to be asked. I was also the gopher boy, as in go for this and go for that. "Benny, run to the woodpile and git me another piece of firewood." "Benny, run down to the barn and git me that square point shovel." "Benny, run tell your granddaddy it's time for supper." I wanted so much to please them, for them to like me, so I tried my best at everything I tried. And I thought I could do anything. I had no appreciation for the fact that there were still a few things, due to size and strength limitations, that a five-year-old could not do. So, I tried everything, even though it was sometimes amusing.

One of those times occurred on a Sunday. This was a special day of the week. And on the seventh day God rested, and so did the Shelfers. Sundays were a day for not only rest and recuperation, but also for reflecting, respecting, and a few other familial edicts that I did not necessarily always agree with. Like the one where you could not fish on Sunday. I could never see the merits of that one. Of course, the animals had to be fed and so did we.

The big event of the day for us was Sunday dinner. This was by no means a day of rest for Grandmother and Aunt Versie, because they prepared and cooked a full spread, with all the fixings. Family and friends had an open invitation and some of them would usually show up. Oftentimes, some of the kids from Jacksonville would come, probably for refresher course on how to cook the best biscuits in the world, as well as some other of Grandmother's specialties. Her siblings, Ford Neel, Son Neel, and Susie Neel, would also occasionally stop by.

The main course of the meal was usually fried chicken. And it was always fresh, because it was walking around in the chicken yard that morning. I would watch Granddaddy go into the chicken yard, catch a chicken and swing him around to wring his neck and throw him on the ground, where he would flop around and be dead in a minute. Simple enough. Then he would bring the chicken back to the house where he would be cleaned and fried to a delicious golden brown. Yummy.

On this particular Sunday it went something like this:

"Harde, run down there and kill me one of them young roosters for dinner," Grandmother said.

"Okay, Laura. I'll be back directly," Granddaddy said. He got up from his gooseneck rocking chair in the living room where I had been listening to him laughing and carrying on with Uncle Hardy and Uncle Verdayne.

I can do this, I thought. I know I can do this.

"Grandmother! Let me do it. I can do it," I said. I ran towards Grandmother, bouncing up and down with a pleading look on my face.

"Please, Grandmother. I can do it," I said.

"Better let your granddaddy do it this time, Benny," she said.

"You need to grow a little, boy," Verdayne said. "You can't kill a chicken when you're just knee-high to a grasshopper yourself." Not exactly the vote of confidence I needed, even though it came from someone I had never seen volunteer to kill a chicken, or do much of anything else to help around the house.

Uncle Hardy didn't say much. He just watched with amusement as I puppy-dogged Grandmother.

"Please, purdy please," I said.

"Let 'im, Mama," Uncle Hardy said. "I think he can do it."

By now, everyone was watching. Aunt Versie came out of the kitchen, where she had been peeling potatoes. Aunt Berta, Uncle Hardy's wife, walked in from the middle bedroom where she had been nursing my new little cousin, Ronnie. "Alright, go ahead, if you think you can do it," Grandmother said. "Just don't mess with them laying hens or the big red rooster."

Before grandmother finished her sentence, I was out the door and racing down towards the chicken yard. After I entered the yard and closed the gate behind me many of the young chickens, fryers we called them, came running towards me, thinking I had more food. The laying hens paid me little mind and continued their scratching and clucking in different parts of the yard. The big red rooster kept his distance, but watched me intently. I reached down to grab one of the young chickens but he just squawked and fluttered away and the others scattered throughout the yard. A little embarrassed, I looked up towards the house to see if anyone was watching. Not only were they watching, but everyone was out on the porch laughing and chuckling to one another. Not to be deterred, I chased that chicken into the corner and grabbed him again, this time tightly around the neck. Now I would do the deed just as I had seen done many times before. Holding him by the neck, I swung him around three times and threw him on the ground, expecting him to flop around and die. He didn't. He squawked and fluttered away, only mildly irritated with a few ruffled feathers.

I didn't have to look up towards the house to know that the family was having great fun watching the entertainment of the day. More determined than ever, I chased the same chicken into the corner and caught him again. With all the gusto I could muster, I swing him around by the neck five times and threw him high up into the air, so he could hit the ground and bounce around and die. He didn't. He just flopped away and scurried to the back corner of the yard, where I immediately caught him again. I stood there covered in sweat, weighing my options. I could hear the laughing coming from up on the porch. I looked up that way and everyone was laughing but Granddaddy who was walking slowly down the steps.

Resolutely, and with a death grip on the chicken, I marched out of the chicken yard and up towards the house.

"What're you doing boy?" Verdayne said. "You taking him for a walk or do you want us to set a place for him at the dinner table?"

"Come here, Son," Granddaddy said. "I'll help you."

Without looking at anyone on the porch, I took the chicken directly past the house to the woodpile. With my right hand I stretched his neck across a block of wood and before he could flounder, with one swing of the hatchet in my left hand, I chopped his head off. Finally, he flopped around, dying, with blood spurting everywhere. No one had ever explained to me that when you were wringing a chicken's neck, you had to hold his head to keep it from turning so that the motion would break his neck. With the hatchet in one hand and the chicken head in the other I looked back towards the house. The looks on their faces had turned from amusement to amazement.

"Well, I guess is more than one way to skin a cat," Aunt Versie said.

"Or, to kill a chicken," Uncle Hardy said. The 'I told you so' look on his face was all I needed to see.

Besides Sundays, there were two other special days of the week that had a different routine, Saturdays and Wednesdays.

Saturdays were a day of work for everyone, until dinnertime. Grandmother and Aunt Versie were usually busy with the cleaning, scrubbing, ironing, sewing, and washing clothes on the inside. Outside, Granddaddy was busy taking care of the yard and the critters, but he spent most of Saturday morning on the woodpile. He had to make sure that we had enough wood for the kitchen stove and the fireplace to make it through the weekend. I always tried to 'help out'. I was big enough to carry the wood, one piece at a time, and stack it on the back porch outside the kitchen door. So, I did.

Dinner was served right on time at noon. Afterwards, it was time to washup, put on some clean clothes and go to town. Besides the occasional fishing trip, this was the highlight event of the week. We took Nellie and the buggy to town for some time after Daddy left for the war. Then I noticed that they were both missing from the barn. When I asked Granddaddy what happened to Nellie, he told me he didn't trust her anymore after what she had done to Daddy, so he gave her and the buggy to Uncle Hardy, who traded them for two mules and a wagon. I don't think Granddaddy had that much use for Nellie anymore and grew tired of her sassy antics.

So now, Uncle Hardy would stop by and have Saturday dinner with us, and take us to town on the wagon. Granddaddy and Aunt Versie would make the trip, but Grandmother seldom went. She always said there was something she had to do around the house. I liked to sit in the back of the wagon with the tailgate down and dangle my feet. The mules were named Scott and Charlie and seemed to be a lot more docile than Nellie. At least they didn't want to rear up or run away with the wagon. I'll bet Daddy could ride either one of them.

We tied the wagon to the hitching post at the community house where Scott and Charlie could wait for us in the shade. The first stop for Granddaddy and me was usually Joe Cogburn's barbershop. There would be a long line waiting in chairs around the wall for their turn, but that was just fine. It was a perfect time for all the farmers to unwind from a week of hard work by trading verbal jousts and insults and solving the problems of the world.

"Hey Harde, did you hear what happened down at Yates's last night?" Some old farmer asked.

"I ain't heard a thing, I just got to town," Granddaddy said.

"Johnny Holland got liquored up and pulled a switchblade on Hubert Edwards. Beings Hubert's mama didn't raise no fool's, he stared at the knife for a while and then said, 'I apologize, if there's been a misunderstanding.' Then Hubert just walked out the door."

"'Least nobody didn't git hurt." Granddaddy said.

"Except they found Johnny this morning dead on the railroad tracks. He was tied up on the tracks and had been pulverized by the 4 AM train."

"Is Hubert in the hoosecow?" Granddaddy asked.

"Hubert said he ain't got nothing to do with it," the old farmer said.

"What 'chu expect him to say?" The man getting his hair cut asked. "That he knocked him in the head with a baseball bat, tied him up and put 'im on the railroad tracks?"

"If he told the truth, I bet that's what he'd say," Granddaddy said.

There were chuckles all around the shop on that one.

"Did y'all hear about the Kemp boy?" Joe asked. The murmuring became silent in the barbershop. The only sound was the snip snip snipping of Joe's scissors, which snapped a continuous rhythm, even when the scissors were not cutting hair.

"The one in the Army?" Someone asked.

"I'm afraid so," Joe said. "The telegram came yesterday. He was killed a week or two ago on one of those islands in the Pacific."

"God bless his soul," the man in the chair said. "And God bless our soldiers everywhere."

Amens echoed around the room. Granddaddy said nothing, but sat there with a solemn look on his face. I inched closer to him, thinking about what Joe had said. My daddy was in the Pacific and I wanted so much for him to come home.

When it was our turn to get a haircut, I was first to get in the chair. Or, maybe I should say on the chair. Joe would place a board across the arms of the chair, so I would sit tall enough for him to cut my hair.

"Cut it the same, Harde?" Joe asked.

"Yep. High and tight," Granddaddy said. "And Versie Mae said 'no bowl cut'."

The snipping and the chatting at the same time made me nervous, so I tried to sit very still. Especially when Joe picked up the straight razor to shave the back of my neck and around my ears. Soon it was over and Joe splashed me with a sweet-smelling aftershave lotion that burned the back of my neck. Before I could register a complaint, he engulfed me in a cloud of talcum powder, popped the cloth he had tied around my neck, lifted me to the floor. "Next," he said.

Granddaddy sat in the chair and said he only wanted a shave. Joe lathered up a brush from a mug and painted Granddaddy's face and neck with soap. He sharpened the razor on a leather strap that was attached to the back of the chair. The banter had returned to the barbershop and soon Granddaddy was also doused with the sweet-smelling stuff. He stood up and looked in the mirror and ran his hand over his chin and cheeks.

"Joe, how much was that shave?" Granddaddy asked.

Joe probably knew what was coming, but he answered anyway. "The shave was two bits, Harde, just like always."

Granddaddy look back in the mirror and rubbed his hand over his face again, for effect. Making a move to get back in the chair he said, "Well then give me another one."

"Benny! Where are you?" Grandmother yelled.

"On the front porch," I yelled back. I was sitting in one of the rocking chairs practicing shooting rocks with my new slingshot. Granddaddy made it for me with a piece of wood he had carved with his pocketknife and strips of rubber from an old inner tube he had found on the road in to town. I was shooting at bumblebees that were swarming on the wisteria vine beside the porch. They were hard to hit, but every now and then, spat. One would fall to the ground. Grandmother came through the front door and gave me one of those 'what are you into now' looks. I thought for sure I was in trouble.

"Do you know what day it is?" Grandmother asked. I didn't know if that was a loaded question, so I responded with a meek little shrug. "It's Wednesday," she said. "Do you remember what your Wednesday job is?"

58

"Yes ma'am. I'm a watchin'," I said. I sat back in the rocking chair and stared up River Road.

"Good. Let me know the minute you see it coming." Grandmother started back through the front door, then turned and stared at me for a moment. "If you make them bumblebees mad and one 'em stings you, don't come running to me."

"Yes, ma'am," I said.

Even though it was before dinner time, it was already very hot day. Granddaddy would say, "it's 95 in the shade," talking about a day like this. There was no breeze at all, not a leaf was shaking. And it was quiet, except for the sounds of nature which seemed to be amplified. The occasional gnat buzzing around my ear would sound like a dive bomber. Fortunately, most of the gnats were drawn to Fido who was sitting beside me with a happy hassle to keep cool. His eyes were closed to avoid the gnats. He seemed to enjoy the occasional pat on the head, and I was grateful that he was keeping most of the gnats off of me. The usual serenade of birds was the background noise of the morning. The crows in the cornfield, the mourning doves in the woods across the street, the sparrows and wrens in the fence jam, the blue jays in the oak trees above, the cardinals in the peach tree, and my very favorite, the redheaded woodpecker hammering on the old dead pine tree, all chirped in. The soloist of the feathered symphony, the mockingbird, sang continuously in the wisteria vine right there beside the porch, oblivious to the hundreds of bumblebees buzzing around. And they were oblivious to me, the slingshot sniper on the porch, who would launch an occasional rock their way.

The morning stood still amidst all the chirping and the buzzing and the hassling. If I had been a napper, this would've been the perfect time for a late morning siesta. But I wasn't a napper, and I certainly didn't want Grandmother to catch me sleeping on the job. And then I heard it, long before I saw it. The deep growling of a big engine being shifted from one gear to another, followed by a low, steady hum, when it finally reached high gear, was distinctive. The subtle rattling sound caused by the washboard bumps in the red clay road left no doubt. The rolling store was coming.

"Grandmother! Aunt Versie! It's coming!" I dashed through the house repeating myself several times.

"Okay, Benny," Grandmother said. "Run out and flag 'im down. We'll be there d'rectly."

"Yes, ma'am," I said.

As I ran through the front gate, I could hear the rolling store rattling past Dog Bottom and then the engine strain to climb the hill up the road in front of us. It was an old truck, larger than normal, and really needed a paint job, or at least a good washing. It looked like a poor man's moving van. The back bed of the truck was totally enclosed and overbuilt, with extensions off both sides and forward over the cab where the driver and passengers sat. At the rear of the truck were two steps leading to a narrow platform for the customers. The brakes squealed and the rolling store pulled into the circular driveway in front of our house and the engine went silent. Moments later, Mr. Tipton appeared at the window to the platform in the back of the truck. I had already bounded up the steps and was standing there.

"Hey there, young man," Mr. Tipton said.

My reply was a timid little wave because I was eyeing the different colors of the jawbreaker bubblegum that filled a large, clear pickle jar sitting near the window. Grandmother and Aunt Versie crowded onto the tiny platform behind me, so I moved over to give them room to stand.

"Mornin', Ms. Shelfer, Miss Versie Mae," Mr. Tipton said.

"Howdy," Grandmother said.

"Mornin', Mr. Tipton," Aunt Versie said. "We're much obliged to you for stopping by, 'cause we don't have a chance to get to town much. Any news from the war?"

"I did hear some good news…our boys finally took Iwo Jima."

"They did?" Aunt Versie asked. Her voice was heightened with excitement.

"Yes ma'am. Looks like we turned the corner and got them Japs on the run in the Pacific."

"Any word on casualties?"

"I'm sorry to say we lost almost 7000 men, with nearly 20,000 wounded," Mr. Tipton said. "I hope you folks don't have any family over there."

Aunt Versie stared down towards the floor and said, "Yes sir, we do." She shifted her eyes to glance at me. "But we have no idea where they are."

"Mr. Tipton, do you have any sugar?" Grandmother asked.

"Yes ma'am, I have a few five-pound bags left."

"How much you git fer it?"

"It keeps going up. I have to get $.33 for it," Mr. Tipton said. "And a number 30 ration stamp from book number four."

The total fight for survival of our country in World War II meant that our natural resources and assets had to be conserved and directed to the war effort. There was a rationing program in place that restricted the amount of certain goods and commodities each family could buy. The big items on the list were automobiles, bicycles, gasoline and fuel oil, and typewriters. Those items didn't affect us because we couldn't afford them anyway. And most of the food items we either did without or made or raised them on the farm.

Grandmother pulled a ration stamp booklet from her apron pocket and handed it to Mr. Tipton. He tore off a stamp, scribbled something in the booklet and handed it back to her. "Now, Ms. Shelfer," he said, "remember you cain't get no more sugar for three months."

"Then I s'pose we'll just have to be sweet enough on our own," Grandmother said. "You got any coffee?"

"Got plenty of Maxwell House," Mr. Tipton said. "It goes for $.30 a pound."

"Do we need a stamp?"

"No, ma'am. Coffee came off the ration list a while back."

"Good. Let us have a pound please," Grandmother said. "Would you trade for some eggs, Mr. Tipton?"

"I reckon I could use a dozen, Ms. Shelfer. Give you $.50 in trade if they're fresh and they ain't broken," he said.

"Benny, run get that basket of eggs from the kitchen," Grandmother said.

I ran to the kitchen, then hurried back, being careful not to trip and fall with a basket full of eggs. When I climbed back up the steps of the rolling store, I saw Grandmother had also selected a few bananas and a box

61

of vanilla wafers. That could only mean one thing. We were having my favorite dessert, banana pudding, for supper.

"Versie, you want anything?" Grandmother asked.

Aunt Versie looked around at the items on the shelves inside the rolling store, then looked my way with a very sympathetic expression.

"Benny's been such a good boy, I want to get him a piece of that bubblegum he's been looking at." She glanced at me again knowing she would see a big smile on my face. "And give me one of those Baby Ruth candy bars, too," Aunt Versie said to Mr. Tipton.

Aunt Versie handed me the jawbreaker bubblegum and I gave her a great big hug. "We better wait 'til another time to have the Baby Ruth. You cain't eat and chew gum at the same time," she said.

I ran back to the front porch and hopped up in the rocking chair and plopped the golf ball size piece of bubblegum in my mouth and started chewing. I knew I had to work on it at least a half an hour before it would be soft enough to blow a bubble. But that was okay. The rolling store had come and I got bubblegum and candy, and was having banana pudding at supper. My mother had left me, my daddy was gone off somewhere in the Pacific, the world was at war, but for me, life was good on the farm.

Chapter 10

Not much had happened in our sleepy little farm town during the next year or so, except for a few funerals. Several soldiers who were killed in battle were laid to rest, but I didn't know any of them. The one I remember was the death of my aunt Susie, my grandmother's sister. She was the first dead person I'd ever seen. She was laying there like she was asleep, all gussied up in her best Sunday go-to-meeting dress and powdered up white as a ghost. It made me sad, not so much that it was Aunt Susie because I'd only seen her a few times, but because she looked so much like my grandmother. And they were close to the same age. I realized that old people die. They just do. And seeing my granddaddy and grandmother at the funeral made me worry about them. And, I worried about me, and what would I do when someone else I loved was gone.

But the rest of the country and the world were seeing epic, life-changing events. President Roosevelt had united the country into a well-oiled war machine. Along with the help of our allies around the world, he had led a coalition against the enemy dictators and the momentum was turning in our favor. Sadly, Pres. Roosevelt never saw the greatness of his efforts. In April 1945, he suffered a stroke and died at his retreat in Warm Springs, Georgia. Vice Pres. Harry S. Truman, a former haberdasher and judge from Missouri, was sworn in as the 33rd president of the United States. In May 1945, Germany surrendered. Italy had surrendered previously and had switched sides in the war. In June 1945, the three-month battle for the Japanese island of Okinawa was won at the cost of 12,000 American lives and 50,000 wounded. The United States was winning the war it had to win, but the loss of the lives of our soldiers was staggering.

This is the point in history where the world as we knew it changed forever. For the war to end, Japan had to surrender unconditionally, or they had to be totally defeated. We were completing successful bombing raids to many cities in Japan. Pres. Truman made them an offer to cease the raids if they would surrender unconditionally. The Japanese refused.

Meanwhile, President Truman was aware of a top-secret undertaking called the Manhattan Project. A group of scientists had found a way to split the atom and develop a weapon, the atomic bomb, 1000 times more devastating than anything previously known to man. President Truman knew the use of this weapon would destroy Japan, and immediately end the war, but would change the world forever. On the other hand, a Japanese invasion force was being assembled in the Pacific to attack Japan. The estimated loss of such an attack was one million American casualties. President Truman was weary of war. The American people were weary of war. The common sense, no-nonsense president made the decision that to save one million American casualties, and indeed millions of Japanese lives. He would end the war.

On August 6, 1945, an American B-29 bomber dropped an atomic bomb on the Japanese city of Hiroshima, resulting in the immediate death of over 80,000 people. President Truman called for another unconditional surrender from the Japanese. They refused. Three days later, August 9, 1945, another atomic bomb was dropped on the city of Nagasaki, resulting in 70,000 dead. August 15, 1945, President Truman announced the unconditional surrender of Japan. The invasion force was given orders to stand down and the troops were diverted to other destinations for peacekeeping duties.

Sometime after that, we finally got a letter from my daddy. He had been on a ship that was part of the invasion force of Japan when the atomic bombs were dropped. He had been diverted and was now part of the occupying force of the Philippines, and didn't know when he might come home. We were just glad to hear he was still alive. And we were so thankful that President Truman made the decision that surely saved my daddy's life.

Park Verdayne Shelfer, the youngest of the 12 siblings, left school and our house on the farm to join the Army to do his part for the country. He hadn't yet graduated, but was an outstanding student and would be given his diploma on merit when he returned from the war. He was really smart, but I didn't like the fact that he was also a smart aleck. When granddaddy wasn't around, he would sass my grandmother and make fun of her when she didn't use proper English. I didn't like him at all for that. And I didn't like him teasing me and trying to scare me all the time. He regaled himself telling me stories like this:

"Hey, boy. Guess who I saw last night?" Verdayne would ask. We would usually be at the breakfast table after he came dragging in late the night before. He would walk several miles to a farm south of Sneads, near Shady Grove, to see his girlfriend, Minnie Lee Dennis.

"Were they there?" I would ask. I knew who he was talking about and that he was going to tell me anyway.

"Yeah, they were there, down in the branch a Cat Springs. Splitfoot and Saucer Eyes. It was rainy and dark and I could barely see them, but they were there. Old Splitfoot was sitting there on the fence staring at me with his beady little eyes. He was long and lanky and scraggly looking, with gnarly brown teeth poking out of his mouth every which way through a whisker shrouded, tobacco-stained grin. But that's not the worst part. Blood was oozing from one of his feet that was split wide open all the way up to his knee."

I covered my eyes trying not to visualize what he was telling me, and braced myself for the second part of the story that I knew was coming.

"The other was short and shabby and not very big. He looked like a dark blob back in the woods and you couldn't tell much about him, except he had monster eyes. They were as big as saucers. I wanted to run, but one of those eyes was looking at where I was going and the other at where I'd been."

"You're just teasing me. You're just making that up," I said.

"No, they're there waiting on you boy. They'll get you for sure. You'd better stay away from Cat Springs."

So, that's the way it would go. Verdayne had told me another story, and my nightmares were guaranteed for several nights to come.

"Much obliged for the ride, Hardy," Aunt Versie said.

"You're welcome, Versie. Anytime you need to go someplace, just let me know," Uncle Hardy said. "You want me to come back and pick you up, or you want to meet up downtown?"

"How about when we're done, we just meet you at Mr. Cecil's?"

"Sounds good," Uncle Hardy said.

That sounded good to me, too. I was already thinking about that strawberry ice cream cone. I watched Uncle Hardy drive away in his 1940 wood paneled Ford station wagon. He and Aunt Berta and Ronnie, my little cousin, had moved from Jacksonville and were building a house on some acreage they had bought just up the road from us. Ronnie, who was four years younger than me, was running all around but didn't talk much, yet. Still, for me, it was like having a little brother, and I had fun playing with him.

The building was so big. It was the biggest building I had ever entered, except for maybe the hospital where I was born, which I didn't remember. And I felt small holding on to Aunt Versie's hand climbing the steps, even though she told me I was a big boy now and growing like a weed. That didn't seem like a complement to me because I knew weeds were nuisance plants that needed to be eliminated from the garden and the yard. She could have just as easily said I was growing like a flower. Even if she had, I wouldn't have felt any less intimidated as she led me, almost dragged me, down the hall towards the office of Sneads School.

The office door was open and I could see a man sitting at the desk engrossed in a stack of papers he was holding. Aunt Versie knocked lightly.

"Come in." The man rose from his chair as we entered the room. The plaque on the desk said, "Roy M. Deloney, Principal." He was a very distinguished looking man with a slight build, but was taller than Aunt Versie, which meant he was almost 6 feet tall. He wore a blue, striped tie, and a starched white shirt with gold cufflinks. His jet black, wavy hair was parted right down the middle and his seemingly rimless spectacles were so clean and clear you barely noticed them. He had a unique smile. It wasn't exactly a "cat that ate the canary smile," but more like a "show some teeth but not the chewing gum" smile. "I'm Mr. Deloney," the man said. "How may I help you?"

"I'm Versie Collins, and this is Bennett Shelfer, who we would like to register for first grade."

Mr. Deloney stepped around from behind the desk and shook hands with Aunt Versie, then patted me on the head. "Welcome Bennett. We're glad to have you join us here at Sneads school." Then to Aunt Versie he asked, "Mrs. Collins, you are Bennett's mother?"

"No, sir. I'm his aunt and his legal guardian. His daddy is in the Army overseas, and his mother…well, that's what I wanted to talk to about."

"How's that, Mrs. Collins?"

"Please keep this between us, Mr. Deloney." Aunt Versie glanced over at me. I was standing on my tiptoes looking out the window at the big playground and the baseball diamond down below, pretending not to hear what they were saying. "Bennett's parents were divorced for the second time a couple of years ago and my brother was granted custody. We haven't heard from his mother since then. And while we have no reason to believe that she would try to come take Bennett away and disappear, we don't want to take any chances. Could you please make sure that no one takes Bennett from the school except members of the Shelfer family that you know personally?"

"Of course, Mrs. Collins. I'll tell the office staff and I'll have a talk with Maggie Pate, who will be his teacher. She just married Harvey Pate. You might remember her from your days at Sneads High School as Maggie Hunter."

"Yes! I do remember Maggie Hunter. She was about three years behind me in school. She's wonderful." Aunt Versie called to me at the window. "Benny, you're going to love your teacher. She's a nice lady and a friend of mine."

I walked back over to where they were standing. I gave it my best effort to twist a little smile on my face, even though I was not at all sure about this teacher, principal, school thing.

"Thank you for everything, Mr. Deloney. We'll have him here bright and early on Tuesday, the day after Labor Day." She took my hand and we turned for the door.

"You're quite welcome Mrs. Collins," Mr. Deloney said. He reached down and tousled my hair again. "We'll take good care of Bennett and I'm sure he will do just fine here."

We walked through the door and I looked back at Mr. Deloney and managed a more genuine smile, but I think it was only because I was thinking that we were finally on our way to get that strawberry ice cream cone.

The first day of school was my first real exposure to other children my age. I had played with kids in the daycare center atop the King Edward cigar factory in Jacksonville, and then there was Mary Lou, my playmate on 16th

67

St. But that was years ago and really didn't count. Basically, I was an only child growing up with adults. It was disconcerting to see so many children acting like children. They were playing and running around screaming outside and trying not to run around and scream inside, where Mr. Deloney was standing in the hall watching.

"Good morning, Bennett," Mr. Deloney said. He nodded and flashed that unique smile at Aunt Versie who was walking with me down the hall towards the first-grade classroom. I was startled that he remembered my name and responded with my usual shy smile and four-fingered wave.

We entered the door of room number one at the end of the hall. Mrs. Pate knew who I was the minute she saw me standing there with Aunt Versie. She was a gentle lady, tall and thin like Aunt Versie, with brown eyes and long brown hair. Her white dress was covered mostly with a brown floral design and dropped well below her knee. It was gathered at the waist by a decorative wide brown leather belt. The two of them acted like it was old home week for a moment, chuckling about their days at Sneads High School. The bell rang in the hall and Aunt Versie kneeled down and gave me a hug I didn't want, and then she was gone.

My desk was the third one in the middle of five rows of desks. Sondra Hinson was in the desk in front of me, and Dannie McMullian was in front of her. Raymond Walden was in the row next to me, as was Virginia Ann Joiner and Lenora Ann Stephens. I was very shy around the other kids and didn't talk very much. As it turned out that was okay, because it seemed like Sondra was doing most of the talking anyway.

Mrs. Pate turned out to be every bit as nice as Aunt Versie said she would be. I was convinced I was her favorite student. Then I found out that several of my classmates felt the same way. She seemed to be talking directly to me as she taught us how to count and read and write. Sneads did not have a kindergarten, so we had to start at the beginning with everything in the first grade. She didn't even mind that I was different from my classmates in that I was learning to print my ABC's with my left hand.

Mrs. Ivey, my second-grade teacher, was a different person altogether. She was a wiry, middle-aged lady with a narrow face and black wavy hair. She was an adequate teacher, but was very strict and regimented. So much so that she could not tolerate a left-handed student in her class. She insisted that I learn to write with my right hand. So, I did.

Despite being forced into becoming ambidextrous, school days were fun for me. I rode the bus to and from school, and Mr. Cecil was my bus driver. I already knew he was a nice man because of the generous scoops of ice cream he would pile on the cone for me at his store. Most of my classmates were friends and I tried to get along with everyone, even Sondra, "Miss Bossy Boots," who was always telling me what to do. I had a secret little puppy love crush on Dannie, and Raymond had become my best friend.

Chapter 11

It was always an adventure riding the school bus. From a comfort standpoint, it seemed to be too hot or too cold, depending on the season. Usually too hot. Then there were usually one or two of the older boys in the back of the bus that wanted to pick a fight, just for something to do. Or, to perfect their bullying skills. Mr. Cecil would not tolerate such shenanigans, but to stay out of the fray, I tried to sit close to the front. My bus stop was in front of Margo Rigdon's house, which was about a hundred yards from our house and halfway to Ernest Sneads' house, a little further down the road. It was a hot Friday afternoon and the brakes on the bus squealed us to a stop and Margo, Ernest (we all called him Pap) and I hopped off the bus.

The short distance from the bus stop was always a quick sprint for me. I knew Fido would be waiting for me at the front gate and one of Grandmothers biscuits with some sugar cane syrup would be waiting for me in the cupboard on the stove. Aunt Versie, Granddaddy and Grandmother were sitting in rocking chairs on the porch when I bounded up the steps petting and playing with Fido. I gave them a quick glance and started through the front door, headed for the biscuit.

"Benny," Aunt Versie called to me. I stopped dead in my tracks and looked at her. She said nothing, but just nodded towards the swing on the other end of the porch. I turned to look at the man sitting in the swing and my eyes filled with tears.

"Daddy!" I cried. I ran and jumped into his arms. I had almost forgotten what he looked like, and I was so afraid he had left and would never come back.

The next few days were glorious. Daddy was never out of my sight, and we did everything that was fun. We went fishing several times, and not just to

Rock Pond. Early Saturday morning we dug a big can of wigglers, and collected a bag of Catawba worms from the tree out back. These were black and greenish worms about an inch long that ate the leaves of the Catawba tree. Daddy said he liked them to catch the big bream, but the wigglers were best for the shellcrackers. We walked two miles up the River Road to Blue Springs, the last in a chain of lakes that ran off from the Chattahoochee River. About halfway down the lake was an open area that was convenient for people to fish and have a fish fry and picnic. It also served as a swimming hole in the chilly blue water from the spring in the lake near the shore. Blue Springs connected to the Okie Slough, which connected to the Saddler Hole, which connected to the Tan Vat, which connected to the Bird Song, which connected to the Deep Slough, which connected to the Chattahoochee River.

We had been fishing at the Saddler Hole and had a nice string of fish before dinner time. We had some big red bellies and shell crackers. Daddy called most of them, but I did catch one big warmouth perch, a brown fish with a larger mouth that daddy said Yankees called a poor man's walleye. We had started back home for dinner because daddy couldn't stop talking about Grandmother's cooking, and how much he missed it when he was overseas. We were walking on the old logging road alongside the Okie Slough when Daddy stopped and pointed to something in the in the crystal-clear running water below.

"Look, Benny. See those fish?" He asked.

"No Sir," I said. I was looking really hard but I saw no fish.

"There, see them." He pointed again. "Those two things right there that look sticks."

"I thought they were sticks," I said. We both had a good laugh at that one. "Can we catch them?" I asked.

"They won't bite worms," Daddy said. "But, let me show you an Indian trick."

Daddy put a worm on the hook of one of his cane poles and walked down stream to a shallow place in the Slough. Within moments he had caught a little bream about the size of a small goldfish. He hurried back to where I was standing, still watching the fish that looked like sticks. Daddy unhooked the little bream, then re-hooked him again in the tail and quietly snuck down by the Slough, looking back at me with a mischievous grin. He raised the pole and lifted the little bream into the clear water in front of the fish. Boom! One of the fish nailed the little bream and dashed upstream.

71

With one sweeping motion, Daddy snatched him out of the water and halfway up the bank to where I was standing. I ran down and grabbed the big, long speckled fish, with the colorful stripes and the long nose.

"Watch out for those teeth," Daddy said. "A jack has really sharp teeth."

"That's a jack?"

"That's Mr. Jack," he said, giving recognition to the size of the fish. "Yankees call 'em chain pickerels but 'round here we call 'em jacks. They're a little boney, but still good eatin'."

We put the jack on the string of fish and once again headed towards home.

"So that's an Indian trick?" I asked.

"Yep, but there are lots of Indian tricks. They're just special little ways of doing things that city slickers would never dream of."

We were walking faster and didn't talk much on the way home. I noticed Daddy mentioned Yankees and city slickers a lot, and I was feeling lucky that I was getting to do lots of fun things that they never did. I was so proud of my daddy. He had been overseas to fight the Japs and had made it home safely. He could do most anything, and besides that, he knew lots of Indian tricks. But what would happen now? I had heard them talking about how the city of Jacksonville kept at his job open for him while he was serving in the Army. I knew he would have to leave soon to go back to work. I didn't want to think about that. I didn't want to think about Jacksonville.

"That's a nice mess o' fish you got there, Sing," Grandmother said. "Go clean 'em up, we're having fish for dinner. I've already made the hushpuppies, with some collard greens and rutabagas."

Daddy showed me how to scale fish, and I tried my best. Still, it seemed like he had cleaned all the fish and I was still trying to get the scales off of one red belly. As soon as they were cleaned, I watched Grandmother put salt and pepper on them, roll them in corn meal and drop them in the hot grease in her spider. That's what she called her large iron skillet because in her younger years she cooked in the fireplace and then the frying pan had long iron legs on it to keep it out of the ashes, making it look like a spider.

72

Within minutes we were sitting around the dinner table. Granddaddy was sitting in his place at the head of the table, and Grandmother was sitting across from him. Daddy and I were sitting to his right and Aunt Versie to his left. The fish stories had already started. Daddy told the story about me catching the big warmouth, and then I told the story about how Daddy used the Indian trick to catch the big jack. I saw Granddaddy cut a glance towards Daddy with a smile that told me he also had probably passed down a few Indian tricks along the way, too.

"Sing, when do you have to go back to work for the city?" Granddaddy asked.

"A week from Monday, Pappa," Daddy said. "But I told Hardy I'd stay around 'till then and help 'im with his new house."

"I'm sure he's much obliged to you for that, Son. Do you have a place to live in Jacksonville?" Granddaddy asked.

"Willie Maude said I could stay with her as long as I wanted to."

Granddaddy nodded and nibbled on a hushpuppy. There was a curious lull in the conversation and I was beginning to feel uncomfortable because Grandmother, Aunt Versie, and Daddy were looking at each other and then glancing at me. They seemed to be waiting on the other one to speak first.

"Benny, I hear you're doing real good in school," Daddy said, finally breaking the ice. "How would you like to go to school in Jacksonville?"

There it was. Right there on the table. The conversation I had been dreading since my daddy got back. I said nothing, but shrunk down in my chair into my timid and shy mode. This was difficult because all eyes at the table were on me.

"Benny, your uncle Larry is coming back from overseas and I'm going to live with him at Cherry Point North Carolina," Aunt Versie said. "Would you like to come live with us and go to school there?"

I slouched even further down into my chair and bit down on my lower lip. I was determined not to cry because I had been told I was a big boy and growing up fast. It was quiet again at the table for what seemed like the longest time.

"There's a thing or two I would like to say here," Grandmother said. "I raised twelve of you young 'uns and one more won't make no difference."

She glanced at everyone around the table and then looked directly at me. "Benny, you don't have to go nowhere. You can go to school right here in Sneads for as long as you want to. Besides, you're a big help around here and me and your granddaddy would be much obliged for a little help right about now."

The dilemma for me and my future deepened. And if I slinked any lower in my chair I would be under the table. It never occurred to me that I could have an opinion in this matter. I always thought someone would tell me what was going to happen next to my life and that's the way it would be. But, from the way they were talking they wanted to know what I thought.

Aunt Versie had taken me in and cared for me when there seemed to be no one else available. She had saved me from the vicious dog attack. She had brought me to the farm where I had fun learning to do things I could never have done in the city. Then, when I was old enough, she enrolled me in school. How could I tell her I did not want to go to North Carolina and live with her and Uncle Larry?

Grandmother had been so good to me from the day I arrived in Sneads. She had made me new clothes from my favorite feed sacks, and she always had biscuits and cane syrup around for me to snack on. And she made sure we could sneak off to Rock Pond to go fishing often. She had said to one of her friends in a conversation that I overheard that I was her thirteenth child and her very favorite. And she and Granddaddy needed my help around the place. How could I tell her I didn't want to stay in Sneads and live with them?

Daddy had gone through two divorces with my mother, and maintained custody of me in both cases. He never missed a day of work until he was drafted into the Army, and then he went to fight the war for our freedom, and never complained. And in the few days since he returned, we had been inseparable. We had carried on a non-stop conversation, probably much more than Daddy had wanted to hear. Besides taking me fishing, he was teaching me gun safety and how to shoot his 16-gauge shotgun. I could do it, too. I had shot so many pine cones that my right shoulder was turning blue from the kick of the big gun. How could I ever tell Daddy I didn't want to go to Jacksonville and live with him and Aunt Maude?

My basic problem was I couldn't bear the thought of disappointing anyone. Aunt Versie really wanted me to go live with her in North Carolina. Grandmother really needed me to stay and live with her and Granddaddy on the farm in Sneads. It was comforting to be wanted and needed, even as my fear of being deserted still lingered. But, Daddy...well, regardless of what else was said, he was my daddy.

Chapter 12

Daddy went back to Jacksonville to resume his job with the city and Aunt Versie went to North Carolina to be with Uncle Larry. Daddy and Grandmother had agreed it might be best for me to stay on the farm and continue going to school in Sneads, and that was just fine with me.

It was a cloudy, windy morning in March, 1947. Excitement and anticipation filled the air as people crammed into our little house on the farm in Sneads. I slept later than normal because no one got much sleep during the night before. My aunts and uncles began arriving early in the evening and it seemed like they kept coming all night. It was one round of hellos and hugs and loud laughter followed by another as someone else would arrive. Daddy made it in before my bedtime. Like many of the twelve children, he had about a five-hour drive over from Jacksonville. He didn't own a car, so he hitched a ride with Uncle Bud (Julian Elbert) and Aunt Ruth in their black thirty-nine Ford. My cousin, Faye, who was about a year younger than me was with them.

Daddy had come to sleep with me in my bed, but that didn't last long. Aunt Tots (Norma Ethel Shelfer Moody) and Uncle Charlie wheeled in driving their old Model T Coupe and bumped us from the bed. Daddy went to the couch in the living room and I went to a pallet on the floor behind the couch that Grandmother fashioned from a bunch of quilts. Faye was already sleeping there, like a log. She never budged, despite all the commotion.

When I awakened, the pallet had become even more crowded during the night. Aunt Sis (Laura Zelma), the youngest of the girls, and Uncle Johnny Murphy had arrived and planted my cousins Glenn and Virginia on the pallet beside Faye. Glenn was about a year younger than me and Virginia was about two years old. Sleeping beside me with a light snore and an occasional snort was my older cousin Annie Laura Elliott. She and her mother, Aunt Maude (Willie Maude), the oldest of the five girls of the family, had arrived sometime after midnight with Uncle Leon Elliott. He was not in good health and had a peg leg as a result of being wounded in the First World War.

The entire house was buzzing with laughter and chatter. I peeked over the back of the couch to see Granddaddy sitting in his gooseneck rocker smoking his pipe and holding court. All of his sons were gathered around except for the seventh son, Teeter (Park Verdayne), who would be arriving later in the morning from Tallahassee. He had recently returned from Italy after having been discharged from the Army Air Corps, and had utilized the G.I. Bill to enroll in the first coed class of Florida State University.

"Papa, I heard Old Man Hare couldn't swim a lick," Uncle Shine (Angus Gordon Shelfer) said. "Is that right?"

"He could swim like a rock and dive like a feather," Granddaddy said.

There were chuckles all around the room as the boys anticipated what they knew would be another session of tales from the past about Old Man Hare. They had heard most of them before, but they were just as funny every time. And some of them might have even been true.

"How'd you know he couldn't swim, Papa?" Uncle Dick asked.

Another county heard from. Uncle Dick (Marshall Franklin Shelfer) had wandered into the room with a steaming hot cup of coffee, with chicory. He was the second oldest son, but he looked terrible, like death warmed over. He was very skinny, barely skin and bones, with tallowed, wrinkled skin. He had scabs on the side of his head that gave him the appearance of someone who finished last in a bar fight, which he probably had done. I had heard my aunts talking and they said Uncle Dick had made more money than any other Shelfer, yet he was always dead broke. He had a special talent as a dragline operator, and was one of the best at operating the largest cranes and therefore was very much in demand. But he was also a binge drinker. As soon as he got his paycheck he disappeared, often for weeks at a time. Then he would surface dead broke, sick and hungry, at the home of one of his sisters, who would take him in and nurse him back to health. After a period of time, he would look for another job and do it all over again. This cycle was interrupted once by a brief, rocky marriage to a Puerto Rican girl named Ana. They had two boys, Junior and Lester, born a year apart, who were two years younger than me. They were wild and rowdy kids and I could hear them running around outside playing and screaming.

"I knew Old Man Hare couldn't swim 'cause he said so himself," Granddaddy said.

"When did he tell you that, Pappa?" Uncle Grady asked. He (Grady Tyrone Shelfer) was the oldest of the 12 kids. He had arrived early in the morning with Aunt Lillian and his youngest son, Billy, who was just finishing high school. Uncle Grady was the shortest of all the Shelfer men, but he was tough as nails. Some of his brothers and sisters might say he even had a mean streak in him. That being said, he was the chief of police of Auburndale, Florida, a small but growing town in Polk County, southwest of Orlando.

Granddaddy took a moment to repeat the ritual of tapping a new batch of Prince Albert tobacco from the can into his pipe. He struck a kitchen match on the leather sole of his shoe and after a series of draws and puffs the bowl of the pipe was burning to his liking. "Me and Laura wuz sitting on the bank fishing up at Blue Spring and Old Man Hare and one of his boys wuz fishing in an old bateau on the other side of the lake. All of a sudden there wuz a big commotion in the boat with lots of cussing and screaming. Somebody yelled 'snake in the boat' and then the boy jumped out of the boat into the water. A cottonmouth long as my leg had climbed into the boat and started crawling down towards Old Man Hare. He let out another string of cuss words before he grabbed his old 12-gauge shotgun and shot the moccasin. Everthing wuz fine and dandy and he kept cussin' and giving the dead snake the 'what fer' 'till he realized he'd shot a hole in the bottom of the boat and he wuz sinkin' fast. All of a sudden, the cussin' stopped and he started yelling at the top of his lungs, 'Help! Help! I can't swim…that's when he told me he couldn't swim." All the boys in the room were roaring with laughter.

"Did you have to jump in and git 'im, Pappa?" Uncle Hardy (Hardy Anderson) asked.

"I was fixin' to," Granddaddy said, "but, by the time the boat went under the boy had figured out it was only belly deep, so he just waded over and helped Old Man Hare wade out to the hill." The laughter continued.

"Tell us about the time the hog got in old man Harris' peanut patch," uncle Grady said.

Granddaddy looked around the room at his boys with that little mischievous grin on his face. He saw me peeking over the couch and gave me a little nod. "I 'spect there's somebody here knows little more about that than I do. How about it, Bud and Sang (Sing, Daddy)?"

"I don't know nothin'. I'm innocent," Daddy said.

"You're no such thing," Uncle Bud said. "It was your idea."

"Was not."

"Was too."

Daddy and Uncle Bud were the closest siblings of all the boys. They were next to each other in the birth order, with Uncle Bud being about a year and a half older than Daddy. Growing up on the farm they were inseparable, and were still very close. That didn't mean that at times, then and now, they wouldn't fight like cats and dogs. The other brothers glanced around at each other thinking this might be one of those times.

"Now, now, boys," Granddaddy said. "Why don't you just tell us what really happened?"

"Old Man Hare had this nice field of peanuts," Uncle Bud said. "But he couldn't keep the stray hogs out. So, he went to a lot of time and trouble and hard work and spent a lot of money to put this purdy new wire fence around his peanut patch. He wuz so proud of his crop of peanuts, and especially his new fence. He told ever'body about it, and he would stand there for hours just watchin' the peanuts grow and admirin' his new fence. 'Bout two days after he finished it, me and Sang wuz walking by and we seen this young boar hog, he might'a gone 80 or 100 pounds, standing there looking through the fence at the peanuts. Somebody had this great idea (he looked at Daddy), so we chased the shoat down and hemmed him up in the corner. In a flash, we lifted him over the fence and eased him down on the inside. No sooner than he hit the ground, he started rootin' peanuts. He wuz a happy hog. Well, it wasn't long before Old Man Hare found the hog in his peanut patch. He wuz fit to be tied, cussin' and screamin'. He wuz mad as a wet settin' hen. It took him over an hour to chase the pig around through the gate and out of the field. Then for half a day he walked around the outside of the field looking for the hole in his new fence where the hog got in the field. Finally, sweatin' and give out, he sat down on a stump outside the gate. One of his boys came up and asked, 'Pa, if you cain't find the hole, how'd he git in?' Old Man Hare wiped his brow and finally said, 'Aw hell, I reckon he flew in.'"

There was another crescendo of laughing and knee-slapping among the boys until Aunt Maude, who was standing in the dining room finishing putting white icing on the biggest cake I'd ever seen, gave Uncle Bud a dirty look. "Bud, you watch yore language with these young'uns around. Don't make me wash yore mouth out with some of Mamma's lye soap," she said. Even more laughing.

"Willie Maude, even you ain't big enough to do that," Uncle Bud said. He gave her no slack about the obvious fact that she must've weighed over 250 pounds.

"I'll come over there directly and nub you to your knees, just like I used to do when you wuz little," Aunt Maude said. To show that she met business, she held up her right hand to show about half of her thumb was missing.

"I ain't scared," Uncle Bud said. "I got Grady, here, to take up fer me. Grady, maybe you better tell Willie Maude how that big mouth got her that nub in the first place."

"I ain't saying nuthin'. Pappa might take me back to the woodshed again," Uncle Grady said.

Granddaddy almost chuckled again, and continued puffing on his pipe and gently rocking back and forth in his gooseneck rocking chair. Even though he hadn't been getting around very well lately, I could tell he was really enjoying this day.

"I'll tell you how she got the nub," Uncle Dick said. "I wuz little but I remember it just like it wuz yesterday. Pappa told Grady to take the hatchet and go out to the woodpile and chop up some of the short blocks into small pieces for stove wood. Maude was messin' with 'im, as usual, and goadin' 'im 'bout havin' to chop wood. Grady would stand up a block of wood to chop it and Maude would put her thumb up on the block of wood and snatch it away when Grady swung the hatchet. Grady got tired of her foolishness and told her to move her thumb or he'd chop it off. 'Ha!' Maude said. Then in her little impish singsong voice she said, 'I double dog dare you.' Whack! Like a flash of lightnin', the hatchet came down and Maude was runnin' to the house screamin' and bleedin' like a stuck pig and half her thumb was in the pile of stove wood.

"I ain't got no sympathy for Maude nor Grady," Uncle Hardy said. "They're the ones tried to get me killed."

"If you're talking about the Ferris wheel, Hardy, that was your own dumb fault," Aunt Versie said. She had walked into the room like she was on a mission.

"Tell us the Ferris wheel story, Versie," Daddy said. "You were there."

"Yeah, she was there. And she was part of it," Uncle Hardy said.

"I'll tell you guys somethin'. You gotta break up this little bull session. The stories will have to wait. Besides, the first liar don't have a chance with you guys," Aunt Versie said. "Now, some of y'all get in here and help move these chairs away from the dining room table. The photographer from Marianna's gonna be here in a few minutes and we gotta be ready to take some pictures."

The brothers hopped to it and in a moment the chairs were cleared away from the dining room table. Aunt Sis and Aunt Tots carefully spread the white lace tablecloth, the finest we had, on the table and Aunt Maude and Aunt Lillian replaced the newly decorated cake in the center of the table. Aunt Arcenia meticulously placed the bride and groom figurine atop the four-layer cake. Then she came into the living room carrying a white carnation boutonniere.

"Pappa, you're looking mighty sharp today. Stand up a minute. I want to pin this carnation on your lapel."

"I don't wanna' wear no flower, 'Ceenie," Granddaddy said.

"Now, Pappa, I'm not gonna tell Mama you said that 'cause it matches the corsage that she's wearing. Don't you wanna' look nice for your picture? I mean really, Pappa, today is your golden wedding anniversary. You and Mama been married 50 years. Aren't you happy about that?"

"Yeah, that's nice. But, you younguns' ought not to be making such a fuss about."

"Now, Pappa, this is something we just gotta' celebrate. You just relax and enjoy it. Not only that, this is the first time our whole family, you and Mama and all the kids, have ever been together at the same time," Aunt Arcenia said.

"Huh," Granddaddy said. He had a pleasant look of surprise on his face.

"Look at Mama over there in that beautiful blue dress with the purty flowers. Does she look nice?"

"Purty as the day I married 'er," Granddaddy said.

"I am going to tell her you said that," Aunt Arcenia said. "Looks like the photographer's here. Now, go have your picture made and put on a nice smile for the camera."

Granddaddy, all decked out in his best suit with a white, starched shirt and a tie, shuffled into the dining room to join Grandmother. The photographer and his helper lugged a huge camera into the house and set it on a tripod in front of the dining room table with the anniversary cake. They were getting lots of photography tips about how to take the best picture from all of my aunts, but I could tell the man was listening to Aunt Versie who had hired him. Granddaddy looked at me as the girls were trying to line him and Grandmother up behind the cake and he almost smiled. Finally, after much ado, it appeared that the majority of the daughters were happy with the scene, so the photographer decided to go for it. The helper held up a big flash attachment and the photographer hid under the cloth hood behind the camera. On the count of three I heard a loud click from the camera box and saw a bright flash and a puff of white smoke from the flash attachment. The room had an instant smell like matches burning. But it was done and the picture was in the box. Neither of them smiled, but at least grandmother had a pleasant look on her face. Granddaddy, on the other hand, had the look of someone experiencing his last moments before a firing squad.

Looking around the house, it was almost impossible to find a picture of any of the old-timers in which they were smiling. I heard someone talking about that and suddenly it made sense. It was probably because almost everyone had crooked teeth. Or, some that were missing. Most all of the members of my family fit into that category, so no one wanted to smile for a picture. I was lucky that my permanent teeth had come in fairly straight, because I laughed and giggled a lot.

As soon as the flashbulb fired, Granddaddy begin shuffling back towards the living room. That is, until Aunt Tots stepped up and took charge.

"Wait just a minute, Pappa," Aunt Tots said. Then she looked around the room for her husband. "Charlie, you and Larry go get that box out of the back of the car. And don't drop it." And they did exactly that, and placed a large box wrapped in white wrapping paper with a white bow on the table next to the cake.

"What's that?" Grandmother asked.

"Mama, all us kids have been rackin' our brains trying to figure out what we can get you for the occasion. We wanted to get you something that you don't have and you would never buy yourself. So, we all chipped in and got you this. Go ahead, open it, Mama," Aunt Tots said.

"Y'all ought not've got us nothin'," Grandmother said. I could tell she was very excited to get a present. She carefully took the white bow off the box and opened the wrapping paper without tearing it. I knew she was thinking that she would save the bow in the paper and use it again. She opened the top of the box and peeled back the paper and looked inside. "Dishes? Are all these dishes?"

"Mama, you and Papa ain't never had nothing but everyday dishes, so we wanted y'all to have a nice set of China," Aunt Maude said. "Shore hope you like it."

"Oh! It's so purty," Grandmother said. She held up a plate for everyone to see, then ran her fingers over the plate, feeling it. She hugged it tightly to her chest. "What kind is it?"

"It's a set of Homer Laughlin China, Mama. It's Eggshell Nautilus and the pattern is called Ardmore," Aunt Sis said.

"Thank y'all so much," Grandmother said. "Now, y'all help me get 'em washed up. We're gonna have dinner off of fine China today."

It was, indeed, a day to remember. We ate fine food off of fine China. There was so much food, including my favorites; Grandmother's banana pudding and Aunt Berta's pineapple upside down cake. There were so many people. The men continued telling stories in the living room while the women were telling their stories in the kitchen. I spent most of the day with all the kids outside running and playing. Occasionally I would see some of the men, two or three at a time, sneak out to Uncle Grady's car where they would sip on something from a bottle that was in a paper bag. Daddy was right in there with them. It was obvious they didn't want Grandmother or any of the women to see what they were doing, so I knew they were drinking whiskey. I was afraid Daddy would get drunk, but he didn't. At least not that day. After dinner the photographer braved one more photo shoot, this time a group shot with everybody in front of the house. I even got to be in the picture. It took forever but finally it was over and the adults kept telling stories and the kids kept playing in the yard long into the evening.

Chapter 13

The sun was shining brightly on a crisp, cool Sunday morning. It was December 5th, 1948.

Aunt Versie and Uncle Larry had come over from Jacksonville for a visit. It was not unusual to have some of my aunts and uncles staying with us almost every weekend. Daddy would try to come every month or two, but Aunt Versie came more often than that. She said she just had to get over here to see her little man. And I was honored to be her little man. This time she brought me a new toy, a Duncan yo-yo. After a tour of duty at Cherry Point Marine Air Base in North Carolina, Uncle Larry had mustered out of the Marine Corps and he and Aunt Versie had moved to Jacksonville. They had both taken a job at the Jacksonville Naval Air Station. He was working in aircraft maintenance and Aunt Versie was a clerk at the Post Exchange. They were encouraged to work there by Aunt Tots and Uncle Charlie Moody who had worked at the base for years, even during the war. In fact, Aunt Tots was a real life "Rosie the Riveter" who built and repaired airplanes. She was part a group of millions of women who aided the war effort by doing jobs generally thought to be done by men. But most of the able-bodied men were fighting overseas. Aunt Versie and Uncle Larry had bought a little house on Brent Street in Wesconnett, near the base in West Jacksonville. Aunt Tots and Uncle Charlie were building a house on Lakeshore Boulevard on the Cedar River not too far away.

Grandmother had fixed her usual Sunday morning farmhouse breakfast. That of course included smoked ham directly from the smokehouse out back. So that meant we also had redeye gravy, which I liked to mix with my grits. Also mixed in was my usual one egg, over light, with the runny yolks. Granddaddy liked his eggs over well. In fact, Granddaddy liked all of his food well done, as did most everyone that lived on a farm. I believe the reason for this is no matter what they ate, they had personally killed it, gutted it, cleaned it and cooked it. And after all that, they couldn't tolerate the sight of any food with even a hint of pink because it reminded them of the butchering and the blood.

Granddaddy looked very dapper this morning, all dressed up in his Sunday best. He was in a very good mood, and was wearing his best suit with his favorite white shirt, the one with the thin tan vertical stripes.

"Papa, you want some more coffee?" Aunt Versie asked. She had gone into the kitchen and brought the steaming coffee pot from the stove.

"Much obliged." Granddaddy nodded with a little smile.

Aunt Versie filled his cup. Granddaddy started to take a sip, then realized it was too hot. Without hesitation he lifted the cup and saucer, poured the coffee into the saucer, and began blowing on it to cool it, then drank it from the saucer. This elicited the customary stern look from Grandmother, followed by a loving smile.

Granddaddy finished his second cup of coffee and retrieved his watch from the small watch pocket in the front of his trousers. It was made of yellow gold and had the impression of a locomotive engine etched onto the back of the watch. A heavy gold chain tethered it to one of his belt loops. He never wore a belt. He used suspenders, gallouses as he called them, to keep his pants up on his thin frame. Granddaddy's eyesight was still good enough he didn't need spectacles to tell time.

"I 'spect Hardy'll be here directly," Granddaddy said. On Sundays, Uncle Hardy would usually stop by on his way to Sunday school and church at First Baptist in Sneads. Sometimes I would go with him and Aunt Berta, but not today because Aunt Versie was visiting. Grandmother and Granddaddy would not go with us to church on Sunday. I thought it was because of their age, but then I heard them talking about the fact they thought some of these young preachers were more interested in tithing and money than they were about the 10 Commandments and heaven. Yet, they had strong Christian beliefs and lived the life to back it up. They believed one's salvation was a personal matter between them and God and it was more important to walk the walk than talk the talk. And they did.

Granddaddy inserted his watch back into its pocket and without much ado rose from his seat at the table and shuffled towards the living room to assume his position in his gooseneck rocking chair. There was still a chill in the air so before he sat down, he poked at the dwindling embers in the fireplace and threw on another log. Soon he was resting comfortably in the rocker and seemed to be enjoying the warmth of the freshened flames.

Meanwhile, I was standing on the hearth with my back to the fireplace trying to solve the mysteries of the present Aunt Versie had given me, the yo-yo. I figured out how to loop the string around my middle finger, but I couldn't make the yo-yo go down and come back up. It was something about the timing. It would go down and stay down, then I would have to wind it back up. Or when it went down, I would snatch it too hard and it would become twisted. Frustrating.

"Granddaddy, do you know how to yo-yo?" I asked.

It seemed like the harder I tried the more difficult it became. And now I had a bird's nest tangle in my yo-yo string.

"Granddaddy… Granddaddy…"

I glanced over at Granddaddy sitting in the gooseneck rocker. His head was turned to the side and slumped down slightly like he had dozed off.

"Granddaddy," I said a little louder.

Aunt Versie was watching from the dining room when I called him the second time. "Granddaddy's asleep," I said to her.

"Papa," Aunt Versie said. "Papa!" She rushed into the living room and patted Granddaddy's hand, then shook his shoulder. He did not respond. Grandmother saw what was happening and came running. She leaned down and began kissing Granddaddy and holding him tight. She knew he was gone.

Uncle Hardy arrived a few minutes later. After seeing the situation, he rushed to town and came back with Doc O'Hare. The doctor said it was a heart attack and even if he had been sitting with him when it happened, there's nothing he could have done.

Early the next morning a black hearse arrived and slowly pulled up to the front gate. Daddy, Uncle Hardy, Uncle Bud and Uncle Verdayne helped the two men from the funeral home bring Granddaddy's casket up the steps and into the house. They placed it on a stand next to the windows across the living room from the gooseneck rocker where Granddaddy had drawn his last breath. I stood next to Daddy, his reassuring arm on my shoulder, as they opened the lid to the casket. I'm not sure what I was expecting, but Granddaddy appeared to be just lying there asleep with a peaceful expression on his face. He was wearing the same nice suit he had on the day before.

In a few minutes Grandmother and several of her daughters came out of her bedroom. They were by her side as she approached Granddaddy and gently placed her hand on his hands and stood there in silence. Finally, she turned to walk away.

"He's at peace," she said, with a painful smile on her face. "Don't leave him, boys."

"Don't worry, Mama," Uncle Hardy said. "He won't never be alone."

And so, it was. The brothers made arrangements for one of them to be in the room with Granddaddy at all times until the funeral. Even throughout the night.

The funeral was set for the afternoon of the third day, Wednesday afternoon. It was thought that some of the kids might need the extra day of travel to get back to Sneads. All but two of them arrived on Sunday night or on Monday. Uncle Grady had to drive south from Auburndale to try to find Uncle Dick, who was running a dragline somewhere near Lake Okeechobee. The brothers were worried that Uncle Dick might be on a binge rather than working. Fortunately, uncle Grady found him on the job and they made it to Sneads by dinnertime on Tuesday. And for the second time ever the 12 Shelfer children were all together again.

It was drizzling rain when the pallbearers carried Granddaddy down the steps of the house that he had built as a church, then later converted to our home. They began the journey to Dykes Cemetery. Grandmother rode with all five of her daughters behind the hearse in the black family car, which was provided by the funeral home. I rode with Daddy and Uncle Bud and Aunt Ruth and Faye in

86

Uncle Bud's '39 Ford. We followed in a line of cars that slowly processed up River Road to the 16th hill where it turned to the west. This route took us past Greasy Bottom, the old home place that Granddaddy and Grandmother built on the 750-acre farm where most of the kids grew up. About five minutes later we sloshed off the muddy road onto the green grass of Dykes Cemetery. It was easy to spot the Shelfer plot because of the green tent erected over the mound of red clay of a freshly dug grave, surrounded by flowers and rows of chairs.

"On a hill far away, stood an old rugged cross…" A frail lady that I didn't know stood in the back of the crowd and sang this old hymn, which I did know. The rain continued to pepper down as a preacher I had not heard before began reading a Bible verse that I had heard before. "In my father's house are many mansions: if it were not so, I would've told you. I go to prepare a place for you…" He read a few more Bible verses, but fortunately didn't preach too much. When he was finished the lid of the casket was opened and everyone in attendance was invited to file by to pay their last respects. Grandmother, sniffling softly, was the last approach the casket. She stood there for a moment then began wailing hysterically in grief. In an instant she had climbed onto the casket, bawling and desperately holding Granddaddy close. Daddy picked me up and walked away slowly out into the rain. I watched over his shoulder as Aunt Versie, Aunt Tots and the others, gently pulled Grandmother away. They closed the lid on the casket, and just like that, Granddaddy was gone. He had left her. Who would do the chores? Who would chop the wood, hoe the garden, feed the animals, empty mousetraps, and indeed, shoot the occasional rattlesnake? It had never been discussed, but now that granddaddy was gone, who would be the man of the house? I didn't have to be told the answer to that question. At the age of eight, I was the man of the house.

Chapter 14

We were headed west on the Old Spanish Trail, US 90, the highway that traversed the country from Jacksonville, Florida to Santa Monica, California. I was traveling alone on a Greyhound bus returning to Sneads after spending the summer with my daddy in Jacksonville. I wasn't really alone, because aside from the other passengers on the bus, the driver, Eddie Edmonds, was a friend of Daddy's. I heard them talking and he assured Daddy that he would take good care of me. I guess that's why he assigned me the front seat of the bus, directly across from the driver. The cushioned seat was very comfortable and Mr. Edmonds had showed me how to make it recline so I could take a nap if I wanted. That wasn't possible because I had a perfect view through the front windshield and was mesmerized by the oncoming traffic. The large bus and the narrow, two-lane road, made each car, and especially each truck, seem like a life-or-death adventure. It reminded me of my first trip to Sneads with Aunt Versie years ago. Scary then, and scary now. So, I opened up the new baseball magazine Aunt Versie had given me with a great article and pictures of Stan Musial, my favorite player, and the St. Louis Cardinals, my favorite baseball team. And I began to daydream. About baseball, and fishing, and hunting. And about people, like Daddy, and Aunt Versie, and Grandmother, and about what it would be like to have a daddy and a mother and a normal home like most of my friends. But I would never know, because my mother had left me. But there's one thing I did know. No one could take the place of my grandmother.

It had been another fun summer in Jacksonville. Daddy was living in a spare bedroom at Aunt Maude's house out in Dinsmore, a northwest suburb of Jacksonville. Uncle Leon, her husband, had died a few years back of complications from his leg wound from the war. Annie Laura still lived at home, but she was gone most of the time attending school or working at the hospital. I think Aunt Maude liked the company of having us around. At least she said she did.

Some of the summer days at Aunt Maude's were spent fishing in the creek down the road from her house. It was dark, brackish water, because it flowed into creeks and rivers that eventually led to the Atlantic Ocean. It was different watching the water level in the creek go up and down with the tide. Aside from the usual bream and bass I was accustomed to catching, you could also catch some of the saltwater fish like sheepshead, redfish, and croakers. And then there were the pesky blue crabs. Ugh.

Two days a week on his way to work, Daddy would take me to Wesconnett where I would hang out with Aunt Versie at the drugstore where she worked. Not bad duty because she kept me occupied with milkshakes and banana splits. She also arranged for me to play on the Wesconnett Little League baseball team which was great fun. Because I was the only left-hander on the team the coach had me play first base. Because I had played mostly by myself all my life, playing on a team with other boys was exciting.

Occasionally I would go to work with my dad and spend the day with him. He began his job with the sewer department of Jacksonville as a laborer, digging ditches with a shovel. Soon after returning home from the war, he was promoted to truck driver, and about a year after that he became a foreman. He supervised a crew of men which included a truck driver and about a dozen Negro laborers. He repaired and installed sewer pipes anywhere in the city limits of Jacksonville and soon gained the reputation of being able to handle the most difficult jobs. Although Daddy had only a ninth- grade education, he had the ability direct his men to solve problems, where others had failed. He had a tough management style. He would not tolerate insubordination or slackers, and any workers guilty of that would be fired on the spot. As a result, everyone on his crew would pull their own weight. The thing I didn't like about going to work with daddy was what would usually happen after quitting time at the end of the day. He would meet his boss, Joe Butler, at a tavern somewhere and they would shoot the breeze and drink. If a bar wasn't nearby or convenient, they would buy a half a pint of bourbon, like Early Times, and drink it in the front seat of one of their cars, chasing it with 7-Up. The change in Daddy's personality as they passed the bottle back and forth was sickening for me to watch. And he must've known that, but he didn't seem to care one way of the other. I guess it was something he had to do, regardless of the consideration of others. So, when I went to work with Daddy, I saw him at his best, and then I saw him at his worst. And, so it goes.

Mr. Edmunds wheeled the big Greyhound bus into the busy station in Tallahassee for a half-hour break. After the passengers had departed, he took me into the terminal restaurant with him.

"Benny, I think I'm gonna' have me a hamburger steak for dinner ," Mr. Edmunds said. "Would you like one?"

"No Sir, I ain't hungry," I said. Daddy had given me three dollars for a snack, with instructions to give whatever money was left to Grandmother. As much as we needed the money, I couldn't see wasting a dime on any restaurant food. Hamburger steak? I had never had a hamburger and I had never even seen a steak of any kind in my life, other than my grandmother's country fried steak, but I knew it had to be expensive.

"Growing boy like you gotta eat. At least have something to drink. It's been four hours since we left Jacksonville."

"Could I please have a Coca-Cola?" I asked.

About then a perky middle-aged waitress approached our table. "Hey Eddie. How's it goin'?" She asked. "Who's your buddy?" She tousled my hair and flashed a big smile that showed a lot of teeth.

"Goin' good, Grace. This here is my friend, Benny, who's goin' all the way to Sneads with me today."

"That's nice. You havin' the usual?"

"Yes, please, with a cup a' coffee." Mr. Edmunds looked at me, looked at Grace, then back at me. "And the same for Benny, with a Coca-Cola."

"Got 'cha," Grace said, and she was off to the kitchen.

I was just about to say something when Mr. Edmund said, "Don't you worry about it, young man. It's my treat today. Just enjoy."

And I did. I had a hamburger steak that was delicious, because I was starving.

I was on my big red Western Flyer bike, the one with the chrome handlebars, racing towards Raymond's house. Uncle Hardy was out in his field by the old tobacco barn pulling a trailer behind his new Case tractor. I gave him a big wave as I went speeding past. When he had picked me up at the bus station the day before, he told me had seen Raymond and his daddy, Chester, at the hardware store in Chattahoochee, and told them I was coming home. He said Raymond was so excited and said to tell me to come see him, we would go fishing.

I was growing accustomed to spending the summer months in Jacksonville in the city and the school months in Sneads on the farm. It was exciting to always have a change to look forward to in the not-too-distant future; different places, different activities, different friends. I liked it.

The excitement was mounting and my black lunch pail was rattling in the wire basket of my bike as I accelerated down the last hill before the Walden's place. Grandmother said she didn't want us to be hungry on our fishing trip so she packed my lunch box with two drumsticks, two biscuits, and two dog's juice harps. I have no idea why she called them that. All I know is they were delicious pear tarts made from fresh pears from our pear tree down by the pump house.

I was pedaling downhill in the right-hand rut, the smoothest part of the clay road, and by the time I reached the bottom of the hill I was going about as fast as my bike would go. I saw something laying across both ruts in the road ahead of me that look like a large peanut pole. I was rapidly approaching it and looking for a way around it when I saw that it was moving. I immediately realized it was not a peanut pole. The hair stood up on the back of my neck as I realized it was an enormous diamondback rattlesnake. I was in trouble. I couldn't just run over him because he would surely make me fall or he might just double up and bite me. If I tried to leave the rut of the road to try to go around him, I would most certainly fall and slide into him. And, of course, he would bite me. My only choice was to try to stop, so I stomped back on the right pedal and locked the Bendix brakes on the rear wheel my bicycle. What was probably milliseconds seemed like forever and it didn't look like I was going to stop before I hit the snake. My only choice was to lay the bike down, which I did. I came to a dusty, sliding halt just a few feet from the rattlesnake, who had snapped to a coil when he heard the commotion and was already singing his rattles.

I left my bike laying there and ran back up the hill and begin yelling for Raymond. Finally, the Walden's heard my screams about the snake and came running down the road and around the corner, with Mr. Walden shouldering his shotgun. By the time they got there, the snake had crossed the ditch and escaped into the dense cover of the nearby woods. The wide slithering tracks he left in the dry soil clearly showed his path across the road, but they could never find him.

On the farm, living with the threat of snakes was just part of everyday life. There are five species of poisonous snakes in the United States and Jackson County Florida has them all; the rattlesnake, the pygmy rattler, the cottonmouth moccasin, the copperhead moccasin, and the coral snake. You are always hearing about someone's animal or even about some person being bitten by a snake. In our family alone Aunt Tots was bitten by a pygmy rattler not too far from the house when she was a young girl. Junior Neel, the son of Uncle Ford, Grandmother's brother, was bitten when he was two years old by a big rattlesnake. He survived the bite but was never the same because of mental and physical impairments afterwards. Both Uncle Hardy and Uncle Bud had lost bird dogs to snakebites and it was not uncommon to find a cow or a calf dead from snakebite. Fortunately, snakebites do not affect hogs because of the makeup of their circulatory system. I was not afraid of snakes, but I did not like them. I had a healthy respect for them because they would bite and possibly kill you or your livestock or one of your pets.

Raymond, along with his mother and father and sister, lived in a very old farmhouse with his grandfather and grandmother. I was not surprised to learn that this was actually another house that my granddaddy had built. It had weathered well through the years. The different sections of the house, the living room, bedrooms, and kitchen were connected by covered porches, probably to allow more cross ventilation in the summertime. There was no indoor plumbing at all and the only water came from dropping a bucket into a dug well in the side yard. If you had to "use the bathroom" you went out the back door of the kitchen and followed a trail to the outhouse. There was no toilet paper available but there were plenty of corncobs and the summer edition of the Sears and Roebuck catalog.

After the episode with the snake, Raymond and I were anxious to get on with our fishing trip. We filled a Chase & Sanborn coffee can with some wigglers we dug down by the cow pen, grabbed a couple a cane poles from the front porch, jumped on our bikes and were off to Blue Springs. We made sure to keep our speed up when we passed the place where the snake crossed the road. After a left turn at the top of the hill we passed the Old Double Pen home site where Granddaddy and Grandmother lived a few of their early years and where several of my aunts and uncles were born. We turned right about a half mile down the road at Greasy Bottom where my daddy was born, as well as most of his brothers and sisters. We were both dripping wet with sweat from the sweltering September sun as we turned left on River Road and coasted to the bottom of the 16th hill. We were there.

Raymond led the way as we bumped along on our bikes single file down the old logging road to Blue Springs landing, which was about a quarter of a mile into the swamp. There was not a ripple in the water or a leaf shaking as we left our bikes up on the hill and started fishing in the shade of an old sweet gum tree, which just happened to be my grandmother's favorite fishing spot. It was dinner time but the fish didn't seem to be hungry.

"Who do you think will be our teacher in fifth grade this year? I asked.

"Mrs. Wester, for sure," Raymond said.

"I like her. I think she'll be good."

"Who's your favorite teacher so far?"

"Mrs. Campbell was nice last year, but I think Mrs. King in third grade was my favorite."

"I liked her too. So sad, her getting killed in a car wreck by a drunk driver."

"So sad. Does your Daddy drink whiskey and get drunk? I asked.

"Not that I know of."

"Oh! You would know it if he did...you're lucky."

"What about Mrs. Ivey in the second grade?" Raymond asked. He had a smug little grin on his face.

"No. Not my favorite."

"You don't like writin' right-handed?"

"It's okay. I didn't like her lettin' on like there's something wrong with me because I'm left-handed.

Raymond caught a little bitty brim that wasn't big enough to eat, so he threw him back. I got a bite, but missed him. Probably another little one. The heat from the lingering dog days of summer was bearing down, and we were still sweating even though we were sitting in the shade.

"Guess what I saw in Jacksonville?" I asked.

"What?"

"Television."

"Television? You saw television? I heard about it but I ain't never seen it. What's it like?"

"It's like a little bitty movie screen, not much bigger than a basketball. Me and my cousin Faye and her cousins Joyce and Tony Holton were invited to one of their neighbor's house to watch the Lone Ranger."

"You mean Lone Ranger? Like's on the radio?" Raymond asked.

"Yeah, just like that, only you can see it. Well, the screen was a little snowy but you could still see it good. The Lone Ranger wore a mask and Silver was a pretty white horse and Tonto was a real Indian that wore a feather."

"Wow. I hope I can see television sometime. What's in that black box you got there?" Raymond asked. There was a smug little grin again.

"Grandmother fixed us somethin'. You hungry?"

"Hungry as a bitch wolf suckin' nine to the side," he said. We both giggled, even though I had heard that one before.

We had our own little picnic fishing by the water where the food always seems to taste better. The drumsticks, biscuits, and dogs juice harps were gone in mere minutes and soon we were back to concentrating on fishing. The fish weren't cooperating. Not much happening. We were just sitting there staring at the cool blue-green water of the spring fed lake.

"Let's go swimming," Raymond said.

"Ain't got no bathin' suit."

"Don't need no bathin' suit," he said. "We'll swim in our birthday suits." There was that grin again.

In an instant we were rolling up our fishing poles and took them up the hill where we shucked off all our clothes and laid them on the bikes. We dashed back down the hill and took a running jump as far as we could into the cool water of the lake. It felt so good. We swam around on top of the spring water boiling into the lake, playing and splashing each other. As hot as it was and with the fish not biting, it was a lot more fun than fishing. The thrashing and the splashing continued.

"Wait!" Raymond said. He held his hand up in front of his face and I splashed him again. "No wait," he said. "Hear that?" He looked very serious.

"What?"

"That."

Then I heard it. It sounded like someone turned off the River Road and was coming our way.

"Probably just a loggin' truck," I said.

"Listen," he said. We heard it again bumping along down the road getting closer. "That ain't no loggin' truck," Raymond said. "That's a car. Somebody's comin' down here fishin'!"

We were out of that lake and running naked up the hill faster than if we had seen a gator. The car was getting closer now and sounded like it would be coming around the last bend and into the clearing where we were any moment now. I didn't bother putting on underwear. I jumped into my dungarees and quickly tugged them up over my wet body and snatched up the zipper.

"Yoweeeee!" I let out a bloodcurdling scream. The pain was excruciating, more than I could ever imagine. I had caught my tallywhacker in my zipper. At least some skin on the bottom of it. I couldn't move without it killing me. I looked over Raymond thinking somehow, he could help me. But he was already rolling on the ground laughing so hard he was crying. The pain was intense and with the car coming into site, I had only one choice. I clenched my teeth together and yanked the zipper back down. Nothing had ever hurt so badly or felt so good so quickly as not having that pain. The people in the car paid us little mind as they drove on by to fish further down the lake.

Raymond and I decided that we'd had enough excitement for one day so we put all our clothes back on and headed for home. We retraced our steps passing Greasy Bottom and the Old Double Pen and came to a stop when we reached the road where Raymond would turn right and go down the hill past where I saw the snake and around the corner to his house.

"See ya Bud," Raymond said. "Sorry I laughed that you." He started laughing again.

"I see how you're sorry," I said. Then I began giggling too. "Don't you dare tell nobody."

"Don't worry, I won't tell nobody." Raymond started pedaling, speeding away down the hill and looked back over his shoulder. "Except maybe for Dannie," he shouted. And he was gone.

How did he know I liked Dannie? We had never talked about it. Some secrets are hard to keep from your best friend, I guess. I thought about that as I continued the trek home that would pass Old Man Hare's old place, the Long Pond, Uncle Hardy's place, Dog Bottom, and then up the hill to the house. Maybe Raymond saw me watching for Dannie to arrive at school every morning. She walked the short block down from the house where she lived, which happened to be the old Sneads Hotel building. Or maybe he saw me watching Sondra and Dannie playing hopscotch or jacks at recess. Sondra was such a tomboy, but Dannie was always so feminine, and so pretty, with black hair and white porcelain skin like a China doll. I would never tell her, but someday we would be married and have two perfect children and I would have a good job and Dannie wouldn't have to work and I wouldn't drink and I would take the family for a drive in our new Chevrolet and never go faster than the 55-mph speed limit and we would live happily ever after. I would never tell anyone else either.

"Hey Benny, where you been all day?" Uncle Hardy shouted. He had been out in the field working all day but now he was feeding the cows and the hogs in the holding pens near the road.

"I been fishin'," I said. I stood my bike up on its kickstand and climbed up on the fence to talk to Uncle Hardy. He was pouring some shorts, hog feed, from a bag into a trough for a large sow who recently had a big litter of pigs. She was paying no attention to him, lying prostate on the ground grunting contently and nursing her little piggies. So cute.

"Ketch any?"

"No Sir, too hot, I think. Went swimmin' though. And I saw a big rattlesnake."

"While you were swimmin'?"

"No Sir, saw him crossin' the road just around the corner from the Walden's place."

"Kill 'im?"

"By the time Mr. Walden got there with his gun, he got away."

"Well, just another one for us to have to worry about," Uncle Hardy said.

"Yes, Sir." I understood what Uncle Hardy was saying, but at this moment, as I hung on the fence watching and listening to all these little piggies nudging and nestling and nursing and answering their mama's grunts of affection with their new little oinks, it was hard to believe that all was not right with the world. I was trying to count the pigs in the litter, but the way they were stacked in and around each other made it difficult.

"How many pigs in the litter?" I asked.

"Oh! I don't know, ten or twelve. Want one?"

"Yes Sir! Could I have one? I mean, do you think it would be okay with Grandmother?"

"I 'spect it would," Uncle Hardy said. "Just jump in and grab any one you want, but watch out for that old sow. She can be a mean one when it comes to somebody messing with her babies."

It was going to be difficult to pick a favorite out of this bunch of little pigs. They were all mostly black with occasional spots of white around the neck and head, and the way they were packed in there nursing, they all looked basically the same. Except for one. While the others were nursing with their mama, one little male pig had ventured away on his own and was having the best time rooting around in the mud and exploring. And his color was totally different. His entire body was a beautiful Wedgewood blue.

"That one," I said to Uncle Hardy.

"Better be quick," he said.

And I was. I bounded over the fence and scooped the up the little piggy and was out of the pen in an instant. He didn't even squeal. I'm sure the old sow never realized what was going on because she was looking the other way.

"Atta boy," Uncle Hardy said. "Now you take good care of 'im."

"Thank you, Uncle Hardy. I will. I promise I will."

The bike was only a few feet away. I was rubbing the little pig's head and ears and he began grunting softly. I thought I would just put him in the basket of my bike for the ride home, but then I thought his feet would stick through the wire in the bottom. And, I didn't want him to look around and be afraid, because I was quite sure this would be his first bicycle ride. It was then I realized he was no bigger than a thermos bottle which fit in the lid of my lunchbox. I gently placed him inside, fastened the lid with one latch, eased the lunchbox into the basket, and sped off towards the house.

"Grandmother! Grandmother!" I shouted. I ran through the front door carefully holding the lunchbox in front of me.

"I'm in the kitchen," Grandmother said. "You ketch us a mess of fish?"

"No, ma'am. Look what Uncle Hardy gave me." I placed the lunchbox on the kitchen table and opened the lid.

"Oh! Good Lord. A pig?"

"Yes ma'am. Can I keep it?" I looked at Grandmother anxiously and waited for her answer for what seemed like forever.

"I reckon. But, Benny, he's yore pig, and you have to take care of 'im," she said.

"Yes ma'am, I will. I promise I will."

Grandmother went to the back pantry and returned with a baby bottle with a nipple. She filled it full of fresh milk and handed it to me.

"I 'spect he's hungry," she said.

I nestled the little pig in a feed sack under my arm and fed him the bottle. He had the cutest little grunt of satisfaction and he gobbled up the milk like…well, like a pig.

"What 'chu gonna call 'im? Grandmother asked.

"His name is Ned," I said.

Chapter 15

"Did it come, Benny?" Grandmother asked, yelling from the kitchen.

"Yes ma'am, it did," I said. I had been out by the mailbox waiting on our postman, Mr. Adel Demont, to deliver our mail, as he did every day except Sundays and holidays. Our address was Route 1, Box 4, and we had the standard rural mailbox attached to one of the oak trees in the circle in front of our house.

"Hallelujah. You cain't never tell 'bout them gov'mint checks," she said.

Grandmother had been watching every day for her old age assistance check of $39 to come from the federal government, the money we had to live on each month. Old age assistance was a federal program established in conjunction with the states to give aid to older people who had no money and no means of support. We certainly fit into that category. This was Saturday and the check should have been here on Tuesday, and I knew grandmother was short of a few things in the kitchen.

"Guess what else came?" I asked. I placed the envelope with the check and a medium-sized box on the dining room table.

"What?" She asked. She sounded excited now because we didn't get a lot of mail.

"Your shoes from Sears and Roebuck came."

"Lordy me. All this in one day? Let me try 'em on."

Grandmother sat in her chair at the dining room table, opened the box and scrutinized the new shoes that she would wear for another year. They were exactly like the old tattered pair of size 6 brown leather shoes she was wearing except they were new and shiny and didn't have holes in the bottom. They had no laces, but elastic on either side of the top center of the shoe. She slipped the new shoes on her wide but tiny feet.

"They'll do," she said. Her little nod and half smile signaled her approval.

Grandmother was only able to go to school for a few years before she had to drop out to help her family with the house and the farm. She could read and write, but not very well. It had become my responsibility to help her with those kinds of things. So, once a year we would order the same pair of shoes for her from the Sears and Roebuck catalog. Then, every year or two, she would have me order some cotton underwear and brassieres for her. I couldn't believe all those pictures of women wearing nothing but their underwear in the catalog.

"Benny, if we make a grocery list can you take it to McDaniel's for me?" Grandmother asked.

"Yes ma'am. Can I go to the picture show?"

Sneads actually had a movie theater. It was where I saw my first movie, Bambi, on a field trip from school in the first grade. I remember being afraid for all the animals caught in the forest fire. Going to the movies had become my favorite pastime on Saturday afternoon. The theater was owned by Sondra's uncle, and was called the Hinson. Sometimes, I would see Sondra at the theater, but I was always looking for Dannie, who was never there. For a quarter you could get a ticket to the movie, a Coke, and a bag of popcorn. They would have a Western movie with stars like Roy Rogers, Gene Autry, or maybe even the Cisco Kid. Allen Rocky Lane was my favorite. They would also have a cartoon, a clip on the world news, and a serial, which invariably ended on a cliffhanger to be continued the next weekend.

"You can, if we have the money. Go get my purse for me and let's see what we have," Grandmother said.

Grandmother's purse was totally private and sacred to her. I never opened it, but would fetch it for her if she needed something from it.

"I think it's yore lucky day," she said. She pulled a shiny quarter from the little snap change purse where she kept her money. "Now let's make a grocery list."

She recited to me the items we needed and I carefully wrote them on a #5 tablet: 1 pound of Maxwell House coffee, 1 pound of round steak cubed, 10 pounds of Martha White self- rising flour, one box of kitchen matches, 1 gallon of peanut oil, 1 can of Crisco, 5 pounds of sugar, 1 box of Tetley tea, and one weasel of Railroad snuff. After she mentioned the snuff, I read the list back to her because I knew her snuff was always at the end of the list.

"I think that'll do," Grandmother said. "And ask Mr. McDaniel to get it here sometime today if he can, and bring change for a $39 gov'mint check."

"Yes ma'am," I said.

When I entered the front door after walking home from the movies I was engulfed by a savory aroma from the kitchen. I knew Grandmother had supper ready, and I knew what it was: country fried steak with gravy, mashed potatoes, rutabagas and biscuits, with sweet tea to drink. Delicious.

"Benny, after supper I want you to take ole Tom with you down to the corn crib when you do yor' chores," Grandmother said. "I seen some rat signs when I was down there."

"Yes, ma'am. Can I shoot 'em with my BB gun?" I was a pretty good shot with my Daisy Red Ryder air rifle.

"You can if you want to, but we may as well let the cat earn his keep."

Cats were the only pets allowed inside the house. Ole Tom was a rather large tabby cat and was sleeping on a macramé throw rug in the living room. After supper, I tucked him under my arm, grabbed the slop bucket from the back porch, and made my way down to the barn yard. Ned had become a real pet and was getting bigger every day. He loved me like his mother, and I loved him like my…well, like my pet hog. Anyway, he was a character that was fun to play with, and we always seemed to be on the same wavelength. I'm not sure what that says about Ned, or about me as far as that's concerned. He seemed to be wondering what I was doing with a cat under my arm, until I poured the slops into his trough. Then it was slurp slurp, chomp chomp.

The corn crib was only a few steps away. When I opened the door and quietly placed Tom inside, his ears perked up and he immediately went into his crouched, stalking stance. He crept over to the corner of the crib. Suddenly, he jabbed one of his big paws into a hole between the boards in the floor and pulled out two enormous squealing rats, each the size of an ear of corn. He dragged them out the door and disappeared under the corn crib. Soon the rats were no longer squealing. I had a renewed respect for ole Tom. Earning his keep, indeed.

By the time I completed my chores and returned to the house, Grandmother had finished cleaning up the kitchen and was waiting in the living room. It was Saturday night and she had assumed her position in her favorite chair, an old brown wicker rocker with flattened, flowery cushions.

"Reckon we'll be able to git it tonight?" Grandmother asked. "It's 'bout time." She was looking at Granddaddy's gold pocket watch, which she always kept wound, just as he did.

"Maybe, if it ain't stormin' between here and Nashville," I said.

That was my cue. I walked over to the small table against the wall near the fireplace which held the radio. It was a Zenith model with two knobs and a light-colored oak cabinet, about the size of a small toolbox. I clicked on the first knob and waited for it to warm up. After what seemed like the longest time there was a loud hum and lots of static. I carefully tuned the second knob, the one on the right, to place the pointer just above 600 on the circular dial. I could hear someone talking, although he was cutting in and out of the static. He was saying something about the National Life and Accident Insurance Company, so I knew I was close to the right station. I lifted the radio and rotated it on the table and the reception seemed to get better. The announcer was saying that this was WSM, 650 on the dial, a 50,000 watts Clear Channel station. It still wasn't a very clear channel from where I was sitting. There was an antenna wire attached to the back of the radio that extended up the wall and through the ceiling, through the eve of the house, and was attached to the top of the chimney. I reached up and grabbed the antenna and suddenly the reception was clear as a bell. The man was introducing George D. Hay, the Solemn Old Judge, who said in a very dramatic, monotone voice, "from the Ryman Auditorium in Nashville Tennessee this is the Grand ole Opry let 'er go boys." And the music started.

Grandmother's face immediately lit up and she started patting her foot, because it was Roy Acuff, her favorite singer, with his band, the Smokey Mountain boys. They were singing one of her favorite songs, "The Wabash Cannonball." I kept holding the antenna wire so she could hear it better, because she loved the music so much. I did, too. This was our favorite time of the week.

"Benny, hand me that can of Prince Albert and them matches off the mantle," Grandmother said. The song was over and they were introducing a comedian.

"Yes, mam." I turned loose the antenna. The loud static began again, so I quickly handed her the box of kitchen matches and the tobacco. Grandmother never smoked, but she unapologetically dipped snuff all her life. I thought it was disgusting. It seemed dusty and dirty and she had to spit all the time. And, that created problems, especially inside the house, where she had a couple of Maxwell house coffee cans she used as spit buckets. Nasty.

You always had to be careful not to kick over the spit bucket, which would happen occasionally. The worst spit bucket catastrophe was the one involving the bird. One of my aunts had given us a beautiful, teal blue parakeet and a nice cage, which we hung from the ceiling in the corner of the living room. He was a friendly little bird and very tame. He would sit on your finger and eat out of your hand and walk around on your shoulder and give you kisses and do all the little cutie things that birds do. I didn't like to see him confined to the cage all the time, so when all the windows were closed, I would leave the door open to his cage. He enjoyed the freedom of flying around in the house and having fun getting his exercise and just being a bird. Then one day he launched out of the cage and swooped down and flew directly into the spit bucket. I ran over to rescue him but he was already completely covered in the sickening substance, the color and consistency of dark chocolate syrup. I rushed him to the kitchen sink and tried to clean him up, but to no avail. He died a few hours later. I knew Grandmother felt terrible, but it was not my place to ever mention it to her. She was totally devoted to me and would sacrifice her last penny and her last breath for my well-being, so she would never hear it from my mouth that she was not perfect.

"Howdeeeee! I'm just so proud to be here." I was holding the antenna wire again and this lovable, funny woman, Minnie Pearl, was telling how she had just come over to the Grand Ole Opry from her hometown of Grinders Switch. Grandmother pulled Granddaddy's pipe from her apron pocket and tamped it full of Prince Albert. She struck a kitchen match on the hearth of the fireplace and after a few quick draws and puffs she had the pipe lit and settled back to listen to the radio.

It was pure country humor and Grandmother smiled and chuckled at every story Minnie Pearl told. We listened to Ernest Tubb, Eddie Arnold, Stringbean, Grandpa Jones, and some funny stories from the minstrel comedy duo, Jam-up and Honey. We like them all. I especially liked this new guy on the Opry called Hank Williams, and his songs such as "Move It on Over" and "Lovesick Blues." Towards the end of the broadcast as the tobacco was burning down in Granddaddy's pipe, Roy Acuff returned to sing Grandmother's very favorite song, "The Great Speckled Bird."

I couldn't help but watch Grandmother as Roy Acuff finished the old hymn and the verse about going to heaven on the wings of that great speckled bird. She was the picture of total contentment, gently rocking her chair back and forth with Granddaddy's pipe still clenched in her mouth. It was suddenly a morose, melancholy moment for me. I realized that she too, at some time, would leave me. And while I dreaded that moment, there was no doubt in my mind that she did not. Still, no comfort for me.

"Grandmother, why do you smoke Granddaddy's pipe?" I asked. I had wondered about that for a long time, but was afraid to ask. Somehow, in my glumness, the question just popped out.

"Well…" She leaned forward and tapped the ashes out of the pipe onto the hearth of the fireplace, and settled back in her chair. "Me and your granddaddy wuz married for over 50 years. Ever' night 'fore bedtime me and him would sit together by the fireplace or on the front porch. Amidst all the

106

hard times and the good times, this wuz our time. I would dip my snuff and he would smoke his pipe and we would just talk, and for a while all the problems of the world would disappear. After Harde died, I thought the least I could do would be to smoke his pipe for him. And so, I did. Ever' night. And I found out by doing that he wuz still with me and this wuz still our time together." She sat quietly and stared at the tatty pipe she clutched in her withered fingers. "Does that make sense to you, Benny?"

"Yes, ma'am, it does." It made a lot of sense to me.

Chapter 16

During our fifth-grade year, the floating music teacher at school, for a change
of pace from the usual song-singing in music class, offered those who were
interested the opportunity to learn to play the flute-o-phone. That meant we
would have to learn about music notes and rhythm and time and a lot of new
things. I knew I loved music from listening to the Grand Ole Opry on Saturday
night, so I was very interested. The problem, as always, money. The flute-o-
phone cost $2.50, and I knew we didn't have that to spare. Nonetheless, I
finally got up enough nerve to ask Grandmother if there was a chance we might
buy a flute-o-phone. She thought for a minute and ask me to go to her bedroom
and fetch her purse. She opened it up and with her guarded Mona Lisa smile
gave me what I am sure was her last three dollars. "I like music, too," she said.
"Go do your best."

Playing the flute-o-phone in music class was fun and fascinating. There
was only so much English, math, and social studies you could do, so it was a
perfect way to break up the day. I was amazed that our little ragtag group of
students honking away at the same tune at the really sounded pretty good. Mr.
Hutchinson, our principal, would stand outside our door and listen to us. He
made no secret of the fact that he wanted Sneads High School to have a band.
Then sure enough, a year later when we were in the sixth grade, Mr.
Hutchinson sent a note home with all students that a band was being formed for
the following school year. He also announced that an informational meeting
would be held in the school auditorium. The new band director would be there
and also a representative of a company with band instruments to sell to the
parents who wanted their children to be in the new band. I gave the note to
Grandmother, but I knew that money was scarce, so I held no hopes of being in
the band. She had me read the note aloud to her. When I finished, I handed it
back to her. She looked at the note and then back at me, but said nothing.

For the next couple of weeks many of my friends at school were buzzing with excitement about being in the new band. They were talking about trumpets and trombones and flutes and clarinets and other musical instruments with strange names. I'd never heard of any of them. When they asked me what instrument I was going to play I would just answer that I wasn't very good at music and I didn't want to be in the band. Even though I was sure I didn't reveal my disappointment, I received some funny looks from some of my friends, because actually I was pretty good with the flute-o-phone.

Fridays were my second favorite day of the week. That's because it was the day before my favorite day of the week, which was Saturday. Saturdays were usually fishing and hunting and movies and then the Grand Ole Opry. It doesn't get any better than that. I had banished the thoughts of being in the band to the back of my mind by busying myself with studies and sports and other things. When the final bell rang at school on this particular Friday, I ran for the bus and was very excited to get the weekend started. I bounced off the bus at the designated stop down the road in front of Margo's house and ran towards our place, knowing that Fuzzy would be excited to see me. Maybe because he was thinking what I was thinking. My mind, as usual, was set on my snack of a biscuit filled with syrup, washed down with a big glass of iced tea, and Fuzzy usually got the last bite of my biscuit. To my surprise, there was a car parked in front of our house. After a few more steps I recognized the car, and then I ran faster. I dashed past Fuzzy, who greeted me at the gate, after a quick pat on the head and fluffing of his ears.

"Hey, Benny," Aunt Versie said. She and Grandmother were sitting in the rocking chairs on the front porch.

"Hey, Aunt Versie. I didn't know you were coming." I bounded up the steps and gave her a big hug.

"I thought it might be a good weekend to come," she said. She glanced at Grandmother with a sly little grin.

"Ain't you here early?" I asked.

"I didn't want to be late for the meeting."

"Meeting?"

"That's what it says right here in this note Mama mailed to me." She held up the announcement I had brought home from school. "It says, there's a meeting at 7 o'clock tonight about the new band at Sneads High School. Would you like to be in the band, Benny?"

I was a little bit in shock. I glanced at Grandmother, who had this cat that ate the canary look on her face, but said nothing.

"Yes, ma'am, I would," I said.

My heart raced with excitement as I hurried to finish my chores. The chickens didn't seem to mind, but Ned was clearly disappointed that he only got a bucket of slops without a social visit and the usual serenade of a couple of songs from the flute-o-phone.

"Sorry, Ned. I gotta hurry and get cleaned up and eat supper. I might get to be in the band." Even though Ned tripled his grunts as I walked away, I hustled back to the house because I knew as soon as I finished a quick bath, supper would be ready.

The three of us sat in the back of the school auditorium which was quickly filling with a crowd of people. Aunt Versie had persuaded Grandmother to come along, which was very unusual because she seldom left the homestead. My eyes were immediately drawn to several tables down at the front of the auditorium. They were covered with blue velvet cloths on which shiny new musical instruments of every kind were displayed. They were beautiful. Intriguing. And yet, I couldn't name a single one of them.

Mr. Hutchinson said a few words of welcome and introduced Miss Gamble, our new band director. She said a few words of gratitude and introduced the man who was selling the band instruments. He said a lot of words of a sales pitch until Mr. Hutchinson jumped in and said they would all be available for questions at the tables down front for those interested in being in the band.

Grandmother and I followed Aunt Versie down front where we waited our turn to talk to the new band director. It took the longest time. Or, it seemed that way to me.

"Miss Gamble, I'm Versie Collins, and this is my mother, Laura Shelfer, and this is my nephew, Bennett Shelfer."

"Nice to meet you, Ms. Collins, Ms. Shelfer, I'm Louise Gamble." She shook hands with Aunt Versie and Grandmother, then turned to me. "Hello, Bennett," she said. She extended her hand. I timidly shook her hand and nodded. "Would you like to be in the band?" She asked.

"Yes, ma'am," I said.

"What instrument would you like to play?"

"I don't know," I said.

"Hmm….," she said. She noticed that our music teacher was beckoning for her attention across the room. "Excuse me one moment," she said.

We watched her talking quietly to the music teacher. I had the feeling the conversation was about me because they kept glancing by way.

"Bennett, how would you like to play the French horn?" Miss Gamble asked when she returned.

"I don't know. Which one is that?" I asked.

"Is this one here," she said. She pointed to a shiny, gold, medium-size horn on the end of the table that look very complicated. It swirled around and around and had so many circles that it looked like a colored picture of the small intestine.

"I guess… I'm just not sure," I said. I looked at Aunt Versie, who looked at me, and then at Miss Gamble, who looked at all of us for a long moment.

111

"To be honest, Ms. Collins, the French horn is a little more expensive than most of the instruments. But it is also one of our most difficult instruments to play. We try to pick someone for the French horn who is an excellent student and is not only is a good musician but also has a good ear for music." Miss Gamble glanced over at the music teacher and Mr. Hutchinson across the room. "And Bennett comes highly recommended."

I was cringing at this conversation, but Aunt Versie couldn't hide the fact that she was bursting with pride.

"What do you think, Benny?" Aunt Versie asked. She took me aside and was speaking only to me.

"I guess I could try, Aunt Versie. But, it's so expensive. What do you think?"

"I think you're going to be the first French horn player at Sneads high school. I know you can do this, Benny. I'm very proud of you," Aunt Versie said.

"Thank you, Aunt Versie," I said. I had to struggle to hold back the happy tears, but I did.

Miss Gamble was a new college graduate and this was her first teaching job. And for the students of Sneads High School, this was our first band. It was difficult to imagine how any of our early efforts would ever result in anything that resembled music. Nonetheless, Miss Gamble was very energetic and determined. It didn't take long for her enthusiasm to overcome our naïveté and frustration. With practice, and more practice, each of us began to conquer our fear of making a mistake or playing a bad note. And then it became fun. Miss Gamble began with private lessons for each of us on our individual instruments. Then we graduated to small sections. Eventually, the entire group, almost forty of us, were together in the same room decimating the same song. It was a beautiful thing. All of our individual efforts and exasperations came together to play a single song. We were a unit. All of us felt like we belonged to something. Indeed, we did. We were a band.

"Okay, band. Listen up," Miss Gamble said. "I appreciate the hard work all of you have been doing, and I think it's paying off. I think we're beginning to sound pretty good, don't you?"

There was applause and cheers all around from the band. We were in the middle of a rehearsal in a makeshift band room, which was actually an old house that was formally owned by Mrs. Segrest, one of our English teachers. The sound of all of us jammed in that small room playing our instruments together was loud, if not impressive. I loved it. I loved everything about it. I watched Miss Gamble stand on her little platform at the front of the room conducting the band and I thought what a thrill it would be to do something like that. I finally mustered enough nerve to ask her if I could try it. She told me I should put my efforts into learning to play the French horn before I thought about leading the band. And I did. I worked hard to learn to play the French horn. But I also kept asking her to let me try conducting.

"I think it's time for your parents and friends and the people of Sneads to enjoy the fruits of your labors. I think it's time we gave them a performance."

More cheers and applause came from the band.

"Tell your parents, tell your friends and neighbors…tell everyone that a week from Saturday in front of Mr. Carlisle's store at 2 PM the Sneads High School Band will perform. We don't have uniforms yet, but everyone should try to wear dark trousers or skirts and white shirts. Now, let's keep practicing and let's make it great. Okay?"

The band cheered even louder.

"The last number we will practice today will be "The Thunderer," by Souza." There was a rustling among the students as they put the music up on their stands. "For the first run-through this number today, we're going to try something a little different. We're going to try a student conductor." Miss Gamble looked directly at me. "Bennett, get up here."

I was in complete shock. I had been begging to try this but I had no idea that she would actually let me. I stumbled to the front of the room and stepped up on Miss Gamble's little platform. The looks on the faces in front of me were surprising. They weren't laughing. They weren't smirking. They weren't looking for something to throw. They were actually paying attention and ready to play. I raised my arms and they brought their instruments up in the ready position. I gave the downbeat and the music began. I was thrilled beyond thrilled. Even though it was cut time, march tempo, a basic one, two, down and up, I knew it was my ultimate job to keep the tempo at 120 beats per minute. So, I did. Before I knew it, the song was finished and I stepped down from the platform. The students clapped for me and I clapped right back at them.

"Hmmm…" Miss Gamble said, with a little smile on her face. "Good job, Bennett."

To my pleasant surprise, Grandmother had decided on the morning of our performance that she would like to go into town to hear the band. We finished dinner early to be ready to go on time. Uncle Hardy, along with Aunt Berta and Ronnie, stopped by to give us a ride into town. Grandmother, along with me and my French horn in its big black case, piled into the back seat next to Ronnie. He was four years younger than me and in the third grade. Ronnie was so smart and was doing really well in school and he, just like uncle Hardy, had an abundance of common sense. As we grew older, we grew closer. He was more like my little brother then my first cousin.

The sleepy little town of Sneads was wide awake on this Saturday afternoon. Main Street in front of Mr. Carlisle's store was already blocked off between US 90 and Mr. Watson's store. Cars were parked everywhere and people crowded the sidewalks and even the streets. The Pentecostal preacher was polishing off his fire and brimstone harangue in front of McDaniel's grocery. Uncle Hardy had to drive all the way past the post office and Mr. Cecil's store to find a parking place in front of Mr. McAlpine's house on US 90.

By the time we walked back to Main St., Miss Gamble was busy setting up the formation of the band by sections in a semicircle that covered the street, curb to curb. The bass drum, snare drums and the symbol player were in the back line along with the tuba. Then came the trombones, baritones and the trumpets. The saxophones and the French horns were in the next semicircle. Lastly, were the clarinets and the flutes. I left my French horn case on the sidewalk in front of Joe Cogburn's barbershop and hurried to take my place in the formation. I couldn't help but notice Sondra and Dannie in the clarinet section. Especially Danny. She was so cute. It looked like to me she was even wearing a little bit of lipstick. Wow.

Miss Gamble finally got all of us organized in a formation that she was happy with and stepped up on the curb to get our attention and quiet the noodling. Mr. Carlisle sat nearby on an old patio glider he was trying to sell. He was a large, blustery man and talked with a booming voice, probably because he was hard of hearing. He wore khaki work pants held up by wide suspenders over a white dress shirt that needed ironing, reminiscent of pictures I had seen of Theodore Roosevelt, sans mustache. He was a former schoolteacher at Sneads High School, and some would say a very good one. His handwriting was atrocious. So much so that his entire teaching legacy was sullied by one of his quotes. Mr. Carlisle would be writing something on the blackboard for his students when he would say, "read it fast, boys and girls, because, when it gets cold, I can't even read it myself."

All musicians, young and old alike, noodle. It's what they do when they are alone with their instruments without specific direction. Especially before a performance, they noodle away, making whatever kind of loud noise their instrument makes in an effort to warm up their lips, fingers and hands. When an entire band is noodling at the same time it's a gosh-awful sound. Before practice in the band room is not so bad, but here on the streets of Sneads with the entire town gathered around, it was a dreadful sound.

Miss Gamble raised her hands and the noodling immediately ceased. The little town became eerily quiet. She gave us the downbeat to play our warm-up scale and what happened next was quite unexpected. We may have been just a little ragtag startup band, but to me, it was beautiful. The sound reverberating between the buildings lining either side of the street was incomparable to anything I'd ever heard. Electrifying.

The moment was a blur as we honked our way through the first three tunes. I'm not sure how well we played because I was concentrating on doing my best with my French horn part. What I do remember is we were rewarded with great applause from the gathered crowd. Another new experience for me.

"Ladies and gentlemen," Miss Gamble said, "thank you all for coming to hear us today. We are honored to be your new Sneads High School Band, and very much appreciate your continued support in the future. For our final number today, we have for you a classic march by John Philip Sousa, 'The Thunderer.' And as a special treat, to direct this number, will be a student conductor, one of our seventh graders, Bennett Shelfer."

I was shocked. Or, maybe I was in shock. Miss Gamble never told me she was going to do this. I felt paralyzed.

"Get up here, Bennett," Miss Gamble said. She smiled and waved at me to come forward. Everyone was applauding loudly. I stumbled to the front of the band and then realized I was still holding my French horn. Mr. Carlisle was standing and clapping so I placed my French horn on the glider beside where he was sitting. Miss Gamble handed me her baton. It felt strangely different in my hand than the stick from the oak tree I had secretly practiced with down by Ned's pen.

I stepped to the front of the band and looked up at them. It must've been obvious that I wasn't tall enough to see over the front row, because Mr. Carlisle placed a large wooden crate beside me and before I knew it had lifted me up on the crate. Much better. I could even see Grandmother across the street standing beside Boy Glisson's café with Uncle Hardy, Aunt Berta, and Ronnie. They had been joined by Uncle Verdayne and Aunt Minnie Lee and my little cousin Frank, who was almost two years old. I made eye contact with the percussion section, raised that beautiful conductor's baton, and gave the downbeat. Even though it was exhilarating for me to play an instrument in the band, it was ten times that for me to stand in front of them as their leader. The band played beautifully, the crowd was very appreciative, Miss Gamble said I did a wonderful job, and it was all over in a flash. But I knew I liked to conduct the band. I really liked it.

Chapter 17

Sneads was a sleepy little country town. Most people worked at one of a few places. If someone said they worked at Chattahoochee, that meant they worked at the state mental institution which was located across the river in the city of Chattahoochee. Uncle Hardy and Aunt Berta worked there, as well as Raymond's parents, Chester and Darlene Walden. Chattahoochee was by far the largest employer, so it seemed like almost every family had someone working there. If someone said they worked at Apalachee, that meant they worked at Apalachee Correctional Institution, a minimum- security prison on US 90 between Sneads and Chattahoochee. If they said they worked at the dam, that meant they were working on the construction of the Jim Woodruff Dam, the new hydroelectric generating plant being built just below the confluence of the Chattahoochee and Flint rivers. Uncle Dick, Marshall Shelfer, worked there operating one of their largest cranes, when he was not on a binge or drying out. If someone said they worked at the plant, that meant they worked at the Gulf Power Plant, a new coal burning generating facility on the Apalachicola River just south of US 90. Uncle Verdayne had just started working as a chemist in the laboratory there. Almost everyone, even if they had a day job, was involved in farming to some degree. Uncle Hardy was a prime example of that. After working a full shift at Chattahoochee, he would hurry home to tend to his farm. His cows, hogs, peanuts, corn, and sometimes tobacco and watermelons, would keep him busy until after dark.

The uniting cornerstone and the melting pot of our little community was Sneads High School. Most of the families had either attended the school, or were the parents of someone attending. Regardless of whether you were a Baptist, Methodist, Holiness, or you worked at Chattahoochee,

Apalachee, the plant, or just a farmer, you were connected through the school. The basketball and baseball teams were widely attended and a source of pride for everyone, for better or worse. The music programs with the band and choirs and the occasional school play provided entertainment. All originating through the school.

There were only three churches represented in our area. The Pentecostal Holiness Church was located several miles out in the country northwest of town. The Methodist Church was in the middle of town about a block from the school. That's where Dannie went to church. A couple of blocks from there was the First Baptist Church of Sneads. Uncle Hardy, Aunt Berta, and Ronnie went there. And, so did I. They would drive by and pick me up on most Sunday mornings and take me to Sunday school and church. I would always be dressed in a coat and tie, my Sunday best.

Grandmother would never go to church with us. It wasn't that she was a bad person or didn't believe. On the contrary, she was the most wonderful person I'd ever known and I knew she had a deep, abiding faith in Christ. Somewhere along the way, I got the impression, that some preacher had pressured Granddaddy and Grandmother too hard about money and they became disenchanted with attending church. I found it ironic that we lived in a church, at least the building was a church when my granddaddy built it.

Oddly enough, Brother Wattenbarger, the aging pastor of our church, the First Baptist Church of Sneads, and Grandmother, were good friends. It was not unusual for him to come by for a visit. They would sit in the rocking chairs on the front porch and drink sweet tea while they solved the problems of the world and talked about Jesus. And Grandmother was okay with that. She was at peace.

Brother Wattenbarger was a passionate preacher and a wonderful storyteller. His sermons were straight from the Bible. He made frequent quotes from Scripture and invited the congregation to open their Bibles and follow along, which I usually did. I found it interesting how he could talk about something that happened so long ago and relate it to modern-day problems so that everyone could understand. And in doing so, his message, as it was called, was always a good one. So good that even sinners like us can see the errors of their ways. Brother Wattenbarger knew how to preach and knew when to stop. I liked that, because we were usually out of the church and on our way to Sunday dinner by noon.

Services at the Baptist Church would always end the same way. The choir and the congregation would sing an invitational hymn. Anyone present, who had reached the age of accountability, would be invited to join the church. They could come to the church by professing their faith in the Lord Jesus Christ. Or, they could come by letter, meaning they were already a Christian and a member of another Baptist Church and they wanted to move their membership to the First Baptist Church of Sneads.

"For God so loved the world that He gave His only begotten son…" With tears in his eyes, Brother Wattenbarger would talk over the invitational hymn being sung to quote John 3:16 as he moved from behind the pulpit and stepped down in front of the congregation.

"Believe on the Lord Jesus Christ and thou shalt be saved," he would say.

I did, and I was.

On a Sunday soon after that I was baptized on a very special day for the church. Not because Bennett Shelfer had finally seen the light and become a Christian, but because they were going to inaugurate the long-awaited baptistry that had been installed in the wall of the sanctuary behind the pulpit and the choir loft. I was a little nervous about being baptized, but I was very happy for it to be happening in the church, rather than the boat landing down at Ocheesee Pond. At least the baptistry wouldn't have snakes and alligators around. My apprehension was somewhat mollified by the fact that my buddies Maury Wishnoff and Sondra Hinson were also being baptized. Dannie wasn't there, of course, because she was a Methodist. They didn't baptize at their church, they sprinkled. We got dunked, the full immersion.

There was a smell of new paint and the water was cold as I timidly waded down the steps of the Baptistry. I had brought a change of nice clothes, some that I didn't mind getting wet. The water was all the way up to my armpits as Brother Wattenbarger positioned me so I could be seen by the congregation.

119

"I baptize thee my brother in the name of the Father, Son, and the Holy Spirit," he said. And I was dunked. It wasn't exactly John the Baptist and Jesus and the river Jordan, but it worked for me.

Amen.

Chapter 18

My grandmother was very much a homebody. She would seldom leave our house and our little acre of land except for very special occasions, or a fishing trip. Almost weekly she wanted to walk down to Rock Pond to her favorite fishing spot. And then on weekends when Daddy or Uncle Bud or some of her boys came to town, she could almost always be coaxed into a Saturday fishing trip a couple of miles up the road to Blue Springs, Saddler Hole, or one of the other river lakes that all connected to the Chattahoochee River. Of course, that meant a fish fry on the banks of the lake for dinner. And, for me, that meant hushpuppies. Yummy. Good times.

My aunts and uncles would often comment during their weekend visits from Jacksonville about how well Grandmother was "getting along." Even though she was now well into her seventies, to them, she seemed to be doing well. And really, she was. But I could tell she was gradually slowing down. It was the little things. It was more difficult for her to get up from her rocking chair, and her occasional forgetfulness that made me worry about the day she would no longer be with me. What would I do then? She was everything to me almost as long as I could remember. But also, during this time in her life, I knew how much I meant to her. Because of that, I would never, never, want to disappoint her. I always tried my best at everything I did, especially staying out of trouble. Grandmother would say to others, "Benny's a good boy and he always knows right from wrong." It was an interesting concept. I soon realized if there was a question about something being right or wrong, it was usually wrong. She gave me the freedom to do whatever I wanted to do, and trusted me to do the right thing. It worked for me. After all, I was the man of the house.

In the community I never had the feeling that I was considered the man of the house, but it was more like I was a youngster growing up without a father. It appeared to me that several of the men in the community went out of their way to help me or give me special attention. In actuality, these were just good people who probably went out of the way to help everyone.

Coach Joe Dodson was an honest, decent, hard-working man. I had the utmost respect for him. Not only was he the history teacher in the high school and the coach of all sports, namely basketball and baseball, but on the weekends, to provide for his family, he pumped gas down at GD Malloy's Pure Oil station. A football team was not possible in Sneads because we didn't have enough male students in our little school. And even if we did, there was not enough money around to support a football team. The basketball team had the varsity, or the A-Team as we called it, and the junior varsity, which was the B-Team. Raymond, Maury, George, Lloyd Dunham and a few other classmates went out for the B-Team in the seventh grade, so naturally I did too. It didn't matter that I was not very tall and had no basketball experience. Coach Dodson didn't cut me from the team but I rode the bench for the first several games.

It was a cold night in January, 1953. The Sneads Pirates A-Team and B-team were playing in Carrabelle, Florida, a small town on the Gulf of Mexico southwest of Tallahassee. Rather than going on a school bus, we used individual cars for the hour-long trip. I was happy to be riding with Coach Dodson because I knew he had a radio in his car. We were listening to country music when I heard for the first time the new Hank Williams song, Kaw-Liga. I loved everything Hank Williams did. And now I was deeply touched by his song about the lost love of a wooden Indian.

We were playing in Carrabelle's cold and dimly lit gymnasium. I was sitting down at the end of the bench as usual trying to stay warm, and happy that there were only three minutes left in the game that had long ago been decided by the lopsided score. The clock was stopped after a foul and a Carrabelle player was stepping up to the line to shoot free throws. I was shocked by what happened next.

"Shelfer. Get in there," Coach Dodson said.

Even though I was the only Shelfer on the bench, it was hard to believe the Coach was talking to me.

"Get in there," he repeated. He waved his hand towards the court, with that mischievous little grin on his face.

Awkwardly, I slung my jacket onto the bench and ran out on the court. Within seconds the Carrabelle player missed a free throw and Lloyd Dunham got the rebound. I broke for our basket at the other end of the floor. Lloyd made a great pass, catching me in full stride. There was not another player within 10 yards of me. I dribbled to the basket for an uncontested layup and threw up the shot. Not only did I miss the basket, but I barely even hit the backboard. Welcome to the big time. Even though I felt humiliated and there were many chuckles from our bench, it was a great night for me because I got to play in a basketball game. And I had heard the latest song from Hank Williams.

Another of these men who went above and beyond to give back to the community was Mr. George Spooner, the scoutmaster. His wife, Rebecca, was an algebra teacher at the high school. His son, George, was in my class. His daughter, Cora Nell Spooner, was a tomboy and a real cutie girl. Unfortunately, she was four years younger, much too young for me. Besides, Dannie was my age. Maury Wishnoff, also my good friend in my class, was his nephew.

The Boy Scouts of America, under the mentorship of Mr. Spooner, was lots of fun as well as being a very rich and meaningful experience. We would wear our uniforms to our meetings, which were held in the old log cabin community center. Every time I set foot in that building, I was reminded of Aunt Versie bringing me here to get my rabies shots in my stomach with a big needle on the first day I was in Sneads, many years ago. Mr. Spooner taught us the Boy Scout motto, law, and slogan. By theory and example, he taught us what it was like to be a Boy Scout and an upstanding citizen of our community. We learned to always "Be Prepared." We also learned that a Boy Scout was "trustworthy, loyal, helpful, friendly, courteous, kind, obedient, cheerful, thrifty, brave, clean, and reverent." He implored us to "do a good turn daily."

My friend George Spooner was a rock star among us. During the summer he was lucky enough to attend the National Boy Scout Jamboree in California. That alone would secure his notoriety among in our group. But while he was there, he entered and won the national pie eating contest and a big trophy. That was impressive, but his lifetime rock star status with us was secured when he came back with a picture of movie star Hedy Lamarr presenting him with the winning trophy and kissing him on the cheek.

As it turned out, I was one of a few, if not the only band member in our Boy Scout troop. Mr. Spooner approached me to be the bugler for our group. Of course, I told him I didn't have a bugle and had no idea how to play one. He would not be denied. He said if I could play a French horn, I should be able play a bugle. Mr. Spooner was right. Somehow, a bugle was produced and I learned that it was much easier to play than the French horn. I wasn't the best bugler in the world but I knew as far as the Boy Scouts were concerned being loud and enthusiastic was more important than being a musician. I learned the basic bugle commands of Reveille, Assembly, and Taps. Sadly, I would be asked, and nervously accept, the invitation to play Taps at the graveside funerals of some of our military veterans. Honored.

Chapter 19

"Hey, Ned. Want to hear a new song?"

Ned said nothing, of course, but responded with his happy grunt. He always had a happy grunt when I came down to his pen because I never came empty handed. And he was eternally hungry, which was becoming a problem. My little pet piggy had grown into a hog that weighed over 250 pounds and was still growing. He was eating all of our edible garbage and table scraps but still wanted and needed more. I was worried about what would happen to Ned because I knew we had no money to buy feed for him.

His treat for the day was a sweet potato that I dug for him out of the potato bin. We stored our yearly crop of sweet potatoes from the garden in a large mound on the hill and covered them with dirt and topped them with a sheet of asphalt roofing material. I picked a gnarly, stringy potato, the ugliest one I could find, hoping that Grandmother wouldn't mind. She would probably say she could make a pie out of that repulsive looking thing. Still, I didn't tell her, because I knew that fresh food from the garden had to be saved for people. The left-over scraps, if there were any, could be fed to Fuzzy and Ned. I couldn't help but think of the yummy sweet potato pies Grandmother made when I reached down and fed the potato to Ned. He crunched it down with three quick chomps and quickly looked back up at me, grunting happily, and looking to see what else I might have for him. In my other hand was my French horn, but sadly, nothing else for him to eat.

"Okay, Ned. For your after-snack music, would you like to hear "Barcorolle," or "Flow Gently Sweet Afton?"'

Ned responded with even happier grunting and you would think he was a big fan of music from the 1700s. So, I played away.

The concert I played for Ned would have made any 18th century Italian gondolier proud. He responded with his contented grunting, but the truth is I didn't really know if he was enjoying, or just enduring, my music. After all, he was in a pen and was a captive audience.

"Ned, you're gonna miss me tomorrow. I'm going to Tallahassee with Uncle Verdayne to see something I've never seen. We're going to a football game. The Florida State Seminoles are going to scalp the Stetson Hatters. At least I hope they will, 'cause it's their homecoming game."

It was easy to see that Ned liked the Seminoles by the way he looked at me and kept grunting attentively. Or maybe he just thought I had another sweet potato in my pocket.

"Uncle Verdayne says they have a good team and a good coach named Don Veller. He says they have a good band, too, with a new band director named Manley Whitcomb. He says he came down from Ohio State University, wherever that is. Uncle Verdayne keeps telling me that 'cause I'm in the eighth grade I need to start thinking about going to college. He doesn't know it, but of course I'm going to college. Because then, when I graduate, I could marry Dannie and have two perfect children and I would have a good job and Dannie wouldn't have to work and I wouldn't drink and I would take the family for a drive in our new Chevrolet and never go faster than the 55-mph speed limit and we would live happily ever after. Don't tell anyone about that, Ned. I don't even think Dannie knows, yet.

"Benny, hurry and eat yore breakfast so you can do yore chores. Verdayne'll be here directly and you won't to be ready," Grandmother said.

"Yes ma'am," I said.

I wolfed down a syrup biscuit, two fried eggs, over light, mixed with grits and splashed with redeye gravy. For dessert I had a slice of country ham, fresh from our smokehouse.

126

"And after you do yore chores bring me a bucket full of them sweet potatoes from the bin," Grandmother said. "We gotta be ready for a house full of company next week at Thanksgiving. Ain't no telling how many pies we'll need."

After feeding Fuzzy, slopping Ned, feeding the chickens and gathering the eggs, I went to the potato bin and dug up a bucket full of sweet potatoes. I could see that Ned was watching and I couldn't resist. I found a big, stringy, ugly sweet potato and snuck it to him as I walked past his pen on the way back to the house. I don't think Grandmother saw me. A car horn sounded from the circular drive, in front of the house. Uncle Verdayne had arrived to pick me up in his shiny, maroon, 1949 Ford.

It was a quick trip to Tallahassee down US 90, the Old Spanish Trail, passing through Chattahoochee, Mt. Pleasant, and Quincy. I was very familiar with every peculiarity of the route, because of my many trips to Jacksonville for the summers. There was a new fire tower at Mt. Pleasant. Fire towers loomed high above the countryside at specific intervals and were manned by workers from the Forest Service to watch for forest fires. I noticed just past the fire tower there were a new string of ad signs for Burma Shave. The five signs, one after the other said: "Mug and Brush; Old Adam Had 'em; Is Your Husband; Like Adam Madam; Burma Shave." I never knew what the product really was, shaving soap I suppose, but I loved their little dittys along the highway.

We found our seats high up in the bleachers of Doak Campbell Stadium long before kickoff time. They named it after Dr. Campbell, the president of the university. These college students were crazy. Most of them were either dressed up like Indians or wearing maroon-colored clothes, the color of Uncle Verdayne's car.

"Now I know why you're driving a maroon car. It's Florida State's school color," I said.

"It isn't maroon, boy," Uncle Verdayne said. "It's garnet. It's a precious stone like a diamond, only prettier. FSU's colors are garnet and gold."

"Oh," I said.

Uncle Verdayne went to the concession stand and returned with hotdogs and Cokes. I'd never really had a hotdog before, but this one was delicious, all covered with ketchup, mustard and relish. I wolfed it down as both teams, the Seminoles and then the Stetson Hatters, took the field for their pregame warmups. The rousing cheers for the home team by the crowd immediately turned to a unified "scalp 'em, scalp 'em," when the visiting team appeared. Wow. They took this Indian thing seriously. After about half an hour, both teams left the field and disappeared into their locker rooms beneath the stadium.

In the north end zone, the band was lining up. I was looking forward to seeing them, but I had no idea there were so many of them. More than a hundred, with eight tubas. They even had eight French horn players. The men and women were wearing a different style of uniforms. They were all black, but the men wore coat and trousers like a suit. while the women wore a jacket and a pleated skirt. The men's shoes were black, covered with white cloth that fit around the ankles. The women wore tall white boots with gold tassels. The men had black billed hats, like a bus driver, and the women donned round hats the shape of a coffee can, only much bigger. Everyone's hat was topped with a maroon, excuse me, garnet, feathered plume. And everyone wore white gloves. Very sharp.

The band formation covered the entire end zone and everyone stood perfectly still with absolute straight lines in every direction. I couldn't believe not a single one of them was noodling. From the back of the formation this guy with a baton wearing a garnet uniform with a tall, white, fur hat came dashing to the front of the band. He was lifting his knees high into the air with his toes pointed downward and leaning so far back I thought his hat might touch the ground. I was mesmerized.

A loud voice boomed over the loudspeakers: "The Florida State University School of Music presents Drum Major Dick Mayo and the Florida State University Marching Chiefs." The high-stepping guy stopped in front of the band, did a fancy turnaround, raised his baton high in the air and gave a downbeat. The next sound I heard was magical. Magnificent music filled the stadium and it was indescribable. And if it was a song they were playing, I had never heard it. To me it sounded like the beginning of a movie you see in a theater where the lion is playfully growling. They finished the number with a great flourish.

The guy in the tall furry hat blew his whistle four quick tweets and the band started playing the intro of a spirited song that sounded like a march. Then they all stepped off together and began marching down the field, lifting their knees high in perfect unison. All the students were standing and singing some song I couldn't quite understand about fighting for FSU. My eyes were glued to the guy with the baton doing his back-bending high step down the field.

"Who is that?" I asked.

"They're the Marching Chiefs," Uncle Verdayne said.

"No, who is that guy?" I pointed to the high-stepping guy in front of the band.

"He's the leader of the band. They call him the Drum Major."

"Oh...," I said.

They played a football game that day. The Seminoles even managed to pull out a lackluster win over the Stetson Hatters. But the real winner that day was me. I now had a goal in life. Despite the fact that I was in the eighth grade and had barely learned to play the French horn and our little ragtag band had not yet learned to march, I knew what I wanted to do with my life. I wanted to be Drum Major of the Florida State University Marching Chiefs.

Chapter 20

"What you want, Benny? Fried shrimp?" Daddy asked.

We were sitting at a wooden table that was covered with a plastic red and white checkerboard tablecloth in a little hole-in-the wall restaurant on N. Main St. in Jacksonville, between the airport and the Nassau River. I had made the usual summer Greyhound pilgrimage after school was out to spend the summer in Jacksonville. Daddy had picked me up from the bus station as soon as he got off work. I was happy that he had not been drinking. I don't think he had even had a swig from the half pint of Seagram's Seven he usually kept in a paper bag underneath the car seat.

"Yes sir," I said. "With some sweet tea… And can we get some honey for the hushpuppies too?"

The fried shrimp at this place were the best in Jacksonville because they were always fresh. And the hushpuppies were delicious, especially when you filled them with honey. Almost as good as grandmother's biscuits filled with sugar cane syrup, but not quite. A young waitress who appeared to know daddy approached the table and Daddy ordered the shrimp for both of us, along with Ice-T for me and coffee for him. He did his usual customizing of his cup of coffee by diluting it as much as he could with water. I never knew if he was just trying to cool it off or he just liked weak, watered-down coffee.

"You done any fishing?" Daddy asked.

Daddy, for some reason, seemed unusually quiet. At first, I thought it was because he wasn't drinking, but then I wondered if he was worried about something.

"Verdayne took me fishing on his new boat."

"PV got a boat? Where does he keep it?"

"He keeps it in his yard on a trailer."

"Does he paddle it, or does he have a kicker?

"He got a new 7 ½ horse Scott Atwater outboard."

"That's nice. Did you catch any fish?" Daddy asked.

"Caught our limit of 16 bass within 12 minutes of the time we cut the motor off. Good one's too. All of 'em between three and four pounds."

"Shiners?"

"No, Sir. We caught'em on cane poles using carp as cut bait."

"Sounds like a fish tale," Daddy said. I thought I saw a hint of a smile.

"It is a fish tale, but it's the truth," I said.

In just a few minutes two huge plates of shrimp arrived at our table and we dug in. I was starved because of the long bus ride. We had a rest stop at Tallahassee, but I only had enough money for a Coke. Grandmother had offered to give me more money, but I didn't want to take her last dollar. It would not have been the first time, or the last, but I knew she needed the money for groceries more than I needed a snack at the bus station.

"Your Aunt Sis told me your mama came to see you," Daddy said.

"She did. How did Aunt Sis know?" I wondered if this had been what was bothering Daddy.

"I think they stay in touch. So how did that go?"

"It was okay," I said.

It seemed strange to me that Daddy wanted to talk about this now when he never did before. I could count on one hand the times I could remember ever seeing my mother. Every couple of years she would come to visit for a day or two. Grandmother always welcomed her with open arms, but I found it awkward. I was resentful and afraid. Resentful, because she abandoned me as an infant. And afraid she would try to take me away to live in Philadelphia, although she never attempted or even hinted at that. I honestly had no feelings one way or the other about her. She wasn't bad, she was just so different. Probably because she was a Yankee. I guess I was still secretly hoping that Daddy was asking me for information about how things were going with my mother so he might decide to get back together with her and then I would have a mother and daddy like everyone else. Fading hope. Especially after my mother's last visit.

"I have a sister," I said.

"A sister?"

"Well, Grandmother said she was actually my half-sister, whatever that means."

"What was she like?"

"She was okay. Her name is Sharma. She's ten years younger than me."

The young waitress approached the table again carrying two plates of key lime pie.

"I got a couple pieces of pie for you and Benny, Shep. On the house."

"Thank you very much," Daddy said. The waitress cleared plates and returned to the kitchen.

"How did she know our names?" I asked.

132

"I've been here a few times before with people from work," Daddy said. "And I talk about you a lot."

Daddy was only stating what was obvious to me. Our family called Daddy "Sing," but all of his coworkers at the city of Jacksonville sewer department called him "Shep." And I was not proud of the fact he had a tendency to talk a lot about me when he was drinking, which was most every day after he got off from work. Thankfully, he never, ever, drank on the job.

We left the restaurant and headed back towards town in Daddy's old '41 Buick. I never got into this car without being reminded of the most embarrassing moment of my life. When Daddy first got the car a few years ago he drove it over to Sneads to come see me on the weekend. Uncle Bud, Aunt Ruth, and Faye also came over for the weekend in Uncle Bud's 1940 Ford. Both cars were parked straight into the front gate but daddy's car was blocking the circular driveway. He was going to move it so I asked him if I could do it. He handed me the keys and asked me if I knew where the starter was. I told him I did. On the old '41 Buick the starter was located underneath the accelerator. I got in the car and pressed the accelerator to the floorboard. I didn't realize the gearshift was not in neutral, but in reverse, and I had not depressed the clutch. To my absolute shock, the car started and went to full throttle in reverse, spinning the car around and ramming into Uncle Bud's car. I was devastated. Sobbing. In a single moment I had wrecked not only Daddy's car but Uncle Bud's car too. What happened next shocked me also. Daddy and Uncle Bud were not mad at me, but very supportive. Daddy said it was only a couple of fender benders and he would pay to have both cars fixed as good as new in no time. Uncle Bud said that accidents happen and that's why you had to be careful. I learned something that day about being careful, and about being family.

We continued driving south on N. Main St. Up ahead and to the left I could see the alternating white and green light flash from atop the control tower at Imeson Airport.

I knew that beyond the airport was the Jacksonville Zoo, which was on Heckcher Drive. On a typical Sunday morning, Daddy and I would get dressed in our nice clothes. He was a spiffy dresser and was never shy about wearing a coat and tie, or even a suit. He would take me down to the shine shop at 7th and Main to get a shoeshine. Spiffy indeed. Daddy didn't go to church. It wasn't that he didn't believe, it's just that he didn't believe in going to church. With our shoes shined and looking good we would make our way out to the Jacksonville Zoo. Daddy loved animals, and so did I. We would spend hours watching the different animals and sharing peanuts with them.

Further out Heckcher Drive was the bridge across Nassau Sound, where we would oftentimes go fishing on a typical summertime Saturday. We would park the car down by the water at the end of the bridge then walk several hundred yards onto the bridge to fish in the deep channel. We fished with big salt water reels and rods and used dead shrimp for bait. The fun part about fishing in saltwater was you never knew what you were going to catch, anything from a minnow to a whale. I was reminded of Uncle Grady telling me about a fishing trip he went on with Daddy to Nassau Sound. He recounted, with that gravelly voice and a twinkle in his eye, that daddy was fishing on the beach at the end of the bridge where the car was parked when he hooked into a big one. After fighting him for a while the fish jumped up into the air and started flying around. Daddy continued to fight the fish in the air and reeled him down to the sand on the beach. When the fish hit the ground, he spread legs and started running back towards the water. I asked Uncle Grady what kind of fish could swim in the water, fly in the air, and run on the beach. He said he didn't know. I had already secretly named it a Seagram's 7 Sailfish, suspecting you could only catch one of those at the empty end of a whiskey bottle. Uncle Grady went on to tell me he no longer fished in salt water, because everything you caught would bite you. He had a point on that one.

I was not surprised when Daddy turned into the entrance of the airport and parked the car on the right edge of the parking lot, facing the airport boundary fence. It was interesting, and it was free entertainment to sit there and watch the airplanes, usually Eastern or National Air Lines, land and come sputtering up to park at the terminal. The pilots would get off and walk around and stare at the airplane, as if they were looking for something. The beautiful stewardesses would wave bye-bye to the passengers getting off and smile at the passengers getting on. They would close the doors and crank those big propeller engines, engulfing the entire ramp in white, smelly smoke. Then, they were off again, into the night.

We watched, mostly in silence, as a couple of airliners came and went. Finally, Daddy cleared his throat and turned in the car seat to face me.

"There's something I want to talk to you about," he said.

My body became tense. I never wanted Daddy, or anyone else to "talk to me" about anything, because the subject of that conversation usually meant that something was probably about to change for me. So, whatever he was dreading telling me, I was dreading hearing.

"I want to know what you think about me and Dot gettin' hitched."

Dorothy Mayo Holton was Aunt Ruth's sister. She was a beautiful lady with long, flowing black hair. She reminded me of the movie star, Jane Russell. She worked on the counter at Duval Laundry, the biggest laundry in Jacksonville. She was divorced from a man that drank too much. She had two children, Joyce and Tony. Joyce was a year younger than me and the same age as Faye. Tony was a couple of years younger than them.

"I don't know what to think," I said.

I had plenty to think about but I didn't want to talk about it. The family would occasionally say something about Daddy and Dot going dancing together, or something like that. But I didn't see this coming. The truth was I didn't want to see anything coming. Daddy liked to work, he liked to drink, and he liked to take me fishing and hunting. It was a simple life, but that was okay with me. Especially the fishing and hunting part, because that was my time with Daddy. Why did he suddenly want to make it complicated? I had never given any thought to Daddy ever getting married again to anyone except my mother. I don't know why I ever thought he would marry her for the third time. Now he wanted to marry another woman who was divorced with two kids. On top of that, she was Uncle Bud's sister-in-law. Two brothers married to two sisters... I was not excited.

"Does that mean I have to go to school in Jacksonville," I asked.

"You don't have to do nothin' you don't want to."

"Good, because I don't want to go to school in Jacksonville."

And so it was that my new life with Daddy, Dot, Joyce, and Tony began. We moved into the house that Dot had bought on Brackland Street, in the Springfield area of Jacksonville. It was conveniently just two doors down from Uncle Bud, Aunt Ruth, and Faye. It was a small house, probably less than 900 sq. Ft., with two bedrooms, a bath, a living room, dining room, and kitchen. Daddy and Dot and Joyce occupied each of the two bedrooms. They enclosed the front porch and stuffed it with two single beds to accommodate Tony and me.

The dynamics of the summer in Jacksonville had completely changed for me. I honestly liked it better than staying with Aunt Maude because along with Joyce, Tony, and Faye, there were many kids in the neighborhood to play with. Also, there were several recreational parks nearby which offered numerous activities, namely Little League baseball. My favorite was Panama Park where I played outfield for the Hudson Hornets. We had a really good team and ended up winning the City Championship. Hubert Misell, Charlie Nobles, and George McIntyre were some of my little league friends who were on my team.

It was my hope that with Daddy getting married, it might slow down his drinking. No such luck. In fact, his inebriated behavior was highlighted now because there were others around to witness it. This was even more embarrassing to me. When there were just the two of us, I had learned to mediate his intoxication, until he finally slept it off. Dot was not so tolerant. I don't know if it was because she didn't drink, or because she had recently escaped an unfortunate relationship with an alcoholic. Nonetheless, she would confront Daddy, and the fireworks would begin. He was emboldened by the whiskey and would bristle at her admonishments with loud, vulgar rants. Humiliating. I would retreat behind the closed door of my bedroom on the porch. I had learned long ago that it was impossible to reason or argue with a drunk.

After getting off from work at the laundry, Dot would come straight home and fix supper. The main course would be something like chicken and rice, fried chicken, pork chops, spaghetti with meatballs, and even liver and onions. I had to take turns with Joyce doing the dishes. I wasn't happy about that little chore, but I did it. Scrubbing pots and pans was extremely difficult, especially if they sat around long enough for the food to dry and harden. Sometimes we would dry the dishes and other times we would let

136

the wind dry them. That meant we put them in the dish rack on the drain board and then put them away in the cupboard the next morning.

Sometimes Daddy would make it home for supper and sometimes he wouldn't. If he was late, everyone knew what that usually meant. On those nights, Dot would try to get us out of the house before he came home. At least once a week, sometimes more, Dot would pile us into her car and take us to the drive-in movie out on Main Street. She loved movies, all kinds of movies. And so did all of us kids. By the time we returned home from the movies, Daddy was usually already asleep on the couch. Quiet night. Mission accomplished.

Chapter 21

"Hey, Grandmother!"

It was almost suppertime and Daddy and I had just arrived at the old church farmhouse back in Sneads after the long trip from Jacksonville at summer's end. I ran to give Grandmother a big hug. She was sitting in one of the rocking chairs on the front porch.

"Hey, Benny," she said. "I'm glad y'all are here, I was startin' to worry."

"Hey, Mama," Daddy said. He climbed the steps to the porch and gave Grandmother a hug.

"Been doing any fishing?" I asked.

"It's been almost too hot to fish, but we went a time or two down to Rock Pond. They weren't bitin' too good but we managed to catch a mess. You boys hungry? Supper's almost ready."

"I'm a little hungry," I said.

"I thought you would be. Growing boy's gotta eat," Grandmother said.

One could only hope, I thought. I looked around for who was missing from the scene. I whistled loudly. "Fuzzy! Fuzzy!" I shouted.

"Benny," Grandmother said. "I'm afraid I've got some bad news."

"What?" I asked, but in that instant I already knew.

"We lost Fuzzy," she said.

I felt numb, almost paralyzed. I stumbled back to the front porch steps and sat there, bent over, with my head on my knees and my hands covering my face.

"It was an accident," Grandmother said. "Fuzzy went with Hardy down to the 'bacco barn to feed the cows and when they were done Hardy gave Fuzzy a ride in the trunk of his car like he does sometimes. But he forgot he was in there and drove the car over to Chattahoochee to work the next day where was parked in the hot sun, and Fuzzy suffocated. Hardy feels really bad about it."

Without a word, I walked away, around to the back of the house and down towards the barn.

"Benny!" Daddy called to me.

"Let him go, Sing," Grandmother said. "He needs to be by himself a while."

Grandmother was right. I walked past the pump house towards the barn yard and sat down in the shade leaning back against the old pear tree watching the chickens scratching around in the chicken yard. But I wasn't really alone.

My mind was flooded with memories of Fuzzy, my pal for over half my life. I remembered how the little red ball of puppy fuzz ran under my bed to hide when Daddy brought him to me from Jacksonville. He bit me when I tried to get him out from under the bed, then spent the rest of his life protecting me. He was a crazy mixture of chow and German shepherd. He was the size and color of a chow, yellowish red, with a blackish streak down his back. And, as Daddy would say, his tail was curled up so tight his hind legs would barely touch the ground. On the farm, he was what you would call a "ketch dog," meaning he would catch anything or anyone I told him catch. Rabbits, hogs, or even cows were no problem for him.

Fuzzy would always bark and bristle at strangers. But once we accepted the stranger as a friend, he would never forget them and never again give them a second glance. Still, it was Fuzzy's protective mode that would cause problems. One time, my down the road next door neighbor, Margo Rigdon, brought an out-of-town cousin over to play. He and I were tussling, as boys would, and out of nowhere Fuzzy nailed him on the arm. Fortunately, I grabbed Fuzzy before he did too much damage. Margo's out of town cousin never returned again to play.

I couldn't help but smile remembering the time the black snake crawled across front yard where I was playing. Before I could realize what was happening, Fuzzy was on him, biting and shaking him. The funny thing was, he was trying to bite the snake without his lips touching him. Hilarious, even though I can't say I blame him. I'm just glad it wasn't a rattlesnake.

On the farm, animals were just that. Animals. We had them for a purpose. We would raise them and sell them, or kill them and eat them. The dogs had a utility purpose of being a watchdog or helping control the other animals. Animals came and went, and I understood that. Ned was hard for me to lose and now the loss of Fuzzy, my faithful pal, would be harder. I dried my eyes and returned to the house for supper, and one or two of Grandmother's biscuits, filled with sugar cane syrup, of course.

Transitioning from middle school to high school at Sneads was not complicated. It was the same as transitioning from elementary school to middle school. You simply walked down the hall to a different classroom because it was all in the same building. Even so, returning from this summer in Jacksonville to enter the ninth grade seemed to be a little more exciting. I was anxious to try out for the varsity baseball team after a very successful Little League season in the city, but that would have to wait until springtime. Our school did not have a football team, so there was no decision to be made about that. First, I would play basketball in the fall, and looked forward to being in the starting lineup for the B Team. I was fast and had quick feet, but was vertically challenged.

It was always great seeing my classmates again on the first day of school. Sondra Hinson was still Miss Bossy Boots and Dannie was still as pretty as ever. And taller than ever. Would she ever stop growing? Would I ever begin to grow? She showed little interest in me, but she was clearly interested in several older boys. Should I tell her that someday we were going to be married and have two perfect children and live happily ever after? Maybe I should hold off on that one, at least until I was as tall as she.

There was another reason I was excited to enter the ninth grade. It pertained to my other secret dream, totally different from the one about Dannie. We had a new band director at Sneads High School, Mr. Frank Shupp. I had talked to him when he visited the school before the summer break and told him I would like to be considered to be drum major of the Sneads High School Band. He asked me if I had any experience at marching or conducting. I told him other than the time when I led the band in front of Mr. Carlisle's store, I did not, but I was sure I could do it. What I didn't tell him was that I had persuaded Mr. Funderburk, the music education teacher and choir director, to teach me the elementary fundamentals of conducting. Nor did I tell him that I had made several trips to Tallahassee, not just to see the football game, but to mentally record every move of Dick Mayo, the drum major of the Marching Chiefs. Mr. Shupp didn't tell me I could be drum major, but he said he would think about it.

It was one thing to mentally record the moves of a great drum major, but it was a different thing altogether trying to duplicate those moves. I had attempted to learn to march, conduct, and even strut, but it all felt very awkward and clumsy. My great fear was that it also looked awkward and clumsy, but I had no way of knowing what it looked like. I wasn't going to embarrass myself by being seen doing these crazy things, much less ask anyone's opinion, because they would have no idea what I was doing anyway. Besides, this dream of being a drum major was my secret alone, and I was determined to keep it that way.

During my summer in Jacksonville, Panama Park was my favorite place to hang out, but not just because of our championship baseball team. Ginny Jones was a really cute girl who lived across the street from the park. She would come to watch our games and she seemed to like me a lot. I liked her, too. I didn't think she was as pretty as Dannie, but then who was? At least Ginny liked me, whereas Dannie was totally indifferent. At least so far. After baseball games or practice, I would often hang out with Ginny at the park, or sometimes at her house, until after dark. Then I would jump on my bike, but I wouldn't go straight home. I'd ride down to the other end of the park where there was a lighted recreation area, including a basketball court. I'd ride my bike through the gate and past the lighted area to the darkness of the massive park. There, all alone, I would take my baseball bat from the basket of my bike and begin to practice. Not baseball. I would practice being a drum major, using the baseball bat as a baton. It was there I made a revealing discovery. On one side of me were the lights of the park. And on the other side of me was mostly darkness, except for my elongated shadow. I couldn't help but stare at the shadow. I arched my back and lifted my knees with pointed toes and strutted down the field. I may have been all alone in the dark, but in my mind, I was in Doak Campbell Stadium in Tallahassee leading the Marching Chiefs down the field. I still felt clumsy and awkward, but when I looked at the figure of the shadow accompanying me down the field, I saw a drum major. It was an eureka moment for me. Being able to see what my clumsy awkwardness actually looked like, allowed me to press on with confidence knowing that I was on the right path.

All these thoughts raced through my mind as I took my seat as first chair French horn in the band room on the first day of school. The chaos of the students noodling on their instruments was louder and worse than usual. I wasn't sure if this was because of the new school year or the new band director. Maybe both. In either case, the room became pin drop silent when the bell rang for classes to begin and Mr. Shupp, the first male director of our little ragtag band, marched promptly into the room. Not only was he a man, but he was a military man, having just separated from a stint in the Army. He seemed to be very nice, pleasant enough, but much more regimented than our first band director, loosey-goosey Miss Gamble.

"Welcome back, students and musicians," Mr. Shupp said. "I'm honored to be your new band director, and we have many new exciting things happening this year."

He tried to flash a smile, but seemed to have difficulty overcoming his military bearing. Or, maybe he noticed the principal, Mr. Hutchinson, watching him from out on the front porch of the band building, the old Segrest home.

"We'll be taking two new trips this year," Mr. Shupp continued. "Coming up soon, in a couple of months, we will be going to Tallahassee along with many other bands from the area to attend Band Day, where we will be on the field with the Marching Chiefs for the halftime show."

There was muttering and applause from the band at the thought of taking our first road trip ever.

"Then in the spring, we're going to perform and compete at the district band contest in Fort Walton Beach."

There was more muttering and less applause from the band, probably at the thought of being judged for the first time.

"So, it's going to be a lot of fun, and a lot of hard work. So, let's get to it, starting with a B-flat scale."

Mr. Shupp shuffled some papers and picked up his baton from the music stand in front of his small podium.

"Oh! I do have one more announcement. To help us with all this new marching and performing we'll be learning to do this year, will be our new drum major, Bennett Shelfer."

Needless to say, I was flabbergasted. There was applause from the band and good-natured catcalls from the percussion section. Mr. Shupp gestured towards me. I didn't know what to do so I gave a little smile and a timid wave. The scary thing to me was I realized I would no longer be performing under the cover of darkness. Regardless of whether it felt awkward or how it looked, my moves would be there for everyone to see. Scary, indeed.

"Come in, Bennett," Mr. Shupp said. He had asked me to stop by his office after band practice and was sitting at his desk waiting for me. "We have a lot of work to do in a very short period of time. We have to teach this band to march."

"We... have to teach the band to march?" I asked.

"You still want to be drum major, don't you?"

"Yes sir, absolutely I do. It's just that I'm not sure I know how to march, myself," I said.

"No problem, I can teach you to march in no time," Mr. Shupp said. "When can you start?"

"I can start right now."

"Right now?" Mr. Shupp looked at me for a moment with a sideways glance and a hint of a smile. "I like your spirit, Bennett. Meet me in the playground beside gym in five minutes."

And so, I did. Mr. Shupp started me at the very beginning, teaching me to assume a military bearing, the position of attention and parade rest. We began with the basics of actually marching, like stepping off with your left foot, head up, chin tucked, shoulders back, etc. We drilled, he and I, for over an hour when he finally indicated it was time to stop.

"Good job, Bennett," Mr. Shupp said. "We do have one problem that I need to talk to you about."

The thought of a teacher needing to talk to me about a problem made me cringe. I said nothing, but I'm sure Mr. Shupp could tell he had my undivided attention as we walked back into his office.

"Bennett, unfortunately the band does not have the money to buy you a uniform. The best we can do is come up with enough money for a baton and a shako."

"Shako? I asked.

"Yes. You know, the tall furry hat. Look at this catalog."

Mr. Shupp handed me a catalog of band uniforms and accessories. He had opened it to a page that included several different styles of drum major uniforms and shakos.

144

"This is the shako I ordered for you," he said. "We'll stick a blue plume on it and it'll be perfect. With the tall hat and the baton, you can just wear the coat and trousers from the band uniform and that will suffice just fine for you as drum major. What do you think?"

"Yes, sir, that will be just fine."

Actually, I didn't know what to think. In the last couple of hours Mr. Shupp had told me I was going to be drum major, introduced me to the fundamentals of marching, and then basically apologized to me for the fact that I would have to make do with a makeshift drum major uniform. The uniforms in the magazine were all very expensive so it was easy to see why they were unaffordable to the budget of our little band. Our band student's collective efforts at candy sales, magazine sales, and calendar sales had barely raised enough money for our band uniforms, which consisted of band hats, blue coats, and white pants. What I didn't tell Mr. Shupp was I would wear anything from pajamas to a pirate outfit, I just wanted to be drum major. I stared at the drum major pictures in the catalog and the wheels started turning. I had an idea.

"Could I please borrow this catalog?" I asked. "I'll bring it back tomorrow."

"Sure, Bennett. Just be sure and don't lose it, they only send us one of these a year," Mr. Shupp said.

"Grandmother! I'm home."

"I'm in the kitchen, Benny," Grandmother shouted.

I dashed through the house to the kitchen, practically out of breath because I had run almost all the way home, clutching the band uniform catalog.

"I made it, Grandmother. I made it." I handed her the catalog and went straight to the cupboard for a leftover biscuit to fill with sugar cane syrup for my snack.

"You made what?"

145

"I'm drum major. Mr. Shupp picked me as drum major of the band." I punched a hole in the biscuit with my finger and filled it with syrup.

"That's real good, Benny. I know you'll be a good one. I never seen a drum major, is this what you'll look like?" She was squinting through her old glasses at the catalog. I had left it on the drain board where she was working, opened to the page with the drum major pictures.

"That's what I would like to look like, but all the school can afford to buy for my uniform is the hat."

"I can see they ain't cheap," Grandmother said. "Costs an arm and a leg for them things."

"Grandmother, I was wondering…do you think you could make my blue band coat look like one of them drum major coats?" She cleaned her glasses with her apron and stared at the picture in the catalog for the longest time.

"Well, I cain't see too good no more, and my old fingers ain't so nimble. You might have to thread the needle for me on that old sewing machine, but, I s'pose I could try."

Grandmother was so active it was hard for me to think there might be things that she couldn't continue to do. It occurred to me that I hadn't seen her sew anything on the old Singer for quite a while. It was a subtle reminder to me that time and age march onward together, and then a day comes when time alone marches on.

"I'll help you, Grandmother. What do you need to get started?"

"I think I have a spool of gold thread in the sewing basket," she said. "I'll need a roll of one inch gold braid, and a pair of them gold shoulder things."

"You mean the epaulets?"

"Yep, them things. Do you think the school could order that stuff?"

"I bet they could. I'll ask Mr. Shupp," I said.

And so it was that Mr. Shupp ordered the braid and the epaulets and Grandmother worked her magic with the old Singer sewing machine. And I was a new drum major in a new uniform. It wasn't very expensive, but I felt like a million dollars wearing it. When I checked my shadow wearing my new uniform, shako, baton, and all, I saw that the shadow didn't care what I was wearing. Besides, I already knew it wasn't the uniform that made the drum major, but it was the drum major that made the uniform.

It was exciting to see our little group of fledgling musicians become a band. Mr. Shupp took us down to the baseball diamond to learn to march. It was there we learned that a band, no matter how large or small, is just a group of individuals doing their own thing. Then when thrown together as a unit, standardized and synchronized, it was a beautiful thing. Together, we were so much more than an individual could ever be. And we felt pride in belonging to something greater than ourselves.

Band day at Tallahassee was the first big event for a little band. We had performed in a parade in Sneads for homecoming, but this was different. This was a road trip. We piled into a couple of school buses and made the trip over to Doak Campbell Stadium at Florida State University. We joined dozens of other bands from around the state to perform in the halftime show. I was thrilled beyond belief to be on the same field as the Marching Chiefs. All the bands combined to make a formation of the state of Florida. We played the state song, Suwanee River, conducted by Manley Whitcomb, the director of the Marching Chiefs. I told Uncle Verdayne, who was at the game, that it would be easy to spot the Sneads band on the field. Just look for us at St. Augustine.

A couple of months later our band received another surprise invitation from Tallahassee. We were invited to march in the parade at the inauguration of Gov. Leroy Collins on January 4, 1955. We were excited to be slotted in the parade as the next band directly ahead of the Marching Chiefs. I soon learned that with the tremendous thunder of the Chief's percussion section reverberating off the buildings on Monroe Street, it was difficult to march to our own drummers. I managed to keep our band as far ahead of them as possible and we not only survived but represented well, or at least Mr. Shupp said so. And I saw with my own eyes a real live governor of Florida.

Chapter 22

"Y'all wash up and come on in now, dinners ready," Grandmother said.

Daddy and Uncle Bud had come over from Jacksonville to visit for the weekend and go quail hunting and the three of us were sitting in the rocking chairs on the front porch talking about the morning hunt. It'd been a great day. The dogs had found three coveys of birds, and between shooting the covey rises and the singles we had bagged over a dozen quail. I had three birds, Daddy had a couple, and Uncle Bud had the rest. He was by far the best marksman in the family when it came to shooting quail. I was still becoming accustomed to shooting the 16-gauge Lefever double-barreled shotgun that daddy had bought for me, and Uncle Bud was helping me with that. He was trying to get me to focus on targeting just one bird, so he let me shoot the singles. He said he would "wipe my eye," if I missed. That meant he would back me up and shoot the bird that I missed. And he did, too, because he was a deadeye shot. We had cleaned the birds and Grandmother had cooked them for us. Fried bobwhite quail was my favorite and I loved it as much as chicken.

"Yes Mam, we'll be right there," I called to Grandmother, who had already closed the screen door and gone back inside.

Uncle Bud's bird dogs, Sport and Ginger, were sprawled out on the brick of the front porch steps cooling their undersides after four hours of constant running. Sport was a liver and white English Setter and was by far the best bird dog Uncle Bud had ever had, except maybe for Checkers, who had died too soon from the bite of a rattlesnake. Sport would stick his nose into the air and wind the birds, or put his nose to the ground and trail them. He would hold a point forever, until they were flushed by the hunter. And he was an incredible retriever. If you shot a bird down, Sport would bring him to you immediately and place the bird in your hand with a grip so soft it would hardly ruffle a feather. Ginger was a Lemon Setter and was mostly white with scattered spots of yellow. She was a good bird dog. She wouldn't flush the birds prematurely or run around and go crazy when shots were fired, but she was not the hunter that Sport was.

We all sat down at the big oval table in the dining room. Uncle Bud said the blessing and I was gulping down a glass of iced tea when I heard the front screen door open and close.

"Well, well, look what the cat's drug up," Daddy said. We all turned to see Uncle Verdayne coming through the living room.

"Come on in, yore jist in time. I'll set you a plate," Grandmother said.

"No, thank you, Mama. I just had a sandwich with Minnie Lee," Uncle Verdayne said. "I wouldn't mind a glass of iced tea, though."

"Hey, P. V. How are things in your neck of the woods?" Uncle Bud asked.

It was interesting to me how some men out in the country preferred to be addressed by their initials, i.e. C.J., B.E., W.C., or P.V., rather than their name or nickname. Uncle Verdayne certainly did. I couldn't figure out if they thought it was Southern chic to do so, or they would go to any lengths to avoid being called by their actual gosh-awful names. I think it was certainly the latter with Park Verdayne Shelfer.

"Hey Bud… Sing," Uncle Verdayne said. They all shook hands. "Y'all are here just in time. They are filling the lake."

"Filling the lake?" Daddy asked. "I didn't think there were going to fill the lake for two more years."

"They just finished filling it halfway yesterday," Uncle Verdayne said. "They're going to keep the reservoir halfway full for a couple of years to kill all the undergrowth and let the bottom settle before filling it all the way."

The Jim Woodruff Dam, a hydroelectric generating facility, had been under construction for about eight years on the Apalachicola River, just below the confluence of the Chattahoochee and Flint rivers. The project to harvest all the timber in the area of the coming 37,500-acre reservoir had been completed a couple of years ago. In the meantime, the dense undergrowth was making an effort to regenerate the forest, and trees and bushes were sprouting everywhere. The edge of the new lake would only be a little over a mile from our house and farm.

"The deer and turkey will be running for the hills," Uncle Bud said.

"You're right, Bud," Uncle Verdayne said. "And I know one of the only hills they can run two."

"What do you mean?" Uncle Bud asked.

"You know that high bluff that was on the river, just south of Neal's landing?" Uncle Verdayne looked at Daddy and Uncle Bud, who were both nodding. "With the lake half full, I'm thinking that'll be the only dry land left in the lake. I'll bet 'chu sure as grits are groceries every turkey and deer in the swamp will be heading for that island."

"How does that help us, Teeter?" Daddy asked. I knew that of all the names Uncle Verdayne was called, "Teeter" was the one he disliked the most.

"We'll, B. H., I was thinking…" Uncle Verdayne said. He jabbed back at Daddy for calling him "Teeter" by addressing him by his initials, B. H. "If you and J. E. and the boy, here, want to rest the bird dogs this afternoon and shoot some turkeys, I can take y'all out to that island in the bass boat." Uncle Verdayne liked to call me "boy," and that was okay with me. At this point I was totally expecting to be called, "Little B. H."

"I s'pose the dogs could use some rest, and Mama might like a big gobbler for tomorrow's dinner. I ain't never been turkey hunting on a boat, but that sounds like fun, Verdayne," Uncle Bud said. I noticed he didn't return the jab about Uncle Verdayne calling him J.E.

A couple of hours later the four of us were down at the end of the 16th hill where the new lake began, crowding into Uncle Verdayne's 12-foot wooden bass boat. There were only three seats in the boat, one at each end, and one across the live well in the middle of the boat. Uncle Verdayne had to operate the motor, so he sat in the back. I was the smallest, so I sat in the small seat up front while Daddy and Uncle Bud sat on the middle seat, which was the widest of all. Still, it was crowded and very much overloaded.

We started by putt-putting along out into the new lake. The scene was very surreal, new water everywhere, yet not totally covering the little trees and bushes that had sprouted since the forest was cut two years ago. We motored along, slowly and quietly, following the path of the original chain of lakes passing the Blue Springs, the Okie Slough, and then out into the Tan Vat.

"Ain't this some sight for sore eyes," Daddy said.

"Damnedest thing I ever seen," Uncle Bud said. "Water as far as you can see."

"Except for those trees over yonder," Daddy said. "Is that our island where the turkeys are?" He pointed to a large cluster of trees about two miles out in the lake to the northeast of us, almost to Georgia.

"That ought to be it," Uncle Verdayne said.

"How you gonna get there?" Uncle Bud asked.

"I thought I'd just follow the lakes around and go out the Deep Slough into the river, then double back down to the island."

"That's at least seven or eight miles," Uncle Bud said. "Why don't you take the shortcut and head straight for the island? Looks like there's plenty of water and the bushes ain't so thick that you cain't weave around 'em."

"I'm game if you boys are. Here we go." Uncle Verdayne said. He steered the boat out into the bushes directly towards the island.

Within moments the scene before us went from surreal to unbelievable. Almost every bush, little tree, or stump above the waterline contained some living creature. There were animals like raccoons, possums, skunks, and foxes clinging to bushes everywhere to stay above the waterline. But the real story wasn't the animals…it was the reptiles. More specifically, snakes. Snakes of every kind. Everywhere.

"Good God a'mighty… look at that snake!" Daddy shouted.

I turned around to see that Daddy was pointing at a huge rattlesnake on top of a tree stump about 15 feet away. The snake's triangular head, as big as my fist, was slowly sinking into his tightening coil and the long string of rattles at the end of his tail was lifting towards the sky.

"Shoot that sum'bitch, Benny!" Uncle Bud screamed.

In an instant I loaded my 16-guage double-barreled shotgun with number nine birdshot and blasted the head from the monster diamondback that was clearly over six feet long.

"There's another one, Benny. Shoot 'im," Daddy said. He pointed to some snakes in a thick bush off to the left.

"The black one?" I asked.

"No, that's a cottonmouth. And those two orange-lookin' ones with him are copperheads. Look on that log right behind 'em."

I immediately shot the big rattler Daddy was pointing out, then quickly reloaded and shot two more in the bush next to him.

"How much birdshot you got with you?" Daddy asked.

"I got two boxes plus two in the gun," I said. I knew that because I was still wearing my bird hunting vest from the morning quail hunt. So, in total, I had 52 shells of birdshot in addition to four number four shells for the turkeys.

"Don't shoot nothing but rattlesnakes," Uncle Bud said.

"Why is that?" I asked. "Moccasins are poisonous too."

"I'll tell you why," Uncle Verdayne said. "I'll tell you exactly what's happening here. Every year when the river comes out of its banks and floods this river swamp, all these animals and snakes go up a tree for a day or two until the water goes back down, then all is fine. Except this time, the water isn't ever going down. When all these critters get hungry enough, they'll head for the hill. Now, these moccasins are water snakes, they'll stay with the lake. All these rattlesnakes will eventually head for dry land. Right over there," he said. Uncle Verdayne pointed to the southwest shore of the lake. "Right where we live."

"Make every shot count, Benny," Daddy said. "We ain't never gonna have a better chance to thin out these bastards."

And make it count I did. For most of the next hour the barrels of my gun did not cool off, because I did nothing but shoot rattlesnakes. Snake, after snake, after snake. Finally, as we neared the island, I ran out of birdshot. As for the turkeys, within a hundred yards of where we got off the boat, Uncle Bud and Daddy had already shot four more rattlesnakes. It was then that Uncle Verdayne suggested that maybe we should just have chicken for dinner tomorrow and not worry about the turkeys, because the sun was setting and he was thinking that maybe we should get off the lake and away from these snakes before dark. Indeed, there were no arguments from any of us. Within a minute we were back on the boat speeding up the river to take the longer but safer route home. We followed the chain of river lakes back to the Blue Springs landing. And I had killed 56 rattlesnakes in one day.

Chapter 23

It was a hot, muggy afternoon in April, and I was drenched with sweat. I had
made the varsity baseball team as a freshman, and Coach Dodson had me
playing centerfield. I was running around chasing balls so much, I may as well
have been on the track team. Of course, Sneads High School did not have a
track team. We were playing the Marianna Bulldogs which was a class "A"
high school. It seemed like every Marianna player that stepped up to the plate
hit it somewhere hard and far. And then I, along with the other outfielders,
would be shagging after it, hard and far. Really far, because our baseball field
didn't have any fences in the outfield. Any ball hit over our heads or in the gap
between us went a long, long, way. It didn't help the temperature factor that we
were wearing uniforms of thick wool, including the caps.

With the bases loaded and no one out, Coach Dodson called timeout
and walked slowly towards the pitcher's mound. Finally, I had a moment to
catch my breath. When Coach reached the center of the diamond, he took the
ball from Buddy Lanier, our senior pitcher, and looked out towards centerfield.

"Hey, Shelfer, get in here," he called.

It took me a moment to realize what was happening. Even though I had
been badgering Coach Dodson to let me pitch, I never thought he would do it.
Certainly not against Marianna. He had never seen me pitch. I was an okay
baseball player for a country boy. I had a small advantage and disadvantage.
The small advantage was having played Little League during the summers in
Jacksonville. The small disadvantage was, well, I was small. Still a growing
boy. Nonetheless, I was fast, I had a good arm, a good glove, and I could hit for

average but, not so much for power. And, as a pitcher, I had excellent control. Plus, I had been working on a couple of new pitches. I trotted nervously to the mound.

"Okay, Shelfer, bases loaded and nobody out," Coach Dodson said. He had a wry little grin on his face as he handed me the ball. "Let's see what you got."

"You get eight warm up pitches, son," G. D. Mulloy, the umpire said.

We all knew G.D. Mulloy very well. Some of his notoriety came from the "buck" dances he would do down after he had a few drinks at the American Legion Hall on Saturday nights. His "buck" dance was a combination of tap dancing and clogging, punctuated by enthusiastic foot stomping. Coach Dodson knew him very well because he pumped gas for him on weekends at Mulloy's Pure Oil Station, one of the two gas stations in town. I'm sure the visiting team was not aware of that. I had a different connection to the home plate umpire.

Throwing warm-up pitches seemed to be a bit of an overkill. I was warm, no actually I was hot, long before I left centerfield. My new wool uniform was soaked through with sweat. As hot as it was, I wore it proudly, just happy to be on the varsity. To pay for the new uniforms the school had asked for donations from businesses and individuals in the community. In return for their contributions, the donors could have their name, or the name of their business, on the back of one of our uniforms. I was hoping none of the visiting team noticed that written on the back of my uniform was G. D. Mulloy, number 14.

"Okay, Bennett, bases loaded, nobody out," Lloyd Dunham, the catcher, said. "You're coming home on a ground ball. One's a fastball, two's a curve."

"And three's a…"

"There ain't no three, Shelfer," Lloyd said. "You ain't gonna throw that knuckleball in a game. And remember, G. D. likes 'em low." Without waiting for a response from me, he jogged back towards home plate.

G. D. Mulloy, may not have been the best umpire, but he was consistent. Any low pitch that was over the plate and didn't hit the dirt was

156

usually called a strike. He even called them that way against me, and I was wearing his name on my back. It was good for the home team, because we knew we had to hit low and pitch low. Bad for the visitors, because it took them a while to catch on.

It was a very good day for me and the Sneads Pirates. I struck out the side and pitched shut- out baseball the rest of the game. My control was good enough to keep the ball down low in the strike zone, but my real weapon was one of the new pitches I'd been working on. I discovered I could now pitch the ball fast enough to throw a real good curveball. I could throw it over the top, or I could submarine it. Those country boys had a lot of trouble with it. And then our bats rallied for a most improbable win over the boys Marianna.

After that game, I was the starting pitcher. I wanted the ball every time we suited up and Coach Dodson let me pitch almost every game after that. I ended up with a 4-2 record, which I thought was good for a fledging freshman pitcher.

Chapter 24

My eleventh-grade home teacher was Rebecca Spooner. She was also my algebra teacher and was a dedicated educator, along with being one of the nicest, kindest, ladies imaginable. She was the wife of George Spooner, my scoutmaster, and the mother of my good friend George, the national pie eating champion, and Cora Nell, his cutie tomboy sister. I really liked her, but regretfully, she was four years younger. Mrs. Spooner was also the aunt of Maury Wishnoff, another of my best friends. Maury's mother and Mr. Spooner were brother and sister. So, it was a family affair. Regardless, Mrs. Spooner treated all of her students like family. Lucky us.

Math was not my preferred subject even though I managed to make good grades. I tended to favor English and literature. Frances Segrest was a profoundly strict and proper English teacher. Much needed. Katie Mary Walters was our English literature teacher and she made the subject fun for us. She taught us to appreciate the classics for whatever they were to each of us individually. I was surprised to learn how much I enjoyed prose and verse, especially Shakespeare, Chaucer, and Poe. We laughed a lot in her class. Especially one gut-busting hour the day we attempted a class read-through of the "Miller's Tale" by Chaucer. Hilarious. And Mrs. Walters was giggling as loudly as we were.

Mr. Shupp, our band director, had moved on down the state to a larger school. He was replaced by Mr. John Jamison, a graduate from the music school of the University of Miami. He was an incredible musician who could play all instruments, although his primary instrument was clarinet. His real talent, however, was his voice. Mr. Jamison was not a very big man at all. In fact, he was exactly the size of a man you would expect to be wearing a jockey's outfit and riding racehorses. But when he opened his mouth to sing, he was a booming tenor. He sang "The Lord's Prayer" for us at church one day. It was spine tingling, the most stirring rendition I had ever heard.

Mr. Jamison seemed very happy to keep me on as drum major of the band. In fact, he set aside some money from the budget to buy me a new drum major uniform. He even asked for my input on what style of uniform I would like. Naturally, I picked one similar to what Tony Swain, the new drum major of the Marching Chiefs, was wearing. I did not tell Mr. Jamison why I picked that particular uniform. And I certainly didn't tell him about my secret goal to one day wear the uniform that Tony Swain was wearing.

It was the first Thursday afternoon in April, 1957. The weather was warm, somewhere in the high 70s, but to me it was sweltering. It wasn't so much that I was pitching in GD Malloy's number 14 wool uniform, but mostly because I was getting pounded by the Graceville Tigers. My control was still good but my fastball was no faster than it was in the ninth grade and my curveball had lost some of its zip. Yet, I pitched onward.

The usual nice crowd of townsfolk had gathered for the game. When it was my turn to bat again, I noticed that Uncle Hardy was in the crowd, which was strange, because it wasn't time for him to be off from work. When I caught his eye, he gave me a little wave, but he didn't look very happy.

I was having trouble hitting this pitcher so I laid a bunt down the third base line and raced for first, managing to beat the throw. Raymond Walden was next to bat. In his usual fashion, he fouled off what seemed like a dozen pitches down the third base line. Of course, I was running on every one of those foul balls, so for me that amounted to what seemed like a dozen wind sprints down to second base. Finally, Raymond kept one fair down the left-field line and by the time the leftfielder retrieved it from behind the pecan trees, I managed to score from first base. Not enough though, because the game ended and we were still two runs short. I hated losing, but it was always fun to play.

"Hey Uncle Hardy." I went over to say hello to him after the game.

"Hey, Benny. Good game. Nice hustle," he said. "I've come to give you a ride home." He did not have his usual pleasant, affable look on his face.

"What's wrong?"

"It's your grandmother… She's real sick."

"What happened?"

"We think she might've had a stroke."

"I'm ready," I said. "Let's go."

I started walking immediately towards Uncle Hardy's car. I didn't want to take the time to go back to the gymnasium to shower, or even change out of my uniform. Nothing was said on the five-minute ride up River Road to our house, the old church house. My mind was racing, muddled and confused. I feared what I knew was inevitable. When old people have strokes, they die. Grandmother was seventy-nine, but to me, she was still young. I was 16 years old and she had cared for me since I was three. Why did this have to happen now? Now is never a good time to die.

When we pulled into the circular driveway at the house, I noticed there was a new cream-colored Oldsmobile with a Gadsden County tag parked among a few other cars.

"Oh! Good. I see the doctor's here from Chattahoochee," Uncle Hardy said.

I barely acknowledged several people sitting on the porch as I bounded through the front door. Aunt Berta stopped me before I ran into Grandmother's bedroom.

"Wait, Benny," Aunt Berta said. "The doctor's with her now."

160

Just then, the doctor, a tall middle-aged gentleman with thinning hair and wearing a seersucker suit came out of Grandmother's bedroom. He looked around and recognized Uncle Hardy.

"Mr. Shelfer, I wish I could give you good news," the doctor said. "She has definitely had a severe stroke. It's hard to determine the extent of her paralysis or to give you a prognosis. I'm giving her some medicine and some fluids and we'll just have to wait and see. I'm quite certain she is in no pain. I will be back tomorrow to check on her."

"Thank you, doctor," Uncle Hardy said. I saw him hand the doctor a $20 bill.

The vigil began. Telegrams and long-distance phone calls went out to the family and within a few hours they began to arrive. Uncle Hardy and Uncle Verdayne lived in Sneads, but most of grandmother's twelve children lived in Jacksonville. All of the girls, Maude, Arcenia, Versie, Tots and Sis lived there, as well as Daddy, Uncle Bud, and Uncle Shine. They all dropped everything they were doing and headed for Sneads. They all arrived late Thursday night. Uncle Grady had moved, not too long ago, from Auburndale, where he was chief of police of all things, to Pompano Beach, where he owned and operated a couple of draglines. When he got the news, he closed down his operations on Friday and started driving. He arrived in Sneads around noon on Saturday, after driving all night. Uncle Dick (Marshall) was the problem child as usual. No one knew where he was. Finally, Uncle Grady found out he had a job operating a crane for a vegetable farmer near Okeechobee. Uncle Grady called in a favor from an old friend who was a deputy sheriff, who drove out to the farm to give the Uncle Dick the news about Grandmother. Uncle Dick arrived in Sneads on a Greyhound bus Sunday afternoon, drunk and looking emaciated, as usual.

As the days passed, there was no change in Grandmother's condition. She was never conscious and her eyes never opened. Occasionally she might twitch an arm or leg but that was about it for movement. The doctor came every day to check on her and to give her a new IV. Aunt Versie and Aunt Tots organized a schedule of ladies to watch over Grandmother so that around-the-clock there would always be at least two people with her. Grandmother had never been in a hospital in her life and there was never a thought of moving her to one now. A hospital in either Tallahassee or Dothan was over an hour's drive away.

The house was always bustling with people coming and going. The ladies naturally congregated in the kitchen and the men were usually on either the front or the back porch. The understandable pall throughout the house did not exclude the usual stories and tales and subsequent laughter coming from the kitchen and the front and back porches. Nor did it exclude some of the men, namely Daddy, Uncle Grady, Uncle Marshall, and Aunt Tots' husband, Uncle Charlie slipping out to uncle Grady's car for a little tottie, as they called it. I knew their little tottie was nothing more than a swig of Seagram's 7 chased by a swig of 7-Up. As usual, my concern was that Daddy would get drunk. I didn't really care about the others, because whatever they did would not embarrass me. Fortunately, the attenuating factor here was the fact that the guys did not want to incur the wrath of their sisters, Maude, Arcenia, Versie, and Tots. So, they kept their drinking under control.

It was a dark Saturday night and I was sitting on the back porch steps staring into the obscurity and listening to a dueling duet between the screech owls and the whippoorwills. One sound was hauntingly eerie and the other was soothing and serene. Grandmother had been in a coma for over a week with no change in her condition. I heard the screen door open and close behind me and glanced over my shoulder to see Daddy's silhouette. He walked out and sat on the steps beside me and said nothing, but did what he always did. He lit a cigarette.

"Benny, you know your grandmother's probably not going to make it, don't you?" Daddy finally said. It was more of a statement than a question.

"Yes sir, I do." I said.

"She's a fighter, that's for sure," Daddy said. "The doctor's doing everything he can, but he ain't giving her much of a chance…"

Nothing was said for a while as we sat there pondering the inevitable that I had already pondered. What was it about the living of life that required you to be abandoned by your loved ones? My mother left me. Daddy left me to go fight the war. Aunt Versie left me to go live a life with her husband. Granddaddy died, and now nine years later, Grandmother.

"I suppose you'll want to come back here to Sneads for your senior year," Daddy said.

"Yes sir."

"You know you could come to Jacksonville and go to Andrew Jackson, probably the biggest high school in Jacksonville."

"I know, but here at Sneads I'm on the varsity baseball and basketball teams, I'm drum major of the band, and I know everybody. I think I'd rather be a big fish in a little barrel than a little fish in the barrel." I made a feeble attempt at some levity.

"If you're a big fish, you're a big fish. It doesn't matter about the size of the barrel," Daddy said. "Anyway, both Hardy and Verdayne want you to come live with them, so you don't have nothing to worry about."

"That's good, I guess." It was hard for me to find a silver lining at this point.

It was April 25, 1957, three weeks to the day after Grandmother had her stroke. I rode the bus home from school as usual, trying to maintain a normal routine as much as possible under the circumstances. As I approached the front gate, I saw Aunt Versie motioning towards me trying to get me to hurry up.

"Benny! Get in here! She's calling for you," Aunt Versie said.

"What? What's going on?" I bounded up the front porch steps and through the front door.

"Benny... Where's Benny? Is he home from school yet?" I heard Grandmother's frail but clear voice coming from her bedroom.

In an instant I was at her bedside. Grandmother was lying on her back with her head resting on her favorite feather down pillow. She had a bit of a pained expression on her face and she appeared to be trying to move her head from side to side, and succeeding ever so slightly.

"Is Benny home from school yet?" She said again.

"I'm home, Grandmother. I'm right here with you." In that moment I realized that in her mind she was still back on that Thursday three weeks ago when I went to school and she had a stroke before I came home. "The chickens have been fed and I brought in the eggs. Everything is good, Grandmother. I'm home."

She didn't say or do anything more. After a while I went back out on the front porch to be with some of the other family members and to try, not without difficulty, to maintain my composure. Within an hour I heard sniffling and muffled sobs coming from the living room and I knew she was gone. It was hard for me to comprehend the loss of someone whose entire life was love and total dedication to family, especially me. Despite fighting a valiant medical battle she could not win, in the end she was just concerned about me.

Chapter 25

Uncle Hardy was normally not very talkative. When he did say something, it was usually profound. This is one of those days I appreciated the solace of a quiet car ride. Uncle Hardy was driving, and my mind was racing, trying to comprehend where I had been and where I was going.

It was difficult to convince myself that I should be sad leaving Sneads, because I wasn't. The truth was it was never the same after Grandmother died. For some reason I had decided to live my senior year with Uncle Verdayne, Aunt Minnie Lee, and cousin, Frank. They treated me so well and were very supportive of me and whatever I wanted to do. And there's no doubt in my mind it would've been the same had I spent the year with Uncle Hardy, Aunt Berta and Ronnie. Having a good family is a blessing and indeed I was blessed.

My senior year had been a good one. Even now, though, it seemed a blur, like the longleaf yellow pines flashing by the car window on US 90 between Chattahoochee and Quincy. I had managed to make good grades, even though I was never in the running to be the class valedictorian. Maury Wishnoff and Sondra Hinson fought the battle for that distinction.

My participation in sports never waned. On the varsity baseball team, I continued to pitch and play the outfield. During my sophomore and junior years, I seemed to reach a level of mediocrity that, not surprisingly, I was able to maintain during my senior year. I was fast, good with the glove, and a good contact hitter, but for whatever reason my fastball didn't seem to be very fast anymore. And my curve ball didn't curve as much. Coach

Dodson said he thought I had peaked too soon. I think he was lamenting the fact that my ninth-grade year was probably my best in baseball.

Basketball was always the most popular sport in Sneads. I enjoyed playing three years on the varsity, even though I was vertically challenged. I played guard, of course. My dribbling skills were good and I was an okay shooter from the outside. I was an occasional starter, but mostly played a backup role, coming in off the bench. We had the best team our junior year, making it to the finals of the state championship which was played at the University of Florida in Gainesville, where the Gators play. Big thrill.

My departure from Sneads wasn't without disappointments. I regretted that in the end I was four merit badges short of being an Eagle Scout. It was never a goal of mine to do that. I just enjoyed the scouting activities. But now I realize that being an Eagle Scout is quite a lofty perch and I wished I had buckled down to accomplish that achievement. The main problem was the Camping merit badge, which required something like 50 nights of camping. At the time, I could never justify spending that many nights away from Grandmother and the chores of the house.

The other disappointment was personal. It was obvious that my secret dream of marrying Dannie McMullian and having two kids and living happily ever was probably not in the cards. She was always very nice, but never showed any interest in me beyond being friend and classmate. I wondered if I should have been more assertive. Maybe if I had proposed to her somewhere early on, like around the second grade, things might have worked out differently. I guess I'll never know.

"Benny, you think you'll be marching in that first football game?" Uncle Hardy asked. His question momentarily shocked me out of my reminiscing trance.

"I hope so," I said. "First, I have to make the band."

Uncle Hardy just nodded, and drove onward.

I glanced at the tattered brown suitcase in the back seat of the old Chevrolet. Next to it was the black case containing the vintage French horn

Aunt Versie had bought for me many years before. It occurred to me that all my possessions were in those two cases in the back seat.

My thoughts drifted to the fond memories of my four years as drum major and playing first chair French horn for the Sneads High School Band. Mr. Jamieson had done a wonderful job as the latest director of our little group. During my senior year there was almost sixty of us, which was significant considering the small size of our school. We made up for what we lacked in numbers with dedication and enthusiasm. This was denoted by the high marks we received at district band contests in Fort Walton Beach. I chuckled to myself just thinking of the little stunt I managed to pull on our last trip to band contests.

To put it in perspective, because we didn't have a football team and halftime shows we only had three marching performances a year. We had Band Day in Tallahassee and our homecoming parade in the fall. Then in the spring, we had band contests in Fort Walton Beach. Beach is a primary word here, because we got to stay in a motel on one of the most beautiful beaches in the world. We always stayed at the Gulf Wind Motel, what appeared to be the only place on the beach in a tiny town called Destin. This was a big deal for us. We practiced for months learning the music and the marching of our show, which was performed like a halftime show on a football field. This was difficult for us because we didn't have a football field and we never did halftime shows. Nonetheless, our hard work had paid off and we were feeling good about the progress of our performance.

We had finished our final practice on the day before we were to leave for Fort Walton Beach. For some reason I was not feeling very well at all. For the last couple of days, I had felt fatigued and had a nagging headache. On the way home, my face was feeling hot and I was sure I had a fever. There was something dreadful going around at school and I was afraid I'd caught it. As soon as I looked into the bathroom mirror and saw the red blotches all over my face, my greatest fears were confirmed. I knew I had the chickenpox.

My heart sank into my stomach and I suddenly became nauseous. Not so much from the chickenpox, but from the dilemma of the most inconvenient time for me to catch the chickenpox. What could I do? If I told anyone I had the chickenpox, I would be sent home from school and not be

167

allowed to participate in school activities for several days. And that would mean no trip to Fort Walton Beach. And the band would have no drum major for our only band contest of the year. We had been practicing for months. How could I let that happen? The moment I looked into the medicine cabinet behind the bathroom mirror, I had a plan. There, in plain view, was an almost new tube of Clerasil, an over-the-counter acne cream. Not that I ever needed it, of course. Well, maybe, for that occasional pimple that would pop out in the middle of my face. This usually happened after I had chomped down a Baby Ruth, a Hershey's with almonds, or some other colossal amount of chocolate. I'm not sure the Clearasil accomplished anything medically to mediate the pimples. But cosmetically, because it was skin colored, it sure helped to cover them up.

So, the next morning I took two Bayer aspirin to alleviate the fever and the headache and gobbed generous amounts of Clearasil on my face. Wearing long sleeves, sunglasses, and a baseball cap pulled down low over my face, I slunk onto the bus. I managed to keep my interactions with Mr. Jamison at a distance, but I did get a couple of long stares, like something about me was different. Because it was.

The other long stare I received was on the field at the contest. Before the performance, the band had to undergo inspection. I was standing at attention presenting the band to the judge who was no more than two feet in front of me looking me over from head to toe. My white shoes were shined and spotless. My uniform was creased and impeccable. My shako stood tall atop my head and the blue plume reached towards the sky, unruffled. My face was peppered with red whelps covered with at least three coats of Clerasil. I was sweating profusely, even though we hadn't taken a step. I was hoping the judge would think it was because I was nervous about our performance. In reality, I knew it was because my fever had finally broken. He looked at me for what seemed like forever before he continued to inspect the rest of the band.

We proceeded to the field to do our show and I thought our little band did a really good job. I had tried my best to replicate some of the moves of Dick Mayo and Tony Swain, the Marching Chief drum majors.

Mr. Jamison was very congratulatory and complimentary during band class the following Monday. He told us he was pleased at our

168

performance at contests and was not surprised by the high marks we received. Later, Mr. Jamison made a point of showing me the judge's remarks about our performance. The last sentence was overwhelming to me. It simply said, "Outstanding Drum Major." Validation. Reassurance. The dream was still alive.

After a little more than an hour, Uncle Hardy steered us to the right off US 90. A few minutes and a few turns later we came to a stop at the rear entrance of a large building.

"This is it," Uncle Hardy said.

"Thank you so much for the ride," I said.

"Do good, Benny. I know you will."

"Thank you, Sir."

I retrieved my horn and my suitcase from the back seat. With a quick wave, Uncle Hardy was gone and I was standing there alone. I was seventeen years old, staring at the Music Building at Florida State University.

Chapter 26

The moment I walked through those heavy wooden doors I knew my life
was about to change. This was a happening place. Students were coming and
going continuously. Sounds of musical instruments of every kind
reverberated through the hallway that led past the rear of a large auditorium.
I felt smaller and more inconsequential with every timid step I took
following the handmade signs pointing to Marching Chiefs registration. The
hall made a right-left zig-zag where mirrors covered the walls from floor to
ceiling. Dozens of majorette candidates wearing T-shirts and short shorts
crowded in front of the mirrors nervously practicing their routines. They
couldn't have been more nervous than me. I was petrified.

The signs pointed the way through the halls to where a long table
was set up and student assistants were helping with the registration. The one
processing the S's quickly found my name and with a smile handed me a 3 x
5 card with a number on it. She explained that this was the number of a
practice room upstairs where I would go for my individual tryout. She
pointed me towards the stairs. I could see they wasted no time around here.

The practice room was one of what seemed like hundreds of tiny
cubicles lining the halls of the top floor of the music building. Inside the
room was a piano, a stool, a music stand, and a chair. Cramped quarters. I
fumbled my French horn out of its case and tried to run a few scales,
anything to loosen up my lips and make a respectable sound. I knew this
was the moment it was all on the line. Showtime.

Soon there was a knock on the door and in walked the epitome of a Joe College character from central casting.

"Hi, I'm Scott Harpe. Are you Bennett?" He asked. He extended his hand.

"Yes, Bennett Shelfer." His handshake was firm, assured.

"Great! That means we're both in the right room," he said.

Scott Harpe was tall and handsome and neatly dressed in a brand-name pair of Bermuda shorts and a new Marching Chief T-shirt. He exuded confidence. But he was also very friendly. He asked me about my hometown, my high school, my high school band. And he asked about my football team, which of course we didn't have. We talked for the longest time about sports, the weather, everything, and nothing at all. Before long, without me realizing it, he had put me completely at ease. Then, almost as an afterthought, he said we may as well fill this square and asked me to run a couple of scales and play the three sheets of music he had placed on the stand. I plodded through the Fight Song, the Alma Mater and the Garnet and Gold March. The music from a solo instrument never sounds as good as it does from the entire band, but regardless, I knew I had done my best.

"Okay, Bennett," Scott said. "What happens now is after tryouts, all the assistants will meet with Whit and Brownie. Around four o'clock this afternoon a list of the freshmen that will be invited to join the Marching Chiefs will be posted on a bulletin board outside of Whit's office. Good luck."

Another firm handshake, and he was gone. I knew that the Whit and Brownie he referred to were Manley Whitcomb and Robert Braunagel, director and assistant director of the Marching Chiefs.

The afternoon seemed to drag on forever. I spent a lot of the time on a bench outside the music building watching, in the distance, the majorettes going through their tryouts. They were so good and so attractive. A student pointed out Linda Bean and Penny McArthur. I ran into a couple of the other majorettes at the water cooler during one of their breaks, Joanne Crisp and Lou McGuire.

The hall was very crowded outside of Mr. Whitcomb's office at four o'clock. I was still three deep from the bulletin board when I saw my name. I had never been so happy and so relieved. When I got closer, I saw that I was assigned to Magnolia Hall for lodging and we were to meet at 6 PM in the dining room in Suwanee Hall for dinner. Then at 7 PM we were to assemble in the main rehearsal room back in the music building.

Magnolia Hall was the oldest men's dorm on campus. It was an original army barracks style, a long, narrow building, with rows of single beds on either side. There was a common bathroom and shower area in the middle. Perfect, because when I got to my bed, there waiting for me was my very own Marching Chiefs T-shirt. I donned it immediately and rushed to the bathroom where there was a mirror. Wow. I retrieved the maroon gym shorts from my suitcase along with my new white, low top tennis shoes and thick white socks to complete my outfit. The school colors were garnet and gold, and maroon was as close to garnet as I could find among the shorts at JC Penney's. I knew thick socks would be necessary to prevent blisters from all the marching that was about to come.

Being away from home and totally on my own for the first time, and counting every penny, I was naturally concerned about getting enough to eat. My first visit to the cafeteria that evening relieved those concerns for the time being. All expenses, the lodging at Magnolia Hall and the food in Suwanee Hall cafeteria, were paid for by the university until classes started. We could eat all we wanted. And I did. Three meals a day.

The band room was jumping with excitement the evening of our first rehearsal. I found my place in the row of other French horn players and settled in. I saw that I had been assigned 2nd horn music parts, which was just fine with me. The 1st horn parts contained the upper register notes which were more difficult to play, and therefore the better musicians played those parts. And that group certainly did not include me. I played first French horn in high school, but these folks were a cut above and I was just happy to be sitting among them playing any part. The noodling was loud and intense. I unpacked my horn and tried to loosen up my embouchure.

At the moment of 7 PM sharp the room suddenly fell silent. I looked up to see Mr. Manley Whitcomb had stepped up on to the director's podium at the front of the room. He was accompanied by two other gentlemen.

172

"My name is Manley Whitcomb. I want to welcome you to our freshman preschool session for the Marching Chiefs. This gentleman is the man we affectionately called Brownie. He is Robert Braunagel, our assistant director." He nodded towards a large, burly man, with an ample brown beard and brown tousled hair, wearing a brown plaid shirt and brown pants and brown shoes. Brownie acknowledged us with a sheepish little wave.

"And this young man," Mr. Whitcomb continued, "is Charles Carter, our arranger. Charlie came to us, as I did, from Ohio State University. He arranges almost every piece of music we play and we are lucky to be the beneficiaries of his unique talent." Charlie stood off to the side appearing to be embarrassed by his introduction. He wore thick, coke-bottle glasses with a thin rim. His wrinkled white shirt was worn untucked from his blue leisure pants.

"We have much work to do and little time to do it," Mr. Whitcomb said. "That means we must have your maximum effort and undivided attention at every rehearsal. We expect no more and will tolerate nothing less. Let's get started by playing first what we play the most, the Fight Song. From the top…"

Mr. Whitcomb gave the downbeat and we began playing. The effect on me was immediate, emotional and profound. My eyes glistened. Oh! I had heard the Fight Song many times before, but never like this. I had dreamed of this moment for years and years. Just a few hours ago I was standing alone on the curb with my horn and my suitcase and now I was playing with the Marching Chiefs. Or I should say, a group of freshmen who wanted to become Marching Chiefs. I pinched myself, blinked the tears from my eyes and smiled into my mouthpiece filling my horn with all the air I could muster. F-L-O-R-I-D-A, S-T-A-T-E... Florida State! Florida State! Florida State!

The 6 AM breakfast at the Suwanee Room the next morning could not come soon enough for me. It had been a restless night. It was difficult for me to sleep with all the comings and goings and mutterings of the other freshman boys in the barracks. I lay awake thinking about the first time I had seen the Marching Chiefs and Drum Major Dick Mayo when Uncle Verdayne had taken me to the game. I thought about Aunt Versie buying me my French horn, the same one that was in the old case under my bed. I thought about grandmother making my first uniform for me. I thought about my old band director, Mr. Shupp, teaching me the basics of military style marching. And now the day had come for me to learn how to march like a Marching Chief. I couldn't wait.

We assembled at 7 AM on our practice field, an open area south of the Science Building and to the west of Woodward Ave. It had fresh chalk markings, laid out as a football field. There was a small makeshift wooden tower erected on the north side of the field at the 50-yard line.

We were assigned to row leaders, upperclassman leaders who had returned to school early to help with our indoctrination. It was immediately apparent that these people were spirited, committed. My assigned row, eight of us, included the French horns and some baritones.

On the first day we marched without instruments. It was all about the basics. We learned to stand at attention, parade rest, and the motion of bringing our horns up to our lips. We learned to step off with our left foot, lifting the heel first and then the toe and keeping the toe pointed downward until our thigh was perpendicular to the ground. We learned the arm swing. We learned to never let our heel touch the ground, because it would jar the connection between our lips and our mouthpiece and impact the notes were playing. We also learned the most essential basic, to march 8 to 5, eight steps for every 5 yards. With everyone in the band marching down the field at 8 to 5, the lines would always be straight. Every move we made was under the watchful eye of Mr. Whitcomb from his lofty perch in the tower. We believed he was the best in the country. Maximum effort. Expect no more. Accept no less. Attitude. Marching Chief attitude.

And so, it continued. Five rehearsals a day. Outside rehearsals were scheduled at 7 AM and 4 PM in an effort to avoid the heat of the day. Nice try. It was always hot and very humid during any part of the day in Tallahassee in early September. Many students struggled with blisters on their feet, dehydration, heat stroke and other manifestations of not being in shape. I did not. My physical conditioning was as good as anyone's and better than most. Because of that, and because I loved to march, I felt very confident during our outside rehearsals.

174

Our indoor music rehearsals were at 10 AM, 1 PM, and 7 PM. It was here that I faced my greatest challenge. I was a marcher sitting in a room full of really good musicians. I felt very insecure. But these were my own internal insecurities. No one ever indicated to me that my horn playing was not up to par. Nonetheless, I watched, and listened and learned and tried to absorb every new technique possible.

There was one defining difference about the music I was playing as it related to the French horn parts. This music was arranged by Charlie Carter. In most arrangements I had played in high school, the French horn part was little more than rhythm accompaniment. Um pa, um pa, um pa pa. Most always playing on the offbeat and rarely anything near the melody. Boring. Charlie's arrangements left the rhythm parts to the percussion section. He wrote beautiful melodies and counter melodies for the French horn which usually paralleled the parts of the saxophones or baritones. It was such a pleasure to play this music and hear the French horns resonating and contributing to the incredible sound of this band.

The total immersion training, beginning with the 6 AM breakfast and ending when evening rehearsal was over at 9 PM, did have one positive effect. It solved the problem of not being able to sleep in Magnolia Hall. At the end of the day, I was totally exhausted and sleep came deep and easy until the 5:30 AM wake up the next morning.

On the second morning I departed the cafeteria line with my tray loaded down with scrambled eggs, bacon, grits, biscuits and a large glass of orange juice. I was looking for a place to sit when someone at a table with several other boys beckoned me to join them. He introduced himself as Terry Johnson. I knew who he was because I'd already been watching him. He was the new Drum Major. I enjoyed chatting with him and the others over breakfast. Terry was so friendly and positive with everyone, and made us feel like we were a part of this already great tradition of excellence that was the Marching Chiefs.

Outdoor rehearsals, indoor rehearsals and mealtimes all blurred together for the next few days. We had lost a few of our group who, for one reason or another, did not stick it out. On the fourth day I hurried through lunch and walked over to the purser's office to pay my tuition. I was relieved to learn there was a student bank in the same office. I opened my first ever checking account with the $200 money order I had brought from Jacksonville, which represented all the earnings from my summer job. I had worked for the city of Jacksonville engineering department for one dollar an hour, $32 a week bring home pay. I then wrote a check for my tuition, which was around $150.

After I paid my tuition, I was issued my housing assignment.

"What's this?" I asked. I handed the slip of paper back to the lady behind the desk. I had seen that my housing assignment was Phi Delta Theta, and I had no idea what that meant.

"You been assigned to the Phi Delt house," she said.

"There must be some mistake," I said. "I'm not gonna be in a fraternity." I had heard of fraternities and sororities at college, but knew nothing about them, except they were for the kids who had lots of money.

"There's no mistake. When our dormitories are full, we sometimes assign students to fraternity houses that have empty beds, until a dormitory vacancy occurs. Don't worry, there's no additional charge to you."

"Okay, thank you," I said. I folded the slip of paper and put it in my pocket. Fortunately, I was not going to have to deal with the situation until the day before classes began.

On the afternoon of the fifth day, we had the highly anticipated arrival of the upperclassman. This was a different group that had the benefit of one or two or three years of experience with the band. They were a cocky bunch, with an aura of musical arrogance about them. Nothing or no one escaped their harsh, but good-natured, sarcasm and ridicule, except maybe Mr. Whitcomb. Not Charlie, and certainly not Brownie. Not the student newspaper, the football team or the new coach, Perry Moss. And certainly not any opposing band that might share the field with them at halftime. It was all fair game for their derogatory drudging.

My distant cousin, Helen Clark, was one of the upperclassmen returning. She was the daughter of Hub Clark, who was Grandmother's first cousin. She was a pretty saxophone player and an exceptional student. Truly, the All-American girl. She was so sweet and welcoming and made me feel like I belonged there. Her boyfriend was Tony Britton, who played First French horn and was a music major. He was an exceptional musician.

When I first heard the incredible sound of the combined band, the freshmen and upperclassmen, it was everything I had dreamed it would be. Once again, I pinched myself and played on, feeling blessed to be there.

After two days of giving the upperclassman a chance to knock the rust off and get back up to speed on the basics of being a Marching Chief, we were assembled in the band room for an evening practice. Mr. Whitcomb said we were ready to begin preparing for our first halftime show on Saturday, September 13th. I found it strange that I would perform in a halftime show before I attended my first class in college. Strange, but wonderful.

"Before we begin working on the halftime show," Mr. Whitcomb said, "I'd like to run through a new piece that Charlie's been working on." I noticed Charlie Carter and Brownie were standing on the side of the room. "You should have it there on your stand. Let's put up, 'Hymn to the Garnet and Gold.' And let's take it from the top."

Mr. Whitcomb brought the baton down and the music began. I was concentrating so hard on site reading this new piece of music, it took a few measures for the total sound of the music and the Chiefs to hit me. But then it did. It swept me away like a religious experience. I was certain it was the most moving piece of music I'd ever heard. The more we got into this tune the more mesmerizing it became. When it was over, there was hardly a dry eye in the room. We all rose to our feet and gave Charlie a standing ovation. Mr. Whitcomb nodded to him with a smile of satisfaction in amazement. Charlie just gave a little sheepish wave, looking almost embarrassed. I was honored to be sitting in on the first band reading of this classic. Somehow, I knew the "Hymn to the Garnet and the Gold" would be echoing through this music building long after we were gone.

The marching block that would be the performing band was formed and those making it were given a number. It was another anxious moment for me. I was relieved to see that I had been assigned a number, but surprised to see that it was number 28. I was marching as the eighth person in the second row. There were eight marching in each row, so number 28 placed me on the outside of the marching block. Very visible. I liked it.

That afternoon as I was walking up to the practice field for our first halftime show rehearsal, I couldn't help but notice the brand-new blue and white Oldsmobile 88 that was filled with majorettes parking just in front of me. Out of the driver's seat hobbled Lou McGuire, the cute freshman majorette that I had spoken to in passing a couple of times. The guys were already talking about the majorette from Central Florida with the flashy new car whose daddy owned orange groves.

"Hi," Lou said.

"Hi, what happened you?" I asked. I saw that her left foot was completely wrapped with a bandage.

"I sprained my ankle," she said.

"Are you sure it's sprained?"

"That's what the doctor said."

"What about your marching and twirling?" I asked.

"Oh! I can't do any of that. The doctor said I had to take it easy for 2 to 3 weeks."

"I'm sorry," I said. "Good luck." I didn't know what to say. I walked onto the practice field thinking how devastated I would be if I was unable to march. She didn't seem to be so upset about it. I guess if you're cute and rich, maybe everything else is not too important.

Chapter 27

The next day we were given a break in our practice schedule to register for classes. We were told that this was actually a special preregistration period at the new Tully gymnasium for the athletes, cheerleaders, and the band, so that we could schedule our classes in the mornings, leaving our afternoons open for rehearsals.

Tully gym was crowded. Finally, after wandering around, I found the table that included the S's and queued up in the long line.

"Name, please?" The lady at the table asked, when it was finally my turn. She peered at me over thin rimmed glasses that had slid down on her nose. She looked to be middle-aged with her graying hair pinned back. She wore a high collared shirt with lace on either side of the buttons down the front. She was definitely a librarian. Or maybe an English teacher.

"Shelfer, Bennett Shelfer," I said.

"Okay, let's see…" She thumbed through one of several shoeboxes filled with index cards on the table. "Oh! Here it is. I see you're in the band, is that right?"

"Yes, ma'am."

"Very good. We have tentatively scheduled your required classes like math and English on Monday Wednesday and Friday mornings. Does that work for you?"

"Yes, ma'am. Thank you."

"Good. That leaves Tuesdays and Thursdays available for ROTC. Would you like Army or Air Force?"

"ROTC?" I asked. I was totally perplexed. I had never heard of ROTC. "What's ROTC?" I finally asked, after a very long awkward moment.

"ROTC is Reserve Officers Training Corps," the lady said. "Every able-bodied male student at a land-grant institution such as Florida State is required to take two years of basic ROTC. What would you like, Army or Air Force?"

Her explanation only deepened my quandary. The only thing I was certain about was I was being forced to make an important choice on something I knew nothing about. I stood there for the longest time thinking, trying to decide, before finally grimacing and shrugging my shoulders with oblivious resignation.

At that moment the student in line behind me stepped close and poked me in the ribs.

"Take Air Force," the stranger whispered in my ear. "The Army guys have to polish brass and carry a rifle when they march."

"Air Force!" I almost shouted to the lady. "I'll take Air Force."

"Very well, Bennett. Your schedule is all set."

Little did I know the truth of the words the lady had spoken.

My first few of months of college were a very exciting, yet difficult time for me. The tone was set when the Dean of Students threw down the gauntlet to us during a freshman orientation meeting at Wescott Auditorium. He welcomed us, the Florida State University graduating class of 1962, to the University. He said our journey would be challenging and rewarding. He then said something very profound. He said, look at the person to your right. Now look at the person to your left. In four years neither one of them will be here. I looked at the person on my right and the person on my left. They were both looking at me. Game on.

It was exciting to don the Marching Chief uniform for the first time. The white gloves, along with the white spats over black shoes, accented the uniform perfectly for our high-stepping marching style. And it was thrilling to do the first pregame and halftime show. Wow! It was everything I dreamed of, and more. Terry Johnson did a great job as our new Drum Major. And of course, I watched his every move.

It didn't take me long to learn about fraternity life. The day before classes began, I moved into the Phi Delt house and was assigned a bunk in a room with three brothers. It was a total disaster. They were loud and boisterous and raised hell day and night. The nights were hot and you had to leave all the windows open in hopes of catching a breeze. You could hear every pin drop, much less the continuous yelling, door slamming and loud, raucous music. And they were always drinking. So many sloppy drunks. It's impossible to be sober and have an intelligent conversation with a sloppy drunk. I already had too much experience with that in my lifetime. Additionally, they berated me because I was a Temp living in their house. And I overheard one inebriated brother tell another that I was not Phi Delt material because I didn't have any money. That worked for me.

After three days of this insanity, I went back to the housing office and pleaded my case for a move, citing my impossible situation with fraternity life. The lady listened with a sympathetic ear.

"I understand your situation," she said. "But, unfortunately the only other bed we have available is in another fraternity house."

"I'm in an impossible situation here," I said. "I can't sleep, I can't study…"

"Wait. Wait…" The lady interrupted. "Just hear me out for a moment. First of all, not all fraternities are alike. More importantly, in this particular instance, not all fraternity houses are alike. The bed we have available is in the Kappa Sigma house, the newest fraternity house on campus, and the only one with air-conditioning."

"Air-conditioning?" I asked.

"Yes, air-conditioning," she said.

This was a game changer for me. I had never lived in a place with air-conditioning. My living arrangements could not have been any worse, so what did I have to lose?

"I'll try it. Thank you," I said.

The Kappa Sig house on Woodward Avenue was a totally different experience. I was assigned to a room upstairs with three other guys, Ray Hitchcock, Ray Allen and Dave Reinhardt. They welcomed me and treated me with respect, giving me my space to come and go as I pleased. I was given the last remaining bed, the top bunk above Dave Reinhardt and directly under the air-conditioning duct. Perfect. It was not like these fraternity boys wouldn't be fraternity boys, but with the windows closed and the door closed, the room was quiet. I could study and I could sleep.

Academic classes were little more than a blur to me. I felt like I was in a situation completely over my head. Because I was. The classes were very large, some of them in a lecture hall with what seemed like hundreds of other students. I recognized my professors by site because they were the ones talking in front of the class. I was just another student with a number to them. They certainly did not know me by my name, nor did they care. Bennett, you're not at Sneads High anymore.

During this time when I was switching fraternity houses and beginning classes there was a strange medical problem happening to me. Sometime in the late morning, before noon, my left eye would turn blood red and throb with pain with every beat of my heart. Then later in the afternoon the bloodshot eye and the pain would disappear and everything seemed back to normal. This happened every day. I went to see the doctor at the University infirmary. He said he had no idea what it was but I should definitely have it

182

checked out. He asked me where I was from and when I told him he lamented he was pretty sure Sneads did not have a brain specialist. I told him about my dad living in Jacksonville so he gave me the names of a couple of doctors there. He urged me to see one of them as soon as possible.

The next Sunday morning, after the Furman game and our second halftime show, I boarded a bus to Jacksonville. Daddy had somehow managed to book an appointment for me with a neurologist on Monday. The doctor looked at my throbbing red eye and shrugged. He ran a few basic tests on me and shrugged again. He told me to take two aspirin every day for pain and made another appointment for me to come back and see him in three weeks. He said he was concerned about a tumor or growth that might be blocking the blood flow coming out of my eye. Or, he said, it could be stress-related.

Daddy took me to the bus station and I was on the next Greyhound to Tallahassee. I watched the little towns and farms and forests of longleaf yellow pines fly by the window of the bus. It was obvious to me that I had brain cancer and didn't have long to live. Nonetheless, I was at peace knowing that I was a Marching Chief and I was going to make the best of it with the little time I had left.

After a short week of classes and band rehearsals I found myself on the first of four chartered buses with the Marching Chiefs on our way to Atlanta. I'd never been there. The Seminoles were playing a Friday night game against Georgia Tech. It was so exciting for me to be going on my first road trip. Among all the chaos I was going through on campus with the housing debacle, the classes, and my painful red eye, the Marching Chiefs had been my sanctuary. There was no angst or ambiguity with either the practices or performances of the Chiefs. I loved it.

Two totally insignificant things happened that week. Insignificant, except to me. The first concerned my position in one of the formations of our halftime show. The band spelled out GA. TECH and marched it down the field playing "Rambling Wreck," the Georgia Tech fight song. My assignment was to be the "period" after the abbreviation of Georgia. That meant I was marching all alone, totally exposed, down the field with the formation. I was surprised they would give this assignment to a freshman 2nd French horn player.

The second totally insignificant thing happened on the bus ride to Atlanta. It just so happened, probably not coincidentally, that I was on the same bus with Mr. Whitcomb. A couple of hours into the long trip I awakened from a nodding nap to see Mr. Whitcomb making his way down the aisle of the bus, stopping and chatting with different students. Finally, he reached the back of the bus where I was sitting.

"Bennett, I understand you were a drum major in high school," Mr. Whitcomb said to me. "Is that right?"

"Yes, sir. I was," I said.

"Hmmm…" Mr. Whitcomb said, with a couple of nods.

That's all he said. Then, with a wry expression on his face he turned around and walked back towards the front of the bus. It was a casual off-the-cuff remark from Mr. Whitcomb, but to me it was prodigious. It was validation for all my years of hopes and dreams and hard work. And it was all the motivation I needed to rededicate myself to my secret goal. With this remark and my placements in the marching formations, in my mind, I had Mr. Whitcomb's eye. Validation indeed.

Mr. Whitcomb, along with Brownie and Charlie, planned every show to suit the audience. So, needless to say, the pregame and halftime shows went very well that Friday night at Grant Field in Atlanta. The stadium was filled and the Atlanta crowd was very gracious and responsive to our band. In fact, we received two standing ovations. The first was when we marched down the field in the GA. TECH formation playing the Georgia Tech fight song, "Rambling Wreck from Georgia Tech." The other standing ovation was when we played "Dixie." It was said that in Atlanta the best band was always the one that played "Dixie" the loudest. We did and we were.

A group of us went to Johnnie Reb's BBQ place after the game. I was going to try to eat on the cheap and save some of the per-diem food money from the Chiefs, but I splurged and had the ribs. They were okay but not what I expected. I could've had a hamburger and saved the money.

Another thing happened on that weekend in Atlanta that wasn't insignificant at all, but I didn't realize it at the time. Maury Wishnoff, one of my best friends from high school, was a freshman at Georgia Tech. After the halftime show, he came looking for me in the band block in the stands. We were not leaving for Tallahassee until the afternoon of the following day so I asked him if we could meet for a Saturday lunch. We met at The Varsity, the legendary hamburger restaurant on the Tech campus. It was great to see Maury. He looked funny sporting the mandatory "rat hat" that all freshman were obligated to wear. And I'm sure I looked funny with my bloodshot red left eye which was throbbing with pain. I told Maury that the doctor didn't know what was causing it. I withheld my self-diagnosis of terminal brain cancer. We talked about how difficult our classes were. We talked about girls. He said he really liked the looks of our majorettes. I assured him I did too. We laughed at the fact that he was going to a boy's school that had just recently admitted girls, and I was going to a girl's school that had just recently admitted boys. He lamented that it was hard to find a good-looking girl on the Georgia Tech campus. Of course, I rubbed it in by telling him that you could seldom go to the Sweetshop at Florida State without bumping into a Miss Florida. We talked about the good old days at Sneads High and chomped down hamburgers with all the trimmings. Delicious.

It was hard to say goodbye to Maury. When it was finally time to go, I left him sitting on the stool nibbling on his French fries. He was a dear friend who never changed with time. It's hard to find one of those.

Walking across the campus of Georgia Tech to board the bus home, the pain and redness in my left eye subsided. It never returned. I soon forgot about having terminal brain cancer. Maybe it was stress after all. I'm going with that one.

Chapter 28

On the other hand, if my throbbing, red, bloodshot eye had been caused by stress, it would have exploded many times during my freshman year in college. It was my belief after couple of months with the Marching Chiefs that I would have a realistic opportunity to try out for Drum Major at the end of the next year, my sophomore year. Terry Johnson would be graduating and tryouts would be held. I felt encouraged about my chances to be Drum Major my junior and senior years. The drawback was I had to stay in school. And there were two major obstacles to staying in school, academics and money.

"Mr. Shelfer, why did you come to Florida State?" My faculty advisor asked during an obligatory meeting. "What are your goals in life?"

I was taken aback because I was not accustomed to being addressed as Mr. Shelfer.

"I came to Florida State to be in the Marching Chiefs," I said.

"You're already in the Marching Chiefs. What are your goals in life?"

My two goals in life had always been my secret. I was not that comfortable sharing them with a complete stranger. What would he think? I certainly was not going to tell him about my first goal, the one about marrying Dannie. It was obvious that was never going to happen.

My advisor persisted: "Tell me. That's what I'm here for. I'm here to help you."

"My goal is to be Drum Major of the Marching Chiefs," I finally said.

"Isn't that a rather short-term goal?" He asked. He smiled, but at least he didn't laugh.

"No, Sir. I've had it for a very long time." Then my advisor laughed. We both did, and the tension of our little meeting was broken.

"I'm just trying to determine your major in order to schedule classes. Does that mean you want to be a music major?"

"No, Sir. I don't have a piano background and I'm sure I could never pass a music theory class. So, I don't really know what I want to major in."

"Very well, Mr. Shelfer. I'll place you in the undecided category. You will continue taking core classes for the remainder of your freshman and sophomore year. Concentrate on your academics. Good luck."

My academic advisor could sense, I thought, that I was struggling with my classes. It was becoming apparent that to accomplish any goals I had, or might ever have, I was going to have to focus all my efforts on staying in school. And to do that it was going to be necessary to make good grades. Up until this point all my efforts were focused on doing well in the Marching Chiefs. So far, so good, but those efforts would never be reflected on my report card. My priorities would have to change.

The other obstacle to me staying in school was money. Every Monday at lunch time I walked anxiously to the student center to check my mailbox. Daddy had promised to mail me $20 every Friday after he cashed his paycheck. Usually he did, but sometimes he didn't. High angst. It was not very comforting to try to live on a minimum weekly amount, and then sometimes not even get that. There was, however, another side to this that I understood. While it was difficult for me to live on $20 a week, I knew it was just as difficult for Daddy to send it.

Daddy and Dot always had a fiery relationship. When they were married a few years ago that changed. It became worse. A casual observer might wonder how they ended up together at all. I thought I understood it pretty well. They were both divorced from previous marriages. Dot had two children, Joyce and Tony. And Daddy had me. Daddy's brother, Uncle Bud, was married to Dot's sister, Aunt Ruth. Dot lived in a modest house on Brackland Street in Jacksonville, the same as Uncle Bud and Aunt Ruth, with only one house between them. So, in a way, they were already family.

From Dot's standpoint, Daddy was a nice man with a sense of humor who always had a regular job. She knew about his drinking problem, and I believe she thought she could tolerate it. She always made an effort to collect the weekly household expenses from Daddy on payday before he could waste it on drinking.

From Daddy's standpoint, Dot was a beautiful woman. Impressively so. She had a regular job at the laundry where she had worked all her life. And she had a house.

There was never an attempt to be just one happy family. From the beginning, the kids were a constant problem between them. Dot always put Joyce and Tony first, ahead of Daddy, and made no bones about it. She never gave him the opportunity to be the father figure Joyce and Tony never had. Consequently, Daddy always put me first. I didn't need a mother figure, because Grandmother had always filled that role.

Dot was never a big fan of me going to college. She thought I should get a job, find a girl and get married, and get on with life. And it wasn't just me. Dot never encouraged Joyce and Tony to go to college either. Joyce was the nicest, sweetest, stepsister anyone could ask for. She never caused trouble for anyone and always made really good grades. But by this time, much to Dot's delight, Joyce was already smitten with the son of Dot's best friend from the neighborhood so college wasn't in the plans for her. And Tony was well on his way to being a juvenile delinquent, having already been arrested a couple of times for stealing.

Dot could not believe I was such a goody two-shoes and did not drink and smoke like most of the kids my age. She was convinced that I at least smoked. She smoked like a chimney, almost as much as Daddy. During the summer when I was there working my summer job for the city of Jacksonville engineering department, she thought someone was stealing her cigarettes. In fact, she thought it was me. In an effort to clear the air and to smoke me out, so to speak, she offered to buy my cigarettes for me and give me complete exoneration if I would only admit that I smoked. She couldn't believe I didn't accept her proposal. She might have had a taker had she offered the same deal to Tony.

Daddy led a simple, almost mundane life. He worked, and was really good at his job. He had just been promoted from being a Forman on a crew of a dozen men to being Assistant Superintendent of the Sewer Department for the City of Jacksonville. He smoked. He burned almost 2 packs a day of Marlboro cigarettes. He drank. Probably a six-pack of Pabst Blue Ribbon or Budweiser every night after work. Yet, he never drank on the job or missed a day of work because of it. There was only one bright, shining star in his universe, and that was me. I knew his pride and his love for me knew no bounds, even though he never actually told me so. His actions spoke louder than his words. He defended me and my quest to complete college against any and all criticism. So, amidst all the bickering and turmoil, when Dot suggested that I should leave college, to my dad, that was the last straw.

On that Monday I was relieved to find a letter from Daddy in my mailbox. It was a simple note scribbled on a small piece of tablet paper and wrapped around a $20 bill. Daddy said he had an argument with Dot over me staying in college, so he left her. He moved out. He had moved into a second-story one-bedroom apartment on 9th Street, just west of Main. He said for me not to worry because he would make sure I had the money to go to college no matter what. I was stunned. I slowly slid down the wall of the student post office and sat on the floor and read the note again. I felt immense anguish and guilt. I never wanted to be the source of anyone's problems. But I knew this was my one chance to go to college and make something of myself, even if I didn't know what that something was. I could not let Daddy down. He was sacrificing everything for me. I thought about Aunt Versie and her hopes and dreams for me to be the best that I could be. I thought about Grandmother, my beacon of strength, and what she would say to me about finishing a difficult task. "You can do it," Grandmother would say. "Just keep on keeping on." I slowly rose to my feet and began walking towards my afternoon class… Keep on keeping on.

With Daddy's sacrifice and promise to keep me in school no matter what, I knew it was up to me to make the grades necessary to stay in school. Even though I made good grades in high school, I discovered I really didn't know how to study. In one of my classes I sat beside a girl named Ann, from Tavares, Florida, who always made straight A's. She knew I was struggling and was nice enough to tell me how she studied for the class. She would take thorough notes from the professor's lecture and then outline the appropriate chapter from the textbook. Then to study for the test she would memorize the notes from the lecture and the notes from the book. It worked for her. And it worked for me. I discovered that I could memorize almost anything for a short period of time… long enough to take the test. My grades began to improve.

Time management was something else I had to learn. I had to make a schedule and stick to it, making sure there was time for undisturbed study. There were so many distractions on campus, mainly beautiful girls. Linda Gormley was a beautiful blonde cheerleader from Tallahassee. Karen Ekman was a brunette beauty queen from down around Palm Beach. And then there was Faye Dunaway, the theatrical beatnik beauty from Two Egg, Florida, only about 16 miles up the road from Sneads. In actuality, none of these girls were approachable by me simply because I knew I was never going to be ask them out because I had no money. As the old joke goes: I was so poor I couldn't pay attention. Another one was: I was so poor that if steamboats were selling for a dime apiece, I couldn't buy an echo of the whistle.

Lou McGuire, the cute injured majorette, the rich girl from Apopka, Florida, who drove the shiny new Oldsmobile, was certainly not approachable either. But it was different with her. Lou always seemed to be around after band practice, even though she was no longer practicing with the majorettes. And she appeared to have an interest in me, even though for the life of me I could not understand why. I liked her. What's not to like? So, after band practice when she offered me a ride back to the Kappa Sig house I readily accepted. When she asked if I was pledging Kappa Sig, I told her I had no interest in the fraternity and was only a temporary housing student there. And I knew that I could never afford to ask her out on a date, so I thought that would be the end of it. Not so much. I kept running into Lou McGuire.

The Florida State football team was having a pretty good season, winning more games than they lost. The highlight of the season was the first ever football game played between the Florida State Seminoles and University of Florida Gators. It was not easily scheduled. It literally almost required an act of the state legislature to force the Gators to lower themselves and schedule a game with the former girl's school from Tallahassee. The game was finally set for Saturday, November 22, 1958.

The Marching Chiefs practiced with great enthusiasm to prepare for a trip to Gainesville. We couldn't speak for the football team, but we were convinced that the band that had never lost a halftime show was certainly not going to lose this one. We knew we were better than the Gator band and we couldn't wait to get down to Gainesville to prove it. Mr. Whitcomb, or "the great white father," as he was sometimes affectionately called, picked up on our contemptuous condescending attitude towards the Gator band.

"I want you to remember something," Mr. Whitcomb said. He was addressing us after the final rehearsal on Friday afternoon. "When we go down to Gainesville tomorrow, we will actually be the guest of the Gator band. We're going directly to their band building to practice the music for our combined pregame show. Treat them with respect and let's hope they'll be the gracious host that you would expect them to be. Don't talk down to them or try to rub it in that you are better than they are. They already know it. But you're better than they are for only one reason, you work harder. You prepare. You practice. You perform. They have a good band because they give it a good effort. You are among the best bands in the country because of... well, I just told you. And remember that tomorrow in that town or on the field you are representing the Marching Chiefs and Florida State University. Be on the bus at 8 o'clock tomorrow morning."

The drama began early the next day when Joanne Crisp, one of our freshman majorettes, missed the bus. We waited for only a couple of minutes and then the busses rolled out of town. Speculation buzzed through the band about what had happened, and what would happen to her if she missed this classic game. We arrived in front of the University of Florida music building and were surprised to see Joanne standing there, looking like the Miss Fernandina Beach beauty queen she was. As it turned out she had overslept. She woke up in panic mode and scraped together all the cash she had and hurried to the Tallahassee airport where she managed to secure a seat on the last flight out to Gainesville.

Our fellow musicians in the Gator band were indeed very nice and hospitable. I can't say the same about the student body. On our march across campus to Florida Field, the locals were vicious. We were subjected to many rebukes worse than Gator bait and chomp 'em and they were successful in exposing our beautiful, innocent girls to some new terms of endearment. They even sloshed beer down on us from the upper floors of the dormitories. They were already occasionally ringing their victory bell, a large bell suspended high in a tower, and the game had not even started. So much for hospitality.

The pregame and halftime shows before over 40,000 fans were thrilling. The Marching Chiefs definitely won the day. The football game was much closer than anyone expected. On the game's opening kickoff, Seminole running back Bobby Renn faked a handoff and ran 80 yards before being tackled at the Florida 15-yard line. That led to the Seminoles only score. The Gators won 21-7. Oddly enough, after the Gators big win, they did not ring their victory bell. Even stranger, the bell just happened to surface in Tallahassee on the Florida State campus the next day. I can neither confirm nor deny the allegation that it made the trip in the luggage bin of one of our Marching Chief buses. Representing, indeed.

The disappointment of losing to the Gators was short-lived. With seven wins and only three losses, it had been a really good year of football for the Seminoles. We were thrilled to learn that we had been selected to play in a bowl game. And not just any bowl game. We were going to play in the inaugural Bluegrass Bowl in Louisville Kentucky. We could not have been more excited if it had been the Rose Bowl. Another road trip to a game that was going to be a nationally televised game for Florida State was as good as it gets for the Marching Chiefs.

There was only one problem for the band with the trip. Money. It was expensive to move 150 students, with musical instruments, to and from a game almost 700 miles away. There was no money available from the University. Mr. Whitcomb became very creative and at the last minute found a way for us to travel within the available budget. He made a pitch to a couple of state agencies that the Chiefs would do a halftime show promoting Florida tourism before a national television audience. It worked, and we had the funds for the trip. To further economize, our trip was booked on the train, even though the train did not depart from Tallahassee. This would eliminate the need for hotels, with additional meal costs. On the afternoon of Friday, December 12, 1958, the Chiefs assembled at the music building and boarded Trailways buses for Thomasville Georgia. There, we boarded a passenger train and traveled overnight to Louisville.

Needless to say, it was a wild train ride. We were supposed to get some sleep and arrive in Louisville the next morning rested and ready for the game and our pregame and halftime performances. Not a chance. Excitement and anticipation made sleep almost nonexistent. Most of the Chiefs were from Florida and were excited about the weather as much as being on national television. We were told it was going to be cold and to pack our clothes accordingly. And, of course, to us if it was going to be cold then certainly it was going to snow. I had seen snow once in my life the year before when we got about an inch of snow in Sneads. Still, most of the band had never seen a snowflake. We were fantasizing about building a snowman and having snowball fights.

Norma DeCamp was cute and played the flute. I noticed she was sitting alone near the front of the second train car. My heart skipped a beat when she said I could join her because I had a mini crush on her. I had chuckled at the old joke among the boys in the band that you should date a flute player because they're always puckered up. Not so much with Norma. She was a devout Christian and we talked about Christ. She told me she was dating Tony Romeo, the star tight end on the football team. She told me about the big new car he was driving. The more she talked, the sleepier I became. I fell asleep without telling her about dating Lou McGuire and the big, flashy Oldsmobile she was driving.

We stepped off the train in Louisville with our instruments to walk the few hundred yards to the buses that were waiting to take us to the game. It was immediately apparent that only one thing was important about this trip. Survival. The weather was cloudy and desperately cold, but there was no snow. I was wearing every bit of clothing I had with me. That included the long-johns that I had worn on hunting trips back on the farm, as well as a windbreaker overcoat and some gloves I had borrowed from some of my northern friends at the Kappa Sig house. It was not enough. I was freezing.

At the end of the day, the weather was the real newsmaker. The game was played before only a few thousand shivering people at Cardinal Field, near the old fairgrounds in Louisville. Ironically, it was the first football game for the legendary sportscaster, Howard Cosell. The field was frozen hard as a rock and was so slippery the football players switched to tennis shoes rather than cleats, to keep from slipping down. Mr. Whitcomb warned us about marching on frozen ground advising us to use caution with every step to avoid falling and injury. In addition to that he advised us to use Chapstick or Vaseline on our lips to keep them from freezing to our mouthpieces. The windchill factor was 5°. We managed to do our pregame and halftime shows without a slipup or a slip down. I'm not sure how much of it was shown on the ABC television network, but the few fans that saw our performance live seem to appreciate it, although they could not applaud while wearing gloves and drinking hot chocolate or Kentucky bourbon.

The train ride home was much more subdued. Everyone was totally exhausted and disappointed. Exhausted from the previous train ride the night before and then shivering all day at the game. We were disappointed, not so much that our Seminoles lost to the Oklahoma State Cowboys 15-6, but mostly because it didn't snow in Louisville.

Chapter 29

My grades began to improve during the second semester. The disappointing results of my first semester's report card was a wake-up call. Daddy had demonstrated that he was totally committed to doing what was necessary financially to keep me in school. I knew that I had to be totally committed academically as well. Keep on keeping on.

As the days passed, I found my animosity towards fraternity life was waning. In fact, my roommates had become friends and kept trying to talk to me about joining the fraternity. I repeatedly assured them that I had no interest in their fraternity parties or their mystic goodies and rituals. They persisted, insisting that it really didn't matter to them or the fraternity that I wasn't a party animal and didn't smoke or drink. I told him I did not have the time or the immaturity to tolerate their pledge hazing nonsense. Dave Reinhardt said he would be my big brother and would minimize that as much as possible. This little debate went on for a couple of months.

"Look," I said to Dave Reinhardt, "I appreciate your invitation to be a Kappa Sig, but the honest truth is I just cannot afford it." Finally, I thought this would put an end to the conversation.

"I understand," Dave said. "I know $60 a month is a lot of money, but it is what it is and I can't help that. And I want you to know if I can't call you my brother, I'll be happy to call you my friend. I won't bother you about it again."

"Thank you," I said.

I thought for a few moments and realized I never knew the actual cost of belonging to a fraternity, I just knew it was a lot. Hmmm…

"$60? What does that include?"

"Everything," Dave said. "That's your total monthly fraternity expense."

"What about meals?" I asked. I would oftentimes give a green-eyed glance at the brothers dressed in shirt and tie for dinner in the dining room as I went out the door to scrounge around campus for something cheap to eat.

"All the dues and meals, too. $60 covers everything."

The wheels were turning and I immediately did the math. Daddy sent me $80 a month, hopefully. I could eat all my meals at the fraternity house and still have $20 left over for the month. That wasn't much, but at least I knew I would never go hungry. In my mind, I had just stumbled on a way to stay in college.

"Dave, I think this might work. I think I would like to become a Kappa Sig." I could hardly believe the words I'd just said.

"Really? Are you serious? Are you serious" Dave asked. He was overjoyed. "Welcome, little brother, welcome." He gave me a handshake and then a big hug.

Within minutes our bedroom was full of brothers congratulating me and Dave stuck a pledge pin right on the old T-shirt that I slept in. They thought I was so happy because I had pledged the fraternity. My real happiness stemmed from the fact that I knew where my next meal was coming from.

The fraternity experience proved to have a very positive effect on me. The manners and social skills I learned there were important maturing factors that were very beneficial. I didn't mind the routines and the ritual ceremonies. And I didn't participate in all the hell raising and other hazing nonsense that frat boys did. Win, win. All for $60 a month.

There was another invitation to join another fraternity that I readily accepted. Kappa Kappa Psi was a National Honorary Band Fraternity for men. Many of the Marching Chiefs, mostly music majors, including Drum Major Terry Johnson were members. That was good enough for me. I was honored to be invited to be among the up-and-coming leaders of the band program and to be a part of the service organization supporting band music and Florida State.

Lou McGuire was beginning to wear on me. In a good way. It didn't seem to bother her that I didn't have money. Quite the contrary. The thought occasionally crossed my mind that she might be feeling sorry for me. I hoped that was not the case.

Lou was only 5'2" tall but had a very nice figure. She had beautiful, shapely legs, as did most majorettes. Her eyes were blue, but sometimes looked hazel or even green when the light reflected different hues from her copious head of auburn hair. She was always attired as if she had just stepped out of the beauty shop or off the pages of a fashion magazine, or maybe the spring edition of the JC Penney catalog. I began to look forward to her picking me up in the evening after dinner at the fraternity house for a trip to the library or maybe the lobby of her dorm to study. Maybe once a week we would go downtown to a drive-in restaurant for a black cow, which was a root beer float. If we were going off campus, she would want me to drive. That was fine with me. Driving around town with a perfectly coiffed looker from the pages of a fashion magazine in a flashy new Oldsmobile was something to which I could become accustomed.

The routine of the spring semester, the second semester of my freshman year, proved to be very beneficial. There were no Marching Chief functions in the spring, but I did play French horn in the Concert Band. Even though there was only one concert performance, it was a fun experience and allowed me to keep my embouchure in shape and continue to improve my skills as a musician. I also played in the circus band. The Florida State University Flying High Circus was already world-renowned with performers totally from the University.

Aerospace Science, the fancy name for Air Force ROTC, had become really interesting. And, sure enough, I didn't have to polish brass and carry a rifle when we marched. Much to my surprise, they had an Air

Force ROTC band. Naturally, I signed up for it. It was easy music and I already knew how to march, so drill days on Thursday were fun. Academically, I learned about our cold war nuclear defense strategy of deterrence. It was a simple policy to our adversaries, namely the Soviet Union. Our bombs were bigger than their bombs and if they launched a nuclear attack on us or our allies, they would be annihilated. Seemed to be working. I also learned if you were accepted into advanced Air Force ROTC for your junior and senior years of college, they would pay you a stipend. And not only that, if you qualified, they would pay for you to get your private pilot's license. Interesting indeed.

The semester ended and left me with mixed emotions. Leaving Lou for the summer was more difficult than I had imagined. I departed for Jacksonville to work two jobs in an effort to have enough money to return in September. She left for Apopka to rest up for the fall semester. We were total opposites. Maybe opposites attract, after all. I promised to write her because I couldn't afford a long-distance phone call. She promised to call me, because she could.

With my two jobs, it was apparent that I had to have my own transportation. When I arrived back in the city, Daddy helped me buy my first car, a red and white 1951 Chevrolet two-door coupe. It wasn't mechanically perfect but to me it was a good-looking car.

My summer job with the city of Jacksonville engineering department was waiting. This would be my third year in a row. I would again be a rodman on a survey crew that would provide line and elevation for the installation of sewer and drainage pipes installed by the city anywhere in Jacksonville. I was proud to often work on projects that were supervised by Daddy, the assistant superintendent of the sewer department. The job was easy and interesting, even though it only paid a dollar an hour. My second job was with the Duval County recreation department as an umpire for Little League baseball games. It paid me five dollars a game for only a couple of hours work. The work was easy and fun for me, even with the constant carping of the parents when I would call one of their future Hall of Famer's out. Or safe.

After work I would usually meet Daddy for supper at one of the few restaurants he liked in the neighborhood. By the time I got there, Daddy would be mellowed out from several beers. Webb's restaurant on Pearl Street was one of our favorites. I think it was because the food was similar to what Grandmother used to make. Southern style country cooking. The special was always a meat and three fresh vegetables with biscuits, cornbread, iced tea and dessert all included. If we wanted fried shrimp, we would meet at the seafood place out past Imeson Airport on Main Street. Of course, on the way back we would stop at the airport and watch a couple planes from Eastern or National Air Lines take off and land. Fascinating.

A couple of times a week after supper I would drop by Panama Park where I used to play Little League baseball. Alone in the outfield, with a broomstick as a baton, I would use the shadows from the floodlights of the recreation center to perfect my drum major moves. I knew that by this time next year I would know if my dream would become a reality. Terry Johnson would be graduating and the Marching Chiefs would hold tryouts in the spring to fill his position. I knew this would be my only chance of a lifetime and I was determined to be ready.

Daddy's little one room upstairs apartment on Ninth Street proved to be adequate. And depressing. On the positive side, it was on the southeast corner of the building which favored the prevailing breeze to temper the hot summer nights. It had a small Juliette porch that barely had room for two rocking chairs. We had no television or radio so in the evenings we would sit outside and chat and make big decisions. We would chat about the Seminoles and the Gators, the Yankees and the Dodgers and the beastly summer heat. We would not talk about anything personal because Daddy just didn't want to hear it. I mentioned to him, only in passing, that I had met a girl from Apopka. And he never mentioned Dot. It pained me to know that he was living by himself in this one room apartment because of me and my desire to continue college. I wanted to find a way to tell him to go back to Dot and live his life and try to be happy. I never did, even though I thought I could somehow get through college, even if Daddy couldn't help. In his mind he was standing on principle in support of his son. Stubborn. End of story. And if someone didn't like it, little ducks. In another way I was just as stubborn. I never thought it was my place to tell my dad what to do. He drank too much, he smoked too much, and he cussed too much. But he was a grown man and it was his life. It was my belief that he should be able to live it without critical instructions from me.

The big decisions made on the Juliette porch in the evening usually concerned whether or not to walk the two blocks down to the ice cream store on Eighth Street. We almost always reached agreement in the affirmative on that one. Daddy would have a cone of peach and I would have the walnut. Two scoops each, and all was well with the world, right down to the last lick.

Chapter 30

The dog days of summer were dragging along and it was the last Saturday in August, 1959. As I had done countless times before, I was standing outside of Gate 2 at Imeson Airport in Jacksonville watching a National Air Lines Lockheed Lodestar cackle in and rumble to a stop. I was sweating profusely, and not only because of the heat of the afternoon. This day was different. I was standing there wearing a white shirt and tie and my only suit, carrying a suitcase and a ticket. I was about to take my first airplane ride.

My letters to Lou and her phone calls to me increased in frequency and fervor during the summer. It seemed like the more I was away from her, the better I liked her. Absence makes the heart grow fonder? Maybe. She had been trying to get me to come visit her in Apopka. I had resisted because it was not an easy drive, and I usually could umpire a Little League baseball game on Saturday to make more money. As the summer was drawing to a close, she was saying that she needed me to drive with her back to Tallahassee, so she wouldn't have to make the trip alone. Besides, she said, she wanted her parents to meet me. I thought that was a strange way for her to phrase it, as opposed to she wanted me to meet her parents. I wondered what that was all about.

As it turned out, my car had been acting up. It was needing new brakes but the real problem was occasionally, for no reason, it would not start. It was not a battery problem but it was something else that we couldn't figure out. Daddy wanted to take the car to a friend of his who was a reasonable mechanic, but it was going to take some time for him to work it in. That meant I would not be able to take the car back to Tallahassee at this particular time. So that allowed me, if I could find a ride to Orlando, to come to the rescue of this damsel in distress and drive her back to Tallahassee.

The Greyhound bus schedules to Apopka were not very cheap and not at all convenient. One evening after my shadow practice at Panama Park I drove out to the airport and somehow found the courage to approach a National Air Lines ticket counter and ask about flight schedules and one-way ticket prices to Orlando. The nice man must have given me some special deal because it wasn't that much more than a bus ticket. The more I thought about it, the more I knew it was something I had to do. I was very insecure and apprehensive about this trip for the parents to meet me, anyway. I had no idea what to expect. In my mind, if I was dressed in a suit and flew in on an airplane, I might make a better impression.

The moment the propellers on the engine came to a stop the activity around the old Lodestar rapidly increased. As did the beating of my heart. My excitement and my apprehension were about to max out. An airline worker wearing grease-stained coveralls tossed some blocks of wood in front and behind the big tire of the airplane and gave some hand gesture signal to the pilot. "Airline of the Stars" was painted in script on the plane behind the pilot's window. A gasoline truck roared up to the plane and a man jumped out and began pumping gas into the plane. The passenger door near the rear of the airplane flew open and a tall, gorgeous, brunette stewardess stepped down from the plane and began saying goodbye to the dozen or so passengers that hurried off the plane. They didn't look at all afraid and none of them were kissing the ground as they stepped off the plane, so that bolstered my courage to some degree. It was a difficult concept for me to put my life totally in the hands of these pilots, these absolute strangers. But I knew Lou was already planning to meet the flight in Orlando so I couldn't chicken out now.

My seat inside the airplane was on the left side behind the wing. Through the small window I could see Daddy standing against the fence smoking a cigarette. I wasn't sure he could see me so I put my hand next to the window and gave him a tiny wave. He waved back and flashed a sheepish little smile like he wasn't worried at all. Then he disappeared behind a dense cloud of smoke from the gasping, thunderous engine on the wing that was cranking. The smell of hot burning oil filled the cabin. The smoke cleared when the engine started and the man in the grease-stained coveralls saluted the plane. In an instant we were taxiing away. There was nothing I could do now. I was merely along for the ride.

We roared down the runway and the ground fell away beneath us as we became airborne. I sat there with my nose pressed against the window in absolute wonderment at the new sensations of flight. We had seemed to be going so fast on the ground but once we became airborne the sensation of speed diminished. I could see Trout River and Main Street, where the cars were looking like little ants crawling along. As we turned left and gained altitude I could see downtown Jacksonville, the St. John's River, and eventually Jacksonville Beach and the Atlantic Ocean. The white puffy clouds looked like little cotton balls. So peaceful. So tranquil. I loved it.

Soon the sound of the engines abated to a quiet hum and the beautiful stewardess came by and asked me if I would like something to drink. I was tempted, but I declined. I couldn't keep my eyes away from the window. We appeared to be following the St. John's River southward down towards Sanford. Before long, the stewardess came back again and asked me if I wanted the meal for today, which was steak. I politely declined again. I could barely afford the cost of the flight and I knew I shouldn't be splurging for the cost of a Coke, much less a steak. She looked surprised that I had declined, but returned to serving the others.

In what seemed like no time at all we were descending back down through the white puffies. The pilot made some announcement which I could not understand over the noise of the airplane and the engines. The stewardess appeared to be finished picking up the trays and glasses from everyone else in preparation for landing. She came back to where I was sitting once again.

"Are you sure I can't get you something?" She asked. She leaned in close to me so she didn't have to talk loudly and she was sure I could hear her. "How about a nice cold Coke before we land?"

Maybe it was because I was still glistening from sweat, but somehow, she could tell I was dying of thirst.

"How much is a Coke?" I asked, reluctantly.

"Oh! It's free." I could tell she was trying to be gentle with my naivety. "Everything, meals and drinks, are all included in the price of the ticket."

"I would love a Coke. Thank you so much."

She brought me a Coke and chuckled when I wolfed it down in almost one gulp. So, she brought me another one. Cool.

Looking out the window it was amazing to me how many lakes there were in Central Florida. Lakes everywhere. Seeing the big picture from the air presented a totally different perspective than I could ever have imagined. The little ants crawling along the roads below were getting bigger and our sense of speed increased as we were descending. A couple of minutes later with a little bump, a screech of the tires and the smell of burning rubber we touched down in Herndon Field in Orlando.

Before I departed the airplane, I took a few steps forward and glanced into the cockpit. There were so many round dials and instruments and wires and buttons and switches everywhere. It looked so complicated. There was one young pilot and one old pilot. They looked like they were just regular guys. They had flown this big airplane all the way from Jacksonville to Orlando and they were just regular guys. I thought about that for a moment before I turned and walked away.

Lou was standing all alone there at the gate waiting for me. She was wearing what I was sure was a new pair of aquamarine polyester pedal pushers. The shirttails of her untucked, starched, white, three-quarter sleeve shirt were tied together in a square knot above her waist. I knew she was happy that I had come to see her because she abandoned her normally reserved manner and kissed me like no one was watching. I felt like I was still up in the air as we walked away hand-in-hand. I glanced back over my shoulder for one last look at the incredible flying machine that brought me there, flown by two regular guys and a stunning stewardess. I had a strange feeling that on this day my life had changed.

Lou was aware that I'd never been to Orlando before so she must've taken me on the scenic route back to Apopka. Every road seemed to be going around a lake and every home was landscaped with beautiful lawns

204

and flowers. So many flowers. And orange groves, miles and miles of orange groves. Soon we arrived at the McGuire home, a modern sprawling ranch home that was naturally overlooking a lake. Dream Lake. Of course, what else would it be named? As we pulled into the driveway, Lou pointed out the home of her sister, Jean, next door. It was another modern sprawling ranch home.

My apprehension about the parents meeting me turned out to be wasted energy, but it was an interesting "getting to know you" weekend. The McGuire's were a courteous and polite, yet reticent and reserved older couple. With strange names. It was not difficult to imagine that Orvid Eugene McGuire and Wilma Risner McGuire would name their two daughters Flora Eugenia and Louvenia Elizabeth. It made my given names, Bennett Howard, almost seem normal. However, coming from a family of aunts and uncles with names like Versie, Arcenia, Ethel, Angus, and Park Verdayne, I knew I could never broach the subject of strange names.

The McGuire's met and married later in life, in their middle 30s. Mr. McGuire, originally from somewhere in Georgia, moved to Apopka and began a startup nursery of foliage plants. His dedication and business acumen grew the business through the years until Evergreen Gardens became the second largest nursery in the foliage plant capital of the world. Mr. McGuire had also bought some acreage a few miles out of town to dabble in another of his interests, growing oranges. He became very successful with navels and tangelos, a couple of the newer variety of oranges.

After supper it was customary to gather in what they called the Florida room, which was a sunporch off the kitchen, overlooking Dream Lake. Lou and her mother would sit on a sofa at one end of the room and her father would sit in a recliner down by his desk at the other end of the room. I would sit in a wooden Roosevelt chair between them. I felt like I was on the witness stand. The conversation was almost totally about the weather, their ailments, and their religion. Mr. McGuire would talk about how hot and dry it had been and how the orange grove needed rain. Mrs. McGuire would talk about their ailments and their last doctor's appointment and what he said, and how important it was to do what the doctor said. They both would talk about the goings-on at the First Baptist Church of Apopka and how the new deacons were going to spend them into oblivion with the new sanctuary they were building. Mr. McGuire, a longtime deacon in the church, had been against taking on so much new debt for the larger church. They both commiserated over the long-ago departure of their favorite pastor and good friend, Dr. Finley Edge. He and his wife, Louvenia, now lived in Louisville Kentucky where he was a professor at the Southern Baptist Seminary. And that's how I found out where Lou got her name.

Lou's parents, Mr. Mrs. McGuire, discovered that I was a sophomore in college who went to Florida State to be in the band, and beyond that had no goals in life. I'm sure I underwhelmed them. My only redeeming quality was that I was a Christian, more importantly a Baptist, and a member of the First Baptist Church of Sneads.

By the time Lou had finished stuffing dresses and pantsuits and shoes and every other kind of garment into the massive trunk and backseat of her '88 Oldsmobile it was getting late in the day on Sunday afternoon. I had wanted to start the drive back to Tallahassee sooner, but, the best laid plans… We went to church and came home to a big dinner. Jean, along with her husband Bill Henry, with their three-year-old son Chip and infant daughter Allison, came over from next door. Mr. McGuire's brother, Paul, along with his wife Gordie, stayed most of the afternoon. Paul owned a gas station in town and was an avid golfer. Lou had driven me by his house earlier to show me that his entire front yard was a nine-hole golf course putting green. He had a yard man mow it every day, just as a green keeper would do for a golf course. Incredible.

We finally waved goodbye to everyone at Dream Lake and began the journey back to school. We drove into the darkness, and then into the night, and then into terrible weather. Heavy rain turned to light rain which turned to fog. Dense fog. The visibility on the old blacktop asphalt of US 90 was almost zero. I looked forward to the day when I-10 would be completed across northern Florida, but even that would not have helped with such low visibility. Finally, approaching midnight and totally exhausted, we crept into the town of Monticello, still 30 miles away from Tallahassee. Lou was snuggled up next to me dozing on and off. I was worried too much about running into something or being run over by a big truck, or for me to be sleepy. Suddenly, there was a light piercing the fog off to the right of the road. As we inched forward, I could see that the light was a vacancy sign from a motel. I turned into a parking space in front of the office.

"What are you doing?" Lou asked. "Where are we?"

"We are in Monticello," I said. "The fog is so thick I don't think it's safe to continue. Let's park here and take a nap while we're waiting for the fog to lift."

"Napping in the car after midnight in a strange town in the fog is scary to me. So, I don't think we should stay here." Lou was looking around outside the car as if she was expecting Jack the Ripper to appear. "Unless we *stay* here," she said.

"Stay here?" Then I saw that Lou was staring at the motel vacancy sign. "Oh! I don't know. I'm not sure we can just check into a motel like were married," I said.

"They don't care if were not married. They just want the money."

"Money? That's another thing…" She silenced my conversation with another one of those kisses like no one was watching, while wrapping my fingers around a stack of folding money.

"Now, go check in, Mr. Shelfer. Don't keep Mrs. Shelfer waiting."

The next morning the fog had lifted and we made the easy drive to Tallahassee in time for Lou to drop me by the music building to begin my duties as a row leader for the Marching Chiefs preschool training.

"Thanks for the ride," I said. I gave Lou's hand an affectionate squeeze as I opened the car door.

"Anytime," she said, with a sly expression on her face. "How did that little taste of marriage work out for you?"

"Unbelievable," I said.

"Maybe we should talk about making it believable."

"Maybe we should," I said. I didn't know what else to say.

Looking back over my shoulder as I walked away from Lou to begin my sophomore year in college, I no longer only saw an attractive rich girl in a flashy car. I wasn't exactly sure of what it was, but I knew I saw something different.

Chapter 31

What a difference a year makes. One year ago, I was standing on the curb with a French horn and a suitcase. Now as part of the staff as a row leader I was welcoming the new class of wide-eyed freshmen that were walking into the music building hoping to be a Marching Chief. I was thrilled to be totally immersed in the preschool training regimen of the Chiefs. It was so personally gratifying for me to tell someone how to do something, demonstrate how to do it, and then watch them do it. It was like being a teacher, and I loved it. The freshman class was impressive with so many great musicians, especially trumpets, which made Charlie Carter happy. It also had two exceptional twirlers, Janice Freeman and Beverly Calvert, who Dr. Whitcomb featured as the Garnet and Gold girls. They were stunning in their glittering garnet and gold outfits.

Mr. Whitcomb, the 'great white father,' was now Dr. Whitcomb, having completed his PhD from Columbia University,

Classes began and I settled into the routine much easier than last year. Living and eating my meals at the air-conditioned fraternity house was very nice. Lou would stop by almost every night and take me away to the sweetshop, the library, or the lobby of her dorm to study. Lou wasn't crazy about school and it became increasingly obvious that she was more interested in domestics than academics. That made me uncomfortable.

After a couple of weeks, Daddy brought my car, the old 51 Chevrolet, over from Jacksonville. The brakes and the starter had been replaced, but I soon discovered about half the time it still would not start. Strangely enough that didn't cramp my style too much. The old Chevy was a standard shift, of course. That meant that if you could get the car rolling, either by pushing it or going downhill, you could pop the clutch with the car in gear and the engine would turn and the car would start. The terrain around Tallahassee was hilly so I would just make sure to always park on a hill. If the car didn't start, I would let the car roll a few feet, pop the clutch, and I'd be on my way. You do what you have to do.

"Cadet Shelfer reporting, Sir."

Maj. Goni, my Aerospace Science 201 professor had asked me to report to his office after class. Naturally, I assumed I was in some sort of trouble so I was standing before his desk at strict attention rendering my best hand salute.

"At ease, Mr. Shelfer. Please be seated," Maj. Goni said. He returned my salute and nodded towards a chair at the corner of his desk. I reluctantly sat down.

"Mr. Shelfer, the good work you're doing in class as well as the ROTC band has not gone unnoticed by me. I would hope you're giving some thought to applying for advanced ROTC."

"Yes, Sir, I have," I said. In truth, after my plane ride at the end of the summer I was giving that a lot of thought.

"Excellent. I'm glad to hear it. But, that's not the reason I asked you to stop by," he said. "I understand you're in the Marching Chiefs."

"Yes, Sir. I am."

"Great band. Best I've ever seen... Mr. Shelfer, as you know I'm the faculty advisor for the ROTC band. What you may not know is I'm not at all happy with the progress of the ROTC Band. I think it's falling short of its full potential. What are your thoughts, Mr. Shelfer?"

"I agree with you, Sir."

"What do you think we could do to make it better?"

"I think it's all about talent, getting good musicians to be in the band. And that takes us right back to the Marching Chiefs."

"How so?" Maj. Goni asked.

"The Chiefs have quite a large number of freshmen musicians, especially trumpet players, that haven't signed up for the ROTC band. I think we should go after them."

"What would be their incentive?"

"Musicians just want to play music and have fun. If we make the band a special group for them to play music on Thursdays rather than just spend two hours marching, I think they'll respond. Especially if they realize their participation might help with their ROTC grade."

Maj. Goni leaned back in his chair for the longest time and stroked his chin like he was feeling for a goatee that wasn't there. He appeared to be in deep thought. Slowly, he removed his glasses and placed them on his desk.

"Mr. Shelfer, I would like you to be the new Commandant of the ROTC band," Maj. Goni said.

"Maj. Goni…"

"What, Mr. Shelfer?" He asked.

"It's just that I'm only a sophomore and I'm not even a music major. Are you sure about this?"

"It's not about what class you're in or your academic major. It's about leadership. And I see leadership qualities in you, Mr. Shelfer. Can you do it? Will you do it?"

"I can and I will, Sir. I will do my best."

"I have no doubt, Mr. Shelfer. You will have the rank of Cadet Major, the highest rank in the sophomore class. Carry on, Cadet Maj. Shelfer, we both have work to do."

We both stood and I snapped to attention. I gave Maj. Goni a salute, did an about-face and walked out of the office, in shock, wondering what just happened. But already my mind was racing about how to build a better ROTC band.

My years of experience as Drum Major the Sneads High School Band made it an easy transition for me to be the leader of the ROTC band. The effort to recruit freshmen musicians, especially Marching Chiefs, into the band proved very worthwhile. The additional brass instruments, especially the trumpets and the sousaphones, dramatically increased the overall sound of the band not only in volume but also the quality of the music. The band would regard Thursdays, drill days, as performances. The band would lead the corps of cadets onto the parade grounds playing the Air Force song. We would march around and form a band block with our instruments aimed directly at the reviewing stand to expose our best sound to the dignitaries. We would always play the Star-Spangled Banner and then an array of songs like the Air Force Song, Air Force Blue, and Stars and Stripes Forever. On one occasion a visiting general commented to Col. Arnold, the commander of our ROTC unit, that this was the best ROTC band he had ever seen. Maj. Goni was very pleased.

The Marching Chiefs had a great fall season, even if the football team did not. There would be no bowl game this year. The highlight of our year was a trip to Athens Georgia to play the nationally ranked University of Georgia Bulldogs. It was a thrill to march between the hedges at Sanford Stadium before the appreciative University of Georgia crowd. The Bulldogs, with their quarterback, Fran Tarkenton, administered the obligatory 42-0 drubbing to our poor Seminoles. That's okay, because we won the halftime show and then had a night on the town in Atlanta.

Chapter 32

The days and the weeks of the fall semester passed quickly and in no time, it was Christmas break. The Marching Chiefs, the ROTC Band and my academic classes had kept me very busy. And Lou McGuire had kept me busy, too. It was becoming obvious that she was becoming more interested in me and less interested in school. She hated her classes. She began talking more and more about getting married. This talk of marriage only left me nervous and confused. In her mind when she got married, she would live happily ever after. In my mind when I got married, I would need to have a job to make enough money to responsibly take care my family. How could I do that if I was still a student in school? Lou was never worried about money, because that was never a problem for her. I was always worried about money because not having it had always been a problem for me.

"Look, Lou… We have to talk about something, I mean seriously…"

We were sitting in her car parked on the street outside of her dormitory, Dorman Hall. We had been to the drive-in restaurant downtown for a black cow, a celebratory root beer float, because classes had ended for the holidays. The next morning, she was driving to Apopka and I was driving to Jacksonville.

"Sure," Lou said. "What's wrong?"

"Nothing's wrong," I said. "It's just all this talk about getting married makes me nervous. Actually, it scares me." I was hoping she would somehow think this was funny and make this an easier conversation.

"So, are you trying to say you don't love me?" She asked.

So much for the attempted humor. Love was a strong word to me. It was something that was understood between family, and manifested through actions. It was seldom expressed verbally.

"No, you know that's not what I'm trying to say. What I'm trying to say is we are as different as…"

"Now, wait…" She tried to interrupt.

"No, let me finish. I came to Florida State to be Drum Major of the Marching Chiefs and then graduate from college so I could get a decent job and take care of myself and my family, if I ever had one. I did not come here to get married and trash the only dream I ever had. My dad has made incredible sacrifices, in fact, changed his whole life so I could stay in college. I cannot disappoint him now. And about us… Aside from being Baptists and students at Florida State, we are totally different. I don't smoke or drink. But, to be brutally honest, it's all about money. With my summer job and what I get from my dad, I can barely skimp together enough money to stay in school. There's no way I could support you and continue my education. And then there goes my future. What you're looking at here and now is all me of me there is. I have nothing but my future…"

"I hate this conversation," Lou said. "Now let me be brutally honest. I know exactly what I'm looking at, and that's all I want. I want you, and your dreams, and your future. And think about it, I might be more of your solution than your problem. If we were married you would never have to worry about money again. We could get our own place and I could get a job to pay the bills. You know I hate school anyway. Then, without worrying about money, you could put all your efforts and being Drum Major and graduating and getting that good job you talk about. And do us both a favor. Whatever hang-up you have about money and us, get over it. It's your problem and not our problem. And I do not want to ever talk about it again. Is that a deal?"

"Deal," I said, finally.

My mind was racing but my thoughts were muddled by the long kiss that followed which said good night, goodbye, Merry Christmas and Happy New Year.

Daddy and I were sitting in two unfinished wooden rocking chairs on the front porch of his second-story apartment on 9th Street in Jacksonville. We were relaxing before bedtime after a long day of turkey hunting, with no turkeys to show for it. The night air was cool and the city was quiet, except for the occasional car horn over on Main Street or the siren of an ambulance racing to St. Luke's hospital a few blocks south of us.

It was disappointing to me that Daddy and Dot were still on the outs about his commitment to support me going to college. Nonetheless, like most things, Daddy didn't want to talk about it. There were definitely some things I didn't want to talk about either, but I knew I couldn't put them off any longer.

"Daddy, there's something I want to talk to you about," I said.

"What's that?" He asked.

"Lou and I want to get married."

There, I said it. It was out there and there was no taking it back now. Daddy just sat there for the longest time looking straight ahead, saying nothing. From the glow of the streetlight, I could see something I'd never seen before, the glistening of tears forming in Daddy's eyes. I was dying inside because I knew I'd hurt him terribly.

"Did you ask her?" He finally asked.

"No, I wanted to talk to you first."

More dead silence, for what seemed like forever.

"I always wanted you to go to college." Daddy continued the slow rhythmical rocking of his chair and continued to stare straight ahead.

216

"That's what I want too, Daddy. More than anything. And getting married will not stop me from going to school or getting my degree or anything. In fact, it may make it easier. Lou doesn't want to continue in school, so she could get a job. Between what she would make and the money she already has, along with us living in student housing, we could get by."

"Her parents know about this?"

"No, sir. I wanted to try to do things the right way. I wanted to ask her dad, and who knows what he'll say. And I wanted to give Lou a ring, but I haven't figured out how I will do that yet."

"Well, Benny, if you're old enough to know what you want, you must be man enough to do it."

"Then you don't mind?" I asked.

"If you're old enough to know what you want, you must be man enough to do it."

I'm not exactly sure what Daddy meant, but what he said was good enough for me.

Sleep did not come easy for me that night. Things had definitely changed. Even though daddy was disappointed to hear his 19-year-old son wanted to get married, he stoically accepted the news. He was much more stoic than I was when he told me he was going to marry Dot. I learned something from all of this. In life, time marches on and change is inevitable. Accept it. Deal with it.

The next morning Daddy was up early and wanted to go fishing. Even though I could've slept much longer, I jumped out of bed and put on the same camouflage outfit I had worn on the hunting trip the day before. In the top of the closet, I noticed sitting there was my old coonskin hat, complete with a little face on the front and a long tail on the back. I had gotten it a few years back after Democratic vice-presidential candidate, Estes Kefauver, had worn one on the campaign trail in the presidential election of 1956. He and Adlai Stevenson lost to Eisenhower and Nixon, who were reelected for a second term. It was a chilly morning, so just for grins I donned the raccoon hat and away we went.

After wolfing down a quick breakfast at a diner out on N. Main St. we stopped by a bait and tackle shop out near Trout River to buy some dead shrimp to be used for bait. I found it interesting that they would dump the shrimp and a scoop of ice onto a stack of newspapers, roll the whole thing up like a giant tortilla, and you're good to go. Of course, the ice would melt and soak the paper, which would slowly come apart. If the fish were biting it wouldn't matter.

We continued driving north on Main Street and passed Imeson airport before turning west on a paved road, which led to a dirt road, which eventually led us to Cedar Creek. Daddy parked his sky blue '54 Chevrolet on a high bluff overlooking the creek. We grabbed our cane poles and the newspaper shrimp wrap and followed a narrow trail down the embankment towards the winding creek. The chill lingered in the morning air, making me glad that I had brought my furry raccoon friend to keep my head warm.

The trail led to Daddy's fishing spot, a small opening in the marsh grass beside a horseshoe bend in Cedar Creek. This land was part of a large estuary of Duval and Nassau County where the fresh water streams blended into creeks and rivers that eventually led to the Atlantic Ocean. There were tides and the water was brackish, a mixture of freshwater and saltwater. The species of fish were also mixed. You could catch the freshwater fish like bream or largemouth bass and at the same time catch saltwater fish like sheepshead, redfish or drum. We had a low, but incoming, tide. Perfect.

We started catching fish right away. Large copperhead bream. And then I caught a redfish, over a foot long. Within a half hour we had a large string of fish. I knew that later we would be having a fish fry at either Aunt Versie's, Aunt Tot's or Aunt Maude's house. Yummy.

We continued the great morning of father-son fishing. It had not gone unnoticed by me that, strangely, there's been no mention of our conversation from the night before. Finally, while in the midst of catching big copperhead brown, Daddy broke the ice.

218

"Benny," he said. "You remember what we were talking about last night?"

"Yes, sir." Do I remember? How could I forget? I had disappointed my dad and I'm sure in his mind all his hopes and dreams for my future were fading. I dreaded whatever it was he was about to say.

"I been thinking about what you said about trying to do the right thing…" He paused for the longest time, like he was still thinking. The suspense was killing me. "You know that piece of land up in Sneads?"

"Yes, sir."

"Remember we talked about Verdayne wanting to buy half of it, ten acres, from me? And you said that would be all right with you."

"Yes, sir." I had no idea where this was going.

"Well, as you know, I sold him the north ten acres, leaving the south ten acres for us. I say us, because it will be your's someday. The western four acres are thick with tall virgin pines. But the eastern six acres are different with scattered pines and a few scrub oaks. I been thinking I might want to clear those six acres and someday plant something. Maybe a pasture, or pecans or something. Why don't you go to Sneads and have somebody cut those scattered pines on the eastern acres for timber or paper wood. The money you get from that should be enough to buy a ring from Lou."

"Daddy… I don't know what to say…" Now, I was the one getting misty eyed. I bent over to reach down for a fish I was catching.

Pfsssst pow! Ziing pow! I heard gunfire and the sound of bullets from the rifle zing past my head and saw them splash into the creek below me. Instinctively I hit the dirt behind the marsh grass. Someone was shooting at us. Two shots.

"Hey! Don't shoot!" Daddy shouted up the hill. In an instant he jumped up, waving his hands, and began running up the trail towards the shooter. "What's wrong with you, you crazy sum'bitch!"

The next thing I heard was the sound of two car doors slamming and the motor revving up as a car sped away down the dirt road. Daddy stopped and turned around. Slowly, red-faced and out of breath, he walked back down towards the creek.

"Dumb sum'bitch," Daddy said, before I could say anything. "Don't know the difference between a coon and a coonskin cap and somebody fishin'."

"I know, Daddy," I said. "But what are you doing running up there? He had a gun."

"I was gonna take that gun and stick it where the sun don't shine."

And I think he would have, too.

Chapter 33

It was almost like I had a new lease on life. The coon hunters with the rifle had missed me and I had somehow found the courage to talk to Daddy about my future with Lou. After New Year's, 1960, I left Jacksonville a few days early to go to Sneads and quickly arranged to sell the selected timber on the parcel of land we were going to clear. I was afraid Daddy might change his mind. In keeping with Daddy's wishes, I did not say a word to anyone about the why's and wherefores regarding the reason we were cutting the timber. I certainly did not mention it to Lou.

A couple of weeks later a sizable check showed up in my mailbox at school. The next day I took a break while studying for semester finals to make a quick trip to Moon's Jewelers on N. Monroe St. I knew absolutely nothing about diamonds and was wary about being scammed, so I wanted to be sure to shop with a reputable dealer. My budget was the entire amount of the check. I wanted to give my best effort for Lou to have a ring she would not be embarrassed to show her friends. After looking at dozens and dozens of stones, I settled on a diamond that was a little larger than a half carat and graded high in clarity and color. I thought the solitary stone set in white gold was very nice. Regardless, I knew it was the best I could do.

Final exams were stressful, as always. Under any other circumstances a trip to Central Florida to spend a few days with Lou and her family unwinding would be welcomed. Not so much this time. The talk of marriage had intensified but I kept insisting to Lou that I wanted to do things the right way. That meant having a discussion with her parents. Now that would be stress. It seemed at this time everything was stressful for me:

having enough money to stay in school; Daddy splitting up with Dot; making grades to stay in school; upcoming drum major tryouts; taking Air Force qualification tests if I decided to go into advanced ROTC; whatever I would do with my life after school. Little things to worry about.

We arrived at the McGuire home on Dream Lake just in time for dinner. It was delicious, as usual. There was roast beef, chicken and all the vegetables you can imagine, topped off with red velvet cake and vanilla ice cream. I was starving from the trip so I forced my nervous stomach to take nourishment.

After the meal, while the help did the dishes and cleaned the kitchen, we all conveniently retired to the sunporch. I often wondered if Lou had set this up, because to me it looked almost like an ambush. Mr. McGuire sat in his customary seat, the swivel rocker in front of his desk at the end of the room, packing tobacco into his cherry-bowled pipe. Mrs. McGuire and Lou sat on a sofa at the other end of the room. I sat between them in what to me seemed like the witness chair. No one spoke. I felt like all eyes were on me, especially Lou's. I swallowed hard, several times. I'm sure sweat was beginning to glisten on my forehead. After several matches and a frenzy of huffing and puffing, Mr. McGuire finally had his pipe burning to his liking. Through the smoke I could see he had settled back into his chair with an air of indifference and the pipe hanging out of the corner of his mouth.

"The supper was delicious," I said.

"I'm glad you liked it," Mrs. McGuire said with a smile. Mr. McGuire nodded.

"Lou and I wanted to talk to y'all about something," I said. I knew if we carried on with the small talk I might chicken out. "As I'm sure you know, Lou and I have been spending a lot of time together at school and talking about our future and about how we'd like to get married and spend the rest of our lives together… and we would like to have your blessings."

Mr. McGuire gave a prolonged draw on his pipe and just sat there looking towards Lou and Mrs. McGuire.

222

"We've had a feeling something like this might be in the works," Mrs. McGuire said. "Of course, you have our blessings. We think you're a mighty fine young man."

"We just want Lou to be happy," Mr. McGuire said, finally. "We just want what's best for her."

"We will always support you in any way we can," Mrs. McGuire said. "But I want you to know that if there's ever a disagreement between you two, we will always be on Lou's side."

"Thank you, I'll try my best to never disappoint you." I didn't know what else to say.

Later that evening we made it official when I gave Lou the ring. She was shocked and genuinely surprised. She hurried to show it off to her parents, and then to her sister, Jean, who lived next door. Lou would never know the extraordinary measures and sacrifices that were required to make this ring materialize. It didn't seem to matter now, especially with all the excitement in the air. But I knew I was still just a poor country boy, plagued with naivety, trying to do things the right way. Whatever that was.

It was surprising how quickly the wedding plans were made. So much so that I suspected Lou and her mother had already made the plans and they were just now making me aware of them. It didn't matter to me because I knew I was just along for the ride. The date was set for the end of summer, August 20, 1960. I had told Lou I was already committed to the summer job in Jacksonville, which I needed for my tuition money for next year. That was fine with her because that would give her the whole summer to plan the event. And by then the renovations at the First Baptist Church would be complete. Lou wanted to be the first one married in the new sanctuary. I would have just as soon eloped to Georgia where you could get married by a justice of the peace in thirty minutes. That's what Verdayne and Minnie Lee did. Lou would not hear of it. She wanted the dress with the long train and the church and the parties and showers and pageantry, just like her sister, Jean. Even more so. I was beginning to detect a bit of a sibling rivalry between the two sisters. In truth, it wasn't really a rivalry at all, but jealousy on the part of Lou towards her beautiful older sister.

Chapter 34

It was a damp, foggy springtime Saturday morning in Tallahassee. I walked through the main doors of the Business Building and noticed a handmade posterboard sign that read, "AFOQT." I followed the directional arrow which led me to a large lecture hall where I would take the Air Force Officers Qualification Test. This was not a test you could study for, but to be accepted into Advanced ROTC, all applicants had to pass this test. This would pay me a small stipend for my junior and senior years, and pay for me to get my private pilot's license. Needless to say, I was apprehensive. The test lasted four hours long and was brutal. It would take a period of time to get the results, but I walked out of that room totally spent, and drained of any ideas that the Air Force might be in my future.

The days of the second semester flew by, but I never lost sight of my longtime goal. In the evenings after studying was done, I would walk down to the Marching Chief practice field and practice my moves. Alone, as always, and in the dark. I had watched Terry Johnson do an outstanding job as Drum Major for two years. I knew his every move. More than that I had the confidence I could do them. Especially with the Marching Chiefs behind me. Eventually, the notice of Drum Major tryouts was posted outside of Dr. Whitcomb's office. They would be held the afternoon of Saturday, May 21, 1960. Terry Johnson would be holding instructional classes for all candidates each Saturday for a month before tryouts. Wow. After all these years, game on.

"Cadet Maj. Shelfer, reporting Sir," I said. I was standing at strict attention at Major Goni's desk rendering a hand salute. I had been called to his office, so once again I naturally thought there was trouble.

"At ease, Cadet Maj.," Maj. Goni said, returning my salute. "Have a seat."

Reluctantly, I sat in the chair, trying desperately to get a read from the expression on Maj. Goni's face. It was a tough read. He could've been a poker player.

"A letter arrived in my in-basket this morning," Maj. Goni continued. "A very official letter from Air University Headquarters. The general who made favorable comments about what he observed on his official campus visit last month has taken his comments to a new level. Our ROTC band, your band, Cadet Maj. Shelfer, has been selected to represent all of Air Force ROTC nationwide during the Armed Forces Day celebration at Keesler Air Force Base, Mississippi. You and your band will board an Air Force plane at Tallahassee airport early Saturday morning, fly to Keesler and do the event, and then return to Tallahassee later that evening. It's a great honor, young man. What do you say to that?"

"I'm shocked. I don't know what to say." What I was really thinking was, wow! I'm going to get to go on my second airplane ride, ever. "The credit belongs to the musicians who march and play. I can't wait to tell them the good news. Thank you, Sir, for sticking up for the band and giving us this opportunity."

"No, thank you, young man. This one's on you. Here's a copy of the letter for you to read to your band." He handed me the copy and I began to rise to leave.

"Oh! There is another matter concerning you," he said. "Have you received the results of your AFOQT test?"

"No, Sir. I haven't." Suddenly I was experiencing the same sinking feeling I had when I walked out of the room after taking the test. Some of my friends had received their test scores and I was surprised at some who did not make the grade.

"I have the master list of the results right here." Maj. Goni opened his desk drawer and pulled out some papers. He ran his finger down the list of names. "Shelfer, Jr., Bennett Howard…qualified in all three categories; observer, navigator, and pilot. Congratulations again, young man. I hope this means we'll be seeing you in advanced ROTC next year."

"Yes, Sir. Those are my plans."

I tried not to appear too excited as I quickly saluted and exited Maj. Goni's office. I ran all the way back to the Kappa Sig house trying to digest all the good news I had heard. Somewhere, however, in the back of my mind, something didn't add up. I couldn't immediately figure out what it was.

As soon as I got back to my room, I read the letter again. And then it hit me. Like a ton of bricks. Armed Forces Day, the third Saturday in May, was May 21st. It was the exact same day as drum major tryouts. It could not have been worse. I was on top of the world at one minute and bitterly disappointed the next. What could I do? I couldn't be in both places at once. Maybe something could be changed. It was obvious that Armed Forces Day could not be rescheduled, so that only left me one choice. I had to talk to Dr. Whitcomb.

"Come in, Bennett. What's up?" Dr. Whitcomb asked.

"I have a problem I'd like to talk to you about, Sir."

"Sure, have a seat," he said.

"I'm not sure that you know, but I'm Commandant of the Air Force ROTC Band."

"Of course, I know that, Bennett. Good job with that, by the way. I'm hearing good things about that band this year."

"Thank you, Sir. But the problem is…" I really didn't know what to say, so I just handed him the letter from Air Force. "Here, Sir. Please read this."

Dr. Whitcomb scanned the letter, nodding approval.

"That's great news, Bennett. Congratulations, but what's the problem?"

"The problem is the date," I said.

"Oh! I see," he said. He was now pointing to the date of May 21, 1960, in the text of the letter. "The same date as Drum Major tryouts…" He glanced up at me, then back to the letter. He placed the letter in front of me and looked at me again. "Bennett, I'm not sure what you're asking about here, but there's no way I can change the date of Drum Major tryouts. The date has been on the school calendar all year long and it's been posted on the bulletin board for some time now. It would not be fair to the other applicants to change the date now."

"I understand, Sir. Thank you."

"Life is a constant series of choices, Bennett," Dr. Whitcomb said.

"Yes, it is. Thank you, Sir." I picked up the letter and with as much of a smile as I could muster, I slowly walked out of his office.

Life may be a constant series of choices, but there are consequences to the choices you make. Nonetheless, this was an easy choice for me. And I was prepared to live with the consequences. Now, I just had to do as much damage control as possible. On the way back to Maj. Goni's office, I stopped by the Lambda Chi house and talked to a friend.

"Maj. Goni, I have a personal problem, but I also have a solution," I said. I was seated in the chair beside Maj. Goni's desk after the obligatory reporting, saluting and sitting ritual.

"Tell, me young man. What's the problem?"

227

"It's a long story, Sir. But, the short of it is for many years I've only had one goal in life, and that is to be Drum Major of the Marching Chiefs. It's the very reason I came to Florida State. And after being so excited about our band being selected to participate in the Armed Forces Day celebration, I find out is on the exact same day as Drum Major tryouts."

"I see… I see your problem," Maj. Goni said. Maybe they could change the dates of Drum Major tryouts."

"I have already tried that. Dr. Whitcomb wouldn't consider it…something about the school calendar."

"You said you have a solution."

"Yes, Sir, I do. With your approval, I have asked Cadet Col. Bob Reely to stand in for me as Band Commandant for the trip. He's a senior music major and would be perfect for the job."

"Reely, the Wing Commander?"

"Yes, Sir. The highest-ranking cadet in Air Force ROTC."

"I guess we can't do much better than that. I approve. I'm sorry you will not be able to make the trip. Good luck with the tryouts."

"Thank you, Sir, for your understanding."

Maj. Goni extended his hand and we shook. I departed his office with a great sense of relief and a renewed focus on what I knew would be my one chance in a lifetime.

Saturday, May 21, 1960, came quickly. After a night of apprehensive insomnia, I made an early trip to the ROTC building to be there when the band departed for the airport and the flight to Biloxi. And I wanted to thank Bob Reely for coming to my rescue. The guys were excited and it looked like some of them had even shined their shoes.

The Marching Chief's practice field to the South of the Geology building near the Student Center was beginning to fill with Chiefs, who were there to support the Drum Major tryouts. I sat in the car and listened to the inevitable noodling that was always present when musicians gathered to practice or perform. My mind wandered back in time to the first time I saw the Chiefs, when Uncle Verdayne brought me to the football game. I was mesmerized by the sound of the band and the showmanship of Drum Major Dick Mayo and a dream was born. I thought about how Aunt Versie bought my French horn. I thought about the early days of the Sneads High School Band. I thought about the countless hours of practicing in the dark, alone with my shadow. All for this moment. I saw Dr. Whitcomb, Brownie and Charlie walking towards the tower across the field. I knew the moment had arrived.

There were only two other drum major candidates. They were both music majors and very capable, accomplished musicians. We picked numbers from a hat and I drew number 3, the last to go. The format was set. There was a different piece of music we would each have to sight conduct, then do a basic pregame show.

It was a bit of a worry to me that the previous drum majors, Dick Mayo, Tony Swain, and Terry Johnson, had all been music majors. The fact that my major was "undecided" could not have been a feather in my cap. I was also not as tall as the previous Drum Majors, except for Dick Mayo. I was almost 5' 9" with socks on.

The other two candidates completed their routines and did a good job. Dr. Whitcomb handed me his conducting baton and the conductor's score that I was to sight conduct. The Chiefs were assembled on the sideline between the podium and the end zone. I glanced at the new piece of music while I walked down in front of them. It was one of Charlie's new arrangements and I was relieved to see that it was straightforward as far as conducting was concerned. I brought the baton down to begin the music and it was magic. I had conducted the Sneads High School Band for four years and then the ROTC band, but this was different. This was a Charlie Carter arrangement being played by the Marching Chiefs. As good as it gets. I was relieved to get through the piece without any glaring mistakes.

With the drum major mace, the same baton Terry Johnson used, I headed for the end zone. Dr. Whitcomb gave a signal from the tower and it was showtime. I strutted from the end zone to the 20-yard line with knees high and toes pointed with my back almost parallel to the ground. Max adrenaline. After a snappy leg kick about-face, I brought the baton down on the magnificent fanfare, grander than what you would see at the beginning of a 20th Century Fox movie. I had practiced this hundreds of times, but now I was hearing the Marching Chiefs in my ears and not in my mind. Surreal. I conducted the intro to the Fight Song and after another snappy about-face surged into the air doing the conductor's strut leading the band downfield. I was trying to use all my athleticism, wondering if I was maintaining good form. Then I saw it. The afternoon sun was casting a long shadow beside me, like an old friend, giving me encouragement to keep doing what I was doing.

The remainder of the routine was a blur. I conducted the Star-Spangled Banner and then left the field doing the overhand reverse strut to the Garnet and Gold March. It was over. In an instant, years of dreaming and practicing was over. Many of the Chiefs approached me, saying "nice job." I was satisfied I had given it my best effort. Now the waiting game would start until a decision would be announced. Dr. Whitcomb, Brownie, Charlie and Terry Johnson were still chatting in the tower. Dr. Whitcomb was the first of them down the ladder.

"Bennett, you are our next Drum Major," Dr. Whitcomb said. He stepped towards me and extended his hand.

"Thank you, Sir," I said. I shook his hand in total shock. "I know I have some big shoes to fill." I didn't know what else to say.

"I expect you will make them bigger," he said. And then, with a little smile, he walked away. That simple little sentence told me that in his mind I was Drum Major of the Marching Chiefs and he expected me to own that position and be the best that I could be.

Chapter 35

"Have a seat, Mr. Shelfer," my faculty advisor said. "How are you?"

"I'm doing well, thank you," I said.

"That's good to hear. And how is that short term goal coming?" He chuckled softly.

"Actually, very well. I'm the new Drum Major of the Marching Chiefs."

"No kidding. Congratulations. But, have you decided on an academic major?"

"Not really."

"Well, I hate to tell you, but today is the day. When you walk out of this office, you must have decided on a major. We have to schedule the classes for your junior year. Any ideas?"

"I qualified for Advanced ROTC, so I would like to try that for a semester."

"That's a start. Are you thinking about going into the Air Force?"

"I'm thinking more about the stipend they pay you to go to school, and them paying for me to get my private pilot's license." Actually, now that I was going to be married, I was beginning to think that the pay and benefits of an Air Force officer sounded pretty good.

"There is that," he said. "But ROTC is not an academic major. Let's take Air Force out the equation. Aside from music, is there anything you love to do?"

"I love sports, most all sports." I answered with a quickness and conviction that surprised me.

"Why not major in sports? You could get a degree in physical education. You would learn to play and teach all sports. After you graduate, you'd never have to worry about a job, because teachers are always in demand."

"Sounds like fun. Let's do that," I said. Now that I was planning to get married, I knew I had to graduate from college and get a job with a steady income to provide for my family. Being a teacher and a coach would accomplish that. Good enough for me.

"Very well, Mr. Shelfer," he said. "I'll set your schedule. And I look forward to seeing you on the football field with the Marching Chiefs this fall."

"Thank you, Sir," I said. I walked out of his office with purpose and the satisfaction of knowing my new direction would take me to a job that I would love.

"Dr. Whitcomb, you wanted to see me?" I had gently knocked on the open door of Dr. Whitcomb's office where he was sitting at his desk.

"Yes, Bennett. Come in, have a seat," Dr. Whitcomb said. He motioned towards the chair beside his desk. "Congratulations, again, on being our new Drum Major."

"Thank you, Sir. I can't wait to get started."

"Brownie and I have done most of the planning for next year's shows and Charlie's already working on the music. We would like you to join us for the blocking and charting sessions whenever you can."

"Yes Sir, I'd be happy to. Just let me know."

"Good. Now let me tell you the good news for you. I was able to set aside in next year's budget enough money for you to get a new uniform. And not just any uniform. I want you to have a uniform comparable to any Big 10 Drum Major, including the Ohio State Drum Major. Look at the picture this catalog. What you think about that?" He proudly pushed the opened catalog across his desk to where I was sitting.

It was impossible to hide the look of shock on my face. It was obvious that Dr. Whitcomb, who was instrumental in the development of the great band Ohio State University, wanted my role as Drum Major to mirror the one from Ohio State. I stared at the picture in the catalog…the long heavy coat with tails, the riding britches, and the knee-high, black leather boots. I was crestfallen. My mind was racing to the images I had embedded in my mind of my idols, the previous Florida State Drum Majors, Dick Mayo, Tony Swain, and Terry Johnson. They wore sleek, usually white, outfits with a golden Seminole chief emblazoned on a garnet chest plate, with white shoes. None of them wore heavy coats, black boots and riding britches. And I didn't want to wear them either. But, what could I do? I didn't want to appear to be uncooperative in my first meeting with Dr. Whitcomb.

"Dr. Whitcomb, I don't know what to say," I said.

"What do you mean?" He asked. The tenor of his voice had definitely changed.

"I don't have to have a new uniform. In fact, I don't want a new uniform."

"Bennett, why would you not want to be like an Ohio State Drum Major?"

233

"With all due respect, Sir, first of all, most of our games are played in warm, if not hot, weather. It would be beastly hot to wear a uniform like that in the South."

"Hmmm…" Dr. Whitcomb uttered, considering the point.

"Another problem is the boots. I've never seen a Big 10 Drum Major, but I can't imagine being able to strut all the way down the field, like we do here in the Chiefs, wearing heavy boots. It would be difficult to get off the ground and I couldn't even point my toes. That would be a totally different style." I didn't tell him that I had never wanted to wear a uniform with tails because I thought it made me look short.

Dr. Whitcomb had leaned back in his chair with his hand stroking his chin, staring at the picture in the catalog, and then at me. I thought he would never speak again and then I dreaded what he would say.

"I'm not sure what the answer is here, Bennett. Terry's uniform would never fit you," he said.

I was relieved to hear him mention Terry's uniform. That made it easy for me because I had never expected a new uniform anyway.

"Actually, it would, Sir. I've already thought about it. Except for the length of the sleeves and the legs, Terry and I are pretty much the same size. I could take the uniform with me to Jacksonville. I know a place that is very good at alterations. When I come back in the fall it would fit me perfectly and look like a new uniform. Look at the money you would save, Dr. Whitcomb."

"You drive a hard bargain, Bennett." Dr. Whitcomb closed the catalog and stuffed it back it in his desk drawer. "Stop by the wardrobe room and pick up the uniform. Have a great summer, and a great wedding, by the way. See you in the fall." He extended his hand.

"Thank you, sir, for everything." I shook his hand and walked out of his office relieved. He had never mentioned anything about me getting married before, and I was glad he was okay with that. I was also glad that my vision of being drum major of the Marching Chiefs would not be changed by a uniform. It would be as I had always dreamed.

"Hello."

"Hello this is the long-distance operator and I have a collect call for anyone from Benny. Will you accept the charges?"

"Yes, I will," Daddy said.

"Thank you. Go ahead, Sir," the operator said.

"Hey, Daddy. How are you?" I asked.

"I'm doing good. How are you doing?" Daddy asked. I was able to hear what Daddy was saying despite the constant tingling static on the long-distance line.

"Real good, Daddy. I'm the new Drum Major of the Marching Chiefs."

"That's good, Benny. That's real good."

"Thank you, Sir. And I wanted to let you know I'll be coming home next week to start my summer job with the engineering department. Is that okay?"

"That's good. They're already talking about you coming. And I have some news for you. When you get back into town, just go to the house on Brackland Street. I'm going back with Dot. I hope that's okay with you," Daddy said.

"Of course, Daddy. I want you to do whatever you want to do. Don't worry about me. I'll be just fine."

What Daddy couldn't discern over the phone was the huge sigh of relief from me. I had never wanted him to live alone. And I certainly didn't want to be the reason he lived alone. I had told him that next year he would not have to send me any money for college. I would be married, and with Lou working, along with my ROTC stipend, I could get by just fine. And now it would be even better because I would get a stipend for being Drum Major. So, with the major bone of contention between them eliminated, maybe Dot and Daddy could get along.

Chapter 36

The summer of 1960 passed quickly. I felt like I was just along for the ride. Life was happening. I had no idea what the future was bringing, but it was coming at me at the speed of light.

The drama on Brackland Street had waned. Daddy and Dot's reconciliation seemed to be going well. Daddy didn't seem to be drinking quite as much. That was probably the reason for the calmer waters. Joyce and John A., the son of Dot's best friend, were inseparable, so she wasn't around very much. Tony wasn't around very much either. He was too busy looking for trouble, and unfortunately finding it.

My summer job with the engineering department was a great experience. Even though it only paid a dollar an hour, it was very rewarding working with professionals who made it fun to be at work. It was a little sad knowing that after four summers, this would be my last one working with them. I had learned a lot being part of a survey crew, and not only about setting the line and grade for sewer and drainage pipes. I also learned my dad was held in high esteem among his peers. He was given the most difficult and challenging projects and Daddy and his crew made it look easy. He always took care of business. There was something else that did not go unnoticed by me. Daddy never, ever, took a drink while he was on the job.

In an effort to augment my summer income, once again I was an umpire for Little League baseball. I asked for as many assignments as possible to earn the five dollars they paid for each game. I would get off work at 4:30 in the afternoon and then race to somewhere in the county to umpire a ballgame. I loved baseball and of course tried to do the best possible. My efforts did not go unnoticed. My last assignment was to umpire the city championship game. After the game was over, I took off my mask and started walking towards my car knowing I had umpired my last game. A gentleman who had been watching the game approached me and introduced himself as a scout for the Yankees. He said he was impressed with the job I did and asked me if I had ever considered being a professional umpire. He said he would be happy to sponsor me to attend umpire's school to get me into the system that could lead to being a major league umpire. I was caught by complete surprise. Although I was very flattered, I told him I was not interested. All I knew for sure was at this particular moment my plate was full. I was about to get married and be Drum Major of the Marching Chiefs.

On a few occasions I worked the games for the Glenlea team, which Uncle Shine (Angus Shelfer) coached. It always seemed a little contentious to me. Nonetheless, he always treated me with great respect, even though I'm sure he disagreed with some of my calls, especially when I called one of my first cousins out on a called third strike. Uncle Shine was a great man.

Gordon Shelfer was three years younger than me and Uncle Shine's oldest of five sons. He was in the band at Englewood High School and asked me to help him train to be Drum Major. On many occasions we trained in his backyard. He was very disciplined, worked hard, and became Drum Major of his high school band. I was thinking how nice it would be if he would follow me to Florida State and there could be another Shelfer as Drum Major of the Marching Chiefs.

The wedding was Saturday, August 20, 1960. It was everything that Lou and her mother had wanted it to be. More than 150 guests filled the newly renovated sanctuary at the First Baptist Church of Apopka, Florida. Dr. Findley Edge, the renowned minister from the Southern Baptist Seminary in Louisville Kentucky, presided. Lou's sister, Jean Henry, was the maid of honor. Maury Wishnoff, one of my best friends from high school, was the best man. It was convenient for him because one of his aunts lived in Eustis, Florida, a small town nearby.

Lou was lovely walking down the aisle on the arm of Mr. McGuire.

I only had one request for the ceremony. I wanted Mr. John Jamieson, one of my band directors from high school, to sing "The Lord's Prayer." Lou and Mrs. McGuire, especially Mrs. McGuire, were lukewarm to the idea. They finally caved and allowed it in the program when I told them there's no such thing as a bad rendition of a sincere effort to sing "The Lord's Prayer." Mr. Jamieson, who was now the band director at nearby Kissimmee High School, was a man of small stature, about the size of a professional race horse jockey. He had a booming voice with incredible phrasing…the kind of voice that when you hear it, you must stop whatever you're doing and look to see where it's coming from. By the time he had finished singing the first line, "Our father, which art in heaven," Mrs. McGuire was lost in the music. She looked at me and nodded with a smile of satisfaction.

My side of the family was represented by Daddy and Dot and Uncle Bud and Aunt Ruth, the brother-sister couples, along with Aunt Versie and Uncle Larry. The reception was held at the McGuire home on Dream Lake. There was no music or dancing at the event, and of course no alcohol was permitted. That rule provided a little spark of drama to the occasion when the always mischievous Uncle Bud started a rumor among the groomsmen, much to their delight, that he was going to spike the punch bowl. The rumor spread quickly to the bridesmaids and then to Lou.

"Did you hear anything about your Uncle Bud spiking the punch bowl?" Lou asked me.

"No, but I wouldn't put it past him," I said.

"I wish he would," Lou said. And I could tell from the twinkle in her eye that she meant it.

There were lots of food and punch, sweet tea, soft drinks and coffee. And a huge cake. Mercifully, the time passed quickly. We tossed the garter, cut the cake, and made a timely departure around 10:30 pm to begin a new life.

The honeymoon began about 30 minutes up the road at the Holiday Inn in Ocala. The next morning, we drove to a motel on Panama City Beach for a five-day getaway. There was a slow-moving tropical depression in the

Gulf that poured incessant monsoon rains on the Florida Gulf Coast and kept us pinned in our motel room for almost the entire time. What a shame.

Chapter 37

This was the moment I had been waiting for over half my life. September 17, 1960. The Seminoles were about to play the Richmond Spiders. The pregame warm-ups were finished and the teams had left the field. The Marching Chiefs were in formation in the north end zone, covering the field from sideline to sideline. The opening-day crowd was buzzing with excitement. I strutted through the center of the formation out to the 20-yard line, performed a snappy about face and brought the baton down on a new majestic opening fanfare that Charlie Carter had written. The feeling that came over me was indescribable.

"The Florida State University School of Music presents Drum Major Bennett Shelfer and the Florida State University Marching Chiefs," the booming voice on the PA said. Was this a dream?

After four quick whistles I directed the intro to the Fight Song and did another snappy about-face and strutted down the field leading the Chiefs and Penny McArthur and the eight majorettes into the pregame routine.

It was a moment of surreal redemption. Suddenly, it was all worthwhile. The countless hours of learning to play the French horn, learning to march, and learning to conduct, had led to this moment. The years spent alone in the darkness with only my shadow, learning to strut like former Drum Majors Dick Mayo, Tony Swain, and Terry Johnson had led to this moment. And now, to be the fourth Drum Major of Dr. Whitcomb's Marching Chiefs, directing these incredible musicians with the incomparable sound of Charlie Carter's arrangements, was a thrill of a lifetime. It was a dream. And it had come true.

The completion of Alumni Village, the new married student's housing development a couple of miles south of the stadium, had been delayed a few months. Lou and I had signed up for a new two-bedroom one bath apartment. The price was right, about $60 a month. We were told we would be able to put an air-conditioning unit in the window. In the meantime, Lou spotted a new one-bedroom apartment building just completed on Park Avenue, about two blocks from the music building. Even though it was very pricey, over $200 a month, Lou wanted to live there because it was new. She said we could afford it until our place in Alumni Village was ready. I guess we could, but to me, that was a lot of money.

What a difference a few months make. In the late spring I was a penny-counting sophomore chasing a secret dream of being Drum Major, without a clue about what I wanted for a major in college. Neither did I have any concrete ideas or aspirations about a career. Now, I was living my dream as Drum Major of the Chiefs and as a married man with a young bride always waiting for me in a nearby brand-new air-conditioned apartment. My perspective on the future was coming into focus. I knew I had to graduate from college. It was like a square that must be filled. With a college degree in my newly chosen major of physical education, I could get a job and make a living being a teacher and a coach. I would love that.

One thing I had not really thought about was how much fun it would be to be a physical education major. The core classes of the major consisted basically of the coaching of everything. I had to learn to teach and play each and every sport. I had always thought I was a real jock, but I soon learned I didn't know very much at all about sports. Even in the sports of baseball and basketball which I played in high school, I only had participatory knowledge. It was even more interesting taking the courses from instructors who were the current head coach or had been a head coach of that sport.

Danny Litwhiler, the baseball coach of the Seminoles, taught the coaching of baseball. He was a journeyman outfielder in the major leagues for 11 years, playing for the Phillies, Cardinals, Braves and the Reds. He

242

was the first player in the majors to play an entire season without making an error. He was also the first player to stitch the fingers of his baseball glove together. He was a sidesplitting storyteller. He kept us laughing throughout his classes with some yarn from his past. In the meantime, we learned a lot about baseball from someone who had played it and coached it at the highest levels. He would go on to invent Diamond Grit, a substance used to dry baseball fields after a rain. He also invented the use of the radar gun, the Jugs Gun, for timing pitches, which revolutionized the assessment of pitchers in baseball.

Our football instructor was Dr. Don Veller, the former and first full-time head football coach of the Seminoles. I had watched a few high school games and had seen the Seminole home games with the Chiefs for two years, but I really didn't know much about football. The terminology and the different offensive and defensive plays and formations were difficult at first. Dr. Don, as we called him, was a soft-spoken man and a very patient instructor for those of us who had never played football. He stressed the importance of teaching the basics of blocking and tackling. Old school football. Trick plays or even the forward pass, not so important. One interesting assignment he gave us was to scout local high school football teams on Friday nights. I learned a lot about football from watching a team of complete strangers, then filling out a scouting report and presenting it to Dr. Don. That being said, I probably always learned more about those Friday night bands than I did the football team.

Volleyball was a sport I knew very little about, even though I had always enjoyed batting the ball around. Bill Odeneal changed all that the moment I walked into his class, the coaching of volleyball. He was a pioneer of the sport, and at Florida State he became the first full-time volleyball coach in the history of the NCAA. Under his leadership, the Seminoles had won three National NCAA Championships in volleyball. Then, due to lack of funding, they disbanded the team. Coach Odeneal was naturally disappointed by that, but it never diminished his enthusiasm for the game. We spent more time on the court than we did in the classroom. Even though at 5'9" I was vertically challenged, I learned this was a sport I could play well. I could spike the ball off either side, but because of my quickness and good hands I was a really good setter. I loved volleyball.

With no volleyball team to coach, Bill Odeneal became the golf coach. I was glad to learn that he would be teaching us the coaching of golf. I really enjoyed the class, but regardless of how rudimentary Coach Odeneal presented the basics of the swing for us, it was difficult for me. It was a crazy sport where quickness and strength didn't help very much. Enjoyed it. Difficult. I soon learned that was all I needed to know about golf. The class practiced and played at the little nine-hole par three course on the backside of Doak Campbell Stadium. One early morning on one of those short holes, with the dew still covering the grass, I swung my nine iron, fast and hard, as I was known to do. I skulled the ball along the wet grass. I watched the rooster tail from the dew spewing up from the back of the ball go as straight as a chalk line to the hole. It went in. I chuckled and thought maybe this game wasn't so hard after all. A fleeting thought.

Wrestling was also entirely new to me. My only experience with wrestling was in an occasional playground scuffle, back in the day. It was a sport where, unlike golf, quickness and strength was vitally important. I was exceptionally fast, but not so strong. Size was also important. Best to be bigger. Consequently, you always wanted to be at the upper limit of your weight division. It was interesting to see the lengths of fasting and dehydrating wrestlers would endure to lose enough weight to drop down into the top of a weight division. I made it through the class, even though it wasn't my favorite and I never enjoyed it.

There were other sports that I had never played that weren't my favorites, either. Gymnastics was strange and difficult for me. Sneads High School's gymnasium was only for basketball. I'd never seen a pommel horse, balance beam, parallel bar or still rings before. I soon discovered my body build was not the best for these sports. Because of years of marching and strutting in the band, my legs were strong, whereas my upper body strength, not so much. Most of my weight was also in my lower body. It was difficult for someone with lesser upper body strength to perform most gymnastic events to any degree of skill level. Yet I tried, and filled another square.

Badminton was fun, and much more vigorous than I had ever thought. The same with handball and paddleball. Soccer, as far as I could see, was a complete waste of time. Fortunately, I was in really good

244

condition, so I could run with the other majors, most of whom had played the sport. They could kick and control the ball. I struggled doing that.

Swimming was another tester for me. Swim Coach Bim Stults thought we should be able to swim like his scholarship boys. The only swim stroke I had ever done was the freestyle. Jungle freestyle would probably be a better name for it. I had to refine that stroke to get through the class, as well as learn the breast, back and butterfly strokes. Our final exam consisted of a written test as well as a performance test. The last part of the performance part was sea survival, which required us to jump into the pool and not touch the bottom or the sides of the pool for an hour and a half. I accomplished something that day I would have never thought possible. I survived the ninety minutes in the water without drowning. And in doing so, I permanently embedded in my mind the techniques of sea survival…kick, pull and breathe, kick and float. Repeat, for as long as necessary.

Tennis was another of those foreign sports to me. We had no tennis courts in Sneads, and probably not in Jackson County. In my mind, tennis was a hoity-toity activity undertaken by the country club set who just wanted to flit around in their white outfits. Nonetheless, it was required as part of my major. So, there I was, in my white shorts and shirt, on the red clay courts behind Tully Gym, learning how to teach tennis. It was the first time I ever touched a tennis racket. To my amazement, it was really fun. Speed and quickness. Yes, finally. Mrs. Martin-Vege, a former varsity tennis coach, was our instructor. She taught us the rules and etiquette of the game, along with the basic strokes; namely, the forehand, backhand, volley, overhead and serve. It was difficult for me to learn to volley, but my real shortcoming was my backhand. Finally, out of frustration, I reverted back to my baseball experience and placed both hands on the racket for my backhand. I batted a baseball right-handed, so my tennis left-handed backhand was perfect for that. I thought a two-hand backhand might be cheating, but Mrs. Martin-Vege said while the stroke was very unusual, it was certainly legal. In a short period of time, I went from having no backhand at all to having a backhand as a weapon. At the end of the class Mrs. Martin-Vege asked me to be her partner in a mixed doubles faculty-student tournament. We didn't win it, but I had so much fun and had found a new sport I loved.

Chapter 38

By the end of the first semester our new two-bedroom apartment in Alumni Village, the new married student's housing project, was ready for us. Not a bit too soon either, because we were going to need an extra bedroom. Lou was pregnant with our first child. She was very happy. I was very scared.

For Lou, being pregnant meant there would be no pressure for her to go find a job. She would be too busy with shopping for new maternity clothes, baby showers, etc. And she would have to go to the doctor every month. Lou, like her parents, seemed obsessed with going to the doctor. Then there would be the doctor's orders she would have to follow…the doctor said this or the doctor said that. I suppose the doctor never told her she shouldn't be smoking or drinking while she was pregnant. She had smoked since I had known her, but since the wedding she began developing an affinity for cocktails such as an Old-fashioned or Singapore Sling.

For me, Lou being pregnant meant that I would be a father. And with that came all the promises I had made to myself during my childhood. I had seen disappointment and had endured disappointment. I vowed I would do my best to bear whatever responsibility was required to always be there for my kids and earn the title, "Daddy." In my mind I was halfway there because I'd never tasted a drop of alcohol. All I had to do now was graduate from college and get a job.

The routine and stability of married life agreed with me. I seemed to have more time for everything. I devoted all the time necessary to being Drum Major of the Marching Chiefs. It was the thrill of a lifetime I had always thought it would be. I had plenty of time to study and progressed quickly from struggling to make my grades to the Dean's list. I even had time for a few fraternity activities, including intramurals. This turned out to be quite painful because I dislocated my right shoulder twice. The first time was wrestling, and then again diving for a ball playing volleyball. Each time my right arm was in a sling for several weeks. It didn't really bother me in class because I could take notes with my left hand, just as I did in the second grade before Mrs. Ivey made me write right-handed.

Frank Blount, one of my favorite Kappa Sig brothers who was in the Air Force ROTC program, had graduated and gone on to pilot training in the Air Force. His girlfriend was still in Tallahassee, so Frank had flown an AT-6 trainer into Dale Mabry field for a weekend visit. He knew I was in advanced ROTC so he offered to take me for a ride. I had only been on an airplane once before, my National Airlines flight to visit Lou, so I jumped at the chance. I loved it. We took off late in the evening on a clear night and for about half an hour flew all around the area having fun, mostly doing aerobatics over downtown Tallahassee. Frank let me fly the plane. What a thrill. I was impressed with Frank's professionalism and attention to detail. It got me thinking…

It was the first day of summer session 1961. It was an easy decision for us to stay in Tallahassee for the summer between my junior and senior year. Lou was expected to deliver our first child in mid-July and it didn't make sense to be traveling around that time. Knowing this, I had decided to take the coaching of basketball under head basketball coach, Bud Kennedy, during the summer. This would lighten my course load in the fall so I could have more time to help with the new baby and do my best job as Drum Major of the Chiefs. Now, myself and three other physical education majors, were reporting to Coach Kennedy's office for class.

"Come in, gentlemen," Coach Kennedy said. "It's good to see you." He gave us each a warm greeting at a firm handshake. "I thought with the size of the class we would be more comfortable here in my office." He nodded to another gentleman in the office with him. "This is Coach Elmer McCall, he's a head basketball coach from a college up in Indiana and he'll be joining us this summer." We introduced ourselves to Elmer and sat in a circle of chairs around Coach Kennedy's desk.

"You are all my students, but first and foremost you're all my friends," Coach said. "It's good that there are five of you. That gives us a chance to run some plays and get a good feel for the offense. Be sure and wear basketball shoes to class because we will be spending a lot of time on the court."

"And another thing," Coach continued, "a matter of housekeeping. You will take no tests in this class. No pop quizzes, no final exams, no papers to write. But you will learn a lot about the game of basketball. Your grades have already been assigned. Elmer will get an A because he is a head basketball coach. Everyone else will get a B." He looked around at us as we glanced at each other, then his eyes focused on me. "Bennett, you will get a B unless you show up for class when your wife is in the hospital having that new baby, then you will get an F. Family is more important than a bunch of hard-legs sitting around talking about basketball. Understood?" He was still looking at me.

"Yes, Sir. Thank you," I said. Needless to say, I was astounded, even though I didn't like the fact that I couldn't earn an A. I had met Coach before and had seen him around the building. He knew I conducted the pep band for basketball games, but I had no idea he knew anything about my personal life.

Coach Kennedy loved basketball probably as much as I loved the Marching Chiefs. He had a unique pedigree for the game. He was born in Lawrence, Kansas, where his father was the head football coach for the only undefeated football team for the University of Kansas. Coach was an athlete at Kansas and became a personal friend of the inventor of the game of basketball, Dr. James Naismith, who was a physical education teacher there. After a stint in the Navy during World War II, coach ended up at Florida State as an assistant basketball coach in 1948. He became head coach the following year and began building a very successful program for the Seminoles.

We learned the basics of the offense coach was running at the time, namely the weave and what he called the Auburn shuffle. The shuffle was a fast high-low pick and roll offense that allowed for easy screens for an outside shot or an open cutter to the basket. Fun to run.

"Coach, tell us about your trip to Kentucky last year," I said during one of the classes. We loved to hear him talk about basketball.

"That was really something," he said, smiling. Then suddenly he was almost emotional. "To take this scrappy band of Seminoles into Lexington and beat the team of last year's national coach of the year, Adolph Rupp, was, without a doubt, a personal highlight for me. Especially because Adolph was a mentor and a friend of mine since the days when I watched him play for the Kansas Jayhawks back when I was a kid in Lawrence, Kansas. Since then, he's become a legend of the game."

"He probably didn't like taking a whippin' on his home court," one of the guys said.

"Probably not, but win or lose he is always very gracious to me. We're close friends. In fact, he had me to his home for dinner while we were there and we talked basketball into the wee hours. I'll tell you boys something, just between us. The game of basketball is about to change, and change quickly, because of one thing. Integration. It's coming soon, and it's a good thing. It's the right thing to do. As soon as Adolph can find him a Negro seven-footer that can handle a basketball, the color barrier will be broken in the South. The offense will then gravitate towards more of a basic run and shoot strategy and less planned patterns, strictly because of the incredible athletic ability of the Negro athletes. It will be different, but it'll be fun."

Five years after that unique summertime class with Coach Bud Kennedy, it was he, not Adolph Rupp, who broke the color barrier in college basketball of any predominantly white university in the South. Coach Kennedy recruited Lenny Hall to be the first black basketball player to play for him at Florida State. Sadly, he would never get to see him play. Coach Bud Kennedy died of cancer at age 59.

And, let it be known that Coach Kennedy did not give me an F in the coaching of basketball. I did not attend class in the second week of July, 1961.

Chapter 39

The summer of '61 began very slowly. After final exams there were several weeks before my basketball class would begin. The only excitement would be the occasional premature contraction, just to keep our attention. Most of the time was spent sitting around discussing possible names for a boy or a girl. Lou was insistent that if it was a boy, we would name him after me, the third, because I was a junior. For a girl's name, I loved Angela, because I wanted to call her Angel. Lou wanted a namesake for her sister, Jean, but vacillated among other names as well. We had long ago converted the second bedroom into a nursery for the baby. The crib and the changing table were brand-new, resplendent in gender neutral colors of yellow and green.

It was driving me crazy sitting around the apartment feeling useless and nonproductive, so I began checking the help-wanted ads in the newspaper. With my summer class and the baby coming I couldn't take a job with regular hours, so I answered an ad for sales of Watkins products. Watkins was very similar to Fuller Brush. I was familiar with the product line because Grandmother used them back in Sneads. She particularly liked the black pepper and the vanilla extract. I began working methodically, going door-to-door in the Tallahassee neighborhoods west of the campus. I discovered I was an okay salesman and soon felt very good about making some extra money and contributing, albeit modestly, to the budget of our growing family.

"Mr. Shelfer?" The older gentleman in the surgical scrubs asked. I nodded. It was obvious I was startled when he opened the door to the room in Tallahassee Memorial Hospital where I'd been waiting for over an hour and a half.

"I'm Dr. Dussia," he said. He extended his hand. "Congratulations, you have a beautiful baby girl."

"Thank you, Sir," I said, holding on to his firm handshake. "Thank you very much."

"Mother and baby are doing fine, no complications at all."

"Can I see them?" I asked.

"Your wife is in recovery, so it might be an hour or two for her, but you can get a peek at your baby if you like." Dr. Dussia motioned for me to follow him.

There's nothing like the sound of a newborn baby's cry. In this case the newborn baby was screaming. I heard her long before I saw her. Dr. Dussia pointed behind the plate glass window of the nursery to where a nurse was scrubbing a very unhappy baby. She had lathered up the baby's full head of black hair with soap and was rinsing it out with her head under the faucet of the sink against the wall. The baby caught her breath and continued screaming.

"What is she doing to her?" I asked Dr. Dussia. It's peculiar that my parental protective tendencies were kicking in, even though I had no idea at all how to care for a newborn child.

"The nurse is giving her a good first bath, and she seems to be enjoying it very much," Dr. Dussia said. His wry smile gave me the impression I should not worry. "Good luck," he said. "Enjoy your baby." The doctor walked away.

The screaming stopped as soon as the scrubbing stopped. A few minutes later the nurse had the baby dried off, diapered and wrapped in a blanket. She had seen me standing on the other side of the glass watching her every move, so she brought her over for me to see. The little baby in the pink blanket squirmed around as if she was trying to get comfortable. She had a funny expression on her face and appeared to be trying to open her eyes. Finally, she did, just a little bit. I knew she could not see me, but I could see her. "Hello, Angel," I said.

Angela Dawn Shelfer was born July 12, 1961.

The football season of the fall of 1961 was another year of me living the dream as Drum Major of the Marching Chiefs. We did six halftime shows during the regular season. With each new show, it was exciting to see the brilliant creativity of Dr. Whitcomb manifested on the field playing the incomparable arrangements of Charlie Carter. The best of the best. And I'm sure they brought out the best in me. I maintained superb athletic conditioning and could strut the entire length of the football field, if necessary, leading this incredible group of musicians. Indeed, we never lost a halftime show.

The football team itself was another story. It was the second year of Coach Bill Peterson, a defensive specialist that earned his reputation from coaching the famed Chinese Bandits defense at LSU. Football team won only four games during the season, but it was one more than last year. I guess that's progress. There were a couple of highlights. We beat the Georgia Bulldogs 3-0, and for the first time didn't lose to Florida. We tied the gators, 3-3. Needless to say, the football team did not go to a bowl game, but the Marching Chiefs did.

The Marching Chiefs were invited to perform at the pregame and halftime show of the Senior Bowl game in Mobile Alabama on January 6, 1962. We were very excited because we knew we it meant we were recognized as one of the top bands in the country. Not only that, we would be on national television, a rare treat in those days for a band whose football team never went to a bowl game. We did a compilation of tunes and formations from previous shows that drew enthusiastic applause from a modest crowd. Even though the networks had promised us several minutes of television exposure, I'm not sure how much of our show made it on the air. Nonetheless, I knew I did not want to waste my last opportunity to be on the field leading the Marching Chiefs. I gave it my max effort. I left the field at the end of the final number performing the overhead reverse strut. I was enjoying my final moments as a Chief so much that I became careless and hit myself in the face with the ball of my baton. The good news is I did not knock myself out. Nor did I lose any teeth. I merely continued the strut to the sideline, laughing with joy that I had accomplished a dream and lived it well.

After the game we boarded the chartered buses for the late-night trip back to Tallahassee. It had been a very long day and soon after we were out of town heading east on US 90, I melted into the cushioned seat in the front row the bus and fell sound asleep. A few hours later when I awoke, the road looked very familiar. And then there was a sign illuminated by the lights of the Greyhound bus, "Sneads City Limits." Almost immediately we passed the junction of River Road and US 90. It was surreal, almost like I was still asleep and dreaming. My sullen thoughts were about a mile up River Road, to where the old converted church house where I grew up once stood. I had recently received some shocking news about my childhood home.

Aunt Versie had owned the house since she bought it many years ago so Granddaddy and Grandmother would have a place to live out their years. After Grandmother died over four years ago, the house sat vacant for a couple of years. Eventually, Versie thought it would be better for the house to be occupied rather than just sent empty, so she rented it out. The vagrants she rented it to were always a problem. Eventually, after many months of them failing to pay rent, Aunt Versie asked them to leave. They did, and then they burned the house down. It couldn't be proved, because there were no witnesses. There are bad people in this world.

As the Greyhound raced past GD Malloy's Pure Oil Station and down the hill to the darkness of the countryside and onward towards Chattahoochee, the montage of memories of my life in the past shifted toward the future and Tallahassee where my wife and baby were waiting for me. How lucky could I be?

Chapter 40

My participation in Air Force ROTC was increasingly interesting and rewarding. Maj. Goni had mentored me along the way and I had been promoted to the rank of Cadet Colonel, the highest possible rank in AFROTC, where I was the Air Force representative on the Joint Chiefs of Staff. We met with faculty representatives to plan and coordinate all ROTC activities on campus and in the surrounding communities. Interesting, but easy for me because of my experience with the Chiefs.

The reasons I had joined advanced ROTC when I was a sophomore were strictly monetary. I was paid a stipend, which had been nice, but also the Air Force would pay for me to get my private pilot's license before I graduated. And there was no obligation or absolute requirement that I join the Air Force. In the fall of 1961, it was time to do that. I was going to try to learn to fly an airplane.

It was a chilly day in October, 1962. I made the ten-minute drive from our apartment in Alumni Village to the new Tallahassee Municipal Airport, which had been open for less than a year. Dale Mabry Field, where Frank Blount had taken me on my second airplane ride, was now closed. The Air Force contracted local flying services to provide thirty-five hours of instruction to their advanced cadets. At Florida State it was Seminole Flying Service.

"May I help you?" The lady behind the counter asked.

The office was in the corner of a new hanger beside runway 09-27, to the east of the new control tower. It was a new airport, so everything here was new.

"Yes, I'm Bennett Shelfer. I'm from Air Force ROTC."

"Hi, Bennett. I'm Lucille Shuler," the lady said. She extended her hand across the counter and I gripped her firm handshake. "We've been expecting you. For our records, could I see your driver's license, please?" She recorded the information from my license and handed it back to me. "Go outside and wait beside 86 Tango and the man himself will be with you in just a few minutes. She pointed towards a new Cessna 150 on the ramp outside the office.

The few minutes I waited out by the little aircraft seemed like forever. It was so small and only had two seats. It was hard for me to believe that in a few minutes I would be thousands of feet up in the air in this little thing. It was frightening, in a way. I glanced at the new Oldsmobile in the parking lot and thought about my wife and baby back at the apartment. They needed me, so I shouldn't go kill myself. But they also needed me to earn a living to provide a life for them. I thought again about how lucky I was that the Air Force was paying a lot of money for me to do this. And, as of late, I was very curious to see if I could fly an airplane.

The man himself, Grover Shuler, Lucille's husband and the owner of Seminole Flying Service, hurried out of the hanger towards me. He was a slender man, much taller than me, with a wrinkled face that betrayed his miles more than his years. Even though I found out later he was in his late 40s, he appeared much older. He was also a bit of a legend in the flying community. Rumor had it that he flew P-40s and P-51s with Chennault's Flying Tigers, flying with the Chinese Air Force against the Japanese before the US entered World War II. He was definitely old school, and, as they say, a pilot's pilot.

Mr. Shuler introduced himself with a voice as rough as loose gravel. He got right down to business with the walk around inspection of our little Cessna. He identified the flaps, the ailerons, the rudder, the elevators and several other parts of the airplane before we hopped inside. I stared at the instrument panel. So many dials, so many gauges. How could you possibly look at all of them? Mr. Shuler had no problem checking them out with his own internal checklist. He didn't really seem to be concerned that I wasn't absorbing very much of what he was saying. Even so, I watched him intently because I knew if things went as planned, I would be flying by myself in the not-too-distant future.

The little engine roared as take-off power was set and we rolled down runway 36 at Tallahassee Municipal. Mr. Shuler calmly explained everything he was doing with his hands and feet and soon we were climbing out of the traffic pattern. We leveled at 3000 feet and flew northward for just a few miles until we were over Lake Jackson.

"Okay, you have the airplane," Mr. Shuler said.

My feet found the rudder pedals and my left hand gripped the yoke. The next few minutes were spent with me trying to fly straight and level. I tried my best to hold the controls firm and steady but the aircraft was wallowing up and down and all around. The vertical velocity indicator, the altimeter and the heading control were hopelessly erratic. Mr. Shuler watched with indifferent amusement.

"Let me show you something," he said. "I have the airplane. We simply want to maintain 3000 feet and a heading of 360." I took my hands off the controls and slid my feet down from the rudder petals and watched. The flight path of the little plane became silky smooth and the heading and altitude never deviated. I noticed that the control yoke in his hands was always moving slightly, yet you could not feel the movements in the seat of your pants.

"Flying is a million smooth corrections," Mr. Shuler said.

I didn't realize it at the time, but I had just received one of the most important tips about flying an airplane. My next attempt showed great improvement. After that, we went through a series of stalls to teach me that an airplane needed airspeed to fly, and to show me what would happen if we ran out of airspeed. And then what to do about it. Soon, were returned to the airport where Mr. Shuler showed me how to enter the traffic pattern and bring the plane in for a landing. His touchdown was so smooth you could barely feel it. That was fun, I thought, as we cleared the runway. Then to my surprise, rather than taxiing back to the hangar, we taxied back to the end of the runway for another takeoff.

"Now it's your turn," Mr. Shuler said. "Don't worry, I'll talk you through it."

My takeoff was as rough as his gravelly voice, but I did it. He kept talking and I kept flying, wallowing along, all the way around the traffic pattern and back in for a landing. The landing wasn't a grease job, but it didn't register on the Richter scale, either. Then I was on the ground taxiing back to the ramp, but really, I was on cloud nine. I couldn't wait get home to tell Lou the good news. I knew what I wanted to do with my life. I wanted to be a pilot.

Mr. Shuler handed me off to another instructor, Mr. Smylie, after that first ride. This was the usual policy and was not a surprise to me. Mr. Smylie was an easy-going, jovial guy, with a round face and black, wavy hair. He resembled a slimmer version of Jackie Gleason. We did the usual air maneuvers each day, followed by some work in the traffic pattern. The air work included stalls and an occasional spin. And then there were forced landings. A pilot must always have a plan for where he would land the plane should the engine suddenly quit. To emphasize that, Mr. Smylie would pull the throttle back at any unspecified moment to simulate engine failure. I would have to select an emergency landing place such as a pasture, corn field, golf course or highway, then establish a glide path to a dead-stick landing there. When we descended low enough to determine that we could make the field, or not, Mr. Smylie would push the throttle forward and we would climb away. Oftentimes, not without scaring a bunch of cows and an occasional farmer.

A few flights later, after I had about eight hours of flying time, we taxied out for takeoff on runway 36. It was a cloudy, wintry day, with a chilly Northwest breeze. After an uneventful takeoff, Mr. Smylie instructed me to stay in the traffic pattern to practice touch-and-go landings. I steered the little Cessna around the traffic pattern for an okay landing. Not a grease job, but not bad. On the landing role, when it was time for me to add power for another takeoff, Mr. Smylie reached over and placed his hand on the throttle and said, "Let's make this a full stop." I made two right turns on the taxiways and puttered back down to the end of runway 36.

"Set the parking brake," Mr. Smylie said. "I've seen enough." He opened his door right there on the taxiway and started to get out. He leaned back in and said, "I need a cup of coffee. Shoot two touch-and- goes and a full stop and meet me back in the office." And with that he was out the door and walking away.

The little empty seat beside me was a colossal void without an instructor sitting there. It suddenly hit me that I was alone in an airplane that I was expected to fly all by myself. I knew I would be flying solo, but I didn't expect it to happen for a few more flights. But there I was. I nervously reach for the mic and pressed the button.

"Tallahassee Tower, Cessna 6686 Tango ready for takeoff," I said on the radio. And ready I was. My three solo landings to anyone watching were uneventful. But to me, it was a monumental accomplishment. It gave me confidence. I could be a pilot. And more than anything now, I wanted to be a pilot. I wanted it so badly…

One of the requirements to obtain a private pilot's license is to fly a solo cross-country flight. My assignment was a simple one: fly to Perry, Florida, get the signature of the fixed base operator in my logbook, and return to Tallahassee. I plotted the route meticulously on my sectional navigation chart. All I had to do was fly down Highway 98 keeping the Gulf of Mexico on my right and Highway 27 on my left until I ran into the Perry airport, some 60 miles away.

The day of my flight the weather was cloudy and chilly, much like the weather on the day of my first solo flight. Aviation weather for Tallahassee and Perry was 5000 overcast and 10 miles visibility and forecast to remain that way all afternoon. Those conditions were good enough for me because I planned to fly down at 3500 feet and back at 2500 feet. And with 10 miles visibility I could see all my landmarks to stay on course. After takeoff, I made a right turn and flew over downtown Tallahassee while climbing to my cruising altitude. It was easy to pick up Highway 27 leaving Tallahassee and by the time I reached 3500 feet I was established over Highway 98 and on my way. I could see the Gulf of Mexico off to the right. But another thing I saw was a solid scud layer, a layer of low-level clouds, jutting in from the Gulf and crossing my path ahead. At the same time, I noticed the clouds above me getting closer and closer to my altitude of 3500 feet. I was flying VFR, visual flight rules, and could not be in, or near, clouds.

A strange, uneasy, feeling engulfed me. It was a sixth sense, a gut feeling, which heightened my awareness. Something was wrong. The existing weather was nothing like what had been forecast. Without giving it another thought, I made a left turn away from the weather, descended to 2500 feet, and set course back to the Tallahassee airport. Fifteen minutes later I was walking into the office at Seminole Flying Service, wondering how I was going to tell Mrs. Shuler I didn't make it to the Perry Airport.

"Bennett," Mrs. Shuler said. She was standing inside the door waiting for me. "I'm so proud of you. After you took off, I called the Perry Airport to tell them you were coming and they told me the airport was unexpectedly socked in with fog from the Gulf. I panicked and called the tower and asked them to radio you to turn back. They said don't worry about him, he's already back on final approach for a full stop. That's excellent judgment, Bennett. We'll reschedule this cross-country for another day."

"Thank you, ma'am," was all I could say. But deep inside, I was grateful that I had listened to my gut, and it turned out to be the right thing to do. Lesson learned.

What a difference a day makes. The next day the sun was shining brightly and the skies were clear. My solo cross-country to Perry and back was uneventful. A few days later I completed my 35 hours of training with a final check ride from an FAA examiner. Thankfully, it was also uneventful and I became the proud holder of my private pilot's license.

The spring semester of 1962, my final semester at school, was mostly dedicated to my teaching internship. For degree in education and a certificate to teach school, this was an absolute requirement. Because of being married and having a baby, I requested and was fortunate enough to receive a local assignment, Augustine RAA Junior High School in Tallahassee. It was easy and enjoyable teaching the kids and making sports fun for them. Nonetheless, my heart was not in it. Many times, out on the playground the kids, I caught myself looking towards the skies. I wanted to be a pilot in the U.S. Air Force and I was counting the days to my graduation in June.

There were only three obstacles standing in the way of me becoming an officer in the Air Force. I had to graduate and that was a foregone conclusion. My classes were basically all completed and my grades in my last two years had been mostly Dean's list, probably because I was a married student. The second obstacle was a requirement to pass an Air Force flight physical examination. Lastly, after graduation, I had to complete 28 days of summer camp. This would normally have been completed the summer before my senior year, but I had delayed it because that's when Angel was born.

My flight physical was scheduled at the closest Air Force Base to Tallahassee, Tyndall Air Force Base in Panama City Florida. The ROTC department furnished transportation to those of us scheduled for a physical, but I had opted to drive there myself for several reasons.

We had just traded Lou's car and on a new 1962 Oldsmobile 98 sedan. Bill Durham, was a friend of mine in the Marching Chiefs. (A few years later, Bill Durham started what became the #1 college pregame ritual in college football, Chief Osceola and his horse Renegade.) His father worked for the Oldsmobile dealer in Bainbridge, Georgia. Mr. Durham gave us a very good deal. We paid the difference in cash. It was a different world for me to not have to pinch every penny, but I was adjusting.

The trip to Panama City, the site of our honeymoon, in the new car with Lou and the baby was fun. We stayed with Lou's Aunt, Mr. McGuire's sister, who had a house on the bay. Her husband was a pharmacist and they had a big yacht docked behind their house. They were a very nice couple who enjoyed life to the fullest and took their cocktail hour very seriously. Lou did also, I began to notice.

The flight surgeon at Tyndall Air Force Base gave me the most thorough physical I'd ever had. My physical conditioning was excellent and

I had no concerns about being able to pass a physical. The last part of the exam was a very thorough check of my eyes. The doctor dilated them and then he and I were nose to nose for what seemed like the longest time, with him staring into my eyes with a very bright light. This was after lengthy readings of eye charts and me answering the questions of which is better, this, or this? Finally, it was over and he asked me to come with him to his office.

"Have a seat, Mr. Shelfer," the flight surgeon said. He sat in a big swivel chair behind his desk across from me. "You are in excellent health, except for one thing. I'm concerned about your eyes."

I was stunned. Crestfallen. It was a gut shot. I sat there in silence.

"How bad do you want to be a pilot," the doctor said, finally.

"Well, Sir, it's like this," I said. "If I can't be a pilot, I'm not going into the Air Force."

The doctor sat there looking somewhat impatiently, glancing back and forth between me and my examination results he held in his hand.

"And you really do want to be a pilot in the Air Force," he said.

"Yes, Sir. More than anything," I said. The doctor placed the papers down and edgily tapped his pencil on the desk.

"Okay, here's the deal," he said. "I'm going to pass you, but I want to give you some advice on taking an eye exam. How does that sound?"

"That sounds great. Thank you." I was awash with relief and renewed enthusiasm.

"The night before your next eye exam, do not watch TV or do any reading, and get at least eight hours of sleep. Make an early morning appointment, if possible, and wear sunglasses on the way to the exam. Maybe that will help. Okay?"

"Yes, Sir. I really appreciate this."

"You're welcome. Now, get out of here." He flicked his hand towards the open door of his office and flashed a big magnanimous grin.

As I left the building, an Air Force T-33 jet roared off the runway at Tyndall AFB. I watched it fly out of sight and thought about how fleeting life's opportunities could be. I felt like I had dodged a bullet.

June 2, 1962, was graduation day at Florida State University. I was sitting among the other graduates in folding chairs erected for us on the field at Doak Campbell Stadium. The man himself, Dr. Campbell, for whom the stadium was named, was pontificating about how our class would change the world, but I wasn't hearing the word he said.

My mind drifted aimlessly back to the first college graduation I attended. It was for Uncle Verdayne, the first of our family to graduate from college. I sat with my grandmother in Wescott Auditorium watching the event and vowed to be the next Shelfer to finish college. And now I was. I wished so much that my grandmother could have been there. My thoughts wandered back to Aunt Versie buying me my French horn. And then to the countless hours I spent in the shadows, learning to be a drum major. I fondly reminisced of my four quick years in the Marching Chiefs, two of which I was the drum major, on the very field on which I was sitting. In the stands I could see Lou and little eleven-month-old Angel, who was trying to walk and talk and sing all at the same time. They were sitting with Daddy and Dot, who had driven over from Jacksonville. They seemed to be getting along better, with me out of the picture. I thought about Daddy's loyalty to me, which knew no bounds. I often thought how perfect he would be if he would just quit drinking. Nonetheless, I was grateful he did not appear to be drinking on this visit. I thought about how lucky I was that I would never have this problem. You never have to stop drinking if you never start.

My tassel was flipped from one side of my mortarboard cap to the other and I walked off the stage clutching my diploma as a very excited, enthusiastic 21-year-old, looking forward to turning the page to a new chapter in life.

Chapter 41

"You, there, Mister! Halt!"

In that instant my life changed from civilian to military. My
assignment for ROTC summer camp was Shaw Air Force Base, South
Carolina. I had been on base for about fifteen minutes walking down the
sidewalk following directional arrows, and had finally found the
administration building. It was a large one-story building set back a short
distance from the street. A long straight line of square concrete
steppingstones marked the path from the front door to the sidewalk. There
seemed to be no one around, and I was anxious to check in. Unknowingly, I
had cut the corner slightly from the sidewalk to the steppingstones and had
stepped one foot on the grass. Now, someone was shouting at me, and it was
not a friendly greeting.

"I'm talking to you, Mister." An Air Force captain, wearing pilot's
wings, was in my face sneering sarcasm. I snapped rigidly to attention.
"This grass is government property, Mister. You are guilty of damaging
government property. Do you understand?" He shouted.

"Yes Sir," I said.

"Where are you from, Mister?" He asked.

"Florida, Sir." I could see from his name tag that my harasser was
Capt. Yanchek.

"Do you like South Carolina?" He snarled.

"No Sir," I said, with total conviction.

"Then push it 50 times."

"Yes Sir."

In an instant I was down on the steppingstones, making sure not to touch a blade of grass, doing 50 push-ups. Capt. Yanchek walked away, probably thinking there was no way I could do 50 push-ups, especially on the first day of summer camp. He was wrong. I had done my homework and I knew from talking to those who had gone before me that physical conditioning was paramount. Perfect for me. I had a degree in it.

The fraternities at Florida State had what they called "hell week." During this seven-day period, the brothers harassed the pledges until their heart's content. This Air Force summer camp should have been called "hell month." It was 28 days of 24/7 harassment. There was always a TAC Officer or a Drill Sergeant in our face about some seemingly insignificant something. We could do nothing to escape the nonstop needling of the demeaning demons.

Our mornings would start with a bugle playing Reveille over the loudspeaker at 5 AM. We had to be showered and shaved, dressed for physical training, and assembled in formation at the front of the barracks at 5:15 sharp. That means that within fifteen minutes all forty of us had to wake up, get in and out of the bathroom, get dressed for inspection, and make our bed to exact military standards. The pillow had to be fluffed and placed perfectly against a six-inch collar of the sheet turned down over the brown wool blanket, which had to be tucked tight enough to bounce a quarter. Forty cadets had to do all this in fifteen minutes. Of course, that was impossible. So, we did what we had to do. We got up at four in the morning and did our preparations in the dark. Most of us slept on top of our beds to avoid having the make them in the morning. Sleeping without covers on hot summer nights in South Carolina in a military barracks without air-conditioning was not a problem.

The cadet's first organized activity of each day was a double-time march about a half- mile across the base to the parade ground for PT. This was a half-hour of vigorous physical training exercises under the watchful eye of our four TAC Officers. The cadet leading us in the activity didn't seem to know much about what he was doing. And most of the cadets doing the activity were struggling because they weren't in very good shape. At the end of the session one of the TAC Officers, who I had noticed watching me, approached. Even though it was not Capt. Yanchek, I felt sure I must be in trouble. I braced to attention.

"What's your name, Mister?" He asked.

"Shelfer, Sir," I said.

"Cadet Shelfer, beginning tomorrow, you will command the troops at PT."

"Yes, Sir," I said.

And so, I did. The next day I led the cadets in a precisely organized workout routine. Afterwards, the TAC Officer approached me again.

"Good job, Shelfer," he said. "

"Thank you, Sir," I said. I did not tell him I had a degree in it.

"You will command the Corps' PT for the duration," he said.

And I did.

In the midst of the myriad of misery of summer camp were a few interesting activities. One morning we went to the shooting range where we had to qualify with a 45 pistol. I had grown up shooting shotguns and rifles on the farm and didn't have much experience with pistols, so that was fun. When we finished shooting, we were given our targets to do with as we pleased and ordered to assemble in formation for the two-mile march to the mess hall. As we were milling around before the march began, I realized I was holding the paper target in my hand. I had no need for it so I wadded it up in a ball, almost the size of a billiards ball. It didn't fit very well in my pocket, so to dispose of it I dug a hole in the loamy soil of the dirt road with the heel of my boot. I flattened the balled-up target into the hole with the soul of my boot, kicked dirt over the top of it, and mashed it down. After we arrived at the mess hall and were ready to sit down to lunch, another cadet tapped me on the shoulder and told me a TAC officer wanted to see me outside. I had no idea what he wanted, but I was sure it couldn't be good. I hurried outside to report to the officer and my greatest fears were realized. It was Capt. Yanchek.

"Cadet Shelfer, it's you again," Capt. Yanchek snarled. "Does this belong to you?" He slowly unfolded a piece of paper and held it six inches in front of my face. It was my target from the shooting range with my name written at the top. My heart sank. How could that be? I buried it in the dirt on a trail in the forest and hundreds of cadets in the formation behind me marched over it. Yet, there it was.

"Yes Sir," I said.

"Shelfer, not only are you an embarrassment to the entire U.S. Air Force, but, you're guilty of littering government property and desecrating the state of South Carolina," he sneered. "What do you have to say for yourself?"

"No excuse, Sir," I said.

"Cadet, I'll give you one of two choices. Either ten demerits, or eat it."

That was an easy choice for me. I didn't have any demerits and I certainly didn't want any. For each demerit you had to march around the flagpole square in front of base headquarters for one hour. And all this was done at night after taps, when everyone else was asleep.

"I'll eat it, Sir," I said.

Capt. Yanchek handed me the paper target. I shook as much dirt off of it as possible, wadded it up and put it in my mouth and started chomping away. I think he was amazed that I made that choice.

"Enjoy your lunch, Mister." Abruptly, with a smirk on his face, Capt. Yanchek walked away. After a minute or two passed, so did I, straight to the latrine. That piece of paper would never be found again because I gagged the saggy gob into the toilet and flushed it down.

Another evening they bussed us to Fort Jackson, a large army base nearby, for escape and evasion training. They dropped us on the backside of the base with a flashlight, a terrain map, and a small compass. We had to traverse three miles of swamp and forest in the dark of night and arrive at the base camp undetected and without being captured by the Army guys. I teamed up with Chuck Shipp, another country boy who was from Louisiana. We quickly separated from the group and plotted a parallel route to the base camp through the forest and on the backside of a swamp, far away from any of the main or secondary roads. We would pick a direction using minimum filtered light from the flashlight on the compass, then pick a star in that direction and walked towards it. Following yonder star, just like the wise men. It worked beautifully. And honestly, I was much more concerned about being bitten by a rattlesnake than being captured by an Army guy. In a couple of hours, Chuck and I arrived undetected and uncaptured and thankfully, unbitten, at the base camp. Mission accomplished.

The most fun thing for me at summer camp was the airplane ride. My first ride in a jet. Those of us who were pilot applicants were given an orientation ride in a T-33. Of course, I had to be fitted with a flight suit, helmet, and a parachute. This was thrilling to me. They strapped me into the back seat of the T-bird, making sure that I had a couple of barf bags handy. In the front seat was an Air Force pilot with the rank of Captain. As we rolled down the runway for takeoff I was immediately astounded by the speed of the plane and the G forces on my back as we accelerated. Wow! Welcome to the jet age. The captain asked me what I would like to do and I told him I'd like to see some aerobatics. I wanted to see what it was like to be upside down in a jet airplane. In a very few minutes we were down over Lake Marion, northwest of Charleston, doing aileron roles, loops, and barrel rolls. I enjoyed it so much, even though I almost blacked out from the 4-5 G's we pulled doing the loop. The captain was very generous with letting me fly the airplane. I was amazed at the sensitivity of the control stick. I did some aileron roles and then flew the airplane all the way back to the base, except for the landing. I deplaned with a smile on my face because I knew, more than anything else, I wanted to be an Air Force pilot. And I didn't need a barf bag.

The mundane minutia of the daily routine became almost monotonous as one day of summer camp blended into another. Spit-shining shoes, cleaning latrines, and sleeping on top of the bed covers while all the while being treated like scum, wasn't something that made me exactly love the military. The one thing that kept me going was I knew this hell month would come to an end.

And that day finally came. It was so exciting to me. The handful of us there who were to be commissioned were seated on a stage. Lou, along with little one-year-old Angel, had driven up from Florida for the ceremony. I had missed them terribly and could see them sitting in the audience. Soon enough all the pomp and bluster in the talk by the base commander was over. I raised my right hand and solemnly swore to "support and defend the Constitution of the United States against all enemies... so help me God." In that instant I was an officer and a gentleman. But I was also a husband and a father. I was bursting with pride when Lou pinned the gold bars on my collar for my rank of second lieutenant. My thoughts drifted back to the little town of Sneads, the farm, and my grandmother. I just know she would've been proud.

And what a difference it was for me wearing those little gold bars on my collar. As we departed the stage one of the old salty sergeants that had been giving us holy hell for the last month was at the bottom of the steps.

"Good morning, Sir," the sergeant said. He was standing at strict attention with a smile on his face as he executed a snappy salute. I knew why he was there. It's a tradition that a new officer will pay one dollar to the first noncommissioned officer that renders him a salute. I smiled and returned the salute and handed him a dollar.

"Thank you, Sir," he said.

"And thank you, Sergeant, for all of the uh…training you gave us."

"Just doing my job, Sir," he chuckled.

There was another person that intercepted our path as we were leaving. I gave him a quick salute.

"Good morning, Capt. Yanchek," I said.

"Good morning, Lieutenant," he said.

As he returned my salute, I noticed his demeanor was totally different from anything I had seen. He appeared happy and had a broad smile on his face. He reached out and shook my hand with a firm handshake.

"You'll make a fine officer, Lieutenant," Capt. Yanckek said.

"Thank you, Sir," I said. "This is my wife, Lou, and my daughter Angel." Lou extended her hand and they exchanged pleasantries. Angel looked interested, but unimpressed.

"You have a beautiful family, Lieutenant. Enjoy pilot training and safe travels."

"Thank you, Sir," I said.

With Angel in my arms and holding Lou's hand we walked down the long path to the parking lot. And I must say, I had a different opinion of Capt. Yanchek. Not totally different, but I was getting there. We piled in our new Oldsmobile and headed south to Apopka to await my new orders for pilot training. After twenty-eight days it was wonderful having our little family back together again. We took the long way home.

Chapter 42

There were eight pilot training bases scattered around the southern tier of the United States. The closest one to Florida was Moody Air Force Base in Valdosta, Georgia. I really hoped that Moody would be my assignment because it was close to home and family. There was a base in Alabama, Oklahoma, Arizona, and the rest of them were in Texas. I knew that the old adage of "join the Air Force and see Texas" would probably apply to me. And it did. After two weeks of restless anticipation, I finally received my orders: Reese Air Force Base, Lubbock Texas; Pilot Training Class 64-B. Lubbock, Texas? I had never been further west than Mobile and knew little about Texas and absolutely nothing about Lubbock. Nonetheless, after a couple of months of working in the orange grove and living with Lou's parents in Apopka, it was an adventure I was eager to seek.

The last day of the three-day trip West was all Texas. We drove through the hill country west of Dallas, through the Badlands, and then across the plains and the plains and the plains. Mesquite bushes, sagebrush and tumbleweeds. Someone said driving across Texas was just more and more of less and less. So true. The landscape for as far as you can see in any direction went on forever and was peppered with monster metal machines, bucking up and down like a bronco, pumping oil from the ground. Even if you could not see them, you knew they were there from the permeating stench of the liquid they call Texas gold. The last couple of hundred miles before Lubbock were the flat High Plains country, more than 3000 feet above sea level. The locals called that entire area the Cap Rock. There were cotton fields as far as you can see, still dotted with oil wells, pumping away.

We settled into a Holiday Inn on the west side of Lubbock about sundown on a sweltering day in early September, 1962. Reese Air Force Base was about ten miles west of town so we thought that would be a good location to begin our search for a place to live. Reese did not have base housing available for student pilots so they paid a housing allowance for us to live off- base. Lou was happy about that because she was very picky about where we might live.

The next morning, we drove by several addresses for available rentals that were in the classified ads of the newspaper. Most of them closer to town were absolute dumps. There was one more on the list on the south west edge of town. Patio Gardens was a newly completed apartment complex standing alone in a large field of brown dirt and rocks. Everything in and around Lubbock was brown dirt and rocks, a stark change from the green landscape of Florida. Lou loved it the minute she saw the new carpets and appliances. Out back was a small private patio that opened onto a common path that led to the new pool. The rent was more than our Air Force housing allowance, but it was worth it to me for Lou and Angel have a place to be comfortable because of the long hours I knew I would be spending at the base.

We signed the lease for a year and began settling in. The next day a nice couple knocked on the door to welcome us to Patio Gardens. How nice, I thought, for our new neighbors to be so neighborly. But he introduced himself as Fred McClain, and his pretty wife as LaJean McClain. Fred was the owner of Patio Gardens, so he was my landlord, not my neighbor. Lou was happy that I invited them in for drink. Even though I never drank alcohol, Lou would never pass up an opportunity. Fred was a tall, flamboyant, affable, larger than life Texan. LaJean was sweet and petite, and very lovely. We immediately regarded them as friends, not landlords.

Undergraduate pilot training in the Air Force was a year-long program unlike anything I had seen before. The first six months were spent flying the Cessna T-37 jet trainer, affectionately call the Tweety Bird. Unaffectionately, it was called the double-barreled bug smasher, because of the shrill, high-pitched whine of the engines. The second half of the year was in the T-33 Shooting Star, affectionately called the T-Bird. Unaffectionately, it was called the Lockheed Falling Star, or sometimes the Lead Sled, because it took so long to get off the ground.

At Air Force pilot training, half of each day was spent flying and the other half attending academic classes. Each section of students would either be on early schedule or a late schedule. The early schedule would require reporting one hour before daylight to be ready to fly from daybreak until noon. Then academics would start at 1 PM and be completed at 5 PM. The late schedule would report for academics at 8 AM, break for lunch, then fly until dark. This amounted to twelve-hour days, five days a week. Total commitment. Total immersion.

It was surprising to me to learn that over 90% of my class were graduates of the Air Force Academy. The other 10%, like myself, were from ROTC, with a couple of Air National Guard students. And it was all a competition. Upon graduation you would be able to pick your duty assignment based on your standing in the class. I knew I was at a tremendous disadvantage, especially in academics. To the students from the Academy, courses like engineering, aerodynamics, navigation, and celestial navigation were just to review of material they had already studied. To me, it was all new and difficult. The flying part of the program, on the other hand, was different. I already had my private pilot's license from ROTC at Florida State, so I knew I could fly an airplane. I just had to adapt to flying jets. The Academy students, at the time, while they had many familiarization flights and orientation flights, did not have the hands-on flying experience.

My T-37 instructor was Capt. Wally Fraser, a short, freckle-faced redhead. His call sign was "Little Duke." He was a real go getter with a "kick the tires and light the fires" swagger about him. He was good, and he knew that he was good, and that was okay with me. He liked the fact that I studied intensely and was always prepared for the next flight.

Capt. Fraser also liked the fact that I could fly the airplane. On a hot Indian summer day in October, 1962, after takeoff from Reese. I flew Southwest for the quick ten-minute flight to Abnormal. That was the name given the auxiliary field where the students practiced takeoffs and landings. It was probably named Abnormal because it was an adequate description of many of the student landings performed there. I entered the traffic pattern and began shooting touch and go landings. After a touchdown on the second landing, Capt. Fraser surprised me.

"I have the aircraft," Capt. Fraser said.

"You have the aircraft, Sir," I said.

Capt. Fraser steered the T-37 off the runway and taxied back to the mobile control unit from where one of the instructors in the squadron controlled the airplanes at the field. He set the parking brake, shut down the number two engine, and raised the canopy.

"Lieutenant, you are now Rain Dance 54. Perform all checklists, start number two engine, takeoff, stay in the pattern, shoot two touch-and-goes and a full-stop. Then, come back and get me," he said.

"Yes, Sir," I said.

With my helmet and oxygen mask on and my visor pulled down, Capt. Fraser could not see the smile on my face. He disconnected his oxygen hose and radio cords and seat harness and was quickly in the air-conditioned mobile control unit. After a long stare at the huge vacancy in the seat beside me, I did exactly as he instructed me. I noticed I was the only Rain Dance call sign on the frequency. When I stopped to pick Capt. Fraser up, I noticed he was all smiles. He quickly hopped in his seat and reconnected his oxygen hose and radio cords.

"Congratulations, Lieutenant," he said. "You're the first to solo in your class. Good job."

Two clicks on the intercom and a thumbs up was my only response.

Soloing first as an ROTC student in a class of mostly Academy graduates left me feeling pretty good about myself. That didn't last very long. The next week the weather changed, and so did my inflated opinion of my self-worth.

It was said the weather in Lubbock was the hottest and coldest and wettest and driest in the country, all in one week. The winds were always blowing briskly on the high plains of the caprock, usually from the northwest. Reese was known as a crosswind capital of the world because of these winds. Tumbleweeds would be rolling around everywhere. Dust devils, little whirlwinds of dust, were common. Occasionally, there were dust storms where the forward visibility would be almost zero. Oddly enough, if you are airborne looking straight down at the ground, the visibility wasn't too bad. The dust recovery procedure was to find the runway looking straight down, then make tight descending circles down to the runway and land. If a thunderstorm formed in the middle of a dust storm, it would actually rain mud balls. Strange weather indeed in Lubbock Texas.

The next week after my initial solo flight, a cold front came through the Texas Panhandle that left a chill in the air, with clear skies and a strong wind out of the northwest, as usual. The wind was almost too strong for solos to fly, but there were only a couple of us so they decided to let us go. I was scheduled for a solo sortie where I would, totally on my own, fly out to the practice area and practice maneuvers. Then I would fly back to the field and make a full stop landing. I was really enjoying flying the Tweety Bird. I practiced lazy-8's, chandelles, loops and immelmanns until it was time to return to the field.

"Rain Dance 54, initial," I said, into the radio mic on my oxygen mask.

I was at 1500 feet above the ground lined up on initial approach five miles away for an overhead pattern to runway 35L at Reese Air Force Base. There were three parallel runways: 35 Left, 35 Right and 35 Center. Runways are numbered according to the magnetic bearing of the runway. The procedure was to make the approach at 250 knots until directly above the end of the runway, then make a hard left 60° bank turn of 180°, and then rollout in a descent on the downwind leg. I prided myself on flying exact airspeeds and flying tight patterns, just like my rumbustious instructor, Capt. Fraser. I noticed flying down initial approach towards the field I had to keep turning over to the West to stay aligned with the runway. I didn't quite understand that because the winds were only 15 knots out of the West on the surface. Nonetheless, I pressed on undeterred and at the proper time made an extremely tight pitchout to the left that would've made my instructor proud. I began my descent, lowered the landing gear and soon thereafter begin my turn to final.

"Rain Dance 54, gear check," I transmitted.

As I rolled out on final, I was pleased to see the runway was directly in front of me.

"Rain Dance 54 go around!" I heard the excited mobile controller say.

"T-37 on final for 35 Center at Reese Air Force Base, this is Blue-Chip control on guard, go around, go around!" I heard over the emergency frequency.

"Rain Dance 54, go around and clear left," mobile control radioed.

In that instant my heart was in my throat. My face beneath my helmet, mask and visor, was probably white as a sheet. I looked down and saw that I was lined up perfectly with runway 35 center, currently being used by the T-Birds. In my enthusiasm to be an aggressive pilot, a young stud, I had naïvely disregarded the extremely strong westerly winds at traffic pattern altitude. I should've made a very loose break to the West into the strong wind, then crabbed into the wind on downwind to compensate. But, I didn't, and I knew I was in deep trouble.

"Rain Dance 54, on the go," I answered.

The quick trip around the traffic pattern was uneventful and I made sure to apply adequate compensations for the wind. My mind was racing about my fate. Would I be brought before a board? Would I be washed out of the program? I feared the worst.

Capt. Fraser didn't keep me in suspense. He was waiting for me when I walked through the flight room door.

"Shelfer," Capt. Fraser said. "Follow me."

He led me to the flight commander's office and pointed for me to sit in one of the chairs against the wall. He surprised me when he sat in the chair next to me. He lowered his voice to a gravelly growl.

"Shelfer, you're in the pink" he said. A pink slip is the grade you get for an unsatisfactory flight. "What the hell were you thinking?"

276

He launched into a diatribe of several minutes about wind patterns and how they relate to aeronautical activities such as flying, but most of the time was spent describing the location of where my head was in relation to my rear end. Finally, he stopped talking and just looked at me.

"I have no excuse, Sir. I know exactly what I did wrong and it won't happen again," I said. "What happens now? I asked.

"What happens now is you go home and sleep on this and come back and fly with me tomorrow and we'll try to get you out of the pink."

"Yes, Sir," I said.

"By the way, Shelfer," he said with a smirky smile. "I don't want this to get out, but the guys in the mobile control unit said it's the tightest pattern they've ever seen."

There was no way for me to respond to that, so I didn't. I think it was Captain Fraser's way of telling me that I screwed up, but he wasn't really worried about my ability or future as a pilot. That sentiment was reinforced after I flew with him the next day and my status was no longer in the pink.

Chapter 43

The Patio Garden Apartments proved to be a great decision. Fred and LaJean would come by occasionally for a drink, much to Lou's delight. Besides dabbling in real estate and other things, Fred's main job was being a partner with Mass Mutual Life Insurance in Lubbock. I knew he was a good friend when he never tried to sell me life insurance. Sometimes on weekends they would invite us to their lovely home in a nearby upscale neighborhood for barbecue steaks on the grill. Big steaks on a big grill on the big patio of a big house. It was so deliciously Texas. They were a wonderful couple and we enjoyed their company very much. Lou never gravitated towards the military wives, so I was glad she connected with LaJean.

Angel was a happy, rollicking toddler with a quick smile, bouncing around everywhere. She would never walk when she could run. This incessant, spirited activity was probably the reason she took a dive off the bassinet, falling face first onto the floor. Even though the floor was carpeted she bloodied her nose, blacked her eye and drove her front tooth completely through her bottom lip. It was not a pretty sight, but even that didn't seem to slow her down.

In order to make it possible for Lou to have the car available to her some of the time, I formed a carpool with two other students in my pilot training class who lived in neighborhoods on my side of town. One was Bob McNaughton, former quarterback of the Air Force Academy football team, and the other was Aubrey I. Abrams, from Auburn, Alabama. Both were terrific guys and soon became my closest friends in the class. One Friday evening in November when they dropped me off at the apartment, I was in for a big surprise.

The moment I opened the apartment door, the aroma hit me. Lou had been cooking. It smelled like country fried steak, smothered with onions and gravy, and sautéed squash. My favorites. I could see a freshly baked red velvet cake on the counter. Lou rushed to meet me with a friendly smile and a kiss. This was not her usual welcome home greeting.

"Thank God it's Friday," she said. "You must be starved. Come, let's eat. Would you like a Coke to drink?"

"Yes, thank you." I sat at the table and saw that Lou already had a drink. It wasn't Coke.

"Wow," I said. "What's the occasion? Your birthday is not until next week."

"Well… I went to the doctor today."

"You did? Are you still having trouble with that stomach virus that was bothering you last week?"

"Not exactly," she said. She smiled coyly.

"What did the doctor say?" I asked. Suddenly, I began to get the picture.

"He said you're going to be a Daddy again."

"Ohhh, that's great news," I said.

We stood and hugged for the longest time. I was surprised but not shocked at the news. We weren't exactly trying to have a baby, but we weren't trying not to either. I knew Lou wanted another baby. She loved everything about it; the doting attention, the showers and gifts and especially being under the constant care of a doctor. I looked over at Angel, laughing and jumping up and down in her playpen.

"Little Angel's going to be a big sister," I said.

"Da Da Da Da Da," Angel said.

"I know," I said.

We spent a quiet Thanksgiving in Lubbock because we only had a short four days off. The Christmas break was different whereas the Air Force suspended flight training activities for the two-week period over the Christmas and New Year's holidays. This was a welcomed hiatus for me from the relentless daily 12-hour routine of study, fly, study. Without a doubt this was the most intensive training program I had ever experienced. Our Christmas trip to Florida for a little downtime and some Florida sunshine was greatly anticipated.

Of course, Lou had to ask the doctor if it was okay with him if she rode in a car four days to and from Florida for Christmas. Naturally, the doctor, because she asked, to be on the safe side, said he was not altogether comfortable with her taking such a trip at the beginning of her second trimester. That presented a real problem. But the doctor had said it, and whatever the doctor says…

Airline schedules from Lubbock to Orlando were not at all convenient and very expensive. Finally, after making a few phone calls, I convinced Lou of another alternative. The Fixed Base Operator (FBO) at Lubbock municipal Airport had a new Cessna 172, a four-seater airplane, for rent. After a quick trip around the pattern to show him that I could fly the airplane, he allowed me to book it for nine days for a trip to Florida. Perfect.

The weather was bright and sunny and cold as my little family piled into the new Cessna for our trip to Florida. Being in a new airplane was as nice as being in a new car. Everything is bright and clean and it even has that new car smell. Or, maybe I should say that new airplane smell. Lou, all decked out in a new maternity outfit, sat in the backseat on the right. Angel was strapped into an infant seat which I secured in the back seat on the left. The copilot seat beside me on the right was vacant for my use with maps, charts, etc.

The first leg of my meticulously planned trip was from Lubbock to Love Field in Dallas. This was the busiest commercial airport in Texas. I was not too concerned about that because nothing is busier than an Air Force pilot training base with dozens of student pilots in jets buzzing around the same time. In order to avoid the ire of the air traffic controllers in the tower at Dallas I made sure to keep my speed up on final to minimize any conflicts with airplanes like the DC-6's or DC-7's that the airliners flew. The FBO operation there was very nice. We refueled, ate a snack, used the facilities and I checked the weather.

The forecast for the route ahead over Louisiana and Mississippi was for diminishing ceilings in association with a weak cold front, but no ceilings were forecast lower than 3000 feet. I could deal with that because I was flying strictly visual flight rules (VFR). As long as I had enough forward disability to identify landmarks such as towns, highways and railroads, I felt I would be fine. That feeling was short-lived. Soon after we departed Dallas, we were flying under a solid overcast that kept getting lower and lower. I descended down to 3000 feet, then to 2000 feet, then down to 1500 feet to remain clear the clouds.

Lou and Angel had drifted off to sleep in the backseats. It's just as well they didn't realize the apprehension I was feeling because of the deteriorating weather. I had to abandon navigating by the VOR radial, a radio navigation beam, because I was flying so low that I couldn't keep my landmarks in sight. And I was very concerned about obstructions, such as television towers, which I had noted along my route. I began strictly following an East-West railroad that paralleled my route of flight. I was finding some comfort in the fact I thought they would never build a TV tower on top of railroad. The problem was the diminishing visibility did not allow me to focus my eyes inside the airplane long enough to check my map. I knew I could not continue like this. Auspiciously appearing out of nowhere ahead and to the left of the railroad was a big, beautiful, long concrete runway. It felt like someone had thrown me a lifeline. I grabbed it without hesitation. I made an immediate left turn and landed on the runway, not knowing exactly where I was.

"Are we there already?" Lou asked from the back seat.

"Not exactly," I said. "The weather is deteriorating and I had to land to get my bearings."

As soon as I was able to check my map, I saw that I'd landed at a military maintenance base. I immediately thought I would be in deep trouble for landing there without prior permission. To my surprise there was not a soul in sight anywhere. My only hope was they had gone home for the holidays. In any case I did not plan to stick around there long enough to find out. I determined by studying the map the same railroad I had been following would lead directly to Monroe, Louisiana.

Forty-five minutes later we were parked in front of the FBO at the municipal airport in Monroe. The owner was already closing his operation because of the weather and seemed surprised to see us. Nonetheless, he made a kind offer to drive us to a nearby Holiday Inn. Lou had meticulously packed a small overnight bag for such an occurrence, so I locked everything else in the airplane and we were off to the hotel.

By the time we checked into the hotel and walked to the restaurant next door for dinner, dense fog had descended on the area. The steak was especially delicious that evening. I closed my eyes for the night with the feeling I had dodged a bullet. I felt my naivety had put my family at risk, and I vowed to never do that again. And I had learned a valuable lesson to be skeptical of weather reports. Weather will change and you must always be ready for the worst. Flying Magazine each month had a featured article of personal accounts of pilots called, "I learned about flying from that." I was sure this was my "I learned about flying from that" moment.

What a difference a day makes. The following morning the skies were clear and the galloping cold front had made it all the way to the Florida Panhandle. By the time we caught up with it again around Tallahassee the southern end of the front had whimpered out, allowing us clear sailing down the state. We landed at a little grass strip in Zellwood, Florida that was used mostly by crop dusters that sprayed the orange groves. Mr. and Mrs. McGuire, Pa and Mamma as they were called, came to pick us up.

We had a very nice Christmas vacation enjoying the warm Florida sunshine. The day before our return trip to Lubbock, Pa drove me back to the little grass strip to check on the airplane. When I learned he had never been up in an airplane, I offered to take him on a sightseeing trip. After some arm-twisting, he reluctantly agreed. I gave him an aerial view of his nursery, the Evergreen Gardens, in Apopka, his home on dream Lake, and his orange grove northeast of town. It was fun watching him marvel at seeing these things for the first time from the air. It was his first and probably his only airplane ride.

The trip back to Lubbock was long and uneventful. It was nice to fly a private plane and control your own schedule. I returned with my batteries charged and ready to dive into training program again.

Chapter 44

By the end of February our class transitioned from the T-37 to the T-33. The T-Bird, as we called it, was a trainer version of the Lockheed P-80 Shooting Star, the Air Force's first jet fighter. We would be the last class to train on the T-Bird at Reese because it was being replaced by the brand-new supersonic T-38 trainer. I already had a taste of the T-Bird from my orientation flight during summer training at Shaw Air Force Base and was really looking forward to learning the airplane. It was larger and heavier and faster than the Tweety Bird, with tandem seating. The instructor usually sat in the backseat with a student up front. On instrument training missions the student would sit in the back seat, with the under-side of the canopy completely covered by a canvas hood. With no outside references a student would have to fly the airplane, relying solely on his instruments. Good training.

It was exciting to be training on a new airplane, even if it was really an old airplane, and I hit the ground running. I was emboldened by my surprising ranking in the class at the end of the T-37 phase of training. My grades in academics and military bearing were middle of the pack, but my flying grade, which was the result of my five check rides, had me tied for first in the class. It gave me a goal. A lofty goal, indeed, but to finish first in the class in flying would be quite an achievement for me.

Capt. Wetzel was my T-Bird instructor. He was much quieter and more studious than Wally Fraser, my T-37 instructor. I immediately liked him, and as always, tried my best to be prepared for every mission. He pushed me through the pre-solo phase of training and then scheduled me for my solo ride on the earliest possible date. Our flight call sign was Blue Chip, so my solo call sign was Blue Chip 54. On the date of my solo flight, I hustled out and climbed in that big airplane. The backseat looked so empty without my instructor there. I completed my preflight checks, taxied out and took off and flew out to the practice area for some last 8's chandelles, aileron rolls and barrel rolls. I then flew back to the traffic pattern for two touch-and- goes and a full-stop landing. I secured the airplane and hung my parachute and helmet in the flight shack and reported back to Capt. Wetzel.

"Blue Chip 54," Capt. Wetzel said. "Congratulations, you did it again. You're the first to solo."

"Thank you, Sir" I said. I was not aware Capt. Wetzel knew I was first to solo the T-37. Nonetheless, it made me feel so proud to be the first again.

There are many ugly creatures that inhabit West Texas. Most of them were poisonous and would bite you. The Air Force even scheduled briefings to warn us in case we inadvertently came in contact with any of these locals. They told us about the horned toads, the Gila monster lizards, the sidewinder rattlers and those huge ugly spiders, the tarantulas. They warned us to always thoroughly check our equipment such as our boots, parachutes, helmet and oxygen mask to make sure none of these creatures were hiding there.

A couple of weeks after my first solo flight I was out by myself again. I was on my way, all strapped into my airplane wearing parachute and helmet and oxygen mask with my sun visor pulled down. Everything was normal when mobile control cleared me to go and I taxied onto the runway for takeoff. I was about to apply full thrust to the old Allison J-33 turbojet engine when I felt something tickle my upper lip. It wasn't particularly warm that day and I knew I wasn't sweating. Then I felt it again. My mind flashed to the briefings about the critters that could hide in your oxygen mask. Tarantula! It must be a tarantula! In an instant, with both hands, I snatched the oxygen mask off my face. There he was, sitting there on the mic in my mask. It was not a tarantula but something almost as bad. It was a big red wasp. I knew I had to get rid of him immediately. I unlocked the canopy and powered it open. The wasp flew out of the mask and thankfully the wind swept him away. I closed and locked the canopy and put my mask back on after checking it thoroughly for more critters. All this was done to the consternation of the mobile control unit who wondered what in the world I was doing. I assured them all was well and I took off and completed the mission.

When I returned to the flight room, I had some explaining to do. Capt. Wetzel wanted to know what I was doing on an active runway with my canopy open. When I told him the story, he tipped his hat to me and said I had done a good job and that's what he would've done. All I could think about was how lucky I was to have found the wasp before I began my takeoff. If he had begun stinging me on my face and lips as I was breaking ground on takeoff, I could've crashed and burned and no one would have ever known why. Lucky, indeed. It wasn't my time.

June 4, 1963. Lou loved being pregnant. She enjoyed the frequent trips to her OBGYN, Dr. Arnold. And she enjoyed being given medicine and vitamins to take and instructions on what she could and could not do. Whatever the doctor said. But with the early onset of hot weather and her due date approaching, her stomach had ballooned to the miserable stage of pregnancy. She no longer found it enjoyable. We had spent the weekend of June 1st and 2nd alarming to countless false contractions. Then on Tuesday, June 4, during another false contraction, her water broke. No more false contractions, now they were five minutes apart. She was in hard labor.

The first phone call was to Dr. Arnold, who instructed us to meet him at the hospital. The next call was to my carpool buddy, Bob McNaughton. I asked him to relay the news to my instructor who had ordered me not to come in on the day my wife was in labor. I was two weeks ahead of the class on my flying schedule, so it would hurt me to take a day or two off.

Methodist Hospital was a modern facility, less than ten years old, looming large against the otherwise stark, flat landscape on the west side of Lubbock. Soon after we arrived at the hospital, they assigned Lou to delivery room number two and wheeled her back to the delivery area. I was banished to a nearby waiting room. The wait seemed like forever, but really it was only a couple of hours when the light came on. They had a very unique method of announcing the gender of a baby and when it was born. Either a blue or pink light would illuminate beneath the numerical number of one of five delivery rooms. Finally, the light came on for delivery room number two. It was pink.

Dr. Arnold came through the swinging doors into the waiting room with a big smile on his face. Mother and baby were doing fine. He said it would take a bit of time before Lou was out from under the anesthesia, but I could see the baby if I liked. I certainly did.

"Hi, Karen," I said. "Welcome to this beautiful world."

She was pretty in pink lying there sound asleep in the bassinet behind the plate glass window of the nursery. We had finally decided if it was a girl, she would be named Karen LaJean Shelfer. I had always wanted the name, Karen, and Lou had always wanted a namesake for sister, Jean. The middle name, LaJean, would do that and at the same time honor our new friend in Lubbock, LaJean McClean.

The next day I returned to the base passing out pink wrapped, "it's a girl," cigars. Proud papa, indeed.

Chapter 45

As the blistering hot Texas summer turned into what seemed like an even hotter Texas fall, we were nearing the end of our training curriculum. It was becoming apparent to me that I could actually do this. I could graduate from pilot training and be an Air Force pilot. All I had to do was complete my training without screwing something up. Not only that. With only one check ride to be completed, the simulator check, I was in a virtual tie with one academy student for the best flying grade in the class. I was thinking I might finish high enough in the class to actually have some choices of what my duty assignment would be after graduation. I wanted to be the best pilot I could possibly be. I had always thought if you really wanted to be good at something you should learn how to teach it. The more I thought about it, the more I wanted to be an instructor pilot. If only I could finish high enough in the class to be able to choose one of the few instructor slots.

With the airplane check rides completed the rest of my time in the airplane would be spent "boring holes," as we called it, to complete the necessary flying hours to fulfill the requirements for the program. My last weekend cross-country flight fell into this category.

My instructor and I teamed up with a friend of mine and his instructor for a two-ship formation ride on the first leg of the cross-country trip. The destination was Fairchild Air Force Base in Spokane, Washington. I won the coin flip and naturally chose to fly the wing position. I loved flying formation. It turned out to be a grueling, challenging flight. We were in thick clouds most of the way, which meant I had to stay really close to the wingtip of the other aircraft or I would lose sight of him. And with no reference to the ground or the sky or the horizon you had to put total trust, including your life, with the pilot of the lead airplane. This was difficult because oftentimes, your seat-of-the-pants senses would be telling you you're in a turn or even upside down. Vertigo was common and I struggled with it for most of the flight. Finally, on our descent into Fairchild, we broke out of the weather. My instructor said he would give me a break and take it the rest of the way. Now that I was not flying the airplane, I had a moment to relax and become oriented as to where we were and what we were doing. The plan was to make a straight-in approach and a formation landing at Fairchild Air Force Base. I could plainly see the runway about five miles ahead of us. But when I tuned the ILS (instrument landing system) I could plainly see that we were nowhere near the centerline of the runway. Trust the pilot in the lead aircraft? Something didn't add up.

"Sir. Something's not right. I tuned the Fairchild ILS and we're nowhere near the centerline, even though I can see the runway straight ahead," I said, over the intercom.

"Maybe you tuned the wrong frequency," my instructor said. He was busy flying a good formation, tucked in tightly on the wing.

"No, Sir. I checked the identifier on the station and it's good."

"Don't worry, Capt. Johnson knows what he's doing," my instructor said.

That comment didn't assuage my concerns at all. In fact, I was getting that feeling you get when something's not right. The hair was standing on the back of my neck. Again, I voice my concerns to my instructor. By now were about two miles out on final approach.

"*T-33's on final at Spokane International, this is Spokane Tower on guard. Go around! Go around!*" The controller was screaming on the emergency frequency of our radio. "*Fairchild Air Force Base is eight miles to the southwest.*"

We followed the lead aircraft as he executed a go around. As soon as we got about 2000 feet above the ground, I could see the runways of

Fairchild Air Force Base in the distance to the southwest. We had almost landed at the wrong airport.

"Good catch, Shelfer," my instructor said. "Capt. Johnson is going to have some explaining to do."

We landed uneventfully at Fairchild and assembled in Base Ops for the debriefing. We were met there by the operations duty officer, an Air Force major. He told Capt. Johnson that we should not be in trouble because he had talked to Spokane Tower and no one was going to file a report regarding our mistake. Our instructors were grateful and we all had learned a valuable lesson. And for me personally, it reinforced what I already knew. Whether pertaining to flying, or to life in general, check and double-check. Like Uncle Verdayne would tell me back on the farm… trust everybody, but always cut the cards.

My flying curriculum was complete except for one last solo flight. It was my final day of "boring holes." All I had to do was take off and fly around for an hour and a half and come back and land without screwing up. That's all I had to do to become an Air Force pilot. Easy. Maybe not.

The first forty-five minutes flying solo was spent minding my own business in my assigned practice area doing various maneuvers and aerobatics, basically having fun. It had become ingrained in us to clear the area constantly, looking out for other aircraft to avoid a midair collision. The aircraft you see will never hit you was the mantra. I was about to begin another maneuver when I looked back and was surprised to see a T-33 on my tail. Incredible. One of my hotshot Academy buddies flying solo, I thought, had jumped me, feeling his oats.

Let me explain that rat-racing was strictly prohibited in the training command. Especially prohibited for solo students. Nevertheless, there would be talk in the flight room among the wannabe fighter pilot students about how they could jump someone and stay on their tail because they were such a hot stick. The thought being that fighter pilots generally had to get on the tail of another aircraft before they could shoot it down. Rat-racing was the term used to describe this aerial horseplay.

290

So, there I was with this T-Bird on my tail. He immediately aroused my competitive spirit. I was not going to let this hot-shot go back to the flight room and brag about jumping me. I immediately shoved the throttle forward to the firewall. At the same time, I executed a yo-yo maneuver, a high G turn to the right and then to the left. The T-Bird behind me was still there, trying desperately to hang on. With the throttle still it full thrust, I began a tight barrel roll and simultaneously extended the speed-break momentarily. By the time the barrel roll was completed, and speed-brake was fully retracted, the T-Bird on my tail had slid past me and I was now on his tail, where I stayed for the next several minutes. Finally, he seemed to give up the fight and began flying straight and level. I slid into formation position upon his wingtip. What I saw when I looked into his airplane made my skin crawl. Total shock. There was not a student flying solo in the airplane. The student had an instructor with him. Trouble. Real trouble.

In an instant I did a Split-s maneuver and left them there. It's over, I thought. After all this work and effort and dreaming of being an Air Force pilot, I was sure they were going to kick me out of the program for rat-racing. How could I have been so stupid?

After parking my airplane on the flight line, I walked into the flight shack and hung up my parachute and helmet for what I thought might be the last time. I timidly walked into the flight room waiting to be called onto the carpet by my instructor or the flight commander. I waited and waited. Finally, one of my Academy friends walked into the room with this "cat that ate the canary" grin on his face. He sat at my desk and whispered to me that everything was cool, that neither he nor his instructor would say a word about what happened today. Needless to say, I had never been so relieved in my life. I hadn't stopped to think about the situation from the instructor's standpoint. If word got out, he would be in a lot of trouble, too. But he already had his wings, and I didn't. In two weeks, that would change.

The last check ride of pilot training was in the T-33 procedures trainer. It was a military adaptation of the developing Link trainer. No motion or noise, just a box in a building simulating a T-33 cockpit to allow training and evaluation of normal and emergency procedures. The evaluators were not instructor pilots but a group of a half-dozen Tech Sergeants. It was just luck of the draw regarding who would be giving you the grade.

Normally, taking a procedures check in a box on the ground after all the flying grades were completed, would be anti-climactic, a non-event. Not for me. I knew I was leading, or at least tied for the lead for the prestigious flying award for the class. I prepared diligently.

The evaluation went exactly as I expected. I progressed through all the phases of flight from preflight to shut down without incidents or glitches. I was pleased with my performance. The old salt Sergeant giving me the check was a ho-hum guy, and just sat there looking like he wanted to be someplace else. I never saw him pick up a pencil to make a mark or write a comment. All he said in the debriefing was, "good job, Lieutenant." That was it.

Later that day the procedures trainer grade sheets were returned to the squadron. I found mine in a stack of about a dozen others and instantly had a nauseous feeling in my stomach. Every grade on the sheet was marked "Good." How could that be? There were over a hundred individual items to be graded as Excellent, Good, Fair, or Unsatisfactory. A numerical value would be applied to each of those items. And my performance on every single one of those items was only Good? Impossible. The old salt Sergeant had completely glossed over my entire check ride. To him it was just a fill the square and collect a paycheck event. To me it was the difference of being number one in my class in flying, or not.

My competition for the flying award, an Academy graduate, had a different Sergeant administer his procedures check. His grades were mostly checked Excellent with a few Goods scattered here and there. He had a fair evaluator who took his job seriously, and I did not. No one knew how disappointed I was to not win the award. But personally, it was gratifying to know my performance was good enough to win.

The weather in West Texas had been good. Most of our class completed our flying curriculum ahead of schedule. We still had to show up for work even though there was not much to do. Someone suggested we take written the exam for a commercial license. I volunteered to do that, and passed the test on the first try, although my plans were to be a career Air Force pilot. As such, I would never need a commercial license.

It was the last week before graduation. I walked into the flight room and my instructor, Capt. Wetzel, was smiling from ear to ear. He didn't say a word and just nodded towards a bulletin board at the front of the room where some other students had gathered. Our duty assignments had been posted. My future was on that bulletin board. I dashed to the front of the room.

The previous week we had seen the available assignments available to all the pilot training bases Class 64-B, and had submitted our top three choices. I knew I would have some choice because I'd finished top 10 in my class overall, so I gave this a lot of thought. There were almost 500 slots available. There were only two fighters for the Tactical Air Command, a few fighters for the Air Defense Command, a couple of dozen transports for the Material Air Transport Service, a few instructor slots for the Air Training Command and then over 80% of the class going to the Strategic Air Command to fly bombers, mostly B-52s.

There was one thing I knew for sure. I loved flying and now I was even more convinced that I wanted to teach it. I wanted to be aircraft commander. I didn't want to fly copilot or be part of a big crew on a big airplane. So, my number one choice for assignment was to be an instructor pilot in ATC. My second choice was to be flying a transport in MATS. And my third choice was a fighter slot in the ADC.

When I nudged my way through the crowd of the bulletin board, I couldn't believe my eyes. I had been assigned an instructor slot, a T-33 to Laughlin Air Force Base at Del Rio Texas. I had been awarded my number one choice. I wasn't too excited about the base assignment in Del Rio. My choice would have been Moody Air Force Base in Valdosta Georgia, closer to home. Nonetheless, I was overjoyed. I was going to be an instructor pilot in the U.S. Air Force.

Capt. Wetzel was waiting for me when I returned to my table.

"Congratulations, Lieutenant. You'll make a great instructor," he said. He gave me a big handshake, and almost a hug. He seemed almost as excited as I was.

"Thank you, Sir," I said. "I can't wait to get down to Randolph to get started." Instructor pilot school for the Air Force was a three-month stint at Randolph Air Force Base in San Antonio Texas.

"You'll love San Antonio. And Del Rio's not bad either. I have a friend who's been instructing down there for three years, and he loves it. By the way, we tried to get you back here, but there were no instructor slots available for your class at Reese."

"Thank you, Sir," I said. "And thanks for all your help on the T-bird. It's been a great experience."

Graduation day was very special. Aside from being a dad to Angel and Karen, donning the wings of a US Air Force pilot was one of my proudest accomplishments. It ranked up there with being named Drum Major of the Marching Chiefs and being commissioned as an officer and a gentleman in the Air Force. I sat there daydreaming as I listened to the base commander drone through his speech about the leadership and exceptionalism of the Air Force pilot. My thoughts were far away, back on the farm in Sneads, and my grandmother who raised me, and my Aunt Versie, and my aunts and uncles who supported me. I thought about my mother, who deserted me when I was an infant and I had only seen a few times since. Maybe she had done me a favor. I thought about my dad, who, despite all his faults, was totally devoted to me, despite great personal sacrifice. I thought about Lou and how my life changed when we were married and I no longer had to worry every second about money.

My dad watched with pride as Lou pinned the pilot wings on my chest. He had surprised me by getting on an airplane the first time in his life to fly all the way from Jacksonville for the event. Of course, he was also excited to meet three-month-old Karen for the first time, and to see Angel again. It was a great time of celebration, but mentally, I had already turned the page. I was ready to be an instructor pilot.

Chapter 46

It was a bittersweet day leaving Lubbock. Saying goodbye to Fred and LaJean was sad, but I was ready to move on. The truth was I was ready to be something besides a student. I had been going to school all my life and I was ready to be productive. But, oddly enough, I had one more school to attend, instructor pilot school in San Antonio.

Lou had become more and more apprehensive about the possibility of spending our next four years in Del Rio Texas. I wasn't exactly excited about Del Rio myself, so I promised Lou that we would drive through there on our way to San Antonio, to calm our fears.

We loaded Angel and Karen and all of our possessions into the Oldsmobile and the U-Haul trailing behind it. The seven-hour trek southward to our new home town on the border was uneventful. But more than that, it was uninspiring. The closer we got to Del Rio, the landscape became even more desolate. Typical West Texas. More and more of less and less. Tumbleweeds and oil wells, along with the stifling petroleum odor. Completely unimpressive.

We drove through Laughlin Air Force Base, going past the officer's club and the base exchange, then looked at base operations and the flight training squadrons on the flight line. We left the base and took a slow ride through the little town before turning to the east for the three-hour drive to San Antonio. Still unimpressive.

Darkness had fallen and I had some quiet time as we made our way towards the Holiday Inn near Randolph Air Force Base. I reflected on how fortunate I was to have the assignment I wanted, even though the location for me was less than desirable. I reaffirmed to myself that I was an officer in the U.S. Air Force and I would accept my assignments and carry out my orders without hesitation or complaint. That being said, I had thought of something I would not share with Lou, because it was such a long shot. Randolph AFB was the Headquarters of the training command. They controlled everything and everyone. I had a plan.

Instructor school was not like school at all. Maybe because my instructor was a Captain named Wally Tolson. He was such a nice, easygoing guy that our training missions seemed like just another fun day of flying. He was more like a friend than an instructor. In the meantime, I learned all the finer points of flying and teaching each maneuver of the T-33. You had to be patient when a student is learning his maneuvers. You had to let him fail, for him to be able to realize his mistakes. But you never wanted to let him go so far into a bad maneuver that you, as an instructor, could not recover from it. Probably the best point Wally taught me about being an instructor is this: every student is out to kill you. They seem like nice guys and they're trying their best, but sooner or later they'll try to kill you. Best advice I ever had.

Friday, November 22, 1963. It was a cloudy day in San Antonio. I had flown the early period and arrived back of the apartment a little after noon, looking forward to a long weekend. We had taken a three-month lease on a two-bedroom unit just north of the main gate of the base. Very convenient. I sat at the small dining room table watching the midday news while Lou prepared BLTs and tomato soup for lunch. It was a big day for Texas because President Kennedy had come to visit Dallas. I had eaten a part of my sandwich and was halfway through my soup when there was breaking news on the television. President Kennedy and John Connally, the governor of Texas, had been shot in a motorcade in Dallas. A short time later Walter Cronkite, the CBS evening news anchor, gave us the horrifying news that President Kennedy was dead. It gave me a sickening feeling and I could not eat another bite of lunch. Rather than a nice relaxing weekend, it was a time of mourning and grief. I thought President Kennedy was a great man. He was my commander-in-chief.

With each passing week of instructor school, I became even more convinced of how lucky I was to have earned an instructor slot. I loved everything about it and couldn't wait to get to my base and get started. What I was not looking forward to was living in Del Rio Texas. The more I tried to assure Lou that everything would be okay and we would make the best of it, the more I knew I had to at least give my secret plan a try. Late one morning after completing my flying on the early schedule, I stopped by the personnel headquarters building for the Air Training Command.

"Good morning, Lieutenant. What can I do for you?" The sergeant at the desk asked.

"Good morning, Sergeant," I said. "I'd like to see the officer in charge of personnel."

"That would be Major Bert," he said. "What can I tell him is the nature of your business?"

"I would like to discuss a possible change of assignment from Laughlin to Moody."

His name was Sergeant Ennis. He sat back in his chair and stared at me over the glasses he had lowered down his nose, trying not to smile.

"Have a seat, Sir. I'll tell the major you're here." He pointed at the chair beside his desk.

He walked across the enormous room and stuck his head in the big office behind the big glass. He nodded to the major and came back and sat at his desk.

"The major will see you in a few minutes," Sergeant Ennis said.

"Thank you, Sergeant Ennis."

"You sound familiar, Lieutenant. Where are you from?" He was, of course, referring to my southern accent. I had already noticed his accent.

"Northwest Florida, a small town near Tallahassee," I said. "How about you?"

"South Georgia. Statesboro. So, why do you want to be assigned to Moody?"

"Well, Sergeant, I could say it's because my family is in Jacksonville or my wife's family is near Orlando. Or, I could say it's because I went to Florida State and it would be convenient for my wife to go back to college and complete her degree, or for me to attend graduate school. But really it comes down to this: I've never been to Valdosta, but I have been to Del Rio. I would gladly move, sight unseen, to Valdosta, Georgia, to live for four years, than spend a single day in Del Rio."

"I'm not sure the Air force is concerned about any of that," he said. He was now laughing out loud, even though he was trying not to.

"That's just the point," I said. "I realize that to the Air Force it's just a numbers game. In the grand scheme of things, they don't care if Lieutenant Shelfer or Lieutenant Someone Else fills the square at Moody, as long as the square is filled. But, to me, and especially my family, this is monumental."

"The major will see you now," Sergeant Ennis said. I noticed a small light had illuminated on his desk.

"Lieutenant Shelfer reporting, Sir." I was braced at strict attention in front of the mayor's desk.

"At ease, Lieutenant," Major Bert said. "Why are you here today?"

"Sir, I'm attending instructor school here at Randolph with a T-Bird assignment to Laughlin. I would like to see if it might be possible to switch that assignment to a T-Bird at Moody."

"Lieutenant..." The major sat staring, scowling at me for the longest time. I could see he was a ground pounder, not wearing pilot's wings. He was so angry I thought I could almost see smoke coming out of his ears. "Lieutenant, we have better things to do here at headquarters than kowtow to the whims of you whiny pilots. Orders are orders. Now, get the hell out of my office and follow your orders."

"Yes, sir. Thank you for your time." I saluted smartly, did an about-face and departed the office.

"What did he say, Lieutenant?" Sergeant Ennis asked, as I walked past his desk.

"He said not no, but hell no."

"That's what I thought," Sergeant Ennis said. He motioned for me to come closer so he could whisper to me. "Lieutenant, what I'm about to tell you is between just you and me. Understand?"

"Absolutely," I said.

"Give me your serial number. I can't promise you anything, but call me in a week and I'll see what I can do." He handed me his card.

"Thank you, Sergeant Ennis. My wife and I really appreciate anything you might do to help us." I quickly jotted my serial number on his notepad and bounced out the door.

It was probably the longest week of my life. I had not mentioned my little visit to the personnel office to Lou because I knew it was a long shot and I didn't want to get her hopes up. Finally, on the seventh day I could wait no longer than 9:30 the morning. I dialed the phone.

"Headquarters, personnel. Sergeant Ennis speaking." He answered the call on the first ring.

"Sergeant Ennis, this is Lieutenant Shelfer."

"Lieutenant. I've been waiting for your call. Pack your bags, you're headed for Georgia."

"You're kidding, right?"

"No, Sir. I'm not kidding. I have your orders right here. Stop by and pick them up at your convenience."

"Sergeant Ennis, I'm forever grateful to you. There's no way I could ever repay you, but if I could buy you a drink, what would be your favorite?"

"Probably scotch."

"Thanks again, Sergeant Ennis. I'll see you this afternoon."

Later that afternoon I dropped by and picked up my orders from Sergeant Ennis. I left a case of Cutty Sark in the trunk of his car and hurried home to Lou with the good news. She was overjoyed, probably even more than me. Lou called a last-minute babysitter and we celebrated with a steak dinner at the Barn Door restaurant. It was the best porterhouse I'd ever tasted.

Chapter 47

Valdosta, Georgia, was a sleepy little southern town of approximately 30,000 people that greatly exceeded my expectations. The newly opened I-75 made traveling to Florida an easy drive; one and a half hours to Tallahassee, two hours to Jacksonville, and four hours to Apopka. Valdosta State College was there, but the city was most famous for Valdosta High School and its football team. Its legendary coach Wright Bazemore boasted 15 state championships, three national championships, and a 47-game winning streak.

Lou and I bought a comfortable three bedroom, two bath home on Leone Avenue, in a quiet neighborhood on the north side of town. It was a convenient 15-minute drive for me to get to work at Moody Air Force Base, 10 miles away. We needed a second car so Lou and the girls would not be stranded when I was at work. We bought a new '64 Volkswagen bug for me to drive to work. Cheap, great gas mileage, and very dependable.

My job as a flight instructor was very rewarding. It's very gratifying to teach something new to a student and have them understand. Or, in the case of flying, have them satisfactorily perform the maneuver. There was no doubt in my mind that being a flight instructor was a great beginning for my career in the Air Force.

Each flight instructor was usually assigned four students. We would have them for approximately six months in advance pilot training, after which they would graduate and be given pilot's wings. Flight training in the Air Force was basically a "monkey see, monkey do" program. Each maneuver of every mission would be thoroughly briefed in the flight room before takeoff. During the flight, the instructor would then demonstrate each maneuver, followed by the student attempting it again and again until he performed it correctly. After the flight, each maneuver would be thoroughly debriefed. It was a good system that worked very well.

My first set of students consisted of an American, a Norwegian, and two Iranian students. It was not uncommon during those days for the U.S. Air Force to contract pilot training to foreign governments for their student pilots. Foreign pilots presented a different set of challenges to instructors, not the least of which was the language barrier.

Ali Abrishamian was a nephew of the Shaw of Iran. He was brash and daring and brimming with confidence. He was assured, because of his uncle, if he could live through pilot training and get his wings, regardless of his performance, he would return to Iran and fly fighters. He was a good pilot but his English was very poor.

Siyavosh Mokfi, the other Iranian student, was completely different. He was very timid. Quiet and respectful. Unlike Ali, he had no familial assurances of what airplane he would fly back in Iran. His assignment would be based solely on his performance. He was not a very good pilot but his English was excellent.

Instructor school taught us that each individual student was different and, as such, had to be motivated in different ways. This was certainly a true statement regarding my two Iranian students.

The time came in the program for solo formation flights. This was done in two ship formations with an instructor and a student in the lead aircraft and the solo student on the wing. Inasmuch as Abrashamian was the better of the two pilots, I assigned him to fly the solo aircraft and Mokfi would be in the airplane with me. All went well during the takeoff and the climb out phase of flight. Abrashamian was tucked in tightly on the wing, and Mokfi, in the front seat of my aircraft, was doing a good job of flying lead in the formation. We reached the practice area and performed a series of climbs, descents and turns. So far, so good. The last item we had briefed to accomplish was pitchouts and rejoins. The lead aircraft would turn sharply away from the wingman 180 degrees. The wingman would follow four seconds later and follow in trail, about half a mile behind. To rejoin, the lead would enter a gentle turn and the wingman would establish a cutoff angle by turning inside the lead aircraft to join up again on the wing. When Mokfi established the turn for the rejoin, I was watching Abrashamian very closely. He was ahead of the desired angle of intercept and was coming in high and hot. I thought he would realize what was happening and would make a correction. No such luck. He was on a direct collision course with our airplane. At the last moment, I jerked back on the stick of our airplane and Abrashamian narrowly zoomed directly beneath us. Close call.

On the way back to the flight room for debriefing, the words of my instructor at Randolph, Wally Tolson, kept running through my mind: "Every student is out to kill you."

At the debriefing, I tried to remain calm.

"Abrashamian," I said, "today, your rejoins were very poor."

"No, Sir. My rejoins very good." He bristled at the very thought I should criticize his flying ability.

"Abrashamian, you were ahead of the angle and coming in too fast."

"No, Sir. I fly like tiger. I rejoin like fighter pilot."

It was a battle for me to retain my composure. Rather than shouting, I leaned across the table closer to him and lowered my voice.

"Abrashamian, you were coming in too hot, too high, and too much ahead of the angle, and you didn't have a clue that any of that was happening. You tried to kill your friend Mokfi, and me too. You're only sitting here now because I saved your life by avoiding a midair collision. If that ever happens again, you'll be back in your Persian palace by dark the next day and you'll be a ground pounder the rest your life. Is that understood?"

"Yes, Sir," he said. Finally, I had his attention.

Mokfi's attitude and demeanor was completely at the other end of the spectrum from that of Abrashamian. He would take my critical comments about his flying performance personally. On one occasion during a debriefing, big crocodile tears streamed down his cheeks. He said he was such a poor pilot he was afraid they would make him fly Goonie Birds (C-47's) when he returned home. I explained to him that I was required to tell him what he was doing wrong so he could learn to do it correctly. I assured him we would get through the program. And we did. As a young instructor, my Iranian students immediately reinforced another thing I learned at instructor school: Every student is different and it is incumbent upon the instructor to adapt to these differences to maximize learning.

Problems were beginning to develop on the home front. Lou seemed to be always ill with something. She would complain of headaches, neck aches and backaches, and would frequently visit the doctor for relief. He would, of course, prescribe pain medication. It was difficult for me to determine if she was really in pain, or if she was just taking the hypochondria of her family to a new level.

Lou would experience mood swings from one day to the next. I never knew what I would find after returning home from a day of flying, a warm smile or a cold shoulder and the silent treatment. When it was the latter, I was always the problem. I would beg her to tell me what was wrong so that I could make it right. If she said anything at all, she would only say, "If you don't know I'm not going to tell you."

Generally, Lou did not adapt well to being a military wife. She didn't like the Officer's Wives Club and would not participate in their activities. She seemed insecure in social functions and thought it was all about the clothes she was wearing. In her mind, she could never wear the same dress twice, and God forbid if she happened to show up in the same dress as another wife. The one thing she did like was the Officer's Club, especially when we would dine there by ourselves. That's because she was really liking her alcohol. The stronger, the better. Gin was her favorite. She especially liked the Singapore Sling, a mixture of gin, brandy, another liquor, and some fruit juices. I was no fun to her, because I did not, and would not, drink. I didn't mind her drinking, but it was troubling to me when she drank too much. Sometimes it was a struggle to get her home before she was incoherent and to the point of passing out. It worried me a lot. Why did it seem like the most important people in the world to me drank too much?

Capt. Jones, my flight commander, called me into his office after flying one day.

"Have a seat, Ben," Capt. Jones said. He motioned to a chair beside his desk.

He called me Ben. On the farm, I was Benny. In school, high school and college, it was Bennett. Now, my military friends called me Ben.

"I wanted to review your OER's with you, and talk about your Air Force career," he said. "First of all, I'm very happy at the way you handled those Iranian students and that's being reflected in you receiving an outstanding OER."

"Thank you, Sir," I said. Officer Efficiency Reports was the yearly report card on each officer, grading their performance. As such, it became very competitive because it was the primary indicator of who would, and would not be promoted to a higher rank. And when they would be promoted. In the military, it was all about rank. Not only for the privileges, but also the pay.

"How do you like the Air Force?"

"I love it, Sir. I love everything about it, especially the flying."

"Are you thinking about a career?"

"Absolutely."

"You're a reserve officer, from ROTC?"

Yes, Sir," I said. "That's the only problem. To be a career officer, I would need a regular commission, to avoid being riffed."

ROTC officers were given a reserve commission, and because of that could be terminated if there was a reduction-in-force in the military, even if they only had a year or two until they had earned their retirement. Officers with a regular commission were not subject to be cut and were guaranteed a retirement.

"I'll recommend you for a regular commission as soon as you are eligible," he said.

"Thank you, Sir."

"There's one more thing," he said. "Our squadron is getting T-38s sooner than expected and I want you to be in the first class. Pack your bags, you're going back to Randolph."

"That's awesome, Sir," I said. "Thank you so much." It was difficult to maintain my excitement.

The second trip to Randolph AFB was much sweeter than the first. I had already proven myself as an instructor so my objective was mainly to familiarize myself with the speed and performance of this new aircraft. The sleek, supersonic T-38 Talon, powered by two General Electric J-85 engines with afterburners, was more than I had ever expected. It held the world's climb record to 40,000 feet for a period of time. It was a thrill to light the burners on the runway, take off and accelerate to 500 knots, and be at 40,000 feet in just a few seconds over two minutes. Exhilarating. Going supersonic, on the other hand, except for bragging rights, was almost a nonevent. At 40,000 feet we would light the burners and start a slight descent and soon be going faster than the speed of sound, over 600 knots. You could feel a slight burble on the controls of the airplane, known as control reversal, as you went supersonic. We were prohibited from breaking the sound barrier below 30,000 feet, to minimize the effects of the sonic boom on the earthlings below.

Lou and the girls accompanied me again on the temporary training assignment to Randolph. Angel was nearing the end of her terrible twos and Karen had just learned to walk. Karen didn't have to learn to talk because Angel would say everything for her. They were such a joy.

Lou was a meticulous housekeeper. She prided herself on keeping everything spotless, even the apartment we had rented at Randolph. She liked that it was relatively new, because it was easy for her to keep clean. She was also a good cook. Not very adventuresome with the recipes, but that was okay with me because I was a meat and potatoes and vegetables kind of guy. She knew that I liked country fried steak, meatloaf, and other comfort foods so that's what she prepared. Worked for me.

One evening about three weeks into the assignment at Randolph, I came home after a day of harassing the heavens in my new T-38. Lou, as usual, had the table set and dinner prepared when I walked through the door. We enjoyed a nice meal along with the usual theatrics of trying to bribe Karen and Angel into eating their vegetables. It was entertaining to watch.

Lou's mood swings appeared to have abated in the previous few weeks. I attributed it to the fact that we had been busy relocating for the assignment to Randolph. Nonetheless, the situation seemed to be better. We had finished the meal and Lou had prepared herself the usual after-dinner cocktail. She had taken a sip of her drink when out of nowhere her glass crashed across the table, spilling everywhere. Lou's eyes had rolled back in her head, her back had stiffened and she was shaking violently. I grabbed her to keep her from falling onto the floor. I knew, from some of my studies at college, that she was having a seizure. A grand mal seizure. She had all the classic symptoms, including foaming at the mouth and losing control over bodily functions. I held her, constraining her, for what seemed like forever. Actually, it was probably only a couple of minutes. When the convulsing finally stopped, I checked to make sure she hadn't bitten or swallowed her tongue. I carried her into the living room and laid her down on the couch. She slowly regained consciousness but was lethargic for quite a while. She said she had a headache but aside from that remembered nothing about what happened.

The doctors at Randolph AFB Hospital could find no immediate cause for the seizure. They referred her to Brooks Army Medical Center, also in San Antonio, one of the leading military trauma centers in the country, for a complete neurological exam. After several visits there, the doctors at Brooks could not determine a reason for the seizure. At least they ruled out a brain tumor, which we were worried about. They said it could be the initial onset of epilepsy, and they prescribed medicine for her to take that hopefully would prevent another seizure. She was cautioned against drinking alcohol while she was taking this medicine. Trouble.

Chapter 48

In my mind flying the T-38 was the best job in the Air Force. Two flights a day flying around the flagpole in South Georgia teaching highly motivated young officers to fly a supersonic airplane was as good as it gets. I got to sleep in my own bed every night and had weekends off, and no one was shooting at me.

Speaking of shooting at me, there was a war going on. Vietnam. With each passing day the military buildup to support the war increased. Most of the assignments out of Moody, whether it was the graduating students or the next assignment for pilot instructors, would be to Vietnam or to some base supporting the war in Vietnam. It became personal to us, because we were losing friends who were killed in action. Wally Fraser, my T-37 instructor at Reese AFB, had been shot down in an F-100. Buzz Blackwood, one of my instructor friends from Moody, was killed in an F-105.

There was no doubt I wanted to make the Air Force my career. I had received notice I had been granted a regular commission in the Air Force. As a regular officer I was now guaranteed a 20-year career and therefore a retirement. And for that retirement I wanted to reach the highest rank I could possibly reach, and hopefully retire as some sort of a General. For each promotion I would be competing against exceptional officers, most of whom were Academy graduates. It was very competitive, but I didn't mind that. I was confident of my ability and skills. If I was going to distinguish myself from the others and make the rank of General, I knew if there was a war around, I had to get in it. I had to shoot the guns. Therefore, long ago I had volunteered for an assignment to Vietnam. I was on the list.

The situation on the home front was not getting any better. It was difficult for me to accept that I could not make things better, so Lou would be happy. All I wanted in life for my kids was the one thing I never had. A family unit, Mom, Dad, and the kids. I was determined to do whatever was necessary to make it work. Yet, to Lou, I was the problem. To me, alcohol, as usual, was the problem. And Lou drank a lot of it, and continued to take pills.

Once every few months I would make the short trip down to Jacksonville to see Daddy. He and Dot seemed to be getting along better now that the kids were out of the house. Joyce had married the son of Dot's best friend and they lived in the neighborhood. Tony had taken up with a woman and was living across town. He seemed to be always in trouble with the law for taking something that didn't belong to him. Uncle Bud and Aunt Ruth lived two doors down from Daddy and Dot. Two brothers married two sisters and lived on the same street. Interesting.

Daddy was doing well in his position as assistant superintendent of the sewer department of Jacksonville. He was responsible for supervising hundreds of workers and all the jobs for sewer repair and new construction in the city. As an adult, and having been away from him for a few years, I had a new respect for what he had accomplished. Daddy was a functional alcoholic. He never drank on the job and, in the past, seemed to always drink when he wasn't on the job. Lately, he didn't seem to drink as much. Yet, despite the fact that he started at the bottom of the ditch on the business end of a shovel, 25 years later, he was operationally in charge of the entire department. And all of this on a ninth-grade education.

The highlight of a trip to Jacksonville for me was an afternoon hunting or fishing trip with Daddy. We would hunt turkeys north of Jacksonville in the pine forests of Nassau County, or down south at Camp Blanding, an old army base where Daddy went to basic training before he went overseas. It was now a wildlife management area. I had become an adequate turkey caller using a device that fit in the roof of your mouth. It was almost like playing a musical instrument. At least you hoped it would be music to the ears of an amorous gobbler. I learned about calling and most everything else I knew about turkey hunting from growing up hunting with Raymond and his father, Mr. Walden, back on the farm in Sneads. Now, it was fun to be doing this with Daddy. The challenge and all the fun, was in the hunt. Although wild turkey has a unique taste of its own, and is delicious.

Flying is a non-forgiving activity. Flying the T-38 was such fun that it was easy to lose sight of the fact that on every flight your very life depends on your good skills and good judgment. Occasionally things happen and you just hope that you have the flying ability and the knowledge to handle the situation. One day on takeoff, just as we were breaking ground, there was a loud bang in the cockpit followed by a severe vibration of the aircraft. The number one engine, the one on the left, was compressor stalling. The smell of burning feathers permeated the cockpit. Fortunately, the number two engine was performing normally. We made a quick turnaround and a single engine landing, without further incident. Four blackbirds had been sucked into the number one engine, which had disintegrated.

Another day we were doing aerobatics in the practice area. The student was flying the airplane and while I was watching him closely, I was also clearing the area. Looking for other airplanes. We were upside down at the top of the loop when I caught a glimpse of a flash of light. When I looked closer, I saw it was another T-38 coming directly at us at a high rate of speed. Instinctively, I shoved forward on the control stick and we missed by only a few feet. I knew who it was because I recognized the distinctive helmet of one of my instructor friends. I was lucky to see him coming at the last moment. It wasn't my time. I had avoided my number one concern about flying, a midair collision. Or, in the trade, we called it simultaneous occupation of airspace. Of course, we wore parachutes, and were sitting in rocket propelled ejection seats and could leave the aircraft for a nylon letdown at any time. But not if we had been crashed to smithereens by a midair collision.

It was not uncommon to have cloudy weather days in South Georgia. Weather systems from the north would either stall out be slow moving by the time they got over us, giving us a blanket of low-level clouds. We called it a scud layer. We would use that opportunity for instrument training for our students in actual weather conditions. On one of those days our mission was to fly up to Warner Robins Air Force Base with our students for practice approaches. After we were airborne and checked the weather in Warner Robins, we learned it was below minimums. The ceiling and the visibility were both almost zero. I made the decision to change plans and use Jacksonville Imeson Airport for the practice approaches for my student. It just happened to have a high-altitude penetration to a double arc approach, the most challenging approach in our area. We called it the snake pit because of its difficulty. It was great training for the students. And, flying around the Jacksonville airport brought back fond memories from my childhood of parking out by the fence watching the airplanes come and go. Little did I know…

When we arrived back at the base that day, we receive some devastating news. An instructor friend of mine and his student had continued on to Warner Robins, even though the weather was below minimums, and had crashed attempting to land. Both of them were killed. Myself, and all my instructor friends, were in shock. We had no explanation why this instructor, even though he was young, would attempt such an approach. They had the usual accident investigation which found the cause of the accident was pilot error. That was undeniable. The Air Force's remedy for the situation was something I could not understand. They fired our flight commander. He was an outstanding officer, a war veteran, and a distinguished graduate of every school he had ever attended, including the Air War College. And just because some airman in his command made a poor decision and paid the ultimate price, our boss was relieved of his command. His career was over. He would never be promoted again. I was told this was not an uncommon practice in the military. The broad-brush fix for any accident or problem was simply replace the commander. I said nothing at the time, but that did not sit well with me.

Two of my best friends at Moody were fellow instructors, Howard Batten, and Bill Lenz. They both were exceptional pilots. Howard was a hard-charging, no-nonsense guy who liked to push the performance of the aircraft to its limits. He hated bureaucracy. Bill was more of a low key, under the radar, type guy, who always seemed to be ahead of the program. He was one of the best instrument pilots I've ever seen. Howard and Bill loved the outdoors. Occasionally, they would invite me to go hunting or fishing with them. It was always fun because they really knew what they were doing. And, it was nice for me to get out of the house occasionally, because Lou didn't seem to want me around anyway.

Lou continued to occasionally experience grand mal seizures. Despite the doctor's efforts to determine the cause or find the correct medicine, every month or so she would have an occurrence. It was my belief that the doctors did not have a chance to solve the problem because they did not have the total picture. Lou was not being truthful with them about the other pills she was taking, and the alcohol she was drinking. She would lie to me and everyone else about consuming the deadly mixture of pills and alcohol.

One evening after she had a seizure, I carried her to bed as usual. I was frustrated and disgusted. After I got Angel and Karen off to bed, I cleaned house. I poured every bottle of liquor down the drain and flushed the contents of every pill bottle I could find down the toilet.

The next morning, she seemed perfectly fine and I went to work. When I returned home that evening the car was gone and the house was dark. She left a note on the kitchen table saying that she had taken the girls and gone back to Apopka. She said she wanted a divorce and left me the name and phone number of her lawyer. I was devastated and felt sick to my stomach. I could not accept failure at the one thing in life I wanted, to have a family and to be a family.

Mr. McGuire answered the phone when I tried to contact her in Apopka. He was very cold and said, "She doesn't want to talk to you." Then he hung up and would not answer when I called back.

The days of the week dragged by, and for me it was miserable. I told no one that Lou had left me, not even Howard and Bill. Every evening I tried to call her in Apopka and each time it was the same curt response from

Mr. McGuire. Finally, I called one morning and Mrs. McGuire answered the phone. She wasn't exactly sympathetic to my pleadings but she finally relented and handed the phone to Lou. It was a very long conversation with me doing most of the talking, mostly begging her to come home. The next day, after another similar phone call, Lou reluctantly agreed to come back. I promised to do everything possible in my power to make her happy and make the marriage work. And I promised not to trash her liquor and her pills again.

Lou had returned with the girls by the time I arrived home from flying the next day. It was great to see Angel and Karen. I had missed them so much. And Lou seemed almost normal for a while.

A couple of months later she suddenly had a problem keeping food down and went to the base hospital to see the doctor. She returned with shocking news. She was pregnant with our third child.

Chapter 49

Bennett Howard Shelfer, III, was born shortly after midnight on February 28, 1966 at the Moody AFB hospital. A tired looking Air Force doctor, Capt. Barnes, came to the waiting room to tell me I had a son, and mother and baby were doing fine. I was excited that it was a boy and secretly very much relieved that he reported they were both healthy. Lou had not exactly attenuated her bad habits during the pregnancy. She continued to smoke and drink and abuse prescription medications. She also experienced several seizures while carrying Skip.

Lou insisted, as she had done with Angel and Karen, that if the baby was a boy he would be named after me. I relented, if we could call him Skip. One of my favorite fraternity brothers back at FSU was Skip Sewell, and we both liked him and his name.

Meanwhile, back at the squadron, I had been promoted to the rank of Captain. The commander offered me the opportunity to move to Check Section. That meant I would no longer be responsible of carrying a load of students as an instructor, but would primarily be giving check rides to evaluate the students on their performance. I was honored to be asked to do this and jumped at the chance. In had never forgotten the experience with the simulator evaluator when I was a student at Reese AFB. I vowed to always do my utmost to give a fair and honest evaluation to each student, in fairness to them, and also those competing against them.

One of the other instructors in Check Section, Alvin A. Aikens, was a short timer. He was getting out of the Air Force and already had a job lined up at United Airlines. It was difficult for me to understand why such an outstanding officer and pilot wouldn't want to make the Air Force their career. He told me for him it was an easy decision because of working conditions, no foreign assignments or extended tours, and money, the total career earnings of an airline pilot.

Then another thing happened to a friend of mine who was a Major. He was a great pilot and had distinguished himself with 100 missions over the North in Viet Nam. Yet, he was passed over for promotion to Lt. Colonel. He told me he believed the reason he was snubbed was a mediocre efficiency report from one of his commanders in Vietnam who didn't like his gung-ho attitude about the war.

Second thoughts about a military career began to creep into my mind. I loved my job as a T-38 instructor at Moody and I couldn't imagine another assignment that would be better. I saw an ad in a magazine stating if you would come and be hired as a pilot for Eastern Air Lines, they would pay you over one million dollars during your career. To a country boy who had worn hand-made shirts from feed sacks to school, that sounded like a lot of money. Lou and I discussed the career dilemma for hours at a time. She was lukewarm to me flying for the airlines. Her jealously was stifling. She thought I just wanted to go to the airlines to fly with the good-looking stewardesses. Yet, she didn't want me to have a yearlong tour in Vietnam, which was certainly going to be my next move. In fact, I was thinking our discussions may be a moot point, because they were taking six instructors every two weeks with a Vietnam assignment. And I was now number 12 on the list. That meant I could be gone in a month.

It was understood that Lou and the kids would move back to Apopka if I had to go overseas. Being proactive, I placed a For Sale sign in the front yard of the house. We also bought for Lou a new '66 Oldsmobile, the sporty Toronado with the innovative front wheel drive technology. It was maroon, but to me it was close enough to be called garnet, like FSU's colors, garnet and gold.

Then a strange thing happened. I was down to number six on the list for assignment to Vietnam when a message from ATC headquarters came down freezing all instructor assignments to Vietnam until further notice. ATC had dropped below critical manning and no further instructors could be spared for Vietnam in order to maintain the necessary output of pilots for the Air Force.

My life was now in limbo. My original obligation to the Air Force would be over in September of '67, about a year away. But I knew if I received a Vietnam assignment, that would be extended a year for the training commitment associated with being trained on a new airplane.

It had been a while since I had seen Daddy, so one weekend I put that new sweet-driving Toronado on the newly opened I-75 and less than two hours later I was in Jacksonville. Before visiting Daddy and Dot, and Uncle Bud and Aunt Ruth on Brackland Street, I stopped by Imeson Airport. I reminisced about Daddy taking me to watch the planes takeoff and land, and about getting on the National Airlines Lodestar for my first airplane ride to visit Lou in Orlando. This time I was on a different mission.

Flashing my military ID, I talked my way into the airline operation offices, behind the ticket counters. Pilots, mostly from Eastern and National Airlines, would come and go to complete their paperwork and maybe grab some coffee or a cold drink before their next flight. I engaged every airline pilot that would talk to me, asking them how they liked their job, were they in the military, would they do it all over again? And also, if they were in my shoes, would they get out of the Air Force and work for the airlines? I was shocked at their responses. To a man, they all said they loved their job, and I should separate from the service as soon as possible and go to work for a scheduled air carrier.

Some of the pilots explained to me the importance of getting hired as soon as possible because all the airlines used the seniority system, based on your date of hire. This was the single determiner of everything you do in the airlines. Where you were based, the airplanes you flew, whether you were Captain or Copilot, or Flight Engineer, even your monthly schedules, were governed solely by your date of hire seniority. I asked one of the pilots about working in a system where promotions were based on a number and not merit and excellence. He said it worked very well because you always knew exactly where you stood. If your number was next, you would get the assignment you wanted, if you had put in a bid for it. He reminded me that military promotions were not always based on merit and excellence. He said the seniority system takes personalities and favoritism out of the equation. Point made. I immediately thought of my friend back at the base who had been passed over for promotion.

Nearing the end of my visit to the airport in Jacksonville, a grandfatherly type, gray-haired captain for Eastern Airlines pulled me aside for a chat.

"Young man," the old captain said, "let me give you some advice." He looked around to make sure no one else was listening as he pondered for a moment, taking a long drag on the cherry bowled pipe he was smoking.

"If I were you," he continued, "I'd go down to Miami and get a job with National Airlines. They've just ordered a bunch of 727's and they're gonna be hiring pilots, lots of pilots. If you can get on at the front end of their big hiring spree, you can gain seniority quickly. Not only that, they still have professional flight engineers. That means you would be hired directly into the right seat to fly copilot, and you would bypass a third of the seniority list you would have to contend with on other airlines. There is one catch, though. National only has one base, so you would have to fly out of Miami." He glanced at his watch. "Good luck, kid. I gotta run."

"Thank you, Sir. Thank you very much." That was all I had time to say. I shook his hand and he was gone.

For the longest time I sat in the back of the pilot's lounge trying to digest all the information I had learned from my visit. There was not a single pilot I had talked to with any airline that wasn't happy with his job. Most were former military pilots and were gloriously happy about their decision to leave the military and fly for the airlines. Then the old Eastern captain told me to go get a job with National Airlines because they were buying jets and hiring pilots directly into the right seat to be based in Miami. Having been a flight instructor, and therefore aircraft commander for years, I could not imagine sitting in a cockpit at a seat without flight controls. And being a Florida boy, married to a Florida girl, living in Florida, even if it was Miami, was significant. National Airlines was the only major carrier that met those criteria. I was beginning to see some clarity. And I had a plan.

Chapter 50

It was a little after six o'clock on a January morning in 1967 when I pulled in to the parking lot at Denny's restaurant on 36th Street in Miami, Florida. I was tired and hungry after the all-night drive from Valdosta. My only suit was hanging in the back seat of the Toronado and I needed a place to change and freshen up. After driving around the perimeter of Miami International, Denny's looked like the perfect place. Their coffee was fresh, the breakfast was good, and I knew that chances are, their men's room would be cleaner than any of the neighboring gas stations. That could be debatable.

After the chat with the old Eastern captain at the Jacksonville airport, I had obtained a pilot employment application from National Airlines. Even though I had returned it months ago, I had heard not a word from them. I was curious about what was going on, so there I was, shaving and changing into a suit and tie in a Denny's restaurant men's room.

At eight o'clock sharp, I walked into the personnel office of National Airlines. It was already bustling with activity. When I told the lady at the desk what I wanted, she said I would have to talk to Mr. Field, pointing to a middle-aged gentleman at the back of the room. She walked back and whispered something to the man. He glanced up and saw me standing at the counter and came forward.

"Hi, I'm Al Field," he said, extending his hand. "What can I do for you?"

"I'm Ben Shelfer," I said. I gave him a firm handshake, trying not to appear nervous. It occurred to me that I had never really applied for a job before. Not a real job. Selling Watkins products in college didn't count, and when I entered the Air Force, I merely met the qualifications and signed on the dotted line. "I'm an Air Force pilot and I mailed in a pilot application a few months ago. I haven't heard anything and I just happened to be in the area and thought I'd stop by and check on it."

I was hoping my excitement would more than compensate for the fatigue I was feeling from my all-night drive.

"Shelfer?" He asked. "Spell it for me please." And I did. "If you don't mind waiting, please have a seat and I'll be glad to check on your application. It may take a few minutes."

"Thank you very much," I said.

From where I was sitting, I could see Mr. Field had gone to a table at the back of the room. There were two stacks of applications on the table, each one over three feet tall. Mr. Field was painstakingly sorting through them, one by one. Finally, over ten minutes later, he pulled one aside and read it over, casting occasional glances in my direction. When he finished, he brought the application back to the front counter.

"Captain, we have your application right here," Mr. Field said. "Would you have the time to take a couple of tests for us this morning?"

"Yes, I have some time," I said.

Mr. Field took me to a vacant room where he gave me a basic aptitude test, followed by some strange psychological exam. I thought the test was weird because it had questions like, 'which parent would you rather have die first, your mother or your father?' That was an easy one for me because my mother left me and Daddy was still around. That's another story, but it is what it is. It took over three hours to complete both tests and I was asked to come back after lunch for the results.

The company dining hall was Jerry's cafeteria, a building adjoining National's headquarters. It was a beehive of laughter and smiles. Everyone was dressed to the nines. Gorgeous stewardesses were everywhere, each more beautiful that the other. It affirmed to me something I had heard from someone, that National hired stewardesses for their looks. Wow.

Mr. Field was waiting for me when I returned to the employment office.

"Captain Shelfer, the test results were good," he said. "All our pilot hires must be approved by Mr. Amos, the head of personnel. Unfortunately, he is in meetings all day and is unable to meet with you until after five. I hope you will be able to hang around until then."

"Absolutely. Thank you for your help." It appeared that Mr. Field liked me and I was grateful for his personal attention to my application, even if was after he retrieved it from a stack of thousands.

Mr. David Amos, the head of the personnel department had a corner office with a large window. I was there at five o'clock, but Mr. Amos was not. His secretary, a stylish lady that may have been in her fifties, did not seem to be irritated that I had only just arrived in her office at the time she should have been going home. She told me the boss would be there soon, lamenting that it had been a busy day for him. I told her it was not a problem, and at the same time promising myself to not fall asleep while waiting in his office. Twenty minutes later, a portly, dapper man, with a healthy salt and pepper mustache, dressed in a light gray suit with a red paisley tie, strolled into the office. He nodded at his secretary, followed by a glance and a curt nod in my direction. He paced directly into his office. The boss was in the house.

Five minutes later I was sitting across Mr. Amos' mammoth desk looking at a man that appeared to be more exhausted than I was. I was hoping I wasn't giving him the same impression.

"Young man, I see you only have about two thousand hours...not much time for someone with almost five years in the Air Force," he was lamenting.

"Yes, Sir. But most of that time is aircraft command time as an instructor or check pilot in a supersonic jet," I said.

"No heavy aircraft experience..."

"No, Sir."

"No multiengine time…"

"Sir, most of my time is twin-engine, although the T-38 is a centerline thrust aircraft."

"Hmm…We're thinking about a new hire class going directly into 727 jets. How would you feel about that?"

"I'd feel very good about that, because almost all my flying time is in jets."

"You're still in the Air Force…"

"Yes, Sir. My commitment is up in September."

If Mr. Amos was at all impressed with my application, he wasn't showing it. He continued to routinely "ho hum" back and forth through the pages. He appeared to keep returning to one item that concerned him.

"Here it says, you dislocated your shoulder in college. I'm worried about that being problematic. Does it ever bother you?"

"No Sir. Not at all."

"Do you play sports?"

"Yes, Sir. I play most sports."

"Do you play golf?" he asked. He had placed the application on his desk and was now totally focused on me.

"Absolutely, I love golf."

"Do you swing hard?"

"Mr. Amos," I said, "in golf, it's not important how hard you swing, just so you make sure both feet leave the ground."

He tilted his head slightly and studied me closer, but now I saw a little twinkle in his eye. He burst out laughing. Then I began to chuckle. Then he leaned back in his huge swivel chair and roared with a whole-hearted full-belly guffaw.

"I like you, young man. This is the highlight of my day. You're hired," Mr. Amos bellowed. "Go tell Al Field the date in September you can separate from the service and you'll be in the next class. Congratulations."

"Thank you, Sir. Thank you very much." I was deliriously dumbfounded.

"Oh! By the way," he said, as I was walking out the door. "If you can get out earlier, let us know. We need you as soon as you can get here."

When I left Mr. Amos' office, I was floating on air. I rushed to a pay phone I remembered seeing near Jerry's Cafeteria and placed a collect call to Lou, back in Valdosta. She didn't seem to be nearly excited as I was about the possibility of me having a job with the airlines. She also had reservations about living in such a large town as Miami. She had only been there once a few years ago, when the Marching Chiefs went on a road trip for the Seminoles to play the Hurricanes. I didn't share her concerns about the big city, I only saw a rare opportunity for a country boy to have an exciting, lifelong career.

Lou's lukewarm reaction to my phone call didn't quell my excitement. I celebrated by treating myself to the prime rib dinner with all the trimmings at the Miami Springs Villas. A few minutes after I paid my bill, I checked into the Miami Skyways Motel, where I collapsed for 12 hours of sleep.

The long drive back to Valdosta the next day went by quickly. My mind was racing faster than my sleek Oldsmobile Toronado. My trip to Miami had confirmed to me that I now had only one career goal; I wanted to spend my life as a pilot for National Airlines. The departing words of Mr. Amos kept echoing through my brain. "If you can get out earlier, let us know. We need you as soon as you can get here," he had said. Earlier? How could that be possible? A few months ago, at the officer's club I had heard someone remark about separating early from the Air Force with an "early out." I couldn't remember any of the details of the conversation, or even who had said it. I thought nothing about it at the time, but now that I had a job waiting for me at National Airlines, I knew I wanted to separate from the Air Force as soon as possible. I wondered…

Chapter 51

The next morning following my arrival back from Miami, I slept later than usual. As late as you can sleep with three little ones in the house. Angel and Karen were bouncing around and always up to something. Even though Skip had taken a few steps, he still preferred to crawl because he was so fast on all fours, he could keep up with the girls. If there was trouble around, Skip would find it.

The kids were such a joy and provided a ray of sunshine to me in the gloom and doom atmosphere that was Lou McGuire Shelfer. I never knew from one moment to the next whether she would be happy or sad, glad or mad. Whatever mood she was in, to her, it was a reason to drink. She would drink during the day, and then after the kids were in bed, she would stiffen the content of her cocktails until she passed out for the night. Alcohol, combined with the drugs she was taking presented a great problem. She never wanted to discuss her drinking with me because I was a goody two shoes teetotaler and would never understand. This situation, in my mind, heightened the urgency of a move to Miami. My hopes were that Lou would find a better life there.

The headquarters building in Moody Air Force Base was like most of the others. Very banal. Featureless, inside and out. These buildings had been painted every year since Moody was an Army Air Corps training base in the early 1940s. Still, they looked old. And smelled old.

The lady behind the counter at headquarters was a civil service worker, a civilian employee, who appeared to be in her late 50s. From her confident demeanor, it was apparent that she had worked there a long time. She directed me towards the Air Force regulations book I was seeking, regarding resigning commissions and separating from the Air Force.

If an officer wanted separation on the date ending his commitment, it was a straightforward request. However, I kept reading paragraph after paragraph until there it was. An actual early out program for early separation did exist, if certain criteria were met. There were the usual reasons for health of the officer, or any of the officer's family in which the officer was the primary caregiver. Then I read paragraph 16c, which gave me pause. "If an officer has been accepted to an institution of higher learning, they may separate from the service up to 90 days earlier from the date their commitment is completed, but no sooner than one week from the date classes begin." I read the paragraph several times, with thoughts going a mile a minute through my head. I confidently closed the book and, with a big smile, handed it back across the desk to the lady.

"You getting out of the Air Force?" The lady asked.

"Yes, ma'am. I'm hoping to," I said.

"Good luck to you," she said. "I'll be happy to take your application and forward it on to ATC when you're ready."

"Thank you, ma'am," I said. "By the way, does anyone ever apply for an early separation from the Air Force?"

"I haven't seen it. The way things are with Vietnam and everything, it would probably be a waste of time."

"Are the regulations in this book current?"

"Yes, they are. But I've never seen an early out approved."

"Thank you, ma'am. Thank you very much."

The following Monday I was on the road again. The Oldsmobile Toronado was steady as a rock with its powerful front wheel drive and huge Michelin tires gripping the crown of the lightly traveled turtle-backed country road in South Georgia. I was zooming past miles and miles of farms that were being planted with peanuts, tobacco, corn and soybeans. In less than two hours I would be in Tallahassee and once again on the campus of my alma mater, Florida State University.

In the Air Force, as in every branch of the service, the regulations are the law. It applies to the government as well as the personnel. I had read the regulations pertaining to early separation several times. The lady had verified they were current and up-to-date. Regardless of the lady's pessimism towards the idea, I could see no reason why I shouldn't apply for an early out, if I met the criteria of the regulations.

My first stop on campus was the registrar's office. I had called them earlier to learn the summer session of graduate school would begin on June 19th. I also learned it was too late to accomplish the application process by mail. It just so happened that one week prior to June 19th, June 12th, was exactly three months prior to my scheduled separation date of September 12th. Unbelievable. I saw that not as a coincidence, but a sign. And a challenge.

Fortunately, the registrar's office still had a copy of my college transcripts from my graduation in '62. I was thankful that during my senior year I had taken the GRE exam and had scored well enough to be accepted into graduate school. I had brought the results of that test with me. I sat at a table in the office and completed the entire graduate school application. The one thing that caught me by surprise was I needed was a faculty recommendation. I'd had no contact with anyone at the school since graduation, but one of my favorite professors immediately came to mind. I grabbed the application and headed to Tully Gym.

As I entered the gymnasium, the first thing I noticed was the name on the closed door of the office of my old friend and FSU basketball coach, Bud Kennedy, had been changed. Sadly, Coach Kennedy died of cancer the previous year. The name on the door was now Hugh Durham. He was a player when I was in school, and was now probably the youngest college basketball coach in the country. I had known him from a couple of classes and I wondered if he might sign my application. I continued down the narrow hallway and was relieved to see the door was open to the office of Dr. Peter Everett. He appeared surprised and genuinely happy to see me. We chatted for a few minutes. When I told him why I was there he said he would most certainly sign my application recommending me for graduate school. I thanked him profusely and he wished me the best, and I was on my way again.

The registrar's office accepted my application and told me I would be notified by mail of my acceptance or rejection.

Springtime was always a wonderful time of year in Valdosta. The Bradford pear trees and the dogwood trees would proclaim the new season, followed by a kaleidoscope of blooms and blossoms of every variety. Then around the first week in April, the bursting azaleas would claim their territory. Even with all the apprehension about my future it was hard not to be optimistic with all the beauty of nature around me.

After several weeks of nervously watching the mail the letter from Florida State University arrived. I had been accepted into graduate school, to begin classes on June 19, 1967. The very next morning I returned to the headquarters building at the base with a Xerox copy of my acceptance letter to Florida State. I completed the paperwork to separate from the Air Force June 12, 1967, under the early out program, paragraph 16 c, having been accepted to an institution of higher learning. The lady behind the desk wished me luck, even though she reiterated she had never seen such an application approved. She was smiling and shaking her head at me as I walked out the door.

It looked out of place. I saw it from all the way across the room. The large envelope, stuffed into the pigeonhole that was my mailbox, was obviously not the usual bulletins from headquarters. Then I saw it was from ATC headquarters. My orders had arrived. I sat at my desk, trying to be calm, and nervously opened the envelope. I could not believe my eyes. My request for an early out was approved and I was going to be a civilian on June 12, 1967. Against all odds… Unbelievable.

There were two phone calls that I had to make immediately, so I left the building and went to a pay phone booth near base ops for privacy. The first call was to Lou to give her the news. She seemed to be happy. At least she wasn't mad. The next phone call was to Al Field, at National Airlines in Miami. I gave him my date of separation.

"That's great news," he said. "Can I put you on hold for a few minutes?"

"Yes, that's fine," I said. Even though I was paying for a long-distance call, I didn't mind. He sounded like he was glad to hear the news about my separation date.

"Capt. Shelfer, we have a class beginning on June 19th," Mr. Field said when he finally came back on the line. "Could you possibly make it to Miami in time to be in that class?"

"Absolutely, I can be there." I could barely contain my glee.

"Great. Congratulations, young man. We look forward to seeing you at the headquarters building in Miami at 8 AM on June 19th."

"Thank you, sir. Thank you very much."

The next three months seemed to take forever. I made an extra effort not to get complacent at my job, even though it was difficult to not be looking ahead of the challenges of flying a big airplane for the airlines. A few of my fellow instructors tried to counsel me on the bad decision I was making to separate from the Air Force, but most of them wished me well. It didn't matter to me what any of them thought, because I had turned the page. I was certain that I had made the correct decision in the best interest of my wife and three children. Beyond that, nothing mattered.

One evening after I had finished debriefing my last student of the day, I was shocked to see the person who walked into my office. Col. Adams, the base commander, dressed in his flight suit, came directly to my desk. I snapped to attention and saluted.

"At ease, Ben. Sit down and take a load off," Col. Adams said. He sat down himself and promptly propped his feet up on my desk. "I hear you're separating from the service," he said.

"Yes, sir. I have my orders." I was not looking forward to being hotboxed by the base commander over my decision.

"Going with the airlines?"

"Yes, sir. I have a job at National Airlines."

"Ben, don't worry, I'm not here to try to talk you out of it. I just want you to know that I think you're an outstanding officer, you've done a great job here, and if you change your mind about getting out, even until the last day, you just give me a call and I'll take care of it as if nothing ever happened."

"Thank you, sir. I appreciate that." Needless to say, I was in awe. I had flown with Col. Adams a few times, always at his request, and I really admired and respected him. However, I never expected this kind gesture from him.

"Good luck to you, Ben, in whatever you do," Col. Adams said. He offered his firm handshake and then he was gone.

About a month before my separation date, we were having an instructor meeting and the squadron commander came in to make a few announcements. He told us that general orders have been issued that morning and all regular officer's tour of duty had been extended one year. He pointed to the bulletin board where he had posted a piece of paper. I sat there, numb. I didn't hear a word he said after that. In an instant, all my dreams had been dashed by the broad brush of bureaucracy. When the meeting was over, I rushed to the bulletin board to read the edict. Down at the bottom of the page it stated that for those officers that had received their orders for separation, these orders would be honored. I was never so relieved in all my life. I was now counting the days to begin our new adventure.

Chapter 52

My first week as a civilian was frantic. Tuesday, July 13, 1967, Lou and I piled Angel, Karen and Skip in the Toronado and headed south. We were pulling a U-Haul trailer filled with kid's stuff and immediate necessities. We dropped the kideroos and the trailer with Lou's sister, Jean, in Apopka, and continued to Miami the next day. I was hoping that Lou would be happier in Miami so I wanted to find the best house in the best area for her. I had remembered staying at my fraternity brother Ray Hitchcock's house years ago in the Kendall area south of the airport. Lou would love the modern Dadeland Mall nearby. It would be a good place to start.

We found a realtor near Suniland on South Dixie Highway who began showing us homes. Dozens and dozens of homes. Finally, we settled on a house that I was sure Lou would love. It was a spacious three-bedroom, two bath, with a large pool, near Killian Drive and SW 71st Ave. It was in the highly regarded Palmetto school district. It was very expensive, $41,000, and was so new it would not be finished until another four or five weeks. Perfect. We bought it. We then rented a two-bedroom apartment off Kendall Drive for a place to stay until our home was finished. We hurried back to Apopka to retrieve the kids because my new adventure would begin at 8 AM on Monday.

June 19, 1967, I began my career as a civilian pilot. I reported for work with a fresh haircut, a flat top, to be more specific, and wearing a suit and tie. I was in a class that totaled 15, all former military pilots. Mr. Field welcomed us to the company and was followed by several others from personnel for indoctrination talks.

"Gentlemen, welcome to National Airlines. This is the last job you will ever have," one of the speakers told us.

It was difficult for me to comprehend what the man had just said. I felt so grateful to be sitting there. I knew I had a coveted job and I had to do everything in my power to keep it. Most of the major airlines were buying airplanes and hiring pilots. They wanted career pilots and at that time would not hire someone over the age of 30 for a pilot's job. My thoughts drifted again to the ad in a flying magazine stating that pilots hired would be paid one million dollars in career earnings. Difficult to comprehend, indeed.

My first day at National Airlines was not without its surprises. I found out that in a pilot's class where everyone began employment on the same day, seniority was determined by age. Being 26 years old, I was the youngest in the class. Therefore, I was the junior man placed at the bottom of the seniority list. Seniority was important because every choice the pilot could make, such as what airplane you would be flying, when you took your vacation, and even your monthly schedules, would be put up for bid by the airlines and then awarded to the pilots according to seniority.

The next surprise of the day came when I dropped by publications to pick up my airplane manuals. The lady pushed a knee-high stack of books across the counter to me. Written in magic marker on the brown cover of the top book was L-188.

"What's L-188?" I asked.

"That's the Lockheed Electra," she said. "Your class will be the last class on the Electra."

That news was a total shock to me. Since my first day of interviews with Mr. Amos, head of personnel, I had thought we would be the first class to fly the Boeing-727 jets. Instead, I learned we would be the last class on the old workhorse, the four- engine prop-jet Lockheed Electra. It quickly occurred to me that I would be the last man in the last class on the Electra at National Airlines, and as such I would be flying reserve for a year. Most of the pilots had a regular monthly schedule they would be awarded, according to seniority, every month. A small percentage of pilots, those at the bottom of the list, would be reserve pilots. They would be on call and have to respond within an hour to cover unforeseen contingencies such as weather, aircraft mechanicals, sickness, etc.

The news of having to fly the Electra and being at the bottom of the list did not dampen my enthusiasm for the job. The thought of going to new places with new people at a moment's notice was exciting. And I knew better times were ahead. National was hiring a new class of pilots every month to man the new B-727s they were buying. That meant in a year, when my probationary period would be over, I would have over a hundred pilots below me on the seniority list, then I could bid to fly the B-727 with a regular monthly schedule. Also, I would get a pay raise and no longer be making $575 a month.

The next day our class began three weeks of ground school on the Lockheed Electra. Instructors lectured to us from 8 AM to 5 PM, with only an hour for lunch. We had to learn all the intricacies of all the systems on the airplane. That included reading all the voluminous manuals and memorizing the important facts in order to pass a test on each of the systems. It was a daunting task, but it was easier for me because I had been through aircraft engineering classes during my Air Force pilot training.

After ground school was completed, we were assigned to a National Airlines check pilot for our training and qualification on the Electra. Tim Locher and Neil Sapp, two Navy guys, and I, were assigned to Capt. Bob Davenport, a rough and tough ex-Marine enlisted man, for our training. National Airlines did not have flight simulators for the Lockheed Electra. For us, that meant we had to train in the airplane when it was not being utilized to fly passengers. We would show up at the Miami airport at midnight and fly up to Fort Lauderdale or West Palm Beach and practice takeoffs, approaches and landings for the next three hours.

The Lockheed Electra was much bigger and slower than the T-38 supersonic jet I flew in the Air Force. I had to become accustomed to sitting much higher off the ground in the pilot's seat of the Electra. You also had to be aware of those four large engines on the wings, each with four large and dangerous propellers. Unique problems. The fact that the Electra was slower

334

than my Air Force jet presented no problem at all. Everything seemed in slow motion to me, so flying the airliner, in comparison, was easy.

The dreadful part of pilot training on the Electra for us was the post-flight debriefing. After arriving back at the Miami airport around three in the morning, we would leave the airplane at the National Airlines maintenance hangar. Bob Davenport would take us to Jerry's Cafeteria and ask us aircraft systems questions for the next hour or two. I can remember each of us having to draw a diagram of the complete electrical system of the Electra on a napkin several times. Torture. Finally, after several nights of this, we were released to fly the line.

My first adventure into airline flying was a three-day observation trip. I sat on the jump seat in the cockpit behind Capt. Rod Gaines, watching everything that happened. I focused most of my attention on the copilot because I knew I would be in his seat, doing what he was doing, on my very next trip. All of our training in the last few weeks was centered around learning the systems of the airplane and how to fly it. Now, I had to learn everything else about the job of being an airline pilot. It wasn't difficult. It was just different, with so many aspects of delivering a plane load of passengers from point A to point B, safely and on time. The copilot had to confirm the flight plan, check the weather, do a preflight walk around on the outside and inside of the airplane, preflight the instruments and equipment in the cockpit, tune the communication and navigation radios, check and complete the aircraft logbook and the pay sheets for the crew, obtain the air traffic control clearance, execute the preflight checklist, and be ready to go at departure time. It was a daunting task at first, but repetition soon made it become routine, and it became easier.

There was nothing I didn't like about this job. The people of National Airlines were so friendly and helpful. The crew schedulers, dispatchers, gate agents, stewardesses and the other pilots were very welcoming. It was one big happy family.

Unfortunately, it was not one big happy family at home. Lou was miserable. My hopes that moving our family to a new home in a new city where we would find happiness had failed. In her mind, I was the problem. Yet, she could not tell me what I was doing wrong or how I could fix it. It was devastating to me. My only guess was I was too much of a goody-two-shoes. I guess I didn't drink and smoke and raise hell enough for her. My childhood dream of having a happy, normal family of mom, dad and kids, was shattering. I began to look forward to the phone ringing for crew scheduling to take me away. Back to the happy family of National Airlines.

After a couple of months, I returned home from a trip to find for the second time in two years I was being served with divorce papers. This time was different for me. As hard as it was for me to accept failure, I knew I'd done my very best to make it work. I did not want to be the obstacle to Lou finding happiness, so I agreed to everything she wanted; the house, the car, and $250 a month child support. I knew I would always be there for my kids.   And   then   I   turned   the   page.

Chapter 53

October 18, 1967. 1:30 AM.

The predawn scene at Miami International Airport was always surreal. My view driving along Perimeter Road reminded me of a scene you might see in a James Bond movie. Dark, starry night. Nothing moving. Dead silence, except for the purring engine of my '64 Volkswagon Beatle. The airport runway lights, the green and white flashing beacon atop the control tower and the illuminated fingers of the concourses extending from the main terminal packed with airplanes awaiting their passengers, all painted the portrait. There was no expectancy of what would happen next, but with such a dreamlike setting it was obvious this picture was about to change.

Crew scheduling had called me at my apartment an hour ago to assign me a trip. I was living in the only thing I could afford, a one room studio down South in Perrine. The papers were signed only yesterday and the divorce was final. I had secretly vowed to never get married again. I was a 27-year-old single pilot, working for an airline that hired stewardesses for their looks. Why would I ever marry again?

My trip would begin with a deadhead on a Delta flight to Jacksonville, and then continue operating a two-day trip. The big four-engine Delta Convair 880, my ride to Jacksonville, was clearly visible at the end of the G concourse, as I made the curve to the left on Perimeter Road toward National's new headquarters building.

The check-in window at scheduling was at the west end of the building, at the end of a wall that contained all the pilot's and stewardess' boards displaying their monthly schedules. The lone scheduler on duty sat behind the glass.

"Good morning, Flo," I said. "Shelfer, for the Delta deadhead." Florence Webster sat behind the glass with a pencil in her hand.

"Hi Ben. You're flying with two Bobs on this one, Bob Patton and Bob Degroat.

"Oh! Great. Good crew."

"Here are all the Delta tickets with the seat assignments," Flo said.

"Thanks, Flo. Who are the afterburners?"

"Wilson and Billson," she said.

"Wilson and Billson? I don't think I've met them. Sounds like a Vaudeville act." Flo cracked a wry smile, but it was much too early to laugh at my corny jokes. She pointed to a stewardess behind me.

"There's Billson," Flo said, "over there by the mailboxes."

"Thanks," I said. I placed the tickets in my new uniform coat pocket.

The stewardess had her back to me as I approached her at the mailboxes. I did not expect, nor was I in any way prepared for what happened next. She turned slightly to face me, with blond hair and blue eyes and full red lips framing a slight smile. She took my breath away. I was absolutely certain I was looking at the most beautiful creature I had ever seen.

"Hi, I'm Ben Shelfer, I think we might be flying together," I said. I was just trying not to say something stupid. She extended her warm hand with a firm handshake, which I'm sure I held a moment longer than I should have.

"I'm Baxter," she said. "Baxter Billson."

A couple of minutes later our complete crew boarded the crew bus for the short trip to the terminal. Bob Patton, the Captain, was a great pilot and one of the nicest gentlemen you would ever want to meet. When I had flown with him before I learned his home was in Graceville, Florida, just a few miles from my hometown of Sneads, in Jackson County Florida. Bob Degroat was a very affable and extremely competent flight engineer. Karen Wilson, the senior stewardess, grew up in Panama City, also in the Panhandle of Florida. Baxter Billson, the new girl, I knew nothing about, except she was probably a beauty queen and obviously a cover girl. Our scheduled layover on this trip was in Pensacola, Florida. Somehow, I just knew this had to be a good trip.

When we arrived at the terminal and disembarked from the crew bus, I handed a deadhead ticket with a first-class seat assignment to each member of our crew and kept one for myself. When we arrived at the gate for the Delta flight to Jacksonville, the boarding process had already begun. I placed my suitcase and my flight kit in the overhead rack and sat next to the window in seat 2A. The others in the crew boarded and took their seat. Lastly, Baxter Billson walked on looking for her assigned seat. She discovered she was sitting in seat 2B. I tried to act surprised at the coincidence of us sitting together when she grabbed a pillow and blanket and settled into the seat beside me. She never knew that when I passed out the tickets, I made sure her seat would be next to mine.

Baxter and I chatted with small talk for a few minutes after takeoff, then she snuggled in, clutching her pillow and blanket, and was soon sound asleep. It was hard for me to take my eyes off her. She was not only drop-dead gorgeous, but from talking to her, I could tell she was also very kind and sweet. I did not sleep a wink.

The Delta jet made the quick trip to Jacksonville in less than an hour and arrived at Imeson airport at 4 AM. When we deplaned and walked across the ramp towards the terminal building, we noticed our equipment, the Lockheed Electra we would be taking on our trip, was not there. Bob Patton told us the airplane was being used for pilot training and would be at the gate at 6 AM, one hour before our departure. There was something else we noticed, high up into the dark sky. The moon was well on its way towards a blood moon total eclipse.

We all proceeded to the National Airlines operations lounge to wait for our airplane to arrive. I was very familiar with the old terminal building at Jacksonville. It was very special to me. After all, this is where it all began. This is where my Daddy brought me so many times through the years to watch the airplanes come and go, just to pass the time. This is where I came to seek the career guidance and wisdom from the aspect of airline pilots.

And of course, Daddy and Dot, Uncle Bud and Aunt Ruth, and Aunt Versie and many others in my family still lived in Jacksonville.

There was an observation deck on top of the old terminal. I pointed that out to the crew and invited them to accompany me up there to watch the eclipse. Bob Degroat, Karen and Baxter joined me climbing the steep stairs to the top of the building. The view was stunning. There was only a sliver of moon left as the earth occluded the light from the sun. I didn't have a camera with me, but the picture in my mind of Baxter Billson silhouetted against the eclipsing moon was unforgettable.

Our flight left on time and we puddle-jumped our way westward, making several stops out to New Orleans, and then back to our layover city of Pensacola. We arrived at our layover hotel, or in this case motel, in the early afternoon. We were totally exhausted because of the early hour of our report time. Bob Patton invited the crew to accompany him to the state fair, which was in full swing at the fairgrounds nearby. Karen and Baxter said they would love to go, but begged for a couple hours of nap time beforehand.

Bob Patton bribed the crew bus driver to take all five off us to the fairgrounds at 4 PM. After the turmoil of finalizing my devastating divorce last week, this was just what I needed. It was a breath of fresh air. It was an inexpensive afternoon with good friends and two pretty girls. There were no airs or expectations from anyone. Just good, clean fun.

We visited the arts and crafts exhibit where we saw a blue ribbon on the prize-winning quilt. I told Baxter that I grew up on a farm not too far from here, where I would help my grandmother make quilts just like that one. If she thought that was strange, she didn't say so. We continued on to share a big wrap of cotton candy. Later, Baxter joined me to ride the Ferris wheel. Thrilling. Not so much the Ferris wheel, but being with this beautiful creature, sitting alone on top of the world. Later, as we departed the fair. we went through the livestock exhibition. The moment you breathed your first breath in this building you knew it was different because of the inescapable pungent aroma. Every imaginable farm animal was there. We saw the cows and the sows with their calves and their piglets. I told Baxter the short story about Ned, my little pet piglet that Uncle Hardy gave the back on the farm. I didn't tell her of the story ended, about Ned getting so big we could not afford to feed him.

We met the crew bus driver at the appointed time for pickup and he dropped us off at Martine's, a happening restaurant across the street from our Howard Johnson's. We were all seated at a table together in a huge dining room. At the end of the room was a dance floor next to a bandstand where a four-piece rockabilly band was really rocking it. Impressive for a town in the Florida Panhandle on Wednesday night.

Martine's menu was very diverse, but they specialized in seafood, mostly fresh from the Gulf of Mexico. I was starving from the long day and the trip to the fair. I knew I was going to order the fried shrimp, my old standby. But when I saw their appetizer special, I knew I couldn't pass it up. I also ordered a dozen fresh Apalachicola oysters on the half shell. I knew they would be good in October, a month that contained an "r". I wanted to replicate the dish I had so many times growing up in Sneads; oysters from the half shell placed on a saltine cracker with a toothpick, topped with a shot of Tabasco sauce, and chased with an RC Cola. I was disappointed Martine's didn't have an RC Cola, so I settled for a Coca-Cola instead.

I chomped down a couple of the oysters, and I must say they were plump, firm and delicious. The others in the crew admired my zest for this delicacy, except for Baxter. I plopped one on a saltine, covered it with Tabasco, and offered it her, but she wouldn't go for it. In fact, the more she looked at it, the more she had an expression on her face like she smelled something, even though the oyster had no odor at all. So, Baxter doesn't like raw oysters. I guess no one is perfect.

After dinner while we were waiting on the check, the band settled into an old standard slow tune. On a whim, I asked Baxter to dance. Surprisingly, she said, yes. I held her hand and led her onto the dance floor. Within a few steps she settled in closer to me and laid her head on my shoulder. It was breathtaking. The song ended much too soon and we had to leave because we had an early pickup for tomorrow's flight.

The next day we hippity hopped over to Jacksonville and then up the East Coast, eventually ending up in New York at JFK. The trip ended with a deadhead on a National flight back to our home base of Miami. Baxter did not appear to be surprised or disappointed when, oddly enough, she found herself sitting in first class next to me once again on a deadhead flight. This had been a great trip for me and I hated to see it end. It had provided a ray of sunshine to the darkness of the divorce that had consumed me. It reinforced my belief that there were nice people out there who would be fun to be around. And there were thousands of beautiful stewardesses, and I looked forward to maybe dating some of them. Just dating. I would never get married again.

After our flight reached cruising altitude, we were served dinner. I had the steak. I always had a meal on the airplane when it was available, because that was a meal I didn't have to buy. In the meantime, Baxter and I chatted more small talk. After dinner, we were served dessert and coffee. Baxter had hot tea.

"This has been a nice trip," I said.

"Yes, it's been fun." Baxter looked at me with those blue eyes and a wry little smile, seemingly recalling the interesting things of the trip; moon eclipse, the State Fair, the dinner and the dance.

"You must be much older than you look," she said, out of the blue. "Can I ask you how old you are?"

"Of course. I was 27 on Monday."

"I knew you had to be an old man," she said with a teasing chuckle. "Happy birthday."

"Thank you." I knew better than to ask about her age, but I could tell she wasn't very old, probably not even 21.

"If you're that old, then you have to be married…"

"No, actually I'm not. I just finalized my divorce papers on Monday, my birthday."

"I know I'm young, and I may be blonde, but that has to be the biggest lie I've ever heard."

"It's true," I said. The fact that I was chuckling probably didn't make me sound very convincing. "And I have three kids."

Baxter wasn't exactly chuckling at that comment. "Awww, that's nice," she said, finally.

Even though it was my nature to always try to put my best foot forward, there was no reason to sugarcoat my past, or who I was. It was obvious this young stewardess was way out of my league. I had no thoughts or illusions that she would ever go out with me, even if I'd had the money to take her. Yet, she was so much fun to be around and so easy to talk to…almost like having a really good friend.

"So, what does your boyfriend think about you flying with the airlines?" I asked.

"What makes you think I have a boyfriend?"

"A beautiful girl like you has to have a boyfriend, if you want one."

"I do have a boyfriend. We've been dating for five years… and I'm not sure he likes me flying."

"I can understand that. What does he do?"

"He's going to college," she said. "He plays football for Wake Forest."

"Does he want to play pro football?"

"I don't think so. His dad is in the nursery business down in Perrine. He'll probably work for him after graduation."

"That's a moneymaking business," I said. "My ex-father-in-law owns a big nursery called the Evergreen Gardens, in Apopka, Florida."

"Yes. I think his dad does pretty well, too."

Our chatting reverted back to small talk as our airplane began the descent into Miami, and soon the trip was over.

We said goodbye as we departed the crew bus at the employee parking lot. Baxter walked away, leaving me thankful for my job which allowed me to work with such beautiful people. Our time together was unpretentious, non-threatening. It was easy being with her, like we had been friends forever. Nonetheless, I knew I could never have a serious relationship with someone like Baxter. I was divorced, with three kids and she had a boyfriend of five years she was obviously going to marry. That didn't keep me from thinking it would be just fine if crew scheduling placed us together on the same trip again.

Chapter 54

The next few months were very busy for me. The crew schedulers knew I loved to fly and could always report within an hour of getting the phone call. I was the go-to guy for most of their quick calls, aside from the fact that I was the last copilot on the list flying the Electra. And, the longer the trip the more I liked it. The number of hours I flew did not matter, because during the year of probation we were on a flat salary. What did make a difference to me was the per diem pay. When we were on a trip, we were paid expenses for breakfast, lunch, dinner, and a midnight snack. So, when I was out flying, I always made some extra money on the expenses because I always tried to eat at least two meals a day on the airplane.

Meanwhile, on the domestic front, Lou had sold the house on 71st Ave. and moved back to Apopka. She rented a small house in a neighborhood not too far from her parents. This made it much more difficult for me to see the kids, especially with my work schedule. The term reasonable times and places, as stipulated in the divorce degree, turned out to be a problem because Lou would use almost any request to see the kids as an opportunity to harass me. Finally, we agreed I would see the kids from Saturday morning to Sunday afternoon, every other weekend. Crew Scheduling was very helpful in arranging my red days, my guaranteed days off, to be on the weekends I could visit the kids.

A typical visitation trip for me was to fly to Orlando on early Saturday morning, rent a car, drive to Apopka to pick up the Angel, Karen and Skip, then drive to Howard Johnson's on I-4 in Orlando. There was a pool there and they gave me a substantial airline discount. It was still pricey, but it was the best I could do under the circumstances. It was always great fun. And it was so different being alone with the kids, without the drama that was always present when Lou was around. Then, Sunday afternoon, I would take them back to Apopka, return the car to the Orlando airport and fly home.

Being apart from the kids under these circumstances was very difficult. My hopes that Lou would find happiness if we were divorced did not materialize. In fact, she appeared to be more miserable and vindictive than ever. And she was still drinking. A lot. It was impossible to have a discussion about this with Lou, so during one visit I voiced my concerns about the welfare of the kids to her mother, Mrs. McGuire. She reluctantly admitted to me that she was also concerned. I knew this was a situation that could not last.

The fall of 1967 passed quickly into winter. It was during this time I received my first real experience of flying into snow-covered airports with icy runways. Most of the problems occurred during the landings, keeping the airplane from sliding off the side of the runway or from running off the end. The Electra was a good airplane to be flying during these conditions because of the excellent aerodynamic breaking from the four engines with those big props, out there on the wings. It was interesting, fun flying. As always, the key to being safe was to never exceed your personal limitations, or the limitations of the airplane you're flying.

Mercifully, crew scheduling kept me working. Because I was at the bottom of the list, I flew on Thanksgiving, Christmas, and New Year's Day. That was okay with me because I didn't miss the kids as much when I was busy.

The third week of January, 1968, I was assigned a trip with Capt. Sam Belieff. He was a large barrel-chested, barrel-bellied grumpy guy who smoked a big-barreled oak pipe. He appeared to me to be a little grumpy and set in his ways. I could understand why the other pilots affectionately (or not) called him Sam, the Beef. Even so, none of these old cantankerous captains ever bothered me because I just did my job, which was save the ship. I went along to get along, but my instructor experience always meant that in every situation I strived to be ahead of the airplane and therefore ahead of the other pilot. I would never cower to a belligerent captain to sit quietly by and allow the airplane to be in jeopardy.

The third day of the five-day trip had a layover in New York City on Thursday, January 25th. We flew into JFK in the early afternoon and took the limo into the city. We stayed at the Belmont Plaza Hotel on 49th and Lexington, a great location across the street from the legendary Waldorf Astoria. When I signed in at the crew desk, I checked the menu and she wasn't on the list. The menu was our name for a registry of all National Airlines crew members in the hotel, pilots and stewardesses, that was available only to other crew members to see the room numbers of their fellow employees. She hadn't checked in yet.

It had been over three months since I met Baxter Billson. I hadn't crossed paths with her, even though I thought of her often. How could I not? The very next month after our trip together, she was on the cover of The National Reporter, our company magazine, touting our new Sunburst logo, and the new citrus colored stewardess uniforms. My initial thoughts about her were right. She was indeed a cover girl. She was the one in orange. Still, she hadn't arrived at the hotel. In the operations office of every station, there was another list of crewmembers assigned to every flight of the airline, for each day. I knew she was coming.

What would she say if I called her? What would I say if I called her? I couldn't afford to ask her out for dinner and drinks. Maybe I could just talk to her on the phone. Would she be the sweet, congenial girl I had remembered? There was only one way to find out. After another hour, I left my room and went back downstairs to check the menu again. There it was, Baxter Billson. I couldn't wait to get back upstairs to call her.

"Hello," Baxter said. She answered after the third ring.

"Baxter?"

"Yes. Who's this?" She sounded suspicious. Maybe she thought I was crew scheduling calling with a disrupting reroute to her trip. The recent weather had been horrible in the Northeast.

"This is Ben Shelfer."

"Who?"

"Ben Shelfer. We flew a trip together back in October. We went to the fair together, and you hate oysters."

"Of course, I remember. How are you?"

We chatted for a few minutes and Baxter seemed to be the same charming girl I remembered. The more we talked, the more I wanted to see her in person. What did I have to lose?

"I was wondering," I said. "I know it's freezing outside, but there's a diner just two blocks down Lexington that has great hot chocolate. Would you like to join me for a cup? Or, I'm sure they have hot tea if you prefer."

"Yes, yes I think I would," she said, finally.

We met downstairs. She was even more beautiful than I had remembered. She wore her uniform topcoat with a scarf and ear muffs and gloves. I had only my black London Fog uniform topcoat and a pair of leather gloves. It was freezing outside. Desperate. It was 20° and the wind was 20 mph, whistling through the canyons of the sky scrapers of the city. I offered Baxter my hand crossing the icy street and navigating the snowbanks on the sidewalk. She took it, and then we went arm in arm, shivering down the sidewalk to the diner.

We both had the hot chocolate, and I must say it hit the spot. We talked our way through one cup, and then another. We talked about everything. She told me about her parents and her brother. She told me about going to school at Mercer University in Macon Georgia for year. I reaffirmed to her I had indeed been divorced since my birthday, and now my ex and kids had moved back to Apopka. We talked about my dad living in Jacksonville.

Eventually, we were hungry. We each ordered a hot bowl of soup, and then another refill on the hot chocolate. Too soon, we had to go back to the hotel. I paid the bill with my American Express card because, naturally, I was short of cash.

Even though it was colder outside, we walked slowly back to the Belmont Plaza. When we reached the door to Baxter's room, I looked down into her beautiful blue eyes to tell her good night, but I said nothing. I kissed her, instead. And then we kissed again. I was no longer feeling the effects of the cold. At this moment, all was right with my world. I was almost speechless.

"Would you mind if I call you when we're back in Miami?"

"Sure, that would be fine," she said.

We kissed again.

Chapter 55

The day after I arrived back in Miami was Sunday. I awoke early and was unable to go back to sleep. I lay there on my single bed in my stark little apartment in South Perrine looking at the ceiling and thinking about the one thing on my agenda for the day. Call Baxter Billson. I had memorized the number she gave me when we were in New York, and I couldn't wait to dial it. Still, I knew I shouldn't call her at 7 AM.

It happened that I had two black days off so I didn't have to hang around and wait for a phone call from crew scheduling. I had to kill a few hours without spending money, and I knew just how to do it. My grandmother had taught me well. I could always go fishing. Except on Sunday. Grandmother never allowed me to fish on Sunday. Fortunately, Daddy and Uncle Bud never held to that rule, and these days, neither did I.

After a bitter cup of coffee and a bowl of frosted flakes, I grabbed one of the few things I managed to retain after the divorce; my old Shakespeare rod and reel and a couple of Dalton Specials, fishing lures that were spotted to look like a frog. To the south, between Perrine and Homestead Air Force Base, there were acres and acres of vacant land, dissected by freshwater canals everywhere. I just knew they had to be filled with largemouth black bass.

It was fun to fish with top water lures and be able to see the bass attack the lure with a huge splash. The problem was I couldn't get a black bass to strike my lure because it seemed like every cast into the canal, this funny looking trash fish would just devour my lure. Even though they put up a tremendous fight, they were a real nuisance because I was fishing for bass. I must've caught a dozen of those silvery things with the large thin mouth and the narrow black stripe down the side. Finally, I fished my way down to the end of the canal where an old gentleman was sitting on the bank fishing with a cane pole.

"Hey," I shouted to him. I didn't want to get too close because I would disturb his fishing area.

"Howdy," he said. "How you doin'?"

"No good," I said. "These trash fish won't leave me alone."

"Man, them ain't no trash fish you catchin'. Them are snook. They landlocked in these canals and they some good eatin' fish."

What a surprise. I had no idea. What he was trying to tell me was these snook, a saltwater species gamefish, had been somehow trapped in these canals, due to their close proximity to lower Biscayne Bay. It didn't matter to me that they were a delicacy to eat because I was catching and releasing anyway. Still, a fun way to spend the morning.

It was midmorning by the time I arrived back at the apartment and called Baxter. She answered, after the third ring. She was her usual, sweet self, but appeared to be talking in hushed tones. I was assuming her parents were nearby and she didn't want them to hear her conversation.

"I would love to see you again," I said. "Would you like to go for brunch at the Pancake House, the one near Howard Johnson's on Dixie Highway?" She had told the she lived with her parents on 97th St., West of US 1 between Sunniland and South Miami.

"That sounds wonderful. I love the Pancake House."

"Great. How about I pick you up at noon and we can get there before the Baptists?"

"How about I just meet you there?" She asked. "Would that be okay?"

"Perfect," I said.

And she did.

During the next few months, we developed this wonderful, strange relationship, Baxter and I. There were absolutely no expectations from my standpoint. She was Cinderella, and I was certainly no prince. I had nothing to offer her but the truth. I was a divorced Baptist with three children who didn't drink or smoke and was never going to get married again. And I told her so. She was a carefree Catholic, a movie-star beautiful 20-year-old, sampling the world as an exemplary stewardess for a glamorous airline. And she had this football playing boyfriend from a well-to-do family waiting in the wings to marry her when he finished college. Our relationship was obviously going nowhere. That was fine with me because I was living in the present, taking it one day at a time. I was not looking to be a couple. I was looking to be a friend. But surprisingly, I also found a friend.

Baxter, in her sweet, naïve way, was unlike any woman I'd ever known. She was totally nonjudgmental of anything about me, or my past. I wondered how she could be so understanding and supportive about my children and my alcoholic ex-wife. Wisdom beyond her years. I wondered.

Crew scheduling kept me busy during the spring of 1968. National began the process of phasing out my airplane, the Electra, and replacing it with the Boeing 727-200, which we called the stretch 727. It was exciting to see several new airplanes arriving on the property from the Boeing plant in Seattle each month. I was really looking forward to flying these new jets, whose cockpits even had a unique new airplane smell, similar to the smell of a new car. Dozens of pilots and hundreds of stewardesses were being hired almost every month to crew our rapidly growing fleet. By the summer, I would be flying the 727 and no longer be on reserve, meaning I would have a set work schedule every month. In the meantime, I would toil around the country on the old workhorse Electra, and I didn't mind it at all.

Most of my time was spent out of town, either on a working trip or in Orlando every other weekend to see Angel, Karen, and Skip. Baxter's flying schedule was also busy. I knew this because I could see her rotations posted on the boards in crew scheduling. If, by chance, we were both in town at the same time, I would call her and ask her to do something, anything, just to be with her. She was easy on the eyes, and easy on the mind. We would go to the beach on Key Biscayne, and to the Crandon Park Zoo. Baxter would even go fishing with me in the canals near Homestead and out West on Tamiami Trail in the everglades. She even said she liked it, until this happened. One day we were fishing out in the glades at the beginning of a drought. The water, along with the fish, alligators and other creatures, was emptying from the vast flatlands of the glades into the canals. We were really catching largemouth black bass near a culvert that carried water under a service road beside the Trail. I glanced over at Baxter, who was a few feet away from me down by the water's edge.

"Don't move," I said to her.

Baxter froze. She could tell by the tone of my voice that something was not right. Crawling across her foot was this blackish, brownish colored snake with a triangular head about three feet long. I knew it was a cottonmouth moccasin. Fortunately, when I began taking the few steps towards her, the snake quickly slithered off into the water. Baxter began shaking with fear and I was very relieved. If the snake hadn't departed the scene, I don't know what I would've done. I probably would've broken a perfectly good fishing rod because that's the only thing I had at that moment that might kill a snake. Needless to say, the fishing was over for that day and Baxter was never excited about going bass fishing in the Everglades again.

For a city girl, Baxter was a good sport about all the things I dragged her into, just to pass the time. One afternoon I asked her to go dove hunting on some vacant land near 136th street, just West of US 1. There was a freshly dug lake called E Lake, because from the air, its shape looked like an "E". Baxter was game for learning to shoot my 16-gauge double barrel shotgun, so we started with target practice on beer cans. I was surprised that for a little girl with a big gun, she was pretty good. There were a few doves flying around, but none had been within shooting range.

"Shooting a flying bird," I explained Baxter, "is a little more difficult than shooting a beer can. You can't just aim directly at the bird and pull the trigger, because by the time the pellets from the shotgun get there, the bird would have flown on. You need to swing the shotgun along the flight path of the bird. When the sites of your gun extend slightly in front of the bird, you pull the trigger, so the pellets and the bird arrive at the same place same time."

Looking up I saw a bird approaching.

"Here, I'll show you," I said.

I brought the shotgun up to my shoulder, pulled lead with the sites of the gun in front of the bird and pulled the trigger. The bird tumbled in the air. And then, I saw the bright green and yellowish orange colors of its plumage glistening in the sunlight. To my shock and dismay, the bird I had shot was not a dove, but a macaw parrot. It was not uncommon to see these birds flying in the wild in South Florida. Many of them lived free range around the Parrot Jungle in South Miami, usually returning there to roost at night. It was, of course, totally illegal to shoot this protected species of birds. We left the premises immediately. I was so ashamed and humiliated.

During the next few months, Baxter and I were together quite often. To my surprise, she even picked up several of my trips. It was very exciting to leave town with a beautiful girl, fly around the country to a different city every night, and get paid for it. She was so easy to be with, and never boring. It was almost like we were an item, even though I knew we were not. And I didn't want us to be. Besides, she had that five-year boyfriend thing going and I had vowed to never get married again. I had already failed at marriage, resulting in the biggest disappointment of my life. It would be devastating for me to go through that again, both financially and mentally. I was determined to live in the present and enjoy the moment, and I must say those moments with Baxter Billson were very enjoyable.

May and June of '68 were very busy months for me. It was finally my turn to check out on the B-727 and I entered ground school in late May. Subsequently, because of my total immersion into the training regimen, I saw less and less of Baxter. It was probably just as well, because I thought her boyfriend would be home from college for the summer.

There were over a hundred pilots below me on the seniority list, so I would be able to hold a decent monthly schedule, and no longer be on call. Also, as of June 19th, I would no longer be on probation. And I would get a considerable pay increase because I would be paid equipment pay for the hours flown on the 727, as opposed to the flat rate first year pay.

The new airplane was everything I had hoped it would be. It was great to be back in the jets, flying high and fast again. We were basically flying the same routes as we did on the Electra, except occasionally we would also go westward past Houston to Las Vegas, Los Angeles, and San Francisco. They were all fun cities, each with their individual charms.

The summer passed quickly. Because I was getting paid by the hour, I tried to augment my regular schedule by picking up flying time from the open board to a maximum of 85 hours each month.

My trips to Apopka to see the kideroos continued every other weekend. There was nothing happening there to alleviate my concerns about their well-being while they were in the custody of Lou. It was frustrating to not be able to do anything about it.

It was fun to fly the puddle jumpers on the 727. I enjoyed the ups and downs and the takeoffs and landings. The National Airlines gate agents and all the people in operations at the stations around the country were wonderful people, and soon became almost like family.

On a trip in early September, there was a small town on the southwest coast of Florida that I was really looking forward to transiting. From checking the menu in operations, which I did on almost every trip, I saw that when we landed in Fort Myers, Baxter Billson would be on an airplane parked on the ramp next to us. Maybe, I thought, I would have a chance to see her.

We landed at Fort Myers a few minutes late because we had to circumvent some weather along the way. As we taxied to the gate, my heart was beating a little faster than normal because I could see Baxter's airplane, also a 727, was still parked on the ramp. I could see their gate agent taking the paperwork up the stairs to them as we pulled into our parking place. They would be leaving soon. After the captain shut the engines down, I quickly accomplished the shutdown checklist and bolted out the door, down the stairs, and across the ramp. Baxter was standing in the doorway of her airplane talking to the gate agent, who was about to close the door. She saw me dashing across ramp and gave me a wave and a big smile. I flew up the stairs to her airplane taking two steps at a time. To my surprise, she jumped into my arms. I held her tightly and I knew I had missed this girl more than I wanted to admit.

"Hey! We gotta go," the gate agent said.

"I know, just one second," I shouted to him, trying to be heard over the noise of the APU and other airplanes.

"Let's get together soon," I said into Baxter's ear.

"Let's do," she said.

"Pick up my next trip, Flight 180 on Sunday the 15th."

"I don't know… I don't know… We gotta go," she said.

Begrudgingly, I squeezed her hands and turned away and ran down the stairs. I looked back to see Baxter blow me a kiss as the agent closed the door. And then she was gone.

Baxter Billson did, indeed, arrange with crew scheduling to pick up my next trip on September 15th. And then, she picked up my next trip too. And the one after that. Because of her seniority, she was able to be awarded my trips for the entire months of October and November. Flying with Baxter was not like work, it was like a vacation. We would be in a different city every night, with different restaurants and nightlife.

I truly loved New York layovers because of the arts and the theater, especially musical theater. One night I splurged for two tickets to take Baxter to see Man of La Mancha on Broadway. She loved it, and I was blown away by it. I was so impressed by the professionalism of the entire production. The music, the set design and lighting, and especially the performers were incredible. Richard Kiley, who originated the starring role of Don Quixote on Broadway, was unbelievable. The personal irony of it all did not escape me as I sat there with Baxter Billson by my side and Richard Kiley singing "The Impossible Dream."

What was I thinking? The more I was with this girl, the more I wanted to be with her. It was just happening. I was really liking her…a lot. Nonetheless, I couldn't really think of a future with her because I was such a case of damaged goods. Her life was also complicated, even though, much to my surprise, she said she had broken up with her boyfriend. And I had made a vow to never consider marriage again. The pain was still there but without really knowing it, my defenses seemed to be weakening. The words of Alfred, Lord Tennyson were beginning to reappear in my mind: "tis better to have loved and lost, than never to have loved at all."

Chapter 56

November 17, 1968. Baxter and I were sitting beside the pool after dinner at the Lake Wright Motel in Norfolk, Virginia. We were on the last day of a four-day trip that had layovers in Jacksonville, New Orleans, and Norfolk. It was a pleasant evening, cool, but not cold. We were chatting away, small talk about anything and everything.

We had flown every trip together for almost the last three months. It was like a fairytale that was too good to be true. I kept waiting for the bubble to burst, followed by the inevitable disappointment.

In the meantime, after my pay raise, I had traded my Volkswagen Beetle in on a new, aqua, Oldsmobile Toronado. I loved it. And I began looking for a better apartment closer to the airport.

Recently, I had also met Baxter's parents, Mark and Anne Billson. It was obvious they didn't care for me very much. I gave them the benefit of the doubt and chalked it up to the fact that I was seven years older than Baxter, and damaged goods. Nonetheless, they were a strange pair. Mark was a go along to get along milquetoast sort of a guy who was completely domineered by Anne. She was a complete narcissist with a mind and persona trapped in an era of the old "Gone with the Wind" South, which no longer existed. And to me, both her parents appeared to be alcoholics. Alcohol, again.

A few weeks ago, Baxter went with me to Jacksonville to meet Daddy and Dot. She had agreed to go turkey hunting with us. She was deadly on beer cans with a 16- gauge double-barrel shotgun, so I thought that a turkey sitting in a tree would be an easy target for her. Sadly, it was not to be.

Daddy, Baxter, and I left the little house on Brackland St. in Jacksonville in Daddy's old '64 Chevrolet. We were all decked out in camouflage outfits and hunting boots. We also had some rain slickers, because there was a chance of rain. Camp Blanding Wildlife Management Area was about an hour's drive south, where Daddy had roosted a flock of turkeys. We were passing through the little town of Middleburg, or Historic Middleburg, as the city limits sign read, when the old car began running rough. We just happened to be passing a service station/auto repair shop when the engine stopped running together. We coasted up to the dark building. So much for the hunting trip, I thought to myself. Daddy and I had just got out of the car and raised the hood when an old codger came around from behind the building. He appeared to be the owner of the place and had heard us arrive. Daddy talked to him about our car trouble. The old guy put on his mechanics hat and fifteen minutes later he had cleaned some trash out of the carburetor and we were on our way.

There was a light drizzle when we parked the car in our hunting spot, deep in the woods. We donned our rain gear as the three of us began the trek even deeper into the woods in search of the turkeys. Baxter looked so cute in her outfit. She could've been a cover girl for Field and Stream. I'm sure Daddy didn't know what to think. The rain intensified as we reached our hunting spot. The daylight and the thunderstorm arrived at the same time. It was intense. Heavy rain. Buckets of rain. And there was no hint of the storm subsiding anytime soon. It was obvious there would be no way to see or hear a turkey under these conditions. I thought it was funny that it was raining so hard that neither Daddy nor Baxter could light a cigarette. Finally, Daddy decided it was time to get out of there, so we sloshed back to the car. Fortunately, the car started, and half an hour later we were having grits and eggs with ham and red-eye gravy at a diner back in Historic Middleburg. Baxter may have been a city girl, but she was a real trouper.

Baxter and I snuggled closer together in the chaise lounge beside the pool at the Lake Wright. It was quiet and peaceful, with no one around. I leaned over and kissed her softly on the lips.

"I love you," Baxter said.

357

For some reason, I was totally unprepared for what she said. She couldn't possibly love me. After all, I was damaged goods. I had strong feelings for her, but I could never tell her. It wouldn't be right for me to lead her on or make her think I actually thought we might have a future as a couple. Most of all, I didn't want her to naïvely get into a relationship she might regret later. I knew it would spoil the moment, but there was something I had to tell her.

"Listen," I said, squeezing her hand tightly. "I like you a lot. In fact, I'm crazy about you, but there's something you must know about me, and what's in my future. You've met my kideroos a couple of times. You know I'm deeply concerned about their safety and well-being with the life they are living with Lou. If she keeps mixing pills and alcohol, there's no way this situation can have a happy ending. The way this is going, I'm pretty sure that sometime in the future I will go back to the divorce court and bring a suit against Lou for custody of the kids. If I do, I expect to win. Then, it would be me and the three kids. I just wanted you to know that."

Baxter sat silent for the longest time with a very pensive look on her face. Looking into my eyes, she leaned over and kissed me on the lips.

"I knew that," she said. "Your devotion to your children is one of the things I've always liked about you." She kissed me again. "Now, there's something I must tell you…"

Tears began running down her cheeks and for the next fifteen minutes Baxter told me the most incredible story. I held her tightly and became misty-eyed myself as she struggled to recount every heart-wrenching detail of this mind-boggling experience. Finally, there was nothing more to say and the talking and the whimpering stopped. All I could do was hold her close to me because at that moment I knew I was probably going to break a vow.

"I love you, Baxter Billson," I whispered. "So very much."

It was Thanksgiving Day, 1968. I was standing on the observation atop the international arrivals building at Kennedy Airport. A chilly northeast wind watered my eyes as I watched airplanes arrive from

358

all over the world. My interest was only on one airplane, a TWA Boeing 707 arriving from Paris, France.

It had been a busy week for me. I had flown three trips, all without Baxter. She was on a long-planned trip to Europe with her mother. In between trips, I squeezed in a trip to the credit union and to Carroll's in Coral Gables. Thanksgiving morning, I hopped on the first flight to Kennedy to meet Baxter and her mother as they arrived back in the states.

The big TWA jet arrived right on time and began deplaning passengers onto the ramp. From there they would walk directly towards where I was standing to go into the terminal building to clear customs. Finally, I saw them coming down the stairs. My heart was in my throat. I had missed this girl so much. Baxter was wearing this short, green, Scottish plaid skirt, with knee high socks and a red sweater. I waved exuberantly trying to get Baxter's attention over the distance. She saw me, and waved back vigorously. She blew me kisses and held up three fingers, meaning I love you. At that moment, the entire trip had been worthwhile.

Baxter and I were settled in to the last row of first-class on the National DC-8 for the trip back to Miami. Her mother, Anne, was seated three rows ahead and across the aisle. Perfect. Soon after the plane leveled off at cruise altitude, we were served a full Thanksgiving dinner, with turkey, dressing, and cranberry sauce. We both passed on dessert.

Baxter was little miss chatterbox, chatting about the things she did in Europe with her mother, their flight across the Atlantic on TWA, and everything in general. I thought she would have been tired after the ordeal, but that was not the case.

"I can't believe you flew all the way up here, just to turn around and fly back with me," Baxter said.

"There's no place I'd rather be," I said.

"Awww, that's sweet," she said. And then she laid her head on my shoulder and started rambling on again about taking her mother to the Louvre Art Museum in Paris. I interrupted her in midsentence...

"Baxter Billson, will you marry me?" I asked. I produced the ring from my coat pocket, the solitaire diamond I had meticulously purchased from Carroll's, and presented it to her. She looked at me for a moment like she was in shock. I wondered if I'd made a terrible mistake until she kissed me on the lips, long and hard.

"Yes," she said. "Yes, I will marry you."

She kissed me again. And at that moment, it didn't matter that I was divorced with three children. It didn't matter that she was Catholic and I was Baptist. It didn't matter that I was 28 and she was 21, and her parents hated me. We felt intense, total love for each other. After that, nothing mattered.

Chapter 57

The next few months were exciting. Baxter had bid the monthly line I was flying, so we were together almost every trip. That was great because we had a wedding to plan, or maybe sort out, as it happened to be. There were so many factors to decide.

Baxter wanted a church wedding. I didn't care, I just wanted a wedding. The Catholic Church wouldn't marry us unless I paid them a lot of money, became a Catholic, and had my previous marriage annulled. I could not see those things happening. The Baptists would be happy to marry us, but Baxter knew her parents would strenuously object, inasmuch as they hated me anyway. So, we looked for churches of other denominations to perform the ceremony. I teased Baxter, telling her if we could only find a Batholic church, it would be perfect. Baxter mentioned she always thought the nearby little church, Concordia Lutheran, on the corner of Galloway and 124th St. was cute and charming.

We made an appointment with the Concordia pastor, Rev. Samatinger, and he said he would be happy to perform the ceremony. We set the date for March 29, 1969. This would be after Baxter's 22nd birthday and at a time when both of us could arrange a few days off for a short honeymoon.

Baxter's best friend from high school, Leslie Kehoe, was her Maid of Honor. A good friend of mine and fellow National pilot, Mac Mull, agreed to be my best man. It was a lovely ceremony. Baxter was movie-star beautiful coming down the aisle. She wore a white empire ankle length sheath dress, with a custom-made sheer wide-brimmed organza hat, trimmed with matching lace.

We wanted a simple service. And it was, until Rev. Samatinger got to what he called the homily. He droned on and on. I thought he would never stop talking, and I wasn't hearing a word he said. I just wanted to get to the I dos and the I wills, because I did. I really did. Mercifully, the homily and the ceremony finally ended and I scurried Mrs. Shelfer down the aisle and out of the church.

The reception was hosted by the Billson's at their home on 97th St. It was a very nice, intimate affair. Daddy and Dot and Uncle Bud and Aunt Ruth had driven down from Jacksonville for the wedding and it was nice to visit with them for a bit. Uncle Bud didn't have to spike the punch bowl. It was already spiked.

After a couple of hours Baxter and I left for the airport to begin our honeymoon. We boarded the last flight to San Francisco where we spent our wedding night at a hotel near the airport. The next day, after getting bumped from the first flight because it was full, we were lucky to find two seats on the second Pan Am flight to Honolulu.

It was my first trip to Hawaii and I was very excited to see it. Honolulu reminded me a lot of Miami Beach with a few exceptions. The hotels appeared to be less grand and more casual, and the waves in the ocean were a lot bigger. And the tourists appeared to be mostly from Japan rather than from New York.

Marcus Billson, Sr., Baxter's grandfather, lived in Honolulu not too far from the airport with his current wife, Lee. Baxter hadn't seen him in years, and had never met Lee, so she wanted to pay them a visit. His first wife, Baxter's grandmother, they called her Tutu, had died years earlier. Mr. Billson was an affable old gentleman enjoying his retirement years. We accepted their invitation to stay with them overnight before proceeding to our final honeymoon destination.

The old man told us the most incredible story about Baxter's great, great, great, grandfather, Capt. James Makee. In 1843, he set sail on the 95-foot whaling vessel, "Maine," from Kennebunkport, Maine into the port of Lahaina in Maui. While he was there a steward, angered because he was not permitted shore leave, attacked Capt. McKee, striking him twice in the head with a hatchet. The assailant ended up overboard and was never heard from again. Capt. Makee barely survived the onslaught, but made it to Honolulu for medical treatment and extended convalescence. While there he established a very successful shipping and trading company. A decade later he returned to Maui and developed a 15,000-acre sugar plantation in

Ulupalakua, on the slopes of Haleakala. He tended cattle, orchards and vineyards and even imported vegetation and established a dense rain forest on Maui's southeastern slopes. Capt. Makee was quite the party animal and was known to host celebrities, dignitaries and even heads of state, including the King of Hawaii, to his famed bashes on Rose Ranch. This was quite an impressive story I had not heard. The Islanders even wrote a song about him, "Hula O Makee."

The next day we hopped on Hawaiian Airlines for the quick shuttle over to Kauai, the Garden Island. It was a much quieter and gentler place than Honolulu, as evidenced by thousands of acres of sugarcane blowing in the breeze surrounding the airport where we landed. We hurried to the Kauai Surf Hotel, a fairly new resort on Kalapaki Beach.

We had four wonderful days of paradise at this little spot of heaven relaxing, sunbathing, and touring. There were Hula dances every night at sunset, followed by lounge music that lasted into the night. It seemed like every male singer had to play the ukulele and sing "Tiny Bubbles," a song that had been recently made popular by the Hawaiian singer, Don Ho. We cruised on a party boat up the Wailua River to the picturesque Wailua Falls. It made a perfect memory for a honeymoon trip. And yes, they did sing "Tiny Bubbles." They did not, however, sing the song about Capt. Makee. Or, maybe they sang it in Hawaiian and I just didn't know it. Another daytrip was up to Hanalei Plantation, where they made the classic film, "South Pacific." I think Baxter knew the words to every song in the movie. And she now also knew the words to "Tiny Bubbles."

It had been an incredible week. We were married on a Saturday, had taken three flights to Kauai, honeymooned, and had taken three flights back to Miami, returning on the following Saturday. We had to do that because we were flying together for the month of April and our first trip began early Sunday morning. We were totally exhausted but it didn't matter because we were together and nothing else mattered. Our new adventure had begun.

Chapter 58

Baxter and I thought it was a good omen that our first trip together as a married couple had a long layover in Pensacola. We made the most of it by going to a late lunch at Della's, the little Mexican restaurant next door to Howard Johnson's, our layover hotel. They catered to airline crews and their food was delicious. Their chicken enchiladas were great but I especially loved the sopapillas. They were a sugary pastry dessert that were scrumptious, especially if you filled them with honey. I told Baxter they reminded me of my days back on the farm when I would come home from school and poke a hole in one of Grandmother's biscuits, and fill it with sugarcane syrup. Equally scrumptious.

After a long nap, we walked across the street to Martine's, the seafood restaurant, for a late evening of dining and dancing. Once again, I ordered my favorite, fresh fried shrimp from the Gulf. And once again, even though Baxter passed on the oysters, I did not. I ordered a dozen fresh Apalachicola oysters on the half shell, knowing this would be the last month they would be in season. Besides, I thought they were good for me and I needed them.

The house band had been rocking once again, playing many of the old favorites. They did not, however, play "Tiny Bubbles." We were dancing our last dance and as I held Baxter close, I could not help but think how much had changed since our first dance here on the day we met. We had had a rocky past and I had no idea what the future would bring, but I knew that today, the present, the one I was holding in my arms, was like a fairytale.

Baxter and I settled into a relatively new apartment complex on Miller Road and the Palmetto Expressway. It was a great location, fifteen minutes from the airport with no traffic. It was also like the Taj Mahal to me, compared to my first apartment down in Perrine. There were many young people renting there and numerous other airline employees. John Grout, a new hire copilot for National, lived in our building.

For the better part of the next year, we settled into a blissful routine. We flew almost every trip together. Every other weekend we continued our visits to see Angel, Karen and Skip. Unfortunately, the situation with Lou and her abuse of alcohol and pills was not getting any better. It was obvious that her mother and her sister were deeply concerned. Baxter and I tried to make the best of the situation by just having fun with the kids during our visits. Nonetheless, Lou was always browbeating me about something when we picked up the kids on Saturday morning and dropped them off on Sunday afternoon.

Our world changed dramatically on January 31, 1970. The union representing the reservationists, station agents, and ticket agents voted for a strike against National Airlines. Overnight, the airline ceased operations and both Baxter and I were furloughed and out of a job.

We knew there was always a possibility of a strike because there were so many different unions on the property, each representing a different segment of the workforce and negotiating their own work agreement. Employees jokingly called National Airlines "Cobra Airlines," because they said they would strike at anything. Bud Maytag and the management of National were never too concerned about a strike because they belonged to the airline Mutual Aid Pact. In this agreement, the member airlines would pay the airline being struck approximately one third of their monthly pre-strike revenues. They did this to help the management of the struck airline hold the line against union demands for increasing wages and benefits. Maytag would immediately shut the airline down, eliminate most expenses, take then mutual aid money and be none the worse for it. He would even pay dividends to the stockholders during the period of time the airline was on strike. This was a good news, bad news situation for the employees. The good news was we knew the airline would survive the strike and at some point in time, we would be able to return to our jobs. The bad news was we never knew how long the strike would last and how long we would be without a paycheck.

The first thing that Baxter and I did when we received our letter of furlough was file for unemployment benefits. To our surprise, we even qualified for food stamps. Every little bit helped, but I knew with rent, car payment, and child support, we could not survive for very long without me earning more income. It was a daily ritual for me to peruse the help-wanted and business opportunities ads in the Miami Herald. There weren't many part-time or temporary jobs available.

In the meantime, one of my pilot friends told me about a Saturday afternoon cash poker game down in Perrine. He said he would be glad to give me an introduction. I remembered playing poker back in Valdosta and thought this might be one way to supplement my income. Baxter was not at all in agreement with me playing poker, but she finally agreed to let me try to see what would happen.

The game was in the upstairs office of a warehouse in the industrial section of Perrine. The players were mostly good old boys from every facet of life. You meet some interesting characters at the poker table. One of my favorites of the characters was an old guy named Toby, a tomato farmer from Homestead. To look at him, his appearance and the way he dressed, you would think he was just one meal short of being homeless. He was an okay poker player, but I could read him pretty well. Occasionally, after taking a bad beat on a hand, he would go on tilt, playing wild, losing several hands in a row. When he would have to dig for more money, he didn't go into his pocket or his wallet. He went into his sock. Toby kept a roll of 100s, 50s, and 20s the size of a softball, thousands of dollars, tucked away in his sock, covered by his trousers. The players at the table, myself included, were amazed to see this.

My poker patience and discipline paid off. Each of the first two Saturdays I played I was able to leave the game with almost $100 profit. Nice, I thought. An extra hundred dollars a week would certainly help get us through the strike. The third Saturday I was not able to play because we had to attend a party with friends. When I returned to the game the next week, a few of the players were chatting at the table before play began. I sat down and they realized I had no idea what they were talking about.

"You weren't here last week, were you?" One of the players asked.

"No, what happened?" I asked.

"Two hoodlums wearing ski masks busted through the door with guns and robbed us. They took all the money off the table and made us empty our pockets and our wallets. They even took our wallets. It was terrifying."

"That's terrible," I said. I immediately thought of Toby and noticed he was not sitting at the table. "Did they get Toby's wad?"

"No, they didn't. They didn't check our shoes and socks."

"Thank goodness," I said.

Before the game started, I made an excuse to leave and never returned to that game. I felt like I had dodged a bullet and no matter if it was easy money, it wasn't worth getting shot in a robbery. I would have to find another way to pay the bills.

After several more days of scouring the newspaper classifieds I found something that looked interesting. The ad was seeking a door-to-door Fuller Brush salesman, selling household supplies. I thought this might be something I could do because I remembered making extra money selling Watkins products when I was in college in Tallahassee. It was one of those jobs that paid in direct proportion to the amount of work you did. I decided to give it a try.

The district manager agreed to give me as my area a middle to upper-class neighborhood in South Dade, east of US 1, between Suniland and Perrine. I tried to be presentable, dressing in khakis with a short sleeve white shirt and tie, and began knocking on doors. Within a few days I was amazed at how much product I was selling. The problem was the amount of time required to deliver the product. I was selling more than I could deliver. Baxter began helping me by taking the car and making deliveries while I continued selling. Even that was troublesome, so to solve the problem, I hired two furloughed pilots and paid them an hourly wage to deliver for me. The district manager was ecstatic. After four weeks he told me I was the number one Fuller Brush salesman in Dade County. That was nice, but what I really wanted to do was fly airplanes. Fortunately, a couple months later the strike was over Baxter and I were back living the dream.

Then, out of nowhere, Baxter was pregnant. She was thrilled and I was thrilled. I wasn't determined to over populate the world, but Baxter was always so great around my kids, I knew it was important for her to have one of our own. The bad news was we would no longer be able to fly together. She would be fired as soon as the company found out she was with child. Also, I had been awarded a Copilot's bid to fly the DC-8 and would begin

367

ground school at the end of June. We made the best of our trips together after the strike, but sadly, our flying honeymoon was coming to an end.

Baxter flew as long as she could. Then, in October, she went into the office and told them what they probably already knew, and she was terminated.

It was obvious we were about to outgrow our little apartment so Baxter had been on the lookout for a house. She liked some of the models of Pine Acres, a new development out west on Kendall Drive. Prices were increasing almost weekly, although still reasonable. I learned I qualified for a VA loan, with no money down, so we signed the contract for a three-bedroom two bathhouse on 120th St. and moved in the last week of October.

Chapter 59

October 30, 1970.

This was a trip I did not want to take. It was almost 11 o'clock on a Friday night when the big DC-8 airliner that was National Airlines Flight 43 taxied into takeoff position on runway nine left at Miami International Airport. Carl Greenwood, a veteran Captain, was in the left seat at the controls. I was the copilot in the right seat.

During the previous week I had tried desperately to avoid flying this four-day trip. Two days prior, my pregnant wife and I had moved into a new house in Pine Acres, a development in the West Kendall area of Southwest Miami. The house was newly constructed and, other than a bed, we had no furniture. We had taped newspapers to the windows for privacy, until we could purchase curtains. My presence was needed at our new house to make it a home.

There was another reason I didn't want to be on this trip. The Florida State University Seminoles were playing the Miami Hurricanes in the Orange bowl on the very Friday night the trip departed. My beloved Marching Chiefs were in town and I did not want to miss this rare opportunity to see them. Nonetheless, despite all my efforts, I was unable to swap or drop this trip.

"National 43, wind 070 at 10, cleared for takeoff runway nine left," the tower operator said over the radio.

"National 43 rolling, nine left," I answered.

"Takeoff power," Capt. Greenwood said. He pushed throttles forward and the four Pratt & Whitney turbojet engines roared to life.

Vance Stanley, the flight engineer, leaned forward from his seat behind me and trimmed the throttles to the takeoff setting.

"80 knots, airspeed checked," I called out. "V1, rotate, V2."

Capt. Greenwood pulled back on the controls and gently lifted the big jet into the air.

"Positive rate," I said, announcing that the aircraft was climbing.

"Gear up," Capt. Greenwood commanded.

I lifted the gear handle to the up position and the landing gear retracted. Up ahead, below me to the right, I could see the lights of the Orange Bowl. My thoughts immediately drifted to the game I was missing. I had checked the score in operations before boarding the airplane and was so happy that into the fourth quarter my Seminoles were trouncing the Hurricanes.

"National 43, Miami Departure 119.5," the tower operator transmitted.

"119.5, National 43. So long," I said.

When I switched the radio to departure control frequency, there was chatter on the air so I waited my turn to check in. We retracted the flaps from the takeoff position so the aircraft was in a clean configuration as we continued to climb past the Orange Bowl. Staring down, I could see the players on the field and was once again sorry I couldn't be there for this great victory.

The cockpit door opened, then closed, behind me. I didn't look around because I knew it was Terri Martindale, the good-looking blonde stewardess working First Class, coming in to make sure our coffee cups were full. She knew it was going to be a long night by the time we got to San Francisco.

"Captain…." Terri said in a meek voice. Carl was busy flying the airplane. We had now entered a cloud layer with a little bit of turbulence.

"Captain…" Terri said, again.

This time there was something different about her voice that made me turn around to look. The first thing I saw was the barrel of the gun aimed right between my eyes.

"Habana! Habana! No trouble!" the man screamed. His finger was on the trigger and the gun was shaking in his hand. He had a chokehold on Terri's neck with his left arm as he stood behind her, using her body as a shield. He was a slightly built man with a dark complexion, wearing a narrow-brimmed Panama hat. He went on a tirade, waving the gun around and shouting commands in Spanish. Even in the dim light I could tell his face was flushed and his eyes showed a look of desperation and fear.

Carl connected the airplane to the autopilot and turned to face the hijacker, showing both his hands in a calming manner.

"Hey, hey… Calm down," Carl said. "It's okay. We'll take you to Havana. Just put the gun down."

The hijacker either didn't believe him or didn't understand him, and proceeded into another tirade of shouting and gun waving. The turbulence from flying in and out of the clouds continued. I was afraid he might even accidentally shoot someone. I knew if the gun fired, someone would have to go after hijacker, no matter what. Very quietly, I slid my right hand to my waist and disconnected my seatbelt and shoulder harness. If the gun went off, I would lunge for him. I knew Vance, the flight engineer, would help me, if he had not been shot.

"Let's go to Havana," Carl said to me.

"You want me to tell departure?" I asked.

"Yes, tell them."

I had no idea how the hijacker would react to me talking on the radio. Reluctantly, I picked up the mic, not knowing if I was about to speak my last words.

"Miami Departure, this is National 43, we have a man with a gun in the cockpit that wants to go to Havana, and were going to take him," I said.

"National 43… Say again. Confirm you have a hijacker on board," Departure said.

"That's affirmative, National 43."

"National 43, turn right heading 180, climb to one 17,000."

"Roger, 180, leaving 5000 for 17000," I said.

When I turned back around the hijacker once again had the gun inches from my face, pointed directly between my eyes. There was a look of contempt and hatred in his eyes. This time the gun wasn't shaking and his aim was steady. I could see his finger tightening on the trigger…

"Si vamos a La Habana, debemos comunicarnos con el control del trafico aereo," Carl said to the hijacker, in his best attempt at Spanish. I understood no Spanish, but I thought he was trying to tell the hijacker that if we were going to Havana, we would have to communicate with air traffic control. I was relieved Carl spoke up because the hijacker took the gun away from my face and seemed to relax slightly when he heard Spanish being spoken.

Air traffic control gave us a clearance direct to Key West, then direct to Havana, at 22,000 feet. We found clear skies and smooth air over the Florida Keys at that altitude. The hijacker remained skeptical. He thought we might try to trick him by landing somewhere in the states, rather than Cuba.

"Cayo Hueso," Carl said to the hijacker. He pointed down to Key West, the southernmost city in the United States. The hijacker wasn't totally convinced. We made a slight turn towards Havana, now less than 100 miles away.

"Ladies and gentlemen this is Capt. Greenwood," Carl said to the passengers over the PA system. "You may have noticed some unusual activity in the front of the airplane after takeoff. We have an individual who forced his way into the cockpit demanding we take him to Havana, Cuba, and that's what we're doing. We want you to know we're doing whatever is necessary to ensure your safety. The authorities have been notified and we'll be on the ground in Havana in about twenty minutes. Thank you."

Operationally, once the guy stopped waving the gun around, this was just another normal flight to us pilots in the cockpit. Havana was just another airport to us. Hijackings were not all that uncommon in the airline industry during the previous few years, so National Airlines always planned for that eventuality. Before Fidel Castro came into power, National had three nonstops a day from Miami to Havana. Many of our pilots, Carl Greenwood included, had flown that route many times. When operating in the South Florida area, we always carried enough extra fuel to go to Havana. Cuban airport charts and maps were standard issue for our flight kits.

The skies had cleared and we could see the lights of Havana and José Marti International Airport from many miles away. As we were descending, Carl briefed me on one peculiarity about the runway there. He said don't be surprised to see railroad tracks running across the runway through the middle of the airport. We landed straight in on Runway 24, and sure enough, there they were, railroad tracks running directly across the middle of the runway. Strange.

The hijacker once again appeared nervous and agitated as we came to a stop in front of the small terminal building. He appeared to be more at ease and a wry smile came on his face when we shut the engines down and a large group of armed militia immediately surrounded the airplane. They brought the portable steps up to the front door of the airplane and within seconds several gunmen were in the cockpit. They snatched the gun from the hijacker and lifted him off the floor and out of the cockpit.

It was over. It was such a relief to not be under the gun anymore. It must've been even more so for Terri because she had to endure the hijacker's physical abuse. It was impressive to me how she was able to keep her composure.

The shutdown checklist was completed and Carl and I deplaned to see how fast we could file a flight plan and get out of there. The stewardesses and passengers were asked to remain on board, in hopes of a quick turnaround.

When we got to the bottom of the stairs, one of the Cuban ramp agents approached us with a big smile on his face.

"Ahhh… Capt. Greenwood, they got you again," the agent said.

"Hi Manny. How are you?" Carl asked.

The two of them had a cordial exchange of pleasantries like old friends.

"Who was that?" I asked. We continued walking towards a small terminal building.

"That was Manny," Carl said. "He used to work for us when National had the Havana route."

"You were hijacked before? I asked.

"Twice. This is the third time."

"Wow. That must be some sort of a record."

"I'm not sure that's a record you would want," Carl said.

It was approaching midnight on a Friday night in Havana and there was not much happening at the airport. No airplanes taking off or landing. No passengers coming and going. It was eerily quiet. The lobby of the small terminal building was empty, except for one agent. Most of the military junta had dispersed. There were about half a dozen men in a small room, adjacent to the lobby, with raised, angry voices. I could not understand what they were shouting in Spanish, but I knew it wasn't a friendly conversation. The hijacker was undergoing a vigorous interrogation.

We advised the agent in the lobby we would like to file a flight plan to depart as soon as possible. He said that might not be possible, because Castro would have to be notified and give his approval. He went on to say Castro was at a gala at one of the embassies and would be consulted when the event was over. It was already after midnight. I wondered how long could these parties last?

"It sounds like they're giving us the runaround," I said to Carl.

"Unfortunately, we would have no choice but to be patient," he said. "It's a communist regime, and we are totally at their mercy. The Swiss embassy will intercede on our behalf, but that could take a while. We may as well deplane the passengers and the stews. I'll go make an announcement."

All the passengers and our girls filed into the lobby with their carry-on items from the airplane. All except six passengers, a Cuban woman and her five children. We learned the hijacker had his pregnant wife and five kids with him and the authorities had already boarded the airplane and whisked them away.

A representative of the Swiss embassy arrived at the airport about an hour and a half later. He explained how it was unlikely we would be released before spending the night, because now, on the island, it was all about the greenback dollar. He said the Cuban government would try to extract from us as much money as possible by piling on the fees for goods and services while we were there.

It was almost 3 o'clock in the morning and exhaustion was setting in for all of us in the crew and the passengers. Carl decided we had no choice but to play their game. He consented to staying overnight and we all boarded a bus to the hotel that had been arranged.

The Habana Riviera Hotel was located on the Malecon, a curving drive along the waterfront in Havana. It had twenty-one floors and over three hundred rooms and in its day was probably a five-star resort. Unfortunately, its day had passed. The carpets were threadbare, the air conditioning did not work, everything needed painting and was in general disarray. The large room adjacent to the lobby that was previously a casino was now a large bar. It appeared no maintenance had been accomplished on the building since Castro had taken over in 1959, eleven years ago.

There was a large room adjacent to the lobby that was previously a casino and was now a large bar. We informed everyone this would be our place to assemble for information on our departure the following day.

My room on the eighth floor had a musty mildew smell from high humidity and lack of ventilation or air conditioning. I opened the window to allow the fresh night air to enter. Sleep did not come easy. The sheets were old. The bed was old. My mind was churning about the events of the last few hours. It was very unsettling to not be in control, at the mercy of an unknown desperate individual with a gun. Eventually, I drifted off to sleep for a few hours. I was awakened by the daylight and the noise of the loud cars that sounded like they needed mufflers, motoring along the Malecon.

My trip downstairs to find some coffee found Carl and another diplomat from the Swedish Embassy talking in the bar, which was our rendezvous room. It wasn't easy, but I finally added enough milk and sugar to the strong Cuban coffee to be able to drink it. I also choked down a couple of the sugary, fruity pastries that was provided on the buffet set up exclusively for us.

The Cubans had originally given us a takeoff time of 10 AM, but now it had been pushed back to 12 noon. Then later we were told the next update for any further information would be at 2 PM. They gave no reason for these rolling delays which made it very disconcerting for us and our passengers.

Besides Terri Martindale, the other stewardesses on the trip were Nikki Shirley, J. E. Lee, and Alice Miller. After a make-your-own sandwich lunch at the buffet in the bar, myself and some of the girls decided to go for a walk. Anything to escape the hurry up and wait funk atmosphere among the crew and passengers in the bar would be helpful, I thought. We were told to stay close to the hotel and be back in half an hour. We were also told that someone would probably be watching our every move.

We exited the front of the hotel and walked to the north across a large plaza, then across the Malecon to the sidewalk along the seawall. We stood there for a moment, soaking in the hot sun and the cool sea breeze, watching the waves crashing against the rocks below. I thought about Baxter, home alone in a new house with only a bed and no telephone. I wondered if she knew we had been hijacked and were being held against our will on a communist island. Most recent hijacked flights were quickly turned around and sent on their way back to the states. Why were we different? Were we pawns in a bigger picture? I looked to the north across the Caribbean Sea knowing that Key West was only 90 miles away. I wondered if they were going to hold us as hostages for some reason if the US Marines would come rescue us. I wondered.

We crossed the large plaza again on the way back to the hotel. There were a few people around, but I noticed this one particular young man who appeared to be near our age walking near us, attempting to be inconspicuous. Out of the blue he spoke to us without even looking in our direction.

"You're the Americans from the plane, right?" The man asked in a hushed tone. He spoke almost perfect English.

"Yes," I said.

"Please tell them hello for me at the University of Georgia. I'm a doctor who went to medical school there. I miss it very much."

"I will," I said. "Maybe you can come back and tell them yourself."

"That will never be possible," he said. "They would never allow me to leave the country. I have to go now. Good luck." Without looking, he turned away and was gone. It was a very interesting encounter. And vividly revealing about the culture of fear and suspicion on the communist island.

Finally, the Swedish diplomat told us their Embassy had paid all our hotel fees and airport fees on behalf of National Airlines. He also told us a bus had been scheduled for us to leave the hotel at 4:30 PM. That was one pickup I did not want to miss.

The sun was still above the horizon as the old bus weaved its way to the airport. The streets had many potholes and were in great need of repair. The cars on the road were mostly old American cars, Fords and Chevrolets from the 1950s. Nothing newer. The buildings we passed were old and dilapidated. From the storefront and façade of one particular building it was obvious it was a grocery store. People were lined up around the block to the front of the store. When they reached the front of the line, they approached a table. They were not allowed to enter the store but were given what looked like a bag of sugar, a bag of flour, and a bag of beans. No shopping. They would get what they were given, and nothing more.

When we reached the airport, at the Captain's direction, myself and the rest of the crew went over the airplane with a fine-toothed comb. We wanted to make sure the plane had not been sabotaged and no unwanted items or people had been hidden aboard.

The passengers were boarded and the girls did a headcount, only to find that two of our passengers were missing. Two Cuban-Americans were not on the plane. There was a terse conversation between Carl, the Cubans, and the Swiss that lasted for several minutes. Basically, Carl was telling them we were not leaving without all of our passengers, except for the hijacker and his family. The Cubans finally relented and the two Cuban-American passengers were boarded.

Dusk was falling as we finally departed at 6:45 PM. It was my turn to be at the controls and as we lifted off the runway. it was the first time I'd ever heard a rousing round of applause coming from the back of the airplane. The passengers were so happy to be leaving the communist island. And so was I. The general consensus was they delayed our takeoff until after dark so we couldn't photograph the Cuban missile sites on the island. It's not as if our F-101's and U-2's weren't taking pictures of the island every day.

Forty minutes later we were on the ground in Miami. We were met at the gate by a wall of TV cameras and a large crowd of people, including reporters and law enforcement personnel. The seven crewmembers were interrogated individually by FBI agents from the Miami field office of the FBI. After we had told our stories, the crew attended a press conference. Capt. Greenwood did most of the talking, as it should be. I couldn't wait for it to be over so I could go home to Baxter.

About a week later, Baxter and I were hanging drapes to cover the sliding glass doors of our family room. There was a knock at the front door. Standing there in the warm Florida sun was a tall, distinguished, blonde haired gentleman, with a crew cut and a narrowly trimmed mustache. He was wearing a gray suit.

"Bennett Shelfer?" The man asked.

"Yes," I said.

"I'm Jerry West, FBI. May I come in?"

"Of course," I said. "Please come in."

I already knew he was with the FBI. Otherwise, he wouldn't be wearing a suit in this Florida heat. We walked into the family room and I introduced him to Baxter.

"I won't take too much of your time. I would like to see if you can identify your hijacker from a group of pictures," the agent said.

"Sure," I said.

We still had no furniture in our house, so Agent West spread half a dozen pictures in a row on the kitchen counter. I did not have to look at them very long.

"That's him," I said, pointing to one of the pictures.

"You're right, that's him. We've identified him as L. Rosas, but that's probably an alias. He recently robbed a convenience store in Little Havana where he shot and killed the owner. He was on the run when he hijacked your airplane. We going to charge him with air piracy, but we will never have to put them on trial."

"Why is that?" I asked.

"Because our intelligence tells us Castro shot him."

"Wow. Castro was the judge, jury, and executioner. He would've been much better off to face the music here in the states," I said.

Jerry West, Baxter and I chatted for a long while. Oddly enough, later we became good friends and tennis buddies with he and his wife, Judy. Small world.

Chapter 60

November 14, 1970.

The excitement from the hijacking had waned and in between my trips we had been working hard to make our little house a livable home. We had managed to get window coverings and had moved the newspaper from the windows everywhere except the two guest bedrooms. The table in our family room was a large wooden electrical cable spool that had been discarded from the construction going on all around us. It worked for us. Furnishing a home was a long process. Especially with limited funds.

Baxter and I flew to Orlando to visit Angel, Karen and Skip. We picked them up from Lou at the house she was renting on Saturday morning. She gave me the usual admonitions of how she would take me back to court if I didn't do this or did that, concerning the kids. I didn't understand her outrage because I'd never been late with a child payment or returned the kids late after a visit. Then again, there had always been a lot of things I didn't understand about Lou.

We made our usual trip to Howard Johnson's on I-4 in Orlando. Skip, who was three, thought that was where his daddy lived. We had a great time as usual and on Sunday afternoon, at Lou's request, returned the kids to her parent's house on Dream Lake in Apopka. The old man, or Pa as the kids called him, had suffered a stroke a while back and was partially paralyzed. Wilma McGuire, Lou's mother, had her hands full. She was in her late 60s but appeared to be in good health. The kids called her Mamaw.

Mamaw had heard about the hijacking so I told her the entire story. She listened intently and lamented that the good Lord was looking out for me. I agreed.

"The kids are telling me that Lou has been sick a lot and she sleeps all the time," I said. Mamaw cut her eyes to me with a disgusted look.

"She's not sick, Ben. She's taking pills and drinking 'till she passes out. I'm really worried about her."

"That's what I was afraid of. I'm worried about her too. And I'm really worried about the kids."

"Me, too," she said.

"Ma'am, you told me a long time ago that if Lou and I ever had a disagreement you would be on her side, no matter what. Still, I think I need to tell you this. Because of the current situation and my concern for the welfare of the kids, I think I have no choice but to take Lou back to court and sue for full custody of the kids."

"She's not going to like that."

"If I do that, do you think she'll take it out on the kids? Would she harm them?"

"Who knows, Ben? I don't know what she will do anymore," Mamaw said.

"I know you love the kids like I do. And I appreciate your honesty. I just know what I have to do. I'm going back to Miami and contact a lawyer. I'll let you know what's going on and ask you please do not tell Lou what I'm doing."

Mamaw said nothing, but looked at me with misty eyes.

The next day back in Miami I contacted the only lawyer I knew, the one who had handled my divorce. I told him about the current situation and how I wanted to take Lou back to court to sue for custody. He listened intently and finally told me he could not

381

represent me because he had represented the both of us during our divorce. I told him I had no idea how to proceed and asked him for his advice. After thinking about it, he gave me a name and a number.

Jim Nelson was a young attorney who had recently opened up an office in downtown Miami. After working his way through the University of Florida as an undergraduate, he then completed law school at the University of Miami. He had worked construction full-time during the day and attended classes at night. He was only a few years older than myself and grew up in Gainesville Florida. Like me, he was a down to earth country boy. I called him, mentioning the referral, and he agreed to see me right away.

It took a while to recount the entire story about the marriage, the kids, and the divorce. Jim wanted to know not only the present situation, but also the entire journey to that point. I had always been embarrassed to talk about Lou's problems. Not now. The welfare of my kids was on the line. I told him Lou was in the midst of a perfect storm battling drug addiction and alcoholism while being a hypochondriac.

Jim seemed to sense the love and concern I had for my children as he listened intently. He told me it was an uphill battle because, regardless of the circumstances, it was extremely rare for a father to be awarded custody. I told him because of her irresponsibility I had no choice but to go forward, despite the odds. I also relayed to him my concern that Lou might harm the kids if she found out I was taking her back to court.

"So now you've taken this case from the unlikely to the impossible," Jim said, with a wry smile.

"What do you mean?"

"So now you not only want the judge to give you custody, but you want him to give you no-notice custody. Who's the judge?"

"Judge Harold Vann."

"Ugh. He's a tough judge. Fair, but tough. Proving a mother to be unfit without even a hearing is a tall order, especially without other witnesses or corroborating evidence."

"What about Lou's mother, Mrs. McGuire."

"Would she testify? Or at least give a statement showing concern for the children?" Jim asked.

"She might," I said. It was more of a hope than a statement.

"Ben, I can see your concerns and your commitment to this. I'll take the case but I can offer you no guarantees of success. What I can guarantee you is I will give it my very best effort."

"Thank you. I might not be able to afford you. My wife and I just bought a house and…"

"Let's not worry about that right now," Jim interrupted. "I'll make the fee reasonable. If you can give me a retainer of five hundred dollars, you can pay me the rest monthly over time. Does that sound reasonable?"

"Yes, it does. Thank you very much," I said. I liked this guy.

After I got home and told Baxter what was happening, I made a phone call to Mamaw. She reluctantly agreed to talk to Jim Nelson. When he called her, Mamaw confirmed to Jim her concerns for the welfare of the children and affirmed Lou's neglect of the kids pretty much as I had described it to him. Somehow, I don't know how, Jim persuaded Mamaw to write a letter to the court delineating her allegations and concerns.

Jim scheduled a meeting with Judge Vann in his chambers early the next week. He filed for a hearing on the custody issue and then, with Mamaw's letter in hand, petitioned the court for an order of no-notice custody, pending the hearing. The judge took the matter under advisement.

The waiting was excruciating. Thankfully, I was busy flying a four-day trip which helped keep my mind occupied. The morning after I returned home, the phone rang.

"Ben?"

"Yes."

"This is Jim Nelson. We got it, buddy. The judge granted no-notice custody."

"That's incredible! Thank you. How long is the custody for?"

"Until the hearing," Jim said. "Let's hope she doesn't fight it."

"Oh! She'll fight it," I said. "You can be sure of that."

My regular visitation was scheduled for the next weekend. With the judge's custody order in hand, Baxter and I left our Pine Acres house in Miami early Saturday morning to drive to Apopka to pick up Angel, Karen, and Skip. They were ready to go when we got to Lou's rental house but, of course, I couldn't leave without the obligatory browbeating and admonishment tirade from her over what would happen if I didn't have the kids back on time Sunday afternoon. Little did she know, I thought. Little did she know.

On the way out of town, we made a stop by Mamaw's house on Dream Lake. She gave the kids extra tight hugs. When the kids were back in the car, I thanked Mamaw profusely for her help and the noble stand she had taken demonstrating the love for her grandchildren. And we drove away.

On the way out of town we joined up with I-4 to connect with the Florida Turnpike southward to Miami. We went flying past the Howard Johnson's motel where we had spent most of our weekend visitations.

"Dad, turn around. You missed our Howard Johnson's," the kids were all screaming from the backseat. I had not yet told him what was going on.

"Kideroos," I said. "I have some really good news to tell you. We're not going to Howard Johnson's. We're going to Miami, and you're going to live with us and your little brother or sister when they arrive in February."

The kids were super excited and I was glad to see none of them were disappointed. They had tons of questions about school and friends, etc. They were worried about what their mother would do when she found out. I explained to them, as best I could, that the judge had given me temporary custody and I hoped he would make it permanent custody after a hearing in a few months.

The kids then had one more question. Would Baxter be their mother? And if so, what would they call her?

"Your mother will always be your mother," I said. "But now that we have custody, Baxter will be a wonderful mother to you. I think you need a special name for her." I looked over at Baxter in the passenger seat. "What do you think they should call you, Darlin'?"

"Well…" Baxter said, as she turned around smiling at the kids in the backseat. "Maybe they could call me Ma mere."

"Mom Air?" Angel asked.

"What's that?" Karen asked.

"Ma mere," Baxter said. "It's French for my mother."

"Oh! Ma mere," said Karen.

"I like Ma mere," said Angel. "Skip, can you say Ma mere?" Angel asked.

"Ma mere, Ma mere, Ma mere," little Skip said, making his hilarious funny face.

We all laughed, and the trip to Miami passed quickly. And Baxter had her new name.

The next day, Sunday, we spent the afternoon shopping at the Dadeland Mall in Kendall, a part of South Miami. The children had only packed their usual overnight bags consisting of one outfit and a bathing suit, so they needed everything; clothes, school supplies, and personal items. At 5 PM, the time I was supposed to return the kids, I went to a payphone in the mall and called Lou. After her usual bombastic barrage of threats and obscenities, I simply told her the judge had granted me custody of the kids and she would be served with a copy of the decree on Monday. I told her she could contact her lawyer or the judge for confirmation. She assured me with another salacious rant that she would be doing just that.

It was a bitter court battle that consumed almost a week. Jim Nelson was masterful in laying out a compelling case for Lou being an unfit mother. I testified for the longest time. There were documents supporting our case from not only Lou's mother, but also her sister, Jean. Then Baxter was called to the stand. She was twenty-three years old and looking like she was eighteen, and ten months pregnant. She wore little makeup, simple jewelry, and a straight, plain maternity dress. She looked so innocent, and drop dead gorgeous. When asked how could she even think she would be qualified to take care of the children she said simply, "I have been a stewardess for National Airlines flying all over the country for over three years. Next month we are expecting a child which will be our fourth. I just feel that God has a plan for our family and I'm excited to see what it is."

Lou had hired Ben DuBois, a local attorney from Apopka to represent her. It was surprising to me that he didn't seem to be more engaged in the facts of the case. Instead, he seemed to be more engaged with Lou herself. There was definitely something going on. He would awkwardly wink and smile at her and kept touching her unnecessarily. They were even rubbing legs and playing footsies under the table. Even a casual observer, and Judge Vann was certainly no casual observer, might conclude that Ben DuBois had an altogether different interpretation of attorney-client privilege.

After another agonizing week of waiting, hoping, and praying, Judge Vann issued his final order. We won. We won it all. I thought Jim Nelson was a genius. I was granted full custody. Lou was allowed reasonable visitation rights at my discretion. That would work just fine because I vowed to never harass Lou the way she had harassed me about visits with the kids. She was not required to pay child support, nor did I want any. I just wanted the drama to end and for us to live the life of a normal family, whatever that was. Besides, we had to prepare for our next child who would be coming soon.

Chapter 61

February 10, 1971.

    The kids were all asleep and Baxter and I were snuggled in bed after midnight watching Johnny Carson. I was trying to stay up long enough to see Nancy Sinatra appear, hoping she would sing her hit from a while back, "These Boots Are Made for Walking." We chatted about the busy day and the occasional mini contractions Baxter had been having. She was already over a week late and we wondered if she could make it to the 14th for a Valentine's Day baby. From the looks of that enormous tummy on petite little Baxter, I saw no way of that happening. We, especially Baxter, were ready for this little one to make an appearance. The swinging maple bassinet we had purchased for the baby was nestled in the corner of the room, fully adorned with gender neutral colors.

    We had a babysitter on standby. It was not Anne and Mark Billson, Baxter's parents. They despised me for being divorced, marrying Baxter, getting her pregnant, and then bringing my kids to live with us. Maybe understandable. Nonetheless, I was trying my best to have the complete family that I never had, and give Baxter the happy home that, in my opinion, she had seldom had.

    "Feel this," Baxter said with a grimace. She took my hand and placed it on her tummy. It was as hard as an overinflated basketball, and twice the size. The contraction finally relented, but I could tell this one was different from the others and much more painful. Five minutes later another pain returned, even more intense. The time had come.

    By the time we arrived at Baptist Hospital the contractions were more frequent and painful. There was no way this could be false labor. Dr. Joseph DeCenzo arrived soon after we did and confirmed our baby was on the way. An hour and a half later, I had to leave Baxter because she was being taken to the delivery room. Spouses were not allowed to accompany their wives for the birth, so I was shown to the maternity waiting room.

It seemed like forever until sometime after 4 AM Dr. DeCenzo came through the door. "It's a boy," he said. "Mother and baby are doing great.

Benjamin Scott Shelfer was a big baby, over eight pounds. From the very beginning he had a quick smile. When I first saw him, he was in the nursery getting his first bath. He wasn't objecting until the nurse started shampooing his thick head of black hair. Even then, it was only a token newborn cry. So cute.

Baxter and I had discussed dozens and dozens of baby names. We even bought a book containing hundreds of baby names. We could have saved the money because Baxter always liked the name Benjamin. And I had always thought Scott was a great name for a boy. So, Benjamin Scott was an easy choice for us, and we would call him Scott.

Baxter and baby Scott came home from the hospital the morning of the fourth day. It was an unusual homecoming because all three kids at home, Angel, Karen, and Skip, had suddenly come down with a stomach virus, with all the ugly trappings. After discussing the situation, Baxter and I decided we would bring them home and be as careful as possible. The Billsons vehemently disagreed, saying Baxter and the baby should come to their house. Despite the drama, it was not their decision and they only despised me more for bringing Baxter and the baby home. It turned out just fine. Despite their curiosity, we kept the older kids away from the baby until they were had recovered from the virus. The baby was never sick. Our family was home and all was well.

We loved our little house on 120th Street. The development was called Pine Acres. Probably because before they built our homes the land was acres and acres of pine forest. In fact, directly across the street from us was nothing but pine trees and palmettos for as far as you could see.

The neighbors were very nice. There were many National pilots in the development. A few doors down, was a Delta pilot, Bob Larson, who just happened to be a bass drum player for the Marching Chiefs and one of the first guys I met when I was a freshman at Florida State. Larry Seiple, the punter for Don Shula's Miami Dolphins, lived a few streets away. George Coates, an executive with GMAC, lived two doors down on the corner with his wife and three kids. Between us, next door, were Jack and Darlene Groover, a doctor and a nurse. Jack and I helped each other install our irrigation wells, sprinkler systems and landscaping. Together we bought and shared lawnmowers, edgers, and tools. The Shelfers had a standing invitation to use their pool whenever we wanted. If any of the kids got sick, they would come over as doctor and nurse and check them out. The Groovers were great neighbors and even better friends.

With Baxter not pregnant and feeling normal again, and little Scotty adding weight and perfecting his cute little giggle, we settled in as a nice normal suburban family. As normal as a family could be with kids that went from newborn to ten. The loose cannon in the group was little Skip, who had just turned five years old. He was always getting into trouble. Skip made Dennis the Menace look like a cherub.

Our neighborhood was all new homes, some of which were just being finished and had no one living in them. One day our neighbor George Coats knocked on the door, telling me there was something I needed to look at. It appeared that Skip and two of his kids had been up to no good. We started walking down the sidewalk and running to meet us was little Skip. He had bright apple green paint daubed on all of his clothes and most parts of his body. Even on his face and in his hair.

"I didn't do it! I didn't do it!" Skip screamed.

One of the newly finished houses a couple of doors away had its garage door open. Skip and two of the Coates' kids had found a can of leftover apple green paint in that garage with some used brushes and rollers. They smeared paint everywhere. It was all over the bright white walls of the garage. They even painted the water heater. Skip was still proclaiming his innocence, even though on the side wall of the garage in knee-high primitive green lettering was written, SKIP. It would've been comical had I not been so furious. It took George Coates and me an entire day to repaint that garage with several coats of new white paint.

There was another day I was working inside the house when I heard the distant sounds of sirens. The sounds kept getting louder. I walked out the front door to see what was going on and I saw there was dense smoke coming from a fire back in the woods across the street. To my left, two fire trucks were coming down 120th St. They turned left into the woods towards the fire about a block away. I hadn't seen Skip in a while, so I was naturally curious about his whereabouts. A few moments later, there he was. Fifty yards down the street to my right, Skip darted out of the woods and crossed the street and ran down the sidewalk towards our house. His face was flushed bright red, he had markings of ashes and soot on his shoes and clothes and a mostly used box of matches in his pocket. Once again, he was screaming he didn't do it. To me, by now, hearing that from Skip, had come to mean a full confession.

Fortunately, the fire department was able to contain and extinguish the fire across the street before it spread to other areas. Fortunately, also, they never saw Skip dashing from the scene. We had tried to warn Skip about the dangers of playing with matches, but that only seemed to increase his infatuation with fire. Baxter and I decided to take a more direct approach. We put Skip in the backyard with a full box of wooden kitchen matches. We had him take one match out of the box at a time, strike it, hold it, and watch the flame until the entire match had burned down to his fingers and he could no longer hold it. It took hours. Baxter and I took turns watching him until he finished the entire box. It worked. The mystery of the fire was gone and Skip no longer wanted to play with matches.

Even though Skip was only a small tyke, I could tell he was a good athlete. He was a fast runner with quick feet and could throw and catch like kids much older. He was zipping around the Groover's pool like a jitterbug. There was only one problem. He was still wearing a bubble. A couple of years ago, I strapped a styrofoam bubble swimming device on him so he could paddle around the pool with Angel and Karen. They had started with a bubble also, but they soon both gave it up and were swimming on their own. Skip would not give it up. He would not go near the pool without his bubble. If I took him into the pool without it, he had a death grip around my neck and would scream bloody murder if I tried to break him loose to let him see he could swim. I could think of only one thing to do. With Skip still in my arms I walked up the steps and out of the pool. He finally quit screaming and released the chokehold he had on my neck. I was walking alongside the pool still carrying him. I'm sure Skip thought I had relented and was going

390

to get his bubble. Instead, I suddenly tossed him as far as I could toss him into the middle of the pool. He screamed until he hit water. He came up swimming and continued screaming until he reached the edge of the pool and climbed out of the water. He realized what he had done and at the same time I was laughing and telling him, "good job." He wanted to do it again, and again, and again. And we did. Despite the early drama it was a great day. Skip could swim.

Our little three-bedroom house was very confining for our four kids. Scott was a joy of a baby boy, but I knew Baxter also wanted a baby girl. And I wanted her to have her little girl, for so many reasons. We began thinking about a bigger house.

At the same time, along with the bigger house I had another idea in the back of my mind. I had been physically active all my life, however the constraints of family life and trying to be a good husband had greatly curtailed those activities. I played left field on the National Airlines softball team because most of the games were at Suniland Park, or another park with a playground where it could be a family outing. I enjoyed golf, but it was much too expensive and time-consuming. Tennis was great fun and vigorous exercise in a shorter period of time. I kept thinking how nice it would be to have a tennis court in the backyard.

Lennar Homes, the developer of our community, Pine Acres, kept expanding. They bought the tract of pine forest land across the street from us, the same one Skip had set afire, and mapped out new streets and lots to build new houses. On the first day the new development was open for preconstruction sale, I stopped by the sales office to check it out. The blueprint survey of all the streets, houses and lots, covered an entire wall of the office. Using the scale of the survey, I cut a small rectangular piece of paper to scale, matching the exact size of a tennis court. As soon as I began fitting it on all the lots with four-bedroom houses it was obvious my choices would be few. In fact, there were only two lots where a full-sized tennis court would fit, and on only one of them would the tennis court be facing the desirable north-south direction. On an east-west tennis court someone is always looking into the sun. That new lot happened to be on a cul-de-sac on 110th Ave., only two blocks south of where we now lived on 120th St. Even though it would not be completed for almost a year, I immediately placed a deposit on the house.

Chapter 62

In the spring of 1972, it was a short but exciting move into the new house at the end of the cul-de-sac on 110th Ave., two blocks away. We had watched with great interest as it was being built, block by block, day by day. We knew we would be closing on the property soon when we saw the workers sodding the yard with pallet after pallet of lush St. Augustine grass.

Real estate prices in South Miami were skyrocketing. We sold our three-bedroom house for several thousand dollars more than we paid for it, and our new house was already worth several thousand dollars more than the price we locked in less than a year ago. Win, win. All I had to do now was get to work and make this new house the home we wanted it to be.

The first thing I had to do was save the newly laid grass in the yard. It was not yet the summer rainy season and without water the new sod would never survive. It was difficult dragging hoses around the yard and expensive using city water to irrigate the grass. A pilot friend of mine, Sandy Hutchinson, had a sideline business of installing irrigation wells. I employed him to drop a well for us and connect it to an irrigation pump. I rented a small trencher to cut small ditches in the coral rock and installed sprinklers to cover the entire yard. The grass was green.

The tennis court project proved to be more problematic than I had anticipated. I discovered I needed a zoning variance to build a tennis court within 7 ½ feet of the property lines. That meant I had to fight City Hall, or County Hall as it was in this case, for permission to install a tennis court. That was troubling because you never knew how that would turn out. I managed to get on the docket for the next County Commissioner meeting and with waivers from my neighbors in the hand, I went downtown and pled my case to them. I decided to seek a variance for lights for the tennis court also, even though I had no intentions or money for the installation of lights. I made my pitch to the commissioners and managed to get them into a discussion about what time I should turn off the lights, rather than whether or not I could have a tennis court. They finally approved everything, but decreed I would have to turn the lights off by 10 PM. I guess you can't have everything. But, in my case, I did.

The tennis court went in quickly after the approval of the County Commission. I saved money by subcontracting the asphalt, the surfacing and lines, and the fencing. Topline materials were used all around, including reinforced heavy-duty fencing. A generous amount of silicone sand was added to the surface paint to give the hard court a slower play and a softer feel. A shaded sitting area beside the court was an absolute necessity because of the tropical sun. In keeping with the Florida theme, I hired Roy Cypress of the Miccosukee Indians in the Everglades to install a chickee hut, framed with cypress poles, complete with a thatched roof weaved from palmetto palm fronds. I still remember Roy's phone number. It was Frog City, station 19. The installation of an electric water cooler beside the chickee hut made the rest area complete. Let the games begin. And they did, with regular games among a large group of tennis playing friends. It was especially fun also to teach the game to Baxter and the kideroos.

It was somewhere between spring and summer of 1973. In Miami that meant that the weather had been hot for months and was about to get really hot. I awakened to the aroma of freshly brewed coffee wafting down the hall from the kitchen. The time was 9:15 AM, according to the clock on the bedstand. That was late for me to be sleeping, but I had arrived home at midnight the night before after a DC-10 trip to the West Coast. I padded out of the bedroom following my nose towards the coffee pot. Baxter was in the kitchen emptying the dishwasher.

"Good morning, Darlin'," I said.

"Good morning, my love," she said. She gave me a good morning hug and a kiss.

"How are you?"

"I'm just fine. Except that, well, I do have that pain."

394

"You have that pain. *That* pain?"

"Yes, *that* pain," Baxter said. She placed her fingers against her lower tummy to show me.

In my mind, in an instant, it all became very clear. I smiled as I recalled the loving welcome home reception I received from Baxter the previous evening.

"Guess what, Darlin'," I said. "You're pregnant and it's a girl!"

"How do you know that?" Baxter asked.

Trying not to laugh, I explained to Baxter what had happened, according to my limited knowledge of reproduction.

"Last evening, there were millions of boy and girl swimmers trying to race up the canal to get on the boat," I said. "The boy swimmers were very fast and frantically raced up the canal, but the boat wasn't yet there. They were all spent from the sprint, and died from exhaustion. Meanwhile, the girl swimmers paced themselves and swam patiently methodically all night up the canal. They had plenty of stamina and life remaining after the swim and waited patiently for the boat, which just now arrived when you felt the pain. The strongest of the girl swimmers hopped on the boat a moment ago, and you are now pregnant with your little girl."

And it happened just that way. Blakely Spencer Shelfer was born nine months later on March 30, 1974. Baxter was absolutely thrilled to be holding her little girl. We were so sure it would be a girl that we only picked out girl's names. Baxter loved Blakeley from the beginning, and Spencer was an old family name. We would call her Spencer.

Later that year, in the summer of 1974, National Airlines was shut down again by another strike. This time it was the mechanics union. Regardless of which group was striking, the other unions would not cross their picket line, so the result was always the same. The airline was shut down and the employees were out of work. Bud Maytag, the owner of National Airlines, was a shrewd businessman and a tough negotiator. Buoyed by payouts from the Airline Mutual Aid pack, a strike insurance corporative amongst airlines, Maytag would reduce the airline to a bare-bones operation on the first day of a strike, then hold firm on the demands of the striking union. We never knew how long the strike would last.

It was obvious to me I was going to have to find a job, and find it quickly. I had been making a nice paycheck as copilot on the DC-10, but with all the kids, the new house, and the new baby, we had not been able to accumulate any savings at all. I scoured the help-wanted ads of the Miami Herald every day. In the meantime, I applied for unemployment.

The Fuller Brush job was available, but I could not get excited about doing that again. I was afraid that by the time I built a profitable route, National would be flying again. Then, I saw an ad in the paper for something I thought might be interesting and fun. I couldn't resist. I could be an ice cream man.

The next day I drove to Miami Beach to talk to the ice cream distributor. I ended up renting the ice cream truck, buying the assortment of ice cream treats to fill the freezers, and driving back to the Kendall area to start my route. There's no denying it was fun, seeing all the smiles on the children's faces. Especially my own children's faces.

In my mind, my life up to this point had been nothing really special. On the other hand, it wasn't exactly void of accomplishments. From a small country town, I went on to be drum major of one of the best bands in the country. I was a college graduate, only the second one ever in my family. I was an instructor pilot on supersonic jets in the Air Force. And I was now flying the newest, largest airliner coast-to-coast. Nothing special. Particularly to my kids. But, when I came down our street driving that truck with the music playing and the bell ringing as the ice cream man, I had arrived. The smiles on the faces of my kids told me I had finally amounted to something. Priceless.

Unfortunately, the bloom on that rose faded quickly. It soon became apparent no matter how hard I worked this venture was doomed. By the time I had paid for the truck rental, paid for the gas, paid for the ice cream, I could only make a profit of $25 a day. That was not nearly enough to pay the mortgage, keep the lights on, and feed five kids. At the end of the day, I would lay down and close my eyes to rest, but the rest wasn't there. I could still hear the bell ringing and the singsong music of "Pop Goes the Weasel" playing in my head, interrupted by some little kid yelling, "Stop! Stop!" After seven days, I was no longer an ice cream man.

My next venture at making money during the strike was almost like an answered prayer. We had a new tennis court in our backyard and I had a degree in coaching that included teaching tennis. A few people had even asked me to teach them tennis. I decided to give it a try.

My first tennis lesson was to a group of four housewives. Baxter had told her best friend Sue Nichols I was going to be teaching tennis. She not only spread the word, and I might say no one can spread the word like Sue Nichols, but she also recruited three others, all dear friends of ours, to join her in my first class.

So, there they were, these four lovelies, the sexy housewives of South Miami, all wearing the newest tennis outfits from the Burdine's boutique, lined up on the baseline of my home tennis court, ready to learn to play tennis. They were all absolute beginners.

"Ladies," I began, addressing the group. "The first thing I need to demonstrate is the ready position. Holding the racket in front of you with a relaxed grip and slightly bent elbows, you stand on the balls of your feet, which are spread a little wider than shoulder width apart."

Looking at the group of girls front of me, and thinking about what I was saying to them made me smile, almost laugh. The more I thought about it, the more I knew I had to do what I was thinking.

"So now, ladies, leaning forward, with your knees slightly bent, you are ready... Ready to assume the ready position."

In an instant I threw my racket aside and dropped to the court lying flat on my back with my legs spread wide and my feet above my head. The girls howled. They laughed and laughed. My little stunt broke the tension and set the tone of the lesson. The first thing they learned was not the ready position, but that tennis, even tennis lessons, should be fun.

Little did I know what my ready position demonstration had accomplished. Sue Nichols, Miss Sue as we lovingly called her, and the other ladies in the class spread the word far and wide about the ready position. Within three weeks my calendar for tennis lessons was full. I felt fortunate to be able to put food on the table during the four-month strike without going into debt. After the strike, I didn't want to leave my students hanging, so I continued to teach tennis on my days off. I did this until 1977 when I finally had enough seniority to check out as Captain on the 727.

Chapter 63

The pay structure for airline pilots is determined by several factors, the largest of which is the weight of the airplane. The heavier the plane, the more money you were paid to fly it. That's why I always bid the heaviest airplane as soon as my seniority would allow, regardless of working conditions. And I also kept a standing bid in for a Captain's position. In the summer of 1977, I was surprised to be awarded the bid. I was one of the first pilots in my hiring class to check out as Captain because I didn't mind being on call for most of the month as a reserve pilot. In my mind there was no such thing as a bad trip if I was Captain.

A couple of months later my training to be Aircraft Commander was fast and furious. There were a couple of weeks of ground school, followed by an oral exam, given to you by one of the Check Pilots. In my mind, this was the most difficult hurdle in the entire check-out process. After one of my check rides as Co-pilot on the DC-10, Capt. Bill Archer, a senior check pilot told me, "Shelfer, you fly a lot better than you oral." He was trying to tell me that in the future I should be better prepared for the oral part of the exam. I knew I would have to recite all the critical action procedures word for word, but I'd also have to demonstrate a complete knowledge of all the aircraft systems. It was intense. Fortunately, I'd taken Capt. Archer's advice and made it through the oral exam just fine. After that, the simulator check was routine and uneventful, if you can call engine fires on takeoff and low visibility engine-out approaches uneventful.

Actual aircraft training was a requirement. In September, I spent an hour and a half in the left seat doing takeoffs and landings at the Jetport in the Everglades, or TNT as it was called. The runway was originally built to be part of the largest airport in the world serving both coasts of South Florida. It would accommodate mammoth jumbo jets and SST's, the trans-oceanic supersonic jet liners. When the development of the SST's failed to materialize, the existing runway was the perfect place for aircraft training. It was a safe place away from populated areas, and the snakes and alligators didn't seem to mind the noise.

The next day after the training flight my FAA rating ride in the airplane was scheduled. When the FAA examiner boarded my flight, I was aghast to see it was none other than David (Pink Slip) Potter, the hatchet man from the local FAA office. He was called Pink Slip because he was known to fail someone for the most insignificant reasons. Nonetheless, here he was sitting on my jump-seat. It was the fastest ninety minutes I'd ever seen. Pink Slip sat quietly throughout the flight and left afterwards without any derogatory comments. I was happy with that.

The next week, I was excited to be in the left seat of a B-727 getting my line check. My Check Pilot was Capt. Pat Ledford. He was a great aviator, very mild mannered, and one of the finest gentlemen you'd ever want to meet. We flew around the Northeast for a few days until it was time for my final FAA signoff. Each new Captain is required to be observed by an FAA examiner in the normal work environment before being released to fly the line. I would be observed on a round-trip flight from Miami to Washington National Airport.

When the FAA examiner boarded my flight in Miami, it was none other than my old friend, Pink Slip Potter. It was comforting to have Pat Ledford in the right seat.

The weather at DCA was clear skies, but there was a brisk wind out of the northwest. I knew we would be landing to the north on RW36. I also knew from flying into Washington during my copilot years, when the traffic was heavy, the tower controllers would offer you RW33 as an option to land. The good news was it was more into the wind. The bad news was it was a much shorter runway. And, sometimes, the aircraft might be too heavy to legally land.

Sure enough, we were about five miles out of final for RW36 when the controller called.

"National 106, can you extend for 33?" the tower controller asked.

Pat Ledford, who was operating the radios while I was flying, looked over at me from the right seat. He was probably worried about what I might say. He didn't know I'd already checked the operations manual to confirm we would be at a legal weight to land on the shorter landing strip.

"Yes. We'll take 33," I told him.

"That's affirmative, National 106," Pat replied to the tower.

"National 106, extend for RW33, you're cleared to land, wind 310 at 16, gusts to 25," the tower controller said.

Without hesitation I made a sweeping turn to the right and then back to the left while descending to align with the short runway. In an instant we were on the ground with a smooth touchdown followed by moderate braking to turn off at the end of the runway.

Pat Ledford remarked to me with a chuckle in DCA operations after the flight that when we were on short final approach, he glanced over at Pink Slip who was sitting behind me. He said he looked like a white-knuckle flyer staring at that short runway with wide eyes and a death grip on the jump seat. Pink Slip probably did not see that approach very often, but to us National pilots, it was a routine operation.

The takeoff from DCA for the trip home required special procedures to comply with security and noise abatement concerns. After taking off to the north we immediately made a left turn to follow the Potomac River to the northwest for 5 miles. This guaranteed proper clearance from the Pentagon to the south and the White House to the north. It was a precise, demanding departure procedure, but easy for us because we did it so much.

The weather was beautiful for the trip back home to Miami. Pink Slip had been very quiet throughout the trip, so naturally I was wondering what his comments would be after the flight. Pink Slip lessened my concerns as I was taxiing the aircraft towards the terminal to park it at the gate.

"Shelfer," Pink Slip said, leaning over my shoulder and whispering in my ear. "If you can park this thing without hitting the terminal, you'll be the newest captain at National Airlines."

I did, and I was. At thirty-six years of age, I was proud to be an airline captain flying big jets for a major airline.

Chapter 64

Living the life of an airline pilot turned out to be better than I ever thought it could be. It was one of those rare jobs that paid enough money for a comfortable living and yet allowed enough time off to enjoy it. I was also lucky to have a wife like Baxter, a former stewardess, who totally understood every aspect of my job. Unlike many of the pilot wives, she was not at all the jealous type. I guess that comes with the territory of being the best-looking girl in the world.

It was also good for me, personally, to be able to mentally leave my job at the airport. I rarely talked about flying when I was home and most of our friends were not airline people. Oftentimes my schedule would allow me to be home several days in a row. That made it convenient to see the kids in many of their school activities and sporting events. Playing and teaching tennis on the home court was a fun way for me stay in reasonably good physical condition.

When I wasn't flying, there were different, interesting things always running through my mind. As my grandmother would say, I was always chasing rabbits. What she meant by that was I was always dreaming of this and that, some pie in the sky idea or scheme, and trying to make it happen. The thing about a country boy chasing rabbits is you knew you would never catch one. My dog, Fuzzy, could catch a rabbit easily, but I could not. Still, the chase was fun. When I grew up (if I ever did) the rabbit chasing didn't stop. Fortunately, Baxter was as tolerant of my dreams and schemes as my grandmother. They both just humored me and smiled.

Since the days of my English and literature classes with Frances Segrest and Katy Mary Walters at Sneads High School, I'd been interested in the arts. I loved poetry. I loved the rhyming, rhythm and reasoning of poems. It was interesting to create a thought or mood with rhyming words. It was definitely right-brain activity.

After my days at Florida State, my time was consumed with learning the finer points of aircraft engineering, navigation and operating various aerospace vehicles. Basically, a left-brain overload. My right brain wanted to be heard.

It began in my early copilot years with a trip to San Francisco. The weather always seemed to be gorgeous there, with bright sunshine and beautiful flowers blowing in the wind. In my hotel room, inspired by the beauty of the area, I began writing what I thought would be a poem. Without thinking about it, I began putting music to the words. Before the crew bus picked us up for the trip to the airport for our flight back to Miami, I had completed "San Francisco Sunshine", my first song. Words and music. I could hardly wait to get back home to the old upright Grand player piano Mamma had given us. I plinked out the notes of the melody and wrote them in a musical notebook to be sure I wouldn't forget them. This was so exciting to me to know I could actually compose a song.

Within a few days, I wrote another song, then another. The musical compass for my songwriting definitely favored country music. My musical roots began at an early age back on the farm listening to the Grand Ole Opry, the home of country music, 650 on the dial of our old Bendix radio. Country music out in the country was a Saturday night ritual for me and my grandmother. Later, from playing the French horn and my time at Florida State and the Marching Chiefs, I developed a love and appreciation for most kinds of music. I loved many classical pieces and almost all the Broadway tunes. Nonetheless, now that I was dabbling into songwriting, I learned whatever ditty was bouncing around in my head usually had a country flavor. And it was usually in the voice of a country music star.

It was obvious to me from the beginning that I was at a severe disadvantage as a songwriter. How could anyone hear my songs? We were much too poor for me to have piano lessons when I was growing up so I was never exposed to music theory or any instrument that played chords, such as a guitar. The French horn, the only instrument I could play, except the flutophone, was not exactly an instrument on which I could accompany myself and sing one of my songs. And singing was another issue. I was terrible. If I had to sing for my supper, I'd starve to death. But as I heard my songs in my mind, they were as pitch-perfect as the notes I had written on the lines of the staff.

The time period was the early seventies, the same time frame when Baxter and I were settling in to our Pine Acres houses and welcoming baby Scott and Spencer to our family. One Sunday morning there was an article in the Miami Herald about the origins of a new hit song vaulting up the Billboard pop charts, "Treat Her Like a Lady," by Cornelius Brothers and Sister Rose. I was surprised to learn it was produced at a local studio near downtown Miami called The Music Factory, by a fellow named Bob Archibald. I was even more surprised that after a couple of messages back and forth through Flo, his secretary, that Bob Archibald agreed to see me.

The Music Factory was located near I-95 just north of downtown Miami. Bob Archibald was an interesting chap. He wore a glitzy suit with a silky looking shirt. His thick, black, horn-rimmed glasses accentuated a full head of slicked-back dark hair, so black it looked like it had been dyed. He showed me around the fully soundproofed studio, including his big swivel chair at the control board, where he mixed the recordings. It didn't appear to be that grand, but nonetheless, I was impressed.

The walls of his office were filled with gold records and pictures of famous people. Most of the pictures were from the big band era. Harry James appeared to be his favorite. By now he knew that in my day job I was an airline pilot. He seemed to be intrigued with that, and especially the story of my recent hijacking to Cuba.

The conversation finally got around to the reason I was there. There were two of my recently written songs I really liked, both country and Johnny Cash type tunes. "Lord Help Me Walk Alone" was about someone who sought freedom from dependencies such as drugs and alcohol. "Take Me Back to That Old Town" was about reclaiming the life and values of the old hometown. I handed Bob the lead sheets, with the words and music. He asked me to sing them. Gulp. Remember, I can't sing. But I gave it my best shot, with the obligatory apologies. He wanted me to sing them again. He hadn't thrown me out of his office yet, so I did.

Bob removed his large horn-rims and placed them on his desk. He leaned back in his big cushy chair, closed his eyes and rubbed his temples.

"I have an idea," Bob said, finally. "I like these songs, especially the lyrics. I'm trying to break in this new kid named Bill Acosta who is the son of a preacher. He has incredible pipes. This material may work for him. Let me think about it I'll be in touch."

A few days later, Archibald called me back. He wanted me to come in and sign a contract. He wanted to work up the songs and release them as a single for Bill Acosta's debut record. "Lord Help Me Walk Alone" would be the A side of the record and "Take Me Back to That Old Town" would be on the flipside. I was shocked. I raced down to his office and signed the contract. I was skeptical about him having total control of the songs. He specifically did not even want me to be present for the recording sessions. But the truth was, he had gold records hanging on his wall and I was an airline pilot. I decided to trust him.

Several weeks later I found myself sitting in the big room of the Music Factory recording studio with a very happy and upbeat Bob Archibald. He turned up the sound and played the songs for me. I was totally shocked. The songs, my songs, were not country. They were not even pop songs. The sounds I was hearing was somewhere in the gospel rock genre. It wasn't that it was bad, or I didn't like it, it was just so different than anything I had imagined. It was then I learned that a piece of music, like a painting or any form of art, is interpreted differently in the eye of the beholder. I had to be able to turn it loose and let it happen.

And happening it was. Bob Archibald had a plan. The records, 45s, were already being pressed. A pre-release publicity blitz was being planned. Bill Acosta's concert tour was in the works. All I had to do was fly airplanes and watch it happen.

A few weeks later I received another exciting phone call from Bob Archibald. Variety Magazine had reviewed "Lord Help Me Walk Alone" as a pick to be a hit. So exciting. It also said "Take Me Back to That Old Town" was another solid side. All this happening, and all I had to do was fly airplanes.

And now the rest of the story. Along about this time, Bob Archibald and the singer, Bill Acosta somehow became involved in a vicious contract dispute. This resulted in the two of them parting ways, and Archibald canned the record. My record. Oh, well. At least I was still flying airplanes.

My years in the early 70s were spent flying copilot on the DC-8, and then the DC-10, mostly to the West coast. National Airlines was formally known as the "Airline of the Stars," because of our nonstop route from Los Angeles to Miami, two popular destinations of television and movie stars. It was not unusual to have famous people on the airplane. I had the pleasure of chatting through the years with many stars who were my passengers; the Beach Boys, Country Joe McDonald, Frankie Laine, Bob Hope, Flip Wilson, Keith Jackson, Chet Atkins, Ann Margaret, and Connie Stevens, to name a few. I talked with Connie Stevens the longest time when we were on the ground in Las Vegas, having diverted there because of bad weather in Los Angeles. She is one of the few people I've seen that I thought was prettier in person than on the screen. Andie MacDowell is another of those people.

There was one of my star encounters that was particularly interesting. I was flying copilot on a trip from Miami, nonstop to Los Angeles. The captain was someone whose name I don't necessarily want to mention, but it sounded a lot like Whitlow. At cruise altitude, after passing Houston, with me flying the airplane, the captain left his seat to go use the blue room. He returned a few minutes later and I turned around to see the person climbing into the captain's seat was Glen Campbell. For the next hour, as I kept the airplane headed towards Los Angeles, it was just a kid from southern Arkansas and a kid from northern Florida making small talk about airplanes and music. Glen Campbell was a really nice guy. I liked his voice, but in my mind, he was one of the best guitar pickers on the planet.

Most of those trips were to Los Angeles which required a long layover to comply with the rest requirements for the trip back to Miami. Our layover facility was the Huntley House, a grand, old hotel in Santa Monica. It was a favorite layover spot for National and many other airlines because it was in a few blocks of popular restaurants, the Pacific Ocean, and the famous Santa Monica Pier.

The California scene was a different world to this farm boy from Sneads, Florida. I seized every opportunity to visit the Hollywood and Beverly Hills area. I toured as many of the television studios and movie lots as possible, with the limited time available on a layover. I saw Lee Majors filming the "6 Million Dollar Man." At CBS, I saw Doris Day arriving to make a guest appearance on a show. She was not yet wearing makeup. Yikes. I saw the NBC studio of the Johnny Carson Tonight Show. And while I was at NBC, I applied to be a contestant on the new game show,

Wheel of Fortune. To my surprise, they accepted me on the spot for a filming on the same day the next week. As luck would have it, I was scheduled to be back in town on another layover on that day.

In the early days of Wheel of Fortune, the contestants were not playing for cash prizes, but for merchandise, vacations, etc. Chuck Woolery was the host and Susan Stafford was the pretty lady who turned the letters on the board. I didn't come away empty handed. I solved one of the puzzles with the name of Ludwig van Beethoven. My appreciation of classical music finally paid off. I won one of the prototype models of a portable television that was powered by batteries. I also won a year's supply of Rice-A-Roni, the San Francisco treat. During the lunch break I was seated with Chuck Woolery. He was from a small town in Kentucky and had recently married another television star, JoAnn Pflug. So, there we were, two country boys, about the same age, having lunch at a television studio in Hollywood, California, during the filming of a television show. Chuck Woolery was a good man. An experience like this only reinforced something I learned long ago: people are people, regardless of fame or fortune or station in life. You usually get what you give, whether it's respect, kindness or love.

Lincoln Park was a public facility on Wilshire Boulevard in Santa Monica about five blocks down from the Huntley House. It was convenient for me to exercise there on my layovers because they had six tennis courts. There were lots of players there, which made it easy to find a game. It also cost nothing to play there, a pilot's dream. The only downside was the surface of the courts was comprised of hard, slick concrete, typical of most California courts, making it hard on your knees and ankles. Nonetheless, I loved the place. I played there so much I believe they considered me one of the regulars. The people there were very welcoming and nice. And interesting.

One of the locals that was usually at the tennis courts when I was there was Irv, an older gentleman. When I say older, I mean he was older than me. He was probably in his 50s, but in good physical condition. One day we were chatting after we played tennis.

"Irv," I said. "I notice you're out here playing tennis every day. Don't you know that the tennis courts here are for only the housewives and airline pilots during the week? What do you do that allows you to play tennis every day?"

"I'm retired," Irv said.

"Retired from what?"

"I wrote a song."

"A song? What song?"

"Unforgettable," Irv said, almost apologetically.

"Wow. That's awesome, man," was all I could say, as the unforgettable music and lyrics of the old Nat King Cole standard drifted through my mind.

It just goes to show, you never know. Irv Gordon was a demure, unassuming man. Yet, he had written one of the greatest songs of all time. Admirable in every way.

Another interesting chap from the tennis courts of Santa Monica who became a good friend was a fellow named, Jon Troy. He was a record promoter on the West Coast. He called on radio stations to ensure airplay on records released by the labels he represented. I had shared with Jon my interest and passion for writing songs, and he seemed genuinely interested. Especially after the Music Factory produced and recorded a couple of my songs. One day when I arrived at the tennis courts, Jon chased me down.

"Hey, Ben," Jon said. "I have a friend in town from the East Coast staying at my place for a while I'd like you to meet. After tennis, why don't you stop by for a sandwich and a glass of iced tea?"

"Sure," I said. "That would be great."

We finished our game and walked the few blocks to Jon's modest two-bedroom flat, without him mentioning his guest again.

When we entered the apartment, Jon invited me to take a seat in the living room pointing to a chair near an old upright piano. I settled into the chair and Jon continued into the kitchen to make the iced tea. A few moments later, the bedroom door across the room opened and a young man sauntered out. He had very long black, scraggly hair, and an untidy growth of facial hair. He was not very tall. He was wearing absolutely nothing but a pair of whitey-tighty underwear.

"Hi, I'm Ben," I said.

"I'm Billy," he said.

We begin chatting a bit as he sat down on the stool at the piano. Jon had told him I was a pilot and I also had an interest in music. I knew absolutely nothing about him. As we talked, he swiveled the stool towards a piano and began to noodle away. I immediately noticed that what he was doing was not your ordinary, everyday, piano plinking noodling. The rich symphonic progressions coming from the old piano were impressive and inspiring. I quit talking and just listened. There was an undeniable classical depth to the mesmerizing music I was hearing. A couple of minutes later, Jon returned from the kitchen with a pitcher of iced tea.

"I see you have met Billy Joel," Jon said to me.

Indeed, I had. We visited for a while before I had to return to the Huntley House to get some sleep before flying the red-eye back to Miami. Billy Joel was from the Bronx, New York. He had recently released his first album, Cold Spring Harbor, with little acclaim or financial success. Billy blamed the failure on the producer for technical errors during the production and lack of promotion afterwards. They had parted ways, and were involved in bitter legal battles. Billy was in a bad place financially and mentally. He was severely depressed. Columbia records, Jon's employer, asked Jon to reach out to Billy to see if he could help him make a new start. Billy had accepted Jon's offer to come to Santa Monica and stay with him while sorting things out. Jon's plans were for Billy to work night gigs in Los Angeles, decompress, and write more material and get back in the recording studio.

During my short walk back to the Huntley House that day, my mind was filled with gratitude for the interesting world my occupation, flying, and my hobby, tennis, continued revealing to me.

About a year after I met Billy Joel in his whitey-tighties in Santa Monica, my phone rang in Miami. It was Jon Troy. He asked a favor of me. He wanted to borrow a car.

As the months had passed, Jon and I had chatted occasionally at the tennis courts. With Jon's help, Billy had found some stability in his life. He was writing songs again. For a while he played a regular gig at The Executive Room, a bar on Wilshire Boulevard in Los Angeles. While there, he wrote "Piano Man," the title song of his second album, which was rocketing up the Billboard charts. With Jon Troy now acting as his manager, Billy Joel's career had taken off.

Jon had booked Billy to do a concert at the University of Miami. The expenses for air travel, food and lodging for Billy and the band were covered. The ground transportation expenses were not. Jon wanted to borrow a car from me for Billy to use while he was in Miami. My airport car was a small Toyota station wagon that was several years old. With profuse apologies, I told Jon that he was welcome to it, expecting him to decline my offer. He did not.

I'm sure it was quite a sight with Jon and Billy Joel arriving to check in at the Fontainebleau Hotel on Collins Ave. in Miami Beach, driving my old Toyota station wagon. Baxter and I visited them at the hotel the afternoon of their arrival, where we were given VIP passes to the concert later that night.

The performance was exhilarating. Billy, now already known as the Piano Man, owned the University of Miami crowd from his first song until hours later at the end of his several encores. After the show, the backstage scene was wild. Baxter and I visited for a while with Jon and Billy and the band in their dressing room. I knew it was time for us to go when the smoke filling the air was smelling a little strange. It was definitely not coming from a Camel or a Marlboro. As an airline pilot, one that did not smoke or drink, I certainly could not take the chance of being part of a drug scene. Baxter and I said our goodbyes and good lucks. We knew a star had been born.

My creative juices were always flowing. Regardless of how a song would turn out, it was always fun to write. I knew most of them were bland and amateurish, but not all of them. After all, Variety magazine had said so. Soon, I had a shoebox full of songs that had never been, and would probably never be heard. "Please Ask Me Back Again," "The Lady Loves Love Tonight," "If the Shoe Fits, Wear It," "Love Revolution," "Coming Home to Home," "Make Me A Memory," "I Live with Santa Claus," and "How Many Miles To Miles City" were just a few of the titles.

And then there was the time I thought I'd finally written a couple of songs that would be sung forever. Scott and Spencer attended a fairly new school, one that did not as of yet have an Alma Mater or a Fight Song. So, I wrote "Hymn of Trinity" and "Fight Mighty Titans" which were eagerly accepted by the board of the school and Head Master, Dr. Ned Dougherty. The very next year, the school merged with a larger school that already had their school songs. So much for my songs being sung forever. I'm beginning to see a pattern here.

Without being able to sing or play the guitar or piano, it was a challenge to get a demo tape produced so my songs could be heard. That doesn't mean I didn't try. Frank Shelfer, my cousin from Sneads, called me from Tampa, where he was living at the time, telling me about a group of musicians who would get together on Thursday nights and jam at a small studio there. Frank said they would try to do some demos for me. I flew to Tampa and this wild and crazy gaggle did four demos for me in about three hours. They were rough and raw, but they were my songs on tape for not much money. I loved it. The young guy who was playing piano and doing the cat herding on the group was named, Dave. He also sang vocals on a couple of songs. I found out later his last name was Bellamy. The rest of the story is Dave Bellamy with his brother, Howard, soon became known as the Bellamy Brothers, one of the most famous pop-country musical duos of all time. One never knows…

Chapter 65

About a year after I checked out as Captain when I returned from a flight, I had another of those ominous notes in my company mail box: "Please stop by the Chief Pilot's Office at your earliest convenience." Of course, in that instant, all the events of the previous four-day trip flashed through my mind. Did I violate any FAR's, federal aviation regulations? Were there any unusual flight delays or incidents with air traffic controllers, dispatchers, gate agents, passengers, or other crewmembers? None that I could recall. Yet, here I was being summoned to the Chief Pilot's Office.

"Come in, Ben. Come in," Jimmy Meyer said when I knocked on his door. "Have a seat. How are you?"

"I'm good. Real good," I said. I liked Jimmy Meyer. He was on our softball team for a while and I'd flown several maintenance test-flights with him on the DC-10.

"How's Baxter? You know we still can't forgive you for taking her off the line."

"As I recall, it was the company that fired her because she was pregnant."

"Touché," he said. "Touché." Now we were both chuckling.

"Ben, I'll get right to the point," Jimmy said. "We've heard nothing but good things about the job you're doing for us here at National. Everyone likes your professionalism and your personality. I've flown with you myself and I know you're a hell of a good pilot. I know that you were an instructor and a check pilot in the Air Force. I'd like to offer you the same job at National Airlines."

"Thank you. That's very nice, thank you," was all I could say.

"Go home and talk it over with Baxter, if you like," he said.

Jimmy discussed with me the aspects of the job. The Check Pilots at National were called Flight Managers. They trained and checked pilots in the simulators, the airplanes during training flights, and the airplanes on the line. Additionally, they flew particular charter flights, maintenance flights, and other special operations flights. They were involved in every facet of the airline operation. There were two major benefits of the job: schedule and money. You could generally, within reason, get any days off that you wanted. This was important to me with the kids active in sports and afterschool activities. As for the money, we were paid a guaranteed flat monthly salary of the max possible hours plus an override. I liked that. And I knew this was something I didn't need to discuss with Baxter.

"Thank you, Sir. I'm honored. I gladly accept your offer and will give it my best.

It was so much fun to be an instructor pilot again. Teaching was my passion, especially when the students were highly motivated airline pilots. Crew Scheduler Glen Miller did most of our scheduling. He was so easy to work with. If I needed a day off to attend an event for the kids, I could usually get it.

On the home front, we had joined, for a while, the Briar Bay Tennis Club down on SW 136th St., by the new Falls Shopping Center. The kids were enjoying tennis and I really liked their clay courts. Another member there happened to be the FBI agent who investigated my hijacking to Cuba. It was nice getting to know Jerry and his wife, Judy, and his two girls.

From our experience at Briar Bay, Baxter and I knew tennis was a great sport we could enjoy as a family. We decided to spend the money to join Royal Palm Tennis Club, the premier, old school, traditional tennis club in South Florida. It was a private, member owned club, where the players had to wear all white attire. The exceptional new pro there was Don Petrine, Jr. Skip, Scott, and little Spencer who had taken to the game at a young age, really enjoyed Don's summer tennis camps. Don's father, Donald Petrine,

Sr. was the director of the Junior Orange Bowl tournament, one of the largest international junior tennis tournaments in the world.

One of the legendary members of Royal Palm was Doris Hart. Doris had won the Boxed Set of Grand Slam titles: Wimbledon, the French Open, the Australian Open, and the U.S. Open in Singles, Doubles and Mixed Doubles. She was one of only three players, all women, to ever do so. It was my good fortune to play with her on several occasions. On the first day I was her partner, I was very nervous, trying to make a good impression. I was hitting the ball very hard, but making way too many errors. Doris finally turned to me and said, "Ben, just hit it back. Maybe something will happen." Enough said. That stuck with me and I learned a lot about tennis from that.

Another member of Royal Palm who taught me a lot about doubles was Phyllis Tiktin. She was a fireball, very competitive, and I loved playing with her. Phyllis liked to win, but more than that, she hated to lose. Fortunately, she didn't lose very often. We partnered to win many tournaments together and was eventually ranked #1 in Florida in our age group.

There were many interesting doubles games with another good friend, publisher Karl Wickstrom. His products included "Aloft," the inflight magazine of National Airlines. My pilot friend, Bob Mitchell, was his advertising editor. Karl also started the popular magazine, "Florida Sportsman."

Karl Stenstrom, an industrialist, was another good friend from the club. He was a Swede who married a Brazilian beauty and they had recently moved to Miami. His friendly banter along with his competitive spirit was contagious. Our kids were about the same age and we enjoyed many family get-togethers. Karl introduced me to a close friend of his who had also recently moved to Miami, Jeb Bush.

Chapter 66

In the early 70s, my dad finally retired after working thirty-four years for the city of Jacksonville. He began on the business end of a shovel digging ditches and ended in the position of Assistant Superintendent of the Sewer Department. Remarkable. Especially, for someone I would call a functional alcoholic. He drank every day, but never on the job. And I never knew him to miss a day's work for any reason.

Baxter and I were enjoying our new four-bedroom house in Pine Acres. But now, with number five, little Spencer, toddling around, it was obvious we needed more room. We sketched some plans on a dinner napkin. We wanted to build a huge family room, or great room as it was called, complete with fireplace and a bar that would be completely open to the kitchen and dining room. Off of that room, we wanted to add a bedroom to the existing pool bathroom (even though we didn't have, nor did we want, a pool), making it a five-bedroom, three-bath house. The only problem was money. I could never afford an architect to draw up the plans or contractor to do the work. Baxter said I was cheap. I would rather say I was frugal. Besides, I would never pay to have something done if I could do myself.

In the back of my mind, I had a plan. I was not afraid of hard work, but I did not want this to be one of those penny-wise and pound-foolish stories. I was also not afraid to ask for help. There were two people whose advice and assistance I really needed to be able to complete this project.

The first person was my good friend and fellow pilot, Tom Batten. Tom was quarterback for the Florida Gators at the same time I was drum major for the FSU Marching Chiefs. We often joked about how we were on the football field at the same time so many years ago. His team won the football game, but my band won the halftime show. During the summers of his college years, he worked construction, learning how to build things.

After college, Tom went on to be an Army pilot in Vietnam, flying L-19's as a forward air controller. Tough job, but he was a tough guy. Now, back in Miami and flying for National Airlines, Tom wanted to get his contractor's license and continue to build things. After all, pilots at National (Cobra Airlines, strike at anything) needed a contingency plan to put food on the table during a strike. Tom was good at building things, as he was at everything he did, and he generously offered to help with our addition. Invaluable.

The other person whose help I needed for the project was my dad. I flew to Jacksonville for a quick visit with him to see how he was enjoying retirement. He wasn't. Dot was still working at Duval Laundry and Uncle Bud, two doors down, was still working for the Electrical Department. During the week Daddy would spend his time was sitting around drinking and smoking. Not good. Even so, I never nagged my dad about the drinking or the smoking. It was my belief that he was a grown man and it was never my place to tell him what to do. Fortunately, when I explained our home addition project and asked for his help, he eagerly volunteered. I think he would've done anything to get out of the house and get out of town.

The next four months proved to be extremely frantic, yet, very therapeutic. Tom Batten would tell me the materials to buy and where to buy them, and then do the difficult part of getting me started on each phase of the project. I would then do the work with my dad by my side every step of the way to make sure I had the items I needed, and was doing the job properly.

We rented a trenching machine to dig the ditch into the coral rock where the concrete truck poured the foundation. We laid every concrete block of the walls, and tied them together at the top with a poured concrete tie beam. We made sure to deeply anchor the new updated hurricane straps that would hold in place the wooden beams of the roof over the family room. We nailed the plywood on the roof and then covered it with tarpaper so it would be protected from the rain. We even built a brick fireplace in the family room. It was unique because we built it from a type of brick called Old Chicago. These particular bricks came from an old train station in Chicago. Interesting. Recycling at its highest price. Even so, we liked the look so much we also used the old Chicago brick for a patio outside the family room.

The family room and bedroom addition turned out so much better than we could have imagined. But more than that, it was an invaluable experience with my dad. The kids got to see him as a quiet man, a kind and gentle soul. When it came to common sense, he was a genius. His advice on the feasibility and functionality of practical things was seldom wrong. His patience was admirable. If I became frustrated with something, or even smashed my thumb with a hammer while laying bricks and walked away, he would be waiting there with the next brick and a board of mud (wet concrete) when I returned. As long as he had a carton of Marlboros and a six-pack of Pabst Blue Ribbon, he was happy. The kids got to see that too.

Daddy had the kids conditioned to bring him something to drink.

"Angel, the bear's about to get me," he would say. Angel knew that meant he was hot and thirsty and needed a drink. She would bring him a beer. Angel told me later that when we were building the concrete block wall, she would sneak off to watch Daddy finish his beer and then giggle as he would hide the empty can in the holes of the block in the wall. I suppose that would make it a Blue Ribbon wall. The kids didn't miss much.

One morning during the renovation, June 7, 1977, we received a tragic phone call from Sneads. Uncle Hardy had suffered a massive heart attack and died. We were shocked. Even though he was 70 years old, uncle Hardy appeared to be in excellent health. We dropped everything and went to Sneads for the funeral and to be with Aunt Berta and Ronnie and the family. The First Baptist Church, the same church where I was baptized, was packed for a fitting tribute to one of the kindest and most honorable men I'd ever known. His passing affected me profoundly.

After spending a lot of time with Daddy working on our addition in Miami, I was concerned about his well-being. He was retired with nothing to do, living where he no longer wanted to live. It weighed on my mind. While we were in Sneads for the funeral, I asked Daddy to come take a walk with me to visit our piece of land there. I say our piece of land, but actually it was my land because Daddy had deeded it to me a few years previously. He had bought 20 acres after returning home from the war. With my approval, years ago he had sold the northern ten acres to Verdayne, who had built a nice two-story house in the tall pines on the west end of the property.

We walked the land beginning at the River Road where Grandmother's house, the house where I grew up, once stood. We continued through the six acres of a sagebrush field, to the four acres of tall long-leaf virgin yellow pines to the west. It was there I made a proposal to Daddy. I proposed that I would build him and Dot a nice place to live among those magnificent pines. They could come home to Sneads and make a new start to live out their years. I offered to plant a pecan orchard on the sagebrush field for Daddy to tend, if he wanted something to do besides go fishing. He contemplated the offer in his usual deliberate fashion. He stood there, looking up and listening to the wind whistling through the pines. He finally nodded. "I'll talk to Dot," he said.

"Hello," I said.

It was early evening a few days after we had returned home from uncle Hardy's funeral. I answered the phone on the first ring thinking it might be crew scheduling assigning me a Captain's trip.

"Hey Benny. How's everybody?" Daddy said.

"Everybody's good. Has everybody up there?"

"Good... Good. Me and Dot been talking about what you said when we were back home, and we're really interested."

"That's great, Daddy. We'll have to get together soon and talk about what kind of house you would like."

"I think Dot has already found something she likes."

"Something we can build in Sneads?" I asked.

"No. It's already built. We just have it delivered to Sneads."

"What? You mean a Jim Walter home?" I thought Daddy might be talking about a pre-fab house where you bought a package of all the parts and it was assembled onsite.

"No, not that, Benny. When me and Dot started talking about what you said, she drug me over to Phillips Highway to look at house trailers. Now before you say anything, hear me out a minute, Benny. These new double wide trailers are really nice… And big, too. They're bigger than our house. Dot likes 'em, and I have to say, I do too. I need you to come up here and look at 'em."

"I don't know, Daddy. I hadn't thought about a house trailer."

"It don't even look like a house trailer. The good thing about it is we wouldn't have to bother with building a house, which would take a lot of time and aggravation. We could move sooner than later. 'Cause, you know, Benny, I'm not getting any younger."

The next week I went to Jacksonville on one of my days off. To my surprise, I could see the merits of Daddy's argument. Once a new double-wide was assembled, it looked nothing like a house trailer at all. It was spacious, and everything was new. I could see Dot was excited, but she was afraid the one's she liked were too expensive.

During the next month, the search was on. Now that I knew what we were looking for, I began looking at availability and price, and not only in Jacksonville. Daddy and I, with little Scott tagging along, went on a shopping road trip to Tallahassee, Panama City and Dothan, Alabama. It was finally in Dothan where we found exactly what we wanted, and it happened to have the best price.

We went to work clearing the property, drilling a well, installing a septic tank, and having electrical service established. It was exciting to see the new home arrive. It was a three-bedroom, 2 bath, with a laundry room, kitchen, dining room, and a great room with beamed ceilings and central heat and air. Nice. Dot and Daddy loved it, and so did I. Nestled in the tall pines, it was perfect.

Daddy was anxious to get started on the orchard. Naturally, I thoroughly researched every variety of pecans available. I finally decided on two varieties, the Desirable and the Wichita. The former because it was the sturdiest and most popular, and the latter because even though it required the greatest care, it was the fastest to bear fruit. And I wanted Daddy to be able to see the fruits of his labor. The Desirables and the Wichitas were also perfect for cross pollination. Who knew?

We ordered the trees from a nursery in Monticello, Florida, which was the pecan capital of the area. While waiting on the trees to arrive, we mowed the six acres of sagebrush field and staked out the rows for the pecan trees. We installed irrigation pipe down the rows with a drip sprinkler head for each tree. The system was connected to the new submersible pump which was in the new well, 120 feet deep. The new trees were planted and the young seedlings sprouted in the springtime. It was beautiful.

Soon after that, Uncle Bud retired from his job with the City of Jacksonville Electrical Department. He and Aunt Ruth sold their house on Brackland Street, bought a new double wide trailer, and placed it on their land about a quarter of a mile up the River Road, across from Uncle Hardy's house. It was nice for Daddy and Uncle Bud, the closest of all the seven sibling brothers, to be together again for their retirement back in the country where they were born and raised.

Daddy changed his lifestyle a bit when he moved back to Sneads. It might've been because he was getting older and slowing down, but he didn't drink nearly as much. And never to the point of intoxication. He even started going to church and became a member of the First Baptist Church of Sneads and was baptized, like I was so many years ago. Amen and amen.

Chapter 67

Baxter was an unbelievable wife. She was easy on the eyes, and easy on the mind. And she was also extremely tolerant of all my screwball dreams and schemes; chasing rabbits, as she would say. Little did I know what a wild rabbit I would be chasing when the phone rang one night in our Pine Acres home as we were finishing dinner in the spring of 1979.

"Hey Benny," Daddy said. "How y'all doing?"

"We're good, Daddy. How are you?"

For the next few minutes, we engaged in the usual chitchat about the weather, both in Sneads and Miami, and the kids and how they were doing in school and in sports. Then Daddy got to the real reason for his call.

"Benny, I need you to come up here and talk to P.V."

"What about?"

"You know how the A-rabs have us over a barrel about this oil. Remember those long lines at the gas stations?"

"Of course. I remember the only station that had gas around here was out on the turnpike. I waited five hours and when I finally got to the pump, they would only let me have five gallons. What's that got to do with P.V.?"

"Well, I'll tell you…"

Daddy described in detail that P.V., Ronnie, and Frank had been examining a theory that P.V. had been studying. It involved the production of ethanol, motor fuel alcohol, from corn. Ethanol, 198 proof alcohol, essentially free of water, will burn in cars. He said if a mixture of 10%

ethanol is added to 90% gasoline, it can be used normally, without having to modify the American automobiles. The critics of ethanol contended it takes more energy (BTU's) to produce it than is derived from the resultant product. It was a valid argument. The few ethanol plants in production used either coal or natural gas to fuel the plant, both expensive fossil fuels. The Shelfers of Sneads, Florida, were suggesting a new renewable energy process, totally independent of fossil fuels. The essence of their argument was the energy contained in the shuck and cobb of a single ear of corn was more than enough BTUs to fuel the distillation process of the corn from the cobb.

There's no doubt I was skeptical. P.V. was known for espousing wild and crazy ideas about different subjects. Nonetheless, if they had stumbled across a process that Daddy was describing to me over the phone, the ramifications regarding our fuel shortages and energy independence would be tremendous.

"Daddy, how do they know it will work?" I asked.

"They've done it in the lab."

"What's this have to do with me?"

"They want to do something with this, and they want you and me to be a part of it," Daddy said. I could tell he was excited about this.

"I'd have to see it to believe it."

"Come to Sneads and they will show you."

It had been a while since I'd been to visit Daddy, so this excuse was as good as any for me to go.

"Okay, Daddy. Pick me up at the Tallahassee airport at four o'clock fast time tomorrow afternoon."

It had been many years since I'd been back to Sneads High School and the building where I attended school for twelve years. Not a lot had changed.

The chemistry lab in the science room looked exactly the same. Daddy and I met P.V., Ronnie and Frank there. They had made arrangements to borrow the school lab for this little project because P.V. didn't want a possible conflict of interest with Gulf Power where he worked, even though he was the head of the lab there.

When Daddy and I walked into the chemistry lab, the demonstration was well under way. On the countertop there were glass tubes and vials and beakers connected together with other vessels that included a vacuum pump and a flaming Bunsen burner. There was a distinct odor filling the room, the likes of which I hadn't smelled since I stumbled onto that liquor still, while turkey hunting in the swamp up the River Road as a teenager. At the end of the line of the fluky experiment was a clear liquid dripping into a large beaker. Anhydrous alcohol. Virtually no water, 199 proof. Motor fuel alcohol of the finest grade.

We spent a couple hours in the lab with P.V., Ronnie and Frank walking me through the process, and explaining how it was a better and cheaper way to make motor fuel alcohol. The essence of their claim was by accomplishing the distillation process under a vacuum, it significantly reduced the energy required to the point where corn stover, the shuck and cob of an ear of corn, would supply more than enough energy to complete the process. I listened and asked many questions. The biggest question was, so what? How can that involve us? They explained how they wanted to build an ethanol plant, a prototype, in Sneads, to prove the process. I was intrigued. They had my attention.

In the overall picture, this is how it would work. The farmer plants a crop of corn. He knows how to do that because he has done it for many generations. We would contract with the farmer in the spring for the price we would pay him for his corn in the fall, a totally new concept the farmer would easily embrace. The corn would be harvested in the field by a corn snapper, instead of a corn shredder, rendering an ear of corn, with the grain and shuck still on the cob. The farmer would bring it to our plant where it would be stockpiled. We would put the ears of corn in a shredder where the grain would be separated from the shuck and cob. The corn would be ground into bits and forwarded to the vats for fermenting. The shucks and cobs would be shredded into thumbnail size pieces and forwarded to the boiler where it would be burned for energy. At the end of the process, we would have three products, almost equal by weight; anhydrous alcohol, dark distiller's grain (the residual from the corn), and carbon dioxide, captured form the distillation process. We would even cogenerate our own electricity to power the plant and have an overage to sell to the electrical grid.

The by-products of the distillation process were a surprise to me. We buy one commodity, corn. We sell three products; ethanol, distiller's grain, and carbon dioxide. Plus, free electricity. The revenue from the ethanol alone would more than pay for the corn. The revenue from the sale of the distiller's grain and the carbon dioxide would all be profit. It seemed too good to be true, and that made me extremely skeptical. But not so much that I didn't want to give it a good look. It was such an All-American project. We would be buying a local product, creating local jobs, selling a locally produced, totally renewable, energy source that was completely independent of Middle-Eastern oil cartels. When Daddy took me back to the Tallahassee Airport that night, I boarded the last National Airlines B-727 to Miami secretly knowing that this was a rabbit I desperately wanted to chase.

And so, the quest began. The next couple of years were busy and exciting. What were the odds of our family actually building an operational ethanol plant? Overwhelming. But, as I heard P.V. say many times through the years, "Nothing beats a trial but a failure..." an undeniable truth.

It took many day trips to Sneads for me to grasp the scope of the total project. It was convenient to depart on the first National Airlines flight from Miami to Tallahassee, spend the day with Daddy, and meet with P.V., Ronnie and Frank when they got off work. Then I would rush back to Tallahassee for the last flight to Miami. At least I was sleeping in my own bed.

It became immediately obvious the problem with this project was not the science or the process, but the funding. Where would we get the almost five million dollars for an ethanol plant, and where would we build it? We were all working, except Daddy, who was retired. We weren't poor, but none of us were exactly affluent either. The only collateral we had for a loan was our homes, and we agreed not to put those at risk for this project. We also agreed not to give up operational control of the proposed plant to obtain funding. Basically, we did not want to work for someone else.

Because I had the ability to travel economically, and had days off during the week, it was obvious to me I would be the one doing most of the work promoting this project. I knew we had to protect our personal assets, perfect our process and protect our discovery, and then somehow, fund the plant. Somehow.

To protect our personal assets, one of the first things we did was to form a corporation. We hired another Shelfer, from the group of Shelfers in Havana, to help us. Jim Shelfer was an attorney in Tallahassee. It was nice to meet and get to know him. With his counsel, we formed Southern Ethanol, Inc.

We also asked Jim Shelfer about protecting our new process for distillation of motor fuel alcohol. If we could obtain a patent on our new discovery, it would be a game changer. Jim advised us to seek a patent attorney in Washington to make the claim.

The politicians in Washington from President Jimmy Carter on down were talking big about the newly formed Department of Energy and how they were all supportive of renewable fuels and the contribution of biofuels in the battle for energy independence. They touted government guaranteed loans for energy related projects. If you were able to get approval for a government guaranteed loan, then funding would be almost certain. It was obvious to me we would need some such assistance.

In August of 1979, I wrote a letter to the Washington office of Sen. Lawton Chiles, asking his office for direction and assistance. I never received an answer.

Locally, I had a better response. Doyle Conner was the Florida Secretary of Agriculture. His office assigned a staffer, Jim Lee, to look at our project. He made the hour-long drive from Tallahassee westward to Sneads, where we gave a presentation for him explaining our process. Dog and Pony Shows, we called them. He seemed genuinely interested and didn't try to discourage us. In fact, he said he would make Secretary Connor aware of our project.

At this point we had a pretty good idea of the scope of the project and the size of the ethanol plant we wanted to construct. The question remained, where would we build it? We thought we needed at least twenty acres. We could always build it on some of the Shelfer's property. The problem was, our land had only road access, meaning everything coming and going would have to be by truck. Very restrictive. We were aware of a tract of land owned by the state of Florida, consisting of approximately 170 acres east of the town of Sneads, between US 90 and the L&N railroad. The property was only a short distance from the port of Sneads on the Apalachicola River and would give us unique river, road, and rail access to the site. We asked Sec. Connor's office about the possibility of purchasing some of the property. They suggested they might be able to support a different plan, which was to establish an industrial park with Southern Ethanol as the first tenant. This would require approval from the Jackson County commissioners and the Governor and cabinet of the state of Florida.

On February 18, 1980, supported by the other Shelfers, I made the initial presentation to establish a Jackson County industrial Park to the Jackson County commissioners in Marianna. They approved our petition.

Three months later, on May 20, 1980, we were at the capitol in Tallahassee. After a grandiose introduction by Sec. of Agriculture, Doyle Conner, I made a presentation to Gov. Bob Graham and his entire cabinet. The petition asked for the establishment of an industrial park on 164 acres east of Sneads, with Southern Ethanol being the lead tenant on the eastern 30 acres of the land. I was surprised by the interest of the cabinet members, especially Gov. Bob Graham, who recorded copious notes in a small, hand-held note pad he kept in his shirt pocket. I was thrilled when the cabinet approved our request. Two months later, the Jackson County Commissioners gave their final approval and we had the perfect site for our ethanol plant.

In the meantime, I was a traveling man, mostly to Washington, DC., in search of funding avenues for our project. The first was with Jim Lee, from Doyle Conner's office. We visited someone in the Department of Energy in several of their other contacts in Washington, all to no avail. We were seeking any types of grants or government guaranteed loans. There appeared to be a big difference in what was being reported out in the country and what was actually being done in Washington. I thought the administration of Jimmy Carter, the peanut farmer from Southwest Georgia, not too far from Sneads, would be in favor of putting the farmer in the business of producing energy with a totally renewable process. Not so much.

Several other trips to Washington were to meet with the prestigious law firm we had engaged to pursue the patent on our unique distillation process. In this case, prestigious law firm means it was very expensive. Nevertheless, if we could prevail on this application, it would be a game changer, whether we funded the plan or not. We were dealing with a senior partner in the firm who seemed to think our application had merit and had a chance to prevail. We proceeded onward, paying the toll as we went.

Another trip I made was to Houston, where I had made appointments with executives of several oil companies. We were exploring the possibility that they might want to be a partner with us in our new totally renewable energy process. They had no interest at all except to say if we could build and operate our plant, they would be extremely interested in buying our ethanol.

The most personally gratifying trip for Southern Ethanol for me was to Brazil. For years Brazil had led the world in the utilization of alcohol for motor fuel. Most of their cars burned 100% alcohol. They used sugar cane juice as the feedstock and the spent cane stalk, bagasse, as the fuel. Similar to our process of corn and stalk. They had ethanol plants dispersed among immense farm lands, and we were interested in observing this operation first hand. The real reason this trip was special for me was because I took my dad. It was his first trip out of the country since he returned from the Philippines in World War II. I remembered that day, seeing him waiting on the porch for me when I returned home from my first-grade class. Now here he was, sitting beside me in the First-Class seat of a 747 flying out of Miami to Rio de Janeiro. Surreal. From Rio we continued onward to São Paulo, and then caught a commuter flight to our destination, Ribeirao Preto, a couple hundred miles inland to the northwest.

We were met there by representatives of one of the largest alcohol producers in Brazil. For two days we toured their fields and their plants and were wined and dined. Every vehicle we were in was powered only by alcohol from the sugarcane fields, and there was no public or corporate resistance to that concept at all. Refreshing.

It was funny to me watching Daddy react to the different foods and drinks of Brazil. Every time we went to a different place and met or met another person, it was customary for someone to pour a shot of special Brazilian coffee into a small cup. It was to be wolfed down with one gulp. The problem was, it seemed to have ten times the caffeine of a normal cup of American coffee, and you'd be offered one or two of these, every hour or so. We finally had to comically decline the coffee shot. Daddy was extremely selective of the Brazilian food. He would eat chicken or beef, if he could be sure that it was chicken or beef. We were treated to a quail lunch that was very tasty. We both passed on the pickled quail eggs, even though they were highly touted as an aphrodisiac.

Daddy was impressed at the lush farms with workers everywhere, busy as an anthill. Of course, they were on a totally different pay scale than farm workers in America.

We flew back to Miami tired and jetlagged, but we had learned we had reason to be excited about the plant we wanted to build. The Brazilians were doing it on a national scale. We also learned that we could, if necessary, buy all the components of an entire alcohol plant in Brazil and have it delivered to us on a barge to the Port of Sneads. Interesting. Nice to have options.

Along with assistance from Doyle Connor's office, for the better part of a year and a half, we had immeasurable help from Bob Wattles, a young attorney from the Orlando area, and Cliff Hinkle, a young investment banker from Tallahassee. We explored every option for funding our plant that even seemed remotely possible. We were stonewalled by the government, but after a presentation to a group of engineers in Atlanta, we were approached by an individual that told us if we could bring fifty thousand dollars cash in a plain paper bag to a location in Atlanta, we could secure a government guaranteed loan for our project. I felt sick to my stomach and I immediately began to regret my last vote in the general election. We jumped in our car and drove non-stop back to Sneads.

It began to appear our only option to fund the plant would be the issuance of industrial revenue bonds. At long last, after our project survived an independent process audit by a regional engineering firm and an independent financial audit by national accounting firm, we were approved for an industrial revenue bond issue by a major financial house. Months later, January 1, 1981, bonds were on the market to fund an all-or-nothing amount of 6.7 million dollars. The interest rates we would be paying were astronomical, over 12%, but it was a sign of the times. And the operation of the plant would cover it. Unfortunately, the bond issue did not fully fund, so there was no deal. We were of course disappointed, but I knew we had done our best. As P.V. often said, "nothing beats a trial but a failure." He was right, again.

Chapter 68

The rules of the game for the airline industry were established randomly beginning in the 1930's as commercial use of the airplane expanded rapidly. Pan American World Airways had blazed the trails and set the standards for air travel around the world. Domestic airline companies sprang up to connect the cities of the U.S. for passenger travel, and more importantly, the transport of mail. Every aspect of the operation became highly regulated by the federal government, especially the routes that were flown. These routes were assigned, as air mail routes, to specific carriers and protected from infringement by competition from other carriers. The airlines could then buy the necessary planes and hire the necessary people to service the route. They could also charge what they wanted for a ticket, almost assuring profitability.

In the late 1970's after the election of President Jimmy Carter, there began a public outcry to deregulate the airline industry with regard to domestic routes. This would mean any airline could fly, or not fly, to any domestic city at their discretion. Unregulated competition.

Bud Maytag, major stockholder and CEO of National Airlines, was vehemently against deregulation. He had bought controlling interest of National from its founder, George T. Baker, in 1962. Maytag had shunned the family business of his grandfather, the Maytag washing machine magnate, to become an innovator in the airline industry. National became the first domestic airline with an all-jet fleet. Under his "keep it simple" business style, National blossomed into a very competitive and profitable domestic carrier.

Maytag, a bachelor, was enamored of the National Airline stewardesses. He named all the airplanes with female names. Following that, Maytag directed the launch of the controversial but highly successful "Fly

Me" national advertising campaign. Beautiful stewardesses would appear in television commercials and full-page newspaper ads saying, "I'm Anne, Fly Me," or "I'm Jo, Fly Me." The saucy ads with the beautiful girls were the talk of the town. Every town. Mission accomplished. Bud Maytag dated numerous National stewardesses. Eventually, he ended up marrying one, a friend of Baxter's named Wisty Mixon, from Perry Florida. Predictably, I suppose, it was a marriage that didn't last.

After a long, successful run, the "Fly Me" ad campaign had run its course. Everyone wondered what would replace it. One day when I checked my company mailbox at the end of a trip, I had a note to please contact a lady in the advertising department. She invited me to try out for a television commercial shoot for the new advertising campaign. For the casting call, we were in uniform and given lines to say, such as "Were National Airlines! Watch us smile!" We were told those words did not relate to the actual campaign theme, which was a closely held secret. The session was lots of fun and I certainly gave it lots of energy and my biggest smile.

To my surprise, they called me the next day. I had the part for a television commercial for National Airlines. The shoot was on Concourse F at Miami International, late at night after all the flights had departed. It was there we learned the new advertising slogan was called, "Watch Us Shine." My role was actually just playing myself, a National Airlines pilot. There were three pilots, Ray Foglia, Howard Morgan and myself walking down the concourse. My line was "Watch us shine with the most non-stops to New Orleans," then Howard would say "Houston," and then Ray would say, "and San Francisco." We did it countless times. Then we ran it again changing the names of the cities. It was interesting and fun being under the bright lights of the camera. That wasn't the best part. I learned that we were actually going to be paid money for this. National Airlines cut a deal with the Screen Actors Guild to use nonunion actors, company employees, for their commercials, provided they pay them union scale wages. Sweet. It's always good to be paid money for something you would do for nothing. I felt the same way about flying airplanes.

Soon after that, the new ad campaign was launched and the new commercials featuring many National Airlines employees began airing. It was thrilling to see the product of our efforts randomly appear on the television screen, even if our clip was only a few seconds long. It was also thrilling to be occasionally surprised at the mailbox with a check for acting.

432

Mailbox money. It wasn't life-changing, but with a wife and five kids it really helped.

On another occasion, I was selected to be part of a National Airlines Orange Bowl commercial, that was to be shown nationwide only once during halftime of the annual Orange Bowl game on New Year's Day. This commercial was different from the others, in that, it was filmed in NYC. National flew myself, with Baxter and the kids, to New York and booked us into the Waldorf-Astoria Hotel for the weekend. Aside from six hours of filming on Saturday morning, we had the entire weekend to be a tourist and enjoy the city. We visited Rockefeller Center, the Empire State building, the Statue of Liberty along with a tour around Manhattan on the Circle Line. It was a great time. And for all that, more mailbox money.

In the latter years of the 1970s, the dynamics of a struggling airline industry was crushing in on Bud Maytag and National Airlines. National had a simplified route system and a simplified fleet of airplanes that were mostly paid for, making them virtually debt-free. Their success led to their downfall. National was a prime candidate for a hostile takeover. Texas International Airlines, led by Frank Lorenzo, made the first unsuccessful attempt. Eastern Airlines also made a takeover attempt and failed. Others made overtures. Eventually, Pan American World Airways won the day with an offer of $437 million. Maytag took his money and quietly retreated back to Colorado and retirement. I was now a Pan Am pilot. Strange. Very strange, indeed.

Out of the blue, my mother came to see me. I was surprised and shocked. More than that, my kids were surprised and a little confused. They had no idea who she was. To them, their grandparents on my side of the family were Granddaddy and Grandma Dot. I had never seen the need in putting all the pieces in place beyond that. Until now.

My mother had been mostly suppressed in my mind. She had tried through the years, I suppose, in her own way, to keep in touch with me. She had called when my grandfather, David Van Meter, died in 1972. Baxter and I flew up to Philadelphia for his funeral where Baxter met my mother for the first time. Baxter got along with her splendidly, just as my grandmother had done so many years ago. Baxter also met my sister, Sharma. Despite the circumstances, it was a good visit. Yet, there was no denying I still harbored deep resentment towards my mother for leaving me as an infant. A cross I still bore.

Chapter 69

It was totally different being a Pan Am pilot. In every way and on every level, from top to bottom. The corporate headquarters for Pan Am was in the historic, picturesque, Pan Am building, a skyscraper atop Grand Central Station on Park Ave. in Midtown Manhattan. Pan Am transported passengers on routes they had pioneered around the world to six continents and over 80 different countries. They had numerous bases for pilots and flight attendants, domestically and abroad. It was hard not to be impressed with Pan American World Airways.

One thing about working for a major airline is, you're just along for the ride. As long as you do your job, pass your check rides, stay healthy and pass your physicals, your fate rests with the economic health of your company and decisions made by others. My new uniform with the distinctive white hat did not bring me peace of mind at all. On the contrary.

As part of the newly merged company, many former National employees were puzzled by what was happening. Pan Am had paid over $400 million for a domestic root system they could've essentially had for nothing in the new deregulation era. And they were still losing money, a million dollars a day. That was mind-boggling to us, coming from a company that was always profitable, regardless of the circumstances. The original Pan Am employees, Blue Balls as they were called, didn't seem to be concerned. "Don't worry about it," they would say. "We've never missed a paycheck," they would say. "There's always been a Pan Am and there will always be a Pan Am." To use an airplane analogy, this is how the old National employees, Orange Balls as we were called, felt about the situation. It's like we found ourselves strapped into the cabin of this huge airplane with all of these Pan Am employees. Immediately, we had this feeling of uneasiness. "Are we descending," we asked. "Are we going down? Who's flying this thing?" No one seemed to know the answer or to be concerned. I was concerned. Very concerned.

After the merger, before we had begun mixing Pan Am and National airplanes, crews and procedures, I was in the check pilots office in the old National building at Miami International. Don Blackburn, one of our supervisors walked in and said that a scheduling emergency had arisen. A Blue Ball captain had been injured in an automobile accident on the way to the airport. There was a Pan Am B-727 filled with passengers bound for Guatemala City sitting at the gate in Miami without a Captain. Pan Am had no short-call reserve captain available, so the flight was about to be canceled. Don Blackburn wanted me to postpone the line check I was scheduled to perform and take the flight to Guatemala.

My mind was racing. All of my flying experience had been domestic flying within the United States. Except, of course, that little trip to Cuba a few years ago. That hardly counts as international experience. I knew Guatemala was a city in Central America with lots of mountains. Beyond that, I knew nothing about it.

A short time before, I had done some publicity touting the merger of National and Pan Am. I suddenly realized it would be an honor to be the first National pilot to fly with an original Pan Am crew. Fifteen minutes later, wearing my new Pan Am uniform, white hat and all, I was walking into the cockpit of the B-727 bound for Guatemala City.

Needless to say, the copilot and the flight engineer were very curious and skeptical about my sudden appearance on the flight. All the rumors and innuendos and apprehensions about the merger were thrust upon them without notice in the form of an Orange Ball Captain. And I'm sure, in their minds, a boy captain at that. It was obvious to me I was the youngest crewmember on the airplane, including the flight attendants (we no longer called the cabin crew stewardesses because they were now also hiring males for that position). Not only that, I was also the most junior in seniority of all the crew members aboard with my June, 1967 date of hire.

Regardless of the awkwardness of the moment, we all had our roles to play and our jobs to do. As Captain, I did my best to establish a friendly,

436

confident atmosphere in the cockpit. The other crewmembers, professionals that they were, immediately bought into it. Soon I found myself flying across the Gulf of Mexico to a foreign country I had never been to, in an airplane with a blue ball on its tail with six other crewmembers I had never met. It was thrilling and one of those special moments that made my job as a Check Pilot exciting; doing those special assignments that would not be available to me as a regular line airman.

Guatemala City was called the city of eternal spring because it had a temperate climate throughout the year. The temperature usually reached the 70s or 80s Fahrenheit during the day and would cool to somewhere in the 50s at night time. The city itself and La Aurora International Airport were cradled in a valley with an elevation of approximately 5000 feet above sea level. It was surrounded by mountains on all sides except to the south, where there was a large lake in the distance. There was an active volcanic mountain clearly visible to the southwest. For all these reasons, it was a difficult airport for an approach and landing. Especially at night, or bad weather. I was happy my first trip there was in the daytime with beautiful weather and an experienced crew.

The first thing I noticed upon landing was "security" was everywhere. Everywhere you looked there appeared to be a 15-year-old kid wearing a camouflage jacket and carrying a machine gun. Very ominous. Fortunately for me, my crew took me under their wing and assured me I didn't have to worry about the "security." They told me the Guatemalan people were very passive and pleasant towards Americans, and I went on to find this was true. We were welcomed at the El Camino hotel downtown, probably the nicest hotel in the city. My interest peaked when I saw they even had red clay tennis courts attached to the hotel. Very impressive.

After checking into the hotel, I was anxious to take a walk to get a feel for the city. The copilot, who spoke a little Spanish, graciously offered to show me around. The afternoon was sunny and warm following a brief rain shower, and the city was bustling with people everywhere. There were vendors selling something at every turn, in the shops and on the streets. We had walked what seemed like several miles in the hot sun and with the altitude, we were naturally very thirsty. We had reached the edge of one of the parks of the city and came upon an old farmer sitting on the curb proudly displaying his wheelbarrow full of fresh pineapples. The copilot was really interested, so he bargained for a slice of pineapple. I declined, even though my mouth was parched. He chomped it down, regaling about how sweet and fresh it was. The old farmer, seeing the copilot's delight, offered to cut him another slice from a fresh pineapple. When the copilot readily agreed, the old man reached down and picked up a shiny machete from the dirt next to him, rinsed it off in the stream of rainwater trickling down the gutter, and proceeded to slice that pineapple like he was a master chef at Benihana's Japanese restaurant. The copilot suddenly lost his appetite. I was glad I had declined. Fortunately, we found a vendor selling Coca-Cola. I had two of them because I knew I wouldn't be drinking the water in Guatemala. We stopped for lunch at an upscale steakhouse on the way back to the hotel. The steak and potatoes were very tasty. Along with two more Coca-Cola's.

During the following years with Pan Am, I flew to Guatemala quite often. It was deemed a special airport, mainly because of the surrounding mountains. As such, a check pilot had to be in the cockpit for any captain's first trip into the airport. After the integration of the Pan Am and National flight crews, all of us in the check section were busy until the Orange Ball captains were airport qualified into Guatemala.

They were fun and interesting trips for me. The tennis pro at the hotel became a friend of mine and arranged for me to play tennis on almost every layover. It was the first time I'd ever had a ball boy fetching balls for me in a friendly game of tennis. Soon I realized the young Mayan kids were destitute and were trying to do anything to earn few American coins.

Regardless of the nice hotel and the gentle people in the city of eternal spring, for me my antennas were always up because there was always a hint of uneasiness about flying into Guatemala. It was there I felt my first earthquake. That one was only a few gentle jolts because the epicenter was quite a distance to the southwest. Nonetheless, for me it was like a shot across the bow about the possibility of what could happen.

There were always safety concerns because in many places outside Guatemala City the rebels and gangs controlled the countryside. Kidnappings were not uncommon.

During the morning of my last trip to Guatemala I was awakened in the hotel by distant gunshots from somewhere in the city. I wondered what that was about. Downstairs, I noticed a distinct difference in the attitude of the hotel staff. They were very businesslike, not their jovial selves. The crew

438

bus driver hurried us into the van and began racing to the airport, following what looked like was an armed escort. The streets were filled with the military kids carrying their big guns. When we asked what was going on, no one seemed to have an answer. At the airport we were hurried onto the plane for an expedited departure. After takeoff, immediately below me to my left, I could see the presidential palace was totally surrounded by tanks and armored vehicles. La Aurora airport control tower then advised us that the airport was closed. When we arrived at the gate in Miami, the news media met our flight wanting our reaction to the coup d'état that had taken place in Guatemala City. Fortunately, we didn't know much about it. That being said, it was obvious to me they had waited for our departure to close the airport and execute the coup. I was happy about that.

Chapter 70

For me, a former National Airlines pilot, working for Pan American World Airways wasn't necessarily better, just different. National had been lean and efficient and profitable. Pan Am was none of those things. It was large and bulky and bogged down in bureaucracy. And it was still losing $1 million a day. Hard to imagine.

There was no shortage of angst and animosity between the employee groups of the two airlines. There were many grievances and lawsuits, usually over the integration of the seniority list, and especially so in this case. I had been a B-727 Captain at National for a few years, but pilots with my date of hire at Pan Am were still furloughed and not working. Naturally, with this merger, they had high hopes of taking my job. The case went to arbitration and the arbitrator basically decided that a pilot would take away from the merger what they brought to the merger. To my great relief, on the newly merged seniority list, I kept my position as a B-727 Captain.

The National pilot's retirement fund was another highly contested item. Pan Am wanted our money to be folded into the Pan Am pilot's retirement fund, which was part of the Pan Am general revenues account. With National, our retirement money was individual and separate, and we fought to keep it that way, because in a bankruptcy the Pan Am money would all be up for grabs. Due to the efforts of Charlie Caudle and other pilots, we won that battle, and our funds remained in our named accounts, controlled by each pilot. That was an important victory.

My position as a check airman was also secure with the new airline, even though the role was more narrowly defined. Pan Am check pilots only gave checks in the airplane, whereas at National we did everything, including the simulators. At Pan Am, they had first officer instructors doing all the simulator work at the Pan Am Flight Academy on 36th St. in Miami.

Operationally, as far as flight operations were concerned, Pan Am was very strong. Its system of airplane and training manuals were by far the best in the industry.

Pan Am had a bustling charter division based out of JFK in New York. They would operate special flights for both college and pro athletic teams and many other entities that required a special airplane at a special time. Many of these trips were placed out for bid by the line pilots. There were some trips that were assigned to supervisory pilots, due to the nature of the mission.

One of the charter clients Pan Am had served for many years was the White House. Whenever the president travels, they are usually accompanied by the White House Press Corps. A few of the press are sometimes invited to travel on Air Force One. Most of them, along with staff and some Secret Service, travel on the press plane. For each of the president's trip, the White House travel office would place a bid among the airlines for the trip. The airline with the lowest bid and the capabilities of accomplishing the flight would be awarded the bid. Pan Am was usually the winner of those bids and had been for many years. Pan Am even carried the White House Press Corps on the day President Kennedy was assassinated in Dallas. A storied past.

Even though I was over 40 years old, I had never seen, in person, a president of the United States. It seemed like such a stretch for a farm boy from Sneads, Florida. Nonetheless, there I was, standing on the ramp at Andrews Air Force Base watching President Ronald Reagan climb aboard Air Force One. Surreal. He even waved in my direction. I immediately realized he was waving at the beautiful Pan Am flight attendants standing beside me. He probably recognized them because the same girls were on almost every trip. They told me the president always smiled and waved at them when the first lady, Nancy, was not with him.

It was interesting meeting the presidential pilot, Col. Bob Ruddick, the quintessential professional Air Force pilot. We chatted for a while and I learned that my old fraternity brother from Florida State, Frank Blount, was a former presidential pilot. The same Frank Blount who gave me my second airplane ride over the night skies of Tallahassee.

The White House Press Corp plane had a very interesting mission. Our passengers, the press, would report on and film the departure of the president, including the takeoff of Air Force One. Then they would run and climb on our airplane. We would hurry and takeoff and perform an interchange, pass Air Force One in the air enroute to our destination, so as to land 10 minutes before them. The press could then film the landing of Air Force One and report on the arrival of the president. It was a demanding task, usually flying into different and challenging airports. And there was no room for error. It would not be good to be involved in an incident on the presidential mission with seventy-five reporters on board. It would certainly make the news. The entire mission was different and interesting. I considered myself very fortunate to be a part of it.

Meanwhile, back on the home front, life was coming at us, ready or not. Baxter, was a wonderful mother to our kids. Different, but beautiful in my eyes. In life, you have to play the hand you are dealt, and Baxter was hanging tough. The kids weren't necessarily bad, they were just kids, five of them with all the associated problems. Baxter's parents, Anne and Mark Billson, were no help at all. Not even moral support. They still hated me for us getting married and never forgave Baxter for the same reason. And they constantly reminded her of those facts, in an effort to control her. Baxter was playing a difficult hand, indeed. Definite qualifications for sainthood.

The kids were playing a lot of tennis. Skip and Scott were involved in other sports as well, but little Spencer had really taken to the sport. In an effort to keep them involved, we joined the premier tennis club in the area, Royal Palm Tennis Club. It was easy to go there in the afternoon where the kids could participate in tennis activities with other kids, and I could easily get in a game with other adults of my age. Most of these people were very accomplished tennis players and that made it very enjoyable.

Karl Stenstrom had introduced me to another tennis player and close friend of his who had recently moved to Miami, Jeb Bush. Strangely enough, his father was Vice President of the United States. Aside from that, Jeb was just a regular guy who loved tennis and the give and take bantering of playing in a game with the likes of Karl Stenstrom, Karl Wickstrom, and Dean Colson. It was always a fun time.

Jeb and I became good friends. We played tennis and golf together and would occasionally get together for lunch or dinner. Sometimes he would come over to our house for a game of tennis, followed by impromptu snacks or dinner, thrown together by Baxter. Eventually Jeb and his wife, Columba, bought a house very near Royal Palm tennis club.

In the fall of 1984, we were having a check pilot's meeting in Miami discussing the manning of the White House Press Charters. President Reagan's reelection campaign was heating up and the White House had decided to charter an airplane to accompany Vice President Bush on all his campaign trips until election day. I immediately volunteered. This was a surprise to the others, because I had been flying fairly often with President Reagan. They were not aware of my friendship with Jeb. Even so, I prevailed and was given the assignment.

The first trip I had with the Vice President was an out and back to Savannah Georgia. After an interchange enroute, we arrived at Savannah with ample time for myself and the entire crew to be standing behind the rope line when Air Force Two taxied onto the ramp. After deplaning, the Vice President greeted the dignitaries at the bottom of the stairs, then hurried directly over to where I was standing. He extended his hand to me.

"Good morning, Mr. Vice President, I'm Ben Shelfer." I gripped his firm handshake.

"Yes, I know you are," he said. "Jebby's told me about you. We'll have to play tennis sometime."

"That would be great," I said. All the time I was thinking there's a fat chance that will ever happen. The Vice President was a very gracious and considerate man. He continued to greet our entire crew and all the others who were standing by to see him.

It just so happened the next weekend our crew was scheduled to layover in Washington, DC. Saturday was a bright day with lots of sunshine and a bite of fall in the air. The leaves were near peak color. Spencer was 10 years old and Scott was 13 years old at the time. Growing up in Miami, they had never seen the leaves change. I had persuaded Baxter to bring them up for the weekend to show them the colorful foliage and all the magnificent sites of Washington. Their flight was arriving at Washington National around noon on Saturday and I had departed the hotel in my rental car to pick them up.

While I was gone, I received a phone call at the hotel. When I didn't answer in my room, the gentleman left a message for me, but then called back and asked if there were other crew members from Pan Am registered in the hotel who he might be able to reach. The front desk rang the room of Sam Cannato. Sam was another check pilot who flew a lot of White House charters and a good friend of mine. He was also a tennis buddy and had a tennis court at his house in South Miami, where we had many great games. Sam was a great pilot and while he was very nice and polite, he was a very matter-of-fact, no nonsense type guy when it came to the company, procedures, etc. When Sam's phone rang, I have it on good authority the conversation went something like this:

"Hello," Sam said, answering the phone.

"Could you please tell me if Ben Shelfer is in town?" the gentleman asked.

"Who's calling?"

"I'm just trying to find out if Ben went back to Miami or stayed in town for the weekend?"

"Who's calling?" Sam asked, more emphatically.

"The Vice-President," the gentleman said.

By this time, Sam was losing patience and became very indignant.

"The Vice President of what?" He shouted into the phone.

"This is George Bush," the gentleman finally said.

Needless to say, Sam immediately had a change of attitude and assured the Vice-President he would get a message to me as soon as possible. And that's exactly what happened when I returned to the hotel.

The front desk clerk flagged me down as we walked by, saying I had an important message. He handed me a hotel message note which said Vice President George Bush had called and wanted to see me today for a game of tennis. I called the number and the White House switchboard operator answered. When I told her who I was calling and gave her my name, the Vice President picked up the phone on the first ring.

"Hey Ben, are you in town," he asked.

"Yes sir, I'm here for the weekend."

"Got a game for us this afternoon. Got an old Yale buddy, and the Swedish Ambassador…they're pretty good, but I think we can take 'em. Are you up for it?"

"I'd love to play, sir. There's just one problem. My wife and two kids are in town. I just picked them up at the airport."

"Bring 'em… bring 'em. They would enjoy this place," the Vice President said. Of course, I knew he was right. It would be an unforgettable experience for Baxter, and especially Scott and Spencer.

The Vice President's mansion was on the grounds of the Naval Observatory located on the Potomac River, about two and a half miles northwest of the White House. I'd seen it many times while flying the approach down the river to National Airport. It was a grand old Queen Anne style home on about 13 woodsy acres of the Observatory property. The tennis court was tucked away in the tall trees, down a long trail to the southwest of the residence.

George Bush, always the gentleman and consummate host, made a big fuss of meeting Baxter and the kids. He wasted no time in introducing Scott and Spencer to C. Fred, their cocker spaniel. They found him to be more independent and more rambunctious than Europa, our female dachshund at home. The Vice President made apologies for the Second Lady, Barbara not being there. She was visiting their daughter, Dora.

When the other players arrived and it was time to play tennis, the Vice President invited Scott and Spencer to bring C. Fred and ride in the limo with him down to the courts. It wasn't that far, but the secret service security detail required the Vice President to ride in the protective limo. His simple act of kindness made a lifetime memory for the kids.

The tennis game was interesting and different, and not only because of the ever-present secret service detail. The Ambassador and the Yale buddy weren't just the Vice President's friends, they were also really good tennis players. I found myself being the new guy in a very competitive game. Almost immediately I relaxed, listening to the constant good-natured teasing and bantering taking place on the court. And the Vice President was giving it with the best of them. I knew George Bush had been captain of the Yale baseball team and was a good athlete. I quickly learned he was a classic serve and volley tennis player, seldom being caught out of position. He was tall, had a great wing span, and had all the shots. His favorite shot was his "falling leaf" service return, a soft spinning angle shot that went to the server's feet, making a return difficult. And for being 60 years old, he was in great physical condition, even though he was a busy man, only a heartbeat from the Presidency.

The Vice President and I partnered to win a couple of close sets, then we switched around for the third set. Afterwards, the kids and the dog and the Vice President jumped back in the limo for the ride back to the mansion. As I was walking back with Baxter and the others through the tall trees with the golden leaves, I knew I had just played tennis with not just another politician, but a very special man. Was it because I was friends with his son that he immediately treated us like family? Little did I know.

There was another reason I wanted to fly with the vice president, and that was the mission itself. President Reagan had what was called a rose garden strategy. He would leave the White House at 8 o'clock in the morning, helicopter to Andrews Air Force Base and board Air Force One. He would fly to a city or two during the day, but would be back in the White House by 5 PM. For the crews of the press plane, that meant we had to be at Andrews Air Force base at 6 AM and would not return until 6 or 7 PM. Then we would have a short layover in Washington DC and do it all over again the next day. The Vice President, on the other hand, would leave Washington on Monday and lay over in several cities across the country during the week and be back in Washington by Friday. We would usually be in our layover city by three or four PM, with plenty of time for a nice dinner and rest

446

before we left the next morning. As far as I was concerned, this was by far the most interesting mission.

Chapter 71

Pan Am had a bustling charter division based out of JFK in New York. Aside from the White House Press Charters, they would operate special flights for both college and pro athletic teams and many other entities that required a special airplane at a special time. Many of these trips were placed out for bid by the line pilots. There were some trips that were assigned only to supervisory pilots, due to the nature of the mission.

One of those assignments proved to be very intriguing. After returning from a trip there was a note from Don Blackburn, the Manager of Flying for Pan Am in Miami. Don was a great pilot and a consummate gentleman and I was glad to see him in this job. He wanted me to stop by his office as soon as possible. I walked down the hall and knocked on his door.

"Come in, Ben," Don said. "And please, close the door behind you."

Oh! Dear, I was thinking. Somebody must be in trouble, and I hope it's not me. Don chit- chatted for a few minutes before finally getting to the point of the meeting.

"Ben, what I'm about to say is private and confidential and does not leave this room. Are you okay with that?" Don asked.

"Absolutely," I said.

"And if at any time you're not interested in what I'm about to tell you, you can walk out the door and this conversation never happened. Understood?"

"Yes."

"There are many tentacles to this company we now work for. I got a call from the charter department in New York. They have contracted a series of secret 727 charters for the Defense Department to be used by our military for research, development, and training. I have no idea where you would be going or what you'd be doing with the airplane. You would be gone for about a week at a time. And like I said, it's top secret, so you can't tell anyone, not even your wife and family, where you're going or what you're doing, other than you're flying a charter. Would you be interested in doing something like that?"

"Who would I be flying with?"

"Leo Unzicker would be the other pilot," Don said.

Leo, a former Navy guy, was an exceptional pilot with great attention to detail. And besides that, he was a good friend who lived in Pine Acres, just a block over from our first house on 120th St.

"That sounds very interesting," I said. "Count me in."

"Great," Don said. "I was hoping you would say that. I don't care to know what you guys are doing, just don't get hurt and don't bend metal."

After that ominous farewell from Don and a good luck handshake, I returned home to Baxter, where I could not tell her about my new assignment. How is that going to work? I wondered.

A short time later, Leo Unzicker and I had a discreet meeting in Miami with a military liaison officer from the defense department. He gave us some perspective on the objectives of the charter. After the Iranian hostage crisis that plagued the last year of the Carter administration, President Reagan had vowed, never again. There was a max effort to rebuild the military to establish a doctrine of peace through strength. And in specific cases of Americans in peril, the commander-in-chief wanted the ability to intercede with a superior force. And that meant training and preparation. They wanted Pan Am because after Coca-Cola, the Pan Am blue ball was the second most recognized logo in the world. A Pan Am jet could be seen in most places without arousing undue suspicion. Few people would suspect they might be carrying special forces, instead of commercial passengers. We were shocked to learn the reason they wanted a B-727.

A decade earlier, a man who became known as D. B. Cooper hijacked a Northwest Airlines B-727. After extorting $200,000 cash from the airline, he ordered them to take off again, then lowered the rear stairs of the airplane and parachuted into the night sky to an uncertain fate. He was never found and the crime has never been solved.

As the meeting progressed, two unknown guys walked into the room. They looked like they were in their thirties. They had long hair and were wearing jeans and faded golf shirts. They could have belonged to a rock-and-roll band or a motorcycle gang, except they appeared to be in excellent physical condition. We quickly learned they were Navy Seals, from the newly formed Seal Team Six, which was the Navy component of the Joint Special Operations Command (JSOC). The two were also pilots who had flown into Miami in a twin-engine Beechcraft King-Air airplane. They got right to the point about the primary reason for the charter. They wanted to train and become proficient at parachuting out of a B-727 like D. B. Cooper had done, down the rear stairs. And they wanted to begin the next week at a discreet location in Texas. Leo and I glanced at each other probably thinking the same thing… what on earth have we signed up for?

The next week Leo and I boarded a Pan Am jet in Miami for our deadhead flight to Houston. Along with us was Paul Loux, our flight engineer for the trip. He was an interesting chap, much older than us, and a veteran of the U.S. Army in WWII. For years he had flown the private airplane for the Los Angeles Dodgers and its owner, Walter O'Malley. I was glad that he was with us because of his common-sense attitude and can-do spirit. We were going to need a lot of that.

The B-727 assigned to us for the special charter was waiting for us on the maintenance ramp at Houston Intercontinental, where it had undergone numerous discrete "modifications." After the infamous hijacker escaped through the rear stairs of the B-727, the FAA mandated an air vane be installed on all B-727s, that would prevent the rear stairs from being lowered in flight. The D. B. Cooper switch, as it came to be known, had to be deactivated. The other two warning systems, which automatically deployed the passenger oxygen masks and sounded a warning horn above approximately 10,000 feet, also had to be deactivated. In addition, all the seats in the rear of the airplane had to be removed. When the three of us climbed on the airplane wearing baseball caps and blue jeans, we got some strange looks from the mechanics. They had probably been sworn to secrecy also, because they knew better than to ask us anything about what we were doing.

After a careful preflight of the airplane and all its modifications, we took off and flew west into the Texas sun. Using our unique radio call sign and special ATC clearances, we soon arrived at our U.S. Air Force Base destination and were escorted to an isolated parking spot on the ramp. We secured the airplane for the night and were driven to our off-base hotel by the defense department liaison officer. It was a strange feeling checking into a hotel and not being in my airline pilot's uniform. Incognito. Strange feeling, indeed.

It was an even stranger feeling climbing aboard the airplane the next day knowing everything we were about to do would normally be something for which we would usually lose our jobs. My thoughts drifted back to another time I was doing something I should not have been doing, like rat-racing with another airplane on my last solo flight in pilot training. Luckily, no one found out about it. And then I remembered the last words from Don Blackburn, "Don't get hurt and don't bend metal." I was shocked back into the moment when an Air Force motor pool bus arrived and Seal Team Six began coming up the rear stairs, all with their parachutes and jumping paraphernalia.

We had met that morning in a planning meeting with team leader, Dick Marcinko. He was a tough looking hombre with the size and physique of a linebacker for the Chicago Bears. He had a legendary record in Vietnam with the Navy's underwater demolition teams and had been handpicked to lead this unit by the Chief of Naval Operations. Marcinko had then personally selected the unit's members from all across the other existing naval special forces and underwater demolition teams. They were selected not only for their demonstrated physical abilities, but also their areas of expertise, such as explosives, communications, sharpshooting, etc. These men were the elite fighting force in our nation's military. It was obvious we were about to be pushing the performance limits of man and airplane in a strange and hostile environment, performing maneuvers that had never been attempted in a B-727. I felt privileged to be working with these guys, yet I had a healthy respect for the limits we were testing. Don't get hurt and don't bend metal.

We took off and climbed to 10,000 feet heading towards the designated jump zone. This was a military area restricted to all civilian aircraft. At 10,000 feet we would not be required wear our oxygen masks. The airplane was not pressurized, so we would be able to open the rear door. Paul Loux, the flight engineer, left the cockpit and walked back to the

451

airplane and opened the rear door. The noise was deafening. He activated the lever to lower the rear stairs. The noise became much worse.

The rear stairs only lowered a couple feet. It was immediately obvious there were a couple of problems. The first was the slipstream, the air rushing past the aircraft. Even though we had slowed to minimum clean speed, the wind pressure was a hindrance to the stairs lowering to their normal position. The second problem was the hydraulic actuator on the rear stairs was there to lift the stairs to the closed position. The force to lower the stairs was mostly gravity freefall. We extended our slats and flaps and slowed to minimum approach speed and the stairs finally lowered enough for the jumpers to barely squeeze through the opening. They made a jump, but it was not the best of situations. The jumpers not only had to get out of the airplane carrying a lot of equipment, but they had to do it all together and quickly. Otherwise, at the speed we were traveling, there would be too much separation between them, making it difficult for the entire team to assemble on the ground together at the target together. Back to the drawing board.

After a brainstorming session with Marcinko and a few of the other Seals, we came up with a couple of solutions. To deal with the stairs not fully extending into the airstream, it was suggested that a common hydraulic jack could be used to force the stairs down. The other problem, getting the entire team out of the airplane quickly, required a little more imagination. The best solution was to build a slide device that, when in place, would extend from the rear door to the bottom of the extended stairs. Paul Loux, with funds from the Defense Department, stepped up and took on the development of that project.

A couple weeks later, we found ourselves at another military base out west, ready to test the new procedures. Several jumps proved the devices worked very well. The hydraulic jack allowed complete extension of the rear stairs and the slide allowed the jump team to exit the airplane within seconds. Marcinko said the guys were like kids on a playground going down the slide. With those obstacles behind us, it was time to face our most challenging task, high altitude jumps.

There are many operational uses for the procedures we were developing. Most of these possible scenarios involved the secret insertion of the good guys into an area without being detected. For instance, we could be flying along at high altitude on a normal air route as a Pan Am passenger jet, but with Special Forces aboard. Without changing altitude, we could slow down, lower the rear stairs and exit the jumpers, then resume cruise speed, all without arousing suspicion. The advanced horizontal distance capabilities of the newer parachutes would allow them to glide to a target many miles away. Think Cuba, or more realistically, Grenada.

They called it HAHO. High-altitude jump, high-altitude parachute opening. Operating at the higher altitudes brings a whole new set of problems into the equation. We knew all our flights would be unpressurized, so we'd have to wear oxygen masks and breathe oxygen anytime we were above 10,000 feet. We also knew it would be extremely cold. We would be operating above 30,000 feet where temperatures of 30 below zero were not uncommon. Heavy jackets and gloves were the uniform of the day. The unknown part to us was the performance of the aircraft. Would the engines provide enough thrust to operate at high altitudes and low air speeds, unpressurized, with the rear stairs down? The flight manuals couldn't answer the question.

To prevent parachute opening failure at high altitudes, we knew it would be necessary to reduce the speed of the aircraft as much as possible. Yet, it was not recommended to use flaps above 20,000 feet on a B-727. The reason was as you moved the flap lever out of the up position, the trailing edge flaps would begin to extend, but all the leading-edge devices would immediately fully extend. At higher altitudes, the forces would be too great on the leading-edge devices and they would fail, and in extreme cases separate from the aircraft. This was illustrated by the infamous TWA Captain, Hoot Gibson. Hoot, with a plane load of passengers at 39,000 feet, wanted to try a trick to make the airplane fly a little bit higher. When the copilot had gone to the restroom, Hoot pulled the circuit breaker to disable the leading-edge devices. He carefully extended the flaps slightly. The aircraft began a very shallow climb. About this time, the copilot returned to the cockpit and observed the popped circuit breaker. He pushed it in to reset it. All the leading-edge devices immediately extended and began to bend, fail, or separate from the aircraft. The aircraft began a violent roll and dive towards the earth. After a complete barrel roll and passing 5000 feet, they lowered the landing gear as a last resort and finally managed to gain control of the badly damaged airplane and bring it in for a landing.

Leo Unzicker consulted with the engineers at Boeing for us. We didn't want any part of the Hoot Gibson scenario. Don't get hurt and don't bend metal. They confirmed for us, off the record, that we may be able to gain a slight performance advantage by using a few degrees of trailing edge flaps, as long as the leading-edge devices were not extended. Food for thought.

The subsequent training flights were interesting and uncomfortable. Flying unpressurized, even though we were dressed for it, we were freezing most of the time, because of the temperatures outside the airplane. The noise inside the airplane when the rear stairs were extended was deafening. All communications had to be via the interphone. We had to continually wear oxygen masks. The Seals were on supplemental oxygen before and after they jumped. It occurred to me that Leo, Paul and I were the only ones aboard the airplane that didn't have a parachute. Hmmm...

We managed to push the operational limits of the B-727 in every direction. We had to take off with absolute minimum fuel to reduce the weight enough to operate at their higher altitudes with the rear stairs extended. Even then, it would take maximum power to fly at the necessary low air speeds with some of the flaps extended to be able to maintain altitude. Maximum power equated to maximum fuel burn. That's a problem, especially when you take off with minimum fuel. As soon jumpers were away, we would turn and head back to the base with our low fuel warning lights glowing. It was a beautiful sight to look down and see the glistening parachutes of Seal Team Six gliding towards their target. I felt privileged to work with them and I was just glad those fearless warriors were on our side.

Side note: Many years later I ran into Dick Marcinko signing books at a bookstore in Louisville Kentucky. He had retired from the Navy and was a successful author of a series of shoot and loot books he called the Rogue Warrior series. I had read his books and found them to be shockingly realistic from the times I had worked with his team. He had even mentioned working with Pan Am in one of his books. Surprisingly, he recognized me immediately and we had a nice chat about our training experiences. He signed a book for me and mentioned the slide we built to exit the rear stairs of the B-727. He called it the "slide for life." Small world.

The customer of another secret Department of Defense charter was the JSOC, Joint Special Operations Command. Leo, Paul and I landed our B-727 in an overgrown World War II abandoned landing strip somewhere in the middle of nowhere forests of South Carolina. We were met there by our military liaison contact who chauffeured us to our motel in the nearest small town, several miles away. Once again, we were dressed totally incognito. None of the locals had any idea who we were or what we were doing.

We were there to provide our airplane to be used as a hostage rescue training platform for special operations combat units from the Army, Air Force, and Navy. Included were Delta Force from the Army, the 24th Special Tactics Squadron from the Air Force, and of course Seal Team Six from the Navy. These units spent the better part of a week not jumping out of our airplane, but learning how to get into it. Hour after hour they developed and practiced procedures for how they would enter an airplane, eliminate the bad guys, and rescue the hostages. It was amazing to watch. I would be sitting on the airplane listening and watching, knowing they were coming. An instant later, there would be a rescue warrior coming in every door and window opening of the airplane, including the cockpit windows. Formidable and fearless.

Another aspect of the training on this Carolina trip that was highly classified was the use of NVGs, night vision goggles. I had heard about them, but never before had a need to use them, and therefore never a need to know about them. As an introduction to their use, we were taken in the dark of a moonless night to the isolated strip where our airplane was parked. Standing there on the ramp it was so dark it was difficult to see person standing next to you. There were no lights or sign of activity anywhere. Suddenly there was a loud roar from a huge plane that had landed on the strip. Then there was the sound of helicopters whizzing by overhead. You could see nothing because none of them were displaying any lights at all. Then we were handed our night vision goggles. When we powered them up and fit them to our eyes, the results were amazing. Truly like night and day, as they say. We could see everything. A few yards from us on the runway was an Air Force C-141. Special forces troops were repelling down from an Army Black Hawk helicopter that was hovering near us. All of this was in plain view with the night vision goggles. Impressive. We were instructed in the techniques for using the goggles in the cockpit while flying in blackout operations. I couldn't imagine ever being in a situation where we would be required to do that. Then, you never know.

Chapter 72

January 4, 1985.

It was a cold, wintry morning in Cincinnati. I glanced outside as I walked through the lobby of the downtown Holiday Inn on my way to breakfast. The snow was still coming down. The big flakes. We were beginning the second day of a three-day trip. After an exciting fall season of flying the Bush patrol during the election, and the secret missions of Seal Team Six and Delta Force, it was very relaxing to start the new year flying a regular trip, with a regular crew, as a regular airline pilot. Refreshing and rejuvenating, as it should be.

By the time we boarded the crew bus, the snow had mostly stopped. There were seven of us; Captain, Copilot, and Flight Engineer, with four Flight Attendants. The normal crew staffing for a 727. The sun broke through the clouds as we crossed the bridge over the Ohio River. By the time we arrived at the Cincinnati airport, which was actually located in northern Kentucky, the skies had cleared and there was a strong, chilling wind from the north. And everything was covered with snow. Unfortunately, so was our airplane.

When we arrived at flight operations, we learned there was an hour delay posted for our departure time. We had leased deicing equipment from another airline and had to wait our turn to use it to clean our airplane. Patience required, but difficult under the circumstances. Our flight, Pan Am 558, operated every afternoon from Cincinnati to Cleveland to JFK. Its primary purpose was to carry international passengers to JFK for the evening push, connecting to flights around the world. Too much of a delay would threaten those connections and cause major disruptions and inconvenience for the passengers and Pan Am.

The deicing was finally completed and we managed to push back only an hour and fifteen minutes late. I had briefed the crew that once we pushed back, we would do everything possible to make up some time on the flights to JFK. We would fly max speed, and then try to make a twenty-minute turnaround in Cleveland. If we could do that, our passengers would make their connections.

We took every shortcut and flew fast and landed on runway 06 at Cleveland Hopkins International Airport a few minutes before 3 PM. We made a right turn off the runway and hustled in to Gate 5 on Concourse A, a short distance away.

Pan Am had a very small presence in Cleveland, operating only 3 flights a day. As such, it was more economical to contract other airlines to service the few flights we had to Cleveland. You have to do everything possible to save money when you're losing $1 million a day, every day. Every single day. But, that's a story for another time.

U. S. Air was our contracted provider for ground services in Cleveland. We used their gates, their operations, and their agents to service our flights.

After completing the shutdown checklist, in the jetway, I ran into our US Air agent, Jeanette Rivera. We chatted about the need for a quick turnaround, and she was ready for it. She would begin pre-boarding two mothers with infants as soon as the Cleveland passengers had deplaned and the flight attendants were ready.

The copilot, Bill Weiler, followed me down the jetway steps onto the ramp and into the operations office, only a few feet away. Ron Rupp, the flight engineer, was already doing the walk around inspection beneath the aircraft.

Meanwhile, back in the terminal at the entrance to Concourse A, a big, tall woman, wearing a hood and a long overcoat, walked through the security checkpoint with her hands in her pockets. The alarm sounded.

"Wait just a moment," the airport security agent said. "Step over here please. Do you have anything in your pockets? We'll have to check you out with our wand." He lifted his handheld metal detecting wand.

The woman took her right hand out of the pocket holding a pistol. She pointed it directly at the agent. He ducked behind the counter and the woman put the gun back in her pocket and began running down Concourse A. An alarm was sounded and a policeman came up the stairs from a position below the security checkpoint and began running after her. About 50 yards down the concourse, she approached Gate 5, Pan Am 558 to

Kennedy Airport. There was no agent at the gate, and the door to the jetway was open. The woman ran down the jetway towards our airplane.

Jeanette, the gate agent, had preboarded a lady carrying a small baby and placed them in seat 12F, the 3rd row of economy class, on the right side of the airplane. Jeanette was leaving the airplane to go back to the gate to continue boarding when the woman with the gun in her pocket rounded the corner of the jetway and saw her. The woman appeared to be out of breath and sweating.

"Wait," Jeanette said. "You don't have to hurry, were not boarding yet. Let me see your ticket."

The woman pulled a gun from her pocket and thrust it towards Jeanette's face. With a quick motion the young agent dodged to the left tried to grab the gun, knocking the woman's hand down. The woman fired a shot and hit Jeanette in the side at her waist. Jeanette screamed and lunged out the jetway door and ran down the steps.

The woman with the gun entered the airplane and immediately looked left into the cockpit, where the door was open. Brook Hunt, the male purser, was sitting at the flight engineer's panel, completing some paperwork. He had a startled look when this huge form of a woman darkened the door of the cockpit. She pointed the gun at his face and pulled the trigger. *Pow!* Brook had jerked his head to the right and she missed him. *Pow!* She fired again. He had jerked his head to the left and she missed him again. At that moment, the policeman who had been trailing her down the concourse rounded the corner of the jetway. The woman saw him and ran down the aisle of the airplane, through the first class section, and hid directly behind the class divider between first class and economy. Brook dashed from the cockpit out the front door. After saying something to the policeman, he ran down the jetway stairs.

In the back of the airplane, the other flight attendants were taking care of the catering in the rear galley. The galley door had been opened to accommodate the catering truck and the rear stairs were down, as was standard operation for the 727 on the ground parked at the gate. The effect of the doors being open resulted in it being very noisy on the airplane. It was so loud that anyone around the rear galley couldn't hear the shots fired in the front of the airplane. Two of the flight attendants in the back, Delsa Amundson and Karin Busse, seeing the woman standing behind the class divider, sensed that something unusual was taking place. Karin urged Delsa to go check it out. Delsa walked up the aisle towards the front of the plane. Karin followed a few feet behind her.

When they reached the front of the economy section, the woman hadn't noticed them. She was standing there looking toward the front door of the plane with one hand in her pocket and the other holding what Delsa thought was a walking cane. A young mother, Cynthia Shisler and her infant baby, Laura, were slumping in the seat behind the woman. Across the aisle from them, Delsa, noticed an older couple, Frank and Bonnie Esterquest, seated in 11A and 11B. They were trying to shield themselves with magazines, cowering down and staring at the woman. Delsa, surveying the situation, looking back and forth between the couple and the woman, said to the couple, "What's going on here? Is she bothering you?" She motioned toward the large woman standing there. Bonnie Esterquest whispered, "I can't talk right now."

Delsa knew this was a situation that required security. She began walking forward past the woman when the woman turned and saw her and raised her hand that held not a cane, but a gun. Delsa raised both her hands up in a disarming manner and immediately continued walking slowly up the aisle. *Pow! Pow!* The woman fired two shots at her, missing her both times. Delsa exited the plane through the front door. The other flight attendant, Karin, upon seeing the woman brandish the gun, dove in between the seats to take cover, and did not move

Meanwhile, Bill Weiler and I were at the counter in the operations office completing the paperwork for the flight to New York. There was a door behind me to the break room for the ramp rats and the baggage smashers. That's what we, and even they themselves, affectionately called the ramp workers and the baggage handlers.

We had only been at the counter a short time when I heard a strange sound coming from the break room. It almost sounded like a woman squealing. I thought perhaps it was some of the ramp rats being rambunctious on their break. I heard it again. This time I could tell it was definitely a woman with a muffled scream of anguish and pain. Out of curiosity, I stuck my head into the room to see what was happening.

"Captain," Jeanette screamed. She was leaning across the picnic table in the break room, pressing both hands to a spot on her side. "There's a woman up there shooting people on your airplane. And I've been shot."

Jeanette was obviously in great pain, and looked like she was about to faint. I ran and grabbed her to try to stabilize her and keep her from falling from the table. Bill Weiler dashed in to help. Jeanette exhaled a large breath and moaned again as she turned and sat on the bench and leaned back against the picnic table. She pulled up her bloodied blouse and we all stared at the wound. I saw where the bullet entered the pinch-an-inch area on the side of her waist. Thankfully, it was not bleeding too badly. Surprisingly, a few inches back, I saw another wound hole where the bullet had exited. It too, was bleeding very little.

"Hang on, Jeanette," I said. "We're gonna get you some help and you're gonna be just fine. Hang tough for just a minute."

There's a woman up there shooting people on your airplane. The image of what Jeanette had said was chilling. I could not imagine anything worse than someone walking down the aisle of an airplane, my airplane, indiscriminately shooting passengers in their seats along the way.

"Jeanette's been shot!" I shouted through the door to operations, pointing towards the wounded agent. "Sound the alarm! Call the police to gate five. Someone's shooting people on the airplane." I dashed out the door, and across the ramp to the jetway stairs, followed by Bill. Running down the stairs was Brook, the purser.

"What's going on up there?" I asked.

"There's a woman up there shooting a gun, but she's shooting blanks," he said.

"Shooting blanks?"

"Yes. She's gotta be shooting blanks. She put the gun between my eyes and pulled the trigger twice, and I'm still here."

"Brook, she's not shooting blanks. She shot the gate agent. I saw the bullet hole in her side." The color appeared to drain from Brooks' face and I turned and continued up the stairs.

There was a small window in the door at the top of the jetway. I peered through it and saw a policeman just standing there, looking towards the airplane. I opened the door and stepped into the jetway. The policeman glanced back at me. He appeared to be out of breath and was sweating profusely. He was sadly obese, like the proverbial cop who never met a doughnut he didn't like… Or eat. He didn't even have his gun drawn.

Pow! Pow! Two shots were fired from inside the airplane.

"What's happening? Is she shooting passengers?" I asked the cop.

"Aww, it's just some crazy woman in there shooting blanks," the cop said, in a very casual manner. It was hard for me to comprehend what I was seeing. I guessed Brook had told the cop the woman was shooting blanks and he bought the story.

"She's not shooting blanks," I said.

"Really."

At that moment, Delsa exited the front door and screamed, "She's got a gun! She shot at me. She's right in there. Somebody do something."

"Are there any passengers shot?" I asked her.

"I don't know," she said. Delsa ran out the jetway door and down the stairs to the ramp.

"She's not shooting blanks," I said again to the cop. "She shot the gate agent. I saw the bullet hole in her side. If she's shooting passengers, I want you to go get her."

"What?"

"If she's shooting passengers, I want you to shoot her. I want you to take her out. Do you understand?" The manner of my speech left the cop no doubt what I expected him to do.

"Oh! Okay," he said, finally.

It was like a Barney Fife moment for the policeman. Or maybe it was like why me? Why now? Or, I didn't sign up for this kind of thing. In any case he finally pulled his gun and appeared to be taking the situation more seriously. I was beginning to think I was going to have to get the cop to give me his gun so I could go after the woman myself.

At the moment, there were no more sounds coming from inside the airplane. I didn't know if that was good or bad. I crept to the entry door and peeked inside the airplane through a small space between the partition at the front of the first-class cabin and the outer fuselage. The woman was standing there behind the class divider at the beginning of the economy section. Her attention was totally towards the front of the airplane where she had seen the policeman. She didn't see me watching her through the sliver of a crack. I listened carefully and looked around the cabin as best I could to try to determine if anyone else had been shot. If there was, I couldn't tell from my narrow vantage point.

The seconds dragged by. The woman just stood there, doing nothing. Several other Cleveland airport policemen rushed down the jetway. They told me the Cleveland SWAT team and the FBI were on the way. That was a relief to me because I knew there were at least 25 passengers still trapped on the plane.

Bill Weiler, I knew, had a personal interest in this operation. He was extremely concerned about his girlfriend, Karin Busse. Delsa had told him Karin had ducked between the seats only a few rows back from the woman with the gun. Bill raced back down the jetway stairs to the ramp and met up with Brook Hunt. They went to the back of the airplane and began the tedious process of quietly sneaking passengers, one or two at a time, out the back door and down the rear stairs to freedom.

A short time later, much sooner than I expected, the Cleveland SWAT team arrived.

"Hi Captain, I'm Jim Gnew of Cleveland SWAT. What's the situation here?" The team leader asked.

"We have a woman with a gun standing in the middle of the airplane down the class divider. She shot the gate agent and fired at two of our flight attendants and has fired several other shots in the cabin. Sounds like a small caliber pistol. I can't tell if anyone else is injured. It could be as many as 20 passengers still on the plane. If she's shooting passengers, I want you to take her out," I said.

462

"No problem, Captain. That's what we're here for. Where can we get eyes on her?"

"Only two places. The front door and the rear stairs."

In an instant, I knew these were the men for the job. Jim Gnew placed a sniper on the floor of the entryway where he could get a shot at the woman if she stepped out from behind the partition. I took another sniper down the jetway to the rear stairs of the airplane. From there, he had the woman in the crosshairs of his scoped rifle. The entire SWAT team was wired for sound. They all had earpieces and headsets were taking orders from Jim Gnew. I felt a small sense of relief believing that, if necessary, they could end it before the woman could do much more damage.

When I arrived back at the front door of the airplane, the FBI negotiator, Roger Dennerll, had arrived. Like Gnew, Dennerll was also extremely professional. We chatted for a moment to bring the negotiator up to speed on the situation.

"I'll try to talk to her to see what she wants. We'll see if we can have a little give-and-take dialogue. Maybe she'll release some or all of the hostages, or maybe even surrender," Agent Dennerll said.

"Just so we understand each other," I said. "You can tell her anything you want and promise her anything you want, but this airplane is not moving."

"Got it," Dennerll said.

The frigid wind continued to howl and the temperature dropped into the teens as the lengthening shadows gave way to darkness. Bill and Brook had managed to get everyone off the airplane via the rear stairs, except 8 passengers and Karin Busse.

The woman with the gun did not budge. The crisis negotiator tried desperately to no avail to get her to talk. Even if she talked, it would have been difficult to hear or understand her because of all the airplane and airport noise. Eventually, Dennerll managed to push a telephone with a long cord down the aisle to her, using a telescopic pole. He rang the phone and the woman answered. Denerll turned to look at me and muffled the telephone with his hand.

"She wants to talk to the pilot," he whispered to me.

"I can certainly talk to her, if you like," I said.

"No, I think we'll do it this way," Dennerll said.

"This is the pilot," he said to the woman on the phone.

The woman did not believe Dennerll, so he borrowed Bill's hat to show her. When she still didn't believe him, Dennerll donned Bill's uniform coat. It was freezing in the jetway, so Bill slipped on Dennerll's FBI jacket. From my standpoint, I'm not sure which one of them look more out of place. It would've been comical at the situation not been so dire. Dennerll finally convinced the woman she was talking to the pilot. She told him she wanted to go to Brazil. Rio de Janeiro.

When I heard about Brazil, I thought to myself this poor woman had already committed two basic hijacking flaws: she commandeered an airplane that had no pilots on it, and she picked a 727, which would not possibly hold enough fuel to fly to her destination. This could not possibly turn out well for her.

Dennerll told her he would take her to Brazil, but it would take some time to get approval from the chief pilot, file the proper flight plans, clear it with customs, etc. In the meantime, he asked her to show some good-faith and release the hostages, because they didn't want to go to Brazil. She bristled at that request. A short time later, she agreed to release the woman and the baby sitting in first class, Marie Westerfeld and her 21-month-old son. The snipers watched the woman carefully as the mother scurried off the airplane with her baby.

The FBI had been trying desperately to identify the woman. They even entertained the possibility that she might be a man, because of the way she was standing and her large physical stature. The FBI team finally identified her as 42-year-old Ornetta Mays. She had been diagnosed as a paranoid schizophrenic and had recently escaped from a nearby mental facility. Dennerll subsequently talked to her psychiatrist and learned the woman was delusional. She thought everyone in authority was conspiring against her, especially the FBI. Strangely, it appeared that her hostile actions at the Cleveland airport had made this delusion a reality.

The night was cold and dark and the minutes and hours ticked by. The power on the airplane was being supplied by the APU, the auxiliary power unit. There was a concern the continuing strain on the APU would cause it to shut down, creating darkness on the airplane and chaos in the cabin. To prevent that from happening, maintenance people wanted to switch the power source to external power, a power source separate from the airplane. There was only one problem. The power had to be manually switched by someone in the cockpit, and at that time there was no one there. And the woman was becoming more agitated and was still standing in the airplane with a gun, looking towards the cockpit.

When I explained to Dennerll that I needed to go into the cockpit to switch the power source, he didn't like the idea. Nonetheless, we worked out a plan. I took off my uniform coat and hat and slipped into a bulletproof vest, furnished by the Cleveland SWAT team. Ornetta Mays had become very methodical and predictable about when she would look around the partition to stare towards the cockpit. She would peek out for about five seconds and then wait sometimes as much as a minute before she would look again. Dennerll watched her and gave me a thumbs up when to go. I took three quiet steps into the cockpit and closed the door. Mays did not see me. And more importantly, she didn't shoot me.

The light on the flight engineers panel told me the external power was available to the aircraft. I nervously flipped the switch, because sometimes when the power is transferred, the external unit is not compatible and the lights will go out. Thankfully, after a quick blink of the lights, the power stayed on. I watched the woman through the peephole in the cockpit door, wondering if the thin door would stop a bullet if she began firing at me. Probably not. When the woman glanced forward and predictably looked away, I got the thumbs up from Dennerll and retraced my three quick steps to the jetway.

The conventional strategy of delay, delay, delay, didn't seem to be exactly working on Ornetta Mays. The plan was to keep promising her we were trying to meet her demands, yet obstacles, one after another, beyond our control, would keep appearing. The hopes were, she would become tired and thirsty and hungry or sleepy and become disillusioned with this debacle and give herself up. Not so much with this woman.

Dennerll had told Mays he was trying to get approval for the trip to Brazil but the chief pilot didn't have the authority to approve it. She became more agitated and demanded a letter from the president of Pan Am giving full approval for the trip. Dennerll assured her Ed Acker, the president of Pan Am, was aware of the situation and might be persuaded to provide such a letter if she would show some good-faith by releasing the hostages. Mays reluctantly agreed to release three hostages. Only four hostages would remain: the elderly couple, Frank and Bonnie Esterquest, and Cynthia Shisler and her baby, Laura. A few minutes later two men and flight attendant, Karin Busse, scurried off the back of the airplane. Bill Weiler met Karin at the bottom of the rear stairs for a long embrace on the dark, freezing cold ramp. Soon after that, almost as if by magic, Mays was provided a letter signed by "Ed Acker," directing the flight operations department of Pan Am to take all steps necessary to transport Ornetta Mays to Brazil. *You can tell her anything you want and promise her anything you want, but this airplane is not moving.*

Concourse A had been closed shortly after the ordeal began. All the other gates had been emptied of airplanes, passengers and employees. When the night came, the lights on the entire ramp had been turned off, so Mays could not look out the window of the plane and see the first responders gathered at the scene. I found a brief moment during a lull in the negotiations to retreat back to the concourse to use the restroom. I looked back up the concourse towards the terminal. There was bedlam at the security checkpoint where the concourse was closed off. There was a crowd of TV cameras, photographers and reporters being kept at bay by the airport police. An agent told me CNN was streaming live coverage of the hostage standoff. It then occurred to me that Baxter and the kids could be watching. They might be concerned, even though I was pretty sure they wouldn't know it was my airplane.

Baxter answered the phone on the first ring, which surprised me. She knew it was my airplane and she was very worried and glad to hear my voice. She said she and the kids were glued to the television. My boss, Ken McAdams, the chief pilot in Miami, had personally called Baxter to tell her it was my flight involved in the Cleveland hijacking and he believed I was okay. I assured her that was the case and I loved her and the kids, but I had to go. I hung up the phone and hurried back down the jetway.

At the door of the plane, Dennerll and Gnew were in a deep discussion. They had continued to consult with May's doctor, in light of her increased belligerence. Mays had a letter directing she be flown to Brazil, but nothing seemed to be happening. She was rapidly tiring of the false promises of the negotiators. The general consensus of the professionals was the fear Mays would continue to tire of the ordeal and choose to end it, not by giving herself up, but by shooting all the hostages, then herself. They devised a plan.

Jim Gnew of the Cleveland SWAT team took the lead. He wanted to take the woman alive without shots being fired, if possible. The safety of the hostages was paramount. The plan was for Gnew and Robert Patton, also of Cleveland SWAT, to sneak into the airplane and hide in the first-class galley when the woman wasn't looking. Then, when everyone was ready, thunderous flash bombs would be exploded in the back of the airplane to divert the woman's attention toward the rear of the airplane while Gnew and Patton rushed down the aisle from the first-class galley to subdue her.

Gnew thought the plan would work, but his lack of familiarity with the interior of the airplane left him uncomfortable. He asked me if Pan Am had another airplane available where he and his team could practice the exact steps required for the rescue operation. As luck would have it, there was another Pan Am 727 on the ground in Cleveland. Our concourse was closed so they were operating on the adjacent concourse nearby. I hurried with Gnew and his team to the airplane, which was almost ready for departure. I began explaining to the captain of the flight what I was doing at the door of his airplane with a SWAT team dressed in dark clothes and he just laughed. He told me that he and everyone else knew we had a problem and to go ahead and do what we had to do. He asked me to make an announcement to his 140 passengers, which I did. Gnew and Patton practiced their entrance to the first-class galley, and then counted the exact number of steps it would take to reach the partition where the woman was standing at the back of the first-class section. An FBI agent practiced his entrance where he would follow them down the aisle and use his body to shield the elderly couple sitting across from the woman. After a couple minutes, the lawmen had perfected their moves and knew exactly what was required. We rushed back to the standoff.

It was after nine o'clock at night and the ordeal had lasted over six hours. Ornetta Mays had become even more distraught and continued to make threats to her hostages, even the woman and her baby. The SWAT team and the FBI knew they had to go get the woman. It was time.

Jim Gnew and Robert Patton were ready. The FBI agent was ready. The flash bomb diversion fireworks in the back of the airplane were ready. Everyone was wired for sound, with ear pieces all tuned to a common frequency. Gnew and Patton timed the glances on the woman and tiptoed into the first-class galley. Gnew gave a thumbs up to Dennerll, who signaled the operation to begin.

BaBOOM! BOOM! BOOM!!! The flash bomb charges detonated at the rear door of the airplane with earsplitting explosions and blinding flashes of light. Gnew and Patton charged down the aisle. Gnew rounded the partition to grab the woman, but she did not fall for the diversion. *Pow!* Ornetta Mays shot Gnew in the chest. Right in his bulletproof vest. *Pow!* Robert Patton shot Mays in the chest with a large caliber handgun. She was not wearing a bulletproof vest. Ornetta Mays collapsed on the floor. It was over.

In an instant, the FBI agent escorted the Esterquest couple and the Shisler mother and baby off the plane to safety. The agent had thrown himself on top of the old couple to shield them from harm, until the shooting stopped. They had survived the ordeal fairly well, even though they were certain they were going to be shot. They had displayed amazing ingenuity by stuffing magazines they had brought on board, and those from the seat-back pocket, beneath their shirt and blouse as a makeshift bulletproof vest. Unbelievable. Cynthia Shisler revealed the reason the baby had been so quiet was because she was breast-feeding her throughout the entire ordeal.

Jim Gnew suffered a grazing bullet wound to his knee. The bullet fired from Mays' 22 caliber handgun had ricocheted off his bulletproof vest to cause the injury. None of the other law enforcement personnel or the hostages were physically harmed.

The medical first responders rushed on board to attend to Ornetta Mays. After treating her at the scene, they rushed her to a hospital. I was standing there as they carried her out on a stretcher. She did not look good. There was blood everywhere. She looked like a goner to me. Understandable, after taking a point-blank round to the chest.

At that moment I was overcome by an immense sense of relief. My crew and my passengers had been under the gun of a crazy woman for 6 ½ hours. Mays had haphazardly fired over a dozen rounds aboard the airplane in the midst of crew and passengers. Miraculously, only the gate agent, Jeanette Rivera, was injured to begin the ordeal, and Jim Gnew sustained a flesh wound to end it. There is no doubt we were lucky and had dodged the bullet, so to speak, in so many ways. I gave a silent prayer of thanks, because someone was definitely watching over us.

Back in the real world, the show must go on. Or does it? After the dust had settled and the ordeal was wrapping up, our flight dispatcher in New York called for me on the phone. He wanted me to leave as soon as possible that night to bring the airplane back to JFK. I told him, in language as plainly as I could speak, that we would not be flying anywhere that night. I told him I was taking the entire crew to the nicest restaurant I could find for a meal of comfort food and adult beverages, all on the company's dime. And then we would be going to a hotel for our legal rest. We needed time to unwind and count our blessings. And that's just what we did. I personally thanked the crew for their exceptional performance, bravery and valor under life-and-death circumstances. Well done, team.

As it turned out, the aircraft could not be moved anyway, because the FBI had designated it a crime scene until further notice. So much for that.

The next morning our entire crew was in uniform again for a press conference at 10 AM at the airport. Jeff Kriendler, from Pan Am corporate communications in New York, had flown out to supervise the event. I had met Jeff from previous Pan Am publicity events. The press conference went well and lasted over a half-hour, with basic questions and answers. During this time, I was able to publicly tout the exceptional professionalism of our entire crew.

The FBI finished their crime scene investigation at noon and released the airplane back to the company. They had found 10 spent bullets from Mays' pistol lodged in the plane. Most of them were near the front of the airplane in the wall to the cockpit. Sure enough, they found two slugs in the flight engineers panel, where Mays had fired a point-blank range at Brook Hunt and missed him…twice. *She's not shooting blanks.*

Two Pan Am mechanics had flown in that morning from JFK. They examined the aircraft and declared it airworthy. Bill Weiler, Ron Rupp, and myself looked it over closely and determined there's no reason it wasn't safe to fly. The inside of the airplane looked like a disaster area after the ordeal and the FBI's investigation. There was only one bullet hole in the fuselage that we could find and that was at the edge of the front entrance door. It was not large enough to affect pressurization. That afternoon, with our flight attendants, Jeff Kriendler, and the two mechanics on board, we ferried the airplane back to JFK for maintenance.

A few weeks later our crew gathered together one last time. Ed Acker, the CEO of Pan Am, invited us with our spouses or significant others

469

to a dinner at Joe's Stone Crabs restaurant on Miami Beach, as a personal thank you for a job well done. Baxter and I had been to Joe's several times before, but never like this. We got a glimpse of how the other half lives. There was a big crowd outside the door waiting to get into the restaurant. But, not for the Ed Acker party. We were escorted to a private table off to the side of the restaurant and feted to anything we wanted. For Baxter and me, that would, of course be the stone crabs. And Baxter did have a couple glasses of Mr. Aker's fine wine. It was a wonderful evening and a nice gesture from Mr. Acker towards our crew. We didn't talk shop at all. No airline business was discussed. We certainly didn't talk about the elephant in the room. Ed Acker was doing everything he could to save our struggling airline. *And they were still losing money, a million dollars a day.*

There were kudos and commendations for everyone after the hijacking. I certainly received my share of kind words for whatever part I played in the ordeal. They were humorously summed up by the last letter I received from my Chief Pilot, Ken McAdams:

Dear Ben:

Inasmuch as you have already received commendations from the President of the United States, the Vice President of the United States, the Chairman of the Board, Pan American World Airways, and the Vice President of Flight Operations as well, enclosed you will find a further note of appreciation from the Office of the Mayor of Cleveland, Ohio.

Somehow with that lineup of kudos preceding my own, I feel totally outgunned. Nevertheless, a few more meager words of appreciation for your excellence and professionalism certainly should not hurt. On behalf of all of us that Chief Pilot's office, let me extend these for your many jobs well done, at this stage becoming too many to enumerate.

Best

Regards,

Ken   McAdams

Chapter 73

Pan Am's charter flights were moneymakers, because generally the deal was signed and the money was paid up front for every flight. Guaranteed profit. Pan Am had long-term contracts with professional baseball and football teams and several colleges for their football teams. And then, occasionally out of the blue, would come a strange one, like the one to which I was assigned in early April, 1986.

The New York Hall of Science in Queens, New York contracted Pan Am to provide a charter flight from JFK for 150 science buffs, politicians, and businessmen, to see Halley's Comet. In 1705, English astronomer Edmond Halley determined the comets which had been appearing every 75 years since before 240 BC were in fact the same comet. Hence, it was named Halley's Comet. It consisted of a coma, or nucleus, and a tail of comet dust, ice crystals and other elements. It is the only comet that can be seen from Earth with the naked eye.

The passengers, a strange sampling New York notables and upper crust of New York society, began boarding the airplane at 1 AM for our 1:30 AM departure. They were grasping for what would probably be their only chance to see the comet in person. The lights from the city and the New York weather made stargazing difficult. There were several familiar faces among the boarders, the most recognizable of which was Tom Brokaw, NBC anchor of the evening news. Also. there was a gentleman on board who was one of the few people to have seen Halley's Comet on its last visit in 1910.

Flying in the right seat with me on this trip was Dan Condon, who was the chief pilot in New York at the time. More on Dan Condon later.

471

Everyone in operations at Pan Am were very concerned about the success of this flight. These people had already paid $250 for a flight to nowhere, what if it was also a flight for nothing? Would the comet be visible? Would clouds obscure the comet? Could the passengers see it from inside the cabin? So many questions.

Condon and I had formulated a plan with our dispatchers and meteorologists. The view of Halley's Comet was far better in the southern hemisphere than the United States. Therefore, we decided to fly south over the Atlantic to a point approximately 150 miles east of Savannah Georgia to improve our viewing chances. The weather at that location was forecast to be favorable, although there was a possibility of a layer of clouds below 30,000 feet.

The departure from JFK was mostly in the weather as we climbed through 20,000 feet flying southbound. At 31,000 feet, our cruising altitude, we were mostly in the clear. In the back of the airplane, the party was on. Flight attendants wined and dined the collection of Halley hawker hopefuls with first-class food and beverage service throughout the airplane.

We reached our destination at 31,000 feet over the ocean east of Savannah about 3 AM. Sadly, our greatest fears were realized. We were in a cloud layer making visibility impossible. We climbed to 33,000 feet. We were still in the weather, however, intermittently we could see a few stars and clear skies above. The problem was we were pushing the altitude limits of the airplane. We consulted the performance manuals and determined that 35,000 feet would be the absolute upper limits of our capability at that particular weight and temperature. Carefully, we pushed the throttles forward and nursed the 727 to 35,000 feet.

And there it was. Halley's Comet. At least we thought it was. About 45° up in the southeastern sky was this fuzzy looking star with a fuzzy looking tail. Was that it? We had to be sure before we announced to the folks that we had found it. We invited the elderly gentleman who saw the comet in 1910 to come to the cockpit. He stared up at the sky for longest time. He had to wait for his old eyes to adjust to the dark cockpit after leaving the bright lights of the cabin. In a minute or so, he became very emotional. We knew we were looking at Halley's Comet. He remarked he never thought he would see it again. Even though it wasn't as bright as he remembered it 1910, he was grateful to see its return. At that moment, to me, the trip was a success.

In the back of the airplane, the cabin meal service had been cleared and the cabin lights were turned off. For the next 40 minutes, above all the clouds, we flew a rectangular pattern over the Atlantic with 10-minute legs, so passengers could take turns at the window seats on each side of the aircraft to view the comet. Success.

The party continued on the flight back to JFK. The passengers were treated to bagels, Milky Ways, and Mars bars. And of course, champagne. Some said they were underwhelmed with the appearance of Halley's Comet. And truthfully, so was I. Maybe it was because the comet may have been overhyped by the news media. Or maybe it was because I had seen the fireworks on Key Biscayne on the 4th of July. In any case, I thought it was nice to be able to take advantage of my only opportunity to see Halley's Comet in such a special way. The next visit of the comet to Earth will be in 2065.

More about Dan Condon. Dan was appointed Chief Pilot in Miami in Miami not too long after the National-Pan Am merger. He was a Navy guy, having graduated from the Naval Academy where he was known as a sharp guy, but had the reputation as a bit of a prankster. As the new Chief Pilot, he was my boss, because I was a 727 Check Pilot in Miami. Dan, for some reason, decided to give the check pilots various odd-ball assignments to test the depth of our administrative skills. He wanted me to draft a letter for his signature to respond to an inquiry from a college student in Texas regarding being a Pan Am pilot. I thought this was absurd. I was teaching, checking, flying the line and also some of the White House press Corps missions. I didn't need to be spending time on busybody make-work projects that should be done by the personnel department. Rather than confront Condon directly about this ridiculous request, I decided I would confront this ridiculous request by pranking the prankster. I drafted the following sanitized version of a letter to Tidwell and persuaded the secretary to type it on Pan Am letterhead for the chief pilot's signature:

Mr. John Tidwell
7002 Sand Castle
Houston, Texas

Dear Mr. Tidwell:

We at Pan Am are pleased to respond to your inquiry regarding a career in commercial aviation. It is refreshing to know that there are those, such as yourself, that are preparing diligently, even today, to carry our industry into the 21ˢᵗ century.

Surely, you must realize as we soar into the future, that there are a few clouds on the horizon. Not lack of business; more people are flying today than ever before. Indeed, not lack of equipment; our aircraft get safer, more efficient every year. The storm clouds are in the hemisphere of labor... the workforce. You see, John, deregulation (the AIDS of the airline industry) was perpetuated by the replacement of experienced professional pilots, making wages commensurate with their many years of training and experience, with young inexperienced "would be" pilots that will work for nothing, just to wear the uniform and get out of town with the flight attendants.

John, you're not trying to be one of those "B" and "C" scale company busters, are you? The fact that you're from Houston makes me believe that you must know that sucker Lorenzo. Why didn't you write him for a job? He'd put you directly into the right seat, you being a college sophomore with an interest in aviation. Then, before you get old enough and smart enough to think of a career, family, etc., He'd replace you with another inexperience, naïve, nonunion a****** like yourself.

In closing, f*** you Tidwell, and the nonsked you rode in on. We'll never hire another Parker 51 f***** such as yourself as long as I'm chief pilot.

Sincerely,

D. J. Condon
Regional Chief Pilot

P. S. If you are in need of additional career guidance, pi** up a rope.

Later, upon recalling reading the letter again, Condon commented: "Reading it brought back that morning in stark detail… I was impressed that it was typed, seemed well-organized and I was just going to say send it out – and then I finish reading it! It took a couple of seconds until I could decide if Ben was either stark raving mad or had a great sense of humor. I'm still not sure."

Mission accomplished. He never asked me again to write a letter for him.

Chapter 74

The B-727 was my favorite passenger airplane to fly. With three engines in the rear of the airplane it was very quiet in the cockpit. Eastern Airlines called their 727 the "whisper jet." It was very responsive on the controls and was easy to handle. For decades it was the workhorse of the airline industry and was often called the DC-3 of the jet age.

There was only one peculiarity about flying the 727, and that was the landing. With most airplanes you would fly the airplane to a hundred feet or so from the runway, then retard the power and pull back gently on the stick and the airplane would settle in for a nice landing. Not the 727. With that airplane you have to maintain the same angle of attack and the same power setting until you are a few inches off the runway. Then you slowly push the stick forward and retard the power for a grease job. Failure to keep the power on, especially in a crosswind, would result in free fall to a very hard landing. Or worse.

As an instructor pilot, when we had a new pilot checking out on the airplane who was having difficulty with landings, we had the perfect solution. We would take them up to fly the New York shuttle. After a few days and a dozen or so landings at LaGuardia, Washington National, and Boston, they were usually good to go. Such was the case with this one new student I was training.

Our first flight was from JFK to Washington National, where we would begin a couple days of shuttle flying from there. When we boarded the aircraft in New York a Pan Am special rep pulled me aside to tell me about a VIP who had been pre-boarded. After I stowed my flight kit in the cockpit, I walked back to First Class and welcomed her aboard. I would have recognized her right away, even without the entourage traveling with her…this soft-spoken, diminutive lady, wearing off-white with a matching scarf. The flight attendants were doting over her, so I knew she was in good hands.

The flight out of JFK was uneventful. My new copilot in the right seat was doing a good job and seemed to handle the airplane well. So far so good. A cold front had moved through the Northeast overnight and the skies were clear in Washington. There was a brisk, gusty wind from the northwest. The approach and landing would be to the north, beginning near Mount Vernon and following the Potomac River to the airport. During the approach briefing, I cautioned the new guy about the possibility of wind shear under these conditions. I suggested it might be prudent for him to keep the power up and carry a little extra airspeed near the ground to be on the safe side.

We were bouncing around in moderate chop throughout the final approach. Passing through 500, 400, 300 feet, the turbulence continued. The copilot was wrestling the airplane in the tough conditions as best he could, even though he was see-sawing with the throttles, over controlling them much more than necessary. I knew from experience such a strong wind from the northwest swirling over the terminal and hangers on the airport, could create a dangerous downdraft closer to the ground.

Passing 200 feet, I first felt it in the seat of my pants. It was like the bottom fell out. The airplane was sinking rapidly towards the ragged rocks of the Potomac River. I also noticed the throttles were retarded lower than they should have been and my new guy wasn't reacting to correct the situation.

"I have the aircraft." I commanded to the copilot.

"You have it," he replied. He lifted his hands from the controls.

Without hesitation, I jammed the throttles forward and pulled back on the stick and was able to arrest the sink rate. I nursed the airplane back on the proper glide path, established a little right rudder, left wing down crosswind correction, and rolled it on for a nice landing.

Not a word was said about what had just happened until we were parked at the gate and the shutdown checklist was complete. I spoke first.

"What happened out there?" I asked. "What were you thinking? Do you know you could go straight to hell for that?"

"What?" The copilot asked. "What did I do?"

"You just tried to kill Mother Teresa," I said.

It took the new guy a few moments to realize I wasn't mad at him at all. It was just my way of breaking the ice, so we could have a real discussion about the perils of crosswind landings with the possibilities of windshear.

The system worked. As an instructor pilot, you must allow the student to make a mistake, but never to the point that would compromise the safety of the flight. Lesson learned. After a couple of days flying in gusty conditions around the Northeast, he was doing a very nice job with the entire operation, including crosswind landings. He was released to fly the line.

And I claimed bragging rights forever that I saved Mother Teresa's life. And Mother Teresa never knew.

On Sunday, April 27, 1986, I was watching the television news in my hotel room in Berlin, West Germany. I was on a required day off after I had spent the prior week administering line checks to various 727 pilots who were flying Pan Am's Internal German Service, the IGS. One of the stories reported on the news caught my attention.

The news anchor noted there had been sketchy reports of a problem at the Chernobyl nuclear power plant in the Soviet Union, near the city of Kyiv. This caught my interest because the next Tuesday, April 29th, I was scheduled to be the Check Captain on Pan Am's first flight into Moscow in eight years. Commercial service had been suspended during a period of the Cold War. During the Geneva summit of 1985, President Reagan and Leader Gorbachev agreed to resume flights between the two countries. The reporter went on to say officials of Moscow, while admitting they were performing routine maintenance at the Chernobyl facility, denied experiencing any abnormalities.

The next day, Monday April 28th, I deadheaded from Berlin to Frankfurt to be in position for the trip the next day. I was excited to be going to Russia. For dinner that evening I went to the usual spot near the hotel, the Basseler Eck Restaurant, a.k.a. the Gas Station. Naturally, it was so named because it was located behind a gas station. I loved the place because the owner, Gerd Hitzeger, welcomed all Pan Am crewmembers with open arms. I ordered the same dish every time, the schweinshaxe, a traditional German pork hock recipe. Not exactly like Grandmother made when we butchered hogs back on the farm in Sneads. It was better.

After dinner, back at the hotel, I turned on the television and tuned in the international channel for the news, which was spoken in English. They were talking about the Russian nuclear plant. A facility in Sweden had detected unusual amounts of airborne radiation streaming into their country from the Soviet Union. This created massive speculation about what was really happening at the Chernobyl power plant. Did they have an accident? Was there a meltdown? Was the atmosphere being contaminated with nuclear radiation? Were there injuries? Deaths? The report from Sweden was very concerning to me because our route of flight the next day would take us directly through the area between Kyiv and Sweden. I believed what the Swedes were saying, and I was very skeptical about the Russian's denials.

Before going to bed, I used the phone beside the bed to call our dispatcher at flight control in New York. The dispatcher was responsible for the operational planning of the flight, such as route of flight, fuel required, weight and balance, etc. He said it was all over the news in the states, but our station manager in Moscow had heard absolutely nothing about Chernobyl from the local news or the authorities there. We discussed the wisdom of operating the flight, notwithstanding all the hype and fanfare from the company and the government about our first trip back into Moscow. The dispatcher said he would attempt to gain some assurances to assuage our concerns by departure time the next day. I said goodbye, hung up the phone and went to bed. I did not sleep well.

The next day, Tuesday morning, April 29th, I arrived in operations at Frankfurt to learn that the trip to Moscow was definitely a go. The evening before, a Pan Am 747 had departed JFK nonstop to Frankfurt to begin the Moscow service. On board were politicians and dignitaries, including a Pan Am VP and the US ambassador to the Soviet Union. It had arrived on time to connect with our 727 in Frankfurt, continuing on to Moscow. The dispatcher in New York told me the Russian ambassador to Germany would meet me at the departure gate of our flight to discuss our concerns about Chernobyl.

When I arrived at the door of the aircraft he was standing there, the Russian ambassador. By his appearance he was right out of central casting for any middle-aged Politburo politician. He was short and stocky with a bad haircut and a tousled beard. He wore what appeared to be a brownish secondhand suit with a second day shirt and a snow shovel tie. Needless to say, I was underwhelmed by this gentleman.

The ambassador and I exchanged pleasantries. He spoke broken English and I spoke no Russian, so he had me on that one. I got right to the point.

"What about the news reports about a possible nuclear accident at Chernobyl?" I asked.

"Cap tan, ve haf no problem in Russia," he said.

"The Swedes report high levels of radiation in the atmosphere streaming across from Russia. What about that?"

"Cap tan, yo haf my word. Ve haf no problem in Russia."

I could see where this was going. I'd heard it from the horse's mouth, the Communist Party line of full denial.

On board the aircraft I huddled with the crew. The line Captain and the copilot were excellent pilots and had prepared well for the trip. The flight attendants aboard were all Russian-speaking girls from Poland. They all spoke fluent Russian and perfect English, and were drop-dead gorgeous. I relayed to the crew what the Russian ambassador had said. We all agreed to take him at his word and not worry about the things we could not control, and concentrate on giving these notable passengers the high level of Pan Am service they were expecting.

Flying into the Soviet Union was different. From the moment we entered Russian airspace it was obvious the controllers were not there to help us, but to harass us. They required us to navigate using radio beacons, a very primitive form of navigation for us. These beacons along our route of flight were very close together. A radio call with a position report was required at every station, resulting in a frequency change and position report every five minutes, or so. Completely unnecessary, because we were sure they had us on radar the entire time. Or, maybe they didn't. Another thing, the altitude assignments were in meters, not feet. This required consulting a conversion chart at every altitude change. Different.

The landing pattern at Sheremetyevo, the airport in Moscow, was also totally different. We circled north of the airport to land to the Southwest on runway 24L. Rather than flying a straight-in approach, as would be done at most airports in the world, the flight pattern required a descending turn during the entire approach until you were on short final. You wouldn't expect the Russians to do it the easy way.

After landing, when we pulled up to the gate, we were greeted by a huge crowd of people. An entire marching band was in formation nearby on the ramp, playing away. After the airplane was parked, I donned my coat and hat and stepped out of the cockpit. In a few moments the cabin door opened and a monstrous man in a Russian military uniform stepped right up into my face. He stood there towering over me, bearing the expression of a robot which had never heard a kind word. I thought maybe he needed a little southern charm.

"Good afternoon," I said with a smile. "On behalf of Pan American World Airways and the United States of America, we are excited to be returning to Moscow."

The Russian's expression never changed. He inched even closer to me, tilted his head slightly to the side and gazed down directly into my eyes. He held the gaze for a long, uncomfortable moment.

"Ur pay-pers, plz," the soldier finally demanded. Not so much a hello, or a welcome, or a how do you do. "Ur pay-pers, plz," he repeated.

Welcome to the Soviet Union. So that's how it was, and how it was going to be. It was a rude awakening to life behind the Iron Curtain.

It wasn't like we had not been briefed. A Pan Am liaison for the trip warned us to not expect the same courtesies in the Soviet Union that we as crewmembers enjoyed in the United States and other parts of the world. She said Big Brother was alive and well in Russia, watching everything we did and listening to everything we said. There were even rumors that the hotel rooms might be bugged with listening devices. The Soviets were notorious for enticing Americans into compromising positions, then blackmailing them into turning over sensitive information or even being a communist spy.

Even though the Pan Am station manager accompanied us through customs, the harsh, brash, adversarial attitude towards us continued. We were thoroughly searched and patted down. They emptied out my flight kit. They went through all my clothes in my suitcase and even fingered through the toiletries in my Dopp kit. Infuriating.

Sheremetyevo Airport was almost 20 miles northwest of the city of Moscow. It was springtime in Russia and all the vegetation had that new green grass color. The countryside reminded me of Oklahoma, mostly flat, sparse trees and an occasional rolling hill. Along the way we passed a spot called the Last Defense Line Moscow – Memorial "Ezhi." This memorial marks the line which was the furthest point the German army was able to advance during its December 1941 offensive on Moscow, before the attack was stopped by Soviet resistance.

Our rooms were waiting for us at the Intourist Hotel in downtown Moscow, about two blocks from Red Square. The hotel was appropriately named because it catered mostly to foreign visitors. It was adequate, but nothing special. When I stepped out of the elevator to go to my room, I noticed a matronly woman, a true-life babushka, sitting at a desk at the end of the hall. She had no purpose being there whatsoever, that I could tell, except to observe what was going on in the hall. Big brother. Big sister. Same difference. Once I closed the door to my room, I looked around wondering where were the little cameras and microphones? I saw none, but it didn't matter, because I had nothing to hide.

That evening, the entire crew was invited to a banquet sponsored by Pan Am to celebrate our inaugural flight. Naturally, we all attended, because it was free food and drink in a strange city. The fete was held at the Cosmos, a very modern, futuristic hotel about 20 minutes away in the northeast section of the city.

The station manager chaperoned our group for a subway ride to the hotel. During the short walk to the subway station, I noticed people on the street were very indifferent and had this indifferent and impersonable straight-ahead stare. Not a smile among them. We passed a grocery store. I glanced in to notice that the shelves were about three quarters empty. It reminded me of the grocery store I saw in Havana, empty shelves. Not much of a testament for communism. The subway, on the other hand, was surprisingly quick and efficient. And very clean. There was no graffiti on those walls.

When we arrived at the Cosmos, I was introduced to a high-ranking Soviet military pilot, in uniform, who would act as my host. Finally, a little hospitality, I thought. He was a nice enough guy. His English was good, but he was very guarded in what he said. Nonetheless, from our conversations, I began to form some impressions about life in the Soviet Union. The central government owns and controls everything. Everyone works for the government and fears the government. Everyone basically does the minimum to accomplish their job, and nothing more. There's no incentive to excel, because they will receive the same meager needs of food and shelter and healthcare from the government anyway. There aren't many dissidents, because dissidents have a way of disappearing to Siberia, or worse. Socialists control at its best. I learned the government even restricted travel of its citizens within the Soviet Union. If someone from Moscow wanted to go to St. Petersburg, for instance, they would have to state a reason and a specific need to go there. Then, if approved, they would be issued a visa from the government for the travel. Unbelievable. And to think, these were the people we Americans feared for all those years of the cold war. The iron curtain was there to keep freedom out of the country and the people locked in. These poor souls had never known, and would never know, freedom.

My Soviet pilot friend bluntly denied having any knowledge of a problem with a nuclear power plant in Chernobyl. He inferred that if there was a problem in Chernobyl, he would've heard about. I wasn't convinced.

The banquet affair was predictable, with politicians and corporate bigwigs droning on about how our very presence there demonstrated the openness of leader Gorbachev's Perestroika and the strength and stability of Pan Am. There was occasional polite applause, but I didn't hear any "amens" from our group. Certainly, none from me.

The food was not remarkable, but there was plenty of it, and I was hungry. I ate mostly steak and potatoes. I was hoping it was beef, but I couldn't be sure. Regardless, it did the job. The vodka was flowing, but not for me, Ben the Baptist from Sneads, Florida. I drank my usual overseas beverage… Coca-Cola. Never the water.

All the speeches had been made. It had been a long, interesting day for all of us. Even though the night was winding down and it was getting late, there was one more bucket list type item I really wanted to do. I had seen the changing of the guard ceremony at Arlington Cemetery and at Buckingham Palace. I wanted to see the changing of the guard at Lenin's tomb in Red Square. I couldn't be sure I would ever return to Moscow so I wanted to make it happen that night. In talking with the others on the crew, the Polish flight attendants also wanted to visit Red Square. That was good for me because they were Russian speakers. I bid farewell to our hosts and my dinner partner, the Soviet pilot, and departed the banquet hall with the four girls to hail a taxi for the midnight changing of the guard at Red Square.

The Polish girls were an interesting group. They hated the Russians. Their entire life had been spent under Soviet domination, with the Russian language and culture crammed down their throats. Even though they had never been to Moscow, they were very knowledgeable about its historical sites, especially Red Square, because it was forced on them in school.

The five of us walked through the lobby of the cosmos and out the front door to look for a taxi. There was a queue of people at least 50 yards long lined up on the sidewalk. To my surprise, as we approached the driveway, a taxi whisked up and the driver hopped out and opened the doors for us. I hopped in the back seat with three of the girls and the fourth girl rode shotgun in the front with the driver.

The taxi driver slammed the accelerator and screeched away from the hotel like we had robbed the place and he was the getaway driver. Even though it was late at night, I was about to get a rude awakening to traffic on the streets of Moscow. Basically, it appeared to me, the only traffic law in the city was the law of the jungle. Every beast for himself. It wasn't about courtesy. It wasn't about safety. It was about speed and competition. And our driver thought he was the Russian Dale Earnhardt. This made the traffic in Mexico City, which was the worst I'd ever seen, look like a kiddy car parade.

As the four of us in the backseat held on for dear life, the girl next to me discreetly pointed to the driver up front and whispered in my ear.

"KGB," she said.

"Noooo," I whispered. "How do you know?"

"Did you see that taxi line? We walked out of the hotel and he pulls up just for us?"

The expression on my face told her I wasn't exactly convinced of what she was saying.

"KGB," she whispered again. "For sure."

Red Square was impressive but it wasn't exactly square. It was more like a large rectangular athletic field that had been covered with stone pavers. The Polish girls were excited to be seeing in real life the Soviet symbols which they had only known from pictures and literature. We walked around the perimeter of the so-called square and they pointed out to me the significance of each building along the way. We passed the State Historical Museum, the Kazan Cathedral, and the most colorful of all, the brightly-domed St. Basil's Cathedral, which was at the end of the square. I glanced at my watch to see that it was 11:45 PM. I knew from their conversation that the girls wanted to stay a few minutes longer at St. Basil's. I wanted to be in a good position to see the midnight changing of the guard, so I told the girls I would meet them at midnight at Lenin's tomb, which was centered on the southern side of the square.

The venue was surprisingly crowded for such a late hour. As I made my way across the square directly towards Lenin's tomb, I noticed someone off to my right angling towards me and matching me step for step. Closer, I could see it was a girl. She was wearing a red blazer, with white pants and a cute red beret. She was tall and strikingly attractive, which I had noticed was not uncommon with pre-babushka Russian women. By the time I reached Lenin's tomb, she was standing beside me.

"Hellooo," the girl said in broken English.

"Hello," I said.

"Yu 'Merican?"

"Yes."

"Wher yu frum?"

"Miami."

"Ahhh, everyone frum Miami very rich," she said.

"No, not everyone," I said.

By now, my antennas were out and on full alert. *Everyone in the Soviet Union works for the government.*

"Why you come Russia?"

"Business," I said. "What about you? What do you do?"

"I student athlete."

"Really? What's your sport?"

"I pole vaulter."

I smiled, but I was laughing inside. Here's this gregarious, engaging young beauty in Red Square near midnight, telling this American she's a pole vaulter. What could possibly be wrong with this picture? *The Soviets were notorious for enticing Americans into compromising positions.*

"Where you stay?" The girl asked.

"I came down from the Cosmos," I said.

It was the truth, but I didn't exactly answer her question. I was looking for a way to get away from this girl when, fortunately, I saw the Polish girls approaching in the distance.

"Do you see those four girls over there?" I asked, pointing to the girls. The tall girl in red peered at the flight attendants, and nodded. "The brunette on the left is my wife," I said.

"Oooooh," the girl said.

"Bye-bye. Good luck," I said. I turned and walked away.

When I reached the flight attendants, I linked arms with the brunette, who had been sitting next to me in the taxi. I asked her to walk with me for a minute, and we trailed along with the others.

"I see you made a friend over there," she said. The cute little smirk on her face told me she knew exactly what was going on.

"I told her you were my wife."

"KGB," she said.

At this point, I was beginning to believe her.

486

We heard them before we saw them, the staccato clapping of the leather boots slapping the pavers. The three soldiers of the honor guard goose stepped half the length of Red Square on our left to the front of Lenin's tomb. At that point, after a series of precision drill maneuvers, two of the soldiers replaced the couple guarding the tomb. Then, the three of them, the retiring guards and their commander, goose stepped away, concluding the ceremony.

The pageantry of the changing of the guard at Red Square didn't have the pomp and circumstance of Buckingham Palace, or the impeccable precision of the Tomb of the Unknown Soldier, but I was glad to be able to see it. At this point, I was totally exhausted. It was time for rest.

The girls and I walked the short distance from Red Square back to our hotel. When I reached my floor, I noticed they also had had a changing of the babushka's. It was a different woman, but there she was. Sitting. Watching. Big Sister never sleeps.

The next day, after another round of deep pocket searches and pat downs at Sheremetyevo Airport, we boarded our airplane for the flight back to Frankfurt. I noticed we had a surprisingly heavy load of passengers with us on the trip. We roared down the runway and lifted the nose of the airplane for takeoff. When we separated from the ground the strangest thing happened. There was a loud roar from the back of the airplane. It took me a moment to realize nothing was wrong with the airplane, but the sound was coming from the passengers. There were loud cheers and thunderous applause from an airplane full of people that were ecstatic to be on a flight leaving the Soviet Union. Oddly enough, I recalled, the last time I'd heard such an ovation on takeoff was leaving another Communist country, Cuba, after my first hijacking.

A few minutes later, the brunette flight attendant, my borrowed wife from my Red Square moment, came into the cockpit to offer us beverages. She said it was an unbelievable scene in the passenger cabin. Although they couldn't talk about it while they're in Russia, they were talking now. They were saying there was indeed a nuclear accident at Chernobyl. They said a reactor had melted down at the plant and was leaking deadly radiation into the atmosphere. There were people dying in the area and they were evacuating Kyiv. The government was still in full denial and the people were not allowed to publicly discuss it. Yet, the news on the grapevine was spreading faster than the leaked radiation.

This news became very concerning to me. Were we affected? Did we have passengers suffering from radiation sickness on board? Was our airplane contaminated? Would we be flying through the contaminated jet stream again? Logical questions.

When our flight had cleared Soviet air space, I made a call to our dispatcher in New York. I explained our situation and told him I was apprehensive about the possibility of bringing a contaminated airplane full of people up to the terminal in Frankfurt. He shared those concerns.

Upon landing in Frankfurt, we taxied to an isolated area on the ramp where the ground crews conducted a radiation sweep of our airplane. Fortunately, they found none. We dodged a bullet that day, but the people of Chernobyl and the surrounding areas of Ukraine were not so lucky. The immediate death toll was 31 people, but eventually thousands died and hundreds of thousands were ill with the effects of radiation poisoning for generations to come. I felt fortunate not to be one of them.

Chapter 75

The spring of 1988 was a busy time for White House Press Charters. It was the last year of President Reagan's second term in office and the presidential primaries or his successor were in full swing. Vice-President Bush was the favorite candidate for the Republican nomination, but Senator Bob Dole, the war hero from Kansas, was mounting a strong challenge. On the Democratic side, Governor Michael Dukakis was leading the way in a field that included Jesse Jackson, Al Gore, Gary Hart, and David Duke, former Grand Wizard of the Ku Klux Klan.

The Bush Patrol, the Vice President's press charter, arrived back at Andrews Air Force Base late on a Friday evening. We had been crisscrossing the country with several campaign stops a day for the last four days, and would be doing the same the next week. Because we had to pre-position the airplane for the next charter to Andrews Air Force Base on Sunday, I had decided to spend my one day off in Washington rather than meet myself coming and going to Miami for just one day.

When I arrived at the hotel that evening, I called Baxter at home in Miami. She told me my Aunt Virginia had called. Aunt Virginia was my mother's younger sister, a very nice lady whom I had met a couple of times. She wanted to get a message to me that my mother had been hospitalized in Philadelphia and was very ill. She and Sharma, my half-sister, were deeply concerned about her. Baxter gave me the name of the hospital in Philadelphia and the room number where my mother was staying.

My dad had died not too long ago at age 69 from lung cancer, and now my mother was critically ill. Daddy's passing at a relatively young age was profound for me. But, now my mother, critically ill at age 67… I mean, it wasn't like we had ever been close. How could she leave me alone in a crib at 11 months old and just disappear? What about me was so bad it made me intolerable? I could never understand that. I just knew I never wanted to feel that hurt, that rejection, again. Through the years my mother had made what I considered an obligatory effort to stay in touch. I was always congenial and pleasant during those times, but kept my distance. I would never allow her to hurt me again.

Surprisingly, Pan Am had two flights a day each way between Washington National and New York's Kennedy airport, with a stop in Philadelphia. The next day I donned my suit, we were required to travel in coat and tie those days, and rode on a pass on the first flight to Philadelphia. There, I rented a car and drove to the hospital.

The hospital room was dark and depressing and my mother was indeed very sick. She had tubes running from bottles to everywhere. She was on oxygen. I hadn't seen her in years and she looked old. Very old. It had been at least 20 years since I'd seen Sharma, who was now an adult. She was a cute young lady and very quiet and shy.

My mother stared at me intently as I approached her bedside. Maybe it was because she couldn't see me clearly. Or maybe she didn't recognize me. Or both. She tightened her squint and tilted her said slightly to the side for the longest moment. Then she knew.

"Benny," she said. Her labored voice, with the heavy Philadelphia accent, was barely above a hoarse whisper. "Benny, I can't believe you're here."

"I heard you were sick, and I wanted to come to see you," I said.

"You look so much like your father."

"I'm not sure if you heard, but Daddy died about five years ago… Lung cancer."

"Lung cancer. That's bad stuff. This emphysema's bad enough… Giving me a fit."

From her reaction I couldn't tell if she knew about Daddy's passing, or not. I changed the subject. I told her about Baxter and the kids. I told her I'd been a captain for over 10 years. I told her about my hijackings. I told

490

her about flying the White House press Corps, and about being friends with the Bush family, and about playing tennis with Vice President, hopefully soon to be president, Bush.

Eventually, she changed the subject back to my dad, but not in a good way. She seemed suddenly desperate to tell me her version of what happened back in the day, when I was an infant. She wanted to tell me things that my dad did, or did not do, to cause things to work out as they did. I immediately recoiled. I was not going to sit there and listen to someone, especially my mother who had deserted me, talk about my dead father, the one who stayed to raise me. I knew my father wasn't a saint, far from it. I didn't need to hear that from her. My dad was fiercely loyal and supportive to me until the day he died. As I was to him.

"I don't want to hear it," I said to her, probably too abruptly. "I don't want to hear it. It's okay. Everything has turned out just fine. It's okay."

Soon after that I said my goodbyes. I looked back at my mother as I left the room and an unexpected rush of deep sadness swept over me. Somehow, I knew I would never see her again.

I'm not sure what I wanted to accomplish with that visit to Philadelphia but, whatever it was, it didn't happen. My mother wanted to unburden her heart and find comfort by talking to me about what happened almost 50 years before. I could not listen to her and give her comfort because I only saw her as the person who deserted me as a baby. Sadly, a cross I still bore.

My mother died a short time later. For whatever reason, I wasn't notified of her passing. I never knew why. My mother died with regrets, and oddly, I now lived with regrets. I vowed no one would ever know.

Chapter 76

In the spring of 1986, I had the title at Pan Am of 727 Standards Pilot. The ominous title was just a name for the guy who supervised the dozen or so 727 check pilots at Pan Am's Miami base. I'd held this position for couple of years. In addition to this I had been flying a steady diet of White House Press Corps charters. It was a busy time.

Out of the blue I received an urgent message to call Tom Batten. Tom and I had been good friends since the early days at National Air Lines where we were teammates on the company softball team. He grew up in Miami and went on to play quarterback for the Florida Gators. And then he was a pilot in the Army and flew 100 missions as a Forward Air Controller in Vietnam. Tough duty.

When I returned Tom's call, he had a surprising and interesting proposition. He had accepted the job to be the new chief pilot for Pan Am's Miami base. He wanted me to be the Manager of Flying, a position in the chief pilot's office that was responsible for all flying operations of the Miami base and direct supervision of the approximately 750 pilots who were based there.

It was a tough decision. I told Tom I needed 24 hours to talk it over with Baxter, and he consented. There was nothing about an 8 to 5 office job, five days a week, that interested me. The job also required that I get rated on the B-747. That meant I would have to maintain a dual qualification on the 727 and the 747, in addition to my office duties. Triple busy. On the plus side, I would be paid for the max hours you could fly, plus an override, which would be a nice pay increase. Also, even though I would be working office hours five days a week, I would usually be able to control my own schedule. This was very appealing to me because the kids were very active in sports and theatrical events, things I didn't want to miss. Scott was attending South Center for the Arts and performing at Southwood Junior High School, and Spencer was number one in the state of Florida in tennis for her age group. Additionally, Spencer was a principal in a syndicated TV show called, Kidz Biz, featuring exceptional kids from all genres of adolescent life. Exciting times.

Baxter liked the idea of me being home every night, so she urged me to take the job. That was good enough for me. The next day Tom welcomed me as the next Manager of Flying for Pan Am's Miami base. I told Tom my only concern was I would not be able to fly the White House press charters, or even get enough flying time in general. He assured me I would get plenty of flying time and fly an occasional White House trip. And I did.

For the next couple of years, I would leave our Pine Acres house in Kendall at 7:15 AM every weekday to be in the office at the airport at 8 o'clock. Working with and for Tom Batten was good duty. We had a mutual trust through our long friendship that prevailed through our working relationship. Lou Colangelo, Director of Flight Operations, and Larry King, Manager of Flight Engineers, were also in the office and a joy to work with.

The problem with this job was just that, problems. With 750 Miami based pilots flying all around the country and to so many parts of the world, every difficulty, every FAA rule that was bent or broken, eventually ended up on my desk. If a pilot was involved, usually with an inadvertent infraction, I tried to protect the airman by assuring the FAA we would deal with the party involved in house. In most cases we would be able to prevent a fine or certificate action by the FAA against the airman. Other issues would include procedural changes, airport notices and changes, and countless other items which might affect the day-to-day operation of an airline. The discouraging part about the job was, I was usually stomping out brushfires all day long. At the end of the day, I oftentimes went home feeling as if nothing had been accomplished. Frustrating.

Frustrating also was watching this once great airline continue to deteriorate as a corporation and the helpless feeling of not being able to do anything about it. In 1981 they had sold the Intercontinental Hotel chain for $500 million and the landmark Pan Am building in Manhattan for $400 million. In 1986 they sold the Pacific routes to United Airlines for $700 million. In January, 1988, in a desperation effort, Ed Acker was replaced as chairman of Pan Am by Tom Plaskett, a young airline executive from American Airlines. Still $1 million a day, every day, down the drain. How could this last? I knew it could not. I knew sooner or later the fiddler would be paid.

One of the most difficult jobs I had as Manager of Flying was making the final decision on someone's flying career. In the uncommon instance a B-727 pilot failed to perform up to standards on a simulator check ride, they would be retrained and given another opportunity. If they failed that check, more training and a recheck. If a second failure occurred, more training, and then I would be the one to administer a third check ride, the final one. These elimination flights were highly visible, and always monitored by a representative from the FAA and ALPA, the Air Lines Pilot's Association. Most of these rare checks turned out okay, but some did not. And sadly, those pilots had to be terminated. There's nothing more important to an airline than safety, and that starts with pilot proficiency. I slept well at night knowing I had given the airman every chance to succeed, yet never compromised the high safety standards of the company.

December 21, 1988, Pan Am suffered another devastating loss. Clipper 103, a flight from London's Heathrow airport bound for New York disintegrated from a bomb explosion at 31,000 feet over Lockerbie Scotland. All 243 passengers and 16 crew members perished. I was

494

working at my desk in Miami when I heard the news. For the next few hours, Lou and Larry and I gathered in Tom's office listening as the updates dribbled out from Pan Am headquarters in New York. This loss was personal for me. I had met Jim McQuarrie the captain, but the flight engineer, Jerry Avritt, was a friend of mine whom I had flown with many times on the 727. Another reason it was personal was I had piloted a 747 out of London to New York only three days before and in five days I was scheduled to do it again. And I did.

The investigation of the bombing went on for years, but it was an instant death knell for the recovery efforts of Pan Am. Eventually. it was determined that a bomb was placed in a cassette player inside a suitcase and on board a Pan Am airplane in Malta. From there it went to Frankfurt, then to London, where it was transferred to the baggage hold of flight 103, where it exploded on the way to New York. Even though several former Libyan intelligence officials were later charged with the crime, the damage had been done.

Chapter 77

Busy times are often fun times. It was certainly that way for me in the late 1980s. My flying and check pilot duties with Pan Am, flying the White House trips and other special flights, were exciting. Notwithstanding the bankruptcy cloud that was always there, casting doubt on the future of the company, and my job. A million dollars a day. And there was nothing I could do about it. Besides, the kids were growing up fast and that was enough for me to worry about.

Scott was immersed in the drama program at South Center for the Arts at Southwood Junior High School. He had prominent roles in musicals such as The Music Man and Oklahoma, under the direction of Rick Adams, who established and headed up the drama program there. Rick was one of those teachers. One of those that years later, students would look back and say Mr. Adams made a difference in their education, and their lives.

Baxter and I loved theater and the arts and tried to support the Southwood program as much as we could. Baxter would help with makeup and costuming and occasionally I would have an opportunity to sling a hammer or paintbrush to build sets and backdrops for the theatrical productions. It was in that capacity that I met Michael Callahan, who was on the staff at Southwood as a lighting and set designer. Mike was an interesting and talented young man, He was very pleasant to work with, and of course had a love for the theater. While working with Mike, he casually mentioned he had always

496

wanted to write a musical based on his favorite movie of all time, "It's a Wonderful Life." Everyone, myself included, loved the old Christmas classic starring Jimmy Stewart and Donna Reed. He confessed he never tried to write it because he didn't know much about music or writing songs. Mike went on to say the copyright protection of "It's a Wonderful Life" had recently lapsed into public domain.

The conversation piqued my interest. I loved writing songs. I especially liked the challenge of writing situational songs, such as creating a musical would require. When I chatted about my passion for composing songs and my appreciation for musical theater, Mike became very excited. "Let's do this," he said. "Let's write a musical. I'll write the book and you write the songs."

There were a thousand reasons for me not to get involved in something like this, aside from the fact that I'd never been busier in my life. I didn't know much about Mike, except he was really young, barely old enough to vote. Yet, he was very pleasant to work with and was exceptionally adept at set design and lighting for the stage. And another thing about Mike was evident from the start: his youth and inexperience was greatly overshadowed by his exuberance and enthusiasm. I didn't reject the idea of writing a musical with Mike, but I was reticent.

During the next few weeks, I bought a VHS tape of "It's a Wonderful Life," and watched it intently for content and emotion, trying to conceptualize songs for the major scenes. So many exciting possibilities.

At the next painting and hammer-slinging set building session, I asked Mike if he had jotted down any scenes from the musical he wanted to write. He said he had a few scenes on legal pads here and there, but he had the entire storyline in his head. He proceeded to give me a fascinating account of his thoughts on the complete musical, from opening to finale. He generally followed the plot of the movie, but included some very interesting twists, including some different characters. Interesting.

One thing led to another and Mike's passion for this project finally carried the day. I agreed to give it a try, but only for one scene and one song, just to see if it might be possible for us to work together.

Mike described to me the opening scene, set in the post-depression era, in the early days of World War II, in the boardroom of the bank. The Board of Directors and the bank were in total disarray following the death of their beloved bank president. Everyone wanted the president's son, George, to take over the bank, believing he was the only one who could prevent the conniving curmudgeon of the town from swindling his way into owning the bank. George had turned down their offer in favor of his dream of going to college. In the upbeat opening number, members of the Board of Directors are making ridiculous motions such as giving a set of pots and pans to new customers, hiring security guards, or installing drive-through windows. The chairman nixes these suggestions as insane in an attempt to deal with the crisis at hand, as stated in the chorus of the rousing, upbeat song I pitched to Mike a few days later:

This Board of Directors needs direction
Someone who could give us some protection
This is not a satisfactory projection
Well this is not the time for dejection
There's a man for whom we all have affection
He has only brought to us a rejection
Nevermind let's get on with the election
This Board of Directors needs direction

Mike loved the song. He thought it was exactly the opening number we were looking for. A song for each scene of a musical must set the tone, enhance the mood, and further the plot. We both felt this song met those requirements. This was exciting. So, we agreed to continue the journey. No promises, no obligations. Mike began writing the book that was so vivid in his mind and soon gave me the next scene. A short time later, I gave him the next song. And that's the way it went for about a year until the first draft was completed.

In no way do I want to insinuate that writing a musical is easy. But the truth is, it was so much fun and so interesting, it seemed that way. When I needed a new song for the musical, it usually happened like this: I would study the scene, the characters, their mood, and what they needed to say. Then, over a period of time, maybe days or even weeks or months, I would visualize it in my mind as a scene from a movie. At some point, out of nowhere, the song would come to me. Oftentimes it would be in the middle of the night like a dream from the twilight of my sleep. When this happened, I learned not to fight it, just get up and write it down. The music and lyrics would usually come at the same time, each yielding to the other until they meshed together to find their purpose for the musical.

There was one particular song that was especially vexing for me. We were dealing with the part of the plot for the Jimmy Stewart character meets the Donna Reed character. Mike had given me the task of writing what he called a "like" song. "We can't have a love song," he said, "because the characters haven't met." I had written many songs, including several for this musical, but I was struggling to find my way with this one. One day while checking into operations for a trip, I bumped into an ornery old Captain, Boots Shaw. Boots was a big man who had played college football and towered over me like hundred-year-old sequoia. He was gruff and crotchety and rough around the edges and many copilots hated to fly with him. I didn't really mind it because I found him to be a rough tough creampuff. We chatted for a moment and I recalled a similar meeting I had with Boots years ago when I was assigned to be his copilot on a trip.

"Hey Ben. Where you going?" Boots had asked.

"I'm going with you, Boots," I said.

A genuine, giant smile stretched across his face.

"Ben," he boomed. "You've made my day.

He had grabbed my hand with his mammoth meat-hook and gave me a bone-crunching handshake.

At the moment I remembered that encounter with Boots, I knew I had it. When I reached the Huntley house in Santa Monica for the layover, I sat down and wrote what is probably my favorite song. I believe in love at first sight, so for me it really is a love song. And it was inspired by none other than Boots Shaw. And he never knew (RIP, Boots).

Here's the chorus:

You've made my day
Just a simple little smile
Seems to say
Could we visit for a while
Could we share some feelings too
Telling me and telling you
I feel special when you look at me that way
You've made my day
You've made my day

The immediate problem I had from the musical end was getting the songs I had written into a format from which they could be performed. I had plunked out the melodies on a piano, as I did with all the songs I had written, to make a lead sheet and obtain copyright protection. It was difficult for me to personally demo a song because I was vocally challenged. I couldn't sing a lick. In my mind it was pitch perfect, but out of my mouth, not so much. Sadly, I had never learned to play the piano. Creative challenges.

An exhaustive search for a music arranger led me to a private residence in North Miami Beach. Mike Lewis was a music composition major at Florida State, where he preceded me by couple of years. He'd had a rewarding career in music since college, mostly in Nashville. Now, because of some health issues, he had moved back home to Miami and was working as a freelance arranger. His client list represents a Who's Who of everyone famous in the music business.

When I introduced myself to Mike, he said, "Yes, I know who you are. I arranged a couple of your pieces for Bob Archibald over at the Music Factory." I was shocked. He had done the arrangements and supervised the recording sessions for "Lord Help Me Walk Alone" and "Take Me Back to That Old Town." Small world, indeed. That was the release that had been picked as a hit by Variety Magazine, only to go down in flames with a lawsuit between the producer and the singer.

Mike Lewis was hired on the spot and did a great job to produce an arrangement of each song with the feeling and vision I portrayed to him. It was such a pleasure to work with this gentleman, a true professional.

Michael Callahan and I were anxious to see our new creation performed on stage. We tried pitching it to regional theaters, the Goodman in Chicago, Playwrights Horizons in New York, and even the Coconut Grove Playhouse locally. The problem was always the same. Too many actors. We had a cast of over 30 actors, which made it dead on arrival for houses paying union scale wages. We had never considered the number of actors while we were writing the piece. We just wanted something that would be fun and entertaining.

It was Mike's idea to cut to the chase and put it up at South Center for the Arts. It was, after all, friendly territory because he worked there. In the fall of 1987, he persuaded the administrators to allow us to use their facility for a run of nine performances in February 1988. We would charge admission and designate opening and closing nights as charity events for American Cancer and the ALS Association, respectively. The remaining revenues would be used to pay the primary actors and essential production staff.

By keeping the production local, it was our good fortune to hire Rick Adams as director. Without his extraordinary theatrical talents and management skills, the show would've never been possible. Another heaven-sent hire was Ted Grab as musical director. Ted was Musical Director of South Center for the Arts. His talent and tenacity were invaluable the development of the show. Playing piano

501

in the pit with Ted Grab was a kid from Southwood named, Alex Lacamoire. Little did we know he would become a Broadway legend. Michael Duetsch, who was a teacher at Southwood, did a brilliant job as choreographer, tailoring each scene to the level of talent available.

We called our musical, "What Might Have Been." It was loosely based on the movie, "It's a Wonderful Life," but Mike took many liberties with the story. He renamed and changed many of the characters, and added a few. The angel, Clarence, who came down to save the Jimmy Stewart character from self-destruction by showing him what might've been if he had never been born, was actually a lady of the evening trying to earn her wings. The old antagonist curmudgeon's henchmen were his comedic nephews, new characters, called Dirk and Dack.

We held auditions for the show in November and December, 1987. The resulting cast was an unbelievable cross-section of our community. There were pros and amateurs from every corner of the cage coming together to demonstrate their love for the theater and make this show happen.

The part of George, (Jimmy Stewart) was played by Chris Gardner, a fledgling young actor trying to make it in the tough business. He was tall dark and handsome, perfect for the part, and didn't disappoint with the avalanche of script and music he had to learn.

Denise Randall was cast as Peggy (Donna Reed). She was a lovely, demure young soprano voice major who had recently moved to Miami from northern Michigan.

Jim Herron was perfectly cast as Joe Gibbs, chairman of the Board of Directors. In his day job, he was Executive Vice President and General Counsel for Ryder Trucking Systems. He was drawn to the stage by his love of opera. He had performed leading roles in the St. Louis Opera Theater or ten years.

In the small world department, Jim Herron was good friends with my first cousin, Gordon Shelfer, who had recently moved to Miami as a Vice President of Ryder Systems. Gordon was my cousin from Jacksonville whom I had trained to be a drum major, with hopes that he would come to Florida State and succeed me as drum major of the Marching Chiefs. But alas, he went to the University of Florida and went on to be drum major of the Gator Band. Even stranger, Gordon's son, Andrew Shelfer, attended college locally at the University of Miami, and was drum major of their marching band, the Band of the Hour. Unbelievable. A drum major of the marching bands of the top three universities of Florida from the same family. On a sad note, my cousin Gordon, would die of a heart attack two years later at the age of 46.

The part of old man Marley (Henry Potter, played by Lionel Barrymore in the movie), was played by Roy Smart, who had retired from the Air Force and was also retired as a teacher. The old cantankerous curmudgeon's career and his character were defined in the opening song.

I'm not loved but I'm legal
I'm not righteous but I'm right
I like law to the letter
And I'm known to fly by night
Just sign that second mortgage
And build that brand-new barn
But miss one teensy payment
And I'll take your house and farm

Mystery mortgage
Sign right here
You can trust folks like us
You have no need to fear
Mystery mortgage
The finest print
There's no need that you read
I can tell you what it meant
Mystery mortgage
A deals a deal
And although it's some dough

You'll see that it's a steal
Mystery mortgage
Those payment plans
You miss those
We'll foreclose
And take it off your hands

Old man Marley's dirty work was mostly done by his nephews, the comedic cousins, Dack and Dirk. Dack was brilliantly portrayed by the choreographer of the show, Michael Deutsch. Dirk was played by my son, Scott Shelfer, who did an amazing job with song and dance and comedy. Obviously, those skills came from Baxter's side of the family. Michael and Scott working together gave a virtuoso performance and brought magic to every scene they were in. Their characters were trapped working for Marley, when all they wanted was to escape and join the circus, as described in one of their songs.

I need a change of pace
This job is quite depressing
To put on another face
Indeed would be refreshing
I want to travel with the crowd
Where laughs and drills abound
Dear Mr. Barnum & Bailey
I want to be a clown

I want to take a frown
And make a million smiles
I want to stretch some happiness
Across a million miles
I'm ready to paint my face
With a big nose red and round
Strike up the band and shoot the cannon
I want to be a clown

Louise Gramling was a fortunate find for us as the head of the bank tellers. She was a drama teacher who was a drama major at Florida State University. We had originally wanted our dear friend Jennie Block for that role, but she had a scheduling conflict.

The bank tellers were played by standouts who had attended South Center for the arts, Amy Langer, Britt Hamre, Andrea Roth, and Linda Emm. They lament their boring job and uncertain future the beginning of their opening song.

Why can't a feller get a teller
Must we go through life alone
Just a simple man with money
That could give a girl a home
It's not important that he's handsome
Personality doesn't count
It's just the bottom line
On his savings account

Business as usual um umm
Nothing unusual
Business as usual
Everything's just fine
Be courteous and polite un umm
Do it fast and get it right yea
Business as usual
Working hard all the time

For the Shelfers, it really was a family affair. Scott played the song and dance comedian. Skip, my oldest son, played a cameo role as the auditor of the bank. He made a real character of his character and the result was a persona I could have never thought of, but would never want to change. Baxter, along with our dear friend, Sue Nichols, beautified the stage with several appearances as townspeople, townies as we called them. They had way too much fun. We never had to interrupt their backstage conversation to tell them it was time for them to walk on. Well, maybe once. Or twice.

Spoiler alert. Everything turned out just fine in the musical, as it did in the film. The angel saved George from self-destruction by showing him what it might have been like in the town if he had never been born. The glorious feelings of triumph and redemption were captured in the grand finale.

To be able to see tomorrow
As if it were yesterday
To be able to see your failures

505

Before they come your way
To be able to right the wrongs
That happen now and then
To be able to change your destiny
When you know what might have been
I've followed the footsteps of angels
I've seen what's around the bend
I'll follow life's journey until the end
I saw what might've been
I'll follow life's journey until the end
I saw what might've been

There was another musical to come. I'd been thinking about it for a while. In a few years, it would be 1992, five hundred years after the discovery voyage of Christopher Columbus. There were already talks of festivals and celebrations. Congress had established the Quincentenary Jubilee Commission in Washington to sanction and coordinate these observances on a national level. Replicas of Columbus's three ships, the Pinta, the Nina and the Santa Maria, would tour over 50 cities around the country over a two-year period to highlight the accomplishment. My vision was to write a musical that would piggyback the tour of the three ships with performances in the cities where they stopped along the way.

There was one daunting problem that tormented me. I enjoyed writing songs, especially situational songs, but I had no performance skills. Whatever musical piece I created had to be played and sung by someone else. I knew those shortcomings would present a huge problem with a musical about Christopher Columbus. With any hopes at all of getting the musical written and produced by 1992, I needed a collaborator who could perform and demo the material.

Working with Mike Callahan on the previous musical had been a wonderful experience. I deeply regretted my shortcomings would not allow me to work with Mike again on the Columbus project.

506

Christopher Bishop (Bish) was a graduate of West Point and a Dade County school teacher who had dabbled in acting and performing. He played piano and guitar, and could sing. His wife, Polly, was a teacher at South Center for the Arts, where Scott and Spencer attended. At a chance meeting at the school, I shared with Bish my vision of writing an original musical about Columbus. After some consideration, he agreed to attempt the project.

During the next few months, despite being time limited due to our regular jobs, we outlined a plot and decided to call our musical "1492." We composed a song we knew would be the closing number of the musical, "Discovering America," and a few other songs.

Bill Lane, a friend of ours from South Miami, was an alumnus of Duke University in Durham, N.C. He was intrigued with "1492" and worked with his charitable trusts to fund a production at Duke University in 1992.

During the next couple of years, the musical was completed to the point of attempting a production. Bish and I went to Washington where we presented our work to the Quincentenary Jubilee Commission. Subsequently, they designated "1492" as the official musical of the Quincentenary Celebration and "Discovering America" as the official song.

With the funding from Bill Lane and Duke University, we cast the show with Broadway actors in New York for a production at the Bryan Center at Duke University. It was performed there with the Broadway cast from February 21-March 7, 1992.

It was thrilling for me, but bittersweet. The events of the last year had consumed me with not only trying to launch a musical, but also trying to save an airline and thousands of jobs, including my own. The musical at that point, could not be my main focus. I hoped it would go well.

It did not go well. The reviews of the show were scathing. And by this time there were outspoken critics of Columbus in the press, demonizing him as something other than an explorer. Subsequently, our show stopped there. I'm glad I kept my day job.

Chapter 78

The entire year of 1988 was like a blur. The Presidential primaries started early in the year. Vice President George H. W. Bush was the heir apparent to the dynasty of President Ronald Reagan, the populist movie star turned politician, who was completing his second term in the White House. The Vice President was challenged in the primaries by Senator Bob Dole of Kansas, and television evangelist, Pat Robertson.

The Vice President loved campaigning. And he was good at it. He enjoyed meeting people and seemed to connect with everyone he met on a personal level. Probably because he had the uncanny ability to remember what seemed like thousands of names. Either that or he could read name tags using his peripheral vision. Whichever, this came in very handy at fund raising events.

The decision was made by the White House Press Corp to have a group of reporters follow the Vice President everywhere on the campaign. And I mean everywhere. Every state in the union. Our crew and the ragtag group of reporters on the campaign became known as the Bush Patrol. We flew reporters such as Britt Hume, Chris Wallace, Ann Compton, Bill Plant and Susan Spencer. We gave them a home away from home on our plane and treated them like family, catering to their every need. That's why they preferred Pan Am. I was fortunate to fly most of these flights, along with my good friend and former Gator Quarterback, Tom Batten.

Another close friend, Dusty Rhodes, was not able to fly the charters the last part of the campaign because he was recovering from a serious automobile accident. Dusty, a former Navy pilot and graduate of the Naval Academy, had moved to Jacksonville a few years previously. He was one of those likable, affable guys who never met a stranger. He was an exceptional pilot and had a keen, quirky sense of humor, which made him the perfect flying partner. He had returned to the University of Miami for his law degree during the strikes at National Airlines and was also a practicing attorney. Dusty's wife, Nancy, happened to be the Duval County Chairman of the Bush campaign. Naturally, Dusty and Nancy became friends of the Bush family. And also, favorite friends of the Shelfer family.

A typical week for the Bush patrol during the campaign of 1988 would start early on a Monday morning at Andrews Air Force Base near Washington DC. Operationally, that meant that the cockpit crew had to leave Miami Sunday afternoon to pick up the B-727 aircraft, usually somewhere in the Northeast, and ferry it to be in position at Andrews. Then for each of the next several days we would make several quick stops in cities across the country, then reach our layover city around three or four in the afternoon. It was fun flying, streaking into strange and different airports. It was also very demanding flying with no room for error. You had to get it right the first time, every time. And we did.

Occasionally, at the layover city, our crew would be invited to the evening event. The Bushes were very inclusive and loved mixing groups together. This gesture was welcomed by us, especially if there happened to be free food and drink or entertainment involved. And then for me personally, every once in a while, the Vice President would include me in a tennis match. It was always an honor to be asked to play with the man who would become the leader of the free world. He would usually pick me as his partner. We were both lefties and I was almost as competitive as he was. Sometimes we would win, and sometimes not. It was always vigorous, fast-paced tennis, and always fun.

The Republican national convention of 1988 was held in the Superdome in New Orleans. Vice President Bush was never really threatened by Senator Dole and Reverend Robertson and had long before wrapped up the nomination. The mystery of the moment was who would the Vice President pick to be his running mate? In a surprise move, on the second day of the convention, he picked 42-year-old Senator Dan Quayle from Indiana to be his running mate. He then gave a compelling acceptance speech at the convention where he advocated for a "kinder, gentler" nation. He also vowed to not raise taxes with the catch phrase, "read my lips, no new taxes." This would be a statement that would come back to haunt him.

The Democrat ticket for the primary election consisted of Governor Michael Dukakis of Massachusetts, and his running mate, Senator Lloyd Benson of Texas. After Labor Day, the race was on. The press charters resumed at a torrid pace, crisscrossing America, sometimes five and six days a week, ending up in Houston on election night, November 8, 1988.

It was thrilling to be in the election headquarters ballroom and witness the announcement that Vice President Bush was now President-elect Bush, having won a landslide victory of 40 states and over 53% of the popular vote. The President-elect gave a humble speech of gratitude, expressing thanks and giving credit to everyone responsible for the victory. He pledged to unify the country and reach across the aisle to work for the betterment of all Americans. Lastly, he especially thanked President Reagan for his friendship and leadership. The President-elect caught my eye in the crowd, as often happened when I was able to attend his events, and acknowledged with a nod and a smile. I was honored to be in the room as history was being made.

The period of time between election night and the inauguration of a new president is an exciting time. President-elect Bush was busy forming his new administration with the selection of his new cabinet and thousands of other appointments across the wide spectrum of government agencies. Not an easy task.

President Reagan was keeping a lower public profile, but behind the scenes he was mellowing into the sunset, looking forward to heading back to his ranch in California. I had not flown on a trip with him lately because I was busy with the Bush Patrol. So, I was a little surprised to receive an invitation to a reception with President Reagan at the White House in early December, 1988. He had invited the entire Pan Am team that had participated in the White House Press Corps program. There were almost 40 of us there from the Pan Am's charter and flight operations. Billy Dale, the head of the White House Travel Office, had organized the event which culminated with a ceremony in the Oval Office.

President Reagan was a very affable guy in person, and a great storyteller. He loved to spin humerus yarns that would have been funny and interesting, even if he had not been the one telling the story. He visited around with all of us, but he especially enjoyed chatting once again with our female flight attendants, inasmuch as the First Lady wasn't in the room. The

President addressed us all with sincere remarks of gratitude to Pan Am for eight years of loyal service to his press corps. Then myself, along with Tom Batten, were honored to represent the group in a special presentation to the President. Included in my words were: "Mr. President, for over half a century Pan Am's Clipper Ships have blazed the trails of aviation around the world. On behalf of the 46,000 employees of Pan American World Airways, we are pleased to present you with your very own 'Clipper Gipper'." It was the biggest model airplane I had ever seen, a Pan Am 747 with "Clipper Gipper" written in script on the fuselage.

Another surprise invitation in December 1988 was from President-elect Bush and Mrs. Bush. They invited the entire fight crew from the Bush Patrol, with our spouses or significant others, to attend a special thank you brunch at their residence at the Naval Observatory. It was a unique gathering. Along with our crew attending were a couple of cabinet members, a couple of astronauts, a Supreme Court Justice and a couple of Ambassadors. Baxter and I were seated with former US Ambassador to the United Nations, Jeanne Kirkpatrick. This no-nonsense lady was passionate about her anti-Communist beliefs and her politics. A few years before she had switched from the Democratic to the Republican Party. It was obvious she had great respect for the President and the President-elect. Baxter tried to get the ambassador to talk about her husband and her three kids, but she was very guarded about her personal life. She was an interesting table mate, nonetheless.

After all the guests had completed the main course, the room suddenly became suspiciously quiet. The front doors opened and surprisingly, men and women in uniform begin filing into the area. The group, about a dozen and a half of them, formed a semicircle around the front of our dining area and began singing. Heavenly voices were exalted by the perfect acoustics of the large room of the observatory. Ambassador Kirkpatrick whispered to me, "it's the Sea Chanters. It's George's favorite group." For the next half-hour we were treated to a special, personal Christmas concert by the official U.S. Navy Chorus, the Sea Chanters. Among the Christmas carols, in deference to the President-elect, they inserted a spirited rendition of "Anchors Away." The finale was "Silent Night." It was magical.

After the dessert plates were cleared and the other guests had said their goodbyes, President-elect Bush pointed me to a room upstairs in the living quarters where I could change into my tennis clothes. He had conveniently scheduled a game for us after the brunch. The weather was a little chilly, but otherwise nice, and soon we were down on the tennis court for another competitive match.

While we were playing tennis, Baxter was visiting with Mrs. Bush. This special lady, affectionately called the Silver Fox by her family, had a unique personality that personified the no-nonsense New England woman that she was. She ran, to use a maritime expression, a tight ship. Baxter had noted that all the pictures in the downstairs area of the old mansion were of leaders, politicians, and dignitaries. Baxter asked Mrs. Bush, where were the pictures of her family? Mrs. Bush escorted her upstairs and showed her dozens and dozens of pictures of the Bush kids and grandkids displayed on the walls and in the bedrooms. Baxter was amused by some of the earlier pictures of Jeb, and deeply touched by the pictures of Robin, their infant daughter who died suddenly in 1953 from leukemia.

After tennis, the President-elect and I were sitting in rocking chairs on the front porch chatting and enjoying a beverage. Mrs. Bush walked by and whispered to me. "Ben, you married well," she said. I smiled as she walked away because every day, I appreciated the wisdom of her words. Still, to have the matrimonial blessings of the Silver Fox was special.

After the holidays and before inauguration day in January, 1989, there appeared to be a lull of activity in Washington. Behind the scenes, however, the President-elect and his team were busy forming the new administration and planning the January 20th celebration. And there was one more trip being planned before the inauguration.

Around the middle of the second week in January, I received an urgent call from our charter division asking about the possibility of flying a 727 on a press charter into the little Marathon airport at Islamorada, in the Florida Keys. Just one week before the biggest event of his lifetime, President-elect Bush wanted to go bone-fishing.

The Marathon airport was small, with only about a 5000 foot long and a 100-foot-wide asphalt runway, with a narrow taxiway and a tiny ramp. I had flown over it many times, but had never paid much attention to it. Performance data indicated that landing there would be no problem. Takeoff weight would have to be limited, depending on the outside temperature. Still, even though no one could recall a 727 flying into Marathon before, I could see no reason not to do it. It was just another interesting airport for the Bush patrol.

Friday morning, January 13, 1989, one week before inauguration day, we picked up the White House Press at Andrews AFB. A couple hours later and after an airborne interchange with Air Force 2, we were on final approach to Marathon. Below us was water everywhere. Linked together by US 1 was a narrow string of connecting islands stretching ahead of us to the southwest towards Key West, some 90 miles away. Even though the runway ahead of us appeared ridiculously short, I had to remind myself it was only a couple hundred feet shorter than runway 33 at Washington National airport, and that was part of our everyday operation. Paralleling a runway was a skinny taxiway, and paralleling the taxiway directly next to the airport boundary was highway US 1. We landed without a problem and roared to a stop well short of the end of the runway, using Max reverse thrust and medium breaking. No problem. We navigated the small taxiway and taxied onto the postage-stamp sized ramp to be in position for the arrival.

Air Force 2, a DC-9 on that flight for the short runway, screeched in ten minutes later and pulled onto the ramp. The President-elect was all smiles and in good spirits as he bounced down the stairs and into the Florida sunshine. He greeted the dignitaries in the welcoming party and then waved me over for a chat. We talked about fishing. He knew I shared his love for the sport. He told me in one hour he hoped to be on the bone-fishing flats. We talked about Jeb, and about tennis. He then told me something that was overheard by some reporters and turned out to be the news item of the day. He told me their dog, Millie, was pregnant, and they were looking forward to puppies in the spring. National news from a hungry press on a slow news day.

The departure for the flight back to Andrews Air Force Base on Sunday afternoon proved to be exciting. Not so much for me, but, strangely enough, for Baxter and a couple of the kids. Scott and Spencer who were in high school at Palmer Trinity Episcopal School in Miami, were on a weekend retreat to Key West. Baxter, who worked at the school, was a chaperone for the event, and later told me what happened. They just happened to be driving back from Key West and were caught in traffic in Islamorada caused by the President-elect's motorcade. They knew I would be flying out of Marathon airport on Sunday afternoon, but did not know what time.

My kids never thought much about my job as a pilot. They would see me put on a uniform and leave for work, and then return later, but they never saw me do my job. Their favorite job I ever had, I'm sure, was that week when I was the ice cream man during a strike of National Airlines. Until that Sunday afternoon in Marathon. They just happen to be stalled in traffic on US 1 directly adjacent to the airport boundary when we thundered down the runway for takeoff. We were, of course, at the max takeoff weight for the short runway and were using absolute maximum thrust from those three Pratt & Whitney engines, with 15,000 pounds of thrust each and probably generating an outside noise level of over 140 decibels. Baxter said the entire island was shaking as we roared into the air. She said the kids were in awe at the sight of the 727 with the Pam Am logo streaking into the heavens, knowing that their dad was flying the plane. But for me, it was just another of the tens of thousands of takeoffs, validating the miracle of flight that for me never became old. And after that flight, even my kids might agree, it was much better than me selling ice cream.

Chapter 79

Growing up in Sneads, Florida, a presidential inauguration was something you only saw on the evening news, or maybe on the newsreel at the theater on Saturday afternoon. I had never known anyone who had attended an inauguration. Events like that were far removed from anything I could imagine growing up on the farm. Yet, there it was in the mailbox. Baxter and I had received an invitation to attend the inauguration of George H.W. Bush as the 41st president of the United States on January 20, 1989. And I actually knew the man. I knew his family. He was a friend. Full disclosure, I may have been one of George Bushes' 10,000 closest friends. Nonetheless, I was honored to accept the inauguration invitation.

Scott and Spencer, who were 17 and 14 years old respectively at the time, accompanied Baxter and me on the trip to Washington. We were met there by Dusty and Nancy Rhodes, even though Dusty was still hobbling from his automobile accident.

Hotel rooms in Washington DC during a presidential inauguration are always at a premium. Even more difficult than trying to find a place to stay in Tallahassee on a Florida State University homecoming weekend. Fortunately, Dusty and I had a friendly relationship with the staff at the State Plaza Hotel, one of the regular layover hotels for our White House press charters. They agreed to reserve us a couple of rooms and even gave us a decent rate. The hotel was conveniently located near the White House within easy walking distance of all the inaugural events. Easy for us, not so much for Dusty.

January 19, 1989, we checked in early at the State Plaza. Afterwards, I walked over to the inauguration headquarters which was in another hotel near the White House. There were countless inauguration events planned for the celebration, all of which required a specific ticket for admission. Jeb had arranged for our tickets and his office had advised me to pick up the tickets to our selected events at the VIP desk at the headquarters hotel. There were a few people in the VIP line and the man next to me looked so friendly and familiar. I thought he was a politician or someone I'd met along the way while flying the press charters during the campaign. We exchanged smiles.

"Hi," I said to the man. "I'm Ben Shelfer."

"Hi, I'm Ben Crenshaw," he said. He chuckled as he extended his hand for a robust Texas handshake.

No wonder the guy looked familiar. He was the famous professional golfer who had won the Masters a few years back. (Little did I know he would go on to win it again in 1995) I knew he was a friend of our new president, so we chatted about the president's love for golf and tennis. Nice guy, Ben Crenshaw.

This was the bicentennial presidential inauguration. It had been 200 years since our first president, George Washington was inaugurated in 1789. Much ado was made about the 200 years from George to George, Washington to Bush.

The opening ceremonies to the inauguration were held at the Lincoln Memorial. It was an impressive backdrop for the event. The renowned statue of Abraham Lincoln seated in the chair faced the vast reflecting pool which stretched from the steps of the memorial to the east, towards the Washington monument. We arrived early enough to secure good seats not too far from the front on the right side of the reflecting pool. When we went through security to get to the site, each of us were given a small commemorative flashlight. We thought that to be a strange souvenir at the time.

The entire Bush family, kids, grandkids and all, arrived at their seats on the terrace at the foot of the steps of the memorial. Vice President-elect Dan and Marilyn Quayle were seated there also. To kick off the program, there was a flyby of 21 Navy F-14's to commemorate the new president's Naval service. They looked pretty sharp for Navy pilots. There were speeches and entertainment. Willard Scott, the famed weatherman on the NBC Today Show, emceed the evening. The entertainment had a definite country music theme, starting with the Gatlin Brothers. Sandy Patty also performed, along with the Beach boys. Their music is timeless. I remembered years ago the Beach boys were on board my airplane where I had an interesting chat with Brian Wilson. The last entertainer to perform was Lee Greenwood, who of course sang his trademark, "God Bless the USA." The song touched me deeply, even after I'd heard Lee Greenwood sing it so many times in the past year across the country on the campaign trail.

The sun set behind the Lincoln Memorial and darkness followed, bringing a chill to the air. Fortunately, the temperature was not beastly cold, only in the low 40s, as the President-elect strode to the podium. He gave a heartfelt address of unity and vowed to be president of all the people for a kinder, gentler nation. He ended his talk promoting his theme of volunteerism, communities helping communities and people helping people. He called the program a "thousand points of light." It soon became evident why we had been given a flashlight. President-elect Bush lit a torch on the podium and, along with Mrs. Bush and the Quayles, turned on his flashlight and raised it into the air and asked us all to do the same. It was a phenomenal site as the band began playing patriotic music. It was 40,000 points of light covering the grounds across the reflecting pool. And then the fireworks began. It was the most breathtaking fireworks demonstration I'd ever seen. A fitting end to the beginning of an unforgettable couple of days.

We attended the reception for the new First Lady, Barbara Bush, at the John F. Kennedy Center for the Performing Arts. It was an impressive venue. I remembered it was almost exactly a year ago a picture of Mrs. Bush and I chatting at a campaign stop ended up in the magazine, "US News and World Report." And here she was, the rising First Lady, in all her splendor.

Mrs. Bush was presented by a tearful, heartfelt introduction by Marilyn Quayle, the wife of Dan Quayle, the new vice president. The Silver Fox, attired in a dress of her trademark color, royal blue, was on her game with her forthright remarks and unpretentious humor. Her quick wit lampooned her hair, makeup, and the designer dress she was wearing. Vintage Silver Fox.

The main event, the inauguration ceremony, took place at noon on January 20, 1989. It was quite a hike for us to get there, especially dragging Dusty, who was trying to graduate from crutches to cane in the rehab process from his accident. That meant he was recovering well enough that we could tease him about being a gimp. And we did. Relentlessly.

Over 300 voices of the Mormon Tabernacle Choir were warming up the crowd as we reached our "VIP" seats. I'm sure that every member of Congress and every government worker inside the Beltway along with all of George Bush's 10,000 closest friends were seated in front of us. But that was okay. We could easily see the podium on the steps of the capital. Jeb and Columba Bush and their kids, along with the entire Bush family were there. Barbara Bush and Marilyn Quayle were introduced, followed by President and Mrs. Reagan, then President-elect Dan Quayle and lastly, the man of the hour, Vice President George Bush.

Rev. Billy Graham gave the invocation. I recalled the day I welcomed Rev. Graham and his wife, Ruth, on board my airplane leaving St. Croix on a flight to Miami. I was touched by what a nice, generally interesting man he was. Today, however, he had his game face on. He touched all the bases before finally ending his prayer. Amen.

The Harlan Boys Choir from Harlan Kentucky sang "This is My Country." Vice President Dan Quayle was then sworn in by the first woman to serve on the Supreme Court, Associate Justice Sandra Day O'Connor. There was another song. A baritone Staff Sergeant from the US Army Band, sang "God bless America."

The Chief Justice of the US Supreme Court, William Rehnquist, came forward to administer the presidential oath of office. The Vice President placed his hand on the same Bible used just to swear in our first president, George Washington. At that moment, my tennis friend, the tall lefty who played the backhand side of the court and had the famous falling leaf service return, was sworn in as the 41st president of the United States. Very surreal.

President Bush gave an inspiring speech continuing the theme of peace, prosperity, and independence. He vowed to be the president of all the people. If only that were possible.

The Reverend Billy Graham returned to give the benediction. Fortunately, it was short and sweet because everything had been said at the invocation. Amen and hallelujah. The ceremonies ended when the Army Staff Sergeant returned and sang the national anthem.

Our little party, the Shelfers and the Rhodes, were hobbling back towards the parade route when a Marine helicopter lifted off from behind the capital. It carried President and Mrs. Reagan on a farewell flyby of all the Washington Monuments and the White House, before taking them to Andrews Air Force Base. There they would board the jet, usually called Air Force One, and fly to the Reagan Ranch near Santa Barbara, California. Mission accomplished. A job well done.

On an operational side note, I knew that Colonel Bob Ruddick, the presidential pilot for the entire Reagan administration was flying President Reagan home. It was also Bob's last flight because he was retiring from the Air Force. Another job well done. Colonel Danny Barr was the new presidential pilot for President Bush.

"I Love a Parade," or so the old song goes. But the truth is most people that had ever been in a marching band, including myself, hated parades. That's because it was like carrying your instrument for miles on a forced march for only about 60 seconds of showtime as you pass the reviewing stand. Yet, some parades are memorable. I was honored to march as Drum Major of the Marching Chiefs at the inaugural parade of Governor Ferris Bryant of Florida. Later that same month John F. Kennedy was inaugurated as president. I would have gladly marched in that one without complaining, but the Chiefs were not invited.

Our little group, the Shelfers and the Rhodes, limped along the bleachers erected along Pennsylvania Avenue until we finally found our "VIP" parade seats. They were located on the south side of the Avenue, but almost a block before the reviewing stand at the White House. Dusty was grumbling about the seats we had been assigned when we noticed we were in the same section as Reverend Jesse Jackson and country music star, Lee Greenwood. And then we thought perhaps our seats weren't so bad after all.

It was surprising, yet thrilling, to see President and Mrs. Bush get out of the presidential limo and walk the parade route in front of us, waving cheerfully to the crowd. I thought about my friends in the Secret Service protective detail and how they must've been frenzied trying to protect this vulnerable scene. It all went well, and so did the parade. For the next three hours we were entertained by over 200 units representing every state and territory and all the service academies. There seemed to be extra entries from Texas, Indiana, and the U.S. Navy. It was impressive. And I must admit, I really did love that parade.

And then there was the inaugural ball. Actually, at this inauguration, there were eleven inaugural balls. They were divided into different demographics. And somehow Florida had an inaugural ball of its own. And so did the young people. We thought Scott and Spencer might have more fun at a party without us, so they attended the Young People's Ball at the Washington Armory.

Dusty and Nancy and Baxter and I, of course, went to the Florida Ball. Baxter looked stunning in her sheer white blouse accented by a black collar and a pleated, floor-length, silk skirt. Baxter was always a head turner, but especially so on that night in Washington.

Nancy, being the Republican chairman of Duval County, and Dusty, being Dusty, knew many of the people at the ball. They arranged for us to sit with the Jacksonville delegation. Their good friend, Bob Martinez, the governor of Florida, stopped by and visited with us. We said hello to Jeb and Columba Bush, who were at the party for a while. Jeb was in good spirits after working so long and hard on his father's election campaign.

We danced and dined for a couple of hours, waiting for the main event. President and Mrs. Bush arrived at the party with great fanfare. The Silver Fox look dazzling in her Navy sapphire velvet and royal blue satin gown. She was wearing her trademark necklace of three strands of white pearls, which matched her hair perfectly. The president made a few light remarks of gratitude to all of us. He joked that he had been able to spend a couple of hours at his new residence, and found the accommodations quite satisfactory. He then whisked the First Lady onto the dance floor and whirled her around for a couple minutes, and then they were gone. Off to repeat the process at the next presidential ball.

It was the perfect ending to an unforgettable experience. It was an honor for Baxter and me to be there with Scott and Spencer to witness a sliver of our history. And it was especially nice sharing this with our dear friends, Dusty and Nancy Rhodes.

Chapter 80

February 17, 1989, was a typical winter's day in St. Louis, Missouri. The sun was trying to break through the clouds and the temperature was in the 20s as Air Force One touched down at Lambert field and taxied to the secure ramp away from the passenger terminal for the 9:55 AM arrival. Danny Barr was the new presidential pilot, and I knew he would not be late for this one. He would set the parking brake at the exact time of arrival and within 30 seconds the cabin door would open. And that's exactly the way it happened. Precision. Dependable.

Myself, along with my entire Pan Am group were waiting as the new president bounced down the steps from Air Force One. He was met by the usual contingent of notoriety, including John Ashcroft, the governor of Missouri, a congressman or two, and others. After all the greetings had been said, President Bush looked towards the ramp where I was standing. He knew I would be there because I had left a note to be placed on his desk in Air Force One. I had done that, at his invitation, since his early days as Vice President, and it continued when he was President. I think he just wanted to know when I was on the trip, in case he needed me for a tennis game. Regardless, I knew leaving him a personal note was a special privilege, and I never took it for granted.

"Hey, Ben," the President shouted my way, waving me over. "Get over here."

Normally, I would never leave my position on the ramp in that situation and approach the President. He would usually come over to where we were standing to chat. Fortunately, I was known to the Secret Service detail, and friends with some of them. And I was wearing an "A" pin, given to us by the Secret Service permitting access to the area. I walked to where he was standing.

"Hey Ben, how are ya? How's Baxter and the kids?" The President asked, extending a firm handshake.

"All is well, Sir, everyone is well. And we all sure enjoyed your little party last month," I said.

"Yes, I did too," the President said, with a wry smile and a twinkle in his eye. "I wanted to ask you, Ben. Have you played with Jebbie lately? How's he hitting 'em?"

"Jeb's hitting good. I played with him a couple days ago and he's playing tough."

"Do you think Jebbie and Marvin could take Chris Evert and Pam Shriver?"

That question took me totally by surprise. In an instant, I had a lot to process. Jeb was playing really well, 6'3" tall and in his 30s. I had played with Marvin a few times at the White House and I knew he was taller, younger, and probably a better tennis player than Jeb. On the other hand, Chris Evert was Chris Evert, the Ice Maiden, one of the best female players in the history of the game. She was still ranked in the top 10 in the world. Pam Shriver, 6 feet tall, was a top player and one of the best doubles players ever. Normally, a professional woman tennis player will beat an amateur man player any day of the week. Somehow, I thought this particular matchup would be different.

"Wow. That would be a tough one, Sir," I said. "But I think they could do it."

"You think so, huh? Chrissie's been busting my chops about how the boys would be lucky to win a game off of them. I'm gonna crank up the rhetoric with those girls and we'll see what happens. Gotta run… See you, Ben." And he jumped into his limo, the beast, and the motorcade departed.

Tuesday, May 16, 1989, Baxter and I, along with Jeb Bush, boarded the early morning Pan Am flight out of Miami nonstop to Washington, DC.

Several weeks before, the President had informed me first dog Millie had delivered a fine litter of pups. He then told me Chris Evert and Pam Shriver had taken the bait and the tennis match was on with Jeb and Marvin, to be played at the White House. With tongue-in-cheek, the President had also given me the task of making sure Jeb was ready to play. That was not difficult for me. Jeb was already a really good player, having been a walk-on for the tennis team at the University of Texas. It was just a matter of him hitting enough balls to be in good physical shape. We were already playing often in a game at Royal Palm tennis club in Miami with other really good players such as Stenstrom, Wickstrom, and Colson. We increased the frequency of those games to several times a week. Mission accomplished.

And then came the surprise. Jeb had told me his father had invited Baxter and me to accompany him to Washington to stay at the White House for the tennis match and all the associated festivities. We were honored and grateful to accept this once-in-a-lifetime opportunity.

When we landed at Washington National Airport, Baxter and I followed Jeb to where a government car was waiting. We were chauffeured directly through the West gate to the south portico of the White House. During the short ride, Jeb talked to his dad via the secure car phone. We were all invited for lunch with the President at noon at the Oval Office. Wow.

At the south entrance of the White House the chief usher was waiting. He already knew us by name and escorted us to the elevator that took us to our room on the third floor of the residence. We were issued a picture ID on a lanyard they gave us exclusive access to the White House, including rare access to the residence area. Jeb was also staying on the third floor. We later learned that Pam Shriver and her mother would be there too, and that Chris Evert and her husband Andy Mill would be sleeping in the Lincoln bedroom on the second floor of the residence. That was the room with the ghosts.

We had a few minutes to freshen up in our room, then we walked with Jeb to the West Wing. The president's secretary, located just outside the Oval Office, acknowledged to Jeb that he was waiting for us. President Bush arose from his desk and came to greet us as we entered the room. He could not have been more cordial. I could tell he was in a particularly good mood. He showed us around the office explaining the history of each item, picture, and portrait. I noted that his desk seemed to be the same one President Reagan used. He told us it was the legendary Resolute Desk, built from the timbers of the HMS Resolute, an abandoned British ship discovered by an American vessel and returned to the Queen of England as a gesture of goodwill. In 1880, Queen Victoria commissioned the construction of the desk from the retired ship's white oak and mahogany, and presented it to President Rutherford B. Hayes. The President told us even though many presidents had used the desk, including John F. Kennedy, he was going to swap it out for one he liked better when the Oval Office was to be redecorated in a month or so. He said he had to get some blue in the drapes and carpets, because the Silver Fox is partial to blue. It was quite a history lesson, in real time.

The conversation soon turned to lunch. The President suggested we have lunch in his private study, which was directly adjacent to the Oval Office. We followed him the few steps from the Oval Office to the study. He pointed out his private bathroom nearby, and invited us to use it at our convenience.

The President's study was not a large room, but it was bigger than one might think. It was tastefully decorated with beautiful furniture, including a long white sofa. Beautiful paintings with ornate frames adorned the walls. There were several arrangements of fresh flowers placed around. In the center of the room was a small, round mahogany table, which also had a centerpiece of fresh flowers. There were four chairs and four place settings of White House crystal and China. It was lovely. And it was lunch, indeed.

Baxter was her sweet and charming self and looked adorable sitting at the table chatting with the President. She was wearing a smart, Navy blouse, dotted with small red flowers, and an ankle-length blue, Scottish plaid skirt. I was sitting directly across from the President wearing my Wedgewood blue daytime suit with a favorite silk tie of light raspberry. Jeb was wearing a light cream sport coat, but no tie.

The waiters were there immediately to take our drink orders give us a luncheon menu. The President highly recommended the egg-drop soup as an appetizer. I fell for it, and it was actually pretty tasty. Unlike the nonalcoholic beer he had recommended that I try earlier, after one of our tennis matches, which I didn't care for it all.

"Ben," the President said, "have you looked at the weather?"

"Yes, Sir, I'm afraid I have," I said. "I stopped by our dispatch before leaving Miami and our meteorologists are calling for that weather system to move into our area beginning about 2 PM."

"That's what I was afraid of, we may have to execute Plan B. Let me make a phone call," the President said.

Almost as if by magic, and aide placed a small table with a telephone beside the President's chair. Within moments, the President was connected to a certain senator and just as fast he learned that the very private, exclusive tennis court on the fifth floor of the Hart Senate office building on Capitol Hill had just become available for his use. It's nice to be president.

The chicken salad croissant and the ice cream dessert were delicious. After lunch, we all stepped outside the Oval Office to get a firsthand look at the weather. Sure enough, the clouds were moving in, and Plan B was definitely going into effect.

On the way back to our room on the third floor, Jeb took us on a detour to the East Room located on the State Floor of the White House. We noticed public tours were in progress and there was a crowd of people around something in the East Room. There, in a small cordoned off area, was the first family's English Springer spaniel, Millie, proudly showing off her litter of six pups. They were the cutest things. Jeb had a personal interest in the litter, because his mother was emphatic that he would take one with him back to Florida. She had said each of her kids would get a puppy and Jeb would be no exception. I'm not sure Jeb was happy about that, but the Silver Fox had spoken.

After the President's workday had ended, we all met at the back entrance to the White House. It was there Baxter and I met Chris Evert and her husband, Andy Mill. Pam Shriver was there also. Baxter met Marvin Bush for the first time. When it was departure time, the tennis players braved the drizzling rain and jumped into the limo with the president. Directly behind them, of course, was the Secret Service vehicle with all the firepower. Baxter and I were in the next vehicle. I'd been in several motorcades, but this was a first time for Baxter. It was thrilling. With traffic stopped, lights flashing and sirens blaring, we arrived on Capitol Hill in a very few minutes.

At the Hart Senate office building we were whisked to a special elevator normally reserved for senators only that took us to the fifth floor.

Within a few steps we were at the makeshift tennis court. There were several factors immediately apparent that would affect the game of tennis. The court itself was an afterthought. This building was never designed for the construction of a tennis court. The dimensions were tight on both sides and at the ends of the court, which could be problematic on wide or deep shots. The playing surface was merely concrete that had been painted. It reminded me of some of the California courts I'd played on, such as Lincoln Park in Santa Monica, or the early days of Balboa Park in San Diego. That meant the court would play extremely fast. Other factors were the lower ceiling and the dim lighting, neither of which were on par with a normal indoor tennis facility.

Word travels fast in Washington. Folding chairs were placed along the walls in an effort to accommodate the gathering crowd, which was already about 50 people crowding around to watch the pros play the Bushwhacker's. Game on.

This was a difficult situation for Chris and Pam. They were the pros. They were supposed to win. Yet, the Bush boys could actually play, and didn't appear to be intimidated. The balls were hit hard and the points were short and the match was even through the first four games. At that point, all the press were asked to leave the building. Then the girls, with strong groundstrokes and consistent play, quickly took the next four games to win the first set.

Jeb gave me a questioning look during the break between sets. I told him that he and Marvin had to get to the net. There's no way either one of them could trade groundstrokes with Chris Evert, the best ever in the women's game. And Pam Shriver's backhand slice deep in the court was always problematic skidding off the slick court. I told Jeb he had to serve and volley on the serve and chip and charge on the service return. They didn't have to worry a great deal about the girls lobbing because they were both so tall. That, along with lower ceiling made lobbing a difficult option. Basically, my advice was for both of them to be very aggressive.

Aggression it was. And surprisingly, even though the next two sets were extremely close, Chris Evert and Pam Shriver found themselves bushwhacked by Jeb and Marvin. Frankly, I was shocked. I never really thought the boys could pull it off. And it wasn't as if the girls weren't trying their best. There's no one on this earth more competitive than Chris Evert. It was just on that day, under those conditions, it was not to be. Chris was a gracious sport, but there is no doubt she did not like losing. The President had that "told you so" twinkle in his eye after it was over. I would've liked to have been a fly on the wall in the presidential limo on the ride back to the White House.

Dinner that evening was in the President's dining room in the residence of the White House. There were no press photographers present. And the number of guests had increased. President Bush was always abundantly inclusive with invites to his events, and this was no exception. In addition to Chris and Pam and our tennis group, there was Commander David Walker and his crew of astronauts. They had just returned from space on the shuttle Atlantis after deploying the Magellan spacecraft, which would go on to map the surface of Venus. One of my favorite country singers, Moe Bandy and his wife Margaret were there, along with Moe's country band. Also, there were a few other members of Congress in attendance.

After a delicious dinner, the president invited the entire group across the hall to a large oval room. There were chairs for everyone spaced around the room, but the group was standing around talking like an after dinner social mixer. I enjoyed chatting with Pam Shriver and Chris Evert and her husband. Andy Mill was a happy-go-lucky likable soul. Chris was cordial, but I think she was still feeling a little heartburn from the afternoon's tennis match. Did I mention she was competitive? I chatted with the astronauts, including their commander, David Walker. He was a very nice, bread-and-butter type of guy who had attended the Naval Academy. I really enjoyed talking with Moe Bandy. I was proud of myself for showing great restraint in not trying to pitch Moe Bandy one of the many country songs I had written. He just smiled when I told him his song, "Bandy the Rodeo Clown" was one of my favorite songs. A few minutes later, I would realize why he was smiling. Baxter spent the most time talking with Margaret Bandy. They talked about their love stories and their kids. Baxter learned they were staying overnight in the Queen's Room, a couple of doors down from where we were standing.

After some time had passed the White House usher got everyone's attention and indicated we should be seated. The President had some gracious remarks of welcome and gratitude to everyone there. With the familiar twinkle in his eye, he made a few subliminal quips about the tennis match, without mentioning who won, or the score. Chrissy was trying to smile. The President then said he had a real treat for us. He introduced his good friend, Moe Bandy and said Moe had agreed to do a few songs for us. Indeed, it was a treat, and I was thrilled. Moe's first song was my favorite, "Bandy the Rodeo Clown." After a couple more songs he closed with what I knew was the President's favorite, "Americana." What an evening. Life is good at the White House.

At the end of the evening, the President came over to say good night to Baxter and me. He thanked me for getting the big guy ready for the match and for us coming to cheer them on. He then apologized that, because of his schedule, he would not be able to have breakfast with us the next morning. He suggested we have a leisurely private breakfast in the solarium, which was accessed from the third floor, near the room we were staying. We said good night, thanking the President for his incomparable hospitality and the unforgettable experience of staying at the White House.

Baxter and I retired to our bedroom. Baxter noticed that, once again, the bedroom was in perfect array. Even though we had showered before dinner, every washcloth and towel had been replaced, the pillows on the bed had been fluffed and the entire room looked exactly as it did when we first walked in. How do they do that? Baxter wondered.

We turned off the lights and got into bed. I snuggled up to Baxter, put my arms around her and gave her a familiar nuzzle.

"Don't even think about it," she said.

"Why not?" I asked, a little surprised.

"There are people everywhere. Every time a towel is used, it's replaced. If a pillow needs fluffing, it's immediately fluffed. How do they do it?"

"Darlin, that's ridiculous. Besides, they've all gone home now."

"How do you know? And you know this room is probably bugged. There are probably cameras everywhere. I can't do it."

End of story. Shot down in flames. Paradise lost. Baxter later admitted one of her greatest regrets in life was not making love at the White House.

The next morning, Baxter and I walked the few steps from our room to the solarium. It was immediately evident why some call it the hidden gem of the White House. The bright sun of the crisp spring morning warmed the room through the wide panoramic windows. Looking south we had a picturesque view of the Washington Monument and the mall which led to the Lincoln Memorial. Beyond that was the Potomac River which curved its way past Washington National Airport, where we would be in a couple of hours. Airliners were taking off flying directly towards us. They then immediately turned left to follow the Potomac to the northwest to avoid the prohibited airspace around the White House. I had flown up and down that river hundreds and hundreds of times.

Soon after entering the room, we informed an attendant who just happened to be nearby we would be having breakfast there. Two place settings were set and coffee, juice, and pastries miraculously appeared. I ended up having the Western omelet. It was every bit as good as the Western omelet at the Wagons West restaurant in the Suniland shopping center in South Miami. And the service and the view were incomparable.

Before we left the White House, Jeb picked his Florida pup from Millie's litter. He had been issued stern instructions by the Silver Fox to take the puppy in the cabin with him during the flight to Miami. She didn't want the dog to be placed in the cargo bin. I assured Jeb Pan Am would allow him to place his new puppy, which was in a carrier, underneath his seat. Jeb would not hear of it. He didn't want to do anything that might be perceived as special treatment. He swore Baxter and me to secrecy, and the dog went in the cargo bin.

And that's how it went. Baxter and I were back home in Miami after a couple of days adventure that seemed like a fairytale. On the bright side, from my standpoint, there were no domestic staff or hidden cameras around our house. Paradise regained.

The next time I ran into Mrs. Bush, she asked me about the trip to Florida with Millie's puppy. I assured her all was well and Jeb made sure the Florida dog arrived in Florida with no problems at all. Jeb's secret was safe with me and once again he had escaped the wrath of the Silver Fox.

Chapter 81

Sometime around Valentine's Day, 1989, the word filtered down from Pan Am's division in New York that President Bush was planning his first international trip. He would embark on a five-day odyssey to Eastern Asia. Of course, the press plane on the long-range trip would be a B-747. At the time, as Manager of Flying in Miami, I was dual qualified on both the B-727 and the B-747. Having recently qualified on the latter, my time and experience in the big airplane was minimal. Bill Frisbie, Pan Am's chief pilot in San Francisco, commanded all the B-747 White House press charters for Pan Am. Bill's experience on the airplane was immeasurable, and he was generally considered the B-747 guru for Pan Am, if not the entire airline industry. I was delighted that Bill invited me to be part of the crew on this historic trip.

We departed Andrews Air Force Base on Wednesday, February 22, 1989 on the first leg of the Asian trip. Over seven hours later, I landed the 747 during snow flurries and a testy crosswind at Elmendorf Air Force Base in Anchorage Alaska. Air Force One, a B-707, landed behind us. It was the first international trip for Danny Barr as presidential pilot. The President braved the elements to make a few remarks to the gathered crowd, while both aircraft were refueled. And then we were off to Tokyo.

The snow-covered mountain ranges northwest of Anchorage, were absolutely stunning. Beautiful desolation, as far as the eye could see. After another flight of over seven hours, we arrived at Tokyo International Airport, traditionally called Tokyo Haneda Airport.

President Bush's primary reason for the Japan visit was to attend the funeral of Emperor Showa, more commonly known as Hirohito, who had

530

died in early January. Scores of other world leaders were also in Tokyo for the funeral and the president would meet with many of them.

There were a couple of things that surprised me upon our arrival in Tokyo. The welcoming ceremony for the President was magnificent. There were military honor guards and marching bands formed on the ramp where thousands of people were waiting. We secured the airplane and the pilots and flight attendants from the charter hurried to a secure location on the ramp, adjacent to the section reserved for White House Press Corps. Air Force One arrived and Pres. and Mrs. Bush descended the stairs and stepped onto the red carpet. Of course, it was a red carpet. They were met by Japanese officials and the American Ambassador and others from the American Embassy. Bands played. Honor guards honored. Very striking.

The second thing that surprised me upon our arrival in Tokyo was personal to Pan Am. Tokyo had always been a major city for Pan Am, who had established routes around the world from the beginning of aviation. During the last decade, the financial difficulties of the once proud Pan Am conglomerate had continued unabated. The only strategy to combat this million-dollar-a-day loss appeared to me to be self-cannibalism. In an effort to generate cash, in 1981 Pan Am sold its Intercontinental Hotel chain, with hundreds of hotels. The same year it even sold the Pan Am building in Manhattan. Then, in 1985, and another desperate measure, they sold the Pacific routes to United Airlines for $750 million. When we deplaned in Tokyo there were couple of dozen people who greeted the flight crew. They were very emotional, many of them crying, at the sight of that beautiful Pan Am 747 pulling up to the ramp. Those people were former Pan Am employees, many of whom now worked for United Airlines. Pan Am had been their life. They loved this company, but now, to them it was gone forever. It was both heartwarming and heartbreaking to see this. Quietly, my empathy for them was very personal. Would I no longer have a Pan Am in my future? How long did I have? We were still losing $1 million a day.

It was my first trip to Tokyo. There were lots of buildings, lots of lights, and lots of people. 32 million people. That was hard to comprehend for me, who had 17 people in my graduating class. We stayed in the heart of town in the same hotel as the press corps, a five-star hotel. It was extremely nice and out of this world extravagant. The restaurant in the hotel was prohibitively expensive, so I ventured out on the street where there were thousands of choices. I had never been one for exotic foods so I had no interest in eels, raw fish and the majority of the Japanese menu. I usually went for a dish of rice and either beef or chicken, hoping it was beef or chicken.

The following afternoon the President and Mrs. Bush were scheduled to visit the American Embassy, which was not too far from our hotel. The President had business meetings and Mrs. Bush wanted to do some shopping. The embassy had arranged for reputable vendors from the city who had been approved by security to come display their wares. The Pan Am crew was invited to drop by the embassy and check it out.

At the embassy we were escorted to a section of rooms where booths were set up by the representatives of dozens of local retailers. The items included accessories, specialty items, watches and jewelry, all quality items at a discounted price. I wanted to find something nice for Baxter and I was hoping this would be to place, but I wasn't sure where to start. I turned a corner to go into another room and almost bumped into Mrs. Bush. We chatted for a bit and I told her I was looking for a gift for Baxter. I think she could tell the task had me baffled.

"Come look at this, Ben," Mrs. Bush said. "This is something I just picked up for Doro, and I think they would look lovely on Baxter." She had stepped down to the end of the counter and pointed to a necklace of pearls. It was simply elegant and the pearls glistened under the lights.

"Wow, that's perfect. Baxter will love it. Thank you so much," I said.

I flipped my credit card onto the counter knowing I not only had the ideal gift for Baxter, but it was also selected specifically for her by the First Lady of the United States. Priceless.

From Tokyo, the President's Asian trip took us to Beijing, China. It was not only an official state visit, but also a sentimental journey for President Bush. He would be renewing old friendships from the days he spent there as ambassador to China. It was interesting that while the entire population of China was well over a billion people, there were only approximately 7 million in the city of Beijing. It was about one quarter of the size of Tokyo.

Bill Frisby had flown into Beijing before, but of course I had not. Communications and reporting procedures were different and difficult in the beginning. The dialect of Mandarin Chinese, or whatever it was, and my southern drawl, was not an easy mix. Persistence made it work. Along with the fact that they probably had their best English speakers working our flight because we were with the White House contingent.

The weather was cold and clear in Beijing. At least that's the way it was above 20,000 feet. As we began our descent approaching the city, I noticed we are about to enter a tobacco stain colored brown haze. Pollution on steroids. I remembered the last time I had seen a site like that was in 1963 flying over the Los Angeles basin in a T-33 on a cross-country during pilot training. That was also a brown pollution haze trapped over the city by the San Gabriel Mountains to the east. Still, it was nothing like the Chinese pollution I saw below us. As we descended into the murk, I felt like I was about to take my last breath of fresh air for the next couple of days. There were no clouds, but the visibility was less than 2 miles with a brown smog as we touched down in China.

Our entire Pan Am crew watched from the press area on the ramp as Air Force One came to a stop in Beijing. President Bush was met by the usual group of ambassadors and Chinese dignitaries. The cadre of military bands and honor guards were present in much greater numbers than in Tokyo. The Chinese bands and honor guards, however, could not hold a candle compared to the Japanese in terms of appearance, music, and military bearing. As a former drum major of the band that never lost a halftime show, I felt I was qualified to make a judgment. The Chinese went through the ceremonial motions of pomp and circumstance, but they appeared amateurish and sloppy, like high school kids waiting for the bell to ring in a class they did not want to attend. Mediocrity at its best.

It took over a half-hour for our crew bus to transport us to our layover hotel in downtown Beijing, the Great Wall Sheridan. It was an exceptional hotel with the finest amenities. Once again, I was happy I didn't have to pick up that lodging tab.

President Bush asked a favor of me, if time permitted. He wanted me to visit a certain tennis club in Beijing and give his regards to the Pro, who was an old friend of his. He knew he was too busy for that stop to be on his schedule. The club was a short taxi ride from the Great Wall Sheraton. The old Pro could not have been more surprised or gracious at my presence. Through struggling English, he conveyed his longtime affection for President Bush and spoke fondly of the days he played tennis at the club, some 15 years before. It was amazing that the President, then, as now, was friends not only with the leaders of the country, but also a cross-section of average citizens as well. I could certainly attest to that.

Two of the most famous, must see, tourist attractions in Beijing are the Great Wall of China and Tiananmen Square. On the second day, the White House travel office arranged for a special tour of those places for the Pan Am crew. It was a typical cold, partly cloudy, always hazy February day in Beijing.

The bus ride to the section of the Great Wall we visited took what seemed like almost two hours. Our tour guide, who doubled as the bus driver, was very knowledgeable and spoke almost perfect English. Once we cleared the bustling city, the topography immediately changed. It was starkly rural. We were on a narrow two-lane road that traversed a countryside of modest mountains and wide, flat valleys. The land reminded me of some sections of our state of Tennessee. Farmlands were everywhere. Every few miles there would be a large cluster of buildings. Our guide told us these were communes, political and economic production brigades to collectivized living and working practices. He said there were almost 100,000 of these units across China. Communism to the max. The workers we saw appeared sad and bedraggled. I happened to notice that, being a farm boy myself. I also noticed a conspicuous absence of small animals, especially dogs.

Surprisingly, a few times along the way, I saw a satellite dish mounted to the roof of the building. I secretly wondered how the Chinese would keep them down on the farm once they've seen Western civilization and freedom. Time would tell.

As we neared our destination, the guide began giving us a few facts about the Great Wall. There were over 13,000 miles of wall averaging 26 feet high built across the northern borders of Imperial China during a period of over 2000 years beginning in the 7th century BC and ending in the 1600s after 300 years of the Ming dynasty. Millions of Chinese people lived and died constructing the wall, including workers, soldiers, peasants, slaves and convicts. The wall's purpose was to provide protection against the various Eurasian nomadic hordes. It was hard to imagine.

After the long ride from the city, I was happy to see we parked nearby a public restroom. That was, until I actually saw the restroom. And smelled the restroom. There was a large stone building with an open entrance on either end, one for men and one for women. There was a fee that amounted to about $0.10 to enter. For that fare you were allowed admission and given one small square of toilet paper. Inside was an early version of the squat toilet that was essentially an open hole in the floor. The stench was unbearable. Much worse than any outhouse I had used growing up on the farm. Have you ever tried to hold your breath and use the bathroom at the same time? It's totally possible.

Another strange observance was cute little Chinese toddlers running around with a large hole built into the bottom of their pants. And they were wearing no diapers. I could only imagine how that worked. I did start paying close attention to where I was stepping.

Our Pan Am group climbed the steps to the top of the wall. We spent a couple hours walking along the narrow roadway on top of the wall taking in the sites. It was mystifying, bewildering. The wall meandered its way through the rolling hills in either direction as far as the eye could see. It was painful to think about the millions of poor souls who for generation after generation, over thousands of years, did nothing but build this wall. And they built it with their hands, every single stone. The question to me was, why? Did they not think this plan through? Did they not think the marauding hordes would find a way over, around, or through the wall? I couldn't get past the fact that to me, it was unbelievable that the wall was built in the first place. Yet, there it was, one of the seven wonders on the earth.

After visiting the Great Wall, we drove to Tiananmen Square, a large area the size of the city square in the center Beijing. We visited the Great Hall of the People, the National Museum of China and several other temples, statues, and monuments around the square. Historically, it was the site of several people's protests through the years. Little did I know the spot on which I was standing in Tiananmen Square would dominate the world news beginning in a couple of months. The People's Liberation Army would advance on the square and kill and wound thousands of students who would stage a democracy protest. Timing is everything.

Even though it had been a long day of sightseeing, there was more. The Air Force One crew had invited the Pan Am flight crew to dinner at their hotel, the Holiday Inn. I found it both strange and comforting that we were both staying in American hotels.

It was a dark night in Beijing, and there were very few streetlights. During the taxi ride to meet the Air Force One crew for dinner, I saw an amazing sight. It was one of those bizarre, dreamlike scenes that, as they say, you can't un-see. There were no other cars around and our taxi made a turn down a dark road. In the narrow beam of headlights that permeated the darkness in front of us were hundreds of people on bicycles. The taxi driver plowed ahead, giving them no quarter. Miraculously, they parted for us to slither through them. It was like a scene from a submarine deep underwater, furrowing through a school of thousands of fish. Very surreal.

It was nice to spend some time with Danny Barr and the Air Force One pilots. We traded war stories and talked about flying. I told them my hijacking tales. Bill Frisbie raised the question with Danny Barr about going nonstop from Seoul to Andrews Air Force Base in Washington on the last leg of our trip, instead of making a fuel stop in Alaska. I wondered what that was about. Danny told him the 707 didn't have the range to do that, especially with the President on board.

It was a delightful, relaxing evening of camaraderie. Once again, I was probably the most conservative one with my menu choices. I didn't fall for any of the slithery selections. I ordered rice and chicken and washed it down with Coca-Cola. It wasn't bad, and I didn't get sick from either looking at it, smelling it, or eating it. Another successful international meal.

We climbed through 20,000 feet on our flight from Beijing and I breathed my first breath of fresh air in a couple of days. Our destination was Seoul, Korea, a little less than three hours away. Once again, we interchanged with Air Force One to be in position for the President's arrival. Seoul, a city of about 10 million at the time, is nestled in the rugged mountains in the very northern part of South Korea, only about 30 miles from no man's land, the DMZ. Our majestic 747 with the Pan Am logo parked on the ramp awaiting Air Force One made a very picturesque setting.

When we assumed our position on the ramp for the arrival of the President, the precision and perfection of the welcoming delegation was astonishing. Unlike the Beijing contingent, the uniforms and the military bearing of the South Korean marching band and the honor guard were extraordinary. It was a proud moment to be standing a few feet from the President as he was honored by the country of South Korea. He accompanied the commander of the South Korean Armed Forces as they 'trooped the line' to inspect the large brigade of troops. And these troops, perfect from head to toe, were ready for inspection.

If you're on a layover in a strange city and are looking for a good restaurant, stick with the flight attendants. They know. I accompanied the cabin crew to a place in Seoul that was perfect for me. It was called the Nashville Club. Ensconced in the shopping area known as Itaewon, behind heavy ornate wooden doors, was an authentic country-western bar exactly as you might find in Nashville, Tennessee. The jukebox was blasting some Merle Haggard and "Okie from Muskogee" when I entered the room. Perfect. The waitresses in their cowgirl outfits, spoke perfect English. The menu was everything Americana, including steaks and ribs. I had been eating in foreign countries for almost a week, so I cut straight to the chase. I wolfed down a huge cheeseburger with all the fixings, a pile of French fries, and two large cokes. My stomach thought we were home.

After a restful night's sleep, I ran into Bill Frisbie at breakfast the next morning. He had in his hands what appeared to be flight planning paperwork. He had been talking with Pan Am's dispatcher in New York and they both agreed if the forecast winds and temperature panned out, a nonstop flight to Andrews Air Force Base might be possible. Billy Dale, the chief of the White House travel office, was all for it if we could do it.

"This is your leg, Captain. What you think?" Bill asked.

He handed me the paperwork. I could see that we would be at absolute maximum takeoff weight departing Seoul, with full fuel tanks. I could also see we would have to ride the jetstream and maintain a 100 to 200 knot tailwind to be able to arrive at Andrews Air Force Base in Washington in a little over 12 hours. The destination weather was good. Everything had to be perfect.

"Let's do this," I said, grinning. I knew if we had a wind bust and were running low on fuel, we would be over North America for the last several hours of the flight with plenty of places to stop to refuel.

"I'll alert the troops," he said. I knew he would tell Billy Dale who would notify all the networks and news agencies of the change of plans.

The 747 is an airplane that handles much better in the air than on the ground. In the air it flies like a big Piper cub. On the ground you're worried about the wing clearances, the tale clearances, the engine clearances, along with the problems of keeping all the wheels of the undercarriage on the narrow taxi ways. And on this day in Korea, we were extremely heavy. I taxied the mammoth clipper ship into takeoff position, pushed the throttles forward, and asked for Max power. The engines roared and slowly we crept forward, gradually getting faster and faster as the runway ahead was getting shorter and shorter. Finally, we reached rotate speed. With one slow, deliberate pull, I nursed the big bird into the air. Landing gear up, and we were on our way.

A couple of hours flying time out of Seoul, it was agreed that I would take the first rest break. On long international flights we always had relief pilots on board so everyone in the crew could stay rested and fresh. At least that was the idea. I went to our rest area, had a bite to eat, and closed my eyes for a couple of hours. When I returned to the cockpit, the two flight engineers and Frisbie were having a concerned discussion. They were telling him that for some reason there, the fuel figures didn't add up.

On international flights it was our procedure to keep a "how-goes-it" chart. Approximately every hour, usually when crossing an even Meridian going East West, we were required to confirm our position, note our fuel, and give a position report to oceanic radio who in turn passed the information to the company. In this particular case, we were on course and on time but the fuel numbers were slowly but surely deteriorating. It didn't appear to be burning in the engines, but yet it was missing from the fuel tank. What was happening?

It was decided we would continue to monitor the situation. And we did. To no avail. Every single position report we seemed to have about a thousand pounds of fuel disappear for no apparent reason. Was it a simple gauge error? Was fuel leaking from the tank?

We were about three hours from Washington, DC when I climbed back into the left seat. I had checked and rechecked the fuel situation. I knew we could probably make it to Andrews Air Force Base but in doing so we would have used all our reserve fuel and would be deep into our emergency fuel when we landed. I also knew a diversion would create major problems for the White House press, especially Dan Rather and the other television news anchors who had planned to be live on the air for the nightly news at 6:30 PM. I also knew there were several airports, such as Minneapolis and Detroit, along our route where we could access maintenance and refuel.

"What do you think, Captain?" Frisbie asked. I knew he probably already had his mind made up and just wanted to see what I would say. I also knew he had his heart set on making the flight nonstop from Seoul to Andrews. I wasn't sure he was going to like what I was about to tell him.

"Better safe than sorry," I said. "Let's go to Detroit."

And that we did. We called Billy Dale to the cockpit and told him the situation and our decision. He notified Air Force One by satellite radio, and other preparations were made with the networks, etc., contingent upon what we learned from our maintenance in Detroit.

We zoomed into the Detroit airport and I quickly taxied to one of our gates at the Pan Am terminal so our passengers could use the telephones. Within minutes our Pan Am maintenance staff had found the problem of the missing fuel. The fuel line to the number three engine had a pinhole leak and was misting fuel overboard. Miraculously, within about a half-hour they had replaced the fuel line and we had refueled and were on our way.

Better safe than sorry. Always.

President Bush's first international trip was memorable to me. I saw sites and cities I had only imagined before. It made me appreciate my country and my president even more. I learned to appreciate different customs and traditions and food. Well, at least customs and traditions. The food, maybe not so much. I couldn't, for instance, get past the flippant remark about dining in China.

"How was the chow in China?" Someone would ask.

"The chow was tough," I would say. "The cocker spaniel, on the other hand, was very tender."

Chapter 82

It was a magical time when President George HW Bush was in the White House. Every week or two, sometimes more often, the President enjoyed boarding Air Force One for a trip somewhere in the country to celebrate a special event or promote an administration policy. Aside from my job as Manager of Flying for Pan Am in Miami, I was able to fly a majority of the White House press charters accompanying those trips. During this time, President Bush was kind enough to continue inviting me into some of his tennis games, as well as other interesting functions and events, both at the White House and on the road. There are so many memories from the special stretch of time.

An interesting fact about President Bush was he loved letters and notes. Especially those that were handwritten. He loved to send them and he loved to receive them. Maybe that's why he continued to allow me to leave personal notes on his desk on Air Force One through the years. And somehow, he found the time to reciprocate. It was exciting to go to the mailbox and occasionally get a note from the President of the United States.

It was fascinating to be in a position to observe the President performing his job at his most public events, and his most private moments. It's in those private moments you see the true measure of the man.

One such time was on a trip to Albuquerque, New Mexico. It was in the dead of winter. We landed with the White House press in a vicious cross wind from the northwest and parked on the ramp about 10 minutes before the arrival of Air Force One. Blizzard conditions had arrived in the area sooner than expected. The pelting of snow and sleet was blowing sideways and the chill factor was approaching 30 below zero. Not surprisingly, none of my crew wanted to brave the elements to be present for this arrival. I would not be deterred. I donned every piece of clothing I had, including some earmuffs I borrowed from one of the girls. When Air Force One came to a stop, aside from the press, I was the only one at the arrival area except a handful of local politicians, Congressmen, and the governor. And one more profoundly different individual. Standing off to the side, away from the others, was an elderly Indian chief, dressed in full ceremonial regalia, including a long, feathered headdress. He draped a thin woolen blanket around his shoulders and his headdress to keep the feathers from flying with the wind. The old chief was a stoic site, a lone soul shivering against the icy wind. The President, wearing a heavy topcoat but no hat, bounced down the stairs and quickly greeted the arrival delegation. Just as quickly, he almost ran to the presidential limo waiting nearby. The old chief stood there motionless as the President jumped in the limo and it started to pull away. Abruptly, the limo stopped. The President walked over and met the old chief with a warm embrace. They talked for the longest time, impervious to the stinging sleet peppering their faces. When the president finally departed, the look on the old Indian's face said it all about the measure of this man, President George HW Bush.

It was my good fortune to play tennis at the White House with the President, and others, many times. My teenage daughter, Spencer, had also played there. She was ranked among the top junior players in the country and the President had followed her tennis progress through the years.

On this one occasion, I was invited to the White House for a tennis match, except, this time I was not invited to play. The president already had a foursome: John McEnroe, Andre Agassi, and Tim Mayotte. Unfortunately, it rained out the tennis, so we enjoyed a lunch reception in the residence area on the second floor of the White House. Interestingly, everyone you meet at the White House is really nice. That includes John McEnroe. I enjoyed chatting with John and his parents who were there with him. I talked with Tim Mayotte about watching him win the Lipton tournament in Florida a few years earlier. Andre Agassi was there with his girlfriend. Andre still looked like a kid with his long hair and wild tennis outfits. We talked about my having watched him when he was 12 years old practice with Poncho Gonzales at Caesars Palace in Las Vegas. He had nice things to say about Poncho. When Mrs. Bush joined our conversation, Andre reached into his tennis bag and handed her what he said was a gift for the President. The Silver Fox held up a pair of long, bright blue tennis shorts that would obviously extend below the knees. "Oh no you don't," she said. "He's not going to be caught wearing these things in public, certainly not around the White House." She had that mischievous smile on her face, the one where you couldn't tell if she was joking or not. I knew.

The President's summer home on the ocean on Walker Point in Kennebunkport, Maine also had a tennis court. Several times I was invited to play there.

When the president made a trip to Kennebunkport, we would accompany him, with the press, to Pease Air Force Base, in Portsmouth, New Hampshire. From there president would take the helicopter, Marine One, to his home on Walker's Point in Kennebunkport. Our mission would be complete, except we would have to ferry the airplane to the city where Pan Am wanted to put it back into service. On this one day, when I had a tennis invitation from the President, we had to drop the airplane at Boston Logan Airport. From there, I hurriedly changed into my tennis warm-up suit and made the hour and forty-minute dash in a rental car back to Kennebunkport. I turned onto the road at Walker's point and sped past the prohibited area, do not enter signs. I immediately encountered a roadblock, with a deputy sheriff's car blocking the driveway. When I came to a stop, a female deputy sheriff stepped out of the car. With both thumbs in her pistol belt and a go-to-hell look on her face, she sauntered towards me.

"Where do you think you're going?" She asked.

"I'm Ben Shelfer. I have an invitation to play tennis with the President."

"Sure, you do," she sneered. She was about to tell me to turn around and go back down the road towards town when I interrupted her...

"Ask the Secret Service."

At this point she was more than annoyed with me. She asked for my driver's license then backed up a couple steps and spoke into a walkie-talkie.

"We got one down here at the checkpoint. Some guy from Florida says he's gonna play tennis with Timberwolf," I heard her say in a condescending tone.

"What's his name?" The voice from the speaker asked.

"Scheffler, something like that. S-h-e-l-f-e-r."

"Tell Captain Shelfer to drive up to the house. The President will be waiting for him." I thought I recognized the voice of one of my Secret Service friends.

"Sorry sir," the deputy said, meekly. "Just follow this road."

At the house the President introduced me to the few guests that were there, who were just finishing a late lunch. Sam Skinner, the Secretary of Transportation was likable and interesting. We had a nice chat about the overall status of the airline industry, and he heard the short versions of my hijacking stories. The President's daughter, Doro, was there. Her son, Sam, was buzzing around. He was a small tyke, who appeared to be a year or two younger than Jeb's youngest son, Jebby.

We had a very fun, competitive tennis match. Afterwards, I had to hustle back to Boston to be on the last flight that night to Miami. I accepted the President's offer to take a quick shower before I hit the road. When he realized, from our conversation, I had no dry underwear to put on for the trip home after tennis, he insisted I take a pair of his. And, sheepishly I did. I returned to Miami to proudly show Baxter I was wearing underwear from the George Bush personal collection. Priceless.

Dusty Rhodes was often the other pilot with me on the White House charters for President Bush. Remember, Dusty was a friend of the Bush family because of his wife Nancy's political leadership in Jacksonville. He is one of those guys who never met a stranger. It was nice to fly with someone with such a pleasant manner and keen sense of humor. More importantly, he fulfilled the first requirement for those trips, he was a great pilot.

On a dark and stormy night flying into Andrews Air Force Base, Dusty had an opportunity to demonstrate those flying skills. We were positioning the aircraft into Andrews to be ready for a press charter early the next morning. We were racing to reach the airport ahead of a vicious squall line ahead of an approaching cold front. Dusty was flying the airplane. We could see flashes of lightning to the west. Coming down final approach landing to the north, the tower cleared us to land and told us the wind was 320 at 35 knots, a vicious crosswind at the very limits of the airplane. I glanced over at Dusty. If the situation hadn't been so serious, it would've been hilarious watching him wrestle the beast.

"Dusty, are you ready for this? I asked.

"Ready as I'll ever be," he muttered.

The touchdown wasn't bad at all considering the conditions. But then it required full left aileron into the wind and almost full right rudder to keep the aircraft on the runway while stopping. At that point the tower transmitted the wind was gusting up to 55 miles an hour, far exceeding our crosswind limits. Thankfully, due to Dusty's exceptional flying skills that night, we were safely on the ground and in position for the next day's flight.

Like myself, Dusty enjoyed attending the Presidential functions when we were invited and able to do so. He had a good-natured mischievous side to him that would sometimes lead the two of us to places we probably should not have been. Special Assistant to the President, Spence Geissinger, often went along with these schemes. It helped that the secret service knew us.

Like the time we were at the christening of the aircraft carrier, Abraham Lincoln, in Newport News, Virginia. We were invited to tour the new aircraft carrier and attend the President's dedication speech to the troops. Before the ceremony, Spence directed Dusty and me to spend some time in a private holding area of the ship. We opened the door and walked in and there was President Bush alone in the room. I think he was more shocked than we were. Nonetheless, he assured us we were not in trouble and we had a nice chat.

There was one surprising phenomenon that happened to us aboard the aircraft carrier. Dusty and I were wearing our Pan Am captain uniforms that included flight wings and our white hat with the so-called scrambled eggs on the bill. They looked much like the uniform of a Naval Captain or Admiral. Close enough for the thousands of sailors aboard the ship, all of whom saluted us on site if we were near. I finally merely returned their salute, out of respect for their attention to duty and their service. I was reminded of the old military saying: "If it moves, salute it. If it doesn't move, pick it up. If you can't pick it up, paint it."

Then there was the time we were in Monterey Mexico. Between the airport and the city there was a soccer stadium where 10,000 troops were in formation to honor President Bush's visit. A Mexican general accompanied the President to inspect the troops. When they finished the troop-the-line inspection, they approached the podium where the president of Mexico awaited. In the gathering, two rows behind the president of Mexico, were Dusty and me, standing out in our white Pan Am hats. President Bush immediately saw us and began laughing, shaking his head. He was probably wondering how did those guys pull that off?

On another occasion we found ourselves at a private reception for major fundraisers in Orlando, Florida. And yet another time we were in Philadelphia. The President had been to an event downtown and had returned to the airport. Awaiting his motorcade's arrival, the Philadelphia Police Department had formed a single line of approximately three dozen police officers who would have the honor of receiving an award presented by the President. The police Commissioner was assisting the President present the commendations, as they made their way down the long line of recipients. Dusty and I couldn't resist. When the president reached the end of the line, there we were standing at attention, trying not to laugh. The President laughed first, commenting to the Commissioner, "I know these two guys…no awards for them."

We weren't exactly like wedding crashers for these events. Well, maybe we were. Fortunately, the President had a good sense of humor and appeared to be amused by our antics. Fun times.

Chapter 83

It was January, 1991. Eastern Airlines, one of the major air carriers in the US, after years of financial struggles, had abruptly ceased operations. They followed a long line of other air carriers over the cliff of bankruptcy, such as Braniff, Southern, Texas International, Air Florida, New York Air, Frontier, Midwest and others.

Following the Airline Deregulation Act, passed under the Carter administration, the airlines entered an era of destabilization which I have called the regurgitation of the airline industry. Because they could fly between any two cities in the US without government approval, opportunist entrepreneurs would either take over or form an airline. They would lease airplanes on the cheap, contract out their maintenance, hire nonunion flight crews for peanuts, and call themselves an airline. They would charge discounted rates on popular routes, taking the profits from established carriers. These entrepreneurs would pay themselves handsomely. Of course, this type of operation could not sustain profitability. After a couple of years, when all the favorable startup agreements ended and the bills had to be paid, they would simply drain the money from the company for themselves and declare bankruptcy. They would then retire or retreat to someplace like Aspen and await the next opportunity. Meanwhile everyone else, including the creditors, the lessors, and the employees were out of luck.

One thing about being an employee for an airline is, in the overall scheme of things, you're just along for the ride. The decision as to whether your company grows or shrinks, is bought or sold, or goes out of business altogether, is made by others. You have absolutely no control over your ultimate fate.

Recently, I had resigned my position as Manager of Flying for Pan Am in Miami. Tom Batten, the Chief Pilot in Miami, was being pressured by flight operations in New York to replace me. It was my opinion, some of the Blue Balls, the original Pan Am pilots, resented someone like me, an Orange Ball, an original National Airlines pilot, using my position as Manager of Flying to do such things as fly a 747 around Europe, or fly the coveted White House press Corps. So, I made it easy for them. I resigned, and returned to being a 727 Check Pilot in Miami. Besides, I was worried about other things, like survival of the airline.

On a late January morning, 1991, my telephone rang.

"Hello."

"Hello Ben, this is Bob Ferrel calling."

"Hi Bob, how goes it?" I asked.

"I guess you heard about Eastern Airlines."

"I'm afraid so. I'm surprised they lasted this long."

"Yeah, me too. That's why I called. I'm afraid we're next," Bob said.

"Yep, we've lost $1 million a day as long as I can remember. We're totally screwed."

"I wanted to run something by you. A few of our National guys were at an ALPA meeting in New York last week venting our frustrations. We said there must be something we can do, even though we don't know what it is. We can't simply crash and burn without trying to do something to save the ship."

"Good luck with that," I said.

My antennas were on alert. Bob Ferrel was a good friend of mine. He was a Notre Dame graduate who went into the Air Force and flew 100 missions over North Vietnam in an F-105. Remarkable. The pilots called that airplane the "thud," because most of them ended up on Thud Hill, near Hanoi. Bob was one of those guys that was good at everything he attempted.

547

He was a scratch golfer and was also an exceptional carpenter and builder. He could remodel anything. Baxter and I visited Bob and his wife, Marion, at their summer home in North Carolina on several occasions. Through the years, Bob had held several positions with our ALPA, our pilot's union. I, had not. Most of my time with the airlines had been spent as a supervisor, on the side of management. I appreciated the work the union had done for pilot's salary and safety through the years, but I didn't always approve of the tactics. I believed in the right to work. I didn't see my employer as an adversary. I came to the airlines looking for a job, and I thought if I didn't like what they were paying me I could always quit. So, yes, I became skeptical of the out of the blue call from Bob Ferrel.

"What we've decided," Bob was saying, "is to form a select committee of Orange Balls to go to Washington to see if there's anything that can be done. We would like you to join us. We're going to meet in Washington next week and…"

"Hang on, Bob," I interrupted. "Let me save you some time. I'm not going to Washington to picket Congress or the White House or be a part of any other demonstrations…"

"I know, I know," Bob said. "I know exactly where you stand. We're with you on that. This is not a union activity. This is beyond that. The only thing ALPA is going to do is provide an office for us at the ALPA headquarters in Washington, and reimburse the airline for our salary and pay our expenses."

"The union and Pan Am flight ops approved that?"

"I think it's more like they tolerated it," Bob said, "just to get us out of their hair."

"I'm gonna have to think about this one, Bob. That sounds like a boondoggle that won't amount to anything."

"Who knows? The meeting is at ALPA headquarters in Washington next Monday at 2 PM. We need your help and would love to have you join us."

"I'll think it over, Bob," I said.

Later that day there was a phone call from Dusty Rhodes, inquiring if I had talked to Bob Ferrel. I told him I was skeptical and thought it would be just another union boondoggle that was a waste of time. Dusty didn't exactly disagree with that, but repeated the familiar refrain, what have we got to lose? Pan Am's daily losses were nearing the $2 million a day mark. The creditors were restless. The vultures were circling, waiting to pick the carcass clean.

"Let's cut to the chase, Dusty," I told him. "In the end, whatever happens to Pan Am, any change in its international routes will have to be approved by the White House. And I can tell you right now I'm not going to badger, or in any way lobby the President, or ask him to do anything."

In my mind I knew the end was near. The once greatest airline in the world, Pan Am, the pioneer of aviation around the globe, would soon be gone. And so would my job. I had never been without a job since college and I dreaded the thought of being 50 years old and unemployed.

"Okay, Dusty," I said. "I'll see you on the morning flight to Washington on Monday."

Monday after lunch the committee convened at ALPA headquarters in Washington. Bob Ferrel was chairman. And there was Sam Butler, Frank Pigone, Dennis DiDonna, Marv Osborne, Dusty Rhodes, and myself. Marv Osborne was the lone Blue Ball member on the committee.

We gathered around a narrow table in a cramped office as Bob Ferrel reiterated the simple purpose of the committee: to see if there was any way to save jobs. We brainstormed for a couple of hours discussing possibilities.

Pan Am was not a candidate for a buyout or a major merger, because with the airline the purchasing carrier would also be forced to assume Pan Am's enormous debt. Dealbreaker. The usual scenario after the bankruptcy and ceased operations of an airline, would be for the surviving airlines to swoop in and cherry pick the routes and the airplanes of the defunct carrier. Very seldom would they take employees also. It appeared this was exactly what was about to happen to Pan Am, and therefore to us as employees.

Pan Am was already down to bare bones. It had already sold or squandered the Pan Am building, the hotel chain, the Pacific Routes to United, and countless other assets. The only resources remaining were its routes and airplanes. And in our mind, it's people. It occurred to us we should be trying for something along the lines of the 1986 sale of Pan Am's Pacific routes to United Airlines. In that case United purchased the routes, the planes, and the pilots to fly them. That means jobs.

The committee brainstormed the idea of taking the root structure of Pan Am, and meshing some of those routes with the individual routes of other major carriers, with the purpose of making a stronger carrier. We would prepare a sales presentation of these routes for the management of each airline that would listen. Our only stipulation would be the purchaser would have to take the planes and the pilots also.

There were a couple of immediate problems with our plan. First of all, we knew no airline CEO, CFO, or any level of airline management would schedule a meeting with us. We were just a handful of ragtag pilots on a self-appointed committee. We had absolutely no authority to do anything, much less represent ourselves as someone who could sell part of the airline that employed us. If we tried to schedule a meeting with any airline, their management would immediately call Tom Plaskett, the CEO of Pan Am, asking who are these guys? It would be necessary to meet with Tom Plaskett and get his approval for us to exist.

The second problem was, by what means could we dictate to a buyer the requirement to take employees along with the deal, rather than just the planes and the routes? That would have to be a political mandate tied to the approval of the routes. That meant Secretary of Transportation and White House approval.

Later that afternoon we met in the office of ALPA President, Randy Babbitt. He had been a pilot with Eastern Airlines, following in the footsteps of his father, Slim Babbitt, who was an Eastern pilot and union organizer. Oddly enough, I had met Randy at a couple of tennis outings in Miami a few years back. I was surprised he made it to this prominent position. Randy humored us along as we stated our intentions. We asked him if he could be of help with us with the Secretary of Transportation. He said he did not know Sam Skinner, and had never been to his office. I thought that was a strange answer for the president of a national pilot's union. So much for his help. Nonetheless, we were grateful ALPA was providing office space and paying our expenses.

Bob Ferrel called the CEO of Pan Am, Tom Plaskett, and asked for a meeting with our committee. He was, of course, extremely reticent. Finally, because he had a previously planned trip to Washington, he agreed to meet with us later that week in the Clipper Club at Washington National Airport.

After Bob reported that we had a meeting scheduled with Plaskett, I made a call to Sam Skinner's office. I told his secretary I had met Secretary Skinner at Kennebunkport. I briefly informed her about our committee and our effort to save Pan Am jobs. I asked for a meeting with the Secretary at his earliest convenience. After placing me on hold for a few minutes, she came back on the line and reported the Secretary would be happy to meet with us the next day at 1 PM.

Bob Ferrel and Dusty Rhodes accompanied me to the Secretary of Transportation's office the next day. Sam Skinner was the same affable, friendly guy he was at Kennebunkport. He and I chatted about our visits there. Bob proceeded to briefly tell the Secretary the purpose of our committee was to effect the sale of Pan Am assets that would include the employees. Our sole objective was to save Pan Am jobs. Skinner looked at us with a wry smile and a gleam in his eye.

"Does Plaskett know what you guys are up to?" The Secretary asked.

"Yes, sir. We have a meeting with him on Thursday," Bob said.

"Good. You tell Plaskett I said there'll be no deal without employees. Tell him don't even think about." We knew he was referring to a deal in which Pan Am recently sold routes to London Heathrow Airport to United Airlines for $290 million, which did not include employees.

Dusty and I exchanged a mutual glance. I'm sure we were both thinking the same thing. Our job is done here.

Bob was a scratch golfer and Dusty had a son-in-law playing the PGA Tour, so when the Secretary began talking about golf, they were on a familiar subject. When it was time for his next appointment, Secretary Skinner wished us luck. We thanked him for his time and his support and agreed to keep him informed of our efforts.

True to his word, Tom Plaskett kept his meeting with us on Thursday afternoon at the Clipper Club at DCA. He recognized me from our meeting at the Pan Am Building in New York a couple of years prior. We had chatted about my hijackings and he was aware I had played tennis with the President and piloted some of the White House press Corps charters. He had previously made a name for himself among the airlines when he was with American Airlines by establishing the first frequent flyer miles program in the industry. It had transformed airline marketing programs.

Our entire committee met with Plaskett behind closed doors. No one else was present. Bob Ferrel got straight to the point, as he was known to do, and addressed the elephant in the room.

"It is our opinion," Bob said to Plaskett, "that it's over for Pan Am. And, in the not-too-distant future, the company will file for bankruptcy and cease to operate."

Tom Plaskett sat there stonefaced. The moment he didn't vehemently deny what Bob had said, I had a sick feeling in my gut. He knew. And now, he knew we knew. I guess I had privately been in denial, hoping there was a white knight out there somewhere that would gallop in and save our once proud company. I now feared the worst.

Bob continued to lay out our plan. We would attempt to entice other airlines to buy routes and planes from Pan Am as long as they took employees with the deal. Bob gave him Secretary Skinner's message, no employees, no deal. I think he was shocked we'd already talked to the Secretary of Transportation. At least we had cleared the air and the stage was set.

The obvious fact was that we, a group of pilots, had no authority to sell or do anything concerning the company. Our only hope was to begin a dialogue with a healthy airline that would create interest in a bargain deal that would benefit them. At that point, the buyer would come to the table with Plaskett and the board of Pan Am to agree on the price and complete the sale. After that, they would await approval from the White House.

Tom Plaskett, to his credit, sensed our desperation along with our sincere intentions, and did not attempt to summarily dismiss us. He agreed if we kept him informed every step along the way, he would not shoot us down. Fair enough. We had an impossible task, but at least we could try.

Before we boarded our flight to Miami that evening, I informed Bob and Dusty I would continue on the committee and chase this rabbit with them with one stipulation: I had to be available to continue to fly the White House Press Charters. They agreed. Game on.

Upon landing in Miami, I hurried to our home in Pine Acres to tell Baxter about the meeting with Plaskett. She met me at the door with a much-needed warm embrace.

"Please don't talk about anything you hear about this committee, but for what it's worth, Plaskett agrees with us that the end is near for Pam Am," I said.

"That's pretty obvious," she said. "What will we do?"

"Don't worry, because our committee is going to do something that has never been done before to save jobs, even though we don't know what it is, or how were going to do it."

Baxter gave me that look. She wasn't buying into my feeble attempt at humor. I noticed she was already in a melancholy mood as usually happens approaching the end of January, nearing January 29th.

"How old will Skippy be next month?" She asked.

"Skip will be 25 on the 28th."

"Wow, 25. Unbelievable."

There was no way to soothe her solace. The only thing I could do was hold her tight, and I did for the longest time.

"Someday, Darlin'… Someday," I said.

The months of February and March of 1991 were critical for the committee. We spent most of the time in Washington doing research on all the routes of Pan Am around the world, including those that were dormant and not being used. We also included other assets such as planes, terminals, gates, and timeslots at different airports. Then we did the same for most of the major airlines, and compared the assets of Pan Am with each of them individually. It was our hope to show them possibilities to expand their company and gain market share in ways that had not occurred to them before. And at a bargain price.

We were working at the ALPA office one morning when a stranger walked through the door. He had his black hair slicked back and was wearing a bright, expensive suit. He chatted it up with us for a couple of minutes and then just as quickly departed. Bob Ferrel seemed to know who he was. He said he was Al Checchi, CEO of Northwest Airlines. Interesting.

We spent countless man-hours preparing and constructing a state-of-the-art slide presentation, with narrative, for United, American, USAir, Northwest, and Delta Airlines. The difficult part of the equation was getting an appointment with the CEOs or upper management of these airlines to make a presentation. It took weeks, sometimes months, to make this happen. Obviously, before taking a meeting with a group of pilots from another airline, someone from each company would probably call Tom Plaskett and have the "who are these guys" conversation. They would also probably check with the chairman of their pilot's union to verify our existence. Fortunately, we had those bases covered.

Our brothers in ALPA who were with other carriers had mixed feelings about our quest to work for their airline. Most airline pilots are very defensive about their seniority number. Despite the fact we would be bringing routes and planes to their company, they did not want some Pan Am pilot to be placed ahead of them on the seniority list. From the Pan Am pilot's perspective, we were more concerned about a job than a seniority number.

During these months when I traveled to Washington to work on the committee, I always brought my tennis racket and my uniform and flight kit. Occasionally, I would be invited to play tennis at the White House. Usually, it would be with the President. And sometimes I would play there with Marvin Bush when he needed someone to complete a foursome for his game.

My uniform was always with me because I wanted to be available for a press charter, should it be scheduled on short notice. I continued to leave my personal notes for the President so he always knew when I was on the trip.

And occasionally, there would be an invitation to play tennis. Usually, the invite would be forwarded to me by the staff. On a couple of occasions, I received the invitation differently.

"Clipper 1000, Air Force One," I heard Presidential Pilot Colonel Danny Barr call over the radio on a discrete frequency. When flying a press charter, we were always in touch with Air Force One when they were airborne.

"Air Force One, Clipper 1000," I transmitted.

"Clipper 1000, there's a gentleman here who would like to know if you're available for an athletic endeavor late this afternoon."

"Air Force One, tell the gentleman, that's affirmative."

"The gentleman says you will depart from his place at 5 PM."

"Roger that," I transmitted.

I knew the President was standing in the cockpit of Air Force One listening to the conversation.

Sometimes we would play at a tennis court at the layover hotel. Other times we would take the "beast," the presidential limo, motorcade and all, to a tennis club somewhere in the area. Those were special moments, just the President and myself in our tennis clothes sitting in the backseat of the most heavily armored and protected automobile in the world, chatting about family, friends, sports, etc. The President had a surprising depth of knowledge and interest in the airline industry. It dawned on me that he was the President and probably knew most of the airline CEOs personally. He was aware of Pan Am's struggles and asked me pointed questions. I always answered truthfully, to the best of my comprehension. He was aware of our committee and why I was spending time in Washington. I think he found it amusing. During all our private chats, I never lobbied the President for anything or asked that anything be done. Moreover, I considered all conversations with the President to be confidential, and therefore kept them private.

Dusty Rhodes, being a graduate of the Naval Academy, a former Navy pilot, a practicing attorney in Florida, and an airline pilot, had an extensive range of friends and acquaintances. Dusty's relationships opened many doors for us in Washington and specifically on Capitol Hill, as we made the rounds looking for any thread of hope to save our jobs. It was Dusty's Naval connections that secured for us a meeting with the new Senator from Arizona, John McCain, even though Dusty had a scheduling conflict and was unable to attend the meeting. McCain was a hero of the Vietnam War and spent many years as a POW. To make a personal connection with the Senator, we mentioned Dusty's name and also the name of one of our friends and Pan Am pilot, Dave Dollarhide. Dave was a close friend of McCain's when they served together on the USS Forrestal, before McCain was shot down. The Senator listened to us with a very sympathetic ear. He assured us he would support any initiative that would ensure the survival of Pan Am and the jobs of its employees.

Members of our committee attended numerous other meetings with various senators and congressmen. None were more interesting than our visit with California Congressman Bob Dornan. He was a former Air Force fighter pilot who was called "B-1 Bob" because of his staunch decade-long support of the development of the B-1 bomber. Dornan, a former actor, was an affable, yet fiery no-nonsense guy who was more conservative than Ronald Reagan. We spent over two hours with him, mostly because he insisted on taking us on a walking tour of the capital. He was also testing the waters about a presidential bid. I think he just enjoyed spending time with other pilots. It was with him as it was with other members of Congress; lots of sympathy, but no ideas for substantial help.

There were hopes among some Pan Am employees, and even some of our committee, that Congress would mount a rescue for Pan Am, along the lines of the Chrysler automaker bailout of 1979. Once again, across the political spectrum, there was sympathy but no action. Totally understandable. How could we expect the American taxpayers to reward decades of corporate mismanagement with billions of bailout money?

Tailored presentations were prepared and given separately by others on the committee to American Airlines CEO, Robert Crandall and United Airlines CEO, Stephen Wolf, along with their CFOs. We called the CFO's the bean counters. They were very interested in the assets of Pan Am, but it was obvious to us they were willing to wait until Pan Am went belly up, and then swoop in to take advantage of whatever was available. We knew that would be planes and routes, but no employees. At the end of each of these presentations, they asked a few questions, but we were done in less than an hour.

My first participation in a presentation was at Northwest Airlines headquarters in Minneapolis, Minnesota. Bob Ferrel, Dusty Rhodes, and I flew out to meet Northwest CEO Al Cheechi and his bean counter. We had met Cheechi earlier when he came into our room at ALPA Headquarters. My second impression of the man was no better than the first. His jet-black hair was still slicked back and it looked like he had on the same shiny suit. I would never buy a used car from this guy. He began pontificating to us as we filed into his office.

"Come in guys… Have a seat," Cheechi said. "Let's get something straight from the very beginning. If we do some sort of a deal here, you guys will never, ever, in your lifetime make the money a Northwest pilot makes…"

"Hold on, Mr. Cheechi," Bob Ferrel said. "We're just here to see if Pan Am has assets that would benefit your company. We not here to integrate a seniority list or to negotiate a pilot's contract."

"That's good. There's no way you can change this. You guys have to look at it this way… The Northwest pilots are just part of the lucky sperm club."

Obviously, Al Cheechi had to know any negotiations of price or wages would have to be done directly with the management of Pan Am, not three rogue pilots. Maybe it was just a shot across the bow to us to set the tone for the meeting. Perhaps it was a defense mechanism to masquerade the financial struggles of Northwest Airlines. Regardless, we knew early on they had little interest in any part of Pan Am because they had no purchasing power or the necessary credit. The result was what, unfortunately, was becoming our usual dog and pony show; a slide presentation and a few polite questions and we were done in less than an hour. I can't say I was unhappy about this particular outcome.

The next month after the trip to Minneapolis, Bob Ferrel and I, and a couple others on the committee, made a pitch to US Airways. We met the CEO, Seth Schofield, and one of his bean counters in a company office in Arlington, Virginia. What a difference a CEO makes. Seth Schofield was an absolute gentleman and could not have been nicer to us, aside from the fact he was in constant labor disputes with the pilots of his company. Our presentation went smoothly and was received well, but everyone in the room knew they were not in a financial position to help us. Once again, 45 minutes and a few questions, and we were done. We wished each other well and departed.

It was difficult for those of us on the committee to remain optimistic. Despite our best efforts to develop creative presentations matching assets and airlines, we had only met rejections. Even so, we pressed onward, leaving no stone unturned. We even started considering foreign airlines. ANA, All Nippon Airways had shown an interest. I was skeptical of a deal with foreign carriers because I knew Department of Transportation approval would be difficult.

There was one last major domestic carrier who was reluctant to meet with us, Delta Air Lines. After sometime, their management agreed to a meeting, when the Delta pilot's ALPA leadership, whom we had met in Washington, persisted we were legitimate.

Whit Hawkins, President and COO of Delta Air Lines, along with several of his bean counters attended the Delta presentation. I was not in attendance, but I was very familiar with the presentation package. Our committee believed the perfect addition to Delta's domestic system would be the addition of B-747s flying to deep South America, and A-300s to the Caribbean, all out of the Miami hub. On paper, for us it was the perfect fit. Not for me personally, because I was currently qualified on the 727. But at least many jobs would be saved. And that's what was pitched in the 45-minute presentation. Then it was time for questions. But, rather than a few polite questions and out the door, the questions continued. For couple of hours of the questions continued. For some reason, Delta didn't seem to be interested in deep South America or the Caribbean. Instead, the majority of their questions centered around Pan Am's Atlantic routes using A-310 aircraft, and the New York, Washington, Boston shuttle operation using B-727s. Who knew? When the last question was answered, Whit Hawkins complemented our committee on its presentation and preparedness. He then said the words we had longed to hear. He said to tell Tom Plaskett that they would be in touch. Miles to go, but the first step had been taken.

If Delta bought the New York shuttle, that could be a game changer for me, because I was currently a 727 pilot. I was cautiously optimistic. When I returned home to Miami that week, I told Baxter not to get her hopes up, but it appeared Delta Air Lines was interested. Neither of us could really believe it. Of all the airlines, knowing what I knew then at age 50, if I had the opportunity to switch flying jobs to any airline, it would be Delta. We had several friends working there and we knew it was a great company. Around the dinner table that night, the kids picked up on the conversation. I told them to keep this a secret, but if Delta did a deal with Pan Am and I became a Delta pilot, to celebrate, I would take the entire family on a cruise. The kids were all ears. They had never been on a cruise. At least it was good to dream.

Ron Allen, CEO of Delta Air Lines, after hearing from COO Whit Hawkins about our committee's presentation, immediately scheduled a meeting with Tom Plaskett at the Pan Am building in New York. After only a few days of negotiations, on July 12, 1991, Ron Allen and Tom Plaskett reached a tentative agreement. With the approval of the bankruptcy court, Delta would purchase Pan Am's European routes, including the Frankfurt hub, along with the New York shuttle, for a price of $260 million. The deal would include B-727 and A-310 aircraft, along with over 6000 employees. Although, our committee was ecstatic, we knew we had to temper our optimism because Plaskett would be looking for a better deal than Delta's $260 million offering. Sure enough, with blood in the water the sharks began circling from everywhere. Crandall from American, Wolfe from United, Checci from Northwest and even Carl Icahn from TWA, came to make offerings. They even combined their efforts to make joint offers. It was their opinion they could roll Ron Allen and Delta out of the deal with enough money. The problem with most of their bids was they did not include employees. From standing on the sidelines, I knew the bids of Crandall, Wolf, and Icahn had little chance of prevailing. Not just because of their questionable financing, but also, I knew Sam Skinner, and the President, would not approve another deal that did not include employees.

In the end, Tom Plaskett got his desired bidding war. In early August, American, United, and Northwest, in an effort to close the deal and end the bidding, made a combined offer of $1.3 billion. Ron Allen was not deterred. It only aroused his competitive spirit. On August 12, 1991, with time running out for Pan Am, Ron Allen made an offer of $1.39 billion, which was quickly accepted by Plaskett and the bankruptcy court. The deal was final.

Dusty and I were in touch with the Secretary of Transportation's office to let them know this was the deal best for our employees. We received no indications that it would not find quick government approval.

It just so happened I was about to fly a White House press charter. The President was taking a vacation trip to Kennebunkport. I was sure the President was aware the recently signed Pan Am-Delta deal was exactly what we had been working for to save the most jobs. I was confident it would meet with quick approval. Little did I know at the time, this would be my last trip as a Pan Am pilot. It would have been so bittersweet.

The work of the Pan Am Select Committee was done. A small group of pilots, starting with nothing but desperation, began a chain of events that saved almost 7000 jobs, including those of 770 pilots, and permanently change the landscape of international air travel. We neither sought nor received recognition for our efforts. It didn't matter. We knew.

Chapter 84

Delta Air Lines made immediate steps to begin the New York shuttle operation without interruption. Every hour, from early morning to late at night, a B-727 would shuttle from New York LaGuardia airport, Boston Logan Airport, and Washington National Airport to each of the other cities. It was convenient for the passenger because no reservation was required. They would just walk up to the counter, buy a ticket, and get on board. Simple and easy. And it was a cash cow moneymaker for the company. Delta was ready to begin cashing in.

A few days after Delta finalized the Pan Am purchase the phone rang in our Pine Acres home. It was Delta Air Lines offering me an opportunity to interview for a job as a Delta pilot. I accepted immediately. I felt like I'd been given a new lease on life.

The next week, the last week of August, 1991, Delta arranged for dozens of Pan Am B-727 pilots to be flown from Miami to JFK for an interview and a fasting physical exam.

My interview was conducted by a genteel southern gentleman who had been a Chief Pilot for Delta in Dallas. He could not have been nicer, and the interview went very well. But then, my resume was more than adequate; Check Pilot in the U.S. Air Force, and at National Airlines and Pan Am, Manager of Flying for Pan Am in Miami... I even served on the panel that hired Pan Am pilots. After telling him the highlights of my two hijackings, we were done and I could continue on to take the physical.

It was now three in the afternoon and I was famished. Because we had to fast for the physical exam, I had eaten nothing all day. It wasn't until

5 PM until the exam began. They drew some blood, and then I had to drink some concoction. I'm not sure what it was, but I do know it made me sick as a dog. I immediately threw it up and gagged with the dry heaves. Finally, I saw the doctor, who looked me over inside and out. I was so relieved to pass the physical, but it was so late I had already missed my flight back to Miami. The food at the restaurant in the airport hotel at JFK had never tasted so good.

The next week, the first week of September, I flew to Delta Air Lines headquarters in Atlanta for company indoctrination and B-727 training and evaluation. I learned how Delta began in 1925 as a crop-dusting outfit in Monroe, Louisiana, and was now striving to be one of the world's major airlines. The employee culture at Delta was different from other airlines. All the employees seem to support one another, and therefore the company. There were no unions on the property except for the pilot's union and the dispatcher's union. It was a refreshingly friendly working environment. It was no wonder the Delta employees loved their company.

On September 10th, I was scheduled for a simulator session to practice the normal and emergency procedures using the Delta checklist. We were in one of the older simulators Delta utilized which was in a training facility off-campus in the Greenbrier shopping center. Except for a few instrumentation differences, the Delta and Pan Am 727 airplanes were basically the same. The operating checklists, however, had many differences. We had one day to learn these procedures, and then take a check ride.

A senior Delta Check Captain and a true southern gentleman, would administer the Delta check ride to myself and the first officer. Bob Stimpson, a sharp young Delta guy who was a graduate of the Air Force Academy, was along to check the third pilot, the flight engineer.

I had been a check pilot on the 727 for almost 15 years, so I knew the drill. The check ride progressed through all the normal procedures and then we accomplished the windshear on takeoff. No problem. I pretty much knew what was coming next, engine failure on takeoff. We called the maneuver the V1 cut, because a critical engine would be failed at the worst possible moment on takeoff when it was too late to abort. Sure enough, as we began to rotate for liftoff, the number three engine failed. No problem. I applied Max power to the other two engines and lifted the airplane into the air. As we raised the landing gear passing about 200 feet, we heard the warning: WINDSHEAR! WINDSHEAR! We were in severe turbulence and the aircraft began sinking towards the ground. Meanwhile, I'm thinking, what's going on with this? It's not legal to combine severe malfunctions on a check ride. I guess this guy doesn't want me to be a Delta pilot. Nonetheless, utilizing all my abilities and experience, I continued to fly the airplane with a failed engine through the windshear. We survived.

There was a lot of muttering going on between the two check airmen back at the malfunction panel. I heard Bob Stimpson say, "wow, I think this guy's gonna make it." The Check Captain apologized to me profusely. He had left the windshear malfunction in the control panel from the previous maneuver, which then combined with the engine failure. I felt relieved he admitted to an honest mistake. And I was happy I had survived.

When the check rides were completed successfully, the old gentleman, my new friend, gave us a ride back to Delta headquarters and walked us directly to the personnel office. On the spot, we were issued a Delta ID card. The saga was over. I stood there as a Delta pilot. The date was September 11, 1991. It was exactly 10 years prior to 9/11, a date that would live in infamy.

Delta wasted no time putting me to work. I was immediately assigned to Delta's New York base to fly the shuttle out of LaGuardia. My first trip departed in three days, so I hurried to pick up my flight manuals and my new Delta uniform and catch the last flight home to Miami.

Baxter and I were not happy that I was now based in New York. And we both knew we would never move our home to that area, so that would make me a commuter. I would be responsible for flying to New York on my own and getting a place to stay while I was there. Not the best situation. But I was now a Captain with a dynamic, profitable airline. That indeed was the best situation.

While I was home for my one day off, the phone was ringing off the hook. It was the kids calling. "Ship ahoy! When do we sail?" They would ask. I thought it was nice that I was now a Delta employee, but they were really excited that we were going on a cruise. I promised them it would happen, for sure, as soon as my new schedule would allow.

My first Delta flight was a dawn breaker, the first flight out in the morning. That meant I had to fly to New York the night before and stay at an airport hotel at LaGuardia. By the time I reached the hotel, it was almost 10 PM. I unpacked my new Delta uniform and placed it on a hanger to be ready for my early morning trip. It was then I realized I had forgotten my uniform black tie. Yikes. Another embarrassing uniform over-sight. It was definitely panic time, because there was no way I was going to show up for my first trip as a Delta pilot without a black tie. I ran downstairs and jumped on the hotel shuttle bus for the ride back to the LaGuardia terminal. Unfortunately, it was so late all the specialty shops or other stores that might have a black tie were closed. More panic. When I jumped on the shuttle bus to go back to the hotel, I asked the driver if he knew any stores in the area that might be open. He said there was only one convenience store anywhere near the hotel in Jamaica Queens that would be open at such a late hour, but he would not recommend me going there. He was trying to tell me something, insinuating the neighborhood might not be safe. I bribed him to take me there anyway. When we arrived at the store, I understood what the shuttle driver was talking about. Nonetheless, I was desperate. And I was relieved when the driver volunteered to accompany me inside the store. We walked straight to the dude behind the cash register at the counter.

"Would you have any black ties in the store?" I asked.

"Ties?" The clerk asked.

"Yes, ties," I said. I was standing there before him in the clothes I usually wore deadheading on a flight, my gray suit with a red silk tie Baxter had given me. I lifted the tie to show it to the clerk. "I need a black tie."

"Naw, man. We don't have no ties." He looked at me like I was from Mars.

I was standing there with a feeling of desperation. I was looking down at the red silk tie I was holding my hand and had a brainstorm.

"How about shoe polish? Do you carry shoe polish?" I asked.

"Yeah, we got shoe polish."

"Do you have black liquid shoe polish?"

"It's over there…" The clerk looked at the silk tie I had in my hand and started grinning, showing a golden grill. "Naw, man. You can't do that. Don't do that to that tie."

But I did. I bought the black liquid shoe polish. Back at the hotel I painted the front side of the red silk tie with the black liquid. I dried it quickly with the hairdryer provided by the hotel. It took three applications, but it worked. The next morning, I began my career as a Delta pilot wearing my new Delta uniform with a customized silk tie. Who knew?

Eventually everyone knew. After my first four days of flying the shuttle, I had become friends with the Delta Chief Pilot at LaGuardia. As I was leaving to commute back to Miami, I confided in my new boss what I had done, and showed him the backside of my tie which was bright red. He laughed and laughed. Then he told me I should've mentioned it to him because he had a drawer full of black ties in his office in case a pilot needed one. The laugh was on me.

It was with a great sense of pride that I wore my new Delta uniform. As I strode through the concourses of busy airports, I was secretly looking for just one man. I had a message for him. That man was Alfred Checchi, the CEO of Northwest Airlines. I wanted to say to him, "Mr. Checchi, I'm sure you don't remember me from that day in your office in Minneapolis, but I'm Captain Ben Shelfer, now of Delta Airlines, and I am President of the Lucky Sperm Club."

Flying the shuttle was great fun. Especially when I didn't have a student with me and wasn't teaching or checking. There were lots of takeoff and landings at interesting airports. Commuting to the shuttle was no fun at all. I didn't like the extra nights out of town and I especially didn't like having to pay for those nights in a hotel. To lessen the costs, I was able to make a deal with the manager of one of the airport hotels near LaGuardia for a highly discounted rate when I rented a room for the entire month. I would then sublet the rooms to other commuting pilots for the nights I didn't use it, at a price cheaper than the rate they would normally pay. The room was full almost every night and it almost entirely offset hotel costs for the month. Sometimes you have to be innovative to survive, especially if you're a commuter.

We had several Delta pilot friends who lived in Miami. One was Bill Arnold. In the small world department, I had known Bill back in ROTC at Florida State. He was also the catcher for the trapeze act and the Flying High Florida State Circus. This was at the same time I was conducting the circus band.

Paul Repp and his wife Stephanie had also been close friends of ours in Miami for years before Paul took a job with the training department and moved to Atlanta in the late 80s. After a couple months of shuttle flying, I got a phone call from Paul. After a few minutes of pleasantries and rehashing old times, Paul got to the reason for the call.

"Ben, I wanted to ask you. Would you be interested in coming to the training department and instructing on the MD-11?" Paul asked.

The question took me completely by surprise. I had only been with Delta a couple of months. And I knew nothing about the MD-11, except it was referred to as a rich man's DC-10, the plane I had flown as a copilot with National. The MD-11 was larger, had bigger engines, and had the modern technology of a glass cockpit which featured electronic flight instruments on large LCD screens, rather than the traditional round dials and gauges. Nonetheless, Paul's question got my attention.

"Wait," I said. "Does that mean I would be working out of Atlanta, rather than having to commute to New York to fly the shuttle?"

"Yes, I'm afraid so."

"Then I'm your man," I said.

"Great. I remember you flew the DC-10 for years at National, and Delta could use your Pan Am international experience with this new airplane."

There was also a pay advantage to being in the training department. I would be paid max hours for the largest equipment my seniority would hold anywhere on the Delta system. For me, that was the B-757. Even though I was losing six years of date of hire seniority, and it would take three years to attain pay parity with the Delta pilots, this was the best way for me to maximize my income.

Delta's training facilities were at the headquarters complex along Virginia Avenue on the north side of the airport in Atlanta. I had to qualify on the new airplane, meaning I had to complete ground school and simulator training, then a check ride in the plane.

Andy Bukaty, an original Delta pilot, was picked as a new MD-11 instructor and paired with me for training. It was fortunate for me, because he was an exceptional pilot and instructor. Andy was also a great guy, a Kansas Jayhawk, and we soon became close friends.

The ground school on the MD-11 at Delta was unlike any I had ever attended. It was totally computer-based training. You just sat at a computer module wearing a headset and pressed go. All the necessary information on the aircraft systems was presented visually and with a voice narrative. At the end of each segment, you would be asked questions to reinforce the lesson you had just learned. I actually liked the training better than having a live instructor in the room, because the information was presented thoroughly and without interruptions or distractions. The proof was in the pudding. At the end of the ground school, Andy and I both passed our written exams and oral exams without difficulty.

MD-11 flight simulator time at Delta was at a premium. To complete our simulator training, Delta leased an MD-11 simulator from Alitalia. And their simulators just happened to be in Rome, Italy. So, Andy Bukaty and I, along with an MD-11 instructor, hopped on an airplane and flew to Rome for our training. We had a simulator session scheduled every other day, so we spent two weeks on the outskirts of the city.

It was my first trip to Rome, and with Andy acting as our tour guide, we made good use of our downtime on our days off. We would hop on the commuter train for the short ride to the city to see the sights. We began with a hop on, hop off bus tour of the entire city. The Colosseum was intriguing, as was the Circus Maximus chariot racing arena. The Vatican however was the most fascinating of all. Andy was a devout Catholic. Myself, not so much. I could probably be best described as a backsliding Baptist, even though I didn't drink or smoke.

It just so happened that Andy had two priest friends who were now assigned to the Vatican. One was the priest who married Andy and his wife Barbara years ago. The other, Andy had known from his days back in the Kansas City diocese. One priest was a Saint maker. He was part of a group who decided who would be a candidate for sainthood. The other priest was working as a lawyer, defending members of the flock who had been charged with sexual abuse or pedophilia. They were interesting and delightful individuals. We dined with them several evenings at their choice of local restaurants, which was always superb. They treated us to a day-long private tour of the Vatican. From the catacombs to Vatican Hill, we saw it all, unencumbered by the thousands of tourists who were there. In my view, the Sistine Chapel, specifically Michelangelo's ceiling, was mesmerizing, and the most interesting site I saw in all of Rome. The priests even had a special treat for us. There I was, Ben the Baptist, at a private mass in the Vatican. Even though I didn't get a cracker and I don't drink wine, it was still very special to me.

After our training in Rome, Andy Bukaty and I flew to Los Angeles, where an MD-11 was available, and completed our rating ride. The entire training experience from beginning to end was wonderful. And I loved flying the MD-11. It could be difficult to land in a crosswind, but I knew that from flying the DC-10, so I had no trouble at all.

Not long after I settled into my new job in the training department in Atlanta, Phil Glenn, who had attended the Air Force Academy, became the Fleet Manager, my new boss. There has never been a better leader. The Pharaoh, as he called himself, was easy-going and soft-spoken. He expected everyone to do their job, and we did. However, he did have one rule. Once a month the entire MD-11 department would have to take an afternoon together and play golf. It was always a fun outing, and great camaraderie.

Phil Glenn's calm, no pressure attitude actually prevailed through most of the company at Delta Airlines. These people were not concerned at all about losing their job from a bankrupt company. I had never realized how much stress I had been under for years enduring the demise of Pan Am. It finally hit me that everything was going to be okay, and if I did my job and could stay healthy, I could work until the mandatory retirement age of 60.

The only downside to my job was it was in Atlanta, and we lived in Miami. I was not a fan of commuting to work, but at least it wasn't commuting to New York. Delta didn't care where I lived as long as I showed up to work. Spencer was still a senior in high school, so I happily made the best of the situation, knowing we would not be moving from Miami soon. My home away from home became the Howard Johnson's on Virginia Avenue. Regardless, I loved my new job. And I was enjoying the

568

new peace of mind that came from working for a company like Delta Air Lines.

True to my word, I booked a cruise for our entire family. Admittedly, it was a short cruise, three days on Disney's big red boat, but it was great fun. It was a celebration of our good life and good fortune, with hopes for even better days ahead.

Chapter 85

The dog days of the summer of 1992 were upon us. It was a steamy hot August in Miami. It was also steamy hot where I worked in Atlanta and elsewhere throughout the South. Time marches on and life kept happening for the Shelfers, ready or not. Angela and Karen had both married and given us our first granddaughters, Stuart and Melissa. We were grandparents. Wow. Skip had recently graduated from Florida State and Scott was a senior there.

Spencer had recently graduated from Palmer Trinity High School. She had continued to play competitive tennis at the national level and was highly recruited by many colleges across the country. After months of deliberation and official visits to several universities, Spencer shocked me by choosing Vanderbilt University in Nashville, Tennessee. I had never been to the Vandy campus. I didn't know much about the school except academically it was outstanding, and the women didn't have a very good tennis team. The previous year, they didn't win a single match in the Southeastern conference.

Even though I had doubts about Spencer's choice of schools, she convinced me to go for a visit and check it out. The next day I flew to Nashville and had lunch with a delightful lady, Peggy Omohundro, the head coach of the Vanderbilt Commodores. She convinced me that Vandy was serious about competing in women's tennis on the national level and recruiting Spencer would be their first step towards that goal. She offered Spencer a full ride to Vanderbilt. The coach then gave me a tour of the campus, including all the athletic facilities. As I left there that afternoon, I told the coach she would be hearing from Spencer soon. I knew that would not be my last trip to the campus of Vanderbilt University.

Friday, August 21, 1992, was freshman move-in day at Vanderbilt University. Baxter and I had loaded Spencer and all the clothes and "stuff" possible into our Lincoln Continental and had driven from Miami to Nashville. We spent the next day, Saturday, moving Spencer into her freshman dorm room. At the end of the day Baxter and I were totally exhausted, so we left Spencer in her dorm room went to a hotel downtown to rest.

The next morning, I was awakened by my mobile pager beeping by the bedside. I thought perhaps it could be my scheduler at Delta, even though I was on my days off. The training department was very accommodating to us about days off for family functions, so I didn't expect it to be them, and it wasn't. It was our daughter Angel, who lived in Orlando. I called her number right away.

"Hello," Angel said.

"Angelll," I said, accentuating her name. Baxter had always said she could tell which of the kids I was talking to on the phone by my manner of speech. My retort was, they were all special so why wouldn't I converse with each of them in a special way.

"Dad, are you watching this storm?"

"What storm?"

"Hurricane Andrew. It's headed straight towards Miami."

"No, I haven't seen the news in three days. Moving a freshman girl into a college dorm a thousand miles from home is hectic. Don't worry, Darlin', it'll turn north and go up and hit the Carolinas like a nice hurricane should."

"Not this one, Dad," Angel said. "This one's a category five that just hit Eleuthera in the Bahamas and is headed due west towards Miami, and it's supposed to hit there tomorrow morning."

"Don't worry, it'll change directions. They always do. Thanks for letting me know," I said. "I'll keep an eye on it. Love you, darlin'. I'll call you later."

"Bye, Dad. Love you. You'd better watch this storm."

"I will. Bye."

It was the middle of hurricane season and I had heard there was a storm out in the Atlantic. But there but always seemed to be a storm somewhere this time of year. Nonetheless, I flipped on the TV. The image on the screen immediately got my attention. The hurricane that days ago had been forecast to drift to the north was currently devastating the outer islands of the Bahamas and heading directly west towards Miami. Not only Miami, but the projected path on the screen was directly over South Miami, where we lived in Kendall. And it was a fast-moving storm, moving due west at 15 mph, with winds over 160 mph. That was trouble.

In an instant I knew what had to be done. We had to get to Miami. Our house in Pine Acres was sitting there unprotected. Years ago, I had purchased supplies for hurricane preparation; plywood to cover the windows and doors, duct tape, and concrete nails, and stored them in the garage. I even bought rolls of roofing felt to repair a damaged roof. None of that would do any good, of course, unless it was installed. And I was in Nashville, Tennessee.

Under normal circumstances, the fastest way to Miami would be to fly. I knew that wouldn't work in this case because airports would be closed and flights would be canceled in advance of the storm like this. There was only one way to get there. I had to drive. A two-day trip had to be done in one day. So be it.

Baxter began packing our bags while I called Angel and told her we were driving to Miami and I would check in with her later. We woke up Spencer and took her for a quick breakfast at the famous Pancake Pantry on 21st Street, near the Vandy campus. I could see why that place was famous. Good food.

Couple of hours later, passing through Chattanooga, Tennessee, I called Angel again, this time on a new thing called a car phone. It was about the same in size and weight as two large bricks tied together. The reception was spotty and it was difficult to keep it charged. Other than that, it was a great device. Even so, we were grateful to be able to communicate during this stressful time without having to stop the car. The hurricane had not changed direction nor diminished in strength. In fact, it was increasing in intensity. It was already after noon Eastern Daylight Time and Angel had taken matters into her own hands. She was convinced there was no way we could drive to Miami and board up the house by ourselves before Andrew arrived. Secretly, I admitted she was probably right. Angel had gone shopping and filled her car with water and other staples to survive the aftermath of a hurricane. Angel's husband, Chuck, and our son, Skip, who was living with Angel at the time, were already in route to Miami to prepare the house for the storm. Skip knew the location in the garage where I kept the emergency plywood. They also had with them Daisy, our little Yorky pup, who Angel was keeping for us while we were on the trip to Nashville.

We joined I-75 and encountered heavy Sunday afternoon traffic through Atlanta and the entire state of Georgia. The southbound traffic lessened after we passed the Florida line. It was around 8 PM by the time we passed Orlando. The storm was relentless. It never changed directions or weakened. Miami was still in its crosshairs. All the toll gates on the Florida Turnpike were open to allow unrestricted access during the hurricane evacuation of South Florida. The opposite direction north bound lanes of the Turnpike looked like a parking lot. The cars were moving slowly, backed up as far as the eye could see. In our direction, southbound, there were very few travelers, except for us. It made us wonder if we were doing the right thing. It was too late at that point to be second-guessing. I increased our speed on the Lincoln to between 90 and 100 mph. We had the road to ourselves. It was an eerily quiet night, truly a lull before the storm.

We made it home before 11 PM. Skip and Chuck had done a phenomenal job of shuttering the entire house with the plywood that was stored in the garage. My old Boy Scout motto of "be prepared" served me well in this instance. They had even taken the windscreens down from the fence around the tennis court. There was nothing left to do but wait. Hurricane winds were expected to begin at or before 2 AM. I was concerned about my airport car, our old Chrysler, which was parked in the Delta employees parking lot near the airport. I knew the area would be flooded, so Skip and I made the trip to the airport to retrieve the car. On the way home, the weather began to deteriorate rapidly. Sheets of rain began to pepper the windshield and the wind began to howl. It worsened. Along the Palmetto Expressway, I saw sparks flying from transformers on the power lines as electricity begin to fail from downed power lines from the falling trees.

When Skip and I made it home to Pine Acres, our electricity was still on. We put Chuck's car and the Lincoln Continental in the garage. The question then became what to do with the Chrysler? We had planted beautiful black olive trees in our yard that had grown quite tall in the last 20 years. I estimated the heights of the trees and measured a place in the front yard to park the Chrysler, so hopefully it would not be hit by a falling tree. We had done everything we could do. All of us were totally exhausted from the long, stressful day. Skip and Chuck collapsed on recliners in the family room while Baxter and I, along with little Daisy, settled into the living room couch. We couldn't see outside the house at all because all the windows and sliding glass doors were boarded up with plywood. I listened to the constant thunder and the heavy rain pounding the roof and closed my eyes. We waited. We didn't have to wait very long. The lights went out. No electricity. No air conditioning. No television. We knew from the last reports the storm was coming almost directly at us. It could slide past our neighborhood slightly to the south, but that would put us in the northeast quadrant, the most dangerous part of the storm. The howling wind, now from a northerly direction, had increased to a constant, omnipotent roar. The sound of unknown objects constantly pounding the outside of the house was distressing.

In fear, Baxter and I, using our flashlights, hurried to join the boys in the family room. Poor Daisy had the hyper-hassles and was shaking uncontrollably. In her short life she had never experienced anything like this. But then again, neither had we. Because of our thorough preparations, we had hoped to get through the storm without much damage to the house. Now, we were just hoping to get through it with our lives. It was a helpless feeling being at the mercy of mother nature.

There was nothing to see in the family room that would give us any comfort. My dad and I, with Tom Batten's help and guidance, had added the family room and the extra bedroom to the original house. I was certain we had strapped down those huge beams according to the new Dade County hurricane building code. I was curious if they would survive the test. What I saw when I shined the flashlight around the family room was chilling. The huge picture window from the family room to the lanai and all the sliding glass doors were actually bending in and out from the pressure of the wind, even though they were covered with plywood. The entire ceiling was being lifted up and down several inches with the cycling of each gust. It looked like it would be lifted off and blown away. And soon.

All of us rushed into the kitchen to avoid the certain catastrophe we thought was about to happen in the family room. The relentless wind with the deafening roar was now coming from the east. Then something rammed the house with a huge crash and the sound of broken glass coming from the bathroom down the hall. I peered around the corner and saw the top of the

574

huge tree, it looked like an Australian pine, had pierced the plywood on the bathroom window like a javelin, and stretched across the entire bathroom. The wind and the water were blowing in through the damaged window, so I rushed down the hall and closed the bathroom door.

We changed our position in the house again as the wind shifted from the south. The safest place at that time appeared to be once again in the living room. The storm continued to rage. There was another colossal crash, this time from the direction of the master bedroom. As I went down the hall to investigate, I got a face full of wind and rain spewing in from the window at the head of our king size bed. I shined the light carefully because I couldn't believe what I was seeing. A 4 x 8 piece of plywood, probably from a neighbor's roof, had sliced through the plywood protecting our bedroom window, shattered through the glass, and was covering our bed. All I could do was close our bedroom door to try to keep the wind out of the rest of the house and thank our lucky stars and the good Lord above we were not lying in that bed.

We continued to hunker down in the living room and finally, after a couple of hours of stark terror, hurricane Andrew began to subside. As that happened, the shock and fatigue were taking their toll on all of us. We drifted off to sleep in the couches and the easy chairs of the living room.

A couple of hours later I awoke. It was weirdly quiet. Daylight was struggling to stream through the still covered windows. I quietly stood up and stretched and began to survey the damage. As I walked to the family room, water squished in the carpet under my feet. I noticed there was water everywhere on the floor. The picture window and the sliding glass doors in the family room were still intact. I stared at the ceiling with a small degree of pride and satisfaction. The roof was still there. It had withstood the storm. The plywood on the windows and doors had done their job. The only broken glass in the house was where the tree came through the bathroom window and the plywood came through the bedroom window.

It was already feeling stuffy inside the boarded house with no air conditioning. I opened the front door for some fresh air and looked outside. Devastation everywhere. Debris everywhere. Not a tree was standing. The mailboxes were gone. The street leading to our house was impassable due to standing water, fallen trees, and debris.

My plan for parking the old Chrysler had worked. The fallen tree nearby had totally missed it. What did not miss it were the shingles and boards and other flying objects which decimated the paint job. That's okay, it was still drivable. Small victory.

Skip and Chuck had awakened and joined me in the front yard to survey the damage to the outside of the house. The two bottlebrush trees near the tennis court had fallen and each had destroyed a section of the white picket fence which connected the house to the tennis court. The cypress frame of the chickee hut beside the court was still intact. Not so much for the Palmetto palm fronds which comprised its roof. They were gone with the wind. The chickee had been erected by Roy Cypress, a member of the Miccosukee Seminole Indian tribe who lived in a place called Frog City in the Everglades. He had been building chickee's all his life. Now, he would have more work to do.

The tennis court itself was a disaster. Even though the windscreens had been taken down and I had insisted on using heavy-duty fence post when I built it, it made no difference. Every fence post was bent and curved in a willy-nilly manner which could not be explained. Long sections of the fence itself had been torn apart and swept across the tennis court surface by the wind countless times, digging deep gashes in the surface of the court with each cycle. Even the net posts were bent. The dense schefflera hedge behind the tennis court was still standing, but now it was only sticks. All the leaves were gone.

We got a ladder from the garage and Skip, Chuck, and I climbed up on the roof. It became immediately apparent why we had so much water on the floor of the house. There were countless shingles and several sections, maybe 25%, of the roof missing. That was trouble. It wasn't threatening rain at the moment, but it was August in Miami and that meant it would rain almost every day. The three of us talked it over and came up with a plan. We had to remove the plywood from the windows so we could ventilate the house with no air conditioning. We would simply use that plywood to replace the missing sections on the roof. Then we would cover the plywood with the rolls of roofing felt I had stored in the garage to complete the makeshift repair and the house would remain dry. Of course, the entire roof would have to be replaced. That would be another day. Until then, dry is good.

The boys began moving the plywood from the windows while I retrieved a bicycle from the garage. I needed to run an errand to make sure the Gogs made it through the storm okay. With the roads impassable, a bicycle might be the only way I could get to their place. The Gogs were

Baxter's parents, who were about 70 years old, and lived in Pine tree Village about a mile away. They got that name when our son Scott was an infant trying to say granddaddy and grandmother. All he could manage to say was GaGa Man and GaGa Mommie. The names stuck. (Note to self: never let an infant grandchild invent a name for you before they can talk. I am Granddaddy.)

Before departing, I walked back inside the house to talk to Baxter. I didn't see her at first, but then I found her in the kitchen. She was at the pantry door, standing barefooted in water, quietly rearranging the spices in the spice rack. I watched her for a long moment.

"Hey Darlin', what are you doing?" I asked.

"Nothing," she said.

The look of hopeless desperation on her face reflected the scene of hopeless desperation all around us. I realized that Baxter was probably in shock. The dread and fear of the last several hours was horrifying, and had taken its toll. I put my arms around her and held her tight for the longest time.

"It's okay… It's okay," I said. "We made it. We survived. Not a scratch. Don't worry about the house and don't worry about stuff. We'll rebuild better than ever and buy new stuff.

Baxter nodded, and tried to smile.

"I'm going to check on your parents. I'll be back soon."

"I'll be okay," she said. "I'll be okay.

As I started out the door, I was surprised to hear the phone ring. The electrical system was decimated and even though we had underground utilities in the neighborhood I never thought the phone would be working. But there it was, ringing away.

"Hello."

"Scheffler, how's it going? We're worried about you guys."

577

It was Dusty Rhodes calling from Atlanta. And he knows my name, but in lighter moments he calls me Scheffler. That's because he knows people tend to call me anything but Shelfer.

"Hey Dusty… we made it through the storm okay, but our place not so much…"

The next few minutes I went on to tell Dusty about the entire experience. Telling him about the tree and the plywood coming through the windows, 25% of the roof gone, water throughout the house, tennis court destroyed, trees down, etc.

"Well, thank God you guys are safe," Dusty said. "And at least you have a roof over your head… Oh wait, sorry..."

And at that we both started laughing. Dusty was always quick with the zapping one-liners. It felt good to laugh and relieve some of the stress of the moment.

The Gogs survived the storm pretty well. They had some roof damage and a huge pine tree had fallen and destroyed their back patio fence and lanai area. Otherwise, they were good. They wouldn't be going anywhere for a while because all the streets were severely flooded and covered with fallen trees and debris. I made sure they had plenty of food and water for a few days, then made my way back to Pine Acres.

It took the rest of the day to remove the plywood from the windows and doors and make repairs to the roof. With the open windows, the house was now ventilated but still beastly hot. Baxter and I slept in the corner bedroom because of master bedroom was a wreck and our mattress was settled and ruined.

Our next task was becoming immediately apparent. The soaked carpet throughout the house was beginning to mildew. And smell. A sickening smell. It took the entire next day for us to rip out the carpet and padding from the entire house and lug it outside. Not a pleasant task. At the end of the day, I'm sure I was smelling worse than the carpet.

On the second day the phone rang again. It was Phil Glenn, the MD-11 fleet manager, my boss at Delta Air Lines in Atlanta. He had called to check on us. He could not have been more gracious.

"Ben," Phil said. "I want you to know I'm clearing your schedule and we want you to take all the time necessary, no matter how long it takes, to take care of your family and your property after the storm. Just let us know when you're ready to come back to work."

"Thanks, Phil. That's so nice of you. But the truth is I don't want you to clear my schedule. Baxter and I are going to secure the house and come to Atlanta. I'd like to be on the schedule every day, starting Monday."

"Are you sure, Ben? Why would you do that?"

"Because Atlanta has electricity, drinking water, hot food, hot showers, and air conditioning. And we're not going to have any of that at our house in Miami for a long time."

"I see your point. Okay, I'll put you on the schedule starting Monday, but if something changes let me know," Phil said.

Hurricane Andrew maintained a westward trajectory across southern Florida and into the Gulf of Mexico. There it turned northward and slammed into the Louisiana coast and inflicted more damage and destruction. Andrew was only the third category five hurricane in history at the time, to impact the continental US. The northern eye wall of the storm passed about 20 blocks south of our neighborhood, where there were reports of wind gusts up to 180 mph when the anemometer failed. More than 63,000 houses were destroyed. Another 120,000, such as ours, were damaged. With over $27 billion in damages, it was the costliest storm ever. Sadly, 65 people died.

The advent of Hurricane Andrew had caused Baxter and me to reevaluate our situation in terms of quality of life. Fortunately, I had a good paying job with Delta Airlines, but that job was in Atlanta. I didn't like having to commute on an airplane to go to work. And I especially didn't like being away from Baxter and staying at the Howard Johnson's at the Atlanta airport.

Baxter and I, now being empty-nesters, decided to go on an adventure. We did, in fact, rebuild our Pine Acres home better than ever and in record time. Everything about the house was replaced. Even the window frames and the sliding glass door frames had to be replaced because they were bent out of shape from the pressure of the wind. The storm created a severe housing shortage in South Florida. We placed our beautiful home, the one in which we had raised our children, on the market and it sold in record time. It also sold for the highest price ever paid for a house in that neighborhood at the time.

We deeply regretted leaving our dear friends in Miami, but our new home would be in Atlanta.

Chapter 86

It was a really good drive. I had swung hard, as usual, and got all of it. At first, I thought it might go into the fairway bunker, but it somehow careened off the berm beside the sand trap and finally came to stop further down in the middle of the fairway. It must've been 250 yards. Could I reach the green in two on this par five, the number one handicap hole on the course? Should I go for it? Was there any doubt? Absolutely not. I grabbed my three wood and gave it a rip. I'm sure both feet left the ground. It reminded me of what I had told Mr. Amos on my job interview with National Airlines almost 30 years before. "In golf, it is not important how hard you swing, just so both feet leave the ground." The ball flew high and far. I thought it might have the distance, but it began drifting more and more to the right. It disappeared down into the trees and bushes to the right of the green. Oh, no… Was it in the river?

There were few golfers playing that day and no one was playing behind me. I was walking alone carrying my own bag. I dropped my clubs beside the green and clumped through the thicket down towards the river. My ball was not to be found, but I did find three others. I noticed there was someone fishing from the sandbar in the bend of the river. He was a big guy who was casting left-handed. Somehow, he looked familiar. I inched closer.

"Rick! Is that you?" I shouted, waving to the fisherman.

"Ben? Ben Shelfer?"

"Yes. Rick, what in the world are you doing here?"

"I was going to ask you the same thing. I live here, over in Brookside."

"Me too. I live just up the fairway there," I said, pointing towards my house.

It was Rick Kerr, my old friend and tennis buddy from the Secret Service. Vice-President Bush introduced us and arranged our first tennis match years ago. He and his wife, Deborah, had moved to Georgia after he was assigned to President Jimmy Carter's security detail. I hadn't seen or heard from him in years. Now we were neighbors. Small world, indeed.

For me, this was the home hole at the Horseshoe Bend Country Club in Roswell, Georgia, a northern suburb of Atlanta. Baxter and I had bought a lovely home in a fairytale setting overlooking the fifth fairway and the Chattahoochee River. It was our Camelot. I thought it more than ironic to be living on the Chattahoochee, the same river I had fished throughout my childhood years near my hometown of Sneads, Florida.

Aside from the championship golf course, Horseshoe Bend had a nice tennis facility. I enjoy playing the team competition of ALTA, the Atlanta Lawn Tennis Association, the largest tennis organization in the world. There were many great matches and I partnered with many great tennis friends such as Steve Tomlinson, Keith Bannister and Joe DeLapp.

Baxter and I enjoyed socializing with other Horseshoe Bend neighbors who became lifelong friends, such as Bill and Mary Ann Wiehe. Bill was the head of advertising for the Weather Channel, which was headquartered in Atlanta. Also, there was Mike and Julie Reilly. Mike was an executive with Procter & Gamble after he played football at Alabama for Bear Bryant and flew helicopters in Vietnam. And then there were the best friends, next-door neighbors, and movie buddies in the world, Dick and Anina Morgan.

The MD-11 training department at Delta was a wonderful place to work. It was our largest and most modern airplane at the time. After two or three months in the department we would be assigned a month to fly the line to maintain our flying proficiency. Most of those trips were to the Orient, leaving from Los Angeles or Portland, Oregon.

My first trip to Bangkok, Thailand was interesting. The other captain on the trip was chairman of the safety committee for ALPA, the pilot's union. Being the nice guy that he was, he offered to show me around the city. He assured me rather than taking a taxi it would be cheaper and faster to take a tuk-tuk. I followed him outside the hotel and we jumped on this tuk-tuk, which was nothing more than a three-wheel motor-scooter, driven by a Thai teenager with death wish. Before I could rethink what was happening, we were zooming in and out of the snarled traffic, racing and cutting off cars, trucks, and tuk-tuks alike, daring any other fainthearted fool to lay a fender on us. We had two speeds, wide open, and stopped. I was sure I was going to die. I could already imagine the Atlanta obituary: "Shelfer dies with the safety chairman of ALPA in a Thai tuk-tuk."

The next day we booked an eight-hour tour of the Thai countryside. We were on a bus, not a tuk-tuk. There was lush green foliage and flowers everywhere. There were miles and miles of rice paddies along our route. We saw countless temples. At one point we stopped and boarded what we called a longboat, an extremely long and narrow vessel with a canvas top. The boat was in a network of canals where we zoomed from one outdoor water market to the next and were invited to purchase flowers and crafts and enjoy culinary delights such as fresh snake, eel or coi. Not me.

Last stop of the day for the tour bus was beside a large circular tent erected beside the road. We were herded inside and seated in folding chairs around a small rink area in the center of the tent. There were several crates with small holes in them stacked a few feet away from me on the dirt floor of the rink. I thought they might contain some small animals, but I soon learned they were filled with snakes. Cobras. We were on a snake farm.

In a moment a couple of the "farmers" appeared. They were young adult males. Something about them was different. Their hands were covered with scar tissue and they had this disconnected look on their face. They reminded me of the banjo player in "Deliverance." They dumped over this crate and a huge king cobra slithered out. The guys did their little show, they caught the snake and milked him of his venom. They then brought the snake over to where we were sitting on the rail and shoved him in our direction.

"You want to touch?" The guy asked.

"Absolutely not," I said.

"It's good luck to touch the king cobra," he said.

At that moment, for some reason my thoughts drifted to my friend, Glen Stalvey, the $20 million man, my pilot friend who had won the Florida lottery. Then I thought about the lottery ticket I had in my wallet and the $50 million drawing coming the next day.

"Let me touch that snake," I said, almost gleefully. And I did.

It didn't work. I didn't win the lottery jackpot. Or maybe it did, I've certainly been lucky in many other ways.

Before long, I became a senior instructor on the MD-11. Then I was an APD, an Aircrew Program Designee, an evaluator who is designated by the FAA to conduct check rides and issue ratings on a particular airplane. It was easy for me, because I always thought that Delta standards were higher than the FAA standards anyway.

In the training department it was easy for me to control my days off. Those were exciting times for us watching Spencer play tennis for the Vanderbilt Commodores. In her four years there, we only missed six matches she played, regardless of where it was in the country. Fun times. Spencer had chosen her college well. Vandy was a great school.

As the old saying goes, time flies when you're having fun. At age 57, the end was in sight. The age 60 mandatory retirement age was looming. I had been an instructor and check pilot for most of my career. I did not want the last flight of my career to be in the simulator. The bottom line was, I only wanted to be a pilot. I wanted to be able to enjoy flying the airplane without having to train or check some other pilot. I'd always said I wanted to simply fly the line the last three years of my career. So, I did.

The airplane I chose to finish my journey was the B-757. It carried a dual rating with the B-767, so I would be flying both airplanes, which ever was at the gate for the trip. I wanted to fly domestically. I had seen enough sunrises over the ocean. I wanted to fly to places I could speak the language, spend the money, drink the water, eat the food, watch television and make a phone call. I appreciated other cultures, but I loved the USA.

The age 60 mandatory retirement for airline pilots was a rule I never agreed with or understood. I always thought retirement from flying should be based on health and proficiency requirements, not an arbitrary birthday randomly picked over four decades ago. In my case, I was in great health and was still performing at the highest standards. I resented the fact my flying career was coming to an end, but it was a fact I had always known and accepted. I was ready to turn the page and move on.

October, 2000, came faster than I would've liked. Delta allowed me to pick any trip I wanted for my retirement trip. I chose a trip from Atlanta to LaGuardia, with a layover in the city. It was truly a family affair. Baxter and all the kids, Angel, Karen, Skip, Scott, and Spencer made the trip. Spencer's husband, Ryan Moorman, made the trip. Our cousin Sabrina and her husband Joe Blanton came along also.

The Shelfers took a big bite of the Big Apple. After we arrived in the city, some of the kids went for a jog in Central Park. Following that, they went to the top of the World Trade Center. Little did they know both towers of the World Trade Center would be gone in less than a year. Before the theater, we dined at Sardi's on W. 44th St. and we had front row mezzanine seats for the Broadway production of The Lion King. It was truly amazing. After the show, we went to Joe Allen's restaurant on W. 46th St. for a late-night snack. The last layover of my flying career was perfect.

The next morning, we rendezvoused at the nearby Stardust Diner for breakfast before pickup. I had rented a shuttle bus from the crew bus company to take us all to LaGuardia. When we arrived at the departure gate, I learned our aircraft was a brand-new B-757. I found it amusing that I, Delta's oldest pilot, would be fly Delta's newest airplane on my final trip. And I was pleasantly surprised that Dusty Rhodes had signed up for the jump seat to be in the cockpit with me for my final journey.

The flight from LaGuardia to Atlanta was absolutely routine. The Atlanta airport was on the west operation and we were assigned runway 26R. Now the pressure was on. It's been said pilot is only as good as his last landing. I knew with my family on board, I was going to have to live with this one for a long time. I rolled it. The first thing to be felt when we touched down were the wheels rolling down the runway. Sweet.

After we cleared the runway, Dusty opened the cockpit door and Baxter walked in and sat on the jump seat behind me. Soon, I was in for another surprise. As I taxied the airplane onto the ramp, there were two firetrucks waiting there to give me a water cannon salute. They each blasted a stream of water in a high arc over our plane as we passed through. It was beautiful and very touching. I knew someone had to pull some strings to make that happen because there had been a moratorium on water cannon salutes due to the severe drought in Fulton County.

As I made the final turn towards the arrival gate, I couldn't believe what I was seeing. Beyond my signal man was a group of men standing at strict attention, rendering a military salute. Baxter was sobbing behind me. I was deeply moved. As we moved closer, I could see Andy Bukaty, Phil Glenn, Paul Repp, and Tom Batten. Art Huckabee and Al Gailey and others may have been among them also. Deep respect. Given, received, and appreciated.

All the passengers congratulated me as they departed the airplane. I had said nothing about retiring on the PA, but I think my kids had spilled the beans and the news had spread through the cabin by word-of-mouth. The Atlanta Chief Pilot met me at the door of the airplane. He then hosted a reception in a private room on the concourse, which was attended by many friends.

The party continued once we got to our home in Horseshoe Bend. More food and more cake and lots of friends and neighbors. It was then Joe Blanton played his guitar and Sabrina and all my kids joined in and sang the song they had written about me on the flight down from New York. It was a hilarious parody of Benny and the Jets.

At the end of the day, I felt immense sadness and deep gratitude. I was sad because somehow, so quickly, it was over. I was grateful because I had flown many different airplanes in challenging situations for over 40 years, and I never bent metal.

Chapter 87

Retirement didn't last very long. Delta had established, through a subsidiary, Delta Global Systems, a cost saving program of hiring non-seniority list instructors to accomplish the majority of their simulator training and checking. They immediately recruited me to come back to the MD-11 training department to be an instructor and check pilot. I would be doing the exact same job I had previously done for years, except, I would never fly the actual airplane. And I would be paid for each training session, as opposed to each hour of flying time. I could completely control my schedule and could work from 10 to 20 days per month. It was an easy decision for me. It was something for me to do in my retirement. After all, one can only play so much golf and tennis.

Baxter and I would sometimes talk about how much we missed our home state of Florida. At some point, we wanted to return there. Not necessarily to Miami, but somewhere less crowded that was south of the frost line. We were not fans of cold weather. We were looking favorably at the West Coast of Florida, somewhere in the Fort Myers, Naples, Marco Island area. While discussing this with various friends, three separate people, who did not know each other, urged us to check out a community called The Landings in Fort Myers. The place sounded familiar.

The summer of 2001, we were invited to the wedding of Hilary Masell, the daughter of our dear friends formally from Miami, Dick and Karen Masell. The wedding was in Naples, where they had resided for many years.

Baxter and I flew into Fort Myers airport on a Friday afternoon. We rented a car and eventually found our way to this place called The Landings.

The minute we went through the guard gate and I saw the fountain in the lake with the tennis courts in the background, I knew we had been there before. Spencer had played a junior tennis tournament there years earlier. I remembered saying at the time those were the best clay courts I'd ever seen. They were hydro courts, watered from underneath, which always provided the perfect moisture content to the clay.

We parked the car at the tennis courts and stepped out into the beastly heat. No one was playing tennis. The only people we saw on the property were four guys sitting in the shade on the porch at the Pro shop. One guy looked familiar.

"Are you with Delta?" I asked.

"Yes, are you with Delta?" The man asked.

"Weren't you on my jump seat a while back?"

"Yes. My name is Paul Istock," the man said, extending his hand.

Another small world moment. Paul was a Delta pilot who had ridden my jump seat on an Atlanta to Fort Myers flight a couple years previously. He had nice things to say about The Landings, and especially the tennis program there.

We visited with Paul for a few minutes, then walked to a real estate office which was conveniently nearby. The agent there, Bill Simmons, gave us a quick tour of the neighborhood and showed us three of the very few condos that were available. One, a three bedroom, had a nice long view of the golf course and lakes, and a glimpse of the marina.

We continued to drive south, making our way towards Naples, and stopped at a couple other newer and much larger communities along the way.

Hillary's wedding in Naples was a wonderful event. It was nice to see the Masells and visit with our friends from Miami, including Sue and Alan Nichols, and Laura and Bill Walker. Driving back to the Fort Myers airport on Sunday we once again dropped in at The Landings.

Bottom line. We went to a wedding in Naples over the weekend, and came back owning a condo in The Landings in Fort Myers.

My Aunt Versie Collins, who cared for me when my dad was overseas during WW II, lived all her years in Jacksonville. She never had children of her own and often said I was the only kid she ever had. I could never repay her for the sacrifices she made on my behalf. But I tried.

After Uncle Larry died, Aunt Versie lived alone, and for many years was doing well. As her health began to decline, I increased the frequency of my visits to see her, I made sure her needs were met in terms of her everyday life. She had a cook and housekeeper and caregiver with her. I made countless day trips from Atlanta to Jacksonville to take her to lunch or to a doctor's appointment.

For the last twenty years of her life, Aunt Versie had a pet gopher, a land tortoise she had named Smokey. She made me promise to make sure Smokey had a good life after she was gone. After Aunt Versie passed at the age of 94, Baxter and I took Aunt Versie, along with Smoky, back home to Sneads. Aunt Versie is resting beside Uncle Larry in the family plot in Dykes Cemetery. I knew the perfect place for Smokey. Baxter and I released him amidst the numerous gopher holes on the hill above Rock Pond. I recalled the day of my first fishing trip with Daddy, Grandmother and Aunt Versie, sixty years previously. It was then I learned gophers carried their own houses with them all the time. And they didn't bite. And how much Aunt Versie loved gophers. Now Aunt Versie was home. And so was Smokey.

Around 2003, Delta made the decision to sell all of its MD-11's. The main reason was fuel efficiency. It had three engines. And all the airplanes rolling off the assembly line now had only two new generation engines that produced more thrust and used less fuel. My training department was being eliminated. Fortunately, I had other choices. I was welcomed to join the B-737-800 training department. It was interesting for me because it was the only airplane at Delta at the time utilizing a heads-up display. The primary flight guidance information was projected in the windscreen which allowed more precise flying to lower weather minimums. I had to go through the ground school and be rated on the airplane, as if I were a real pilot. In the personal trivia department, for me it completed a Boeing straight flush for airplane ratings. Among other airplanes, I was now rated on the B-727, 737, 747, 757, and 767.

Chapter 88

It was a dreary January day, 2004. I had returned home from work to find Baxter sitting in front of the television at the dining room table looking very somber. Tears were streaking down her cheeks.

"What is it? What's wrong, Darlin'? I asked.

"Look at this," she said, nodding towards the TV.

The Oprah Winfrey show was on, as it was every afternoon. They were talking about recent changes to a law in Oregon. It was then I knew the reason for the tears. I held Baxter's hand in mine and we continued to watch the TV.

"I think it's time," Baxter said.

As I squeezed her hand even tighter, my thoughts drifted back to that night in Norfolk when we were dating when Baxter confided in me her heart wrenching story. She told me she dated the same boy through four years of high school. He was a football player and she was a cheerleader. On the night of their senior prom, Baxter got pregnant. Both sets of parents were outraged and wanted Baxter to have an abortion. She refused. Marriage was not in the question because the boy had a scholarship to play college football, and would not abandon that plan. After graduating from high school, Baxter flew to Roseburg, Oregon, where she stayed with her aunt, Jeanne Barnes, to have the baby and give it up for adoption. On January 30, 1966, she gave birth to a beautiful baby girl. Baxter heard her cry, and held her once, and then she was gone.

It was a closely held secret. No one knew, but Baxter did. And through the years she carried in her heart the burden of the unknown, praying that her decision had led to a good life for her little girl. Could she know? Would she ever know? Aunt Jeanne had always sworn she never knew what happened to the baby. But now we were hearing on the Oprah show that the mutual consent adoption registry laws in Oregon had changed and would now allow a birth parent to search for an adopted child.

"If you say it's time, it's time," I said. "Let's do this. But, as we've always said, whatever we find, we have to live with it. We just pray we can find her and she's had a good life."

Throughout the next several months we made inquiries, filled out applications, and paid fees that eventually led to a search. More time passed.

It was August 25, 2004. We were sitting in the very back of an airplane that was taxiing to the gate in Atlanta following a late summer visit to our condo in Fort Myers. I used my new cell phone to check the messages on our land line in Atlanta. There were several, but one was spine tingling.

"This is the Oregon Adoption Search and Registry Center calling for Baxter Shelfer. We have found your little girl, and she would like to hear from you. Please call…"

Needless to say, I was speechless. I quickly wrote the lady's number down and replayed the message so Baxter could hear it. The look on her face said it all.

When we were home in Horseshoe Bend, Baxter called the lady in Oregon. She learned her daughter's name was Diana Gowen and she lived in Tualatin, Oregon. She then wrote down her address and phone number.

When Baxter dialed the number in Tualatin, I left the room. I wanted her to have total privacy for the conversation she had feared she would never have. After a long while, with misty eyes and a happy smile of complete relief, she walked out to join me on the sun porch.

"She sounds lovely," Baxter said. "She said she's had a wonderful life."

Baxter was excited to tell me the highlights of the phone call. Diana grew up in Roseburg. She had one younger brother who was conceived soon after her adoption. She always knew she was adopted, but never thought much about it. She graduated from high school in Silverton, Oregon, after they moved there for her dad to be principal of the school. She graduated from Oregon State University with a degree in sports management. She married Paul Gowen who was from Kansas. They have two daughters, Toni, 7, and Alex, 5. In the phone call, Baxter had relayed to Diana the entire story about her birth father and how she ended up being born in Roseburg. Baxter and Diana agreed to exchange family pictures as soon as possible. Then Baxter had asked if she could come to visit her in Oregon. Diana had said yes.

The exchange of pictures happened quickly. Baxter gathered a few pictures of our family and described each picture with hand-written sticky notes. We mailed them right away. In a few days, we received an envelope from Oregon with pictures of Diana and her family. Diana's resemblance to Baxter was stunning. I thought it was also bizarre that Diana had described each picture with cute little sticky notes. We immediately made plans to visit.

On Thursday, September 2, 2004, Baxter and I boarded a Delta jet from Atlanta nonstop to Portland, Oregon. Upon arrival, we picked up our rental car and headed south towards Tualatin, a suburb about a half-hour away. It was a nervous ride for me, and I could not imagine what Baxter had to be feeling. A moment she had dreamed about and longed for, yet dreaded, was about to happen. Coming ready or not.

We followed the printed directions from the interstate onto winding country roads, and then finally into a nice, upscale residential neighborhood. We found the address, parked the car along the curb, and slowly walked up the driveway to the house. We could see two cute little girl's faces peeking through the glass beside the door.

As we approached the front door, it opened. Toni and Alex had retreated back to where their dad, Paul, was standing in the foyer. Beside him was Diana. She was beautiful. And she was really tall, and looked like an athlete. I was struck that she had almost the same identical haircut and coloring as Baxter. What are the odds of that?

Diana and Baxter locked eyes for a brief instant, then leapt into each other's arms. Tears flowed. It was a moment that stirred the soul. The love emanating from their embrace, for Baxter, seemed to wash away the guilt she carried about a decision she made 38 years ago. Out of pure love, she had given life to this little girl. Out of an even greater love, she had let her go to have a better opportunity for a life of love and happiness of her own. And now, sweet redemption.

The love in the room between the mother and the child was heartwarming. But, then out of nowhere, I was blindsided by a deeply personal revelation. It was about my own mother. She had deserted me when I was an infant. Why did my mother leave me? What about me was so bad she didn't want to have me? I wondered. And I secretly resented her for over 60 years for what she did. And now, seeing Baxter with the child who had a wonderful life because of Baxter's gift of love, I had an epiphany. My mother had deserted me out of love. She knew I would have a better life of love and opportunity with the Shelfer family. And I did. Being with Baxter on her journey made me realize the guilt I'm certain my mother carried throughout her life for the decision she made. I was then aware that her decision was indeed a gift of love. My deep regret is during her lifetime I never told her, "Mom, I love you. It's okay. What you did for me resulted in me having a really good life. Thank you." On that day, standing in the doorway of Diana's home, I forgave my mom. And then, I prayed, somewhere in heaven, she knew. And my heart was not quite so heavy.

The visit to meet Diana and her family could not have gone better. For the next couple of days, the conversations only stopped when we retired to our hotel for the evening. There were lifetimes of stories to tell. We met several of the Gowen's good friends. But more importantly, we met her parents, Bev and Duke Ricketts. They had driven up to meet us for dinner from Silverton, Oregon, which was about 30 miles to the south. They proved to be a delightful couple. We looked forward to meeting them even though we knew they were probably reticent about the entire situation. And understandably so. They had been guaranteed absolute privacy under the adoption laws, and then the laws changed. They probably felt betrayed by what had happened. We wanted them to know that we admired them tremendously and were grateful for what they had done in raising such a beautiful young lady. We also wanted them to know we only came out of love and would never do anything to come between them and their daughter. We knew it would take time.

Epilogue

As the years passed following my retirement from the cockpit, occasionally some of my friends would ask me how long was I going to keep teaching and checking in the simulator? I would always say, I'm not sure, but I'll know when it's time.

Then one day, after I reached age 70, at the end of a simulator period, I turned the motion off and the big machine settled to the floor. And just like that, I was finished. I had often said my goal was not to die with the motion on. Mission accomplished. I hadn't yet reached the point where I was having to study more than my students for a simulator session, but I thought I was enjoying my days off more than I was enjoying my days working. I was gone.

Our five kids, even though they were shocked to learn they had a sister, had totally embraced Diana and her family. Now, we were all just one happy bunch. Due to everyone's busy schedule and our great distances apart it was difficult for us to all be together at once. But when that happened, it was special.

Life in Fort Myers had been going really well. We had sold our condo and bought a standalone house on a lake, also in the Landings development. The extra room and the two-car garage came in handy. I enjoyed tennis, especially playing at the national level with daughter, Spencer. We had partnered to win several National Father Daughter Championships. I also played golf and enjoyed writing. I had written, along with the help of my son, Scott, a screenplay called *Struttin'*. It actually won

594

an award at a screenplay competition. All we need now is a producer with $5 million to get it on the big screen. And more recently I had completed a thriller called *Drawing Dead*. It explores the possibility of there being terrorist hijackers who failed to get airborne on 9/11. It was a fun project and I had pitched it far and wide in an attempt to get it published.

One evening I had been out fishing in the neighborhood lakes. When I returned home, Baxter had already gone to attend a girl's night out at a neighbor's house. I checked my messages and I couldn't believe the news I received. I couldn't wait to tell Baxter, so I interrupted the girl's party and finally got Baxter on the phone.

"Hello."

"Hey darlin', it's me," I said.

"Is everything all right?" She asked.

"Yes. Would you like to sleep with a published author?"

"What?"

"Would you like to sleep with a published author?"

The line was silent for the longest time.

"I'm not talking about John Grisham," I finally said. "The published author is me. I got a book deal. My book is going to be published."

"That's wonderful. I would love to sleep with a published author," she said.

A few months later Baxter and I were riding down US 41 towards Naples.

"So where are we going now?" Baxter asked.

"We going to the Barnes & Noble's at the Waterside Shops in Naples."

"And why are we going there?"

"I got a call from a writer from the Naples Daily News who had seen a blurb about the book coming out next week. She said she would like to do an interview with me for a possible Sunday Feature on the release of *Drawing Dead*. Her name is Sandy Reed, and we're meeting her in the coffee shop at Barnes & Noble's at 5 o'clock."

Sandy Reed was a delightful young lady. Very personable and very professional. Baxter chatted with us for a moment, then excused herself to peruse the bookstore. As she walked away, I was thinking this could be an expensive interview.

"So, Ben. Tell me about your book," Sandy said.

"I'll give you the elevator pitch," I said. "It's about a poker playing FBI agent who battles his obsessions with tarot cards and horoscopes, with the lessons learned from Texas hold'em, while chasing a group of terrorist hijackers who failed to get airborne on 9/11."

"Sounds interesting," she said. "Are any of your personal experiences in the book?"

"Not really. It's all fiction. But it's all totally possible."

"Speaking of personal experiences, it appears you've had an interesting life. Tell me about yourself."

It was a very good interview because I didn't feel like I was being interviewed at all. It was more like I was chatting with an old friend. The more I talked, the more questions she asked. We chatted for hours as Sandy took notes. I told her I was born in Jacksonville and my mother deserted me when I was an infant. I told her about my father being drafted into the Army in World War II and my Aunt Versie taking care of me. I told her about being bitten by the big dog and having to take rabies shots. I told her about growing up on the farm with my grandmother. I told her about playing the French horn and being drum major of my high school band. I told her about my single goal in life was to be drum major of the Florida State University Marching Chiefs. I told her about achieving that goal at Florida State and how I ended up in Air Force ROTC only because of a casual remark by a complete stranger. I told about getting married in college and after graduation going to pilot training in Texas to be an instructor pilot in the Air Force. I told her about the birth of my three kids and subsequent marital problems which eventually led to divorce. I told her about leaving the Air

Force and going to work for National Airlines and meeting Baxter on a night the moon eclipsed. I told her about Baxter and I getting married. I told her about my first hijacking. I told her about the successful custody battle for my three kids at almost the same time Baxter was giving birth to our son, Scott. I told her about writing songs, and meeting Billy Joel. I told her about Pan Am buying National Airlines. I told her about my friend and tennis buddy, Jeb Bush, and subsequently playing tennis with President Bush for many years, as I was flying the White House Press Charters. I told her about my second hijacking. I told her about being on a select committee of Pan Am pilots who affected the sale of Pan Am assets to Delta Air Lines, resulting in the saving of 7000 jobs, including my own. I told her about working for and subsequently retiring from Delta Air Lines. I told her the Diana story.

Honestly, I don't know where the time went, but I looked at my watch and it was almost 8 o'clock. Sandy folded up her notepad.

"Ben, thanks so much for your time. I should be able to write a nice Sunday feature for you. Best of luck with your book. I look forward to reading it and I'm sure you'll do just fine with it. But the book I want to read is the one you just told me. You should write a memoir."

"Maybe I will," I said.

THE END

Acknowledgements and gratitude to those who helped making a memory into a memoir:

I'm grateful to my forever soulmate, Baxter, for her love and insistence that I write this book, and her patience through the years as it happened.

I'm grateful to my kideroos, Angela Smith, Karen Hanna, Bennett Shelfer III, Scott Shelfer, Spencer Moorman, and Diana Gowen for their love, input, and encouragement. And to Carrie Shelfer for the cover design.

I'm grateful to Dusty and Nancy Rhodes for sharing much of this journey with us, and for Dusty's contributions from his vivid recall of fond memories.

I'm grateful to the dozens of friends who contributed to my efforts to complete this book. Included on the list are: Grant Shelfer, Faye Walden, Terri Martindale, Bill Weiler, Karin Busse Weiler, Delsa Amundson, Bob Ferrel, Leo Unzicker, Nancy Scully, Paul Repp, Michael Callahan, and Sandy Reed, who first suggested I write a memoir.

Made in United States
Orlando, FL
02 December 2024

54367037R00326